Psychology AS
for AQA (A)

Jean-Marc Lawton, Richard Gross,
Geoff Rolls

DL DYNAMIC LEARNING

HODDER EDUCATION
AN HACHETTE UK COMPANY

Picture credits

The authors and publishers would like to thank the following for permission to reproduce material in this book:

Figure 1.02 © Kurhan – Fotolia; Figure 1.03 © david hughes – Fotolia; Figure 1.06 © AP/Press Association Images; Figure 1.07 © Tomasz Trojanowski – Fotolia; Figure 1.08 © Earl Robbins – Fotolia; Figure 1.10 © Yuri Arcurs – Fotolia; Figure 1.11 © icholakov – Fotolia; Figure 1.12 © Vladimir Mucibabic – Fotolia; Figure 2.01 © ABACA USA/Empics Entertainment/PA Photos; Figure 2.02 © The Granger Collection, NYC/TopFoto; Figure 2.06 © Alinari/Rex Features; Figure 2.07 © Peter Willi/SuperStock; Figure 2.08 © Alfonso de Tomás – Fotolia; Figure 2.09 From: Ropar, D. & Mitchell, P. (2002). Shape constancy in autism: The role of prior knowledge and perspective cues. Journal of Child Psychology and Psychiatry, 43, 647–653. Photo courtesy of Peter Mitchell, School of Psychology, University of Nottingham; Figure 2.10 © Albo – Fotolia; Figure 2.12 From: Recovery from Early Blindness. A Case Study, By Richard Langton Gregory and Jean G. Wallace. Reproduced in March 2001 from Experimental Psychology Society Monograph No. 2 1963 © 2001 Richard Gregory and Jean Wallace; Figure 2.14 From: Delvenne, J.-F., Seron, X., Coyette, F., & Rossion, B. (2004). Do perceptual deficits always co-occur with associative visual (prosop)agnosia? Evidence from neuropsychological investigations of a single-case study. *Neuropsychologia, 42(5),* 597–612, figure 7. Stimulus images courtesy of Michael J. Tarr, Center for the Neural Basis of Cognition and Department of Psychology, Carnegie Mellon University, http://www.tarrlab.org/; Figure 3.01 © LOU OATES – Fotolia; Figure 3.04 © Alx – Fotolia; Figure 3.06 © János Németh – Fotolia; Figure 3.10 © Monkey Business – Fotolia; Figure 3.11 © Lane Erickson – Fotolia; Figure 3.12 © Monkey Business – Fotolia; Figure 4.01 © EMPICS Sport/PA Photos; Figure 4.02 With kind permission by Prof. Albert Bandura, Stanford University; Figure 4.04 © Alan Heath/Rex Features; Figure 4.05 © Thomas Perkins – Fotolia; Figure 4.06 © Pattie Steib – Fotolia; Figure 4.07 © PA Archive/Press Association Images; Figure 4.08 © Yaroslav Pavlov – Fotolia; Figure 4.09 © Paul Prescott – Fotolia; Figure 5.01 © PA Archive/Press Association Images; Figure 5.02 © Aimee – Fotolia; Figure 5.03 © Food and Drink/SuperStock; Figure 5.09 © Dreef – Fotolia; Figure 5.12 © Ionescu Bogdan - Fotolia ; Figure 6.01 © Lehtikuva OY/Rex Features; Figure 6.05 © Reuters/CORBIS; Figure 6.06 © Andres Rodriguez – Fotolia; Figure 6.07 © iofoto – Fotolia; Figure 6.08 © austinadams – Fotolia; Figure 6.11 © Alexander Raths – Fotolia; Figure 6.12 © LazyTown Entertainment; Figure 6.13 © AVAVA – Fotolia; Figure 7.01 © Image Source/SuperStock; Figure 7.07 © Suchi Psarakos/Earthtrust; Figure 7.08 © Chris Fourie – Fotolia; Figure 7.11 © Kay Holekamp; Figure 7.12 © deanm1974 – Fotolia; Figure 8.01 © razmarinka – Fotolia; Figure 8.04 © Rohit Seth – Fotolia; Figure 8.05 © matka_Wariatka – Fotolia; Figure 8.08 From: Perspective taking in children and adults: Equivalent egocentrism but differential correction (N. Epley et al./Journal of Experimental Social Psychology 40 (2004) 760–768). Photo with kind permission by Nicholas Epley; Figure 8.09 © gemenacom – Fotolia; Figure 9.01 and 9.02 © Terence James Charnley and SANE; Figure 9.03 © greg0637 – Fotolia; Figure 9.06 © ZTS - Fotolia ; Figure 9.07 © Zénoïd – Fotolia; Figure 9.09 © Najlah Feanny/Corbis; Figure 9.10 © Alexey Petrunin – Fotolia; Figure 9.12 © 2009 Tony Overman/The Olympian/MCT; Figure 9.13 © Roger Bamber/Alamy ; Figure 10.01 © Sipa Press/Rex Features; Figure 10.05 The Sims 3 images © 2011 Electronic Arts Inc. All Rights Reserved. Used With Permission; Figure 10.06 © Mikael Damkier – Fotolia; Figure 10.07 © AP/Press Association Images; Figure 10.08 © Richard Villalon – Fotolia; Figure 10.09 © Yuri Arcurs – Fotolia; Figure 11.03 © lala – Fotolia; Figure 11.06 © Sean Gladwell – Fotolia; Figure 11.07 © Andriy Bodnar - Fotolia.com; Figure 11.08 © ivan kmit – Fotolia; Figure 11.10 © AP/Press Association Images; Figure 12.01 © Vladyslav Danilin – Fotolia; Figure 12.03 © Wild Geese – Fotolia; Figure 12.04 © Jason Stitt – Fotolia; Figure 12.06 © DocEver – Fotolia; Figure 12.08 © Nikki Zalewski – Fotolia; Figure 12.09 © Stocksnapper – Fotolia; Figure 12.11 © drx – Fotolia; Figure 13.02 © AndersonRise – Fotolia; Figure 13.03 © Steven Pepple – Fotolia; Figure 13.05 © ITV/Rex Features; Figure 13.06 © Galina Barskaya – Fotolia; Figure 13.11 © vadim yerofeyev – Fotolia; Figure 13.12 © 2004 Donald Miralle/Getty Images.

Every effort has been made to obtain necessary permission with reference to copyright material. The publishers apologise if inadvertently any sources remain unacknowledged and will be glad to make the necessary arrangements at the earliest opportunity.

Orders: please contact Bookpoint Ltd, 130 Milton Park, Abingdon, Oxon OX14 4SB. Telephone: (44) 01235 827720. Fax: (44) 01235 400454. Lines are open from 9.00 - 5.00, Monday to Saturday, with a 24 hour message answering service. You can also order through our website www.hoddereducation.co.uk

If you have any comments to make about this, or any of our other titles, please send them to educationenquiries@hodder.co.uk

British Library Cataloguing in Publication Data
A catalogue record for this title is available from the British Library

ISBN: 978 1 444 12336 4

First Edition 2011
Impression number   10 9 8 7 6 5 4 3
Year   2015, 2014, 2013

Hachette UK's policy is to use papers that are natural, renewable and recyclable products and made from wood grown in sustainable forests. The logging and manufacturing processes are expected to conform to the environmental regulations of the country of origin.

Cover photo © Zenya – Fotolia.com
Illustrations by Barking Dog Art
Typeset by DC Graphic Design Limited, Swanley Village, Kent
Printed in Italy for Hodder Education, An Hachette UK Company, 338 Euston Road, Londo...

Contents

Introduction iv

1 Biological rhythms and sleep 1

2 Perception 42

3 Relationships 79

4 Aggression 121

5 Eating behaviour 159

6 Gender 198

7 Intelligence 235

8 Cognition and development 278

9 Psychopathology 313

10 Media psychology 375

11 The psychology of addictive behaviour 409

12 Anomalistic psychology 446

13 Psychological research and scientific method 480

Index 511

Introduction

This text is aimed specifically at those studying the Psychology A2 AQA(A) specification, though it will also prove useful to any students of psychology.

The book seeks to exist not just as a basic textbook describing the course content as outlined by the AQA specification, but as a learning aid in itself. The book consists of a regular format of features, designed specifically to help you get the most out of your studies and achieve the best possible grade at final examinations.

The book is divided into 13 chapters, which reflect the topics that make up units 3 and 4 of the A2 AQA(A) course. What you will find within these chapters is basic text describing the relevant theories and explanations detailed in the specification, as well as the following regular features. This explanation will enable you to understand and get the most out of them.

In the news
These topical news items illustrate central themes of the issues discussed within each chapter.

Key terms
Concise, clear explanations are provided of significant words and phrases associated with each topic.

Evaluation
This feature tends to occur after a research feature and/or at the conclusion of an explanation/theory. It consists of general evaluative and analytical points useable as AO2/AO3 material in exam answers. This feature is more prominent in this book, as AO2/AO3 marks form the majority of marks awarded in A2 examinations. IDA (issues, debates, approaches) points (see 'IDA' section below) also function as evaluation, and many of the points in the 'Evaluation' feature could easily be transformed into IDA material.

Research in focus
Using examples from the text, this feature focuses on methodological aspects of research studies (how studies are carried out) and asks relevant questions to assist your learning and understanding. Knowledge of research methods is examined directly in the unit 4 paper and can help form evaluative material for answers in all A2 questions. It is often a good idea to reference material in the research methods chapters of this and the AS book in order to get the most out of this feature.

You are the researcher
This is another feature focusing on research methods, but this time from the viewpoint of designing pertinent studies to foster a greater understanding of why and how psychologists conduct research. This helps you to develop the

skills students used to gain through carrying out coursework and is a useful and practical way to learn.

Web support
For those interested and motivated to take their learning further, this feature directs you to websites that provide a goldmine of further information not located in the text. It can be used during or outside of lesson times.

Classic research
As the title suggest, this is a feature focusing on famous psychological studies, taking you through the thinking behind such studies in some detail, as well as the aims, procedure, findings, conclusions and evaluation.

Contemporary research
This is similar in focus and presentation to the Classic research feature, but features cutting-edge research, providing an up-to-date account of the subject and an opportunity for you to include more modern material in your exam answers.

Supplementary learning
Similar to the web support feature, this provides extra learning material to form a useful and relevant source of elaboration for exam answers. This feature is designed for those motivated, interested and capable enough to take their learning further.

Psychology in action
This is an occasional feature focusing on practical applications of psychological research. This is an aspect often overlooked when forming examination answers, and one that helps form a valuable source of AO2 evaluative material.

Strengthen your learning
This feature is found at the end of each element of a topic and is designed to get you to focus on and appraise the material that has gone before. In essence, it is a form of comprehension exercise, for you to use as a means of revision before attempting the exam-based assessment questions that follow this feature.

Assessment check
This feature accompanies and complements the 'Strengthen your learning' feature. These are genuine exam-type questions, covering just about every type of exam question that you can expect to be confronted with in your A2 units 3 and 4 papers. The feature also includes helpful examination guidance, highlighting what is required in an answer, as well as pointing out pitfalls to avoid.

Summing up
This feature concludes each chapter and consists of a review of the main points covered in bullet-point form.

Issues, debates and approaches

This feature is found at the end of each sub-topic of the unit 3 chapters. It details possible material to include in examination questions to cover the requirement to include pertinent information on issues, debates and approaches. Many of the points in the 'Evaluation' feature could easily be transformed into IDA points.

Examination skills

The A2 AQA(A) examination assesses three examination skills: assessment objective one (AO1), assessment objective two (AO2) and assessment objective three (AO3).

AO1 basically assesses your level of knowledge and understanding, and generally does this by asking you to *outline* and *describe* relevant theories/explanations and research studies.

AO2/AO3, on the other hand, assesses your ability to *analyse* and *evaluate* such material – in other words, consider its meaning and worth. This could be achieved through a consideration of what research findings suggest, support/ lack of support from other research sources, methodological criticisms, relevant ethical points, and practical applications and implications of research.

You do not need to immerse yourself too much in understanding the differences between AO2 and AO3, as these marks are assessed collectively. However, AO2 is more to do with analysis and evaluation, while AO3 concerns methodological and ethical issues.

In the unit 3 examination, in which you answer questions from three topics (covered in Chapters 1–8), there is also a requirement to include material on issues, debates and approaches. Marks for this criterion are also covered within the AO2/AO3 mark allocation.

Authors

Jean-Marc Lawton is a senior examiner at AS and A2 for a major awarding body, and has been teaching psychology for over 20 years. He has written several revision and unit guides and makes regular contributions to *Psychology Review*.

Richard Gross is the leading author in Psychology publishing in the UK. His bestselling titles include *Psychology: The Science of Mind and Behaviour*.

Geoff Rolls is Head of Psychology at Peter Symonds College, one of the biggest AQA centres for Psychology. He is also author of *Classic Cases in Psychology*.

Acknowledgements

Jean-Marc Lawton would like to thank Tamara Evgenia Shelepina for her critical astuteness, high-maintenance tendencies and mushroom curries.

Also Ruben at Hodder, Ellie of Tadcaster, Princess Gilgo and the Hills of Rois an Iar.

1 Biological rhythms and sleep

Biological rhythms	**2**
Circadian rhythms	3
Infradian rhythms	5
Ultradian rhythms	6
Endogenous pacemakers	8
Exogenous *zeitgebers*	9
Disruption of biological rhythms	10
Sleep states	**13**
The nature of sleep	13
Lifespan changes in sleep	14
Functions of sleep	18
Sleep disorders	**24**
Explanations for sleep disorders	24
Insomnia	24
Factors influencing insomnia	28
Summing up	**41**

Decoding the specification

The specification outlines what you must study to answer any examination question you might face. Therefore circadian, infradian and ultradian biological rhythms, including the role endogenous pacemakers and exogenous zeitgebers in the control of circadian rhythms, are necessary requirements.

A second requirement is to have an understanding of the disruption of biological rhythms, so you can describe and evaluate them. Shift work and jet lag are given as examples, so wouldn't be named explicitly in examination questions. Any other relevant material would be equally acceptable.

To understand the nature of sleep, you will need knowledge of the stages of sleep and lifespan changes in sleep. There is also an explicit requirement to study the functions of sleep via the restoration and evolutionary sleep theories.

Under sleep disorders, insomnia, sleepwalking and narcolepsy are specifically named, so could form the focus of examination questions. You should be able to describe and evaluate these.

Although these are the basic requirements, other relevant material is featured to further your understanding and help maximise your examination performance.

Biological rhythms

Biological rhythms are cyclical behaviours – that is, behaviours repeated periodically. These are controlled either by *endogenous pacemakers* (internal biological clocks regulating biological functioning) or by *exogenous zeitgebers* (external /environmental cues, like seasonal changes).

IN THE NEWS

Sexual behaviour during sleep: convenient alibi or parasomnia

Jan Luedecke, a 30-year-old landscaper, got drunk during a party in 2003 in Toronto and fell asleep on a couch. Some time later he approached a woman sleeping on an adjacent couch, put on a condom and began having sex with her.

At his trial in 2005 he was acquitted of sexual assault after a University of Toronto psychiatry professor testified that Luedecke was experiencing 'sexsomnia' and was in a dissociative state when the incident occurred.

In February 2008 a Canadian provincial appellate court upheld Luedecke's acquittal. The court did not rule on the prosecutor's claim that if sexual behaviour during sleep is a mental disorder, Luedecke should be declared mentally ill and be required to appear before a mental health review board.

Figure 1.01

This is an example of an increasing number of reported cases of sexsomnia, sexual behaviour during sleep (SBS). The condition often goes unreported and untreated due to embarrassment; many experience SBS for 10 to 15 years before seeking help. SBS not only disrupts sleep, but damages relationships and can lead to allegations of sexual assault.

Reproduced with permission from 'Sexual behaviour during sleep: Convenient alibi or parasomnia', *Current Psychology*. Vol. 7, No. 7, 2008, published by Dowden Health Media.

If you would like to learn more about sexsomnia, go to www. currentpsychiatry. com/pdf/0707/ 0707CP_Article1. pdf where you will find a discussion of the condition, including examples, explanations and research.

Key terms

Circadian rhythms – bodily cycles occurring every 24 hours
Infradian rhythms – bodily cycles occurring less than once a day
Ultradian rhythms – bodily cycles occurring more than once a day
Endogenous pacemakers – internal body clocks regulating biological rhythms
Exogenous *zeitgebers* – external stimuli involved in the control of biological rhythms
Biological rhythms – regular patterns of physiological, cognitive and behavioural activity occurring as circadian, ultradian and infradian rhythms
Shift work – periods of work performed outside regular employment hours
Jet lag – temporary disruption of biological rhythms caused by high-speed travel across time zones

Circadian rhythms

Circadian rhythms are biological cycles lasting around 24 hours, like the *sleep/wake cycle*, which is usually facilitated by time-checks and regular events like mealtimes. There is a free running cycle controlled by an endogenous pacemaker working as a body clock. Another circadian rhythm is *body temperature*, rising and declining as an indicator of metabolic rate, 4 a.m. being the lowest point.

Research: circadian rhythms

- Aschoff and Weber (1962) placed participants in a bunker with no natural light. They settled into a sleep/wake cycle of between 25 and 27 hours, suggesting that endogenous pacemakers control the sleep/wake cycle in the absence of light cues and that light seems necessary to coordinate the biological clock with the external environment.

- Siffre (1975) spent 6 months in a cave with no time cues. Artificial lights came on when he was awake. He settled into a sleep/wake cycle of 25 to 30 hours. After 179 days he thought 151 had passed, supporting Aschoff and Weber's findings that endogenous pacemakers exert an influence on circadian rhythms, though the use of artificial light may have been a confounding variable.

- Folkard *et al.* (1985) isolated 12 participants from natural light for 3 weeks, manipulating the clock so that only 22 hours passed a day. Of the 12 participants, 11 kept pace with the clock, showing the strength of the circadian rhythm as a free-running cycle.

Research in focus

Research into circadian rhythms often uses isolation studies, like those conducted in caves. Why might the data from such studies not be generalisable? What ethical issues are illustrated by such studies and how are they addressed?

Evaluation

Circadian rhythms

- Individual differences exist in sleep/wake cycles. Duffy *et al.* (2000) found that early risers prefer 6 a.m. to 10 p.m., and later risers prefer 10 a.m. to 1 a.m. Aschoff and Weber (1976) found in isolation studies that some participants maintain normal cycles, while others strongly differ.

- Isolation studies have few participants, making generalisation problematic.

- Research suggests that endogenous pacemakers do exist and are regulated by exogenous *zeitgebers*.

- It seems unlikely that humans have evolved with a faulty biological clock running every 25 hours. Animal studies show a 24-hour cycle and it makes more sense for humans to follow this pattern.

- Isolating participants from the environment without controlling their behaviour may be insufficient to reveal the activity of the endogenous circadian pacemaker. Czeisler *et al.* (1999) suggest that participants in earlier sleep/wake cycle studies were inadvertently affected by exposure to high levels of artificial light, skewing the results. Allowing participants to switch on bright lights allowed them to reset their internal clocks. Czeisler *et al.* claim the cycle is actually 24 hours. In their 1999 study, 24 men and women lived for a month in subdued light, with no clues to the passage of time. The participants were placed on an artificial 28-hour sleep/wake cycle, with biochemistry and temperature monitored to mark the action of the body clock. The measurements showed that the human sleep clock operates on a schedule of 24 hours 11 minutes, not 25 hours.

Classic research

Menstrual synchrony studies

Although the menstrual cycle was identified years ago, how it is generated and how it interacts with other factors is not fully understood. There is no doubt it is affected by circadian rhythms, as the secretion of luteinising hormone, which starts ovulation, occurs in the early morning hours. In addition, phase shifts occurring due to jet lag also affect menstrual cycles.

Figure 1.02 Underarm sweat was applied to females' lips to synchronise periods

Aim/hypothesis

McClintock identified the synchronisation of female menstruation when she observed that the menstrual cycles among her dormitory mates became synchronised. After further research, she concluded that the synchronisation of the menstrual cycles among 135 female friends and dormitory mates aged 17–22 was caused by pheromones transmitted through social interaction. Pheromones are odourless chemical substances that, when secreted by an individual into the environment, cause specific reactions in other individuals, suggesting that there might be a female pheromone affecting the timing of other females' menstrual cycles.

Procedure

The research entailed a 10-year longitudinal study involving 29 women aged 20 to 35 years, with a history of irregular, spontaneous ovulation. The researchers gathered samples of pheromones from nine women at certain points in their menstrual cycles by placing pads of cotton under their arms. The women had previously bathed without perfumed products and wore the cotton pads for at least 8 hours. Each cotton pad was treated with alcohol to disguise odours and was frozen. These pads were wiped under the noses of the 20 other women on a daily basis.

Findings

Of the women involved in the research, 68 per cent responded to the pheromones. Menstrual cycles either shortened from 1 to 14 days or lengthened from 1 to 12 days, depending on when pheromones were collected. Pheromones from women in the early phases of their cycles shortened the cycles of the second group of women (between 1 and 14 days) by speeding up their pre-ovulatory surge of luteinising hormone. Conversely, pheromones collected later, during ovulation, lengthened the menstrual cycles (by 1 to 12 days) by delaying the luteinising hormone surge.

Conclusions

It is unclear how pheromones trigger menstrual cycle changes. Because the samples were put on participants' top lips, McClintock admits 'we know absolutely nothing about where the chemical formula is acting, whether it's through the skin, the mucus membranes in the nose, or a pair of tiny pits in the nose'.

Evaluation

- The results found by McClintock concerning synchronisation of menstrual periods can be explained as random occurrences and do not form a significant difference statistically. Also, women's cycles are not universal, which may invalidate findings. What is needed is evidence that women with different cycle lengths show synchronisation.

- A study examining a women's basketball team for an extended period found no correlation between menstrual patterns. However, exercise, dieting and stress can cause changes in women's menstrual patterns and these may have affected synchronisation effects.

- McClintock and Stern's findings have research support (see 'Research: infradian rhythms' opposite).

Infradian rhythms

Infradian rhythms are biological cycles lasting more than 24 hours, like the menstrual cycle, regulated by hormone secretions. Originally thought to be controlled by the hypothalamus acting as an endogenous pacemaker, evidence shows that exogenous *zeitgebers* play a part too. Infradian rhythms include *circannual rhythms* occurring once a year, like hibernation.

Research: infradian rhythms

- Russell *et al.* (1980) applied underarm sweat of donor women to the upper lips of female participants, finding that menstrual cycles became synchronised, supporting McClintock and Stern's findings, suggesting that pheromones act as exogenous *zeitgebers*.

- Reinberg (1967) reported on a woman who spent 3 months in a cave without natural lighting. Her menstrual cycle shortened to 25.7 days, implying that infradian rhythms are influenced by exogenous *zeitgebers* like light.

- Rosenzweig *et al.* (1999) reported on seasonal affective disorder (SAD) (see 'Supplementary research: SAD' on page 6), whereby winter darkness brings about low moods for some. It has been associated with darkness stimulating the production of melatonin, a hormone linked with the regulation of sleep, stressing the importance of light as an exogenous *zeitgeber*.

Research in focus

Research indicates that women living in close proximity develop synchronised periods. However, there are several methodological failings that raise doubts about such findings. What are these methodological failings and how could they be addressed?

Evaluation

Infradian rhythms

- The effects of pheromones on women's menstrual cycles can explain why women living together, like nuns, nurses, and so on, tend to have synchronised periods. Turke (1984) believes that there is an evolutionary significance, allowing women living together to synchronise pregnancies and share child-caring duties.

- Women working in close proximity to men often have shorter cycles, possibly as a response to male pheromones bestowing an evolutionary advantage in giving more opportunities to get pregnant.

- Research into SAD led to the development of successful light therapies to treat the condition.

- The evidence for pheromonal effects in rats is strong and actual pheromones have been extracted and analysed. However, generalising from animals to humans is controversial, as animal behaviour is not always reflective of human behaviour.

You are the researcher

Design a study to test the idea that women working in close proximity to men have shorter menstrual cycles.

For some, this would be a sensitive area to study. How could you gain relevant data without causing distress and embarrassment?

Figure 1.03 Women living together tend to have synchronised periods

Supplementary learning

SAD

Seasonal affective disorder (SAD) is a disorder in which sufferers show seasonal changes of mood and/ or behaviour, most commonly depression, guilt, low self-esteem, lethargy and sleep problems.

The most common explanation is that lack of light during the night causes the pineal gland to secrete melatonin. The increase of light at dawn tells the gland to switch off this secretion to initiate waking. In winter, some people do not experience enough light and imbalances in melatonin cause irregularities with other chemicals, leading to depression. Lewy *et al*. (1980) found that exposure to bright light suppresses night-time melatonin production, supporting the idea that melatonin production is linked to SAD. Support comes from Eastman *et al*. (1998) and Winton *et al*. (1989), both finding that morning bright light therapy is effective in treating SAD.

As SAD occurs mainly during the winter, it appears to be a disorder involving circannual rhythms, which are a subset of infradian rhythms. However, it is argued that SAD occurs because of disruption of the body's sleep/wake cycle, which is, of course, a circadian rhythm. Therefore, SAD could be used in an answer to questions about either infradian or circadian rhythms.

Genetic vulnerability and stress are also involved in causing SAD. The exact cause of SAD remains elusive and unconfirmed.

Ultradian rhythms

Ultradian rhythms are biological cycles lasting less than 24 hours, like the cycle of brain activity during sleep. Sleep has several stages occurring through the night, lasting for about an hour in infancy to 90 minutes by adolescence.

Sleep is a different state of consciousness, where responsiveness to the external environment is diminished. It occurs daily as a circadian rhythm and is composed of an ultradian cycle of separate stages. With the invention of the electroencephalograph, psychologists could investigate brain activity occurring during sleep, concluding that it was composed of identifiably different sequential stages.

- **Stage one** – alpha waves disappear and are replaced by low-voltage slow waves. Heart rate declines and muscles relax. This is a light sleep and people are easily woken.

- **Stage two** – a deeper state, from which people are still easily woken. Shorts bursts of sleep spindles are noticeable, as well as sharp rises and falls in amplitude known as K-complexes. Bodily functions slow down and blood pressure, metabolism and cardiac activity decrease.

- **Stage three** – sleep becomes increasingly deeper and people are difficult to wake. Sleep spindles decline, being replaced by long, slow delta waves. Heart rate, blood pressure and temperature decline.

- **Stage four** – deep sleep, where delta waves increase and metabolic rate is low. People are difficult to wake. Growth hormones are released and incidences of sleepwalking and night terrors may occur.

The sleeper spends about 40 minutes in stage four sleep, about an hour passing in total from stage one to stage four. Stage three is re-entered, then stage two, and then an active stage of sleep called rapid eye movement (REM), about 90 minutes after falling asleep.

After 15 minutes of REM sleep, the sleeper re-enters stages two, three and four in that order, then another cycle begins. It is common to go through about five ultradian cycles in one night. As the night progresses, the sleeper spends more time in REM sleep and less time in other stages. This pattern is fairly universal, though there are developmental differences (see 'Lifespan changes in sleep' on page 14).

Key terms

REM – sleep state where eye movements are noticeable; heart rate, respiration, and so on increases; dreaming occurs

You are the researcher

Design a sleep diary to record the number of hours of sleep participants get each night.

What personal details and types of qualitative comments would be recorded?

How would such qualitative data be analysed?

Why is it necessary to use people of different ages?

What methodological problems could arise with a self-report sleep diary?

Research: ultradian rhythms

- Dement and Kleitman (1957) monitored electrical activity in the brain during sleep using electroencephalogram (EEG) recordings and so could wake participants during the different stages of sleep. Participants reported their feelings, experiences and emotions. People awakened during REM sleep reported dreaming 90 per cent of the time. Dreams were recalled in detail, including elaborate visual images. Only 7 per cent of awakenings from NREM (non-rapid eye movement) sleep led to dream recall. Dement and Kleitman had found the point during the ultradian cycle when people dream.

- Klein and Armitage (1979) tested participants on verbal and spatial tasks, finding that performance was related to a 96-minute cycle, very similar to the sleep cycle.

- Gerkema and Dann (1985) found that ultradian rhythms tend to be correlated with brain and body size, with larger animals having longer cycles.

Evaluation

Ultradian rhythms

- Dement and Kleitman's findings have stood the test of time. However, some studies have found that 70 per cent of participants report dreams during NREM sleep. Foulkes (1967) attributed this to vague, dream-like experiences or muddled thoughts being incorrectly categorised as dreams.

- The artificial surroundings of sleep laboratories, with all the electrodes that have to be worn, suggest that sleep findings may lack ecological validity.

- The development of EEG readings gave psychologists an objective means of studying sleep behaviour.

- Creating lesions to brain areas that control circadian rhythms has no effect on behaviours with an ultradian rhythm, suggesting that circadian and ultradian rhythms have different controlling mechanisms.

- A lot of the research into ultradian rhythms involved animals, creating problems in generalising results to humans.

Endogenous pacemakers

Endogenous pacemakers are rhythms that are not imposed by the environment, but generated from within organisms. As many biological cycles follow a 24-hour rhythm, even in the absence of external stimuli (exogenous *zeitgebers*), there must be an internal biological pacemaker (clock).

The main pacemaker is the superchiasmatic nucleus (SCN), a small group of cells in the hypothalamus generating a circadian rhythm reset by light entering the eyes. A rhythm is produced from the interaction of several proteins producing a biological clock.

Evidence for the SCN being the site of the clock comes from animal experiments.

Research: endogenous pacemakers

- Stephan and Zucker (1971) removed the SCN from rats, finding that the usual rhythmic cycles of activity and sleep were abolished, implying that the SCN is the site of the pacemaker.

- Green and Gillette (1982) found that recording electrodes picked up rhythmic bursts of activity from the SCN that varied according to a 24.5-hour cycle. These rhythms persisted even when the hypothalamus was surgically isolated from the rest of the brain.

- Ralph *et al.* (1990) took the SCN out of genetically abnormal hamsters with a circadian cycle of only 20 hours, transplanting them into rats with the usual 24-hour cycle. Their cycle shortened to 20 hours, suggesting that the SCN is the main endogenous pacemaker.

- Morgan (1995) found that removing the SCN from hamsters caused their circadian rhythm to disappear, but when SCN cells were transplanted in, the rhythm returned, again showing the central role of the SCN as an endogenous pacemaker.

- Hawkins and Armstrong-Esther (1978) found that shift work altered nurses' sleep/wake cycles, but not their temperature cycles, suggesting that different body clocks regulate different circadian rhythms.

Evaluation

Endogenous pacemakers

- Yamazaki *et al.* (2000) found that circadian rhythms persist in isolated lungs, livers and other tissues grown in culture dishes not under the control of the SCN. This suggests that most cells and tissues of the body are capable of activity on a circadian basis.

- It is still recognised that the SCN has the key role as the major circadian pacemaker, but it may coordinate this in collaboration with the cells, tissues and whole organism. Although the SCN sends neural signals as well as neurohormonal signals through the blood to other organs, the specific way in which the SCN 'communicates' to the rest of the body remains unknown.

- The amount of REM sleep people experience as a percentage of total sleep decreases with age, suggesting that age is an endogenous factor affecting the ultradian rhythm of sleep.

- Most research on endogenous pacemakers took place on non-human animals or brain-damaged patients. Such evidence is strong, but is not easily generalised to the wider population.

Exogenous *zeitgebers*

Zeitgebers are external time cues that play an important role in regulating biological rhythms, helping to synchronise and reset them. Endogenous pacemakers need to respond to *zeitgebers*, coordinating the behaviours they regulate with the external environment.

Sunlight is the most important *zeitgeber*. Others include the moon, the seasons, weather patterns and food availability.

If a shift in external cues occurs − for example, after travelling across time zones − the rhythms become aligned to the new cues, a process known as entrainment.

Figure 1.04 The sun and moon are important exogenous *zeitgebers*

Research: exogenous *zeitgebers*

- Campbell and Murphy (1998) monitored the body temperatures of 15 volunteers who slept in a laboratory. They were woken at different times and a light pad shone on the back of their knees. Circadian rhythms fluctuated by as much as 3 hours from their normal cycle, depending on the time the light was shone. The back of the knee was chosen because light applied here would not reach participants' eyes. The results suggest that humans do not rely solely on light entering the eyes, and that blood may be the messenger carrying light signals from the skin to the brain.

- Klein *et al.* (1993) studied a blind man with a circadian rhythm of 24.5 hours, which eventually got out of sync with the 24-hour day. Time cues like clocks did not help and he had to take stimulants and sedatives to regulate his sleep/wake cycle, suggesting that light acts as an exogenous *zeitgeber* in the form of a time cue.

- Luce and Segal (1966) found contradictory results, as people in the Arctic Circle sleep for 7 hours even though it is light all summer long, implying that social cues act as *zeitgebers* here.

Research in focus

The development of measuring tools like EEG and the establishment of sleep laboratories led to a surge in sleep research.

Compile a list of the advantages and disadvantages of conducting research in sleep laboratories.

Aside from sleep laboratories, what other methods are employed to study sleep and what are the strengths and weaknesses of these?

Evaluation

Exogenous *zeitgebers*

- The persistence of rhythms in the absence of a dark/light cycle or other exogenous time signal − that is, a *zeitgeber* − seems to indicate the existence of an internal timekeeping mechanism, or biological clock.

- There is an adaptive advantage in animals having endogenous pacemakers reset by exogenous *zeitgebers*, keeping them in tune with seasonal changes, day/night changes, and so on.

- To rely solely on exogenous *zeitgebers* could threaten survival; therefore internal cues are important too.

- The effect of light on SAD (see page 6) and the role of pheromones in the synchronisation of the menstrual cycle (see pages 4–5) can be interpreted as effects of exogenous *zeitgebers*.

Go to www.bbc.co.uk/science/humanbody/sleep/ for a range of sleep-related activities, including:
- Testing your daily rhythm
- A sleep quiz
- Why do we sleep?

Issues, debates and approaches

- Animal studies, like Stephan and Zucker (1971), are controversial from an ethical point of view, but some justify them in terms of *cost-benefit analysis* – that is, the knowledge gained about endogenous pacemakers outweighs the harm caused.
- Research into circadian rhythms suggests practical applications, like designing timetables around the optimal times to study/work, or when best to take medicines.

Disruption of biological rhythms

Usually, exogenous *zeitgebers* change gradually, allowing time to adjust. However, rapid change disrupts coordination between internally regulated rhythms and external exogenous *zeitgebers*, creating consequences for the ability to function properly.

The synchrony of an organism with both endogenous pacemakers and exogenous *zeitgebers* is critical to well-being and survival; without this, animals may venture into dangerous situations. For example, if nocturnal rodents stray from their burrows during daylight, they are easy prey. In humans, a lack of synchrony within the environment might lead to health problems, such as those associated with jet lag, shift work and the accompanying sleep loss – for example, impaired cognitive function, altered hormonal function and gastrointestinal complaints.

Jet lag

Jet lag is caused by travelling across time zones so quickly that biological rhythms do not match external cues, causing sleepiness during the day and restlessness at night. This lasts until resynchronisation has occurred; best achieved by being allowed to follow exogenous *zeitgebers* – for example, stay awake until night-time. Jet lag is worse travelling west to east, as it is easier to adjust biological clocks if they are ahead of local time (*phase delay*) than behind (*phase advance*). Another reason for jet lag is that the biological clock regulating temperature needs time to reset, causing desynchronised rhythms in the meantime.

Figure 1.05 Jet lag comes from crossing time zones too quickly to adjust

Research: jet lag

- Klein *et al.* (1972) tested eight participants flying between the USA and Germany, and found that adjustment to jet lag was easier for people on westbound flights than eastbound, regardless of whether they were on an outbound or homebound flight, supporting the notion that phase advance has more severe consequences.

- Schwartz *et al.* (1995) found that baseball sides from the eastern USA play better against teams in the west than western sides did playing against teams in the east, suggesting that phase advance has more severe consequences. However, it may be that eastern teams are superior.

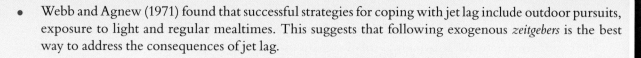
- Webb and Agnew (1971) found that successful strategies for coping with jet lag include outdoor pursuits, exposure to light and regular mealtimes. This suggests that following exogenous *zeitgebers* is the best way to address the consequences of jet lag.

Shift work

Shift work can involve working at times when people are normally asleep, and therefore being asleep at times when people are normally awake, causing breakdowns in the usual coordination between internal biological clocks and external cues. Many shift workers change working hours every week, causing disruption to normal routines of eating, resting, and so on. Workers can be in an almost permanent state of desynchronisation, impairing concentration, physical performance and increasing stress levels that incur long-term health risks. Research shows that shift-work patterns involving phase delay cause less disruption, as does having an adjustment time before changing shifts.

Of employees in industrialised countries, 20 per cent work shifts, requiring drastic change to sleep/wake cycles. Shift workers do not get enough sleep and night shifts affect the body's natural wake/sleep pattern, making it difficult to stay awake at night and difficult to sleep during the day.

Figure 1.06 The Chernobyl nuclear power plant meltdown occurred because of decisions made when lacking enough sleep

The list of accidents blamed on incorrect decisions resulting from lack of sleep is worrying. These include the Three Mile Island and Chernobyl nuclear accidents, the *Challenger* space disaster and the Exxon Valdez oil spill. In addition, workers on night shifts have higher rates of heart disease and diseases of the digestive system. Approximately 20 per cent of shift workers report falling asleep during work, increasing the risk of accidents and decreasing productivity, meaning that shift work diminishes the economic gain it was designed to create.

There are two types of shift work:

- **Non-fluctuating** – where employees work unconventional but constant shifts, like 11 p.m. to 7 a.m.

- **Fluctuating** – where employees work continually changing 8-hour shifts. Three different rotating 8-hour shifts enable a round-the-clock operation to occur, the most common ones being 7 a.m. to 3 p.m., 3 p.m. to 11 p.m. and 11 p.m. to 7 a.m.

These types of shift work produce different effects. In non-fluctuating shift work, the shift in circadian rhythm remains constant once the body adapts to it. Resynchronisation may take a while, but is possible. Fluctuating shifts intensify the severity of circadian rhythm disturbance.

Research: shift work

- Czeisler *et al.* (1982) studied shift workers at a factory in Utah. They found high illness rates, sleep disorders and elevated levels of stress, suggesting that the workers' internal body clocks were out of synchronisation with exogenous *zeitgebers*. The researchers persuaded management to move to a phase-delay system of rotating shifts forward in time, to reduce negative effects. Shift rotations were adjusted to every 21, instead of 7 days, giving time for adjustment. Nine months later, workers appeared healthier, more content and output was up, showing how psychological research can lead to practical applications incurring positive outcomes.

- Hawkins and Armstrong-Esther (1978) studied nurses working night shifts, finding that their performance improved over a week, showing that the circadian rhythm adjusts gradually. However, their body temperature regulation was still desynchronised, suggesting that the temperature body clock takes longer to adjust.

- Monk and Falkard (1983) studied two types of shift: *rapidly rotating*, where shifts rotate quickly, and *slowly rotating*, where shifts rotate over a longer time period. Negative consequences were significantly more noticeable with rapidly rotating shifts, suggesting that they are more disruptive as they do not allow time for biological adjustments.

- Colligan *et al.* (1978) found that workers with shift rotations had more accidents than workers on set shifts. They also drank more alcohol, took more sleeping tablets, had digestive disorders, colds, anxiety, tiredness and less successful social relationships, demonstrating the destructive consequences of disrupting biological rhythms.

Evaluation

Disruption of biological rhythms

- The endogenous cycle is roughly 25 hours, thus it is easier to deal with phase delay than phase advance.
- Research suggests that disrupting biological rhythms affects cognitive and emotional functioning as well as physical functioning, demonstrating the severity of consequences.
- There are large individual differences in the ways people are affected by shift work and jet lag.
- A lot of research utilises naturalistic field studies. These are high in ecological validity, but incur many confounding variables, making the establishment of causality problematic.
- Serious incidents, like the Three Mile Nuclear Plant accident of 1979 and the Chernobyl reactor meltdown of 1986, occurred due to concentration and decision failures in the early hours of the morning, suggesting that the desynchronisation effects of working at irregular hours impairs performance with potentially disastrous consequences.
- The fact that concentration levels are affected by jet lag and shift work supports the idea that these things create disruption to cognitive processes.
- The introduction of modern travel systems and electrical lighting has created a world that evolutionarily determined biology cannot cope with, leading to disruption and negative consequences.
- Research helping to understand the disruption of biological rhythms may have practical applications, like melatonin supplements to address jet lag. Sharkey (2001) reported on the beneficial effects of melatonin in reducing the time required to adjust to shift-work patterns and rotations.

Issues, debates and approaches

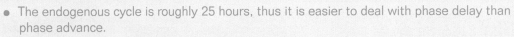

- Much research on shift work only involved male participants, as males tend to be more involved in such work. As such, this research can be seen as gender-biased, with the results not necessarily being representative of females.
- Practical applications of research into disrupting biological rhythms include the phase-delay system of rotating shifts forward to reduce negative effects and thus improve output, and melatonin supplements and strategies to combat jet lag – for example, regular mealtimes.

Strengthen your learning

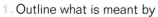

1. Outline what is meant by
   i) circadian, infradian and ultradian rhythms
   ii) endogenous pacemakers and exogenous *zeitgebers*.
2. Use research studies to outline and evaluate one circadian, one infradian and one ultradian rhythm. What other evaluative points can you find for each of these biological rhythms?
3. What have research studies taught us about
   i) endogenous pacemakers?
   ii) exogenous *zeitgebers*?
4. Outline the effects that
   i. jet lag
   ii) shift work
   iii) can have on biological rhythms.
5. Compile an evaluation, in about 300 words, concerning the disruption of biological rhythms, including references to research concerning both jet lag and shift work.

Assessment Check

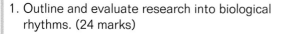

1. Outline and evaluate research into biological rhythms. (24 marks)

2. Discuss the role of endogenous pacemakers and exogenous *zeitgebers* in the control of circadian rhythms. (24 marks)

3. Outline one example of an infradian rhythm. (4 marks)

4. Outline and evaluate the disruption of biological rhythms. (20 marks)

Examination guidance

In question 1, 8 marks would be available for an outline and 16 marks for an evaluation, so the outline should not be overdone at the expense of the evaluation.

With question 2, if only the role of endogenous pacemakers or exogenous zeitgebers was included, this would be adjudged partial performance and access denied to the full range of marks available.

If more than one example was offered in question 3, all would be marked, but only the best one credited.

Only 4 marks would be available for the outline in 4, so the majority of effort should be directed at constructing the evaluation.

Sleep states

The nature of sleep

Sleep is a different state of consciousness where responsiveness to the external environment is diminished. Sleep occurs daily as a circadian rhythm and is composed of an ultradian cycle of separate stages. With the invention of the electroencephalograph psychologists were able to investigate brain activity occurring during sleep, concluding that it was composed of identifiably different sequential stages.

The stages of sleep were described as an example of an ultradian rhythm on page 6, and that material could also be used to answer questions on the nature of sleep, as could the material on page 14 concerning lifespan changes in sleep, as lifespan changes relate to the nature of sleep at different ages. Any answer to a question on the nature of sleep should ensure that the material used is shaped explicitly to the question in order to gain credit.

The physiology of sleep

The brainstem has a role in key functions, like alertness and arousal, but also controls sleep behaviour, with several hormones involved too.

The SCN reacts to different levels of light received by the eyes, stimulating the production of *melatonin* from the pineal gland, which then stimulates the release of *serotonin* in the reticular activating system (RAS). The increase in serotonin levels causes RAS activity to lessen, bringing on the onset of sleep.

The release of *noradrenaline* causes the onset of REM sleep.

Another hormone, *acetylcholine*, is involved with brain activation during wakefulness and REM sleep, sometimes referred to as wakeful sleep.

As sleep has five stages, it is likely that each stage has a different function. Because REM sleep is identifiable in warm-blooded creatures, but not cold-blooded ones, it might be that REM sleep serves the function, by increasing brain metabolism, of keeping brain temperature at a safe level.

Issues, debates and approaches

- Much research into the nature of sleep can be seen as reductionist, such as dividing sleep into separate stages on the basis of EEG readings.
- Descriptions of the nature of sleep can be argued to be deterministic, seeing sleep as a behaviour over which humans have little, if any, control.

Key terms

Sleep – a natural and periodic state of rest during which responsiveness to the external environment is diminished

Evolutionary explanations – theories perceiving sleep as serving an adaptive purpose related to survival

Restoration theory – an explanation of sleep that sees it as a period of rejuvenation and repair

Lifespan changes – alterations in sleep patterns developing over the course of a lifetime

Lifespan changes in sleep

Lifespan changes are a crucial determinant of the amount of sleep people need. Sleep needs vary by age, both qualitatively, in terms of the different stages of sleep, and quantitatively, in terms of how much sleep is needed.

Neonates

Neonates sleep for about 16 hours a day over several sleep periods. After birth, infants display active sleep, an immature form of REM, which gradually decreases, while the amount of quiet sleep, an immature form of slow-wave sleep (SWS), increases.

An infant in REM sleep is often quite restless, with its arms and legs and the muscles of the face moving almost constantly. This is also truth of foetuses, which is why mothers-to-be feel their babies kicking.

Neonates have a different sequence of sleep to adults. Newborn babies often enter REM sleep immediately and it is not until they are 3 months old that the sequence of REM/NREM sleep is established. Over these first few months, the proportion of REM sleep decreases rapidly. A regular pattern of sleeping and waking is rarely established in newborns, but by 20 weeks infants are mainly awake between 10 a.m. and 8 p.m.

One-year-olds

One-year-olds increasingly develop brain activity sleep patterns like those of adults. The proportion of REM sleep declines to about 50 per cent of sleep duration and sleep periods become longer and fewer. Total sleep is about 13 hours a day, with the entire sleep stage cycle occurring every 45 to 60 minutes. Toddlers usually take only one daytime nap at this time.

Five-year-olds

Brain activity during sleep resembles that of adults, though the frequency is different, with REM sleep making up about a third of the total, about 10 hours daily, with boys sleeping slightly longer. Sleep disorders, such as sleepwalking, may be apparent.

Prepubescents

Between the ages of 5 and 12 years, total nocturnal sleep drops to about 9 to 10 hours. Children of this age sleep deeply, particularly in the first half of the night, indicating that thalamocortical brain systems are maturing. REM sleep drops to about 25 per cent of a night's sleep. The increase in NREM sleep drive is also associated with brain maturation and increases in activities like exercise. Pre-teens experience sleep–wake utopia, where during the day they are bursting with energy, and at night they sleep soundly and are wide awake and fully rested from the moment they awake in the morning.

Adolescents

Puberty marks the onset of adolescence, and sexual and pituitary growth hormones are released in pulses during SWS. Melatonin is the hormone determining the biological clock in all cells in the body, but a decrease in melatonin signals to the body to begin puberty. Although sleep quantity or quality does not change much, external pressures on teenagers, like schoolwork, may lead to a less regular sleep cycle. Males may experience wet dreams and both sexes may experience erotic dreams.

Adolescents have less REM sleep than children, and total sleep duration is now about 8 to 9 hours a night.

Young adults (18–30 years)

Young adults sleep less than during adolescence and do not experience such deep sleep. This is not particularly marked and most people would not notice any changes. However, 53 per cent of 18- to 29-year-olds suffer from daytime sleepiness, possibly because external factors, like crying babies, prevent them from getting enough sleep.

Middle age (30–45 years)

A shallowing and shortening of sleep may occur. Increasing signs of fatigue are indicative of middle age. There is a decrease in the amount of deep stage 4 sleep, and it may be harder to stay awake and feel refreshed on waking. Certain factors can contribute to this, like a more sedate lifestyle, consuming more caffeine and alcohol and putting on weight. Weight issues can lead to respiratory problems, including snoring, which can affect sleep.

Late middle age (45–60 years)

Women suffer a loss of hormones due to the menopause, as do men, less noticeably, through the andropause, therefore people of this age go to bed earlier, suffer more from the effects of sleep deprivation and experience a poorer quality of sleep. Sleep duration drops to about 7 hours and stage 4 sleep is minimal. There is a corresponding increase in lighter stages of sleep such as stage 1. The percentage of REM sleep remains fairly constant. Age-related effects on the prostate gland ensure that many men have to get up in the night to urinate, thus affecting the quality of sleep.

Senescence

Sleep at this age is characterised by frequent interruptions and periods of wakefulness. Many have some form of sleep apnoea (see 'Explanations for insomnia' on page 24). Stage 3 and stage 4 sleep are much reduced, possibly because of a reduced need for growth hormones. Elderly people may rise earlier because their circadian dip is not as pronounced as that of younger people, and they require an hour or two less sleep than middle-aged sleepers. REM sleep decreases to around 20 per cent of the total, with stage 2 sleep increasing to about 60 per cent. SWS decreases to around 5 per cent and is non-existent in some cases.

Research: lifespan changes in sleep

- Van Cauter *et al.* (2000) examined several sleep studies involving male participants. Sleep was found to decrease during two life periods: between the ages of 16 to 25 years, and 35 to 50 years.

- Floyd *et al.* (2007) reviewed nearly 400 sleep studies, finding that REM sleep decreased by about 0.6 per cent a decade. The proportion of REM sleep increases from about age 70, though this may be due to overall sleep duration declining.

- Eaton-Evans and Dugdale (1988) found that the number of sleep periods for a baby decreases until about 6 months of age, then increases until 9 months of age, before slowly decreasing again. This may be due to teething problems.

- Dement (1999) reported that over 40 per cent of a group of healthy men and women aged 65 to 88 had some form of sleep apnoea, the majority being frequent 'micro-arousals', which are unremembered brief awakenings lasting 3 seconds or less, which occur between 200 and 1,000 times each night.

- Baird *et al.* (2009) found that infants aged between 6 and 12 months with an increased risk of waking between midnight and 6 a.m. had mothers who had experienced depressive symptoms prior to becoming pregnant. Night waking in the first year of a child's life is associated with sleep disruption at 3 years of age and later behavioural problems and learning difficulties, demonstrating the importance of early sleeping patterns and the mental health of women prior to conception.

- Borbely *et al.* (1981) questioned adults aged 65 to 83 years on their sleeping habits, finding that 60 per cent of them reported taking frequent daily naps. Sleep in the elderly is more interrupted, but they continue to need the same amount of sleep as they did in early adulthood, hence the need for naps.

Evaluation

Lifespan changes in sleep

- Research into lifespan changes in sleep has been conducted in numerous sleep laboratories, using objective measurements. Changes noted in the different stages of sleep involving quantity and quality of sleep were replicated and are well established. This is particularly true with infant sleep patterns, because since the 1970s exhaustive research has been conducted in the hope of discovering the cause of sudden infant death syndrome (SIDS), often called 'cot death'.

Figure 1.07 We spend years co-sleeping, but little research exists on the practice

- There has been little research into normal sleep among the middle-aged. Dement (1999) believes that this is because they are so busy raising families, succeeding at work, and so on, that they find less time to volunteer for sleep research, though their busy lives suggest that they should be studied, as this is the age group in which the greatest number of sleep problems occur.

continued …

...continued

- A major problem with sleep research involves the measurement of sleep. In order to measure the physiology of sleep, participants are connected to a number of electrodes. This can affect the quality and quantity of sleep experienced. It is preferable if participants spend several nights in a sleep laboratory to get used to sleeping with the equipment and wires in place. However, many participants do not have time for this.

- There are numerous external factors affecting the quality and quantity of sleep. Work patterns, children and medication all affect sleep patterns. One under-researched factor is the effect of sleeping with a partner. Many people spend the majority of their sleeping lives sharing a bed with a partner, yet co-sleep effects are under-researched. Co-sleep patterns may be both qualitatively and quantitatively different to sleeping alone.

- The fact that neonates sleep for long periods may be an adaptive response, freeing up essential time for their parents.

- Males over 45 years often have little SWS, which affects hormone production and may explain why physical injuries take longer to heal.

- During senescence the decline of SWS incurs lower levels of growth hormone production, suggesting that SWS is associated with its production.

Issues, debates and approaches

- A practical application of research into lifespan changes of sleep is to issue recommendations to parents on sleep patterns for infants to try to reduce the incidence of SIDS, or 'cot death'.

- Borbely (1986) warns against the use of generalisations about sleep patterns for different age groups. This fits the nomothetic versus idiographic debate – finding laws of behaviour that fit everyone in an age group or focusing on individual behaviour. He reports that studies performed at the University of Florida found consistent findings from the same participant on different nights, but marked differences between different participants of similar ages. This suggests that sleep patterns are determined more by an individual's constitution than the cruder measure of age.

You can view how a sleep study takes place at Stanford University Sleep Disorders Clinic by going to www.talkaboutsleep.com/sleepbasics/viewasleepstudy.htm

Strengthen your learning

1. Outline in bullet point form the stages of and physiology of sleep. Include relevant detail.
2. Outline
   i) quantitative
   ii) qualitative
   changes occurring in sleep patterns throughout life.
3. Compile a list of evaluative points concerning lifespan changes in sleep (this could include relevant material from research studies too).

Functions of sleep

Theories of sleep incorporate biological and psychological factors and humans spend about a third of their time asleep, suggesting a crucial biological function. Sleep is one of the last complex behaviours of which the exact purpose remains unclear. There is no single explanation for sleep; all explanations have their weaknesses and strengths. Good theories should explain the universal nature of sleep, as it is found throughout the animal world. All mammals and birds sleep, and fish, reptiles and amphibians also exhibit periods of quiet restfulness that is like sleep. As sleep is so common in the animal kingdom, it suggests that it must perform some critical function. Although there are wide variations between humans in sleep duration, it is generally seen as necessary, with the average being 6 to 8 hours a night.

Unfortunately, scientists do not agree on what that function is, and the exact purpose of sleep remains an enigma. Countless theories have been proposed, but the two best known are the restoration (or repair) theory and the ecological (or evolutionary) theory.

Evolutionary explanations

Evolutionary explanations see sleep as serving some adaptive function related to survival and therefore occurring through natural selection. Different species evolved different types and patterns of sleep, dealing with different environmental needs, like predator avoidance, conservation of energy and dietary requirements. Thus animal species should vary in their sleep needs depending on how much time they need to search for food each day and how safe they are from predators when they sleep.

Sleep keeps animals dormant when activities vital for survival are not required. Evolutionary explanations therefore see the function of sleep as similar to that of hibernation, conserving energy when the environment is hostile. Similarly, sleep forces individuals to conserve energy at times when they would not function efficiently, and to protect them at night when they are vulnerable to predators. Sleep is thus an *evolutionary stable strategy*, increasing individual and, in turn, species survival.

- **Predator–prey sleep** – Meddis (1979) believes that sleep evolved to keep animals hidden from predators when usual activities, like foraging, are not required.

- **Hibernation theory** – Webb (1982) believes that active animals need larger amounts of food, threatening survival during times of food scarcity. Hibernation conserves energy, thus increasing survival. Grizzly bears hibernate through the winter, living off body fat accumulated during times of food availability.

- **Aquatic mammals** – the precise environmental demands of species affect sleep patterns and behaviours. Aquatic mammals need to breathe, so sleep incurs a risk of drowning. Animals have evolved strategies to cope with this problem.

- **Foraging needs** – evolutionary explanations see sleep duration as affected by the amount of time needed to eat. Grazing animals spend a long time feeding, while predators sleep a lot, only needing to eat periodically.

- **Body size** – smaller animals evolved a greater need to sleep, their metabolic rates being high and energy consumption rapid. Long periods of sleep help to conserve energy stores.

Research: evolutionary explanations

- Stear (2005) reported that sleep saves energy, keeps individuals from being lively at unnecessary times and is an adaptation to ecological factors differing across species, supporting the evolutionary basis for sleep.

- Requadt (2006) found that animals locate warm, safe places to sleep as it minimises energy requirements to maintain body temperature, supporting the evolutionary point of view.

- Siegel (2008) reported that there is less risk of injury when asleep than awake, sleep being a safety device when essential activities are not necessary.

- Pilleri (1979) found that Indus dolphins sleep for a few seconds repeatedly, supporting evolutionary predictions for sleep patterns in aquatic mammals.

- Mukhametov (1984) found that bottlenose dolphins have one cerebral hemisphere asleep at a time, allowing animals to be asleep, alert and breathing simultaneously, supporting evolutionary predictions for the sleep patterns of aquatic mammals.

- Allison and Cicchetti (1976) examined sleep patterns in 39 animal species, finding that prey animals generally sleep less than predators, which suggests that Meddis's (1979) predator/prey sleep theory is flawed. However, Lesku *et al.* (2006) point out that prey animals are usually herbivores, requiring longer periods awake to find and consume sufficient foodstuffs than predators.

Figure 1.08 Bottlenose dolphins have one cerebral hemisphere asleep at a time

Evaluation

Evolutionary explanations

- Sleep deprivation studies (see pages 21–22) suggest that humans can cope with very little sleep. There are case studies of individuals who sleep for as little as 1 or 2 hours per night, seemingly with no adverse effects. Such studies support the 'evolutionary hangover' theory of sleep.

- It makes cognitive sense to suggest that sleep evolved to reduce the danger of predation for prey animals. However, it is not clear why a complex behaviour like sleep should have evolved to do this; simple behavioural inactivity would serve the same purpose. Indeed, many animals freeze and 'play dead' when confronted by predators.

- It is suggested that animals that are preyed on are more vulnerable to predators when asleep, given their decreased sensitivity to external stimuli. Therefore, sleep would not be an adaptive response to avoid predation. Bentley (2000) also points out that snoring is a difficult phenomenon to explain, as it is likely to increase vulnerability to predation by attracting attention while sleeping.

- Giant sloths sleep for 20 hours a day, going against the evolution and body size argument, being large, inactive creatures, with relatively low metabolic rates.

- Sleep may have evolved to suit human ecological needs in the EEA (Environment of Evolutionary Adaptiveness), but has little purpose in the modern world, though it is still apparent.

- The fact that sleep is universal across species suggests some adaptive function, but sleep is so maladaptive in survival terms that it is difficult to see why it evolved. It prevents eating, reproduction and incurs vulnerability to attack. However, sleep deprivation shows that consequences can be severe.

- A lot of research involving evolutionary explanations depends on animal studies, incurring a problem with generalising findings to humans.

Issues, debates and approaches

- Evolutionary explanations are accused of reductionism, reducing complex behaviours to adaptiveness. However, the approach also considers many ecological and physiological factors, reducing the criticism somewhat.
- Evolutionary explanations are also deterministic, seeing behaviour as caused by past environments with no role for free will.

Restoration theories

People generally sleep because they are tired, suggesting that sleep is fundamentally for rejuvenation and repair. Growth hormone is released during sleep, stimulating tissue growth and aiding protein synthesis, used to repair damaged tissues. Waste products are also removed.

- Oswald's (1980) restoration theory: this explanation sees sleep as helping to reverse and/or restore biochemical and/or physiological processes that are progressively degraded during the day. In essence, it suggests that being awake disrupts the homeostasis of the body and that sleep is required to restore it. High levels of brain activity during REM sleep indicate brain restoration, while growth hormone production (and other hormonal activity) during the four stages of SWS indicate bodily restoration and repair.

- Horne's (1988) core sleep model: as many restorative processes, such as digestion, removal of waste products and protein synthesis, actually occur while awake – with some occurring more during wakefulness than when sleeping – Horne concluded that sleep does not provide any repair function in humans, except for the brain. Horne referred to core sleep, which he believed is essential for restoration, whereas other types of sleep he called optional sleep, whose main purpose is energy conservation. Stage four and REM sleep are seen as necessary for the healthy brain functioning required for cognitive processing; during these stages the brain is seen as refreshing and restoring itself, ready for the challenges of the new day.

Research: restoration theories

- Adam (1980) reported that many restorative processes, like digestion, removal of waste products and protein synthesis, do occur during sleep, supporting the restoration explanation.

- Stern and Morgane (1974) believed that neurotransmitter levels are replenished during REM sleep, supporting the idea of restorative sleep. This is backed up by the fact that antidepressants increase neurotransmitter levels, reducing REM activity.

- Cirelli *et al.* (2004) found that during SWS, genes associated with the protein production regulating synaptic connections are activated, supporting restoration theories, especially Oswald's.

- Horne (1988) reported that amino acids, built into proteins, are only available for 5 hours after eating; therefore, for most people, they would not be available during sleep, suggesting that protein synthesis cannot occur during sleep, casting doubts on the theory.

- Shapiro *et al.* (1981) found that long-distance athletes, after running a 56-mile race, slept for longer, suggesting that sleep does aid restoration.

- Everson *et al.* (1989) found that depriving rats of sleep causes increased metabolic rate, loss of weight, and death in about 19 days, possibly due to immune system damage, suggesting that sleep is necessary for restoration. However, the rats are stressed to keep them awake and this may contribute too.

- Horne (1988) performed a meta-analysis of sleep deprivation studies, finding little evidence of reduced physical functioning or stress responses, suggesting that sleep is not primarily for restoration.

- Hartmann (1973) reported that REM sleep is a time for synthesising noradrenaline and dopamine to compensate for the amount used during the day, giving support to the idea of restoration.

Classic research

Gulevich, Dement and Johnson (1966)

The sleep deprivation study of Randy Gardner

One way to find out how important sleep is for both brain and body restoration is to examine the effects of sleep deprivation.

In 1965, as part of a science project, 17-year-old schoolboy Randy Gardner decided to break the then world record of 260 hours of wakefulness as part of a school science project, using no artificial aids or stimulants, including coffee. Randy eventually stayed awake for 264 hours and 12 minutes (over 11 days), a new world record.

Aim

To study the effects of total sleep deprivation over an extended period.

Method

The researchers read about the attempt in a newspaper and decided to collect data during and after the event. Randy was monitored by a medical team at regular intervals throughout his attempt. Data concerning his physical and cognitive state were recorded.

Findings

During the sleep deprivation

By day two Randy had trouble focusing his vision, and by day three he was experiencing trouble with his coordination, as well as emotional fluctuations.

Similar symptoms were reported through days four, five and six, as Randy experienced paranoia, hallucinations, lapses of memory and concentration, as well as feeling physically jaded.

By days seven and eight Randy's concentration problems and memory lapses were more intense, his speech was slurred and he became increasingly irritable and moody.

His condition deteriorated further on days nine and ten; with Randy finding it hard to focus on even mundane tasks and his vision becoming progressively worse. He started to experience disturbing episodes of paranoia.

On the final day eleven, a comprehensive medical revealed that physically, other than a slight tremor, his condition was okay, though he still displayed slurred speech and blurred vision. Psychologically, his concentration was poor and generally his cognitive functions had lessened.

After the sleep deprivation

Randy was monitored by doctors after his ordeal and was quickly back to normal. After his sleep deprivation, Randy slept for 14 hours and soon returned to his usual 8-hour pattern. In all, there were 67 hours of sleep that he did not 'make up'. However, the percentage of recovery sleep varied across the stages. He made up only about 7 per cent of stages 1 and 2, in contrast to 68 per cent of stage 4 sleep and 53 per cent of REM sleep. The phenomenon whereby 'lost' REM sleep is recovered on subsequent nights is called 'REM rebound'. In all, only 24 per cent of total sleep loss was recovered.

Conclusions

- Stage 4 and REM sleep are more important than other sleep stages in terms of restoration.
- It is possible to endure long periods of total sleep deprivation without suffering long-term effects.
- After long periods of total sleep deprivation, only a fragment of the lost sleep is recovered.

continued ...

...continued

Evaluation

- The record Randy Garner broke was that of Peter Tripp, a DJ who endured his sleep deprivation to raise money for charity. Tripp showed more severe negative effects, exhibiting signs of mental instability, like experiencing paranoia (he thought his food was drugged) and enduring hallucinations. At the end of his ordeal, he slept for 24 hours and was soon back to normal. This demonstrates the individual differences associated with sleep deprivation, though Tripp was older than Gardner, being 33 at the time of his event.

- The Gardner study was poorly controlled, with a lack of objective measurements – for example, no EEG readings were taken and micro-sleeps may have occurred.

- Participants in sleep deprivation studies are aware that they are in a study, and being constantly monitored may lead to an increase in stress. Furthermore, the motivation of being monitored is likely to affect people's ability to cope with lack of sleep. Also deprivation experiments involve more than just a loss of sleep. Daily routines, like work and leisure time, are suspended, making results difficult to generalise to more realistic situations.

- Animal studies support restoration theories, as they show that extended sleep deprivation can end in death. For example, Dement (1960) placed cats on upturned flowerpots surrounded by water, and every time they entered REM sleep they fell in the water. The cats went through all stages of sleep except REM and died after an average of 35 days. However, such findings may not be generalisable to humans, as animals cannot be persuaded to stay wake voluntarily, and it may be the stressful methods used to keep them awake that account for their deaths.

Evaluation

Restoration theory

- Patients with brain trauma, either through injury or electroconvulsive therapy, spend an increased amount of time in REM sleep, suggesting that it is the increased blood flow during REM sleep that aids brain repair and restoration.

- Oswald (1980) believed that protein synthesis is dependent on growth hormones secreted during the delta waves of SWS. However, this is not supported by the finding of a decrease rather than an increase in protein synthesis of the whole body during sleep in humans. This decrease in protein synthesis is attributed to sleep being a period of overnight fasting, as protein synthesis remains constant when subjects are fed continuously via intragastric tubes throughout the 24-hour period.

- Studies into the effects on sleep patterns of vigorous physical exercise fail to take into account confounding variables in the form of differences between participants. For example, the ultramarathon runners studied by Shapiro (1981) were incredibly fit athletes who regularly trained and raced over long distances, while the runners studied by Horne and Minard (1985) were of a more variable fitness profile, including fun runners not used to such exertion.

- Young infants have lots of sleep, possibly because of rapid brain and body tissue growth, supporting the idea of sleep for restoration.

- Fatal familial insomnia is a rare human condition, usually starting in middle age, where sufferers cannot sleep and usually die within two years, suggesting support for the restoration theory. However, cases are few and difficult to generalise from, with sufferers also having brain damage that may be responsible.

- Several studies into physical exhaustion and sleep, like Horne and Minard (1985), have found that participants fall asleep quicker after physical exertion, but not for longer, contradicting the findings of Shapiro et al.

Issues, debates and approaches

- Some animal research into the restoration theory can be seen as unethical, such as that conducted by Everson *et al.* (1979), whose work led to the death of rats. Some would justify this in terms of a cost-benefit analysis.

- One practical application of restoration theory is that endurance-based athletes use short sleep sessions after intensive training to promote protein synthesis to repair tissues, lending support to the idea of sleep being for restoration.

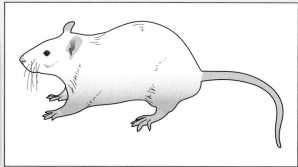

Figure 1.09 Is it ethical for animals to die to discover knowledge about sleep?

Strengthen your learning

1. What are the main points of:
   i) the evolutionary explanations of sleep?
   ii) the restoration theory of sleep?
2. In what ways can evolutionary explanations be supported/not supported?
3. In what ways can the restoration theory be supported/not supported?

Assessment Check

1. Outline the nature of sleep. (8 marks)

2. Discuss lifespan changes in sleep. (24 marks)

3. Evaluate one explanation for the function of sleep. (16 marks)

4. Outline the evolutionary explanation and the restoration theory of sleep. (8 marks)

5. Evaluate one of the theories/explanations outlined in (3). (16 marks)

Examination guidance

Any evaluative material offered in question 1 would not be creditworthy; likewise any descriptive material offered in question 3 would gain no credit.

In question 2 the term 'discuss' means to describe and evaluate, with 8 marks available for the description and 16 marks for the evaluation

A reasonable balance between the two explanations should be attained in question 4 to access the highest band of marks. Question 5 calls for an evaluation of just one theory/explanation, but the other could legitimately be used as a comparison.

Sleep disorders

Explanations for sleep disorders

Insomnia

Insomnia is 'the inability to sleep', where sufferers have a long-term problem initiating or maintaining sleep. Insomnia can take the form of inadequate quantity or quality of sleep, with 50 per cent of humans sometimes having difficulty sleeping, women more than men, possibly because of hormonal fluctuations associated with onset of menstruation and the menopause. However, only 5 to 10 per cent of sufferers are diagnosed with insomnia.

Dement (1999) argues that insomnia is not a sleep disorder, but rather a symptom with different causes. He concedes that it is often easier to refer to insomnia as if it were a single disorder, and, in practice, doctors treat insomnia directly rather than some unknown underlying cause. When insomnia is regarded as an illness in itself it is called *primary insomnia*. If the insomnia is a direct result of another illness, it is called *secondary insomnia*. Insomnia affects both physical and cognitive functioning, with symptoms of insomnia including sleepiness, fatigue, decreased alertness, poor concentration, decreased performance, depression during the day and night, muscle aches and an overly emotional state.

Duration

Insomnia can be transient, lasting a few nights, short-term, lasting more than a few nights, but less than 3 weeks, or long-term (chronic), occurring most nights and for longer than 3 weeks.

Patterns

- Onset insomnia involves difficulty in getting to sleep, often associated with anxiety.

- Middle-of-the-night insomnia is characterised by problems getting back to sleep after waking, or waking too early.

- Middle insomnia involves waking in the middle of the night and/or difficulty staying asleep, often associated with medical illnesses or physical pain.

- Late insomnia involves waking early in the morning, often associated with clinical depression.

Primary insomnia

Primary insomnia is sleeplessness not attributable to a medical, psychiatric or environmental cause. The diagnostic criteria for primary insomnia from the Diagnostic and Statistical Manual of Mental Disorders, 4th edn, text revision (DSM-IV-TR) includes the following:

1. Difficulty initiating or maintaining sleep for at least 1 month.

2. The sleep disturbance, or associated daytime fatigue, causes clinically significant distress or impairment in social, occupational or other important areas of functioning.

3. The sleep disturbance does not occur during the course of other sleep-related disorders, such as narcolepsy or parasomnias.

4. The sleep disturbance does not occur during the course of another mental disorder.

5. The sleep disturbance is not due to the physiological effects of a substance – for example, drugs – or a general medical condition.

There are several sub-types of primary insomnia:

Figure 1.10 Insomnia can bring daytime sleepiness, causing impairments in functioning

1. **Psychophysiological insomnia**

   This is a form of anxiety-induced insomnia sometimes called learned insomnia or behavioural insomnia. The primary component is intermittent periods of stress resulting in poor sleep. This generates two maladaptive behaviours:

   - a vicious cycle of trying harder to sleep and becoming tenser
   - bedroom habits/routines and other sleep-related activities – for example, teeth-brushing – which condition an individual to frustration and arousal.

   People who sleep badly may worry about not being able to function well during the day. Therefore they try even harder to sleep at night, but this makes them more alert, initiating worried thoughts, causing even more sleep loss. Through classical conditioning, some activities associated with sleep, like changing into pyjamas, can become linked with the sleep problems that follow. Through repetition, these bedtime activities trigger over-arousal and insomnia. Some individuals with learned insomnia have trouble sleeping in their own beds, but fall asleep quickly elsewhere – for example, watching TV – possibly because the learned associations are not present in the different sleep environment. Treatment for learned insomnia aims to improve sleep habits and reduce unnecessary worry.

2. **Idiopathic insomnia**

   Idiopathic insomnia was originally called childhood onset insomnia, because it occurs at an early age. It may occur due to abnormalities in brain mechanisms controlling the sleep/wake cycle. Lifelong sleeplessness is attributed to abnormalities in the neurologic control of the sleep/wake cycle, involving many brain areas promoting wakefulness, as well as in brain areas promoting sleep. It is suggested that a brain abnormality exists in the sleep system, causing a person to have high arousal and thus an inability to sleep normally.

3. **Sleep–state misperception**

   People with sleep–state misperception sleep adequately but feel they do not. Such people underestimate their total sleep time and overestimate the time it takes to fall asleep. Sleep researchers suggest that these discrepancies result from an unclear perception of consciousness and difficulty distinguishing sleep from waking.

Research: primary insomnia

- Morin *et al.* (2003) examined the relationship of stress and coping skills, and the role of pre-sleep arousal (doing activities late in the evening that heighten arousal) in sleep patterns for good sleepers and individuals with insomnia. Participants recorded daily measures of stressful events, pre-sleep arousal and sleep for 21 consecutive days, as well as retrospective measures of depression, anxiety, stressful life events and coping skills. Poor and good sleepers reported equivalent numbers of minor stressful life events, but insomniacs rated the impact of daily minor stressors and the intensity of major negative life events more highly than good sleepers did. In addition, insomniacs perceived their lives as more stressful, relied more on emotion-orientated coping strategies, and reported greater pre-sleep arousal than good sleepers. Data showed significant relationships between daytime stress and night-time sleep, with pre-sleep arousal and coping skills playing an important mediating role. This suggests that the key factor in insomnia is the way people appraise stressors and the perceived lack of control over stressful events, rather than the number of stressful events, and this perceived lack of control enhances vulnerability to insomnia.

- Dement (1999) reported on several cases of sleep-state misperception. One case involved a patient who complained of severe insomnia being asked to sleep for 10 consecutive nights in the sleep laboratory. Each morning he completed a questionnaire estimating how long it took to fall asleep each night. He reported times ranging from 1 to 4 hours, with a mean of 90 minutes. However, he never took more than 30 minutes to fall asleep, with a mean of 15 minutes. Another patient reported a total sleep time of 4 hours, yet actually slept for 6.5 hours on average.

- Dauvilliers *et al.* (2005) asked 256 primary insomniacs to complete a clinical interview, psychometric questionnaires and a questionnaire on the family history of insomnia, and to undergo detailed physiological sleep measurements. A control group of non-insomniacs was similarly tested. Of the primary insomniacs, 72.7 per cent reported familial insomnia (a family history of insomnia), compared to only 24.1 per cent of the non-insomniacs, suggesting a familial link to primary insomnia.

Secondary insomnia

When insomnia is caused by psychiatric disorders (usually depression) or a medical disorder (usually chronic pain), it is termed secondary insomnia.

Secondary insomnia is more common than primary insomnia and results from non-sleep-related factors, such as illness, drugs (including caffeine and alcohol), excessive worrying and pain. In patients with secondary insomnia, it is the underlying disorder that needs to be treated. For example, many people suffering from depression experience improved sleep after taking antidepressants, even though these do not affect the sleep patterns of non-depressed people.

There are a number of physical and psychiatric causes of secondary insomnia, including the following:

1. **Hormonal changes in women** – including premenstrual syndrome, menstruation, pregnancy and menopause.

2. **Decreased melatonin production** – the levels of melatonin, the hormone that helps control sleep, decrease as people age. By the age of 60, the body produces very little melatonin.

3. **Medical illnesses** – many medical illnesses disrupt sleep and produce insomnia. Such illnesses include allergies, arthritis, asthma, heart disease, high blood pressure, hyperthyroidism and Parkinson's disease. Treatment of the underlying cause usually results in improved sleep, although sometimes treatment for the insomnia is also required.

4. **Psychiatric disorders** – secondary insomnia, especially awakening earlier than desired, is a frequently reported symptom of depression; it is also associated with other psychiatric disorders, such as anxiety disorders, post-traumatic stress disorders and dementia – for example, Alzheimer's disease. People with psychiatric disorders often sleep badly. Treatment involving drugs and psychotherapy often helps to improve sleep.

There are other lifestyle factors that can cause secondary insomnia, including:

1. **Stimulants** – the most common stimulant is caffeine, and caffeine intake should be restricted prior to bedtime. Even when caffeine does not interfere with sleep onset, it can trigger awakenings during the night. Nicotine is also a stimulant and smokers take longer to get to sleep than non-smokers.

2. **Alcohol** – although alcohol may help sleep onset, it usually interrupts night-time sleep.

3. **Shift work** (see pages 11–12) – many people find it hard to maintain regular sleep patterns when working night shifts or rotating shifts. Establishing a regular sleep routine is the key to healthy sleep.

4. **Environmental factors** – factors such as noise, light and temperature also have a detrimental effect on sleep patterns.

5. **Circadian rhythm disruption** – jet lag and shift work can lead to insomnia.

Research: secondary insomnia

- Monti (2004) found that many cases of insomnia could be treated successfully by treating the underlying cause, such as a medical or psychiatric condition, which suggests that some forms of insomnia are secondary – that is, they are the result of other illnesses – and are not an illness in themselves as primary insomnia is.

- Katz *et al.* (2002) studied insomniacs with chronic medical conditions, such as diabetes, depression, hypertension and heart conditions, finding that 50 per cent of them suffered from insomnia, 34 per cent from a mild form and 16 per cent from a severe form. This supports the idea that secondary insomnia results from other conditions and is a separate type from primary insomnia.

- Lichstein *et al.* (2007) asked participants to complete sleep questionnaires, maintain sleep diaries and list food supplements they took, finding that participants who took vitamin supplements had higher rates of insomnia. This suggests that certain food stuffs, like vitamins, can contribute to secondary insomnia, though it might be that poor sleepers take vitamins.

- McClenaghan (1999) found that low blood glucose levels are a common cause of maintenance insomnia, where sufferers have problems waking throughout the night or waking too early, with stimulants like tea, coffee and alcohol negatively affecting blood sugar levels. Other foodstuffs, like potatoes and bacon, stimulate the production of adrenaline, which can interfere with sleep. However, protein-rich foods assist in the production of serotonin and melatonin, which help to induce and maintain sleep, suggesting there are 'good' and 'bad' foods related to sleep patterns.

Evaluation

Insomnia

- Difficulty in generalisation – there are so many different types of insomnia attributable to so many different causes that it is nearly impossible to make generalisations that describe all cases of insomnia in any meaningful way.

- Physiological support – Smith *et al.* (2002) studied neuro-images of NREM sleep patterns in insomniacs, finding evidence for physiological abnormalities. Patients with insomnia showed consistent and significant decreases in blood flow compared to good sleepers in several brain areas, suggesting that insomnia is associated with abnormal central nervous system activity during NREM sleep that is particularly linked to brain dysfunction.

- Reliability and validity of sleep insomnia measures – there is controversy over the identification of insomnia. Although measures such as the Structured Sleep Interview for Sleep Disorders are reliable when compared to sleep laboratory recordings, there is disagreement between interviewers over the symptom information given by patients, which suggests that subjective self-reports should not be relied on. Vgontzas *et al.* (1994) argue that using sleep laboratory criteria is an unsatisfactory way of diagnosing insomnia, as a study involving 375 insomniacs and 150 non-insomniac controls found that sleep laboratory recordings provide little relevant information for confirming or excluding the presence of insomnia.

- Personality factors and coping strategies – it is evident that personality factors and the way people cope with stress play a significant role in primary insomnia. The main implication is that insomnia treatments should teach effective stress appraisal and stress coping skills to alleviate the condition.

You are the researcher

Sleep hygiene concerns practices, habits and environmental factors important for getting sound sleep, like regularity of bedtime and reduced alcohol consumption.

Design two studies to test the impact of sleep hygiene on sleep patterns – one using an experimental method and one using a non-experimental method. What are the advantages and disadvantages of each method?

Factors influencing insomnia

Apnoea

Apnoea is a medical condition where sufferers have persistent pauses in their breathing lasting for minutes, as well as occasional loud snorts as breathing recommences. This can occur up to 200 times a night. Obstructive sleep apnoea is generally caused by blockage of the airways, often found in overweight, middle-aged males. Central sleep apnoea is caused by impaired brain signals to areas associated with breathing and occurs more infrequently.

Obstructive sleep apnoea (OSA) is defined as the cessation of airflow during sleep, preventing air from entering the lungs, caused by an obstruction. These periods of 'stopping breathing' become clinically significant if the cessation lasts for more than 10 seconds and occurs more than ten times every hour. OSA happens during sleep due to a lack of muscle tone in the upper airway causing the airway to collapse. It is not a problem during waking hours, because people have sufficient muscle tone to keep airways open. When people experience apnoea during sleep, the brain automatically wakes the person in order to breathe again. This waking is usually accompanied by a loud snort. People with OSA experience wakening episodes

many times a night and feel sleepy during the day. OSA ranges from mild to severe. To determine whether someone is suffering from sleep apnoea they first undergo a specialist sleep study, involving a night in hospital where equipment is used to monitor the quality of sleep through brain wave monitoring, muscle tone monitoring, chest and abdomen movements, mouth and nose airflow, heart rate and blood oxygen monitoring.

Sleep apnoea is caused by factors making the throat narrow more than usual during sleep. If the throat is narrower to start with – for example, because tonsils are enlarged – it is easier for throat muscles to close and block the airway. Other causes of a narrowed throat include partially blocked nose, being overweight, having a large tongue and excessive alcohol and/or drugs. OSA also becomes more likely as people age. Treatment includes weight loss and the use of jaw or nasal devices to allow continuous airway pressure.

Research: apnoea

- Chest (2001) found a significant positive correlation between insomnia and OSA, suggesting a relationship between the two conditions.

- Smith *et al.* (2004) found a relationship between insomnia and OSA, with sufferers more prone to depression, anxiety and stress than people suffering from OSA, but not insomnia. Although suggesting a link between the two conditions, it seems that insomnia has more serious side effects.

- Morrell *et al.* (2000) found that sleep apnoea is more common in older adults, with up to one in five sufferers being older, ten times the number of younger people, though the disorder is more severe in the young. It was concluded that the difference in prevalence rates is due to changes in the structure and function of the cardiovascular system in older adults.

- Stickgold (2009) believes that a range of mental disorders, including depression and attention deficit disorder, are caused by sleep apnoea and insomnia. Apnoeac insomniacs had twice the incidence of depression than the normal population, suggesting that the best way to treat such mental disorders is to alleviate apnoea and insomnia.

Evaluation

Apnoea

- Sleep apnoea can lead to insomnia, being more prevalent in older adults. As the population ages, there is an assumption that the disorder will grow, increasing the need for successful treatments.

- The higher incidence of apnoea in older adults is associated with changes to the cardiovascular system as people age, suggesting that sufferers of different ages require different treatments to address the problem.

- Doctors report increasing numbers of younger people with insomnia and sleep apnoea. This may be related to growing obesity among the young, suggesting that addressing obesity may combat these sleep disorders.

- Horne (2009) argues that the claim of apnoea and insomnia causing mental disorders has not been proved and that it is more probable that certain mental disorders lead to insomnia. He also believes that obesity is more responsible for rises in depression levels.

- Research into apnoea and insomnia has seen the development of successful treatments, like losing weight, stopping smoking, reducing intake of alcohol and sleeping tablets, sleeping on one's side and taking up exercise.

Personality

Personality has been implicated in research findings as being associated with the onset and continuation of insomnia. Psychasthenia, a personality disorder similar to obsessive-compulsive disorder, where a sufferer is plagued with unreasonable fears and doubts, excessive anxiety and obsessive compulsions, is especially implicated. Other commonly identified factors include oversensitivity, low self-esteem, lack of autonomy and heightened emotional arousal.

The personality trait of neuroticism is also associated with secondary insomnia, probably due to the high levels of arousal it brings about. Those with anxious personality types are also more vulnerable to insomnia after experiencing traumatic life events.

Research: personality factors

- Lundh *et al.* (1995) found that the predominant factor in persistent insomnia patients is psychasthenia, with high scores on anxiety and monotony avoidance too. Sufferers tend to score poorly on self-esteem and are overdependent on others. The effects of these factors are difficulty in regaining lost sleep, daytime fatigue and lack of concentration, suggesting that personality factors play a role in causing and maintaining insomnia.

- Kales *et al.* (1976) found that 85 per cent of insomniacs had abnormal personalities, characterised by psychasthenia, elevated levels of depression and conversion hysteria. Sufferers tended to internalise psychological disturbances, producing constant emotional arousal, suggesting that a psychophysiological mechanism underpins insomnia.

- Lahmeyer *et al.* (1989) found that insomniacs tend to have borderline abnormal personalities, characterised by traits like manic episodes, supporting the idea that abnormal traits which produce emotional arousal are associated with insomnia.

- De Carvalho *et al.* (2003) found that Brazilian insomnia patients were characterised by heightened levels of anxiety and insecurity, especially among female patients.

- Grano *et al.* (2006) found that male insomniacs are impulsive characters, implying that male and female sufferers are affected by different personality traits.

Evaluation

Personality factors

- Rather than personality traits leading to insomnia, there is a possibility that being an insomniac creates changes in personality. Longitudinal studies following people at risk from their personality profile would settle the debate.

- If it is proved that certain personalities lead to insomnia, this suggests a practical application. Individuals at risk could be identified by personality testing, and targeted for help and advice as a preventative means of treatment.

- Research suggests that treating abnormal personality traits and disorders has more success in reducing insomnia than treating insomnia to try to address personality defects, implying that it is the abnormal personality traits that are the causal factor.

- Furukawa (2009) reports success in using behavioural treatments to address personality-linked insomnia, suggesting that maladaptive learning experiences may be important factors.

- Therapies that reduce anxiety and arousal, like cognitive behavioural therapy (CBT), also successfully reduce the associated insomnia, suggesting that anxious personality types are at a heightened risk of suffering from insomnia.

Issues, debates and approaches

- Research that reveals the physiological and/or psychological contributors to insomnia, like diet and sleep hygiene, can contribute to practical applications in the form of effective treatments for such disorders.
- Overall research into insomnia can be seen to be a lot more holistic in its approach, as it considers a wide range of influences, both physiological and psychological, such as hormonal fluctuations, personality factors, maladaptive learning experiences and cognitive functioning.

Sleepwalking

Sleepwalking is known as *somnambulism* and refers to activities occurring unconsciously when someone is asleep that normally occur when awake. It is a common type of *parasomnia* (abnormal sleep condition) that is more prevalent in childhood, especially among boys, and decreases sharply into adulthood.

Sleepwalkers are usually unaware of their activity and engage in automatic behaviour, like dressing themselves, preparing food, sending nonsensical emails and even committing murder and having sex (see 'In the news' on page 2). Sleepwalkers are hard to wake, and though they have their eyes open they are usually dazed and display incoherent speech.

Sleepwalkers frequently feel embarrassment, shame, guilt, anxiety and confusion when told about their behaviour. They usually suffer from amnesia, remembering little or nothing of sleepwalking episodes.

The exact cause is unknown, though sleepwalking usually occurs during stage three or stage four sleep early in the night. Sleepwalking may occur more frequently during childhood, because children spend more time in deep sleep.

If sleepwalking occurs during REM sleep, it is defined as an REM behaviour disorder. When people sleepwalk they are not acting out dreams, whereas with an REM sleep behaviour disorder, where people might punch the bed, they usually are.

Somnambulism is associated with personality disorders, especially ones relating to anxiety. The disorder places the sufferer at risk of injury or abuse, and causes may be related to genetic and environmental factors.

Sleepwalking is ten times more likely if a first-degree relative has a history of sleepwalking, and it occurs more frequently in identical twins, suggesting a genetic link, while the environmental factors that induce sleepwalking include stress, alcohol intoxication, sleep deprivation, chaotic sleep schedules, hypnosis and several drugs, such as sedatives and antihistamines. Medical conditions like fever, arrhythmia, night-time asthma, night-time seizures and sleep apnoea are also linked to sleepwalking, along with some psychiatric disorders, such as multiple personality disorder, panic attack and stress disorders.

Research: sleepwalking

- Zadra *et al.* (2008) found a link between sleep deprivation and sleepwalking. Participants visited a sleep laboratory and had their sleep patterns monitored during an initial assessment. During a subsequent visit, patients were kept awake for the entire evening, remaining under constant supervision. The next morning participants were allowed 'recovery' sleep, by which time they had been awake for 25 hours. Various measures were taken, including videotapes showing the participants engaging in many different types of sleepwalking, ranging from playing with bed sheets to trying to jump over bed rails. Subjects were evaluated on a three-point scale, based on the complexity of their actions. The results showed that during the first night of baseline sleep, 50 per cent of patients exhibited 32 sleepwalking episodes, while

Psychology in action

Handling nude sleepwalkers

Workers at Travelodge hotels are being given advice on how to deal with naked sleepwalkers following an increase in the number of guests found wandering around, with more than 400 cases in the past year, almost all involving men.

Research conducted in 310 Travelodge hotels found that sleepwalkers wandered all over the building. A number had walked into the reception area asking for a newspaper or saying they wanted to check out.

The biggest reason for sleepwalking while staying in a hotel is probably the stress of being away on business, and working hard between meetings can also increase stress levels.

The study also found that one in ten sleepwalkers had injured themselves on their travels. This is not unusual, as more than 300,000 men and women in the UK who sleepwalk were left with bruises in 1999, and 9,000 were left with broken bones.

After consulting with psychologists, Travelodge issued advice to guests and staff:

To guests

- As 37 per cent of the nation go to bed naked and about 10 per cent of the population regularly sleepwalk, it is advisable to wear something to bed while sleeping in a hotel.
- Get plenty of rest, as being overtired can trigger sleepwalking.
- Remove anything harmful from the room.

To staff

- It is a misconception that sleepwalkers should not be woken. It is not dangerous; it just disorientates sleepwalkers for a short period.
- Sleepwalkers should be accommodated on the ground floor, thereby avoiding stairs. Travelodge windows have restricted opening space, but ground-floor rooms are preferable for sleepwalkers.
- Robes and towels should be kept at reception to preserve guests' dignity.

during 'recovery' sleep, 90 per cent of patients demonstrated 92 behavioural episodes, suggesting that sleep deprivation had increased the amount.

- Bassetti (2002) gene-tested 16 adult sleepwalkers, finding that 50 per cent had a specific gene found in only 24 per cent of non-sleepwalking people. The gene, HLA DQB1*05, is one of a family of genes producing proteins called HLA, involved in regulating the immune system. The same genetic variant of the HLA gene is associated with another parasomnia, narcolepsy.

- Oliviero (2008) proposed a physiological mechanism underlying sleepwalking, finding that during normal sleep the chemical messenger gamma-aminobutyric acid (GABA) acts as an inhibitor, preventing the activity of the brain's motor system. In children, the neurons involved with this suppression are still developing and hence motor activity is not fully controlled, so many children have insufficient amounts of GABA, leaving their motor neurons capable of commanding the body to move during sleep. This may explain why sleepwalking occurs more in childhood. In some children, this inhibitory system may remain underdeveloped, or be rendered less effective by environmental factors, explaining why sleepwalking persists into adulthood.

- Hublin *et al.* (1997) found the disorder to be more common among children, with up to 20 per cent being affected. In adults, the prevalence rate is about 2 per cent. This indicates that the condition is linked to development and maturation.

- Broughton (1968) found that the disorder is heritable, with sufferers ten times more likely than the general population to have a close relative with the disorder, suggesting a genetic factor.

- Lecendreux *et al.* (2003) found a higher incidence among MZ (identical) twins than DZ (non-identical) twins – 50 per cent compared to 12 per cent – suggesting a genetic link, though identical twins also tend to have identical environments, which could be a confounding variable.

Evaluation

Sleepwalking

- The current focus of research is that a group of sleep disorders known as *parasomnias*, such as somnambulism and sleep terrors, share a common genetic cause.
- Children spend long amounts of time in SWS, when somnambulism tends to occur, which may explain why they have higher incidences of the disorder. Also children are observed more during sleep, so episodes are more likely to be detected.
- Somnambulism has been used as a legal defence against charges of murder. Kenneth Parks was acquitted in 1987 of killing his in-laws in Canada due to non-insane automatism.
- Somnambulism can be averted by avoiding risk factors, like excitatory activities, using techniques such as meditation before sleeping and sleeping in a safe environment.

Contemporary research

Lurie *et al.* (2007)

Bruxism in pilots and non-pilots

Figure 1.11

Bruxism is the third most common sleep disorder after insomnia and snoring. It consists of teeth grinding while asleep (though it also occurs while awake) and is a clinical manifestation in 5 to 10 per cent of the population. Thirty per cent of cases occur in stage 1 sleep, 56 per cent during stage two sleep, 6 per cent during stage three sleep, 1 per cent during stage four sleep and 7 per cent during REM sleep, where symptoms are more intense and associated with facial and dental pain. The disorder can also disturb the sleep patterns of non-afflicted partners. There is a particularly high incidence among sufferers of obstructive sleep apnoea, especially during its arousal phase. Smokers are five times more

likely to be sufferers and stress levels and personality factors have been identified as risk indicators. Many studies report a higher incidence of the disorder among males.

The researchers set out to compare the incidence of bruxism among military personnel in highly stressful and less stressful occupations.

Aim

To investigate the potential of work-related stress and personality factors to induce bruxism among military pilots (higher-stress occupation) and non-pilot officers (lower-stress occupation).

Procedure

The study was approved by the ethics committee of the Medical Corp, Israeli Defence Forces.

The participants were 57 Israeli air force officers undergoing routine annual dental checks, comprising 17 jet pilots, 18 helicopter pilots and 22 non-pilot officers.

Participants were healthy, of fairly equal educational and socio-economic status, with an average age of 25.8 years.

All participants received a dental assessment and completed psychological questionnaires to assess two factors:

continued ...

...continued

1. Magnitude of workplace stress – a questionnaire of 11 questions was used with a scale of 1 (very low) to 5 (very high). An average of the scores was used as the 'stress degree'.

2. Coping style – a questionnaire of 68 items was used to assess cognitive and behavioural responses for confronting stress.

Findings

Bruxism was found among 69 per cent of the military pilots (70.6 per cent of jet pilots and 66.7 per cent of the helicopter pilots) compared to only 27 per cent of the non-pilot officers.

The stress degree of pilots was 3.84 compared to the non-pilots' score of 3.59.

Pilots tended to use more emotionally orientated coping strategies and denial in response to stress, as well as fewer problem-orientated strategies.

Conclusions

The results indicate a link between work environment and bruxism, especially the coping strategies for work-related stressful demands.

Evaluation

- Previous studies into bruxism suffered from methodological problems, relying on self-report methods, anecdotal evidence and producing conflicting results. This study is superior, as it uses more objective evidence.

- One possibility for causation of the higher dental damage in aircrew is changes in air pressure and high-altitude conditions. However, this seems unlikely, as there was little difference between the incidence of bruxism in high-altitude jet pilots and the lower-altitude helicopter pilots.

- The research receives support from Goldhush *et al.* (1955), who estimated an incidence of bruxism of 60 to 70 per cent in Second World War fighter pilots, though his findings have less scientific rigour.

- Since bruxism was also found in a relatively high proportion of the non-pilot personnel (27 per cent), it indicates that military occupations in general are stressful and thus a risk factor for developing bruxism.

- The results suggest that the high incidence of bruxism found among smokers is probably due to smoking being used as a strategy to cope with stress, rather than smoking being a factor in initiating bruxism.

- The higher levels of bruxism found among males may be due to males being involved in more stressful occupations. It would therefore be useful to study the rate of bruxism among females working in stressful jobs.

You are the researcher

Design an experiment testing the idea that females in stressful jobs are more likely to develop bruxism.

You will need to consider what types of participants are required in the experimental and control groups. Why would a control group be necessary? How many participants are required for a representative sample? What would the independent variable (IV) and dependent variable (DV) be? Compose a suitable two-tailed hypothesis.

Before the study would be published, it would need to be peer-reviewed. What is peer review and why is it conducted?

A good site for researching more information on various sleep disorders, including advice on coping strategies, can be found at www.parasomnias.com

Figure 1.12 Narcolepsy can strike at any time

Narcolepsy

Narcolepsy means 'seized by sleepiness' and is a sleep disorder characterised by disruption to the sleep/wake cycle, whereby sufferers suddenly fall asleep at unexpected times, often in the middle of activities. It affects approximately 1 in 2,000 individuals, with sufferers feeling sleepy during the day, appearing drunk. The struggle to stay awake is relentless, and whenever narcoleptics relax they fall asleep. However, people with narcolepsy fall asleep regardless of what activity they are doing, hence people have fallen asleep halfway through a sentence, while eating or even while having sex. These sleep episodes typically last 10 to 20 minutes before the person awakes feeling refreshed, only to feel sleepy again soon afterwards.

These sporadic micro-sleeps are common, with the sufferer awaking without realising that he or she has been asleep. Type and severity of symptoms vary between individuals and can improve or worsen over time.

Another common symptom is *cataplexy*, where muscular control is lost, usually as a result of being aroused, for example while excited. Cataplexy takes the form of attacks of muscle weakness or near total paralysis occurring suddenly for a few seconds or minutes and then subsiding. Cataplexics may collapse on the floor, able to see and hear, but completely unable to move. As with REM sleep, the muscles of the heart, eyes and breathing work normally, but arm and leg muscles become limp. Afterwards, muscles operate as usual.

Narcoleptics can also suffer from *sleep paralysis*, which occurs when the brain awakes from an REM state, leaving the body paralysed and sufferers fully conscious. Terrifying hallucinations, *hypnopompic* on awakening, or *hypnagogic* on falling asleep, and a general sense of danger, can accompany sleep paralysis. The experience of narcolepsy is often perceived as a dream, with dream-like objects appearing alongside objects in vision. Sleep paralysis can last from a few seconds to several minutes, and is followed by sensations of panic and a gradual realisation that the hallucinations were not real. Sufferers often wake frequently during proper night-time sleep too.

Narcolepsy appears to be a neurological condition associated with a fault in brain mechanisms controlling wakefulness and sleep. One of the main characteristics of the condition is the intrusion of REM sleep at inappropriate times. During REM sleep the brain is active, with the muscles of the body paralysed. In non-narcoleptics REM sleep does not occur until sleep has commenced. With narcoleptics, REM sleep occurs as soon as they fall asleep or even as they wake up.

The condition usually appears in adolescence and may be the result of a genetic abnormality. Other possible causes are a shortage of the neurotransmitter *hypocretin*, which is involved in the control of wakefulness and sleep, or the result of an autoimmune disease.

Research in focus

As dogs suffer from narcolepsy and cataplexy, selective breeding programmes were devised to breed narcoleptic dogs for research.

Some claim that valuable findings come from such research, while others argue that there is a qualitative difference between humans and animals – for instance, the genetic nature of narcolepsy is different in dogs and humans. Another argument concerns the ethics of breeding and using animals in this way.

Construct an argument for and against that considers the use of dogs in narcolepsy research.

Not all cases are reported, as some are mild afflictions. It is estimated that 0.05 per cent of people in Europe and the USA are sufferers, rising to 0.16 per cent in Japan.

Understanding of narcolepsy stems primarily from research involving dogs, one of the few animals known to develop the condition. This research usually involves Dobermanns and Labradors specially bred in the laboratory.

Research: narcolepsy

- Dement (1999) reported that a sleep research team in Texas found that mice that could not make hypocretin in their brains developed the symptoms of narcolepsy, including sleep attacks and cataplexy, demonstrating the importance of the neurotransmitter in the occurrence of the disorder.

- Montplaisir (2007) tested 16 patients with narcolepsy and cataplexy, finding that they had a higher percentage of REM sleep, though this may be a cause or effect of the condition. Evidence was found of decreased hypocretinergic and/or dopaminergic abnormalities in input to brainstem structures, suggesting that abnormal levels of neurotransmitters are associated with the condition.

- Daniels *et al.* (2001) gave questionnaires to 500 patients of the Narcolepsy Association, finding that they had lower energy/vitality levels, reduced social functioning and lessened physical activity, with 57 per cent of them depressed. The condition put limitations on their educational, work, home and social life, matching results from other countries and demonstrating the extensive impact of the disorder on health-related quality of life.

- Mignot *et al.* (1999) used positional cloning to pinpoint a defective gene called *hypocretin receptor 2*, in dogs, one of the few species suffering from narcolepsy. The defective form of the gene encodes proteins that cannot recognise important signals, cutting off cells from receiving essential directives, including messages that promote wakefulness, suggesting a genetic basis to the disorder, though there is a problem generalising to humans. However, the gene does occur in humans.

Evaluation

Narcolepsy

- Treatments often involve stimulants. The drug Modafinil has proved useful in treatment. It works by activating hypocretin-containing nerve cells and its success lends support to the hypocretin deficiency explanation. Mahowald and Schenck (2005) found that administrating hypocretin to narcoleptic dogs led to reduced cataplexy and more normal sleep and waking durations.

- Finland's National Institute of Health and Welfare (2010) reports that a link between the swine flu vaccine Pandemrix and childhood narcolepsy is being investigated due to increased prevalence of narcolepsy in Finnish and Swedish children after vaccinations.

- Genetic research may lead to the production of drugs compensating for the failure of the hypocretin system. Such drugs may work better than the current regime of stimulants and antidepressants.

- The identification of genes associated with the disorder does not mean that there is a definite genetic cause, and researchers stress the need to identify environmental triggers. Genes need specific environments in which to express themselves.

- The frightening and bizarre hallucinations that are part of the condition have been suggested by Blackmore and Cox (2008) as explaining the experience of alien abduction that people sometimes report.

- Using samples based on patient associations can cause problems with bias, as only certain types of sufferers may join the association.

- Gordon *et al.* (2004) induced narcolepsy–like symptoms in the muscles of mice by injecting them with antibodies from the blood of nine people with the disorder. Mice injected with antibodies from nine people who did not have narcolepsy did not develop such symptoms. The research suggests that in some narcolepsy patients the immune system produces antibodies that inflict damage on brain tissues and trigger symptoms of narcolepsy, implying that some cases of narcolepsy might be caused by autoimmune disease.

Contemporary research

Rose, Blackmore and French (2002)
Paranormal belief and interpretations of sleep paralysis

Sleep paralysis is a sleep disorder involving the frightening experience of being unable to move at sleep onset or on wakening, often accompanied by frightening hallucinations. While sleep paralysis is one of the symptoms of narcolepsy, it also occurs in individuals who do not experience narcolepsy.

In David Hufford's 1982 book, The Terror that Comes in the Night, *he reported on the sleep paralysis myth of 'hag riding' (assault by witches) and wondered if this was an interpretation of the hallucinations associated with sleep paralysis. The researchers set out to obtain first-hand accounts of sleep paralysis and identity the condition's key features.*

Aim

To identify the key features characterising the state of sleep paralysis and to assess how people perceive the experience of sleep paralysis.

Procedure

Two case collections were conducted over a period of two years.

In the first study, adverts were placed in specialist magazines to obtain reports of sleep paralysis. From this, 201 letters were received from respondents aged between 8 and 87 years. There were 119 male participants, 73 female and 9 not identified.

In the second study 184 letters were received, originally sent to a magazine devoted to examining UFOs and paranormal phenomena. Respondents were aged between 9 and 59 years; 106 were male, 66 female and 12 not identified.

From these a database was created, from which key features characterising sleep paralysis were identified and whether respondents were believers in the paranormal. This allowed states and experiences associated with sleep paralysis to be

compiled and rates of incidence among the participant group to be calculated, as well as interpretations of sleep paralysis.

Results

Putting the results of the two studies together, 196 cases of sleep paralysis were identified, with a slight majority of sufferers being male.

The key features were compiled and compared with the figures for non-sleep paralysis (see Tables 1.01 and 1.02 opposite).

The most common features in both studies for sufferers of sleep paralysis were malign presences and vibration/humming noises.

In the first study the majority of explanations given by participants were sceptical (23 per cent), but some respondents claimed supernatural explanations, like spirits and ghosts (16 per cent), and some linked the experiences with extraterrestrial contact (5 per cent). Some respondents identified night working as a predisposing factor (9 per cent). A majority of the non-sleep paralysis cases involved dreams, including episodes of lucid dreaming or apparent dream control.

In the second study explanations for sleep paralysis experiences were more evenly distributed, with sceptical explanations (7 per cent), spirits and ghosts (7 per cent) and extraterrestrial contact (6 per cent) all equally prominent. The majority of non-sleep paralysis cases involved extraterrestrials and strange lights, including UFO sightings.

Believers in the paranormal who had experienced sleep paralysis reported more paranormal features (and more features overall) during the episode than non-believers. Believers in the paranormal who had not personally experienced sleep paralysis were more likely to interpret

continued ...

...continued

Table 1.01: Study 1

FEATURES	PERCENTAGE OF SLEEP PARALYSIS CASES	PERCENTAGE OF NON-SLEEP PARALYSIS CASES
Malign presences	45	11
Vibrations/humming	41	11
Out-of-body experiences	21	21
Pulling/touching	20	11
Nightmares/terrors	19	12
Benign/neutral presences	17	14
Voices/laughter	16	7
Bright/flashing lights	16	14
False awakening	15	16
Pains/pins and needles	11	3

Source: Rose, Blackmore and French (2002)

Table 1.02: Study 2

FEATURES	PERCENTAGE OF SLEEP PARALYSIS CASES	PERCENTAGE OF NON-SLEEP PARALYSIS CASES
Malign presences	59	19
Vibrations/humming	38	10
Nightmare/terrors	37	6
Pulling/touching	26	9
Hallucinations	24	9
Voices/laughter	19	4
Flying/floating/falling	13	3
Pains/pins/needles	13	3
Out-of-body experiences	12	3

Source: Rose, Blackmore and French (2002)

continued ...

...continued

a description of the experience as reflecting a paranormal event and less likely to accept sceptical interpretations.

Conclusions

- There are common experiential features of sleep paralysis.
- Believers in the paranormal interpret the experience of and descriptions of experiences of sleep paralysis as reflecting paranormal events.
- The results offer an explanation for the experience of and belief in the paranormal.

Evaluation

- The fact that, in the second study, the majority of non-sleep paralysis cases offered explanations involving extraterrestrials is not surprising, given the nature of the magazine supplying the accounts.
- The study gives an explanation for Hufford's (1982) detailing of hag-riding myths and a belief in witches, but also suggests that the condition is long-lasting, implying that it may be hereditary. This is backed up by such legends being cross-cultural; Fukuda *et al.* (1987) reports similar myths in Japan.
- The respondents were entirely self-selected, and reports were not standardised in any way. Also the categories used were derived from reading the reports themselves. However, both studies produced similar results with regard to the strongest experiential features of sleep paralysis, and the findings are in line with other survey findings.
- Sleep paralysis shares some symptoms with panic attacks. Paradis *et al.* (1997) reported that therapies used to help sufferers of panic attacks can be employed to help sufferers of sleep paralysis, possibly because a decrease in panic symptoms leads to an improvement in the quality of sleep, which in turn incurs a reduction in sleep paralysis episodes.

Issues, debates and approaches

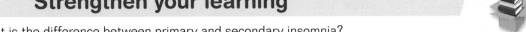

- Much research into narcolepsy concentrates on genetic influences, which can be seen as determinist by failing to acknowledge the influence of environmental triggers, like elevated stress levels.
- It is hoped that research into narcolepsy may help to create an effective and useful practical application in the form of sleeping drugs that mimic natural brain chemistry, rather than the stimulants and antidepressants that are currently used.

Strengthen your learning

1. What is the difference between primary and secondary insomnia?
2. Outline the various sub-types of primary insomnia.
3. What possible causes are there of secondary insomnia?
4. What evaluative points can be gained from research studies of
   i) primary insomnia?
   ii) secondary insomnia?
5. What other evaluative points can be made concerning insomnia?
6. Outline the symptoms and possible causes of apnoea.
7. In what ways can personality factors affect insomnia?
8. For both sleepwalking and narcolepsy, compile a list of
   i) descriptive points
   ii) evaluative points.
9. How might an understanding of sleep paralysis explain a belief in the paranormal?

Assessment Check

1. Outline explanations of insomnia. (8 marks)

2. Outline and evaluate explanations of sleepwalking. (20 marks)

3. Outline one explanation of narcolepsy. (4 marks)

4. Outline explanations of secondary insomnia. (8 marks)

5. Evaluate explanations of sleepwalking. (16 marks)

6. Discuss explanations for insomnia. (24 marks)

Examination guidance

Beware that question 1 requires only an outline of at least two explanations, while question 2 requires both an outline and an evaluation. The outline in 2 would only be worth 4 marks, so most effort should be dedicated to compiling the evaluation.

Question 3 only requires one explanation, if more are provided only the best will be credited. However, the situation is reversed in question 4 where at least 2 explanations are required, quite specifically of secondary insomnia

Question 5 only requires an evaluation. You might be tempted to offer an outline as well, but this would not be creditworthy.

The term 'discuss' in question 6 means to describe and evaluate, with 8 marks available for the outline and 16 for the evaluation.

Summing up

- Biological rhythms are cyclical behaviours – that is, behaviours repeated periodically.

- Circadian rhythms have a cycle of approximately 24 hours, while infradian rhythms have a cycle longer than 24 hours and ultradian rhythms have cycles of less than 24 hours.

- Endogenous pacemakers are rhythms generated from within an organism, while exogenous zeitgebers are external time cues that play an important role in regulating circadian rhythms.

- Shift work and jet lag disrupt biological rhythms, incurring negative effects.

- The nature of sleep includes; the stages of sleep, the content and duration of sleep and lifespan changes.

- Life stage affects the quantity and quality of sleep experienced, with biological and environmental factors contributing to these changes.

- Evolutionary explanations see sleep as serving an adaptive function, keeping prey animals safe from predators, helping to conserve energy, and being related to environmental demands.

- The restoration theory suggests that sleep helps to reverse and/or restore biochemical and/or physiological processes that are progressively degraded during the day.

- Core sleep is essential for restoration, while optional sleep is related to energy conservation. REM sleep is seen as allowing the brain to replenish neurotransmitters used during the day.

- Sleep deprivation studies, like that of Randy Gardner, are used to evaluate the restoration theory and suggest that humans can cope reasonably well with little sleep.

- Insomnia is an inability to sleep and is widespread. Symptoms include sleepiness, fatigue, decreased alertness, concentration and performance.

- Primary insomnia is an illness in itself and not caused by something else. There are sub-types, including psychophysiological insomnia and idiopathic insomnia.

- Secondary insomnia is more common than primary insomnia and is typically caused by psychiatric disorders, such as depression, or medical disorders, such as chronic pain.

- Apnoea is a medical condition where sufferers have persistent pauses in their breathing.

- Obstructive sleep apnoea is the cessation of airflow during sleep, usually caused by a narrowing of the throat due to factors like obesity, age, alcohol or medication issues.

- Central sleep apnoea occurs due to impaired brain signals to areas associated with breathing and occurs less frequently than obstructive sleep apnoea.

- Personality factors are associated with the onset and continuation of insomnia.

- Sleepwalking is mainly a childhood sleep disorder, with an adult incidence of 10 per cent.

- Sleepwalking is associated with personality disorders, especially those related to anxiety. It may be caused by both genetic and environmental factors.

- Narcolepsy affects approximately 1 in 2,000 people and involves excessive daytime sleepiness and sleep attacks. In the latter case, the sudden loss of muscle control is called cataplexy.

- Narcolepsy appears to be a neurological condition associated with a fault in brain mechanisms controlling wakefulness and sleep, with possible causes including genetic factors, a shortage of the neurotransmitter hypocretin or an autoimmune disease.

- Narcoleptics can suffer from sleep paralysis, occurring when the brain awakes from an REM state, leaving the body paralysed.

2 Perception

Theories of perceptual organisation   **43**

Gregory's top-down theory   44

Gibson's bottom-up theory   50

Development of perception   **56**

The development of perceptual
abilities   56

Depth and distance perception   56

Visual constancies   57

Perceptual development   59

**Face recognition and visual
agnosias**   **69**

Bruce and Young's theory of face
recognition   70

Explanations of prosopagnosia   72

Summing up   **78**

Decoding the specification

The specification outlines what must be studied to answer any examination question faced. It begins with a specific and straightforward requirement – to have a knowledge and understanding of two major theories of perceptual organisation, Gregory's and Gibson's. Questions will concentrate specifically on these theories, or a comparison of them, and you will need to be able to evaluate and describe them.

Knowledge of how perceptual abilities develop is required. Depth/distance perception, visual constancies, infant and cross–cultural studies are specifically identified, so there's a requirement to have knowledge and understanding of them and what they tell us about perceptual development, as they may be referred to explicitly in examination questions.

The final requirement is quite clear: a knowledge and understanding of Bruce and Young's theory, and an ability to describe and evaluate it. You should also have a working knowledge of case studies and explanations of the visual agnosia, prosopagnosia.

Theories of perceptual organisation

When a tree falls down in a wood and nobody is there, does it make a noise? (Buddhist proverb)

Eyes do not directly 'see', nor ears directly 'hear'. They are sensory organs that respond to specific types of physical energy, converting this energy into electrical impulses that are relayed by the nervous system to the brain for processing into what is experienced as 'perception'. Yet the brain cannot directly perceive. Shine a light onto the brain and it will not be dazzled; plug an MP3 player into the brain and it will not experience music – it is a silent, unseeing bodily organ. This is because sensing and perceiving are two separate yet interdependent processes, where sensations have no meaning on their own and perception cannot occur without sensations to comprehend. Therefore, when a tree falls down in a wood with no one to hear it, it does not make a noise; indeed the noise only occurs when there is someone there to perceive the sound of the falling tree.

IN THE NEWS

Adapted from the *Daily Telegraph*, 6 July 2003
© Telegraph Media Group Limited 2003

Pilgrims flock to the 'Madonna' in the hospital window

Lorna Dibona, a Catholic grandmother in her mid-sixties is gazing at a third-floor window of Milton Hospital. 'They said it was just condensation between two window panes, but that shape hasn't changed. We've had endless days of rain and now we've had a full week of hot sun, yet she's still there.'

The alleged appearance of a robed Virgin Mary, with child, in the hospital window has provoked scenes described by a Protestant onlooker as 'straight out of a film by Federico Fellini'.

Visitors from as far away as New York City and Washington kneel and pray each evening. Rapt women sing Ave Maria and light candles that, it is said, have continued burning throughout the fiercest thunderstorm.

Not everyone believes. Maintenance workers at the hospital attribute the discolouration on the window to condensation – the result of a ruptured sealant in the frame. This prosaic explanation has done nothing to discourage visitors. More than 50,000 pilgrims have visited the site since the image was noticed last month.

Pareidolia is a type of illusion or misperception involving a vague or obscure stimulus being perceived as something clear and distinct. This often has

Figure 2.01

religious overtones, as with the Madonna seen in the hospital window, and even more commonly involves the perception of faces in mundane objects, like rocks and items of food, with the oldest probably being the Man in the Moon illusion. Astronomer Carl Sagan believed that the tendency to see faces in clouds, buns, and so on, was an evolutionary trait, with babies hardwired to recognise and smile at faces in order to make attachments, as this incurs a survival value. This view has research support: Fantz (1961) found that infants have an innate interest and preference for human faces. And under clinical circumstances, some psychologists encourage pareidolia as a means to understanding patients – for example, the Rorschach ink blot test.

So although some may disagree, it probably is not the face of the Madonna in a hospital window, but the manifestation of a human tendency to see faces in everyday articles.

Theories of perceptual organisation try to explain the relationship between seeing and perceiving. Either, as Gregory believed, inferences (best guesses) are made as to what the world consists of from the sensory information at hand and from previous experience, or, as Gibson believed, the physical world is directly perceived from the properties contained within sensations.

Perception is a cognitive process that concerns how the sensations that stimulate sensory organs are comprehended – in other words, how those sensations are captured, processed and experienced, as touches, tastes, smells, sights and sounds, which are then manifested into meaningful experiences and a predictable world of objects that can be moved about in and interacted with.

Gregory's top-down theory

Gregory was influenced by von Helmholtz (1909), who saw perception occurring through interactions and experimentations with the physical world. Gregory therefore believed that perception was an unconscious, continual process of generating and testing hypotheses, as an active search for the most sensible interpretation of sensory data based on previous experience. The search was *indirect*, as it went beyond the immediate data provided by sensory receptors to involve processing information at a higher, 'top–down' cognitive level.

> *Perception is not determined simply by stimulus patterns. Rather it is a dynamic searching for the best interpretation of the available data … which involves going beyond the immediately given evidence of the senses.* Gregory (1966)

Essentially, Gregory saw sensory information as impoverished, incomplete or ambiguous. For example, the retinal image of a strawberry is unable to convey its taste and density – therefore, perception, rather than being directly experienced from sensations, involves a dynamic search for the best interpretation of stimuli. For Gregory, what is perceived is much richer than the information contained within sensory data; the eye for him is not a camera to view the world directly.

Sensory data is often incomplete or ambiguous, and hypotheses need to be generated about their meaning. A good example of this is found in the experience of reversible figures, like being able to see a woman's face or a man playing the saxophone. Both are perceived, as Gregory believes that separate hypotheses are being generated and tested out, though in real-world situations there is normally ample sensory information to determine which interpretation of information is true. When, as with the reversible figure, confusions occur, visual illusions are experienced.

Perceptual set

Perceptual set is a concept that views individuals as biased in how they perceive, due to previous experiences, cultural factors and emotional and motivational influences. In other words, people see what they want or expect to see and this cuts down on the number of possible interpretations that data may suggest, making perception speedier, though increasing the opportunities for errors to occur.

You are the researcher

A simple method of demonstrating perceptual set experimentally through context can be achieved as follows. In one condition, ask participants to hold identical objects of equal weight, one in each hand. Then ask them whether the objects are the same weight or different. In the second condition, ask the same participants to hold an object of considerable weight in one hand, while simultaneously holding a light object in the other hand. Do this for about 30 seconds, and then replace the objects with those used in the first condition. Participants should report the object in the hand that previously held the heavy object as being heavier.

What advantage is there in using the same participants in both conditions?

What are order effects and how would you control them?

Expectations

One way in which perceptual set is seen as occurring is through expectations, where individuals perceive what they expect to perceive based on previous experience.

Research: expectations

Figure 2.02 Leeper's ambiguous lady – can you see the old and the young ladies?

- Bruner and Mintern (1955) showed an ambiguous figure to participants that could be seen either as the letter 'B' or the figure '13'. Those participants who saw the figure surrounded by the consecutive numbers 12 and 14 perceived it as '13', while those who saw it as surrounded by the consecutive letters A and C, perceived it as 'B'. This suggests that the context in which stimuli are viewed creates an expectation that shapes actual perception.

- Leeper (1935) showed participants an ambiguous picture, which could either be seen as a young or an old woman. Participants previously given a description or picture of a young woman perceived a young woman in the ambiguous figure, and those described or shown an old woman perceived an old woman. This indicates that expectations based on previous experience determine perception in an indirect fashion, as suggested by Gregory.

- Brochet (2002) first gave 54 expert wine tasters an array of white wines, which they described as 'fresh', 'honeyed', and so on. He then gave them an array of red wines to evaluate, of which some were white wine, doctored to look red by the addition of a tasteless, odourless additive. Not one expert spotted the frauds, describing them in terms reserved for red wines, such as 'intense', 'spicy', and so on. Because they had increased knowledge of wine, they were more influenced by colour. The colour created an expectation, which determined actual perception.

Research in focus

Brochet's (2002) experiment was assessing whether wine experts would be fooled by white wine dyed red. What was the purpose therefore of getting them to rate genuine white wines first?

Supplementary learning

The fraud of perceptual expectation

One way in which the role of expectation in perceptual experience can be seen in action in the real world is that of frauds, especially food frauds. It is estimated that the counterfeit food industry is worth about £25 billion a year. Such counterfeiting consists of passing off inferior foods as being of higher quality. For instance, in 2007 two students used DNA testing to prove that 77 per cent of fish labelled as red snapper was actually inferior tilapia, a much less flavoursome fish. An American TV station then tested 38 meals in various cities, finding that 23 out of 38 fish meals were not as advertised. Similar frauds have been exposed in the sale of olive oil and fine wines.

Why do the counterfeiters find it easy to get away with? Maybe people's taste buds are not that sophisticated, but it is more likely that the expectations of what people are consuming have a part to play. If a fish is labelled as red snapper and is coloured to look like red snapper, people expect to taste red snapper and this expectation shapes perception – that is, they actually taste red snapper.

The art fraudster John Myatt created forgeries in the style of famous masters, which were passed as unquestionably genuine by art experts. He was only caught when he fell out with his girlfriend, who informed the police. Sixty of his forgeries have been found, but 140 remain undetected, probably hanging on gallery walls and perceived by an admiring audience as the real thing, because that is what they expect to see.

You are the researcher

Design an experiment to see whether participants would perceive lemonade as cola if they expected it to be so.

One way to achieve this is to have genuine lemonade and ask participants to select from a list of adjectives describing the taste. Repeat the procedure, but with lemonade disguised as cola. If perception is influenced by expectation, the descriptions of the disguised lemonade should be different from the real lemonade.

Why would you also need to have participants rate real lemonade?

In what order would you present the drinks to avoid bias?

How would you compile your list of taste adjectives?

Emotional influences

Perceptual set also occurs through emotional factors, which affect perception by creating a bias to perceive, or not, certain features of incoming sensory data. *Perceptual defence* is important here, where emotionally threatening stimuli take longer to perceive.

Research: emotional influences

- McGinnies (1949) found that emotionally threatening words took longer to recognise than neutral ones, suggesting that perceptual defence influences perception through emotional factors. However, the results may be due to the embarrassment of speaking the words aloud. Bitterman and Kniffin (1953) found no differences in recognition time if the words were written down.

- Lazarus and McCleary (1951) found that nonsense syllables presented so swiftly that they could not be consciously perceived raised anxiety levels if they were previously paired with electric shocks. This implies that emotional factors influence perception unconsciously.

- Phelps *et al.* (2006) manipulated emotion by showing participants, for a brief instance, either fearful or neutral faces in various locations on a screen. An image then appeared briefly and participants selected in which direction it tilted. Participants were more able to do this when the figure was paired with fearful faces, especially those in the same orientation as the tilted figure. This suggests that emotion facilitates perception early in the processing system. This research was extended by Zeelenberg and Bocanegra (2010), who found that the auditory presentation of negative emotional words enhanced the perception of subsequent visually presented neutral target words, but impaired performance when presented visually. This suggests that emotional stimuli affect perception differently in different sensory modalities, possibly due to the focusing of attention.

Motivational influences

Motivation to perceive in certain ways is influenced by factors like thirst and hunger, with images of food seen as more succulent and enticing as an individual becomes more famished. This could have an evolutionary purpose, whereby perception becomes more focused on elements necessary for survival, like the acquisition of food.

Research: motivational influences

- Solley and Haigh (1948) found that children drew a bigger Santa and sack of toys as Christmas approached, but afterwards Santa and his sack shrunk. This implies that motivational factors influence perception.

- Bruner and Goodman (1947) got children to manipulate a patch of light so it was the same size as various coins. All children overestimated the size of the coins compared to cardboard control discs, but poor children even more so, implying that they were more motivated to perceive money as 'bigger'.

- Balcettis and Dunning (2006) briefly flashed an ambiguous figure that could be the letter B or the number 13. Participants told that a letter would get them a nice drink, perceived the letter, while those told that a number would earn them the drink, perceived the number. This suggests that perceptual set influences perception in an indirect fashion and people see what they wish to see.

You are the researcher

Design a correlational study to assess whether pictures of food are seen as more appetising as a meal time approaches.

How would you get participants to rate pictures? How many rating occasions would be needed? Would the same or different participants be used for each rating occasion? Write a suitable correlational hypothesis based on known research.

Cultural factors

Cultural factors influence perceptual set by predisposing individuals to perceive environmental features in certain ways. Thus people from different cultural backgrounds sometimes perceive identical sensory information differently, as they have had different environmental experiences. For example, the Müller–Lyer illusion consists of two equally long lines, but line A appears longer than line B (see Figure 2.03), but is only perceived in cultures where individuals live in a carpentered world of manufactured straight lines,

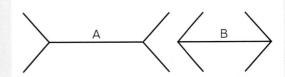

Figure 2.03 The Müller-Lyer illusion

angles, and so on. Those from cultures where buildings are made from natural materials do not experience the illusion. A person from a carpentered world culture experiences the illusion, because they unconsciously read the third dimension of depth into it from experience.

Research: cultural factors

- Segall (1963) found that Africans living in open country, where occasional vertical objects were important features, were susceptible to the *horizontal-vertical illusion*, while those living in dense jungle were unlikely to see the illusion. This implies that physical environment shapes cultural influences, which affects perception.

- Stewart (1973) found that Tongan rural children are less likely to experience a range of visual illusions, including the Müller-Lyer illusion, and the more experienced these children were with an environment of straight lines and rectangles, the more prone to the illusion they were, supporting the idea that environmental experience shapes perception.

- Pettigrew *et al.* (1978) presented a picture of one South African ethnic group to one eye of a participant and another ethnic group to the other eye. White South Africans were not able to distinguish between black and mixed-race people, suggesting that the cultural influence of their racial prejudice affected their perception.

Visual illusions

Gregory believes that visual illusions are experienced because expectations based on previous experience are used to create and test hypotheses from incoming sensory information, but sometimes this is prone to error and false perceptions occur.

In the Kanizsa illusion, an upright white triangle is perceived above an upside-down white triangle with black edges and three black circles. The upright triangle appears ultra-white, with crisp edges, yet it is a perceptual invention. It is not there.

Previous experience of what objects look like when they are superimposed on each other is used to experience the illusion – that is, the third dimension of depth is read into a flat, two-dimensional image. Therefore, individuals go beyond the physical sensory data captured by the retina to perceive something unreal.

Figure 2.04 The Kanizsa triangle illusion

Research: visual illusions

- Gregory and Ramachandran (1992) provided an explanation for the illusion of not perceiving blind spots. The blind spot is found in all eyes, situated in the light-sensitive retina at the back of the eye where the optical nerve connects the retina to the brain, meaning that a black dot should be perceived, but isn't. The brain 'fills in' the information by inferring what should be present from visual data found around the edges of the blind spot. This supports Gregory's view that perception is an active process going beyond available sensory information to perceive that which is expected.

- Myers (2003) explains reversible figure illusions, like the duck–rabbit illusion, where both duck and rabbit are perceived independently, but not simultaneously, in gestaltist terms, whereby individual sensory stimuli are perceived collectively as a whole. This involves formulating and testing perceptual hypotheses, in line with Gregory's theory.

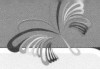
- Gregory (1970) explains the 'hollow face' illusion, where a hollow mask is perceived as a convex face, as due to the indirect knowledge of faces located in memory being pitted against the direct information signalled by the senses, with the indirect, or top–down, processing winning. This implies support for Gregory's theory over Gibson's (see page 50).

Evaluation

Gregory's indirect theory

- Gregory's theory has aided the understanding of perception, stimulating interest and research and creating a wealth of evidence, both experimental and naturalistic, which support the theory.

- There is a logical sense to the theory that inferences based on previous experience would be made when viewing conditions are incomplete or ambiguous. For example, if incomplete features of a creature indicated it could be a duck or a rabbit, the fact that it was floating on water would determine a perception of it being a duck.

- Gregory's idea of indirect processing explains how individuals perceive the same stimuli differently due to different environmental experiences – for example, the Müller-Lyer illusion. If humans perceived directly from sensory information, everyone would perceive in the same manner.

- Gregory's indirect theory explains visual illusions more satisfactorily than direct perception. However, Gregory's explanation is not without criticism; according to Gregory's theory, once it is understood why illusions occur, perception would be modified so they are not experienced anymore. However, they are still experienced, casting doubt on Gregory's explanation. There are other explanations for illusions, like the evolutionary one, which explains the Kanizsa illusion in terms of needing to see form and edges for survival purposes.

- Eysenck and Keane (1990) believe that Gregory's theory is better at explaining the perception of illusions than real objects, because illusions are unreal and simplified and easy to misperceive, while real objects provide enough complex data to be perceived directly.

- Most research supporting Gregory involves laboratory experiments, which are biased to favour his theory, as fragmented and briefly presented stimuli are often used, so it would be difficult to perceive directly from such sensory data. Gregory underestimates how rich and informative sensory data can be and that it may be possible to perceive directly in many real-world situations.

- People's perceptions in general, even those of people from different cultures, are similar. This would not be true if individual perceptions were created from individual experiences, weakening support for Gregory.

- Gregory's theory suggests that memory is constantly searched to find the best interpretation of incoming sensory data. However, this would be time-consuming and inefficient, again casting doubt on Gregory's explanation.

Issues, debates and approaches

- Gregory's and Gibson's theories can be seen in terms of the nature versus nurture debate. Gregory's indirect theory emphasises learning experiences and thus the influence of nurture, while Gibson's direct theory sees more of a role for nature.

- Research into emotional factors, like McGinnies (1949), can be considered unethical by causing psychological harm through exposure to threatening stimuli.

Gibson's bottom-up theory

Gibson believed that there was ample information within the pattern of light reaching the eyes, referred to as the *optic array*, for perception to occur directly, without the need for higher-level cognitive processing or inferring through hypothesis generating and testing. Individuals' movements and those of surrounding objects within an environment facilitate this process. This involves innate mechanisms forged by evolution, which require no learning from experience.

Gibson saw perception as due to the direct detection of *environmental invariances*, unchanging elements of the visual environment. These contain a sufficient source of sensory data to permit individuals to perceive features of their environment, like depth, distance and the spatial relationships of where objects are in relation to each other.

It was while he was preparing training films for pilots during the Second World War that Gibson became interested in *optic flow patterns*, the movement of objects within the visual environment providing information to observers about spatial position and depth. He then researched other forms of sensory information occurring in various environments, publishing his theory in the 1950 book *The Perception of the Visual World*. Gibson's central idea was that texture gradients present in the environment are similar to gradients in the eye, and these complementary gradients permit the experience of depth perception. This idea grew into a general theory of perception containing several key points, including the optic array, textured gradients, optic flow patterns, horizon ratio and affordance.

Unlike Gregory, who relied on research conducted in laboratory conditions involving motionless stimuli and observers, Gibson's research utilised dynamic real-world conditions and he was keen to produce practical applications of his work, having originated from a practically based background. He explained illusions as two-dimensional, static constructions of artificial laboratory conditions.

Gibson saw perception as a 'bottom-up' process, one constructed directly from sensory information. So, different to Gregory, Gibson saw the perceiver, not as the brain, but as the person within their environment. The function of perception, therefore, is to enable a person to function in their environment in safety.

The optical array

Gibson described the optical array as the composition of patterned light entering the eyes. It is an ever-changing source of sensory information, occurring due to the movements of individuals and objects within their world and consists of different intensities of light shining in different directions, conveying sensory data about the physical environment. Light itself does not allow direct perception, but the structure of the sensory information contained within light does. Motion of the body, the eyes, the angle of gaze, and so on continually updates the sensory information being received from the optical array.

The optical array also contains *invariant* elements, providing constant sources of information, all of which contribute to direct perception from sensory information and which are not changed by the motions of an observer.

Optic flow patterns

Gibson described optic flow patterns as unambiguous sources of information concerning height, distance and speed that directly inform perception.

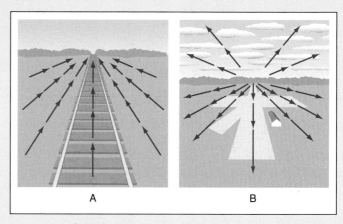

Figure 2.05 Optic flow patterns as seen by a train driver and a pilot

The term 'optic flow' refers to the visual phenomena experienced continually concerning the apparent visual motion that occurs as individuals move around in their environment. A person sitting in a car looking out of the window sees buildings, trees, and so on, appearing to move backwards; it is this apparent motion that forms the optic flow. Information concerning distance is also gained; distant objects like hills appear to move slowly, while objects that are nearer appear to move more quickly. This depth cue is known as motion parallax.

As an individual's speed increases, the optic flow also increases. The optic flow also varies in relation to the angle between an observer's direction of movement and the direction of an object being regarded. When travelling forwards, the optic flow is quickest when the object being regarded is 90 degrees to the observer's side, or when directly above or below him or her. Objects immediately in front have no optic flow and appear motionless. However, the edges of such objects appear to move, because they are not directly in front and thus such objects seem to grow larger. The optic flow provides a rich, ever-changing source of information that is perceived directly from higher-level information processing, without recourse to further such processing.

Research: optic flow patterns

- Johansson (1973) found that a black-clad actor wearing lights on his knees, ankles, and so on, walking in a darkened room, was perceivable as a moving person, but a stationary person was not perceivable if he stood still. This shows how important movement is in determining optic flow patterns.

- Maher and West (1993) filmed the movements of black-clad animals with lights on their joints, finding that the species of animal was recognisable to observers. This demonstrates the strength of information movement in determining optic flow patterns, and shows that there is enough sensory information for perception to occur directly.

- Bardy et al. (1996) asked participants to walk on a treadmill with a screen in front of them, onto which optic flow patterns were beamed. It was found that motion parallax was used to maintain balance by using optic flow patterns to make compensatory movements, supporting Gibson's idea that optic flow patterns are rich enough sources of information to allow direct perception.

Texture gradient

Texture gradients are surface patterns providing sensory information about the depth, shape, and so on, of objects. Physical objects possess surfaces with different textures that allow the direct perception of distance, depth and spatial awareness. Due to constant motions, the 'flow' of texture gradients provides a rich source of ever-changing sensory information to the observer – for instance, as objects come nearer they appear to expand.

Two depth cues are central here to the third dimension of depth being directly available to the senses: motion parallax and linear perspective. The latter is a cue provided by lines seemingly converging as they get further away. These both permit the third dimension of depth to be directly accessible to the senses.

There are several classic texture gradients – for example, frontal surfaces project a uniform gradient, while longitudinal surfaces, like roads, project gradients that diminish with greater distance from the observer.

Figure 2.06 An example of linear perspective. The painting by Vermeer shows that the bricks and other features of the front of the building are mainly parallel and do not converge as they go across the scene. The building is seen as if it were being looked at straight on. It looks flat.

You are the researcher

Art students should have more experience of depth/ distance perception. Conduct an assessment of whether this is true by placing a large piece of card face down and drawing a target 'x' on it. Then get a group of art students and a group of non-art students to reach underneath (without looking) and place a marker (a small adhesive sticker works well) where they think the target is. You will need to mark underneath where the target is to assess accuracy.

How would you determine your data? You could use other groups who differ in degrees of familiarity/non-familiarity with depth/distance perception to assess the role of learning in this perceptual ability.

Figure 2.07 Another example of linear perspective. In this painting by Caillebotte, texture gradient is used in the form of cobblestones that get progressively smaller to show that the street recedes in depth.

Research: texture gradients

- Gibson and Bridgeman (1987) showed participants photographs of surface textures. Participants could correctly identify objects, state their colour, identify the light conditions and say whether they were lying flat, and so on, suggesting that there is sufficient sensory information in surface textures to permit direct perception. This supports Gibson's theory.

- Frichtel *et al.* (2006) presented participants with a film of a car driving through scenery. Evidence was found that infants as young as 4 months old could perceive using texture gradient, implying that the ability is innate, and lending support to Gibson's theory that perception is reliant on innate mechanisms.

Horizon ratios

Horizon ratios are another form of invariant sensory information allowing direct perception. They concern the position of objects in relation to the horizon. Objects of different sizes at equal distances from an observer have different horizon ratios, which can be calculated by dividing the amount of an object above the horizon by the amount below the horizon.

Different size objects at equal distances away have different horizon ratios, while objects of equal size standing on level surfaces possess the same horizon ratio. When nearing an object, it seems to get bigger, though the proportion of the object above or below the horizon stays constant and is a perceptual invariant.

Research: horizon ratios

- Creem-Regehr *et al.* (2003) found that restricting participants' viewing conditions did not affect their ability to judge distances using horizon ratio information, suggesting that this form of invariant sensory information is a powerful tool in establishing direct perception.

- Bingham (1993) asked participants to judge the height of cylinders under various conditions where they were provided with cues in the form of simulated tree silhouettes and a horizon. The heights of cylinders were judged inaccurately when they appeared with the horizon but without trees. Judgements were more accurate when the cylinders also appeared in the context of trees, demonstrating how horizon ratios are used to estimate the height of objects in the visual field.

- Rogers (1996) found horizon ratios an effective source of information when judging relative size of objects in pictures, even when horizons were not provided. Participants could still accurately base relative size of objects by imposing their own horizon ratio based on eye level and the content of the picture, demonstrating the degree to which humans rely on this invariant source of information to perceive.

Affordances

Affordances are the most controversial aspect of Gibson's theory and involve attaching meaning to sensory information. Affordances are the quality of an object that permits actions to be carried out on it (*action possibilities*) – for example, a brush 'affords' sweeping the floor. Affordances are thus what objects suggest or mean to observers and are linked to psychological state and physical abilities – for instance, to a toddler who cannot walk properly a mountain is not something to be climbed.

Gibson saw affordances as giving directly perceivable meaning to objects, because evolutionary forces shaped perceptual skills so that learning experiences were not necessary. This rejects Gregory's belief that the meaning of objects is stored in long-term memory from experience and requires cognitive processing to access.

Research: affordances

- Warren (1984) studied whether participants could judge whether staircases portrayed with differently proportioned steps could 'afford' to be climbed. Whether they actually could depended on the length of a participant's leg. It was found that participants were sensitive to the affordance of 'climbability', and according to Gibson this would be achieved by the invariant properties of the light reflected from the staircases. This, therefore, provides some support for the concept of affordances not relying on experience.

- Bruce and Green (1990) found that the idea of affordances could be used to explain the visually controlled behaviour of animals like insects, lending support to Gibson's theory. However, unlike humans, such animals are not thought to require an internal, conceptual representation of their environment.

- Stoffregen *et al.* (1995) tested the affordances of the actions of others, rather than one's own actions, which most research has concentrated on. Participants observed tall and short actors standing next to an adjustable chair and in motion, to simulate dynamic action that would be present in real-world situations – for example, walking on the spot – and had to make judgements of preferred and maximum sitting heights for each actor. In both conditions, participants provided accurate judgements for maximum and preferred sitting heights, supporting the idea that affordances are available by direct perception.

Evaluation

Gibson's direct theory

- Gibson's theory led to greater understanding and to interest and research into perception. For instance, Gaver (1996) applied the idea of affordances to designing computer displays. Another practical application of Gibson's theory is putting parallel lines increasingly closer together as road junctions approach, giving a false impression of speed to slow drivers down (see 'Psychology in action' on page 54).

- Gibson's theory can explain how perception occurs so quickly, which Gregory's theory cannot.

- There is a wealth of research evidence supporting the elements of Gibson's theory; indeed, recent evidence even generates some support for the controversial element of his theory, that of affordances.

- There may be a biological basis to Gibson's theory. Logothetis and Pauls (1995) identified neurons in the brains of monkeys that seemed to perceive specific objects regardless of their orientation, implying that a biological mechanism allows direct perception. This was supported by Rizzolati and Sinigaglia (2008), who found that the anterior intraparietal brain area is involved in the direct perception of object affordances.

- The idea that the optical array provides direct information about what objects allow individuals to do (affordances) seems unlikely. Knowledge about objects is affected by cultural influences, experience

continued ...

...continued

and emotions. For instance, how could an individual directly perceive that a training shoe is for running?

- Gibson cannot really explain why illusions are perceived. He dismissed them as artificial laboratory constructions viewed under restrictive conditions. But some occur naturally under normal viewing conditions.

- One similarity between Gibson's and Gregory's theories is that they both see perception as being hypothesis-based. While Gregory explains this as a process of hypothesis formation and testing, and sees the flow of information as being processed from the top down, Gibson sees it as an unconscious process created from evolutionary forces, with the flow of information being processed from the bottom up. Another similarity is that they both agree that visual perception occurs from light reflected off surfaces and objects and that a specific biological system is required to perceive.

- Perhaps a combination of Gregory's top-down and Gibson's bottom-up ideas forms the best explanation of perception. Gibson's theory works best for ideal viewing conditions, while Gregory's works best for less than ideal conditions. This approach was utilised in Neisser's (1976) Perceptual Cycle theory.

Psychology in action

The psychology of road markings

Gibson's direct theory of perception was created out of the practical consideration of training aircraft pilots. During the Second World War, Gibson made training films to illustrate the problems pilots had in taking off and landing (see page 50). From this he created his idea of optic flow patterns, a theory that has practical applications to the modern world.

The prime example is seen in road markings. Horizontal lines are painted onto the road surface, becoming progressively closer together as drivers approach junctions or roundabouts. Such markings are common on the exit roads from motorways and serve to create an illusion of increased speed, which causes the driver to slow down before joining a non-motorway road where speeds will be considerably slower than before.

Tan *et al.* (2006) used Gibson's idea of optic flow patterns to investigate the effects of motion on car drivers' perception, where cars travelling towards a viewer appear to increase in speed and size, even though their real speed and size are constant. This perceptual problem is increased by the fact that the viewer is also in motion. A camera mounted on a wing mirror was used to determine real-world speed from two-dimensional optic flow data. The data gained from studies like this are used to determine speed limits and advise on braking distances.

As well as contributing to knowledge of perception, Gibson's theory also saves countless lives in preventing or lessening the impact of road traffic accidents.

There are a number of good sites to reference visual illusions and their explanations, including the following:
http://dragon.uml.edu/psych/illusion.html
www.scientificpsychic.com/graphics/
www.optillusions.com

Issues, debates and approaches

- Gibson's theory has practical applications, like painting road markings progressively closer together to slow traffic speeds, thus saving lives.
- Gibson's theory can be considered reductionist in the sense that it believes perception to be innate, thus ignoring the influence of learned knowledge.

Strengthen your learning

1. Outline the relationship between sensing and perceiving.
2. What is meant by *indirect* (top-down) and *direct* (bottom-up) processing?
3. Why does Gregory see perception as a top-down process?
4. Explain what is meant by perceptual set in terms of:
   i) expectations
   ii) emotional influences
   iii) motivational influences
   iv) cultural factors.
5. To what extent does research support the role of perceptual set in determining perception? Give details.
6. How does Gregory explain the perception of visual illusions? Does research support Gregory's view? Give details.
7. Why does Gibson see perception as a bottom-up process?
8. What is the optical array?
9. Outline Gibson's theory in terms of:
   i) optic flow patterns
   ii) texture gradients
   iii) horizon ratios
   iv) affordances.
10. What degree of research support is there for Gibson's theory? Give details.
11. In terms of evaluation, is Gregory's or Gibson's theory more supported? Construct a balanced argument in bullet-point form.

Assessment Check ▶

1. Outline and evaluate one theory of perception. (24 marks)

2. Outline Gregory's top-down and Gibson's bottom-up theories of perception. (8 marks)

3. Evaluate one of the theories outlined in (2) in terms of research evidence. (16 marks)

4. Critically compare Gregory's top-down and Gibson's bottom-up theories. (24 marks)

Examination guidance

Question 1 gives a choice, so either Gregory's or Gibson's theory could be utilised and the other theory used to evaluate through comparison.

Question 2 requires both theories to be described. You need to achieve a reasonable balance between the two in order to access the top band of marks.

Question 3 is quite specific in that the evaluation should be centred on research evidence, so take care to focus on this requirement and not to stray from the demands of the question.

Question 4 is unusual, but due to the wording of the specification it could easily be set. You would need to outline both theories, for 8 marks, and evaluate them for a further 16 marks. A well-focused evaluation would draw out the similarities and differences between the two theories.

Development of perception

The development of perceptual abilities

Perception is not a single entity; it is composed of several abilities, some of which are learned, and others of which are innate. When babies are born, they need basic perceptual abilities with immediate survival value, which also allow them to interact with and learn from their environment. If all perceptual abilities were fully formed and present at birth, it would not be possible for individuals to adapt to and thrive in different and changing environmental conditions. As everyone's experiences are different, perceptual abilities become shaped to suit an individual's needs and environment, and thus complex abilities are formed more by learning. The fact that perception seems in this way to be strongly linked to survival suggests that perceptual abilities have evolved.

It used to be believed that humans were born with little in the way of perceptual ability, but as research progressed it became clear that humans had more perceptual awareness than had originally been thought. Research has focused on individual perceptual abilities, assessing what proportion of these is learned and what is innate. Various methodologies are employed, each with strengths and weaknesses. The main two areas of research focused on are infant and cross-cultural studies.

Depth and distance perception

Depth and distance perception involve the ability to distinguish the environment as three-dimensional and to judge distances of objects from each other and ourselves. These perceptual skills are fundamental to survival; without them, individuals would constantly be in danger – for example, not being able to cross a road without being run over. Depth and distance perception specifically involve *space perception*, how the distances between objects are assessed, which mainly utilises visual perception.

To accomplish this, there are two types of depth/distance cues: *monocular*, apparent to one eye, and *binocular*, apparent to both eyes. Cues can also be divided into *primary*, which are not dependent on learning, and *secondary*, which are.

Babies have innate abilities to perceive depth and distance by utilising primary cues rather than secondary ones, as these are innate and immediately available. The ability to use secondary cues matures quickly though. More sophisticated forms of depth and distance perception tend to involve secondary cues as these are about individuals learning to interact with their environment. Table 2.01 opposite gives a description of the main primary and secondary cues used to perceive depth and distance.

Table 2.01 Primary and secondary depth/distance cues

PRIMARY CUES	DESCRIPTION	SECONDARY CUES	DESCRIPTION
Retinal disparity *Binocular cue*	Information from both eyes is combined to give an impression of depth and distance.	*Interposition* *Binocular cue*	When objects overlap, the fully visible one is nearer.
Convergence *Binocular cue*	Feedback from eye muscles when focusing on objects informs us about depth and distance.	*Texture gradient* *Binocular cue*	Changes in texture gradients inform us about depth and distance, with surface texture smaller for objects further away.
Accommodation *Monocular cue*	Feedback from the curvature of the lens, which alters shape to focus on objects, informs us about depth and distance.	*Retinal size* *Binocular cue*	The size of retinal images informs us about depth and distance, with distant objects having smaller retinal size.
		Motion parallax *Binocular cue*	Perceiving objects moving at different speeds informs us about depth and distance, with distant objects moving more slowly.
		Arial perspective *Monocular cue*	Sharp images are seen as closer, blurry ones further away.
		Elevation *Monocular cue*	Concerns an object's placement in relation to the horizon. For objects below the horizon, nearer ones seem further from the horizon, with the reverse true for objects above the horizon.
		Linear perspective *Monocular cue*	Lines appear to converge into the distance and objects appear to shrink.

Visual constancies

The whole of an object is never seen at one time; however, because of visual constancies, objects in vision appear to remain constant and unchanging regardless of viewing conditions and the retinal image produced. For instance, as a car approaches, the retinal image of it gets bigger, but the car itself does not. This has an adaptive survival value, as an ordered, predictable world is a safer place to interact with. Relying solely on retinal images would create a perceptual world of constantly elongating and shrinking objects, landscapes and people, with colours forever paling and darkening in intensity – a kind of continually changing mixture of environmental experiences that would be utterly chaotic, nonsensical and ultimately dangerous to move about in.

The characteristics of the main visual constancies, size, shape, brightness and colour, are summarised in Table 2.02 on page 58.

Table 2.02

TYPE OF VISUAL CONSTANCY	DESCRIPTION
Size constancy	Familiar objects appear to have a constant size regardless of the retinal image due to perceptual interpretation of the retinal image.
Shape constancy	Familiar objects retain a constant shape regardless of changes in the viewing angle, with the visual system combining retinal information and the viewing angle to create perceptions of the actual shape.
Brightness constancy	The perceived brightness of a familiar object remains constant despite viewing conditions, which helps in recognising objects as familiar and unchanging.
Colour constancy	Familiar objects appear to retain their colour regardless of lighting conditions, as long as sufficient contrast and shadow are apparent.

Contemporary research

Ropar and Mitchell (2002)

Shape constancy in autism: the role of prior knowledge and perspective cues

Previous research evidence suggested that individuals with autism do not possess typical perceptual abilities, such as not being able to spot anything odd with 'impossible figures', like the Penrose triangle, suggesting that they do not attend to contextual information when processing stimuli. Impossible figures contain contradicting perspective cues that are only evident when comparing different parts of a figure. Therefore, a failure to detect impossibility in those with autism could be due to less influence by prior knowledge or an inability to integrate the component parts of a stimulus.

Aim

To explore the effect of prior knowledge on perception independently of perspective cues with regard to shape constancy. Specifically, the researchers wanted to see if exaggerating a reproduction of a stimulus would occur only when perspective cues were present, or if prior knowledge would be sufficient for exaggeration, even without perspective cues.

Procedure

The researchers used an adaptation of a procedure developed by Thouless (1931), who

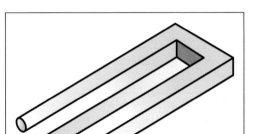

Figure 2.08 Autistics do not see anything odd with impossible figures

asked participants to reproduce a slanted circle, finding that they drew a more circular ellipse relative to the projected image. This occurs because they perceive the ellipse as more circular than it actually is, due to ambient perspective cues.

The researchers asked participants to view a stimulus they knew was a slanted circle inside a chamber that was either lit, so perspective cues were present, or darkened so that only the stimulus was present and perspective cues were absent.

The participants were 28 individuals clinically diagnosed with autism and a control group of 20 individuals with moderate learning difficulties. Nineteen typically developing 9-year-olds and 14 adults also took part.

continued ...

...continued

The researchers constructed a small wooden chamber with a darkened interior and viewing slot in which could be seen either a circular or an elliptical window. Perspective cues could also be produced in the form of black and white vertical lines.

Using a keypad, participants adjusted a shape on a computer screen to reproduce what they saw.

There were three conditions:

(i)   Prior knowledge, where participants knew the stimulus was a slanted circle, but that the chamber was darkened so only the stimulus was visible.

(ii) Perspective plus prior knowledge, which was the same as above, but viewing took place in an illuminated chamber (so perspective cues were visible).

(iii) Ellipse condition, where participants knew there was a non-slanted ellipse inside a darkened chamber.

The order of presentation was varied and counterbalanced between participants.

Findings

All groups of participants exaggerated circularity (drew a more circular ellipse) in the prior knowledge and perspective plus prior knowledge conditions, compared to the ellipse condition. However, only the participants with autism exaggerated circularity to a significantly lesser extent in the prior knowledge condition compared to the perspective with prior knowledge condition.

Conclusions

Individuals with autism are not heavily influenced by prior knowledge of shape when making reproductions in the absence of perspective cues.

Figure 2.09 The viewing chamber with observation slit and perspective cues

If a visual display contains depth cues, shape constancy functions normally in those with autism.

Perception in those with autism is less influenced by prior knowledge and is therefore less top-down or conceptually driven.

Evaluation

- It may be the ability to suppress prior knowledge by those with autism that explains the artistic abilities of 'idiot savants', autistic individuals who possess exceptional talents in specific areas.

- Conceptual and perceptual contexts may influence perceptual processes differently.

- The fact that individuals with moderate learning difficulties performed the same as normally developing individuals, but differently to those with autism, shows that the perceptual difference exhibited by autistics is not due to learning difficulties.

Perceptual development

Neonate studies

Perceptual abilities present at birth are assumed to be innate, as learning experiences have not occurred. But neonate studies present ethical and practical challenges, such as the risk of stressing infants and them being unable to communicate what they perceive. There is also the problem of some innate abilities not being evident at birth, but occurring later on through genetic maturation. However, the earlier a perceptual ability is displayed, the more innate it is presumed to be.

As perception is not a unitary entity, research has focused on separate, individual abilities, with some proving to be more innate and others more learned.

Various methodologies have been developed, including:

- **Preference studies** – where preference for a stimulus indicates discrimination.

- **Sucking and heart/breathing rates** – where change in intensity indicates interest and thus perception.

- **Reinforcement** – where interest in particular stimuli are rewarded to show recognition.

- **Brain scans** – where activation of specific brain areas indicates perception of specific abilities.

Classic research

Gibson and Walk (1960)

The visual cliff

During a trip to the Grand Canyon, married couple Eleanor Gibson and Richard Walk became interested in the depth perception of infants. A domestic row had Gibson fearing that their children would crawl over the edge, while Walk insisted they would not, as they could naturally detect the drop. Gibson's view was that toddlers often fall from high places, such as stairs and cots, and thus learn from experience about depth. Walk was adamant that the ability to perceive depth was part of a baby's hereditary endowment. They subsequently devised, at Cornell University, a laboratory method of testing whether neonates, animals and children could determine depth, to shed light on the nature versus nurture debate.

Figure 2.10 An argument during a visit to the Grand Canyon inspired this classic study

Aims

To determine if young babies had innate depth perception by not crossing an apparent drop when instructed to do so by their mothers.

To determine if the onset of depth perception varies with animals of different species and habitats.

Procedure

A testing device was manufactured consisting of a glass-topped table resembling a 'bridge', with shallow and deep sides, the non-reflective glass covering an apparent cliff with a chequered design beneath the vertical drop.

Participants were put on the centreboard and their mothers called them from the deep side and then the shallow side successively. As neonates cannot crawl, 36 infants aged between 6 and 14 months were used.

The apparatus was also tested with neonate chicks, turtles, rats, lambs, kids, piglets, kittens and puppies.

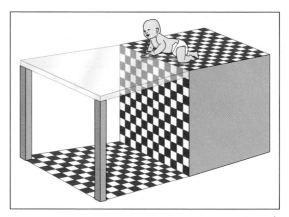

Figure 2.11 The visual cliff

continued ...

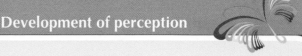
...continued

Findings

Of the 27 infants who crawled off the board at least once, only three (8 per cent) crawled off the brink onto the glass above the chequered pattern. Many infants crawled away from their mothers when they called to them from the cliff side, while others cried when their mother stood there, because they could not go to them without crossing an apparent vertical drop.

The children's behaviour showed a distinct reliance on vision, with many peering down through the glass before backing away. Others patted the glass with their hands, but still backed away.

The behaviour of neonate animals was specific to their species. Newborn chicks never made the mistake of crossing on the deep side, and neither did kids or lambs. Puppies and kittens cannot be tested until a few weeks old, due to their later development of motor skills, and they too refused to cross to the deep side. The centreboard was raised for rats, who tended to use their whiskers to detect the glass. When this was done the vast majority did not cross onto the deep side. Of the baby turtles tested, 24 per cent did cross to the deep side.

Conclusions

Sighted animals develop depth perception before they develop locomotion (movement) abilities.

Depth perception is more innate than learned.

Evaluation

- The development of depth perception in animals appears to be related to the role of vision in the survival of their species – for example, depth perception may not be as important for turtles, as they have less to fear by falling because they are aquatic. This suggests an inherited, evolutionary component.

- We cannot be certain that depth perception is innate in humans, as babies need to be able to crawl to be tested, by which time they have had learning experiences.

- As a rigorously controlled laboratory experiment, the procedure offers an objective method of testing for depth perception.

- It might be considered unethical to distress babies by having their mothers call to them from across an apparent cliff.

- Campos *et al.* (1970) used a visual cliff with 2-month-old babies, finding that heart rates decreased when they were moved across, suggesting depth perception to be innate. Nine-month-old babies had increased heart rates when they moved across, indicating anxiety, which suggests that depth perception is innate, but that recognising the dangers associated with depth is learned through experience.

Original black and white video footage of Gibson and Walk's experiment can be seen at www.youtube.com/watch?v=1VPaBcT1KdY

For a more contemporary look at the apparatus, watch a video of Campos *et al.*'s (1994) study, examining the role of mothers' facial expressions in influencing whether babies will cross. It can be found at www.youtube.com/watch?v=eyxMq11xWzM

Research: neonate studies of depth/distance perception

- Bower *et al.* (1970) found that neonates shielded their eyes at approaching objects, suggesting that depth perception is innate. The findings were identical using only one eye, indicating motion parallax to be an important visual cue in determining depth.

- Slater *et al.* (1984) found that neonates prefer to look at a three-dimensional stimulus than a photo of the same stimulus, even with just one eye. Motion parallax is again important, with the research suggesting that depth perception is innate or develops soon after birth.

- Campos *et al.* (1994) found that 9- to 12-month-old babies would not cross a visual cliff if their mothers simulated a fearful expression, but were more likely to cross if they simulated encouragement. This suggests that infants use learned non-verbal cues to override or confirm their innate depth perception.

- Using a visual illusion involving a cylinder, Sen *et al.* (2001) found that 7-month-old infants (but not 5½-month-olds), using monocular vision, reached for the apparent end of a cylinder. This suggests that the ability to perceive static monocular depth cues occurs around 6 months of age.

Research: neonate studies of visual constancies

Shape constancy

- Bower (1966) used reinforcements to train 2-month-olds to turn and look at a tilted rectangle, finding that they could distinguish between this shape and others, giving support to the idea of young infants having a sense of shape constancy.

- Imura *et al.* (2008) found that 7-month-old infants (but not 6-month-olds) had a preference for an alternating 2D-3D display over a 2D-2D display, suggesting that sensitivity to shading and line junctions as a means of determining shape constancy appears between 6 and 7 months of age.

Size constancy

- Bower (1966) trained infants by reinforcement to respond to a certain cube at a certain distance. Various cubes of differing sizes and at various distances were then presented. The infants mainly responded to the cube of the same size, regardless of its retinal image, suggesting that size constancy occurs early in life. Variations of his experiment led to Bower finding that motion parallax was the most important cue and that texture gradient was not used to determine size.

- Sann and Steri (2007) investigated shape constancy through vision and touch. Neonates could recognise visually an object they had held, but could not recognise by touch alone an object they had seen previously. This indicates that sensory modes used to perceive shape constancy differ in how much they are learned or innate.

Brightness constancy

- Chien (2003) tested 4-month-old infants on a novelty-preference task based on brightness, finding that they could judge the relative brightness of objects and their surroundings, indicating support for brightness constancy being innate.

- Using smiley faces as stimuli, Chien (2006) found that infants displayed brightness constancy even when the level of lighting altered, again suggesting that this constancy is innate.

Colour constancy

- Dannemiller and Hanko (1987) found that 4-month-old infants recognised familiar colours under some conditions, but not all, indicating that some colour constancy appears early in life, but needs time to develop.

- Pereverzeva and Teller (2004) tested infants' preferences to stimuli of various colours embedded in a white or dark surround. The infants preferred stimuli where there was the greatest difference in colour between the stimulus and the surround, suggesting that they did have colour constancy.

Research in focus

What ethical and practical problems are associated with conducting neonate studies? How have psychologists attempted to deal with these?

Evaluation

Neonate studies

- The visual system of neonates is not well developed at birth, making it problematic to identify which skills are innate. For instance, Courage and Adams (1996) found that neonates could not perceive visual detail, with infants having to view objects from a distance of 7 metres to see them in the same detail as adults would at 250 metres. However, the visual system develops swiftly soon after birth.

- Neonate studies can be criticised, as older infants are often used, and they may have learned perceptual abilities from experience.

- There are ethical considerations of informed consent and causing distress with neonate studies. For example, the visual cliff involves mothers encouraging babies to crawl off an apparent vertical drop.

- Making inferences about a neonate's perceptual world may not be accurate and could be vulnerable to researcher bias.

- Neonate research tends to be short-term, as neonates lose interest easily, making findings difficult to validate.

- Many innate perceptual abilities may emerge some time after birth, as a result of biological maturation, which means that neonate studies may not detect them.

Restored sight patients

Cataracts are a clouding occurring in the lens of the eye that can lead to blindness. Some psychologists thought that such patients and other individuals who have their sight restored, usually by surgical means, would prove to be 'windows' through which the perceptual systems of infants could be seen, so the following material could be used as a useful form of elaboration when answering questions about the role of infant research in understanding perceptual development. Their view was that whatever perceptual abilities were exhibited after surgery could be assumed to be innate.

Classic research

Gregory and Wallace (1963)

Recovery from early blindness

Von Senden (1932) reported on 65 cases of cataract patients having their sight restored. These gave valuable insight into the nature of visual perception and its development in infancy. Generally, with cataracts removed, confusion was experienced concerning the visual world; objects familiar by touch were not recognised by sight alone. However, objects could be distinguished against a background and moving objects tracked. Reports of these cases noted disturbingly that many displayed signs of psychological crisis following the restoration of sight.

However, most of these cases were not documented in a scientifically informative way, so the researchers here set out to document more rigorously a case study of a man blind almost from birth, who had his sight restored at the age of 52.

continued ...

...continued

Aim

To provide a detailed account of a case study of recovery from early blindness, using objective tests and measurements.

Procedure/background

The patient, SB, was a Birmingham man born in 1906 to poor parents. He had been blind since the age of 10 months, caused by an infection following vaccination. The only visual memories he retained were the colours red, white and black. He was a resident pupil of Birmingham Blind School, admitted as 'partially sighted' in 1915, leaving in 1923 to work as a boot repairer.

In 1958 he had two operations for corneal grafting, after which he recovered appreciable sight.

The researchers' attention was drawn to the case by a newspaper article, and they first met SB shortly after the operation on his second eye.

His older sister provided information about SB's visual abilities as a child, and use was also made of the blind school's extensive records to verify accounts. SB underwent perceptual tests in the hospital and reported first-hand on the extent of his visual ability.

Findings

SB's sister verified the extent of his blindness, recalling the shocking state of his eyes and the continual wearing of bandages over his eyes as an infant. She recalled his vision being rudimentary at best, remembering his visual abilities being limited to pointing at large white objects. The blind school records back this up, with no mention ever being made of SB having any useful vision.

On meeting SB, the researchers' first impression was of a normally sighted man; he walked through doors without using touch, could name most objects within a room and could tell the time from a wall clock. However, he noticeably did not scan his field of vision, and paid objects no visual notice unless his attention was called to them.

He could determine capital letters, as he had learned them previously by touch.

His colour naming was initially poor, though he could identify red, black and white and had a preference for blue and green, showing that he could discriminate between colours.

Initially he did not find faces 'easy' objects, making nothing of facial expressions.

He experienced scale distortion when looking from high windows, thinking a distance of 40 feet was one he could safely lower himself from by hand.

He quickly learned to distinguish between objects like cars and lorries, and found objects that he knew by sound or touch easier to recognise. His estimates of size were also more accurate for such familiar objects. The only thing about which he showed surprise was that a quarter moon did not resemble a quarter piece of cake, and he was continually fascinated by reflections.

On perceptual tests he showed little, if any, susceptibility to various visual illusions, such as the Müller-Lyer illusion, and he had little appreciation of visual cues present in drawings and pictures. He could produce rudimentary drawings, but was dissatisfied with his efforts. As time went by, SB showed some development of his visual perceptual abilities.

Figure 2.12 Drawing of a bus 48 days after the first operation

Overall, SB found the visual world a drab, disappointing place, with his only interest in moving objects.

continued ...

...continued

Six months after the operation, he was so depressed that he felt he had lost more than he had gained, and the researchers stopped their tests. Subsequently he suffered terribly from a nervous condition and died 2 years after his operation in August 1960, though it was believed that his feelings of inadequacy as a sighted man – for example, not being able to read or drive a car – contributed to his depressed state, rather than a deficiency in visual abilities.

Conclusions

People with restored sight are able to transfer abilities directly from other sensory modalities to the visual modality.

The ability to perceive form, shape and movement and differentiate between colours seems to be immediately available to those with restored sight, though the ability to read depth, distance and other perceptual cues is limited.

Vision can prove of use to those long since blind, but can also be a source of confusion and depression.

Evaluation

- There is some doubt as to whether the visual abilities of adults with restored vision relate to those of neonates. Therefore, they may have limited use as a means of investigating perceptual development.

- Adults such as SB tend to have developed alternative perceptual abilities to deal with the world, like touch and sound, and this may inhibit the motivation and ability to develop perceptual abilities. This suggests that such studies tell us little about the normal development of perception in infancy.

- Many of SB's perceptual abilities may have been intelligent guesses, based on clues he picked up using senses developed while blind, and thus they were not 'true' perceptual abilities at all.

- The view that restored sight cases are 'windows' through which we can view the perceptual systems of infants has not been proved.

Research: restored sight

- Von Senden (1932) reviewed 65 cataract removal cases. Patients tended to be confused initially, and although they learned to track moving objects and distinguish between objects and backgrounds, they generally did not adjust to their new perceptual world, supporting the nature argument.

If you would like to read the full account of the case study of SB, including more of his drawings, school reports and his reactions to visual illusions, go to www.richardgregory.org/papers/recovery_blind/recovery-from-early-blindness.pdf
There is also references to several of von Senden's case studies.

- Sinha and Ostrovsky (2007) tested three Indian adolescents who had had their sight restored, finding that although they possessed basic perceptual abilities, they had problems with more complex abilities, such as not being able to perceive when shapes overlapped. They also tended to believe that each fragment of a shape was separate. However, when shapes were put into motion they were more easily identifiable and, over time, performance with stationary objects became almost normal. The results suggest that movement patterns are important in learning certain aspects of perception.

Evaluation

Restored sight studies

- Instances of people with restored sight are rare and may not be representative. Most patients had visual experiences from before being blind; therefore, perceptual abilities evident when cataracts are removed may not be innate. Other sensory modalities also tend to have become dominant.

- Physical damage to the visual system can occur during the time of blindness and may be responsible for lack of perceptual abilities, casting doubts on the validity of conclusions.

Research in focus

Consider the case studies of SB and those reviewed by von Senden and explain why such studies are criticisable on ethical grounds. In terms of restored sight studies, what are the strengths and weaknesses of conducting case studies?

Cross-cultural studies

Cross-cultural studies involve testing people from different cultures on the same variables. If people from different cultures, living in (usually) very different environmental conditions, have similar perceptual abilities, it is seen as evidence that those abilities are innate. Conversely, if abilities are different, it is assumed that they have been learned.

One popular form of study is to compare people from widely differing cultural environments on their responses to visual illusion.

Research: cross-cultural studies of perceptual ability

- Allport and Pettigrew (1957) found that individuals of a western culture perceived an illusion generated by a rotating trapezoid, as they interpret it as a window. Rural Zulus, with no experience of windows, do not perceive the illusion, suggesting that perceptual abilities are learned through environmental experiences.

- Hudson (1960) showed various cultural groups a 2D picture containing depth cues. Children of all cultures had difficulty in perceiving depth in the picture. Those who subsequently had experience of such pictures learned to interpret depth cues, suggesting that perceiving depth in pictures is learned.

- Turnbull (1961) befriended a pygmy from a dense forest with no experience of long-distance vision. When taken to savannah grasslands he thought that distant buffalo were insects, suggesting that the depth cues necessary for size constancy are learned.

- Segall *et al.* (1963) showed illusions to different cultural groups, finding that Europeans were more likely to experience the Müller–Lyer illusion, while Zulus did not experience it at all, suggesting that Europeans learn to read depth cues present in their environment because they have experience of a carpentered world of straight lines and angles, while Zulus do not.

- Montello (2006) performed a meta-analysis of cross-cultural studies of depth and distance, finding that cultural differences were small, suggesting that perceptual abilities are innate and have evolved because they have a survival value. The fact that some differences were found suggests that the ability has the capacity to be modified by experience.

Evaluation

Cross-cultural research into perceptual ability

- Research from illusions suggesting that environment determines perception can be criticised. Pollack and Silva (1967) found Europeans to be more susceptible to the Müller-Lyer illusion because their retinas permit them to detect contours better, suggesting a biological reason for cultural differences in perception of the illusion.

- Cross-cultural research focuses mainly on visual illusions and 2D drawings, which may not relate to more everyday perceptual abilities.

- The value of using depth cues in pictures as a research tool is debatable, as they do not relate to the actual world. Cox (1992) showed how Aboriginal art is not understood by other cultures unless the 'code' behind it is learned.

- There is a possibility that some sensorimotor learning of perceptual abilities occurs in the womb – for instance, unborn babies respond to external light. This creates difficulties in ascertaining if abilities present at birth are actually innate.

- Early cross-cultural studies were often anecdotal and not conducted under controlled conditions. Later studies have produced ambiguous and even conflicting evidence, making it difficult to assess the relative contributions to visual perception of innate and learned factors.

- It is often difficult to obtain similar samples and replicate methodologies exactly with cross-cultural studies, decreasing the validity of findings.

Psychology in action

Perceptual simulation

Perhaps the most striking use of psychological research into perception has been the development of perceptual simulations, which have applications in several fields, generally involving computer-generated images. The first of such uses was in transportation; Gibson proposed a psychophysical theory of perception for car driving as long ago as 1938, in which he envisaged drivers journeying in a 'field of safe travel'.

Flight simulators for the training of aircraft pilots have been around for a long time, and are also used in the training of astronauts and for developing car-driving skills and assessing the safety of new cars and associated technology.

Renault's driving simulator at its technocentre testing facility provides most of the relevant cues for driving in the real world. The driver operates a real car while interacting with a visual presentation that simulates a multitude of driving experiences. This is made possible by real-time generation of three-dimensional images of the surrounding landscape that correspond to the driven vehicle's position in a computer-simulated virtual world.

Perceptual simulation is also used in computer games, especially games involving the participant's interaction within a world of virtual reality. Such use of psychological knowledge creates huge profits for the gaming industry and gives immense pleasure, though many parents might disagree. However, other uses of simulated perception have undoubtedly done much good, like training surgeons to conduct complicated procedures. Would you rather they learned this way or practise on you first?

Issues, debates and approaches

- The development of perceptual abilities involves the nature versus nurture debate. Those abilities seen as present at birth or appearing shortly after are considered under genetic control and support the nature side of the debate, while abilities that require interaction with the environment support the nurture side of the debate. The more realistic view is interactionism, where perceptual skills result from a combination of innate and learned factors. Basic skills are innate and useful for immediate survival, while more complex skills are learned and can be modified to suit different and changing environments. Neonate and cross-cultural studies indicate that basic perceptual abilities are present at birth, and are then refined and advanced through experience, with some perceptual skills being more innate and others more affected by learning. However, other forms of research can be considered too.

- Ethical issues of distress arise in neonate studies, such as with Gibson and Walk's (1960) research, where mothers encouraged their babies to crawl over an apparent cliff.

- Restored sight studies offer insights into modelling the visual system, creating possibilities for developing computers that can see, as well as helping to diagnose visual disorders and create rehabilitation procedures for visual impairments.

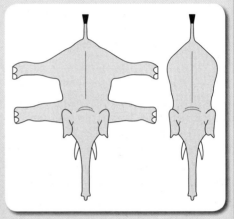

- Cross-cultural studies are susceptible to biased interpretation, especially in terms of the culture of the researcher and using research methods only applicable to certain cultures, a form of imposed ethic. For instance, western-style pictures are often unfamiliar to people of other cultures, who depict objects with all their features showing (see Figure 2.13).

Figure 2.13 A non-western and western cultural depiction of an elephant

Research in focus

Psychologists have shown two-dimensional pictures to people of different cultures to assess whether depth perception is genetic or environmental. What criticisms can be made of this technique?

Strengthen your learning

1. Why is perception composed of several abilities?
2. What is meant by:
   i) depth/distance perception?
   ii) visual constancies?
3a. Why are neonate studies conducted?
3b. What problems do they present?
3c. What have neonate studies revealed about perception?
3d. In evaluative terms, what are the strengths and weaknesses of neonate studies?
4a. Why are studies of restored sight regarded as similar to neonate studies?
4b. What criticisms of studies of restored sight are there?
4a. Why are cross-cultural studies conducted?
4b. What have they revealed about perception?
4c. In evaluative terms, what are the strengths and weaknesses of cross-cultural studies?

Assessment Check ▶

1. Outline cross-cultural studies of the development of perceptual abilities. (4 marks)

2. Outline and evaluate the development of perceptual abilities. (20 marks)

3. Evaluate infant studies of the development of perceptual abilities. (16 marks)

4. Discuss the development of perceptual abilities (24 marks)

5. Outline the role of either depth/distance perception or visual constancies in the development of perceptual abilities. (8 marks)

Examination guidance

Question 1 calls for a minimum of two studies to be outlined. As this question is worth only 4 marks, attention should be taken not to create too much description, as it will not receive extra credit. Question 2 also calls for an outline, which would be worth 4 marks, so most time and effort should be centred on evaluating the development of perceptual abilities, where 16 marks are on offer. A suitable evaluation could be constructed from the degree of research support, as to what extent perceptual development is affected by nature and nurture.

Question 3 only requires evaluation; any description therefore would not be creditworthy. As studies need to be evaluated, it would quite appropriate to include material on methodology.

In question 4, the term 'discuss' means describe and evaluate. Most time and effort should be directed towards the evaluation, as it is worth 16 marks, compared to 8 marks for the description.

Question 5 is an 'either or question'; therefore if both depth/distance perception and visual constancies were covered, only the best would be credited and valuable time that could have been spent on creating a more creditworthy answer would have been lost.

Face recognition and visual agnosias

Face recognition concerns the process by which human faces are interpreted and understood; humans have an innate attraction to faces from birth. Indeed, being attracted to human faces helps babies to form attachments with adults, necessary for survival and development. Face recognition is important in informing individuals as to their level of familiarity and intimacy with each other – for instance, in determining friends, enemies and strangers. This is essential for safe social interactions and group existence and it is not surprising that face recognition is found in other social animals, like monkeys.

Faces contain similarities, such as facial features, like eyes, but also have unique qualities allowing them to be recognised. Being able to read faces is important not just in identifying whether someone is known and what their relationship is to an individual. Faces also convey information about emotions, age, gender, honesty and so on, on which important decisions are based, like whether to trust them, work with them, fear them and so on.

Psychologists have been especially interested in the mechanisms by which face recognition occurs, and whether it is a separate ability from being able to recognise other objects. Research has utilised brain scans to identify specific brain areas, as well as focusing on individuals with visual agnosias, a condition where vision seems normal, but some visual stimuli, like faces, cannot be understood. Such cases may offer insight as to how normal face processing occurs. The major theoretical work in this area is Bruce and Young's (1986) theory of face recognition.

Key terms

Face recognition – the means by which humans faces are processed and made sense of

Visual agnosia – a condition involving an inability to make sense of or use familiar visual stimuli

Prosopagnosia – a visual agnosia where objects can be described, but not recognised

Bruce and Young's theory of face recognition

Bruce and Young's is a stage theory, created from research into case studies of people with brain damage restricting their ability to process faces, and from research into the errors of recognition that normal people make. The theory sees face recognition as involving two different mechanisms:

1. **Familiar faces** – processing occurs by structural encoding, followed by face recognition nodes, person identity nodes and name generation.

2. **Unfamiliar faces** – processing occurs by structural encoding, followed by expression analysis, facial speech analysis and directed visual processing.

A face becomes familiar when it is seen several times so that a firm representation is stored, based on different viewing angles, facial expressions and lighting conditions. Therefore, structural encoding, based on pictorial data, improves.

Face recognition is a *holistic* process, where facial features, involving eight independent sub-processes, work together in sequential fashion. Comprehending faces involves several stages, going from extracting basic information, like gender, through to recollecting meaningful data about the individual, with different processing modules used to process different types of information, such as facial expression.

The theory sees different processing 'modules' being used to comprehend data extracted from faces – for example, expression analysis operates independently of person identity. Table 2.03 summarises the processing modules of Bruce and Young's theory.

Table 2.03 Face recognition processing modules

TYPE OF PROCESSING MODULE	DESCRIPTION OF MODULE
Structural encoding	Creation of descriptions and representations of faces
Expression analysis	Analysis of facial characteristics to infer emotional state
Facial speech analysis	Analysis of facial movements to comprehend speech
Directed visual processing	Selective processing of specific facial data, like the colour of eyes
Facial recognition nodes	Stored structural descriptions of familiar faces
Person identity nodes	Stored information about familiar people, like their interests and talents
Name generation	Separate store for names
Cognitive storage	Extra information aiding the recognition process, like what contexts individuals are known in

Structural encoding involves creating pictorial data that is transformed into abstract or structural representations. Face recognition occasionally occurs with pictorial information only, but generally this is not the case, as pictorial representations cannot represent changes in appearance, such as haircuts. Following structural encoding, other processing modules occur related to physical aspects, for example directed visual processing, where specific facial data, such as colour of eyes, are used to aid identification. The final modules of face recognition are based more on semantic processing of stored biographical details.

The theory believes that two types of information are held about people, helping to identify familiar faces:

1. **Visually derived semantic code** – details related to physical aspects such as gender or race.

2. **Identity-specific semantic code** – biographical details not related to physical aspects such as hobbies or achievements.

It is generally the retrieval of information from the identity-specific semantic code that permits the recognition of faces.

The theory proposes two types of nodes:

1. **Face recognition nodes** (FRNs) – contain structural information on faces.

2. **Person identity nodes** (PINs) – contain identity-specific semantic information, like individuals' relationships.

Recognising familiar faces involves matching structural information describing familiar faces stored in the FRNs, using facial features and their configuration to achieve this. Then identity-specific information from PINs is accessed, which permits specific names and other biographical details to be recalled, helping to confirm true recognition.

Structural encoding, face recognition nodes, person identity nodes and name generation are used to recognise familiar faces, while structural encoding, expression analysis, facial speech analysis and directed visual processing are used to process unfamiliar faces.

Research: face recognition

- Ellis *et al.* (1979) found that external facial features, like hairstyles, are used to recognise unknown faces, while internal features, like noses, are used with familiar faces.

- Malone *et al.* (1982) reported on two case studies: first, a man able to recognise familiar faces, but who could not match photos of unknown faces, and second, a man who could not recognise known faces, but could match photos of unknown people. The results point to damage to different brain areas, suggesting that familiar and unfamiliar faces are processed differently, supporting the prediction of Bruce and Young's model.

- Sergent (1984) presented two identikit faces, differing on either one or two facial features, such as shape of eyes or chin. Deciding whether faces were different occurred quicker when two features varied, implying that facial features are processed collectively (configural processing) rather than independently.

- Young *et al.* (1985) investigated the prediction that as FRNs and PINs are separate types of store, then if just an FRN were activated, an individual should seem familiar, but no information could be provided about them. Participants kept a diary of problems recognising faces and the results showed clear support for the prediction, supporting the theory.

- Diamond and Carey (1986) found that expert dog breeders were not able to identify individual members of a familiar breed if an image of a dog was upside down. This indicates that face recognition requires sensitivity to the overall configuration of a face, rather than just sensitivity to the configuration of facial features. However, Shepherd *et al.* (1981) found evidence that individual facial features are used in face recognition. When describing faces, participants outlined individual features rather than overall shape, contradicting the findings of the previous study, though participants were asked merely to describe rather than to identify faces, and description may be easier and different to face recognition.

- Bruce and Valentine (1988) found that expressive movements, like smiling and nodding, conveyed little variant information to aid identification, suggesting that invariant information is used more to perform face recognition.

Evaluation

Face recognition

- Bruce and Young's (1986) theory allowed predictions to be made, which research has found to be true, supporting the theory. For instance, the belief that familiar and unfamiliar faces are processed differently is backed up by evidence, and the idea that processing of facial information should occur in a *sequential* fashion is supported. The theory is also backed up by case studies of visual agnosias (see 'Case studies of prosopagnosia' on page 74 or details), which show that face recognition consists of independent sub-components.

- The theory's central idea that face recognition is a holistic process, consisting of a series of independent stages, is generally accepted, giving the theory credence.

- Although many parts of the theory are well explained and have empirical support, it is not clear how some of the sub-components work in helping to determine face recognition – for example, cognitive storage. The theory also cannot explain how unfamiliar face recognition occurs or how familiarity is achieved, therefore weakening support for the theory.

- Another aspect not fully understood is the relationship between face recognition and object recognition, and whether they are processed separately using different mechanisms, though case studies of visual agnosia have shed light on this area.

- Although there is a wealth of research evidence to support the theory, there is contradictory evidence too. The theory predicts that names are only gained from relevant autobiographical information stored in PINs. However, de Haan *et al*. (1991) detailed a case study of a patient for whom this was not true, suggesting that the theory has flaws.

- Research generally uses static pictures of faces, rather than dynamic ones occurring in real life, and therefore results do not reflect how face recognition truly occurs.

Issues, debates and approaches

- Bruce and Young's (1986) face recognition theory can be seen as being holistic (the opposite of reductionist), as it sees the recognition of faces as involving independent sub-processes working together in sequential fashion.

- Bruce and Young's theory is a good example of how science works. Since the theory was first proposed it has gone through, and continues to go through, several developments, as other psychologists comment and perform research based on it. In this way, psychology can be seen as a search for verisimilitude, or closeness to the truth.

Explanations of prosopagnosia

Sufferers of visual agnosias, of which prosopagnosia is a type, do not possess damaged visual systems, but cannot use or make sense of certain visual information. Some Alzheimer's patients and some people suffering from strokes and herpes encephalitis exhibit prosopagnosia, with damage to the posterior occipital and/or the temporal lobes of the brain being the main cause. Sufferers can describe objects or faces in terms of features and colours and so on, but cannot name them, even if they are known, like family or friends. There is also a congenital form of prosopagnosia developing without any known brain damage occurring.

There are two broad types of visual agnosia:

1. **Apperceptive** – concerns the inability to recognise familiar objects/faces, though vision is unimpaired.

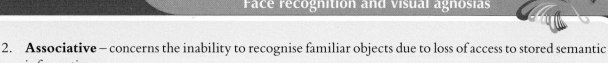
2. **Associative** – concerns the inability to recognise familiar objects due to loss of access to stored semantic information.

The perception of objects and faces was thought to involve processing by the same neural mechanisms, but case studies of prosopagnosia suggests that there are separate systems, with a specific processor for faces.

Prosopagnosia is a visual agnosia where damage is explicit to the fusiform gyrus area of the brain. Objects are recognised, but not faces. The occurrence of different types and levels of prosopagnosia suggests a relationship to different modules of face recognition, supporting Bruce and Young's notion that face recognition occurs as a sequence of stages. The fact that there are different types and levels of prosopagnosia indicates that each module of the face-processing sequence is catered for by a specific brain area, and it is damage to these specific areas that causes the different types and levels of the disorder.

Dailey and Cottrell (1999) suggested how a separate face-processing mechanism could arise based on the idea of the visual system developing a processing sub-system useful for the recognition of faces. This would occur as a natural response to a child's developmental environment, as children need to identify faces in order to form attachments crucial to their survival and development.

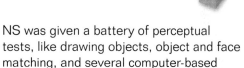

Contemporary research

Delvenne *et al.* (2003)

Evidence for perceptual deficits in associative visual prosopagnosia

Prosopagnosia is a condition where people can describe stimuli in their visual field, but cannot recognise such stimuli, indicating that the brain is unable to make sense of normal visual material. This is thought to occur because sufferers cannot access stored visual memories to categorise articles perceived correctly, with the condition generally manifesting itself as an inability to recognise everyday objects or faces. Case studies of prosopagnosia are especially useful in helping to understand how face recognition occurs. In this instance, a patient with specific brain damage, who was strongly impaired in his ability to recognise objects and faces, was studied to see whether visual impairments accounted for his condition.

Aim

To investigate high-level visual processes of a prosopagnosic patient, to assess whether visual impairments are the cause of prosopagnosia.

Method

The patient, NS, hit by a car while cycling at age 40, was unconscious for 23 days. An MRI scan revealed lesions to his brain in the bilateral occipito-temporal junction area, resulting in various impairments, including a severe visual agnosia for objects and faces.

NS was given a battery of perceptual tests, like drawing objects, object and face matching, and several computer-based perceptual tests.

Findings

NS had a full visual field and no deficits in elementary visual perception. His colour perception was perfect, as was his visual acuity. On object recognition tests he performed well on all perceptual tasks, like length match and size match, and was normal in assessing form, volume and perspective about objects. He could correctly judge photographs of objects as the same or different.

However, in contrast to his normal visual abilities, NS found tasks demanding access to visual semantic knowledge about objects difficult – for example, naming pictures of familiar objects. This deficit of visual recognition proved stable over time. Where he could name objects, it took him an abnormally long time to accomplish this. For example, when shown a salt shaker he said, 'Is that a little bottle? Hmm … one part is like a glass and another contains holes … 15 holes … It might serve to mash fruits, to get orange juice … oh yeah, that's a salt shaker'. Also he could not mime the function of familiar objects.

On tests of face processing, NS could accurately classify whether a picture was of a face or not, could find target features, like a nose or a mouth,

continued …

...continued

could find a target face from ten photographs of unfamiliar faces, despite a change of facial expression, and correctly read emotions on pictures of unfamiliar faces. He could also accurately determine sex and age from facial pictures. However, he was severely impaired in face recognition, being poor in judging whether faces were familiar or unknown.

Computer-based perception tests revealed NS to have deficits in object and face naming at the perceptual level – for instance, he had difficulty in integrating high-level visual processes, like integrating the object parts of three-dimensional structures. In essence, his main difficulty lay in integrating individual features into a whole object.

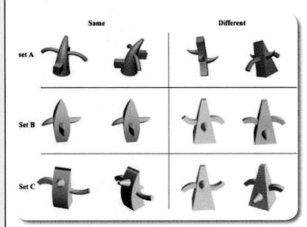

Figure 2.14 The three conditions used in the structural encoding of novel objects task: NS had difficulty integrating object parts of three-dimensional structures

Ten years later, NS was able to work full-time as a laboratory researcher, but maintained severe impairments in visual short-term memory and long-term memory for visual and verbal material. The most striking impairment was his continued inability to recognise common objects or people from their faces.

Conclusions

NH's poor performance at perceptual face processing, the absence of a decrease in performance for upside-down faces and his advantage at processing isolated face parts indicate that his deficit concerned an inability to process objects perceived as a whole.

Prosopagnosia involves a deficit in perception of high-level visual processes necessary to correctly identify individual faces.

Evaluation

- The findings question the idea of separate visual representations for object/face perception and object/face knowledge.

- The circumstances of single case studies are by definition unique and thereby different from other cases. Despite allowing considered knowledge of individual examples, there are problems in generalising to whole populations.

- The study highlights that even with serious perceptual deficits, individuals can live relatively normal and productive lives.

Research: case studies of prosopagnosia

- Bodamer (1947) invented the term 'prosopagnosia' when reporting on three case studies, one of which was of a man with a bullet wound to the head who could not recognise familiar people or his own mirror image; he could recognise people using other senses, however, such as smell.

- Kurucz *et al.* (1979) studied prosopagnosics who could name familiar faces, but could not identify facial expressions. Bruyer *et al.* (1983) had a patient with opposite symptoms, who could understand facial expressions, but not name them. This suggests, in line with Bruce and Young (1986), that facial expression analysis and name generation are separate components of face recognition.

- Tranel and Damasio (1985) measured the electrical skin conductivity of two prosopagnosics, finding that when they were shown photos of familiar faces conductivity increased, even though they claimed that the faces were unfamiliar. No such response occurred with unknown faces, suggesting that although the ability to retrieve memories associated with faces had been destroyed, the memories themselves were intact. This might be why some prosopagnosics recall familiar people from the sound of their voices, by accessing memories using a different sensory modality.

- Campbell *et al.* (1986) found a prosopagnosic who could not name familiar faces, nor identify facial expressions, but could perform speech analysis. This suggests that facial speech analysis is a separate component of face recognition.

- Lucchelli and de Renzi (1992) reported a case study where a patient could not name familiar faces, but could give accurate and detailed semantic information about them. This indicates support for the existence of PINs being an independent sub-component of face recognition, as predicted by Bruce and Young. Also, as the patient had no problems naming objects or geographical places, this indicates that face recognition involves a separate processing system to other objects.

- Bredart and Schweich (1995) studied a prosopagnosic who knew whether someone was familiar, but could not name them or recall any biographical information. His long-term memory and ability to name other objects was fine. He had no damage to his structural encoding, recognising whether faces were faces and knowing whether a picture of a face was complete. His ability to name facial expressions was also unimpaired. In terms of Bruce and Young's theory, he is seen as having damage incurring no problems in the early stages of face recognition processing, but affecting later stages, namely accessing PINs from FRNs, and gaining name codes from PINs. This suggests that face recognition processing occurs in separate stages.

- Kanwisher *et al.* (1997) reported neurological evidence to support face recognition involving a separate processing mechanism. fMRI scans compared brain activity when scrambled faces or hands and houses were presented. The fusiform gyrus was more active in face recognition than in object recognition, implying that this brain area is associated specifically with face recognition processing.

- Duchaine *et al.* (2005) reported on a 53-year-old physicist with two PhDs who had exhibited prosopagnosia since birth. He experienced difficulties with reading expressions, recognising gender and familiar faces, though had no problem in recognising a face as such, suggesting that his recognition difficulties occurred early in the processing system in the structural encoding module. As his object recognition abilities were unimpaired, it suggests that face recognition occurs through a series of face-specific mechanisms.

- Brunsdon *et al.* (2006) reported on a boy, AL, who could not recognise familiar or unfamiliar faces, suggesting that damage was at the level of structural encoding at the beginning of the face recognition process. This suggests that face recognition is composed of sequential stages.

> A good description of what it is like to have prosopagnosia and be able to live a relatively normal life with the condition can be seen at www.youtube.com/watch?v=XLGXAiSpN00 An excellent and well-maintained website that includes links to media items can be found at www.faceblind.org

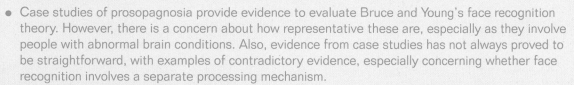

Evaluation

Prosopagnosia

- Evidence shows that prosopagnosia affects face recognition in different ways, implying that face recognition occurs as a holistic process of sequential, independent sub-components.

- Case studies of prosopagnosia provide evidence to evaluate Bruce and Young's face recognition theory. However, there is a concern about how representative these are, especially as they involve people with abnormal brain conditions. Also, evidence from case studies has not always proved to be straightforward, with examples of contradictory evidence, especially concerning whether face recognition involves a separate processing mechanism.

continued ...

...continued

- Humphreys and Riddoch (1987) cast doubt on the idea of object and face recognition having separate processing mechanisms. They suggested that face recognition is simply a more complex form of object recognition. If so, slight damage to a general-purpose recognition system would affect object recognition less than face recognition. Prosopagnosics do tend to have slight damage to object recognition and severe damage to face recognition.

- Gauthier *et al.* (2000) also cast doubt on the idea of separate processing mechanisms. Faces may just be complex objects taking more skill to recognise. This is supported by the fusiform gyrus being activated not only during face recognition, but during object discrimination too. Therefore, the fusiform gyrus cannot be specifically involved in face recognition. Some prosopagnosics also have problems with complex object recognition, including faces, suggesting that a specific face-processing mechanism might not exist.

- Face recognition involves the cognitive approach, a strength of which is its scientific rigour. However, a weakness is that it is abstract, as with the processing modules of Bruce and Young's theory, for which there is no proof that they exist in any objective, physical sense.

Supplementary learning

Research into understanding the dynamics behind face recognition has led to the introduction of face recognition systems. By judging the efficiency and success of such systems, it is possible to assess the theoretical foundations on which they are based, but in real-world environments, rather than the artificial environment of the laboratory, or on the somewhat non-generalisable evidence gained from case studies. Material like this would therefore help to form an effective evaluation of face recognition theory.

Identikit drawings to help identify suspected criminals have been used by the police since the 1940s, but they now use *E-FIT* (electronic facial identification technique), an identification system drawing on a library of computer-stored facial characteristics, with current versions in colour and producing 3D imagery. The system is based on the idea that humans focus on and recognise individual facial features, such as shape of nose. The usefulness of the system is that it allows others to recognise faces originally described by eyewitnesses, and many criminals have been apprehended in this way. It also reduces the risk of wrongful arrest by mistaken identity.

There are now several computerised security systems in operation based on face recognition processes. One such is FaceIt, which picks individuals faces out of a crowd and compares them to a database. This is superior to earlier systems, as it uses 3D imagery and recognises the same face under different lighting conditions and when it is not static, just as a human face recognition system does. However, such systems are not perfect. Boston's Logan Airport found an accuracy rate of 61.4 per cent over a 3-month period and scrapped the idea.

Computerised systems continue to improve and the USA now runs the *US-VISIT* system to check travellers entering the USA. Research is being conducted into the feasibility of introducing face recognition technology into cash machines. Whether such computer-generated systems can ever match the intricacies of the human ability to process and recognise faces is debatable.

Issues, debates and approaches

- Case studies of prosopagnosics could be argued to be unethical by conducting research on individuals that highlight the disabilities in face recognition that they already possess. This could cause long-term distress, though such research may be justifiable if it leads to effective therapies to cope with the disorder.
- Research into prosopagnosia has led to the development of practical applications, like the introduction of computer security systems using face recognition software.

Strengthen your learning

1. What is meant by face recognition?
2. Why is face recognition important for humans?
3. Outline the main features of Bruce and Young's face recognition theory.
4. What research support is there for the theory? Give details.
5. Aside from research, how can the theory be evaluated in terms of its strengths and weaknesses?
6. What is prosopagnosia?
7. Why do psychologists study prosopagnosia?
8. What has research discovered about prosopagnosia in terms of Bruce and Young's theory?
9. What evaluative strengths and weaknesses are there of case studies of prosopagnosia?
10. Does evidence suggest face recognition to be a separate process to object recognition? Give details.

Assessment Check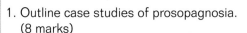

1. Outline case studies of prosopagnosia. (8 marks)

2. Evaluate Bruce and Young's theory of face recognition. (16 marks)

3. Outline Bruce and Young's theory of face recognition. (4 marks)

4. Outline and evaluate explanations of prosopagnosia. (20 marks)

5. Outline and evaluate Bruce and Young's theory of face recognition. (24 marks)

Examination guidance

The wording in question 1 is such that at least two case studies need to be outlined. If more are offered, less detail is expected. Question 2 calls purely for an evaluation, therefore describing the theory is not creditworthy.

Question 3 does call for an outline of Bruce and Young's theory, but it is only worth 4 marks, so you should offer your 'short' version here.

Question 4 also requires an outline, but only for 4 marks, so most time and effort should be directed at creating an evaluation, as it is worth 16 marks. Care should be taken to direct material at explanations; evaluations focusing heavily on research methodology will not score well.

Question 5 is straightforward, but this time you should offer your 'long' outline of Bruce and Young's theory, as it earns 8 marks here. A suitable evaluation could centre on the degree of support from research evidence, including that from case studies of prosopagnosia.

Summing up

- Perception is a cognitive process concerning the comprehension of sensations.

- Sensation and perception are two separate but interdependent processes that theories of perceptual organisation attempt to explain.

- Gregory sees perception as an indirect process where inferences are made from available information and expectations based on previous experience.

- Perceptual set is seen as the major determinant of perception, due to previous experiences, cultural factors and emotional and motivational influences.

- Gibson believes there is ample information in sensory information for perception to occur directly.

- The optic array is the light source that enters the eyes containing invariant, constant sources of perceptual information, like optic flow patterns, texture gradient, horizon ratios and affordances.

- Gregory's theory works best in ambiguous situations or where perceptual information is incomplete, while Gibson's theory works best where there is sufficient information to perceive directly.

- Perception is not a single entity, but is composed of several abilities, some more learned and some more innate.

- Depth and distance perception rely on primary and secondary cues, some of which are monocular and others binocular.

- Visual constancies allow the visual world to remain constant and unchanging regardless of viewing conditions and retinal images produced, creating a safe, predictable world to interact with.

- Neonate studies allow researchers to assess which perceptual abilities are innate, but present practical and ethical challenges.

- Studies of restored sight are a possible alternative means of examining neonate perception, though such a belief is not without criticism.

- Cross-cultural studies compare the perceptual abilities of people from different cultures, to see which are identical and therefore innate and which are different and therefore learned.

- Cross-cultural studies are prone to biased interpretation and contamination from the use of methodologies unfamiliar in some cultures.

- Face recognition concerns the process by which human faces are interpreted and understood.

- Bruce and Young created a sequential stage theory of face recognition, consisting of eight separate but interconnected processing modules, based on physical and semantic characteristics.

- Prosopagnosia is a type of visual agnosia where individuals have normal visual abilities, but find difficulty recognising faces and/or objects.

- Case studies show that there are different types and levels of prosopagnosia, supporting Bruce and Young's idea of different processing modules for face recognition.

- There is debate as to whether face recognition uses the same or different processing mechanisms as object recognition.

3 Relationships

Formation, maintenance and breakdown of romantic relationships   **80**

Formation of romantic relationships   81

Maintenance of romantic relationships   86

Breakdown of romantic relationships   89

Evolutionary explanations of human reproductive behaviour   **95**

The relationship between sexual selection and human reproductive behaviour   95

Sex differences in parental investment   102

Parent–offspring conflict   105

Effects of early experience and culture on adult relationships   **109**

Influence of childhood on adult relationships   109

Attachment styles and partner choice   112

Interactions with peers   114

The influence of culture on romantic relationships   115

Summing up   **120**

Decoding the specification

With romantic relationships, the subject matter breaks down into three separate, interrelated areas of formation, maintenance and breakdown. No specific theories are named; the two given are examples and other relevant examples would suffice, as examination questions are not directed at explicitly named theories. Theories could relate to more than one feature of relationships – that is, to formation, maintenance or breakdown – so it is important to shape the material to fit the demands of the question. Also, an acceptable strategy is to put specific theories together into general theories – for example, combining social exchange theory and equity theory as an economic explanation.

With sexual selection, the emphasis is on human reproductive behaviour and you need to explain sexual selection from the different viewpoints of males and females, especially with regards to parental investment.

Finally, the specification focuses on the influence of childhood on adult relationships. There is also a requirement to have knowledge of the influence of culture on romantic relationships, so that these could be described and evaluated.

Formation, maintenance and breakdown of romantic relationships

Successful romantic relationships are regarded as an important route to happiness. As well as being a means of conceiving and raising children, successful romantic relationships are an important source of self-esteem and personal fulfilment. Many significant factors have been identified in the formation and maintenance of such relationships, and identification of how and why relationships fail helps psychologists to construct strategies to foster successful romantic relationships.

IN THE NEWS

Woman gives up on death row romance

Figure 3.01

Pen pal relationships with Death Row prisoners awaiting execution are not uncommon – over 100 British women are currently engaged or even married to such prisoners.

Divorced grandmother Sandie Blanton is one such woman. In 2008, after flying out to the USA several times for prison visits, she married Chucky Mamou, who is imprisoned on Death Row for abduction, rape and murder of a teenager, although he claims he is innocent.

The wedding was unusual, the bride, as expected, was radiant in white, but there was a noticeable absence of husband-to-be. Indeed Chucky's father was the stand-in groom for the ceremony.

The marriage ended after just six weeks and not because of the lack of a physical relationship, but because Sandie discovered that Chucky was writing letters with sexual content to a married British lady.

Sandie was undeterred and continued to write to up to thirty prison pen pals including Reginald Blanton, who at 28 had been in prison for 10 years for shooting his friend in the head, a charge he denied. The pair became engaged, but, in October 2010, Reginald was executed by lethal injection.

Sandie now says she won't have any more Death Row relationships but she is a campaigner against the death penalty.

Relationships like Sandie's are not uncommon and are an exception to the 'rule' that we become involved with familiar, accessible people. Such relationships are an example of the fact that although there are general theories and explanations of why people form and maintain relationships, these theories do not apply to everyone; there are wide individual differences and therefore always exceptions to the 'rule'.

Formation of romantic relationships

Romantic relationships first require attraction – that is, a preference for another person – and several factors affect whether people will form relationships, as set out below.

(If an examination question asked for an explanation of why relationships form, combining factors of attractiveness could comprise a valid answer.)

1. **Proximity** – the further apart two people live, the less likely it is that they will meet and form a relationship. This only applies to the 'real' world; in the virtual world of the internet, distance is no barrier to the formation of romantic attachments.

2. **Exposure and familiarity** – proximity increases opportunities for interaction (*exposure*), which, in turn, increases *familiarity*. There is evidence that familiarity breeds fondness – the better we know someone, the more likely it is that we will like them. According to Argyle (1983), the more two people interact, the more alike their attitudes towards each other become, increasing the likelihood of further interaction.

3. **Similarity** – evidence suggests that 'birds of a feather flock together'. Key similarities are those concerning *beliefs*, *attitudes* and *values*. According to Rubin (1973), similarity is rewarding because:

   - agreement provides a basis for engaging in joint activities

   - people who agree with us create confidence about ourselves, boosting self-esteem

   - most people are vain enough to believe that anyone sharing their views must be sensitive and praiseworthy

   - people who agree find it easier to communicate with and like each other

   - we assume that people with similar attitudes like us, so we like them too (reciprocal liking).

4. **Physical attractiveness** – it takes time to find out about people's attitudes and values, but physical attractiveness is immediate.

The *attractiveness stereotype* believes that individuals perceive attractive-looking people as having attractive personalities. But what constitutes attractiveness? Different cultures have different criteria, and definitions of beauty change over time.

Facial beauty is more important in women, and men's height and muscularity influence their attractiveness, though there are exceptions to these 'rules'.

The matching hypothesis sees people as attracted to people of similar perceived attractiveness. This was supported by Murstein (1972), who asked participants to compare photos of 'steady' and engaged couples with random males and females put together as pairs. The real couples were perceived as more similar to each other in terms of physical attractiveness.

Key terms

Sociobiological explanation – a theory of relationships based on evolutionary determinants

Reinforcement and need satisfaction – a behaviourist theory of relationship formation based on conditioning

Social exchange theory – an economic explanation of relationship maintenance based on maximising profits and minimising costs

Equity theory – an economic explanation of relationship maintenance based on motivation to achieve fairness and balance

Dissolution – the process by which romantic relationships break down

Classic research

Saegert *et al.* (1973)

The taste of strangers experiment

The mere exposure effect concerns the phenomenon whereby people feel more favourable about things as they become familiar with them. The researchers examined whether this could be applied to attraction between people.

Aim/hypothesis

It was predicted that the more often a participant came into contact with another, the more they would like them compared with those encountered less often.

Procedure

Female students took part in an experiment supposedly concerning the sense of taste, involving tasting and rating various liquids. The experiment was designed so that each student found herself in a closed cubicle with another student either once, twice, five times, ten times, or alone.

Each student completed a questionnaire, but the only question of interest was the one about attraction to the person sharing the cubicle.

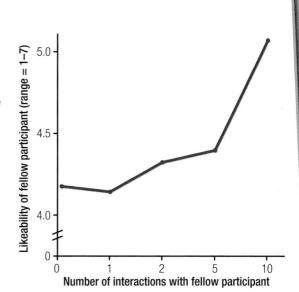

Figure 3.02

Source: Saegert *et al.* (1973), *Journal of Personality and Social Psychology*, 25(2), 234–42, published by the American Psychological Association and reproduced with permission.

Findings

A participant's attraction to another student was directly related to how many interactions they had had: the more interactions, the greater the attraction. (see Figure 3.02).

Conclusions

Consistent with the mere exposure effect, people's degree of familiarity with other people determines their degree of attraction towards them. Familiarity seems to breed liking.

Evaluation

- The participants were female students, and were therefore not representative of people in general.
- It was an artificial situation: people are not usually asked to taste liquids, except as part of market research.
- The experiment is unethical as it uses deception: participants believed it was a study concerning taste.
- Familiarity is operationalised as the number of times interaction occurred, which overlooks the importance of *qualitative* definitions – for example, how familiar another person is in terms of what we have learned about them.
- The study concerns female attraction to other females and thus tells us little about romantic relationships.

The sociobiological explanation

The sociobiological explanation is an evolutionary theory perceiving relationship formation as a form of 'survival efficiency', with a different focus between genders. Males are not certain of paternity (the fatherhood of children) and produce lots of sperm, so their best strategy to further their genes is to have multiple partners. The explanation sees males looking for signs of fertility, like smooth skin; and sexual faithfulness, as they do not want to waste resources bringing up another male's child (*cuckoldry*).

Females produce a relatively small number of eggs, but are certain of maternity (the motherhood of children). Females seek to ensure that children are genetically strong and healthy by being selective in choosing partners and getting them to invest resources. Females look for kindness, which indicates a willingness to share resources. The more a male invests, the more likely it is that he will not desert and will offer further resources to the female and her children.

Males compete to be chosen and females select males on characteristics reflecting genetic fitness. Courtship serves as a period during which competition and selection occur and also to get males to invest resources, increasing the chances of them not deserting and investing more resources in the future.

Research: the sociobiological explanation

- Davis (1990) performed a content analysis of personal advertisements, finding that men look for health and attractiveness, while offering wealth and resources. Females look for resources and status, while offering beauty and youth, supporting the idea of evolutionary-based gender differences in relationship formation.

Figure 3.03 Research supports evolutionary theory: males do seek youthfulness and attractiveness, while women seek resources

- Dunbar (1995) analysed 900 personal advertisements from four US newspapers, finding that 42 per cent of males sought youthfulness, while only 25 per cent of females did. Of males, 44 per cent sought attractiveness, while only 22 per cent of females did, supporting the sociobiological idea that males and females have different reasons for forming relationships.

- Pawlowski and Dunbar (1999) examined the idea that women would hide their age in personal advertisements, because men tend to judge prospective female partners on age, as it correlates with fertility. This prediction was found to be true, especially for women aged 35 to 50, implying that women disguise their age in order to find high-quality partners before reproductive opportunities are ended by the menopause.

- Harris (2005) examined cultures dominated by different religious systems, finding that relationship behavioural patterns either contradicted sociobiological strategies of relationship formation or placed emphasis on cooperative restraint rather than survival through selfish propagation, as predicted by sociobiological theory. This indicates that many human societies have developed relationship systems going against sociobiological predictions.

- Packer (1983) reported that male lions, on defeating dominant males, kill existing cubs and the lionesses then become sexually receptive. This behaviour is adaptive, eliminating competition for the cubs and allowing faster genetic reproduction, supporting the sociobiological explanation.

You are the researcher

Test out Pawlowski and Dunbar's claim that women disguise their age by using personal advertisements from newspapers to see if there is a difference in the number of women and men not stating their age. If the researchers are correct, more women should not state their age. You will need an equal number of male and female advertisements.

Evaluation

The sociobiological explanation

- The sociobiological explanation presumes heterosexuality, that children are wanted and that all relationships are sexual; it is therefore oversimplified. The explanation cannot explain long-distance romantic relationships, like those conducted over the internet.

- The explanation supports gender stereotypes of housebound women and sexually promiscuous males.

- The theory offers a plausible explanation for the evolution of mate preferences and has research support (see 'Research: the sociobiological explanation' on page 83)

- Although relevant to the EEA (Environment of Evolutionary Adaptiveness), the explanation does not suit the modern environment. Many women now have resources of their own and do not need to rely on the resources of men.

- The explanation is deterministic, disregarding the role of free will in relationship formation.

Reinforcement and needs satisfaction

The reinforcement and needs satisfaction explanation is a *behaviourist* or *learning* explanation, perceiving *conditioning* as an explanation for relationship formation.

People may directly reward us (*operant conditioning*) by meeting our psychological needs for friendship, love and sex. Their provision of such needs is reinforcing, and therefore we will like them more and spend more time with them, which ultimately increases the chances of relationship formation.

People may also indirectly reward us (*classical conditioning*) because they become associated with pleasant circumstances, which makes us more likely to form a relationship. If we associate people with being in a good mood, or helping to remove a negative mood, we will find them attractive and will like them increasingly, furthering the chances of relationship formation.

Argyle (1994) outlined several motivational systems underpinning social behaviour and explained how forming relationships satisfies social needs on several levels:

- *biological needs*, like collective eating

- *dependency*, being comforted

- *affiliation*, a sense of belonging

- *dominance*, making decisions for others

- *sex*, flirting

- *aggression*, letting off steam

- *self-esteem*, being respected by others.

Research: reinforcement and needs satisfaction

- Griffit and Guay (1969) evaluated participants on a creative task. If the evaluation was positive, participants expressed more liking for a non-involved bystander than if the evaluation was non-positive, supporting the idea of people being liked who are associated with positive outcomes.

- Griffit and Veitch (1971) found that evaluations of strangers were positive when evaluations were made in comfortable surroundings, supporting the idea that conditioning by association explains relationship formation.

- May and Hamilton (1980) asked females to rate photos of males, while either pleasant or unpleasant music was played. Those with the pleasant music rated the males as more attractive, supporting the theory.

- Hays (1985) investigated student friendships, finding that rather than being focused purely on rewards received, individuals favoured equity (fairness), giving priority to rewarding the other person, thus weakening the explanation.

- Cunningham (1988) asked male participants to watch either a happy or a sad film and then interact with a female. More positive interactions came from those watching the happy film, supporting the explanation that we will form relationships with people whom we associate with pleasant outcomes and circumstances.

You are the researcher

Test the reinforcement and needs satisfaction theory by using May and Hamilton's (1980) technique of showing pictures of opposite sex individuals to participants while playing pleasant or unpleasant music and then asking them to rate the individuals. What experimental design would you use? Why might the choice of music be a confounding variable?

Evaluation

Reinforcement and needs satisfaction

- The theory can explain friendships, as people often like those who are reciprocal with their feelings, but it does not explain the intricacies of long-term romantic relationships.

- A lot of research is laboratory based and lacks ecological validity, as tasks carried out are not the usual ones undertaken, not reflecting real relationships, and therefore not adding to our understanding of relationship formation.

- The theory has a fundamentally selfish view of people as only trying to satisfy their own needs. Many people have genuine concerns for the needs of others.

- The model is supported by the similarity theory, which sees similar people as being suited to form relationships, and that when others have similar attitudes to ourselves it is satisfying, fitting the model.

Issues, debates and approaches

- It can be argued that theories of relationship formation are deterministic, as relationships are seen as having a lack of free will – that is, determined by factors beyond personal control. For example, the rewards and needs satisfaction theory sees relationship formation as an unconscious process based on learned associations.
- The sociobiological explanation is reductionist, seeing relationships as a means of reproduction, therefore disregarding other reasons for being in romantic relationships, like companionship.
- Many non-western cultures feature relationships without regard for receiving rewards or prioritising selfish needs. Therefore the rewards–needs satisfaction theory cannot account for cultural differences and thus can be seen as culturally biased.
- The rewards–needs theory of relationship formation cannot account for gender differences. Women often focus more on the needs of others, and males and females tend to find different things rewarding, suggesting that the explanation is gender biased.

Maintenance of romantic relationships

Social exchange theory (SET)

There are different versions of SET, but underlying all of them is the view that people are selfish.

Homans (1974) believes that people view their feelings for others in terms of profits – that is, the rewards obtained from relationships minus the costs. The greater the rewards and the lower the costs, the greater the profit, and, therefore, the greater the desire to maintain the relationship.

Blau (1964) argues that interactions are 'expensive', as they take time, energy and commitment and may involve unpleasant emotions and experiences. Therefore, what we get out of a relationship must exceed what goes in.

Berscheid and Walster (1978) believe that social interactions involve an exchange of rewards, like affection, information and status. The degree of attraction or liking reflects how people evaluate the rewards they receive relative to those given.

SET therefore is an *economic theory*, explaining relationships in terms of maximising benefits and minimising costs. The 'social exchange' is the mutual exchange of rewards between partners, like friendship and sex, and the costs of being in the relationship, such as freedoms given up. A person assesses their rewards by making two comparisons:

1. **The comparison level** (CL) – where rewards are compared to costs to judge profits.

2. **The comparison level for alternative relationships** (CLalt) – where rewards and costs are compared against perceived rewards and costs for possible alternative relationships.

A relationship is maintained if rewards exceed costs and the profit level is not exceeded by possible alternative relationships.

Thibaut and Kelley *et al.* (1959) proposed a four-stage model (Table 3.01), setting out how relationships could be maintained. It perceives that over time people develop a predictable and mutually beneficial pattern of exchanges, assisting the maintenance of relationships.

Table 3.01

STAGE	DESCRIPTION
Sampling	Rewards and costs are assessed in a number of relationships
Bargaining	A relationship is 'costed out' and sources of profit and loss are identified
Commitment	Relationship is established and maintained by a predictable exchange of rewards
Institutionalisation	Interactions are established and the couple 'settle down'

Research: social exchange theory

- Mills and Clark (1980) identified two kinds of intimate relationship: (a) the communal couple, where each partner gives out of concern for the other; and (b) the exchange couple, where each keeps mental records of who is 'ahead' and who is 'behind'. This indicates that there are different types of relationships and that SET can be applied to some of them, but not universally to all.

- Rusbult (1983) asked participants to complete questionnaires over a 7-month period concerning rewards and costs associated with relationships, finding that SET did not explain the early 'honeymoon' phase of a relationship when balance of exchanges was ignored. However, later on, relationship costs were compared to the degree of personal satisfaction, suggesting that the theory is best applied to the maintenance of relationships.

- Rusbult (1983) found that the costs and rewards of relationships were compared to the costs and rewards of potential alternative relationships in order to decide whether the relationship should be maintained, supporting the social exchange model's idea that people assess rewards by making comparisons.

- Hatfield (1979) looked at people who felt over- or under-benefited. The under-benefited felt angry and deprived, while the over-benefited felt guilty and uncomfortable, supporting the theory by suggesting that regardless of whether individuals are benefited, they do not desire to maintain a relationship that is not fair.

Evaluation

Social exchange theory

- Rubin (1983) believed that although people are not fundamentally selfish, attitudes towards others are determined to a large extent by how rewarding we think they are for us, supporting the theory.

- Sedikides (2005) claimed that people are capable of being unselfish – doing things for others without expecting anything in return – most evident in relationships with those emotionally closest to us. Sedikides believed that individuals can bolster their partners' self-systems when they are faced with failure and other stressful life events. Therefore, the view of humans as being out for what they can get is simplistic and inaccurate.

- Fromm (1962) argued against the theory, defining true love as giving, as opposed to the false love of the 'marketing character', where people expect to have favours returned.

- SET was modified into the equity theory, which concerns balance and stability in relationships and is a logical progression.

- Argyle (1988) criticised methodologies that evaluate SET, declaring them contrived and artificial, with little relevance to real life.

- Research has concentrated on the short-term consequences of relationships rather than important, long-term maintenance.

- The theory applies to people who 'keep score'. Murstein et al. (1977) devised the exchange orientation tool, identifying such scorekeepers, who are suspicious and insecure, suggesting that the theory only suits relationships lacking confidence and mutual trust.

You are the researcher

Conduct a study of the SET by creating two test groups of people in romantic relationships, such as people from different age ranges or different genders, and ask them to record what they give and receive in their relationships. You will need coding units to categorise people's answers. Give careful consideration about how to analyse your data. You should see some interesting results between different types of people's relationships as viewed by SET.

Equity theory

Equity does not mean equality; instead it perceives individuals as motivated to achieve fairness in relationships and to feel dissatisfied with inequity (unfairness). Definitions of equity within a relationship can differ between individuals.

Maintenance of relationships occurs through balance and stability. Relationships where individuals put in more than they receive, or receive more than they put in, are inequitable, leading to dissatisfaction and possible dissolution. The recognition of inequity within a relationship presents a chance for a relationship to be saved – that is, maintained further by making adjustments so that there is a return to equity.

Relationships may alternate between periods of perceived balance and imbalance, with individuals being motivated to return to a state of equity. The greater the perceived imbalance, the greater the efforts to realign the relationship, so long as a chance of doing so is perceived to be viable.

Figure 3.04 Equity theory sees individuals as motivated to achieve fairness in relationships

Walster *et al.* (1978) saw equity as based on four principles, as set out in Table 3.02.

Table 3.02

PRINCIPLE	DESCRIPTION
Profit	Rewards are maximised and costs minimised
Distribution	Trade-offs and compensations are negotiated to achieve fairness in a relationship
Dissatisfaction	The greater the degree of perceived unfairness, the greater the sense of dissatisfaction
Realignment	If restoring equity is possible, maintenance will continue, with attempts made to realign equity

Research: equity theory

- Yum *et al.* (2009) looked at different types of heterosexual romantic relationships in six different cultures. As predicted by equity theory, maintenance strategies differed, with individuals in perceived equitable relationships engaging in most maintenance strategies, followed by those in perceived over-benefited and under-benefited relationships. Cultural factors had little effect, suggesting that equity theory can be applied to relationships across cultures.

- Canary and Stafford (1992) devised the Relationship Maintenance Strategies Measure (RMSM), using it to assess degree of equity in romantic relationships. A link was found between degree of perceived equity and the prevalence of maintenance strategies, implying that equitable relationships are maintained.

- Dainton (2003) studied 219 individuals in romantic relationships, finding that those in relationships of perceived inequity had low relationship satisfaction, but were motivated to return to an equitable state to maintain the relationship, suggesting that equity is a main factor in relationship satisfaction and maintenance.

- Argyle (1977) found that people in close relationships do not think in terms of rewards and costs unless they feel dissatisfied, implying that equity, at least in a conscious fashion, is not a valid explanation of relationship maintenance.

- Murstein and MacDonald (1983) supported Argyle, finding that a conscious concern with 'getting a fair deal', especially in the short term, makes compatibility hard to achieve, especially between married couples.

Evaluation

Equity theory

- Equity theory still portrays people as selfish. Many researchers, such as Duck (1988), prefer to see people as concerned with an equitable distribution of rewards and costs for themselves and their partners.

- Kelley and Thibaut (1978) proposed *interdependence theory*, which suggests that not all social interactions reflect a mutual desire for equity and fair exchange. Intimate relationships are both diverse and complex, and partners' motives can clash as well as converge, producing many outcomes, including aggression, altruism, competition, capitulation, cooperation and intransigence ('digging your heels in'). Interdependence theory goes beyond individual partners, considering the harmony and/or conflict between attitudes, motives, values or goals of people in social relationships.

- Sprecher (1986) believes that close relationships are too complex to allow for precise assessment of various rewards and costs involved in establishing equity.

- Mills and Clark (1982) believe that it is not possible to assess equity in loving relationships, as much input is emotional and therefore unquantifiable, and to do so diminishes the quality of love.

Issues, debates and approaches

- Equity seems more important to females, suggesting that the theory is not applicable to both genders. Hoschchild and Machung (1989) found that women do most of the work to make relationships equitable.

- Some research suggests that equity theory does not apply to all cultures. Moghaddam *et al.* (1983) found that US students prefer equity, but European students prefer equality, suggesting that the theory reflects the values of US society.

Breakdown of romantic relationships

Duck's theory of relationship dissolution

Duck (2001) proposed three broad categories of why relationships break up:

- **Pre-existing doom** – incompatibility and failure are almost predestined.

- **Mechanical failure** – two suitable people of goodwill and good nature grow apart and find that they cannot live together (this is the most common cause).

- **Sudden death** – the discovery of betrayal or infidelity leads to immediate termination of a relationship.

Duck also proposed several other factors as contributing to relationship dissolution:

- **Predisposing personal factors** – for example, individuals' bad habits or emotional instabilities.

- **Precipitating factors** – for example, *exterior influences*, such as love rivals, *process features*, such as incompatible working hours, *emergent properties*, such as lack of relationship direction, and *attributions of blame*, such as perceiving that someone else is to blame.

- **Lack of skills** – for example, being sexually inexperienced.

- **Lack of motivation** – for example, perceiving inequity.

- **Lack of maintenance** – for example, spending much time apart.

Duck believes that the 'official' reasons given to others, including partners, to justify breaking up are more interesting psychologically than the real reasons. The psychology of break-up involves many individual psychological processes, group processes, cultural rules and self-presentation.

As Duck (2001) says:

Truly committed romantic relationships involve the foregoing of other romantic relationships and commitment to only one partner … So, the ending of a romantic relationship indicates two people are now legitimately available as partners for other relationships. This requires them to create a story for the end of the relationship that leaves them in a favourable light as potential partners. Romantic relationships are, therefore, typically ended publicly in a way that announces the ex-partners' freedom from the expectations of exclusive commitment.

Duck (1982) sees breaking up (dissolution) as a personal process, but one where partners regard how things will look to friends and social networks. This suggests an account of dissolution comprising several parts. Duck's explanation begins where one partner is sufficiently dissatisfied with the relationship over a long enough period of time to consider ending it.

The four phases are:

1. **Intrapsychic** – one partner privately perceives dissatisfaction with the relationship.

2. **Dyadic** – the dissatisfaction is discussed. If it is not resolved, there is a move to the next stage.

3. **Social** – the breakdown is made public. There is negotiation about children, finances, and so on, with wider families and friends becoming involved.

4. **Grave dressing** – a post-relationship view of the break-up is established, protecting self-esteem and rebuilding life towards new relationships.

The related thresholds are shown in Table 3.03.

Table 3.03 The main phases of dissolving personal relationships (based on Duck, 1982; from Duck, 1988)

THRESHOLD	PHASE	CHARACTERISTIC BEHAVIOURS
'I can't stand this anymore'	INTRAPSYCHIC PHASE	• Personal focus on partner's behaviour • Assess adequacy of partner's role performance • Depict and evaluate negative aspects of being in the relationship • Consider costs of withdrawal • Assess positive aspects of alternative relationships • Face 'express/repress dilemma'
'I'd be justified in withdrawing'	DYADIC PHASE	• Face 'confrontation/avoidance dilemma' • Confront partner • Negotiate in 'our relationship talks' • Attempt repair and reconciliation? • Assess joint costs of withdrawal or reduced intimacy
'I mean it'	SOCIAL PHASE	• Negotiate post-dissolution state with partner • Initiate gossip/discussion in social network • Create publicly negotiable face-saving/blame-placing stories and accounts • Consider and face up to implied social network effect • Call intervention team
'It's now inevitable'	GRAVE-DRESSING PHASE	• 'Getting over' activity • Retrospective; reformative post-mortem attribution • Public distribution of own version of break-up

Research: Duck's theory of relationship dissolution

- Kassin (1996) found that women are more likely to stress unhappiness and incompatibility as reasons for dissolution, while men blame lack of sex. Women wish to remain friends, while males want a clean break, suggesting gender differences that the model does not consider.

- Argyle (1988) found that women identified lack of emotional support as a reason for dissolution, while men cited absence of fun, again suggesting gender differences that the model does not explain.

- Akert (1992) found that the person who instigated the break-up suffers fewer negative consequences than the non-instigator, suggesting individual differences in the effects of dissolution that the model does not explain.

Evaluation

Duck's theory of relationship dissolution

- The theory has *face validity* as it is an account of relationship breakdown that we can relate to our own and/or others' experiences.

- The view of dissolution as a *process*, rather than an event, is widely accepted. This view applies to the breakdown of friendships as well as sexual relationships, including marriages. However, the theory applies mainly to romantic relationships, because these are exclusive in a way that friendships generally are not.

- The theory does not focus exclusively on individual partners, but takes their social context into account. As Duck (2001) says, 'Break-up involves not only the individual creating the break-up, but the psychological sense of integrity of the person to whom it all happens … But a lot that happens is done with an eye on the group that surrounds the person.'

- The theory does not take into account why dissatisfaction occurred in the first place; its starting point is where dissatisfaction has already set in. Therefore, it fails to provide a complete picture of dissolution.

- As with all stage theories, Duck's four phases do not apply in every case of relationship breakdown; nor do they always occur in the order described.

- The model does not apply to homosexual relationships, which do not involve some of the decisions over children that heterosexuals have to consider.

- The model is simplistic as it does not account for relationships like casual affairs and friendships.

Psychology in action

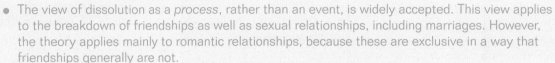

Relationship guidance

Organisations like Relate offer advice, counselling, sex therapy, workshops and mediation for individuals of all ages and persuasions needing help with their relationships, or assistance with separating and divorcing, including counselling for children.

Relate helps 150,000 people a year in Britain, with 80 per cent of respondents reporting that the organisation had strengthened their relationship.

The success of Relate is based on the fact that everything they do, including the training of staff, is based on solid psychological facts established through properly conducted research. Therefore the high profile of Relate and the valuable work they do is a shining example of the practical value that psychology can have in the real world, greatly benefiting and enhancing people's lives. It is worth remembering, though, that practical applications must be based, as Relate's work is, on solid psychology and properly conducted research; otherwise the consequences, however noble the intentions, could be negative.

More information about Relate and the work they do can be found at www.relate.org.uk

Lee's model of relationship dissolution

Lee (1984) proposed a five-stage model of relationship dissolution, similar to Duck's explanation in being a stage theory and perceiving dissolution as a process occurring over time, rather than just a single event.

The theory was reached by analysing data from relationship break-ups.

Table 3.04 Lee's five-stage theory of relationship dissolution

STAGE OF DISSOLUTION	DESCRIPTION
Dissatisfaction	An individual becomes dissatisfied with relationship
Exposure	Dissatisfaction is revealed to one's partner
Negotiation	Discussion occurs over the nature of the dissatisfaction
Resolution	Attempts made to resolve the dissatisfaction
Termination	If the dissatisfaction is not resolved, the relationship ends

Figure 3.05 Duck and Lee both produced stage theories of relationship dissolution

Research: Lee's model of relationship dissolution

- Lee created his theory after conducting a survey of 112 break-ups of non-marital romantic relationships, finding that the *negotiation* and *exposure* stages were most distressing and emotionally exhausting. Individuals who missed out stages, going straight to termination, were those with less intimate relationships. Those going through the stages in a lengthy and exhaustive fashion felt attracted to their former partner after termination and experienced greater feelings of loss and loneliness.

- Argyle and Henderson (1984) asked participants to consider whether rule violations were to blame for personal relationship breakdowns. Rule violations were found to be important factors, with jealousy, lack of tolerance for third-party relationships, disclosing confidences, not volunteering help and public criticism being most critical, suggesting that Lee's explanation is not complete as it does not account for these factors.

- Research studies relating to Duck's model can also be applied to Lee's theory and are a valid means of answering an exam question on the dissolution of relationships.

Evaluation

Lee's model of relationship dissolution

- The theory is simplistic as it cannot explain the whole range of relationships and reasons for dissolution.

- One strength of Lee's research was that a lot of information was gathered and the sample was large. However, it only contained students in premarital relationships and may not relate to other relationships, especially long-term relationships involving children and shared resources.

- Lee's theory is more positive than Duck's, seeing more opportunities for problematic relationships to be saved.

- The theory (like Duck's) cannot explain abusive relationships, where the abused partner may not initiate the stages of dissolution, being reluctant to reveal their dissatisfaction. Instead, the abused partner may simply walk away from the relationship.

- Stage theories describe the process of dissolution, but do not provide explanations of why the process occurs.

Issues, debates and approaches

- Both theories are culturally specific, as there are cultural differences in relationship dissolution that Duck's model does not explain. Many non-western cultures have arranged marriages, which can be more permanent and involve whole families in crises.
- Both Duck's and Lee's models have practical applications in counselling. For example, with Lee's model, if a couple are in the exposure stage, counsellors can concentrate on re-establishing affection in the relationship.
- Both theories can be regarded as reductionist, focusing only on romantic, heterosexual relationships, suggesting that they are not applicable to friendships, homosexual relationships, and so on.

Strengthen your learning

1. Describe factors that influence attraction.
2a. Give a concise outline of the sociobiological explanation of relationship formation.
2b. Do research studies support the explanation? Give details.
3a. Outline the reinforcement and needs satisfaction explanation of relationship formation.
3b. What criticisms are there of this explanation? (Remember, criticisms can be positive as well as negative.)
4. For both the social exchange and equity theories of maintenance of relationships:
    i)   Give a concise outline.
    ii) Compile an evaluation in the form of points for and points against.
5a What *similarities* and *differences* are there in Duck's and Lee's theories of dissolution?
5b. What limitations are there in Duck's and Lee's stage theories?

Assessment Check

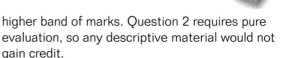

1. Outline two theories of relationship maintenance. (8 marks)

2. Evaluate theories of relationship formation. (16 marks)

3. Discuss theories of relationship maintenance. (24 marks)

4. Outline one theory of relationship formation. (4 marks)

5. Outline and evaluate theories of relationship dissolution. (20 marks)

Examination guidance

There must be a balance between the theories outlined in question 1 to gain access to the higher band of marks. Question 2 requires pure evaluation, so any descriptive material would not gain credit.

The term 'discuss' in question 3 means describe and evaluate. 'Theories' are required, so at least two must be included.

Question 4 requires an outline of one theory. If two were presented both would be marked, but only the best one credited.

In question 5 both an outline and an evaluation are required, but the outline is only worth 4 marks, so most time and effort should be directed towards the evaluation.

Evolutionary explanations of human reproductive behaviour

Evolutionary theory

Animals are grouped into species and within each species there is variation – that is, people are not identical, either in appearance or behaviour. Part of the variation is caused by differences in individuals' genetic make-up (*genetic variation*), 50 per cent inherited from each parent. Genes (strands of DNA) are not always 'switched on'; some are expressed only if combined with other genes, and some undergo *mutation*, a random change affecting the animal's anatomy and, hence, aspects of its behaviour.

Most mutations are harmful and the individuals concerned are unlikely to reproduce and pass mutated genes on to offspring. But sometimes mutations are beneficial. All animals require resources, like mates, food, water and territories, which are often limited. Hence individuals compete, and those surviving may have benefited from a mutated gene, helping them to *adapt* to their environment.

Such individuals stand more chance of surviving into adulthood and reproducing offspring with the mutated gene. Over a long period the characteristic determined by that mutation, if sufficiently distinctive, becomes a permanent feature of particular groups of animals and marks the emergence of a new species. Evolution is the process of *natural selection* by which new species arise from gradual changes to the genetic make-up of existing species over long periods of time.

Darwin's theory of evolution by natural selection is portrayed as the 'survival of the fittest'. This is inaccurate. *Fitness* is not a quality of an individual, like strength or speed, but refers to the capacity to reproduce. Individuals reaching sexual maturity have a better chance of reproducing. Therefore 'fitness' means *reproductive fitness*.

Evolutionary psychology

Evolutionary psychology uses Darwinian concepts to generate testable hypotheses about human behaviour, based on the assumption that individuals act in ways increasing the survival of their genes.

According to Miller (1998), the application of *sexual selection* theory to human behaviour is evolutionary psychology's greatest contribution to understanding human behaviour.

The relationship between sexual selection and human reproductive behaviour

Sexual dimorphism concerns the different characteristics that males and females possess – for example, male humans are larger and more muscular than human females. Evolution explains sexual dimorphism as developing through the process of natural selection, because the evolution of different features bestowed an adaptive advantage – that is, it increased the chances of survival into adulthood and sexual maturity, where genes are passed to the next generation.

Sexual selection involves the selection of characteristics increasing reproductive success. For example, if a male bird's plumage enhances his prospects of being chosen as a mate, the characteristic becomes enhanced as a sexually selected one, as with the peacock's large, ornate tail.

Reproductive success involves the production of healthy offspring, surviving to sexual maturity and reproducing themselves.

Differences between male and female sexual behaviour arise, as they are subject to different selective pressures. These differences occur due to *anisogamy*, differences between the nature and amount of *gametes* (sperm and eggs) produced.

Males produce lots of small, highly mobile sperm, about 110 million sperm per ejaculation – that is, nearly enough to populate Britain twice over – and males can fertilise many females at little cost to reproductive potential. They cannot be sure of paternity, so natural selection favours male behaviours maximising the number of potential pregnancies, resulting in *intrasexual* competition between males, and *polygamy*, where one individual mates with more than one female.

Therefore, a male's best strategy to enhance his chances of reproducing genes into the next generation is to have as much sex as possible with as many females as possible. Various male strategies have arisen, like males seeking females displaying signs of fertility, such as health, youth and childbearing hips, as mating with fertile females enhances the chances of successful reproduction (see 'Male strategies' on page 97).

Females produce a few, relatively large eggs, each one representing a sizeable reproductive investment, though she is always sure of maternity. If females are fertile for 25 years, ovulating one egg a month, then they will have only 300 opportunities to reproduce. Compare this to males, who can, in theory, reproduce about three times a day and remain fertile for longer – indeed, the oldest documented father is Nanu Ram Jogi, an Indian farmer who fathered a child at the age of 90. The oldest documented mother conceiving naturally (without hormone treatment) is Dawn Brooke of Guernsey, who gave birth in 1997 aged 59; her pregnancy was so unexpected that it was misread as an indication of cancer. It follows that females must be more selective about who they mate with, as each mating involves a relatively sizeable part of reproduction potential compared to males.

Natural selection therefore favours female behaviours maximising the chances of successful reproduction through various strategies, like careful mate selection, monogamy and high parental investment. Females seek males displaying genetic fitness, like strength, status and resources. Females indulge in *intersexual* competition, where females choose males from those available. Females also utilise practices like courtship, which help to select the best male from those available and also serve to make males invest time, effort and resources in them and any resulting offspring, thus increasing the chances that the male will not desert and will offer more protection and resources to the female and her offspring (see 'Female strategies' on page 100).

Body symmetry and waist-to-hip ratio

Body symmetry and waist-to-hip ratio are indicators of genetic fitness; they form universal physical characteristics of attractiveness. This means that individuals with body symmetry and a certain hip-to-waist ratio are seen as attractive. Individuals with these characteristics have enhanced chances of reproduction and are perceived as having greater reproductive fitness.

Facial symmetry is the best predictor of body symmetry and is thus seen as attractive (see 'Supplementary research: the importance of facial symmetry' on page 102). Males and females with near-perfect body symmetry report two to three times as many sexual partners as those with the most asymmetrical bodies. It may not be symmetry itself that is directly attractive, however; other characteristics correlated with body symmetry, such as being more dominant or having higher self-esteem, might be crucial.

Moller (1992) explained females choosing males with symmetrical features in terms of the handicap hypothesis (see page 100). Symmetry requires genetic precision, and only good genetic quality males can produce it.

Waist–to–hip ratio is another universally attractive physical characteristic conveying information about female fertility, with a larger waist–to–hip ratio associated with better health status and greater reproductive ability – that is, 'child–bearing hips'.

Physical attractiveness

Males use physical attractiveness to indicate reproductive fitness more than females. Men give a universally higher priority to 'good looks' in female partners, while females give a higher priority to resource provision (good earning potential) in males. This is because men value female partners in terms of *fecundity*, the ability to produce and care for children, and men rely on women's physical appearance to estimate age and health, with younger, healthier women perceived as more attractive and possessing greater reproductive fitness. A preference for large eyes and lips, and so on, is related to estimating women's age, and hence reproductive ability.

Women's reproductive success is less dependent on finding fertile males, for whom age is a less reliable indicator of fertility. Also, male fertility cannot be assessed as accurately from physical appearance. Consequently, women's mate selection depends on their need for a provider during pregnancy and child-rearing. Men seen as powerful, controlling resources that contribute to the mother's and child's welfare, are more attractive. However, although physical attractiveness is less important, females are choosier in selecting mates, as their investment is greater.

Male strategies

Several male strategies have evolved seeking to maximise opportunities and potential for mating success, including the following:

Figure 3.06 Stags evolved antlers as a form of weaponry to demonstrate strength

- **Courtship rituals** – these allow males to compete and display genetic potential, through characteristics and resource abilities. Miller (1997) sees evolution as shaping human culture – that is, language, art, humour and music, to act as courtship displays, attracting sexual partners.

- **Size** – males evolved to be bigger, demonstrating strength for success in competition against other males. Weaponry evolved in some species for the same end – for example, antlers in deer.

- **Sperm competition** – natural selection acted on males, making them more competitive by producing larger testicles, more copious ejaculations and faster-swimming sperm (see 'Contemporary research: Simmons *et al.* (2003)' on page 98).

- **Jealousy** – males fear being cuckolded and spending resources raising another male's child. Buss (1993) argues that men are fearful of partners being sexually unfaithful, while females fear emotional unfaithfulness, illustrating the male fear of cuckoldry and the female fear of partners spending resources on other females.

An excellent website for an overview of attractiveness, including the role of hip-to-waist-ratio, leg length and bust size can be found at www.uni-regensburg.de/Fakultaeten/phil_Fak_II/Psychologie/Psy_II/beautycheck/english/figur/figur.htm There are even some interactive experiments about ideal body shape.

One of the most beautiful sights in nature is that of grebes indulging in their courtship ritual. Resources are presented, behaviour is synchronised and a ballet-like performance can be witnessed by going to www.youtube.com/watch?v=v1XAFo_uVgk

- **Extra-pair copulation** – males mate with females other than their partners if given the opportunity. Women gain from this, as having different fathers brings a wider genetic diversity to their children, increasing survival chances.

Contemporary research

Simmons *et al.* (2003)

Human sperm competition: testis size, sperm production and rates of extra-pair copulations

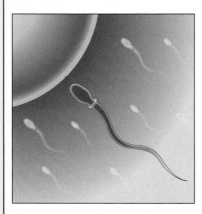

Figure 3.07

Sperm competition sees natural selection as acting on males to make them more competitive by producing larger testicles, more copious ejaculations and faster-swimming sperm. In species where males are promiscuous and mate with many females, such as chimpanzees, testes size compared to body size is relatively large. The researchers were interested in finding whether there was a relationship between human testes size and sexual behaviour, especially in extra-pair copulations (having sex with someone other than your partner).

Aim

To use data on testes size variation, sperm production and extra-pair copulations to assess the occurrence of sperm competition in the human population.

Procedure

Recruits from an Australian university comprised 194 women and 222 men.

Weight and height were measured and participants completed a questionnaire on lifetime sexual behaviour, including occurrences of non-partner sex. Male participants were asked to measure the size of their testes (after receiving instruction and callipers).

Sperm samples were requested from 50 males, after sexual abstinence of 48 hours. To assess reliability, seven participants provided four samples each. The number of sperm present in individual samples was assessed.

The study was conducted with the approval of the Western Australia university Human Research Ethics Committee at the University of Western Australia.

Findings

There were no significant differences between males (27.9 per cent) and females (22.2 per cent) engaging in extra-pair copulations.

Considerable variation in testes size was found across male participants, and sperm production was found to be positively correlated to testes size.

There was no significant difference between testes size and amount of extra-pair copulation, nor a relationship between the number of non-partner copulations and testes size in men who reported indulging in extra-pair copulations.

Conclusions

As the selection pressure from sperm competition risk is taken to lie between 2 per cent (taken as an average from extra-pair paternity data (see Table 3.05)) and 22 per cent, as reflected by the study's behavioural data, male expenditure on testes size is greater than for more monogamous animal species, as predicted by evolutionary theory.

continued ...

...continued

The findings are consistent with the position of humans in comparative analyses of testes size across primates.

The risk of sperm competition in the modern human population is relatively low compared to other animal species.

Table 3.05 Rates of extra-pair paternity in human populations

POPULATION	% EXTRA-PAIR PATERNITY	N	SOURCE
Michigan, USA	1.4	1417	Schact and Gershowitz (1963)
	10.1	523	
Detroit, USA	0.21	265	Potthoff and Whittinghill (1965)
Oakford, CA, USA	0.03	6960	Peritz and Rust (1972)
Hawaii	2.3	1748	Ashton (1980)
France	2.8	89	Le Roux *et al.* (1992)
Switzerland	0.7	1607	Sasse *et al.* (1994)
West Middlesex, UK	5.9	2596	Edwards (1957)
Sykes family, UK	1.3	269	Sykes and Irven (2000)
UK	1.4	521	Brock and Shrimpton (1991)
Nuevo León, Mexico	11.8	396	Cerda–Flores *et al.* (1999)
South America, Yanamo Indians	10.0	132	Chagnon (1979)

N = number of participants

Source: Simmons *et al.* (2004), 'Human sperm competition: testis size, sperm production and rates of extra–pair copulations', *Animal Behaviour*, 68(2), 297–302, reprinted with permission from Elsevier.

Evaluation

- Participants were Australian students and may not be representative of the general population.
- Findings of incidence rates for extra-pair copulations for males and females match those of other studies, suggesting reliability.
- It is uncertain whether extra-pair copulations are an objective measure of extra-pair paternity (where the father of a child is someone other than the male of a pair-bond), though studies of birds suggest that it is a reliable measure.
- Measurements of testes size were reliant on self-reports, which may not be accurate.
- Different studies into human extra-pair copulations found differing figures. Peritz and Rust (1972) found a figure of 0.03 per cent, while Ridley (1993) found a figure of 20 per cent. This may be due to cultural differences, or to the types of samples used – for instance, using DNA data from examples where males had suspicions of non-paternity are more likely to find such evidence.
- There are examples in the animal kingdom of extra-pair copulations in apparently monogamous species. Birkhead (1990) found that 8 per cent of zebra finch offspring result from females' extra-pair copulations with non-partner males.

Research in focus

In Simmons *et al.*'s (2003) research into sperm competition, several males gave multiple sperm samples to test reliability. What is meant by reliability in this context? Explain why reliability is a requirement of validity, but that establishing reliability does not necessarily guarantee validity. Outline one way of establishing reliability.

Figure 3.08 Females choose attractive males as partners so they will produce equally handsome sons

Male bowerbirds build elaborate, often vividly coloured constructions to attract female mating partners. Indeed females select on the basis of which males they judge are advertising best genetic fitness through their artistry. View their amazing behaviour at www.youtube.com/watch?v=GPbWJPsBPdA There are also links to similar videos.

Female strategies

Several female strategies have evolved seeking to maximise opportunities and potential for mating success, including the following:

- **Sexy sons hypothesis** – females select attractive males who will produce sons with the same attractive features, increasing reproductive fitness. Attractive characteristics have an initial adaptive advantage, but natural selection favours their enhancement, until they 'run away', becoming bizarre, like the complex and highly decorated bowers male bowerbirds construct to attract females.

- **Handicap hypothesis** – Zahavi (1975) believes that females select males with handicaps because it advertises ability to thrive despite handicaps, demonstrating superior genetic quality. This may explain females finding males attractive who drink or take drugs in large amounts, as they are demonstrating an ability to handle toxins, a sign of genetic fitness.

- **Courtship** – this strategy is used by females as a means of selecting males on the basis of reproductive fitness, through males demonstrating strength, health and ability to provide resources. Prolonged courtship rituals also benefit females, as they make males invest time, effort and resources, therefore increasing the chances of them not deserting after successful matings, and thus investing more resources in females and their offspring. This occurs through the human practice of dating, with males presenting gifts to females.

Research: the relationship between sexual selection and human reproductive behaviour

- Males of polygamous species are under the greatest selective pressure to exhibit sexual display characteristics. Kirkpatrick (1987) found that this created a runaway process, often resulting in features maladaptive in circumstances other than courtship, supporting the idea of the handicap hypothesis.

- Cartwright (2000) found that women with symmetrical breasts are more fertile than more asymmetrically breasted women, supporting the idea that body symmetry indicates reproductive fitness.

- Singh (1993) used data from 50 years of beauty contest winners and *Playboy* centrefolds to assess waist-to-hip ratios of attractive women. He found that a small waist set against full hips was a consistent feature of female attractiveness, while breast size, overall body weight and physique varied over the years, suggesting that waist-to-hip ratio is an indicator of reproductive ability. Swami and Furnham (2006) found that the optimum waist-to-hip ratio of 0.7:1 corresponds closely to supermodels, such as Anna Nicole Smith (0.69), Kate Moss (0.66) and Cindy Crawford (0.69), supporting Singh's findings.

- Buss (1989) tested participants from 37 cultures, finding that males prefer young, physically attractive females, while females prefer resource-rich, ambitious, industrious males, supporting the gender-based predictions of sexual selection. Davis (1990) performed a content analysis of personal advertisements, finding that men look for health and attractiveness, while offering wealth and resources. Females look for resources and status, while offering beauty and youth, again supporting the idea of gender-based differences in sexual selection. Dunbar and Waynforth (1995) looked at personal advertisements, finding that 42 per cent of males, compared to 25 per cent of females, sought youthful partners, while 44 per cent of males and 22 per cent of females sought physical attractiveness, further supporting the prediction.

- Clark and Hatfield (1989) found that males are more promiscuous, supporting the idea of gender-based differences in sexual selection.

- Boone (1986) found that females prefer older males with access to resources, while Kenrick and Keefe (1992) found that males prefer younger females, supporting the theory.

- Penton-Voak *et al.* (2001) found that females prefer males with greater facial symmetry, an indication of developmental stability that would be passed on to her sons, increasing reproductive potential.

- There is evidence from the animal kingdom to support the idea of sperm competition. Dewsbury (1984) reported that rats have a mating system where multiple males mate with a female, especially at high population densities. Rats have large testicles for their body size, allowing the production of copious sperm, increasing the chances of reproduction.

- Partridge (1980) allowed some female fruit flies to mate freely, forcing others to mate with randomly chosen males. The offspring of these matings were then tested for competitive ability by being raised with a fixed number of standard competitors. The offspring of the free-choice females did better, suggesting that females improve the reproductive success of children by selecting good genes in their partners.

Evaluation

The relationship between sexual selection and reproductive behaviour

- Younger males often desire substantially older women; this is also true of chimpanzees, with males preferring to mate with older females. This goes against evolutionary theory, but may occur due to wanting to mate with females proven to be fertile.

- Cross-cultural replications have not supported the claim that there is a universal preference for a low waist-to-hip ratio, such as 0.7:1. Singh argued that waist-to-hip ratio acts as a 'filter', screening out females who are unhealthy or possess low reproductive capacity, after which face and/or body weight, which may vary between cultures, are used in final mate selection.

- Females often use deception to alter their appearance and lie about their age in order to appear younger and more fertile. Males use deceit to exaggerate their resource provision capabilities and feign love in order to induce females to mate with them. This supports the idea of males and females using different strategies to maximise reproductive potential.

- Evidence suggests that women do not need men like they once did and as predicted by evolutionary theory. Females in western cultures have greater financial security and employment opportunities, and this has occurred simultaneously with a rise in single women having children – 82,000 single women over the age of 30 had babies in Britain in 2006, and 25 per cent of British families are single-parent families (90 per cent are female-led). These statistics are not consistent with women needing male partners to provide for them and their offspring.

continued ...

...continued

- There is a difficulty identifying and separating effects of sexual selection from natural selection, making research problematic.
- Evolution explains male and female behaviour in terms related to maximising reproductive potential. However, the same behaviours can be explained in other ways – for example, female choosiness and male promiscuity by gender role socialisation.
- Evolutionary theory has problems explaining homosexuality and the increasing number of couples choosing not to have children, as it assumes that all relationships are motivated by the desire to reproduce.

Supplementary learning

The importance of facial symmetry

Is a symmetrical face more attractive?

Although individuals vary widely in facially attractiveness, differences vary around a norm, consistent across cultures. Babies spend longer looking at faces that adults consider attractive, and they are too young to have learned cultural standards of beauty.

Langlois and Roggman (1990) used computer-composite images to produce faces of varying symmetrical quality, finding a preference for symmetrical faces, faces identical in shape and form on both sides. This applied to both male and female faces. Cartwright (2000) supported this, finding that men prefer photographs of women with symmetrical faces and vice versa.

It seems that symmetry, which tends to be inherited, equates with fitness. Only individuals with good genes and food supplies develop perfectly symmetrical faces. Langlois and Roggman (1990) believe that individuals whose characteristics are close to the average of the population are preferred because they are less likely to carry harmful genetic mutations, hence the attraction to facial symmetry.

Sex differences in parental investment

Sex differences

Trivers (1972) conceived *parental investment* (PI) – investment by parents in individual offspring – which increases the offspring's chance of surviving and achieving reproductive success, at the expense of parents' ability to invest in other children, either living or yet to be born.

PI includes provision of resources, like obtaining food, teaching offspring and protecting the young. With humans there is a difference between the sexes, with females having an initial investment greater than the male, because female gametes (egg cells) are more costly to produce than male gametes (sperm) (see 'sexual dimorphism' on page 95), and females also carry and nourish embryos for 9 months and breastfeed children for considerable periods. This limits opportunities for further reproduction, as women cannot be impregnated once they are pregnant, making the investment in current offspring even greater.

By contrast, males are not as restricted in their ability to reproduce further, though in many species males provide much parental care – for example, male seahorses carry their offspring in a pouch until maturity.

Trivers (1972) believes there is an optimum number of offspring for each parent. Low-investing males can afford many offspring and favour a quantity rather than quality approach. High-investing females prefer quality rather than quantity, and, consequently, females are more choosy about who they mate with.

Males can produce more children compared to females. Imail the Bloodthirsty (1672–1727), Emperor of Morocco, fathered 888 children, while the female record is a Russian woman who gave birth to 69 children.

The limiting factor for males in maximising reproductive success is the number of women they can impregnate, while for females it is important to choose males with attractive genetic qualities who will provide resources and protection in the long term. This has given rise to male–male *intrasexual* competition and male–female *intersexual* competition.

Women are always certain of the maternity of their children – that is, they are certain that the children are theirs, and by caring for them they are nurturing their own genetic reproductive potential. Men cannot be certain that children are theirs, so it makes sense either to 'sow their wild oats' with lots of women, in the hope that at least some of them mother his children, or to stick to one woman and watch her closely to be certain that she is mothering only his children and has not been successfully impregnated by another man, which would mean the first man is wasting resources raising another male's genetic reproductive potential.

Evolutionary theory predicts that there are a number of ways in which male and female parental investment will differ:

- **Paternal certainty** – with internal fertilisation males are more likely to desert than with external fertilisation, as they are unsure of the offspring's paternity.

- **Order of gamete release** – internal fertilisation gives males the chance to desert and leave childcare duties to the female, while with external fertilisation females have the opportunity to desert first.

- **Monogamy** – in species where offspring are born at an early stage of development or where childcare is intensive, pair bonds are exclusive and long-lasting, increasing the chances of the offspring's survival.

- **Grandparental certainty** – maternal grandparents are certain that a grandchild is genetically related to them, while paternal grandparents are not. Therefore, more care and resource allocation will come from maternal grandparents than paternal ones.

Research: sex differences in parental investment

- Gross and Shine (1981) report that with internal fertilisation parental care is carried out by females in 86 per cent of species, while with external fertilisation parental care is carried out by males in 70 per cent of species, supporting the predictions based on paternal certainty.

- Krebs and Davies (1981) report that the males of some fish species release sperm first in a nest and then the female lays her eggs, meaning that the male has the first opportunity to desert, but the males carry out the childcare, going against the idea of the order of gamete release hypothesis.

- Daly (1979) reports that in some mammals and birds, where offspring are born at an early stage of development and require intensive rearing, monogamy and bi-parental care is often apparent, because the males contribute to feeding and caring for the young, supporting the predictions for monogamy.

- Brase (2006) found that males who demonstrate cues of a positive disposition to parental investment were seen as more attractive by females, supporting the evolutionary explanation of parental investment.

Figure 3.09 As childcare is intensive, birds tend to stay in monogamous pairs

Contemporary research

Pollett, Nelissen and Nettle (2007)

Differences in grandparental investment

Figure 3.10 Do maternal grandparents invest more in their grandchildren?

Evolutionary theory suggests that maternal grandparents will invest more in grandchildren than paternal grandparents, due to the difference between the certainty and uncertainty of maternity/ paternity. Previous tests of this prediction were poor, relying on retrospective ratings by grandchildren. The researchers decided to directly examine grandparents' behaviour to obtain a more objective measure of the prediction.

Aim

To examine whether there is a difference between maternal and paternal grandparents in terms of frequency of contact with newborn grandchildren and gifts and financial benefits given.

Procedure

Data was used from 7,469 participants, drawn from the Millennium Cohort Study, a nationally representative study on pregnancy and child development.

Only participants where all four grandparents were alive were used, and homosexual parent couples were excluded, as were single-parent families. Grandparents with different partners from when sons/daughters were born were also excluded.

All participants received a computer-assisted personal interview, where parents were asked how frequently grandparents had contact and whether the birth of their child had altered the frequency of contact.

Participants were asked if financial assistance/gifts were given and what form/ value this took.

Data were coded into categories.

Findings

Maternal grandparents had more contact than paternal grandparents.

Maternal grandparents increased the frequency of contact after the birth of grandchildren more than paternal grandparents.

Maternal grandparents gave a wider range of financial benefits than paternal grandparents.

Maternal grandparents provided more essential items than parental grandparents.

Conclusions

In line with evolutionary theory, maternal grandparents have more contact, and provide more financial assistance and essential items to newborn grandchildren than do parental grandparents.

Evaluation

- The methodology used allows for a more objective and quantitative investigation of the research area than previously achieved.

- The research allows evolutionary theory to be tested by making predictions based on evolutionary theory and seeing whether they are true in the real world.

- There is a gender difference in the findings, as paternal grandmothers had more contact than maternal grandfathers, going against predictions.

- A confounding variable is that males tend to disperse more widely from the parental home, making visits more difficult for paternal grandparents.

- The study has not considered the role of socialisation – that is, it is a cultural expectation that maternal grandparents will contribute more/have a closer relationship. This could be tested by seeing whether the phenomenon is cross-cultural.

Research in focus

Pollett *et al.*'s study improved on research that relied on *retrospective* (looking back to the past) ratings by grandchildren.

What problems might the use of retrospective data create?

What other research methods are reliant on retrospective data?

Are there ways of overcoming these problems, other than using a different research method?

Evaluation

Sex differences in parental investment

- It is possible to test evolutionary theory by making predictions based on the theory and seeing whether real-life examples support the predictions.

- Daly and Wilson (1988) believe that research findings are inconclusive. Children under the age of 2 are 60 times more likely to be killed by a step-parent, usually the stepfather, than by natural parents. This is what evolutionary theory predicts, as step-parents and stepchildren are genetically unrelated, whereas a child inherits half its genes from each biological parent. However, most step-parents do not kill or abuse, while some biological parents do, which is not in line with evolutionary theory.

- Andersson *et al.* (1999) looked at investments by fathers in the college education of biological children and stepchildren, finding they were highest when a father lived with the biological mother of his children, but otherwise investments were equal, going against evolutionary theory. Maybe men invest in stepchildren to show their ability as resource providers, increasing their attractiveness to females.

- Dawkins and Carlisle (1976) found that in 36 out of 46 species where there is simultaneous gamete release and both sexes have equal chances of deserting, the males provide monoparental care, refuting evolutionary predictions.

- Krebs and Davies (1981) report that it is not always true that external fertilisation leads to increased paternal certainty. In sunfish, cuckoldry occurs during the female's egg-positioning.

- *Neonaticide* is the killing of newborn babies by mothers – not something expected according to evolutionary theory. Pinker (1997) offers the explanation that when it occurs in conditions of poverty, it is an *adaptationist* response. The psychological module that normally induces protectiveness in mothers of their newborns is switched off by the challenge of an impoverished environment, implying that both killing and protecting are explained by evolutionary selection.

Parent–offspring conflict

Trivers's theory of parent–offspring conflict (1974), a direct extension of Hamilton's (1964) kin selection theory, proposed that children desire greater investment than their parents are selected to provide. Parents allocate resources to all offspring to ensure that the maximum number survives. Therefore, conflict occurs, as individual children want more resources from parents than they are prepared to give.

Parental investment includes actions performed by parents for their offspring that increase the offspring's chances of survival, while reducing parents' ability to invest in other offspring, either existing or future ones. When infants are young and highly dependent on parents for care and resources, the cost of investment to parents is relatively low and the benefits to infants high, from the reproductive perspective of both parents and infants. But as infants grow, consume more resources and become more self-sufficient, the cost of parental investment increases, while the benefits to children level out. Parents have equal investments in all offspring, but the amount of resources allocated to each decreases as more are born and as individual children age and are able to fend for themselves.

Investing in new offspring, rather than investing heavily in increasingly self-sufficient children, enhances parents' reproductive success. However, each child regards him- or herself as more important than his or her siblings. Competition between siblings for limited parental resources is inevitable. This is *sibling rivalry*, offspring competing for attention and resources.

Parent–offspring rivalry occurs before birth, with mothers experiencing high blood pressure due to a foetus secreting hormones to gain more nourishment, the resulting high blood pressure bringing more nutrition.

Children use various strategies to try to manipulate parents into allocating them resources, like crying, smiling and regressing to earlier states – that is, behaving in a 'babyish' way so they appear younger.

Older parents will tolerate the demands of young infants more, as they are not compromising their future reproductive potential, because they are not having any more children, which means it makes sense to centre resources on the existing ones.

According to Buss (1999):

- Children wish to delay weaning as long as possible, often in contrast to mothers' wishes.

- Parents encourage children to value and assist siblings more than they naturally would, as this enhances parents' reproductive success. Therefore, parents punish conflict between siblings and reward cooperation.

Figure 3.11 Crying is one strategy that children use to manipulate parents into providing them with resources

Simpson (1999) makes the following predictions based on Trivers's theory:

- Conflict should be increased when half-siblings exist in families, because half-siblings are only 25 per cent genetically similar. Therefore, four half-siblings must survive and reproduce if the genes of an infant are to be fully replicated. So, in blended families, where there are step-parents and two or more half-siblings plus full-siblings, offspring should demand approximately four times as much investment as their parents are willing to give, resulting in long and intense periods of parent–offspring conflict.

- Conflict should be greater in families with young mothers. Because they have many childbearing years ahead of them and more reproductive opportunities than older mothers approaching menopause, younger mothers are less tolerant of the demands of high-cost infants.

Research: parent–offspring conflict

- Daly and Wilson (1984, 1988) reported that cross-cultural research indicates that parental investment is lower in families with at least one step-parent; when fathers question children's paternity; when infants are ill, weak or deformed; during periods of famine; when families are poor or lack social support; when mothers are very young; when families have too many children; and when birth spacing is too short, fitting evolutionary predictions based on parent–offspring conflict.

- Daly and Wilson (1985, 1988) found that even when financial resources and marital status are held constant, younger mothers are more likely to kill infants than older mothers, and older mothers are less likely to abuse or harm infants, in line with Simpson's (1999) predictions.

- Rimm (2002) found sibling rivalry most intense when children are close in age and need more resource investment. Sibling rivalry was also intense when one sibling was gifted – presumably an attempt to stop the talented sibling receiving advantageous proportions of parental resources.

- Sulloway (2001) found that sibling rivalry occurs among spotted hyenas as soon as a second cub is born, with 25 per cent of cubs being killed by the siblings.

- Haig (1993) found that women experiencing high blood pressure have fewer spontaneous abortions, while Xiong *et al.* (2000) found that they have larger babies, suggesting that high blood pressure is adaptive in producing healthier babies. These findings are consistent with the idea that parent–offspring rivalry occurs before birth.

- Trivers (1985) found that herring gulls manipulate parents by appearing smaller than they are (and thus younger), to elicit feeding.

- Goodall (1990) reported that juvenile chimpanzees act in babyish ways to get parental attention, suggesting that juveniles are maximising the amount of resources they receive and delaying the mother from breeding again, as this would be disadvantageous to the juvenile.

You are the researcher

Design an observational study assessing whether children behave in babyish ways to gain parental attention and resources. You will have to construct explicit coding categories of children's behaviour for this to work.

How would you operationalise whether behaviours were successful?

How would you determine inter-observer reliability?

What ethical issues would you need to address?

Evaluation

Parent–offspring conflict

- Evolutionary explanations of parental investment are based on the idea that human behaviour is adapted to cope with life in the Pleistocene era (also known as the EEA – Environment of Evolutionary Adaptiveness), an ancient time of nomadic hunter-gatherers, when most human evolution occurred. Such behaviour is 'evolutionary hangover', which may not suit life in the modern, industrialised world.

- Children have motivation to feel negatively towards siblings, as they are co-competitors for limited parental resources, but are also motivated to have positive regard for siblings as they share 50 per cent genetic similarity, explaining the contradictory behaviour that siblings display to each other.

- Human parents demonstrate a strategy to cope with sibling rivalry by taking them along different developmental paths, maximising each individual's strengths, reducing conflict and producing different individuals.

- The tendency for expectant mothers to feel nauseous is explained by Profet (1992) as induced by the foetus to protect itself from poisonous substances in the mother's diet. Food cravings are explained similarly, as foetuses manipulating mothers' diets to their advantage.

- Children's temper tantrums are seen in an evolutionary light as children seemingly about to injure themselves or attract the attention of predators. Thus parents attend to their demands to reduce risks.

- Evolutionary theory is accused of being reductionist as it reduces human parental behaviour to the single explanation of adaptive fitness, thus ignoring other possible explanations. It is also accused of being deterministic in seeing parental behaviour as driven by biological factors, with no input for free will.

Issues, debates and approaches

- The evolutionary explanation of human reproductive behaviour can be seen as reducing complex behaviours to the level of genes, without any reference to learning experiences or cultural influences.

- Generalising findings of animal studies onto humans is a form of reductionism, because to remove human relationships from their historical and cultural contexts treats them as if they are no different from non-human relationships. For example, women may obtain resources through men because they have been denied direct access to political and economic power.

- Evolutionary explanations can be considered deterministic in seeing human behaviour as determined by genetically preordained factors. It could be argued that females choose resource-rich males, not through evolutionary forces, but because socioculturally they were denied direct access to resources through employment and positions of power, and nurtured children as they could not escape child-rearing duties.

Strengthen your learning

1. What are the main features of evolutionary theory?
2. Explain why differences occur between humans in terms of sexual selection?
3. Why do males favour physical attractiveness in females?
4. Explain what is meant by the following male and female strategies:
    - i)   courtship
    - ii)   extra-pair copulation
    - iii) sperm competition
    - iv) jealousy
    - v)   body size
    - vi) handicap hypothesis
    - vii) sexy sons hypothesis.
5. Explain the varying results found for paternity rates due to extra-pair copulations.
6. Does research into the relationship between sexual selection and human reproductive behaviour support predictions of evolutionary theory?
7. Explain why there are differences in male and female parental investment.
8. In what ways does Pollett *et al.*'s study support evolutionary theory?
9. What is meant by parent–offspring conflict?
10. Compile an evaluation of parent–offspring conflict in 250 words. You may wish to refer to research evidence.

Assessment Check

1. Discuss sex differences in parental investment. (24 marks)

2. Outline research into sex differences in parental investment. (8 marks)

3. Evaluate research into the relationship between sexual selection and human reproductive behaviour. (16 marks)

4. Outline and evaluate the relationship between sexual selection and human reproductive behaviour. (24 marks)

Examination guidance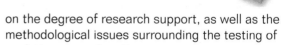

In question 1, 8 marks are available for the outline and 16 marks for an evaluation, which could focus on the degree of research support, as well as the methodological issues surrounding the testing of evolutionary explanations.

Question 2 concerns an outline only, while question 3 concerns an evaluation only. Therefore, putting evaluative material in question 2 or descriptive material in question 3 would not gain credit. The term 'research' refers to both studies and theories, so both are permissible.

Question 4 is quite straightforward, though it is worth considering that the evaluation gains most of the marks, so do not spend too long on the outline – about 10 minutes would suffice.

Effects of early experience and culture on adult relationships

Influence of childhood on adult relationships

This section contains material on the influence of both childhood and adolescence on adult relationships. When using material on adolescence to answer questions concerning the influence of childhood on adult relationships, it would be advisable to justify adolescence as being an extension of childhood due to its non-adult status.

The quality and types of relationships differ between individuals: some are happy with long-term relationships, others prefer more temporary, less passionate relationships. Some individuals seem 'lucky in love', while others go from one disastrous relationship to the next. Psychologists have tried to see whether the quality and pattern of relationships in adulthood is linked to earlier experiences.

Bowlby (1951) believed that the type and quality of relationship that individuals have with their primary caregivers provides the foundation for adult relationships by forming an *internal working model* that acts as a template for the future. This is the *continuity hypothesis*, the belief that similar relationships will occur as an adult.

There are several attachment styles a child can develop in infancy; through the 'Strange Situation', Ainsworth (1971) divided these into *secure, insecure-avoidant* and *insecure-resistant*. Attachment style provides children with a set of beliefs about themselves and others and the nature of relationships. The continuity hypothesis sees attachment types as predicting the nature of adult relationships. Therefore, someone who is securely attached as a child will have similar relationships throughout life, even with their own children.

Hazan and Shaver (1987) applied Bowlby's theory to adult relationships, arguing that early attachment patterns affect three areas of adulthood: *romantic relationships, caregiving* and *sexuality*.

Bowlby made repeated references to attachment being a lifespan phenomenon from which two hypotheses can be made:

- Attachment behaviour characterises human beings throughout life.

- Patterns established in childhood through parent–child relationships structure the quality of bonds in adult relationships.

Hazan and Shaver's (1987) study addressed both hypotheses, as well as other aspects of attachment theory.

Key terms

Adult attachment type – the quality and nature of an individual's relationships with others

Continuity hypothesis – that infant attachment types persist into adulthood, predicting the nature of adult relationships

Peers – people of equal status

Voluntary marriage – a relationship union entered into by both partners on the basis of free choice

Arranged marriages – a union of partners organised by others than those entering into the relationship

Classic research

Romantic love conceptualised as an attachment process

The researchers were interested in examining the idea that the attachment styles established by individuals in childhood explain whether adult romantic relationships are healthy.

Aims/hypotheses

To explore the possibility that attachment theory offers a perspective on adult romantic love, and to create a framework for understanding love, loneliness and grief at different points in the life cycle.

It was predicted that:

1. There would be a correlation between adults' attachment styles and the type of parenting they received.

Figure 3.12 Do childhood attachment types determine the quality of adult relationships?

2. Adults with different attachment styles will display different characteristic *mental models* (internal representations) of themselves and their major social-interaction partners.

Procedure

Respondents to a 'love quiz' in a local newspaper were asked which of three descriptions best applied to their inner feelings about romantic relationships (see Table 3.06). These descriptions related to secure attachments, insecure-avoidant attachments and insecure-resistant attachments.

Participants also completed a checklist describing childhood relationships with parents, relating to the same attachment types.

Two separate samples were tested.

Sample one comprised 205 men and 415 women, between 14 and 82 years of age, with 91 per cent describing themselves as heterosexual; 42 per cent were married, 28 per cent were divorced or widowed, 9 per cent were cohabiting and 31 per cent were dating. (Some fitted more than one category.)

Sample two comprised 108 students, 38 men and 70 women, who answered additional items focusing more on the 'self' side of the mental model (as opposed to their partner), as well as items measuring loneliness.

Findings

Table 3.06 shows the percentage of respondents, classified as either securely attached, insecure-avoidant, or insecure-resistant.

continued ...

...continued

Table 3.06

CLASSIFICATION	% OF RESPONDENTS	RESPONSE
Securely attached	56 (both samples)	I find it easy getting close to others and am comfortable depending on them and having them depend on me. I do not worry about being abandoned or about someone getting close to me.
Insecure–avoidant	23 (sample one) 25 (sample two)	I am uncomfortable being close to others; I find it difficult to trust them and difficult to depend on them. I am nervous when anyone gets close, and love partners want me to be more intimate than I feel comfortable being.
Insecure–resistant	19 (sample one) 20 (sample two)	I find that others are reluctant to get as close as I would like. I worry that my partner does not really love me or will not stay with me. I want to merge completely with another person, and this desire scares people away.

In both samples, those described as securely attached described the most important love relationship they ever had as 'happy, friendly and trusting'. These participants had longer-lasting relationships, and if they married they tended not to divorce.

Securely attached participants expressed belief in lasting love. They found others trustworthy and had confidence in themselves as likeable.

Insecure-resistant participants were more doubtful about the existence or durability of romantic love. They also maintained that they did not need love partners in order to be happy.

Insecure-avoidant participants expressed more self-doubts, compared with both other types, but compared with the insecure-resistant participants did not repress feelings of insecurity.

Both insecure types were vulnerable to loneliness, the insecure-resistant (sample two) being most vulnerable.

Conclusions

The percentages of adults in the different attachment types match those of children in Ainsworth's Strange Situation studies.

The correlation between adults' attachment style and their recollections of the parenting style they received is similar to Ainsworth's findings, where children's attachment styles were correlated with the degree of sensitivity shown by mothers.

Adults' mental models differ according to attachment styles. Securely attached adults are more positive and optimistic about themselves and (potential) love partners, compared with either insecurely attached types.

People with insecure attachment are vulnerable to loneliness.

continued ...

...continued

Evaluation

- The researchers provided a typical account of the processes involved in romantic attachment and an understanding of individual differences in adult relationship styles, as well as a bridge between infant attachment theory and theories of romantic love, which stimulated research in the area.

- The research showed that continuity of childhood attachment style into adulthood is not a certainty – that is, insecurely attached children do not necessarily become insecurely attached adults. Continuity decreases as individuals progress further into adulthood. The average person participates in several important friendships and love relationships, providing opportunities for revising mental models of self and others. Main *et al.* (1985) support this optimistic view, finding that some adults who were insecure in their relationships with their parents produced securely attached children. They had mentally worked through their unpleasant experiences and now had mental models of relationships more typical of the securely attached.

- As attachment patterns derived from the Strange Situation reflect qualities of unique relationships with one person, rather than universal characteristics of a child, so adults' choice of paragraphs describing attachment styles might merely reflect the state of a current relationship. Therefore this may not be a valid measure of adult attachment types.

Attachment styles and partner choice

Evidence suggests that there is intergenerational continuity between adults' attachment styles and those of their children; but what does research suggest about the relationship between adults' attachment styles and their romantic partners?

Research: securely attached individuals

- Belsky (1999) found that observational studies of couples' interactions during problem-solving and self-disclosure tasks indicated that secure men engage in more positive and supportive interactions with partners than insecure men do.

- Simpson *et al.* (1992) found that when female members of college dating couples were confronted with a stressful situation, securely attached women sought more emotional support and accepted more physical contact from their male partners than insecure women did.

- Van Ijzendoorn and Bakermans-Kranenburg (1996) found that securely attached men provided more emotional support, made more reassuring comments and showed greater concern for their partners' well-being, compared with insecure men.

- Belsky (1999) cites studies showing that secure women experienced less conflict with husbands on topics related to time spent together and household division of labour than insecure women. They were also more likely to manage conflict in mutually focused ways, which helps explain why they experience less conflict in the first place and why their relationships are mutually rewarding. This applies to both dating and married couples. Secure individuals were also more committed to relationships and felt greater love for their partners, consistent with Hazan and Shaver's 'secure' description of feelings about romantic relationships.

- Kirkpatrick and Davis (1994) followed a sample of over 300 dating couples for three years, observing that secure males and females were most likely to have stable and satisfying relationships.

- Collins and Read (1990) found that when dating couples were asked about their mental models, the securely attached tended to choose partners who were also securely attached.

Research: insecure attached individuals

Insecure-avoidant types

- Brennan and Shaver (1995) found that individuals classified as avoidant were uninhibited in sexual behaviour, in that they were willing to engage in sex in the absence of strong feelings of love or an enduring relationship. Similarly, Hazan *et al.* (1994) found that such individuals were most likely to report involvement in one-night stands and sex outside established relationships, and they preferred purely sexual contact – for example, oral and anal sex – to more emotionally intimate sexual contact, such as kissing and cuddling.

- Miller and Fishkin (1997) reported that insecure men desired a greater number of sexual partners over the next 30 years, and Kirkpatrick and Hazan (1994) observed, over a 4-year period, that avoidant individuals were most likely to be dating more than one person simultaneously.

- Simpson (1990) reported similar findings of dating college students who scored high on avoidance scoring lowest on commitment and trust, and that they also tended to be attracted to avoidant partners.

- Feeney and Noller (1992) found that avoidant college students were most likely to have experienced relationship break-ups.

- Belsky found that insecure-avoidant types had relationships that tended to be opportunistic and self-serving, rather than mutually rewarding, and were short-lived.

Insecure-resistant types

- The evidence here is less plentiful and objective, but one important finding comes from Kunce and Shaver (1994), who found that resistant women reported the highest levels of 'compulsive caregiving' – that is, they were most likely to agree with statements such as, 'I can't seem to stop from "mothering" my partner too much.'

Research in focus

What ethical problems might arise by questioning people about attachment types, childhood memories and relationship histories?

Are there ways in which these issues could be addressed?

Explain the function of ethical committees in deciding whether research should be permitted.

Evaluation

Attachment styles and partner choice

- Steele *et al.* (1998) found a small correlation of 0.17 between having a secure attachment type in childhood and early adulthood, contradicting the continuity hypothesis.

- Attachment types do not appear as fixed as was first thought. Hamilton (1994) found that securely attached children became insecure as a result of negative life events.

- Having a childhood insecure attachment style does not necessarily equate with poor quality adult relationships. Rutter *et al.* (1999) reported that individuals without secure attachments to their parents went on to form secure, stable adult relationships.

- Levitt (1991) believes that people have expectations of relationships, and although some of these expectations come from previous relationship experiences, not all do; therefore, other factors contribute to the quality of adult relationships. *continued …*

> ### ...continued
>
> - The temperament hypothesis sees the quality of adult relationships as being determined biologically from innate personality, suggesting that attempts to develop better-quality relationships by changing people's attachment styles to more positive ones would not work.
> - Although research shows links between childhood attachment styles and adult relationships, there may be other factors contributing, so causal links cannot be established.

Interactions with peers

Relationships with peers also influence later adult relationships. Peers become more influential as children progress into adolescence, playing a significant role in individuals becoming independent adults, helping to develop social skills, including those needed for adult relationships. Peer relationships do not replace adult attachments; they are just another type of attachment.

Peer relationships differ from attachments with adults, as they are *horizontal relationships* between individuals of equal status.

There are two stages in the development of adolescent peer relationships. First, friendship cliques form of small groups of the same sex around 12 years of age. At about age 14, several cliques of both sexes merge together to form groups. From these groups, individuals will form into romantic couples.

Research: Interactions with peers

- Meier *et al.* (2005) found that both type and quality of adolescent relationships relate to type and quality of adult relationships, suggesting a link between the two.

- Hartup (1996) reported that popular children had positive developmental outcomes, while unpopular children did not, which could contribute to the quality of adult relationships.

- Bagwell *et al.* (1996) found that poor-quality friendships were linked with low self-esteem, while good-quality friendships were linked with high self-esteem, an important factor in having the confidence to build successful adult relationships.

- Hartup (1993) found that popular children with many friends among their peers were more socially able and better at forming relationships.

- Kahn *et al.* (1985) found that students who had not developed strong identities, due to poor attachment experiences in infancy, had less success in later relationships. Males were likely not to be married and females were likely to be separated.

- Collins and Van Dulmen (2006) found that experiences in early relationships with both parents and peers influence the quality of young adult romantic relationships, possessing opportunities to learn expectations, skills and behaviours affecting relationship quality.

- Connelly and Goldberg (1999) found that the level of intimacy in peer relationships laid the foundations for the degree of intimacy in young adult relationships.

Evaluation

Interactions with peers

- During adolescence, attachments with parents can change to more of a relationship of equals, similar to relationships with peers, and the development of these attachments can influence adult relationships. Coleman and Hendry (1999) found that children with close parental relationships during adolescence developed the levels of independence required to form successful adult relationships.

- Hartup (1993) thought it is difficult to calculate the impact of children's peer relationships on adult relationships, as there is a need to differentiate between having friends, who the friends are and the quality of friendships.

- Erikson (1968) believed the topic area is affected by gender differences. He saw female identity development dependent on finding a partner, so female identity development comes after intimacy, with the reverse situation for males, suggesting that attachment patterns have different outcomes on adult male and female relationships.

- Wood et al. (2002) believed that there is a subtle but important difference between the way in which individuals relate to others, resulting from attachment type, and their relationships, which result from the interaction of two people's attachment styles. Therefore, insecurely attached people can have secure relationships if they are in relationships with securely attached people.

- Attachment theories are somewhat deterministic, perceiving childhood/peer attachments as causing later adult relationships. However, it is likely that other factors are influential, such as the different attachment styles that people bring to relationships.

- Furman (1999) believed that because peer relationships are on equal footings, they provide opportunities for cooperation and mutual altruism that are not present in child–adult relationships, and these qualities are important in forming successful romantic relationships.

Issues, debates and approaches

- Measurements of attachment and relationship types and strengths, such as the Strange Situation, are culturally specific and not applicable to non-western cultures; as such, they can be seen to be culturally biased when applied to non-western cultures.

- Research generally does not take into account that male and female peer groups have different influences on adult relationships. For instance, Leaper (1994) believes that girls' and boys' peer groups emphasise different styles of relating, affecting the amount of opportunity for learning skills important for adult relationships. Girls' peer groups emphasise turn taking and mutual decision making and are more influential, suggesting a gender difference in how peer groups affect adult relationships.

The influence of culture on romantic relationships

In western cultures, people choose their own partners on the basis of romantic attraction and date each other, or even cohabit, before making commitments to long-term relationships like marriage. Indeed, many choose to cohabit on a permanent basis rather than get married; the rate of marriages in western cultures has steadily decreased.

Other cultures have a tradition of arranged marriages, where families choose who their children will marry, with parents most influential in partner choice and subsidiary roles played by family members and friends; such marriages are considered unions between families rather than the western model of a union between two people. Such marriages are arranged more on the basis of economic reasons than voluntary marriages, which are arranged more on a romantic love basis. The idea behind arranged marriages is that young people would choose partners on the basis of attraction, which is not perceived as a recipe for success. Young people are perceived as being 'blinded by love', and parents know best who is compatible for their children in the long term. This is backed up by the fact that voluntary marriages have lower levels of satisfaction as time goes by, while those in arranged marriages become increasingly happy and 'in love' with each other.

In the West, arranged marriages can be misunderstood and seen negatively, but in a worldwide context arranged marriages are more common, and there is much evidence showing arranged marriages to be generally successful and, arguably, in some respects more successful than western marriages, certainly in terms of divorce and long-term satisfaction rates. However, divorce rates may be lower in cultures where arranged marriages are practised, because of cultural and practical restrictions on divorce. Pressure from the extended families of married couples for them to try to stay together is greater than in western cultures, so as not to disappoint family members. Such cultures see divorce as bringing shame on the whole family, and divorce may not be practical, especially for females, as opportunities for economic independence, like having a sufficiently paid job, may not be possible, and they simply cannot afford to live without remaining in the marriage. Also there are cultural restrictions on divorced women remarrying, as they are considered 'tainted goods'.

Divorce rates in western cultures where voluntary marriage is practised may be higher because people have the freedom to get divorced. Divorce rates were a lot lower in the West when getting divorced was a more difficult and shameful process.

Cultures where arranged marriages predominate are generally ones where opportunities and rights for women are fewer than for their western counterparts. When such traditionalist cultures become more open, giving more emancipation and freedom to women, numbers of and satisfaction with arranged marriages tends to decline.

In multicultural societies like Britain, where there is a mixture of western liberal attitudes to romantic relationships and non-western traditionalist cultures, which are less liberal and favouring of arranged marriages, clashes can occur. This has led to instances of forced marriages, where young people are compelled to marry against their will, and also the concept of 'honour killings', where family members who are deemed to have brought shame on the family, by marrying against their wishes, are either murdered, usually by male relatives, or are encouraged to commit suicide.

Contrary to what many in the West believe, arranged marriages do not generally mean that the individuals getting married have no say in the process. Arranged marriages rarely take place between individuals totally unknown to each other, and parents make great efforts to pair children with partners they like, find attractive and have feelings for. Those entering such relationships generally have a right of veto – that is, they can decline to marry a possible partner. Internet dating sites, like www.shaadi.com, are popular, not just with young people from traditionalist cultures, but whole families, as they allow for choice in partner selection, but in a manner in line with traditional cultural beliefs and practices (see 'Psychology in action' on page 117).

In two-thirds of the world, a man or his family pays a dowry for his bride, and in return he gets her labour and childbearing qualities. This explains the cultural belief that women have little or no opportunity to get divorced or have an equal role in relationships, as they and their services have been 'bought'. This has given rise to high-profile cases, where western women who enter into marriage with men in more traditionalist cultures and subsequently get divorced find it difficult to have contact with, or custody of their children, as the cultural belief is that such children are 'owned' by the groom and his family.

Moghaddam *et al.* (1993) point out that western cultures are individualistic in nature and this shapes attitudes towards romantic relationships, which are based on the viewpoint of the individual, as voluntary and somewhat temporary. Collectivist cultures tend to be based on the needs of the group as a whole and are more involuntary, as with arranged marriages, and more permanent.

Psychology in action

Internet dating sites for Muslims

The internet dating site www.singlemuslim.com has 100,000 members; it was set up by Adeem Younis when he realised that Muslim men and women were not mixing at his university, as to do so would be frowned on by Islam. People put up a profile on the site, along with what they are looking for, how religious they are, their physical characteristics, and so on.

This and similar sites incorporate traditional aspects, where parents can view and veto potential partners, and chaperones are appointed to attend any meetings between matched individuals. Such sites allow young Muslims to browse through potential partners without breaking any religious rules, and whole families become involved, with responsibility being shared for partner choice that is conducted on cultural lines, but with a more modern aspect to it.

This practice has the blessing of Relate, the relationship guidance service, which states that such websites are an extension of the cultural practice of having family and friends introduce potential partners, but with the added fit that individuals do not have to continue if it does not work out, unlike strictly arranged marriages.

Research: The influence of culture on romantic relationships

- LeVine *et al.* (1993) asked young people from 11 different countries if they would marry someone whom they did not love if they had all the qualities they desired in a marriage partner. More people in collectivist cultures than in individualist cultures said yes – for example, 49 per cent of Indians compared to 3.5 per cent of Americans and 7 per cent of English people – supporting the idea that people from traditionalist cultures marry for reasons other than romantic love.

- Rockman (1994) found that in cultures practising arranged marriages, families often use similar criteria to what individuals themselves would use if they had free choice, and even employ professional matchmakers to facilitate this process. This contradicts the assumption that those in arranged marriages are unhappy with the choice of partners and have no influence in the process.

- McKenry and Price (1995) reported that in cultures where females have become more independent and influential, divorce rates have risen considerably, suggesting that the lower divorce rates often seen in non-individualistic cultures is not a reflection of happy marriages, but of male dominance.

- Umadevi *et al.* (1992) looked at female student preferences for love marriages and arranged marriages in India. Arranged marriages were seen positively as long as the two intended partners consented. However, love marriages were preferred too, so long as there was parental approval, demonstrating the importance of the opinions of the whole family in Indian society.

- Gupta and Singh (1982) looked at 100 Indian marriages of professional, educated couples, 50 of which were arranged marriages and 50 of which were love marriages. Couples were assessed after 1, 5 and 10 years of marriage. In love marriages, loving and liking were initially high, but decreased over time, while in arranged marriages, loving and liking were initially low, but grew and exceeded the level of love marriages after 10 years, suggesting that arranged marriages are more successful over time than love marriages.

- Zaidi and Shuraydi (2002) interviewed Muslim women of Pakistani origin who had been raised in Canada about their attitudes towards arranged marriages. The majority preferred love marriages of their choice, although their elders, especially fathers, were opposed, showing the potential for discord within cultural groups that form minorities within more dominant cultures.

- Mwamwenda and Monyooe (1997) found that 87 per cent of Xhosa students in South Africa supported the dowry system, seeing it as a sign of the groom's appreciation for his bride.

Evaluation

The influence of culture on romantic relationships

- One reason that some cultures may prefer and practise the custom of arranged marriages is that in western cultures there is more social mobility and opportunities to meet potential partners and therefore 'shop around'. In traditionalist cultures, if others did not arrange relationships, there is a high possibility that an individual would never meet anyone suitable and compatible. Divorce can also be seen as an easier option in western cultures, as there will be plenty of opportunities to form more suitable new relationships.

- It may be wrong to think in terms of western/non-western or individualistic/collectivist cultures. Instead it may be more applicable in the modern world to think of urban and non-urban cultures, with urban cultures having greater opportunities to form romantic partnerships on a voluntary choice basis. Indeed, as several traditionalist countries, such as India and Japan, become increasingly urbanised, there has been a shift away from arranged marriages to more voluntary arrangements.

- Simmel (1971) believed that western individualistic cultures have higher divorce rates because individuals are perpetually looking for an ideal partner.

- Xioahe and Whyte (1990) found contradictory evidence suggesting that arranged marriages are superior to love marriages over time. In China, women reported love marriages to be more satisfactory than arranged marriages. However, women in China have developed far more freedom and influence in recent years and findings may be an expression of this.

- Much research into relationships uses data from self-reports, such as questionnaires, and these may be subject to bias, especially in the form of socially desirable answers – that is, respondents will reply in a way that their culture would expect them to, rather than give true answers about romantic relationship satisfaction.

- There is a problem in comparing cultures, as samples are rarely identical, which can invalidate results.

- There are huge variations between cultures in reasons for divorce, and these may be a reflection of cultural norms and practices. In Saudi Arabia a woman can only get a divorce if it is a right stated in her marriage contract, and she would be loathe to do so, as Saudi law states that children remain with the father.

- The dowry system may have a protective value for women, as husbands may be unwilling to abuse wives they have paid money for. However, it is also used to justify children remaining with the husband's family in the event of divorce, the children having been 'paid for'.

- The concept of totally arranged marriages, where the intended partners have no say in the matter, is a rare occurrence. Most partners in arranged marriages have a right to consent and the majority meet each other at social functions or through a third party.

Research in focus

There is a high possibility that the use of self-report techniques to investigate cross-cultural differences in romantic relationships might suffer from social desirability bias. What are socially desirable answers and what effect could they be having on research like this?

Issues, debates and approaches

- Research on the influence of culture on romantic relationships can often involve bias on the part of researchers – for example, seeing arranged marriages as fundamentally inferior to free-choice marriages – or an imposed etic, where western methodologies are applied inappropriately to research in non-western cultures.

- There is an assumption in western cultures that inequity in a romantic relationship is a sign of discord, which, if unresolved, leads to relationship breakdown. However, this is a cultural assumption and is not necessarily true of collectivist societies.

Strengthen your learning

1. What is the continuity hypothesis?
2. Evaluate the continuity hypothesis in terms of how much support/lack of support it has.
3. Outline research into interactions with peers.
4. Provide a concise evaluation of the effect of peers on adult relationships. Try to elaborate your points.
5. What differences are there between voluntary and arranged marriages?
6. Give details of ways in which:
   i) arranged marriages can be considered to be superior/preferable to voluntary marriages.
   ii) voluntary marriages can be considered superior/preferable to arranged marriages.

Assessment Check

1. Discuss the influence of culture on romantic relationships. (24 marks)

2a. Outline and evaluate the influence of childhood on adult relationships. (12 marks)

2b. Outline and evaluate the influence of culture on romantic relationships (12 marks)

3. Outline and evaluate the influence of childhood on adult relationships. (24 marks)

Examination guidance

In question 1, the term 'discuss' means to describe and evaluate. Evaluation could refer to the degree of research support, methodological considerations and the problems of conducting cross-cultural research.

With question 2a. 4 marks would be available for the description and 8 marks for the evaluation, so in a sense this is a mini-essay and therefore about half the time normally dedicated to answering a 25 mark question should be spent here. The same is true for 2b. with 4 marks on offer for the description and 8 marks again up for grabs for the evaluation.

Question 3 is quite straightforward, with most marks (16) available for the evaluation, which could focus on what research has informed about the influence of childhood on adult relationships, along with relevant IDA points that are embedded into the answer and not generic ones tagged onto the end of the answer. If using material on adolescence, be sure to justify its inclusion as an extension of childhood (i.e. its non-adult status).

Summing up

- For a romantic relationship to begin, there must first be an attraction and several factors have been identified that facilitate this, such as proximity, familiarity, similarity and physical attractiveness.

- The sociobiological explanation is an evolutionary theory perceiving relationship formation as a form of 'survival efficiency', with a different focus between males and females.

- The reinforcement and needs satisfaction explanation is a behaviourist or learning explanation that sees conditioning as an explanation for relationship formation.

- Social exchange theory explains relationships in terms of maximising benefits and minimising costs.

- Equity theory perceives individuals as motivated to achieve fairness in their relationships and feel dissatisfied with unfairness.

- Duck and Lee both proposed theories of dissolution describing relationship break-ups as a series of stages to be worked through.

- Sexual selection involves the selection of characteristics increasing reproductive success.

- Differences between male and female sexual behaviour have arisen, as they are subject to different selective pressures.

- Males and females have evolved different strategies to maximise reproductive success.

- Parental investment concerns investment in individual offspring, which increases the offspring's chances of achieving reproductive success, at the expense of parents' ability to invest in other children.

- Evolutionary theory predicts differences between how male and female parental investment differs, and such predictions have generally been supported.

- Parent–offspring conflict concerns confrontations that arise from children desiring greater investment than parents have been selected to provide.

- Offspring demonstrate various strategies to try to maximise parental investment in them at the expense of siblings.

- The continuity hypothesis predicts that infant attachment types persist into adulthood, predicting the nature of adult relationships, and this is supported by research.

- Evidence also suggests that there is intergenerational continuity between adults' attachment styles and those of their children.

- Relationships with peers influence later adult relationships, playing a key role in helping to achieve independence.

- Western cultures emphasise individualism, characterised by voluntary relationships, often of a short-term nature, based on ideas of romantic love.

- Non-western cultures emphasise collectivism, characterised by arranged marriages, generally of a long-term nature, based on ideals of the common good.

- Conflicts can arise in multicultural societies where a range of romantic relationship styles exist side by side.

4 Aggression

Social psychological approaches to explaining aggression   **122**

Social learning theory   123

Deindividuation   128

Institutional aggression   133

Biological explanations of aggression   **139**

Neural and hormonal mechanisms in aggression   139

Genetic factors in aggressive behaviour   142

Evolution and human aggression   **147**

Evolutionary theory   147

Infidelity and jealousy   149

Evolutionary explanations of group displays in humans   152

Summing up   **158**

Decoding the specification

The specification outlines what you must study to answer any examination question you might face. There is a requirement to have knowledge and understanding of social psychological theories. Social learning theory and deindividuation are named are examples, meaning that they could not be named in examination questions and any relevant theories would be acceptable.

There is also a requirement to have knowledge of institutional aggression. Explicit explanations are not specified, so any relevant ones would be acceptable, such as the importation and deprivation models, with a need to be able to describe and evaluate such material.

The focus on biological explanations is quite straightforward, centring on two broad biological areas associated with aggression. Firstly hormonal and neural mechanisms must be studied, as these could be examined directly, with the same situation arising with genetic factors, and you need to be able to describe and evaluate the role they play in determining levels of aggression.

The specification also centres on evolution and human aggression and as infidelity and jealousy are explicitly named, they must be studied. You also need to have knowledge of evolutionary explanations of group display in humans, but as sport and warfare are given just as examples, they cannot feature explicitly in exam questions, so any relevant material would be creditworthy here.

Social psychological approaches to explaining aggression

Social psychological theories focus on the role that other individuals and groups play in eliciting aggression. There are several such theories and two are described here: *social learning theory*, emphasising the role of observation and imitation; and the theory of *deindividuation*, which focuses on the role of losing one's sense of individual identity.

IN THE NEWS

Adapted from BBC Sport, 12 February 2001, http://news.bbc.co.uk/sport1/hi/football/teams/s/swansea_city/1166787.stm

Figure 4.01 The lion started it...

Swans defend lion's decapitation

Swansea City mascot Cyril the Swan has come in for criticism after he pulled off a fellow mascot's head and drop-kicked it into the crowd during the half-time entertainment. The controversial character found himself back in the headlines after Sunday's match against Millwall at the Vetch. But Swansea City have hit back at a wave of criticism, saying it was harmless fun and that Millwall's Zampa the Lion started it. Swansea issued a statement defending Cyril's honour after newspaper reports suggested that his antics had enraged Millwall fans.

Cyril the Swan has been in trouble several times for acts of aggression. Aside from his spat with Zampa, Cyril was accused in October 2001 of assaulting a 46-year-old woman dressed as a dog at the annual football mascots Grand National race, fined £1,000 in 1999 for a pitch invasion, and received a two-match ban for clashing with Norwich's assistant manager. He is not the only one: Wolfie of Wolverhampton Wanderers had a fight with two pigs at Bristol City and a punch-up with West Bromwich Albion's Baggie the Bird, and in November 2001 seven stewards were required to break up a scuffle between Bartley the Bluebird, mascot of Cardiff City, and Bury's Robbie the Bobbie, who was sent off three times in one season, the last occasion being for mooning at Bristol City fans.

From a psychological point of view, such behaviour could be explained by deindividuation, where people are aggressive because their identity is concealed. It could also be viewed as an example of group display in the form of a war dance performed before battle to motivate and intimidate the enemy, and as an example of social learning theory, where violence is observed and imitated by fans.

Perhaps the solution is to be found at Exeter City, whose mascot is Athena, goddess of heroic endeavour.

Social learning theory

Social learning theory (SLT) is defined as learning behaviour controlled by environmental influences rather than by innate or internal forces. SLT is often called modelling or observational learning.

SLT emphasises the importance of observing and modelling behaviours, attitudes and emotional reactions of others. The theory suggests that aggression, like other forms of behaviour, is primarily learned. Humans are not born aggressive, but acquire aggressive behaviours in the same way as other social behaviours: through direct experience or by observing the actions of others.

SLT developed from learning theory (behaviourism). According to behaviourists:

- Behaviour that is reinforced (rewarded) will be repeated and learned.

- Aggression associated with a reward, like praise or increased self-esteem, is likely to be learned.

However, learning occurs indirectly, as well as directly, through observing others. This is learning by *vicarious experience*, by observing others.

Bandura (1977) sums this up thus:

Learning would be exceedingly laborious, not to mention hazardous, if people had to rely solely on the effects of their own actions to inform them what to do. Fortunately, most human behaviour is learned observationally through modelling: from observing others one forms an idea of how new behaviours are performed, and on later occasions this coded information serves as a guide for action.

Observational learning therefore involves individuals observing and imitating others' behaviour. There are four component processes:

1. **Attention** – learning through observation occurs by attending to a model's behaviour. For example, children must attend to what an aggressor is doing and saying in order to reproduce the model's behaviour accurately (see 'Classic research: Bandura, Ross and Ross (1961)' on page 124).

2. **Retention** – in order to reproduce modelled behaviour, individuals must code and recall behaviour by placing it into long-term memory, enabling the behaviour to be retrieved. In the Bandura, Ross and Ross (1961) experiment, children were only able to act aggressively as the information was stored in their long-term memory.

3. **Production** – individuals must be capable of reproducing the model's behaviour, and thus possess the capabilities and skills needed to copy the modelled behaviour. In the Bandura, Ross and Ross study, the children possessed the physical capabilities of hitting and punching the doll.

4. **Motivation or reinforcements** – individuals expect to receive positive reinforcements (rewards) for modelled behaviour and this helps to motivate their behaviour. In the Bandura, Ross and Ross experiment, the children witnessed adults gaining a reward for their aggression. Therefore, the children performed the same behaviour to receive the same reward.

Key terms

Social learning theory – learning occurring through observation and imitation

Deindividuation – loss of individual identity and loosening of normal inhibitions

Institutional aggression – aggression occurring as a result of being in an institutionalised setting

Instrumental aggression – goal-directed non-hostile aggression

Hostile aggression – aggression intending harm, based on emotional response

Importation model – aggressive behaviours are imported into institutional settings

Deprivation model – deprivations associated with institutional life increase potential for aggressiveness

There are several factors influencing imitative behaviour. Individuals are more likely to copy modelled behaviour if:

- it results in outcomes (rewards) that are valued

- the model is similar to the observer – for example, the same sex, age and with similar interests

- the model is charismatic and admired

- the task to be imitated is neither too easy nor too difficult

- the individuals have low self-esteem or are unconfident in their abilities.

Bandura believed that aggression reinforced by family members was the most prominent source of behaviour modelling. For example, the boy who observes his father attack his mother is more likely to become an abusive parent and husband.

Although a model is necessary for imitation, good levels of *self-efficacy* (situation–specific confidence) are also required.

There are many sources of aggression through which social learning can occur, but media influences are perceived as especially powerful sources.

Classic research

Bandura, Ross and Ross (1961, 1963)

Study one – transmission of aggression through imitation: Bandura, Ross and Ross (1961)

Bandura's social learning theory was based on his bobo doll study and the variations that followed. A bobo doll is an inflatable child's toy that bounces back when hit. The researchers were interested in seeing whether children would imitate acts of aggression on the doll in various scenarios.

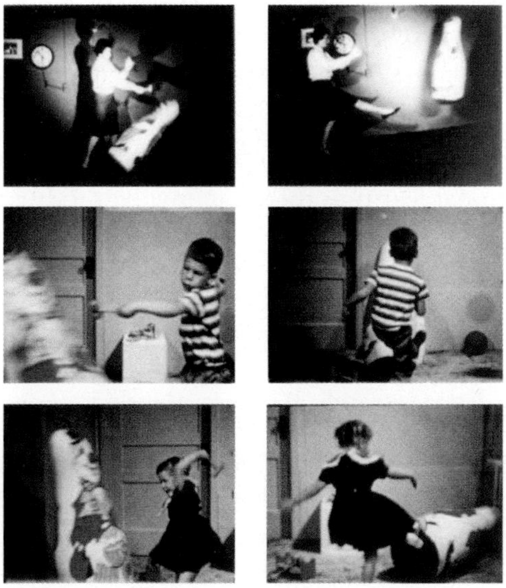

Aim

To see whether aggressive behaviour could be learned through observation.

Procedure

Thirty-six boys and 36 girls, aged between 3 and 5 years, were divided into eight experimental groups of six children each. The remaining children acted as a control group. The children were brought to the experimental room individually, and were invited to play a game; a number of toys were present in the room. An adult 'model' then entered the room and assembled some toys.

Figure 4.02 Original stills from the Bobo doll studies

In the non-aggressive condition, the model continued to assemble the toys in a quiet manner, ignoring the bobo doll. In the aggressive condition, after a minute, the model started acting aggressively towards the bobo doll. The model performed novel aggressive behaviours not expected of children unless influenced by the model's behaviour, including pummelling it on the head with a mallet, hurling it down, sitting on it and punching it on the nose repeatedly, kicking it across the room

continued ...

...continued

and flinging it in the air. Verbal aggression was included, such as shouting, 'Sock him in the nose!' and 'He sure is a tough fella!' Both male and female models were used.

If the children performed similar actions, it would be evidence of observational learning. Merely hitting the doll would not, as that is what bobo dolls are designed for.

Prior to the subsequent test for imitation, all children were subjected to 'mild aggression arousal'. This involved taking them to a room containing attractive toys they were told they could play with; then, after 2 minutes of playing, they were told that they could not play with them after all. They were then taken to a further room where there were a number of aggressive toys, such as a mallet, and non-aggressive toys, such as crayons for them to play with, as well as a bobo doll. The children spent 20 minutes in this room, observed through a one-way mirror. An experimenter rated the different levels of aggressive and non-aggressive behaviour shown by the children. This experimenter had no knowledge as to which group the children had been pre-assigned to.

Findings

Children in the aggressive condition showed much physical and verbal aggression, their scores being significantly higher than those of children in the non-aggressive and control groups. Indeed, 70 per cent of children in the non-aggressive or control groups had zero ratings of aggression.

Both boys and girls were more influenced by the male model. The tentative explanation for this was that physical aggression is typically seen as a more male sex-appropriate behaviour.

Conclusions

Observation of behaviour can lead to imitative learning.

People are more likely to imitate male aggressive models, as physical aggression is perceived as more of a male sex-appropriate behaviour.

Study two – imitation of film-mediated aggressive models: Bandura, Ross and Ross (1963)

Aim

To see whether aggressive behaviour could be learned through observation of a film.

Procedure

A similar method was used in this study as in study one. The children watched a short film in which the 'model' behaved aggressively, both physically and verbally, towards the bobo doll. There were three experimental conditions:

1. 'Model-reward' condition: here the model was rewarded for abusing the doll by being given sweets and drinks, and called a 'strong champion'.

2. 'Model-punished' condition: here the model was punished for abusing the doll, being told off for 'picking on the clown'.

3. 'No consequences' (control) condition: here no reinforcement was given.

After the video, the children were placed in a room with attractive toys and were not allowed to touch them, making them angry and frustrated. After this, the children went to a playroom containing a bobo doll and other toys. Each child was observed for 10 minutes, and an experimenter rated the different levels of aggressive and non-aggressive behaviour shown by the children.

All children were then offered a reward if they could imitate the behaviours they had earlier seen the model performing.

continued ...

...continued

Findings

- Before a reward was offered – children in the model-punished group produced significantly less imitative aggressive behaviour than children in either of the other two groups. There was no significant difference between the 'model-reward' and 'no consequences' groups.
- After a reward was offered – children in all three groups then performed the aggressive behaviours to the same extent. All the children had learned the model's aggressive behaviours.

Conclusions

- Reinforcement is not necessary for the *learning* of behaviours through observation, but the expectancy of reinforcement is essential for the *performance* of these behaviours.
- Both this and the earlier study provide clear evidence for SLT and the modelling influence of both real-life and filmed aggression.
- Other similar studies conducted by Bandura *et al*. demonstrated that children are more likely to model behaviour if they identify with and admire the model.

Evaluation

- The inclusion of other toys and the copying of specific aggressive responses showed that the children had indeed learned behaviour from the model.
- The children used were from Stanford University nursery, so are unlikely to have been a representative sample. Indeed, as only children were used, it is not known if adults would behave in the same way. Stack (1987) reports that the highest number of suicides in New York City came a few days after Marilyn Monroe's death, suggesting that adults also learn from modelling.
- The studies lack ecological validity, as the artificial laboratory situation ensures that it is difficult to generalise the findings to more realistic settings. For example, there was no justification given for the violence portrayed.
- The aggression portrayed was not real and was limited to a doll. Would the children have imitated aggressive acts towards a real person? Johnston *et al*. (1977) found that play aggression correlated with ratings of aggression by peers (0.76) and teachers (0.57), suggesting that play aggression is a valid measure of aggression.
- Demand characteristics may have been present, as some children felt they were expected to perform aggressively towards the doll, though the specific nature of the imitative aggression suggests that modelling did occur.
- The studies may only have shown short-term effects of modelling. However, Hicks (1965) found that 40 per cent of a model's acts could be reproduced up to 8 months after one showing of a 10-minute film, suggesting that the effects were long term.
- The children were deliberately frustrated, and this may have contributed to them being aggressive, rather than observation alone being the cause.
- The studies are questionable ethically: there are doubts about whether informed consent was gained from parents, and, as the children were filmed, there are doubts about confidentiality. The main ethical concern is the possibility of distress and the potential long-term consequences to behaviour in encouraging children to be aggressive.
- Is the number of times a child punches a bobo doll a valid measure of aggression? As a bobo doll is designed to be punched, the number of punches is not really a valid measure of aggression. Some children stated, 'That's the doll we have to hit'.

It is important to remember when answering a question on SLT as an explanation of aggression, and using the Bandura, Ross and Ross study as an illustration, not to spend all your time evaluating the STUDY rather than the EXPLANATION. Such an approach would attract little credit.

Research in focus

One criticism of the bobo doll studies is the possible influence of demand characteristics.

What are demand characteristics and how may they have had an effect in these studies?

What methods of attempting to control demand characteristics have psychologists devised?

Research: Social learning theory

- Bandura (1977) reported that individuals who live in areas with high crime rates are more likely to act violently than those who dwell in low-crime areas, implying that such acts of violence are being imitated. However, there may be other factors involved, such as unemployment and lack of educational opportunities.

- Bandura *et al.* (1963) also demonstrated that viewing aggression by cartoon characters produces as much aggression as viewing live or filmed aggressive behaviour by adults, suggesting that media influences are a powerful form of social learning.

- Williams (1981) found that the level of verbal and physical aggression among children in a remote Canadian community increased after the introduction of TV, again suggesting the media to be an influential source of imitative aggression. However, the study does not show if the rise in aggression was a long-term phenomenon.

- Cooper and McKay (1986) found that after children aged between 9 and 10 had played aggressive video games, acts of aggression increased in girls, but not in boys, suggesting that such sources of social learning affect genders differently.

- Huesmann (1988) reported that children use television models to direct their own actions. Observed aggressive acts are stored in memory, where they are strengthened and elaborated through repetition. They are then used to guide behaviour in situations perceived as appropriate, suggesting that media influences are a source of social learning.

- Charlton *et al.* (2000) assessed the level of aggression in children on the island of St Helena before and after the introduction of satellite TV in 1995. Levels of aggression among the children were initially low, and remained so after TV was introduced, suggesting that exposure to aggression through the media does not necessarily lead to a rise in imitative aggression.

Figure 4.03 Research findings are inconclusive as to whether media sources of aggression are a source of social learning

You are the researcher

Design an experiment that examines whether watching violent cartoons affects the aggression levels of younger children more than older children.

How would you assess changes in aggression levels? How would aggression be measured?

Write a suitable two-tailed hypothesis for your study.

What ethical problems would conducting such a study present?

Would this study be justifiable in terms of a cost-benefit analysis?

Evaluation

Social learning theory

- SLT has much research support, especially concerning the influence of media sources on imitative aggression, though such findings are not without criticism that straightforward observational learning explanations are often too simplistic.

- SLT has been shown to be involved in the development of psychological disorders, particularly phobias, and has formed the backbone of many successful therapies associated with such disorders, like behaviour modification programmes (see page 368). SLT also explains the success of many television commercials, where buying particular products helps people to identify with the models used to promote the product. This indicates SLT to be a powerful learning tool in many areas of human behaviour.

- Social learning can be argued to be more powerful than biology, because there are societies that are non-aggressive, like the Amish communities in the USA.

- SLT does not account for the role of emotional factors in aggressive behaviour.

- SLT can explain people's levels of aggression varying between situations, by means of them being reinforced to be aggressive, and in varying ways, in different situations. If aggression were biologically determined, we would expect aggression levels to be consistent across situations.

- SLT successfully explains individual differences and cultural differences in aggression as resulting from different learning experiences.

Figure 4.04 The Amish are a non-aggressive community of people

Deindividuation

Deindividuation is defined as the loss of a sense of individual identity, and a loosening of normal inhibitions against engaging in behaviour that is inconsistent with internal standards.

Deindividuation theory is a social psychological account of the individual in a group or crowd. It can be applied to aggression as the theory explains how rational individuals become aggressive hooligans in an unruly mob. Festinger *et al.* (1952) coined the phrase 'deindividuation', suggesting that there is a reduction of inner restraints or self-awareness when individuals are 'submerged in a group'. Individuals in groups do not see the consequences of their actions and the social norms usually followed are forgotten.

Le Bon (1895) was the first to recognise how behaviour changes in a crowd. He wrote that an individual in a crowd 'descends several rungs of the ladder of civilisation'. Le Bon proposed a number of factors leading to an individual becoming psychologically transformed in a crowd, the most important being anonymity. Le Bon suggested that the more anonymous the crowd, the greater the threat of extreme action. A 'collective mindset' takes over and the crowd acts as one, with an individual becoming submerged into the crowd and losing self-control.

Le Bon's idea of a collective mindset was criticised, and it was proposed instead that anonymity leads to a release from internal restraints, producing emotional, impulsive and irrational behaviour. Zimbardo (1970) argued that there was more to deindividuation than just anonymity in a group, and suggested that reduced

responsibility, increased arousal, sensory overload and altered consciousness due to drugs or alcohol play an important part.

In the 1980s, new adaptations of deindividuation theory were proposed, as outlined below.

Diener (1980) suggested that people often behave in well-scripted ways, and do so without conscious awareness. When others evaluate an individual, or when behaviour does not follow the script, the individual becomes self-aware. Diener believed that crowds block an individual's capacity for self-awareness and the individual becomes deindividuated.

A key factor in behaviour is social arousal, noticeable at sports events when fans become so involved in focusing on the game they are no longer self-aware.

Prentice-Dunn and Rogers (1982) suggested that there are two types of self-awareness:

- **Public self-awareness** – individuals' concern about the impression presented to other people, knowing that they will be evaluated. Public self-awareness can be reduced by the anonymity of being in a crowd, diffusion of responsibility (the decrease in individual responsibility when in a group) and the fact that other members in a group act as role models to set the social norms or standards of behaviour likely to be copied. In essence, loss of public self-awareness leads to loss of public standards of behaviour or a lowering of inhibitions.

- **Private self-awareness** – the concern individuals have for their thoughts and feelings. This is reduced by becoming so involved in activities that individuals 'forget' themselves – for example, when dancing at a club. In essence, loss of private awareness leads to a loss of internal standards and an over-reliance on environmental cues, such as others in a crowd, as to how to behave – that is, people forget how to think for themselves.

Becoming immersed in a group or crowd causes loss of both private and public awareness.

Deindividuation results in disinhibited behaviour that does not follow usual social norms. The only difference is whether in a crowd individuals are controlled by others or whether they simply cannot control their own antisocial tendencies.

Classic research

Zimbardo *et al.* (1973)

Deindividuation and aggression in a simulated prison

Following a series of media reports into prison brutality and riots, the researchers were interested in examining whether individual characteristics of personality or situational factors of environment were more involved in such acts of aggression.

Aim

To investigate the role of deindividuation in 'total institutions', where people are removed from their normal environment and stripped of their individuality.

Procedure

A simulated prison was created in the basement of Stanford University psychology department, and 24 emotionally stable, male participants were recruited. One group of students were randomly assigned to the role of guards, and the others to the role of prisoners.

Guards and prisoners were deindividuated to become anonymous members of their groups. This was achieved by the prisoners being stripped naked on arrival, and issued with loose-fitting smocks, with an ID number printed on the front and back and a chain bolted around one ankle. They wore nylon

continued ...

...continued

stockings to cover their hair and were referred to by number only. The guards wore military-style, khaki uniforms and silver reflector sunglasses, making eye contact impossible. They carried clubs, whistles, handcuffs and keys. The guards had complete control over the prisoners, who were confined to their cells around the clock, except for meals, toilet privileges, head counts and work.

Findings

Despite being only a simulation, the guards created a brutal atmosphere. Prisoners began to react passively, as the guards stepped up their aggression, which took verbal forms, like abuse, and physical forms, like repetitive press-ups and being pushed into urinals. Prisoners felt helpless and no longer in control of their lives. Every guard behaved in an abusive, authoritarian way, many seeming to enjoy the power and control that went with the uniform.

'Both sets of participants showed classic signs of deindividuation', according to Lippa (1994).

Conclusions

Deindividuation leads to a lowered sense of personal identity and a host of disinhibited antisocial behaviours, such as psychological and physical aggression.

Evaluation

- Both the environment and the behaviour of guards and prisoners were 'realistic'. The findings therefore have ecological validity and can be applied to real prisons. The results were especially surprising given that everyone knew it to be a 'simulation'.

- The forms of aggression witnessed, both verbal and physical, can be considered realistic measures of aggression, increasing the study's validity.

- Many aspects of the study were unethical, such as a lack of fully informed consent and exposure to stress. Zimbardo fully accepted this criticism, claiming that he had been 'blinded' by becoming over-involved in the study in his role as 'prison governor'.

- The sample was unrepresentative, as it included only young, middle-class, male students.

- The findings that deindividuation is an importance source of human aggression have other research support (see 'Research: deindividuation' below).

Research in focus

Zimbardo *et al*.'s (1973) study was subjected to peer review, part of the scientific validation process where research has to be judged, by experts, before being passed fit for publication. However, the peer review system is not without criticism.

In what ways has the peer review process come in for criticism?

Research: deindividuation

- Zimbardo (1970) asked female participants to dress in white laboratory coats and hoods in order to render them anonymous. A control group wore ordinary clothes and had name tags prominently displayed. Participants had to give what they believed to be real shocks to a victim (actually fake shocks and a confederate). Anonymous participants gave more shocks than identifiable participants, suggesting that anonymity contributes to aggression.

- Johnson and Downing (1979) conducted a similar experiment, but participants were made anonymous by the wearing of masks and overalls, similar to those worn by the Ku Klux Klan, or by means of nurses' uniforms. Compared to the control condition, participants shocked more when dressed in the Ku Klux Klan uniforms, but shocked less when dressed as nurses. Although giving some support for the idea of deindividuation, there is also the possibility that the findings are due to the social roles suggested by the uniforms suggested – that is, violence for the Ku Klux Klan hoods and nurturing for the nurses' uniforms.

- Malmuth and Check (1981) found that nearly a third of US male university students would rape if there was no chance of getting caught, supporting the notion of deindividuation increasing a potential for aggressive behaviour.

- Silke (2003) found that people who were disguised perpetrated 41 per cent of violent assaults in Northern Ireland. The more severe the assault, the more likely it was that the attacker was disguised, suggesting that disguises deindividuate people, reducing guilt and fear of punishment.

You are the researcher

Design a study using a repeated measures design that investigates whether people at a fancy-dress party behave more aggressively than when at a party dressed in their normal clothes.

What would be your IV and DV?

How would you solve the problem of order effects?

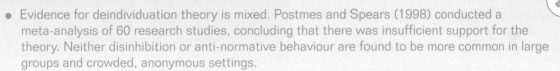

Evaluation

Deindividuation

- Evidence for deindividuation theory is mixed. Postmes and Spears (1998) conducted a meta-analysis of 60 research studies, concluding that there was insufficient support for the theory. Neither disinhibition or anti-normative behaviour are found to be more common in large groups and crowded, anonymous settings.

- There is some experimental support for the theory of deindividuation, but there are other theories with support too. More recent social psychological research suggests a norm-based analysis of collective behaviour, where people follow local group norms if deindividuated.

- Deindividuation does not always lead to aggression; sometimes within crowds deindividuation leads to increased pro-social behaviour. There may be feelings of social identity, and individuals follow the norms occurring within the crowd. This explains how crowds act on moral principles, such as helping behaviour during disasters.

- Ingham (1978) analysed football supporters' behaviour, finding that they follow strictly ritualised rules of behaviour and that acts of violence are not the result of 'mob rule'.

- Research often fails to consider whether the anonymity of the victims of aggression or of the aggressors themselves leads to high levels of aggression.

Issues, debates and approaches

- SLT explanations see aggression as being determined by observation and imitation, and therefore ignore biological factors and the differences that individuals possess in genetics, brain physiology and learning potential, such as differences in levels of testosterone. Bandura acknowledged that biology played a part; however, he argued that aggressive urges/tendencies are biological, but that knowing how and when to be aggressive is learned directly and indirectly.

- One practical application arising out of an understanding of deindividuation is closed-circuit television cameras, such as at football matches, which have reduced violence levels (see 'Psychology in Action' below).

Psychology in action

CCTV and its effects on the incidence of violent crime

One practical application of deindividuation theory is the use of closed-circuit television cameras (CCTV) to monitor public behaviour, especially in places identified as high-risk crime locations.

Deindividuation theory sees people as being aggressive when they lose their sense of personal identity. Therefore, the central idea behind CCTV is to make certain places and populations visible, so that criminals are denied the comfort of anonymity, thus making people accountable for their behaviour.

Figure 4.05

The first CCTV system was installed in Bournemouth in 1985, and about £300,000 a year is spent on installing and maintaining CCTV systems each year in Britain. It is estimated that there are 400,000 cameras currently in use.

However, a Home Office Research Study (2002) found that CCTV led to an overall crime reduction of just 2 per cent and was most effective in reducing vehicle crimes. Most interestingly, the meta-analysis found no reduction in violent crime compared to similar areas where CCTV was not in operation, casting doubts on CCTV being an effective tool, and thus upon deindividuation theory as an explanation of aggression.

Institutional aggression

Institutional aggression occurs in two ways:

1. **Instrumental aggression** – institutional groups sharing a common identity and aims, like the police, the army or terrorist gangs, tend to use aggression in a non-emotive manner, as a calculated means of achieving goals.

2. **Hostile aggression** – people living in institutions, like jails, detention centres or care homes, sometimes use aggression emerging from emotional states, like anger and frustration.

Explanations of institutional aggression tend to be considered as due to *situational factors*, aggression stemming from factors within the social situation, or *dispositional factors*, where aggression stems from personality factors.

Aggression in institutions is a significant problem. In Britain, examples of institutional aggression occur in prisons and the National Health Service. There were 84,272 violent incidents against NHS staff in 2000/1, and in the USA there were 26,000 prisoner–prisoner assaults during 1995. These were reported figures; actual levels are probably five times higher.

Figure 4.06 Is aggression in prison a result of imported personality characteristics or the prison environment itself?

Theories of prison aggression focus on two explanations:

- **Importation model** – aggression occurs due to the individual characteristics that prisoners bring into prison.

- **Situational model** – aggression occurs as a result of factors within the prison setting.

Importation model: Irwin and Cressey (1962)

The importation model suggests that prisoners *import* their social histories and traits into prison, and that these influence their subsequent behaviour.

The aggressive behaviour seen in the prison environment is the same behaviour these individuals demonstrated in normal society.

Cressey (1962) argued that it was wrong to look solely at 'inmate culture' in isolation, and that how it is influenced by elements and experiences outside prison should also be examined.

Many pre-existing factors of incarcerated individuals affect levels of aggression exhibited in prison – for example, alcohol addiction – and two important demographic variables are race and age, possibly because younger and non-white inmates are more likely to be 'separated' from mainstream society's norms and values, which promote pro-social methods of solving interpersonal conflict. Many of these individuals live in subcultures where aggression is valued, respected and reinforced, and such attitudes are imported into prison.

Irwin and Cressey (1962) recognised the importance of prisoner subcultures, identifying three different categories:

1. **Criminal/thief subculture** – these inmates follow the norms and values inherent within the career criminal. Values such as not betraying one another, and being trustworthy and reliable among fellow criminals, are adopted. Such prisoners refer to fellow thieves as their primary reference group.

2. **Convict subculture** – convicts are inmates raised in the prison system who seek positions of power, influence and information within the prison institution. The primary reference group is fellow convicts. Individuals in this particular group are most likely to turn to aggression or other maladaptive forms of coping, and are influenced by deprivation prior to imprisonment.

3. **Conventional or 'straight' subculture** – these individuals tend to be one-time offenders and were not part of a criminal subculture before entering prison. These inmates reject other subcultural groups in prison, identifying more with the prison staff. Such prisoners are not very aggressive while in prison.

Research: importation model

- Mills *et al.* (1998) surveyed 202 inmates newly admitted to a Canadian prison. Using the Alcohol Dependence Scale, they found that higher levels of 'serious institutional misconduct' were associated with more severe levels of alcohol dependence, supporting the idea that many prisoners bring alcohol problems into prison with them.

- Kane and Janus (1981) found that greater periods of unemployment, a lower level of education and a more serious criminal record were correlated with a greater likelihood of aggression while imprisoned, demonstrating how existing factors of incarcerated individuals affect levels of aggression exhibited in prison.

- Irwin and Cressey (1962) reported that one-time offenders were perceived by other prison inmates as 'straights', illuminating the fact that they reject other, more aggressive prisoner subcultures, suggesting that aggression is imported by certain types of inmates.

- Kane and Janus (1981) found that younger and non-white inmates were more likely to be aggressive while in prison, supporting the idea that certain groups are disenfranchised from society's values and import their aggressive norms into prison.

Evaluation

Importation model

- Instead of viewing inmates as influenced by one shared set of values; the importation model looks at subcultures within prisons, a view supported by research, which is thus superior to earlier theories suggesting that inmates imported one 'holistic' criminal subculture into prisons.

- The importation model is accused of failing to provide suggestions for how to manage aggressive prisoners and to reduce prison violence in general.

- Another form of support for the model comes from gang culture. DeLisi *et al.* (2004) studied the prison records of 831 US male inmates in order to assess prison violence records of inmates involved in street and prison gangs, finding a small, but significant relationship between gang membership and prison aggression, suggesting that subcultural values are imported into prisons by gang members. However, other factors, like race, also had importance.

- Further backing for the model comes from Poole and Regoli's (1983) finding that pre-institutional violence is the best predictor of inmate aggression in juvenile correctional institutions, though the results are not generalisable to adult prisoners.

Situational models

Individual factors, as highlighted by the importation model, play a role in institutional aggression, but institutional environments also play a part, with situational factors influencing prisoner behaviour.

Situational factors can be thought of as:

- *organisational* – leadership, management, policies and procedures

- *physical* – security level, level of available resources

- *staff characteristics* – gender, level of experience, relationship to and interactions with prisoners.

The role of situational factors is demonstrated in the deprivation model.

Deprivation model

Early explanations of prison aggression perceived the aggression as originating in the daily deprivations of prison life, which were such that prisoners could not form healthy relationships with people outside prison.

Sykes (1958) argued that the origins of prison subculture emanate from within an institution, not from outside. Sykes outlined five deprivations that arise 'from the indignities and degradations suffered by becoming an inmate':

1. **Deprivation of liberty** – imprisonment informs prisoners that they cannot be trusted to live in the free world. Prisoners are morally rejected by society, with the loss of liberty emphasised by symbols, like the use of numbers and uniforms, with civil rights being lost.

2. **Deprivation of autonomy** – prisoners have no power and few choices to make on a daily basis. Prison officials have control over prisoners' behaviour, leading to feelings of helplessness among inmates, which can lead to frustration and aggression. Prisoners are told what will be happening – for example, 'no exercise today', but not given reasons why.

3. **Deprivation of goods and services** – prisoners are deprived of many of the goods and services normally available. Western emphasis on possessions makes this deprivation hard to bear. Deprivation of goods and services brings about a sense of failure.

4. **Deprivation of heterosexual relationships** – for heterosexual men, female companionship is an important part of self-identity, so denial of heterosexual relationships reduces men's sense of self-worth. In addition, the prevalence of homosexual behaviour in prison leads to greater anxieties for many.

5. **Deprivation of security** – prisoners often fear for their own security, with many inmates perceived as aggressive, leading to a heightened sense of physical threat.

Such deprivations lead to increased stress for prisoners and, as a consequence of suffering deprivations, some inmates act aggressively to reduce stress and obtain resources. Thus aggression in prison is a means of gaining some control over the social order imposed in prison.

Research: situational models

- Blomberg and Lucken (2000) reported that prisoners have to obtain permission to eat, sleep, shower and interact, the latter restricting prisoners' ability to maintain relationships with family and friends. This supports the idea that deprivation of liberty influences prison behaviour, such as institutional aggression.

- Sykes (1958) found that deprivation of goods and services brings about a sense of failure to many serving time in prison, again suggesting that deprivational factors contribute to prison behaviour.

- Cheeseman (2003) found that with much prison aggression there is a lack of real purpose or goals, other than the reduction of stress, outlining how factors of deprivation can lead to stress, which then expresses itself as violence.

- Johnston (1991) found that prison overcrowding leads to increased aggression, due to increased competition for resources and the tendency to adopt violent defensive behaviours, either individually or through the formation of prison gangs with extreme in-group/out-group beliefs, suggesting that situational factors are at play.

- Jiang and Fisher-Giorlando (2002) applied various explanations of institutional aggression to 431 disciplinary reports from an American men's prison, concluding that the situational model was the most persuasive, with the deprivation model best at explaining violence against prison staff.

Evaluation

Situational models

- McCorkle et al. (1995) examined individual and collective acts of aggression in 371 US prisons, finding that the deprivation model was not useful in explaining rates of prison violence; indeed, there was a stronger link between prison administrative practices and levels of violence. Their results suggested that prison aggression occurs as a result of poor management practices, high staff turnover and lack of staff discipline. One positive element of this research was that it suggested that changes in the way institutions are run could lead to decreased aggression.

- Haslam and Reicher (2006) reported in the BBC prison study (based on Zimbardo's study) that participants' behaviour could not be explained as being due purely to allotted roles, and that behaviour was better understood in terms of social identity theory, which sees behaviour due to in-group and out-group reference points (us and them).

- Situational explanations do not explain why prison riots suddenly explode in the absence of new environmental or situational factors. Levels of deprivation remain fairly constant in many institutions, yet violence can erupt suddenly. Recent research has focused on levels of relative rather than absolute deprivation – that is, prisoners' perceived discrepancy between what they receive and what they might expect to receive.

- Research does not suggest a direct relationship between crowding and institutional aggression. Megargee (1976) found that aggression in prisons was negatively correlated to the amount of living space available for each prisoner. It may be that when a prison is overcrowded, management strategies occur to compensate for this, involving fewer opportunities for inmates to interact. Therefore, there is a distinction between social density, the amount of space available when prisoners interact, and spatial density, the amount of space each prisoner has in their cell.

- Much prison aggression has unexplained motives, making it difficult to conduct research and draw firm conclusions. Light (1991) found that 25 per cent of prison assaults had no apparent reason, and Goffman (1961) reported that prisoners often attempt to hide the motives behind aggressive actions.

- After abuses within institutions become public knowledge, it is common for dispositional explanations to be offered – that is, a few 'bad apples' are to blame. However, this can be perceived as an attempt to find a scapegoat, so that the system/institution itself is not seen to be at fault.

The case for interaction

A lot of research into institutional aggression concerns the debate over dispositional and situational factors. The best way to view this debate is from an interactionist viewpoint, with personality and situational factors acting on each other, determining levels and types of aggression. The interaction between the importation and deprivation models is seen as providing a more convincing understanding of the impact of imprisonment on inmate violence than either model separately.

Violence is best viewed as the product of three interacting sets of variables:

- aggressor (personality, needs, concerns, perceptions)

- victim (personality, needs, concerns, perceptions), and

- situation (the human and physical environment in which the incident takes place).

The first two variables relate more to the importation model and the third to the situational model.

Supplementary learning

Terrorism as a form of institutional aggression

Terrorists groups can be seen as institutions, collective groups of people bound together by a common purpose, and committed to using aggression in both an instrumental and a hostile fashion in order to realise their goals.

The main causes of terrorism lie in cultural and subcultural clashes, but can be seen as a form of minority influence, where minority groups seek to affect social change by changing majority views. Their behaviour and beliefs are generally consistent and persistent, leading to gradual changes in public opinion. The IRA in Northern Ireland had growing popular support among the nationalist community, reflected in the large proportion of the electoral vote achieved by its political wing, Sinn Fein.

Terrorism can be seen to justify aggression by the idea of 'collective responsibility', like the targeting of random civilians by the London tube bombers.

Figure 4.07 IRA mural in Northern Ireland

Research

- A Ministry of Defence report (2005) found in a confidential opinion poll that the majority of Iraqis privately (although not publicly) supported the terrorist insurgency, supporting the view that terrorism is a form of minority influence.

- Barak (2004) reported that terrorists are generally people exhibiting suppressed anger who have experienced economic and political marginalisation, suggesting that terrorism has its roots in cultural and subcultural clashes.

- Pyszczynski et al. (2996) asked Iranian and US students to focus on their own mortality and found that it increased support for extreme violence, such as military interventions and suicide bombings, suggesting a degree of similarity in attitudes and behaviour.

Evaluation

- The idea that terrorism results from those experiencing economic and political marginalisation is opposed by the fact that many terrorists, such as the Baader–Meinhof Group and the London tube bombers, were university educated and from affluent families.

- By their very secretive nature, terrorism and terrorists are difficult to study and present many methodological challenges. Most research 'findings' are based on subjective interpretations and are at risk of extreme researcher bias.

- The idea that there is a 'typical' terrorist is rather simplistic; it is more probable that a range of explanations are needed to explain the huge variety of terrorist groups and actions, including instrumental and hostile acts, encompassing both situational and dispositional factors.

- Merrari (1991) found that there was a lack of empirical data and over-reliance on other researchers' results, creating a problem in reaching valid conclusions.

Issues, debates and approaches

- Explanations of institutional aggression can be seen in terms of the nature versus nurture debate. Some explanations tend towards seeing aggression as a product of innate personality traits imported into prison – that is, an influence of nature – while other explanations see the brutalising environment of prisons as contributing to heightened aggression – that is, an influence of nurture.

- Research studies of institutional aggression can be seen as gender biased in concentrating mainly on male prisoners, who may have different profiles to female prisoners. Female offenders often develop strong bonds with other members of their social groups, rather than identify with prisoner subculture. Thus explanations for female aggression in prisons may be qualitatively different to those for male inmates.

- Research permitting a better understanding of aggression in prisons could lead to the formation of useful practical applications, such as prison reform. Zimbardo's research initially led to progressive changes in the treatment of prisoners. However, Zimbardo feels that prison regimes became worse, not better, suggesting that his research cannot be justified in cost-benefit terms.

Strengthen your learning

1. Outline the process by which aggression can be learned through:
   i)   social learning
   ii) deindividuation.
2. Does research indicate SLT or deindividuation to be a better explanation of aggression? Use evidence to support your answer.
3. Outline how institutional aggression could occur through:
   i)   the importation model
   ii) the deprivation model.
4. Assess, using research evidence, whether the importation or the deprivation model is a better explanation of institutional aggression. You may also wish to consider the case for interaction.

Assessment Check

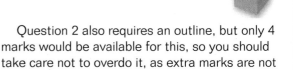

1. Outline one social psychological theory of aggression. (4 marks)

2. Outline and evaluate explanations of institutional aggression. (20 marks)

3. Outline two social psychological theories of aggression. (8 marks)

4. Evaluate one of the theories outlined in (3). (16 marks)

5. Outline and evaluate one explanation of institutional aggression. (24 marks)

Examination guidance

As with all exam questions, the most important task is understanding the requirements of the question. In question 1, you are required to outline just one theory; if you do two, both would be marked, but only the best one would be credited.

Question 2 also requires an outline, but only 4 marks would be available for this, so you should take care not to overdo it, as extra marks are not available . Most time and effort should be spent on the evaluation, where 16 marks are on offer.

Question 3 is similar to question 1, but this time two theories are required, which is reflected in the higher tally of 8 marks. To gain access to the highest band of marks, a balance between the two theories is required. The evaluation in question 4 should focus on just one of these theories, but other theories could be used, even non-social psychology ones, if used as a comparison.

Beware that question 5 focuses on just one explanation of institutional aggression. Therefore, you need to know individual theories in enough detail to be able to answer this kind of question fully.

Biological explanations of aggression

Biological explanations see aggression as resulting from internal physiological causes. Certain individuals may have increased genetic dispositions to be aggressive, but for genes to produce aggressive effects they must express themselves through other biological means, such as hormonal and neural mechanisms. Biological factors can be perceived as sole causes or as working in conjunction with other factors.

Neural and hormonal mechanisms in aggression

Neurotransmitters and hormones are biological mechanisms that play an important role in many areas of human functioning. The neurotransmitter *serotonin*, along with hormones like *adrenaline* and even the female hormones *oestrogen* and *progesterone* have been identified as being involved with aggression. Most research, though, has concentrated on the hormone *testosterone*.

Testosterone is a male hormone, though it is found in low levels in females, and is associated with aggression. Testosterone appears to be influential during two life periods: the 'critical time period' a few days after birth, during which sensitisation of neural circuits occurs, and in adulthood when testosterone modulates neurotransmitter pathways.

Testosterone is associated with human and non-human animal aggression – for example, when testosterone levels peak around the start of puberty, there is a corresponding peak in aggression levels among boys. However, men with high levels of testosterone do not necessarily become aggressive; indeed, high levels of testosterone are also associated with athletic prowess, and there are examples of females with low levels of testosterone who behave aggressively. Clearly the relationship between testosterone and aggression is not a simple one.

Much research identifying links between testosterone and aggression involves animals, with the classic methodology involving hormone removal and replacement.

For example, castration produces a decrease in aggression, and when testosterone is replaced through hormone therapy, aggression is restored to pre-castration levels. Timing of castration can have a marked effect, with animals castrated at birth showing decreased levels of aggression even if given huge doses of testosterone as adults. However, castrating similar animals later on has a much reduced effect on aggression levels. It is believed that androgen stimulation in the early days after birth causes changes in the neural system, affecting aggression levels into adulthood.

During this critical time period after birth, testosterone acts to sensitise neural circuits in the brain. This sensitisation allows for the effects of testosterone that manifest in adulthood.

Testosterone acts on serotonergic synapses, lowering the amount of the neurotransmitter serotonin. Research has identified low levels of serotonin as being involved in heightened levels of aggressiveness. Therefore, it may be that testosterone modulates the levels of various neurotransmitters that mediate effects on aggression.

Sapolsky (1997) argues that high levels of testosterone do not lead to heightened levels of aggression, but instead that aggressive behaviour elevates testosterone levels, with this viewpoint being supported by research.

Overall, it seems that the more testosterone individuals have, the more competitive and assertive they will become, and it is merely a by-product of this that those with heightened testosterone have more chance of behaving aggressively if they are in a social environment that facilitates such behaviour – that is, by the very fact that they are more assertive and competitive.

Research: neural and hormonal mechanisms in aggression

- Klinesmith *et al.* (2006) showed how testosterone levels change as a result of behaving aggressively. Male participants either assembled a gun or the game Mouse Trap™ and were then given a drink with a small amount of chilli sauce in it. They were then supposedly allowed to prepare a drink for the next participant with as much chilli sauce as they desired. Testosterone levels were measured from saliva samples given throughout the study. Testosterone levels increased 100 times more in men who assembled guns than in men who assembled the game, and those assembling guns put three times as much chilli sauce in the drink. This suggests that environmental stimuli like guns increase aggressiveness, partially via increases in testosterone, giving support to Sapolsky's belief that high levels of testosterone do not lead to heightened levels of aggression, but instead that aggressive behaviour elevates testosterone levels.

- Connor and Levine (1969) found that rats castrated after birth had reduced aggression when tested as adults, suggesting a link between aggression and testosterone. However, rats castrated after puberty could be made aggressive with injections of testosterone, while the early castrated rats could not, suggesting a developmental factor.

- Edwards (1968) found that injections of testosterone in neonate female mice made them act like males with increased aggression when given testosterone as adults. However, control females only given testosterone as adults did not react in this way, suggesting that testosterone masculinises androgen-sensitive neural circuits underlying aggression in the brain.

- Delville *et al.* (1997) found that drugs increasing serotonin production lead to reduced levels of aggression, suggesting that low levels of serotonin are linked to increased aggression.

- Linnoila and Virkunen (1992) found a relationship between low levels of serotonin and highly explosive violent behaviours, suggesting that a lack of serotonin is linked to aggression.

- Popova *et al.* (1991) found that animals selected for domesticity because of reduced aggression levels had lower serotonin levels than their wild, more aggressive counterparts, supporting the idea of a link between serotonin and aggression.

- Higley *et al.* (1996) reported that individuals with raised levels of testosterone exhibit signs of aggression, but rarely commit aggressive acts, suggesting that social and cognitive factors play a mediating role.

Contemporary research

Crockett *et al.* (2008)

Serotonin regulates behavioural reactions to unfairness

Serotonin has long been implicated in social behaviour, including impulsive aggression, but the mechanisms by which this occurs were not clear. By manipulating the effect of serotonin on participants playing a game involving fair and unfair choices, the researchers were able to show a causal link between serotonin levels and impulsive aggression, which highlights why people can become aggressive when they have not eaten.

Aim

To investigate how individuals with low serotonin react to what they perceive as unfair behaviour.

Procedure

Brain serotonin levels were temporarily reduced in 20 healthy volunteers by manipulating their diet. The volunteers also participated in a 'normal' serotonin-level condition that acted as a control. A double-blind technique was used so that participants did not know which condition they were participating in.   *continued …*

...continued

Participants played the 'ultimatum game', where one player, 'the proposer', suggests a way to split a sum of money with another player, 'the responder'. If the responder accepts the offer, both players are paid accordingly. If the responder rejects the offer, neither player is paid. Normally, people tend to reject about half of all offers less than 20 to 30 per cent of the total stake, despite the fact that this means they receive nothing.

Offers fell into one of three 'fairness' categories: 45 per cent of stake (fair), 30 per cent of stake (unfair) or 20 per cent of stake (most unfair). Social reward (fairness) and basic monetary reward (offer size) were manipulated by varying both the offer amount and the stake size across trials.

Rejection rates (percentage of offers rejected) were calculated for each subject at each level of fairness.

Findings

Compared to the normal serotonin condition, serotonin depletion significantly increased rejection rates to over 80 per cent, and this effect was restricted to unfair offers, as serotonin depletion did not interact significantly with offer size.

Controlling for fairness, participants tended to reject low offers more frequently than high offers, regardless of whether serotonin had been depleted.

Conclusions

Temporarily lowering serotonin levels increases retaliation to perceived unfairness without affecting mood, fairness judgements, basic reward processing or response inhibition.

Serotonin plays a critical role in regulating emotion during social decision making.

Evaluation

• The results support findings of neuro-imaging studies, as the effects of manipulating serotonin levels through diet mirror those of lesions to the ventral prefrontal cortex brain region, thus indicating a crucial neuro-modulatory role for serotonin and therefore impulsive aggressiveness.

• The results suggest that serotonin plays a critical role in social decision making by keeping aggressive social responses in check.

• The study highlights why some people get aggressive when they have not eaten, especially tryptophan-rich foods, such as eggs and chickpeas, which provide the essential amino acids for the body to create serotonin.

Evaluation

Neural and hormonal mechanisms in aggression

● Simpson (2001) reported that testosterone is implicated only in certain forms of aggression, like inter-male aggression, but plays no part in others, such as predatory aggression.

● Much research indicating testosterone to be associated with aggression comes from animal studies, causing generalisation problems. Human aggression is more complex and is affected by many mediating factors; indeed, the effects of previous experience and environmental stimuli have been found to correlate more strongly.

● Another problem with animal studies is that certain brain structures are involved with different types of aggression in different species. For example, the cingulated gyrus is linked to fear-induced aggression in monkeys, but to irritability in cats and dogs, again creating problems in generalising from animal species to humans.

● It is not always easy to measure testosterone levels accurately, which causes methodological problems. Results from human studies are often subjective, relying on questionnaires and observations. Measurement of cerebrospinal fluid is more accurate, but less easy to conduct on

continued ...

...continued

humans. Castration affects many hormone systems, meaning that the precise effect of any one hormone, like testosterone, is difficult to determine.

- Albert *et al.* (1993) reported that there is a lot of research that does not show a significant relationship between aggression and testosterone. This may be because testosterone is only linked to certain types of aggression, that other factors are involved or that there were methodological issues.

- Various drugs, approved by clinicians, have been associated with reducing serotonin levels and increasing aggressive behaviour. Penttinen (1995) reports that cholesterol-lowering drugs like lopid, appetite suppressors like fenfluramine, and even low-fat diets all produce such effects. Some drugs have been withdrawn because of their potent anti-serotonergic effects.

- Huber *et al.* (1997) argued that reducing serotonic activity in a wide range of species, from crustaceans to humans, has the same effect of increasing aggression, suggesting that this indicates an evolutionary link.

Issues, debates and approaches

- Much research into neural and hormonal mechanisms in aggression involves animals, which creates ethical problems, as many techniques used are painful and irreversible. Some would justify such research in terms of a cost-benefit analysis, where the knowledge gained and the possible practical applications this could lead to are seen as outweighing the harm caused.

- Neural and hormonal explanations perceive aggression as being biologically determined and, as such, disregard the degree of free will, in the form of self-control, that individuals have over behaving aggressively.

Genetic factors in aggressive behaviour

Research indicates that aggression is influenced by genetic factors, with early research concentrating on chromosomal abnormalities, specifically the XYY genotype, but this proved not to be significantly associated with aggression.

Genes determine how much testosterone is produced and how quickly it circulates round the body. Genes also determine the synthesis of testosterone receptors, and how many and how sensitive such receptors are. Testosterone may affect brain function and contribute to aggression, but genes regulate how much testosterone is made and how effectively it works. Genes control our behaviour via the messenger testosterone.

One method used to study aggression genetically is through heritability studies, typically involving animals selectively bred to see whether aggression levels are inherited. Research on mice has suggested that aggression has a genetic component, expressed through the metabolism of serotonin. Other studies, involving mice reared in isolation, indicate aggression to be a natural biological tendency, as the mice had no opportunities to learn such behaviour.

The gene *monoamine oxidase A* (MAOA) attracted interest when, by chance, it was found that mice lacking the gene were excessively aggressive. The enzyme made by the gene mops up excess neurotransmitters, the brain's chemical messengers, so mice lacking MAOA had unusually high levels of neurotransmitters like serotonin, noradrenaline and dopamine. Studies have also suggested that MAOA is involved in human aggression, as high MAOA levels have been found in aggressive males. On its own, the MAOA gene variant has no effect, but if males who carry the MAOA gene were abused as children, there is a greatly increased chance of them committing violent crime. It seems that aggressiveness is influenced by a variation in the MAOA gene, which is sensitive to social experiences early in development; therefore, its functional outcome depends on social context. This indicates that an interaction of genetics and environment is at work in determining human aggression.

Overall, it can be seen that while genetics influences aggression, it is not 'aggressive genes' that cause aggression, but rather that genes trigger a genetic sensitivity to the environment, causing the combination of aggressive genes and an 'aggressive' upbringing to have negative and aggressive results.

Psychologists need to be aware of the reductionist approach of trying to identify a single gene responsible for aggression; recent research indicates that many genes may be involved.

Research in focus

In Crockett *et al.*'s (2008) study, a double-blind procedure was used.

Explain what is meant by a double-blind procedure and what the advantages of using it would be in this particular study.

How does a double-blind procedure differ from a single-blind procedure?

Research: genetic factors in aggressive behaviour

- Cases *et al.* (1995) studied mice genetically engineered to lack MAOA. The mice had a dramatically altered serotonin metabolism and severe behavioural alterations. When adult, they showed enhanced aggression and were aggressive during mating, giving support to human studies suggesting that aggression is a direct result of MAOA deficiency, rather than other genetic influences or psychosocial factors.

Figure 4.08 Studies of mice suggest that aggression is a natural biological tendency

- Bock and Goode (1996) found that male mice reared alone show a stronger tendency to attack other male mice then those reared with others. Other male mice, reared with their parents, had been shown when it was necessary to be aggressive and when it was not, giving support to the idea that aggression is a natural biological tendency shaped by learning experiences.

- Mattson (2003) found that MAOA–deficient male mice (female mice with the defective gene behaved normally) attacked new mice introduced into their cage and failed to establish usual dominant–submissive relationships, demonstrating the influence of the gene on aggressive behaviour.

- Brunner *et al.* (1993) studied a large Dutch family where all the males had a mutant form of the MAOA gene. All had borderline retardation and reacted aggressively when angry, fearful or frustrated, suggesting that abnormal MAOA activity is associated with aggression.

- Moffitt *et al.* (1992) performed a longitudinal study on 442 New Zealand males from birth to age 26, recording which participants, as children, suffered abuse and also what level of activity of the MAOA gene participants had. It was found that those who had suffered abuse and had the low–activity version of the gene were nine times more likely to indulge in antisocial behaviour, including aggression. Participants who had been abused, but carried the high–activity version of the gene, were no more likely to be antisocial than those not suffering abuse, suggesting that the MAOA gene is involved in aggressive behaviour, but is sensitive to social experiences early in development.

- Rissman *et al.* (2006) performed research into the SRY gene, which leads to the development of testes and high androgen levels in males. Both male and female mice with and without the gene were tested, with the SRY gene being associated with high levels of aggression, suggesting that genes and hormones interact with each other; although sex chromosome genes are not the whole story, they seem to play a big part.

- New *et al.* (2003) found that acts of impulsive aggression, such as domestic and work-based attacks, have a genetic component related to the serotonergic system. New found that aggressive patients with personality disorders had a G-allele variant of a serotonin gene, HTR1B, suggesting that many genes may be involved in aggressive behaviour.

- Deneris *et al.* (2003) removed the PET 1 gene, linked to production of serotonin, from mice, finding that these normally placid creatures became anxious and aggressive, especially to intruders entering their territory. The behaviour of the mice was similar to human personality disorders characterised by anxiety and violence, suggesting that over-aggressive people may be missing this gene.

Evaluation

Genetic factors in aggressive behaviour

- The genetic basis of aggression has proved elusive, and it appears that numerous genes are involved. These interact with environmental stimuli to cause aggression, with each genetic variant having only a small impact on an individual's overall predisposition to aggressiveness.

- Many studies have used animals, which have practical advantages, such as quicker breeding cycles, allowing for intergenerational effects to be seen relatively quickly. Much research has involved mice, as they provide a useful model for human behaviour because they have genes and proteins that serve similar functions. However, there are many qualitative and quantitative differences between mice and humans, making generalisation difficult – for example, mice lacking the HTR1B gene, associated with serotonin production, had elevated levels of aggression, but this is not true of humans. Animal studies also raise ethical issues for many people, including breeding animals with elevated levels of aggression.

- The effects of the MAOA gene on aggression are not so noticeable in females as the gene it is found only in the X chromosome. Females have two X chromosomes and it may be that the version of the gene found in one of their X chromosomes cancels out the effects of the other.

- One-third of males carry the low-level activity version of the MAOA gene, suggesting that it bestows adaptive advantages. Also associated with risk taking, it may have beneficial qualities in certain occupations, such as working in the stock market.

- From research into genes related to the serotonic system, New (2003) hypothesised that multiple genes and environmental factors contribute to an individual's degree of susceptibility to impulsive aggression, suggesting that an interactionist explanation utilising biological and environmental factors works best.

An interesting article from the *New Scientist* concerning a convicted murderer who had his sentence reduced as he had 'aggressive genes' can be found at www.newscientist.com/article/dn18098-murderer-with-aggression-genes-gets-sentence-cut.html

Psychology in action

Anger management

Figure 4.09

Anger management is a practical application of psychology that refers to a system of psychological therapeutic techniques and exercises, whereby someone with excessive or uncontrollable anger can control or reduce the triggers, degrees and effects of their angered emotional state. Indeed, in some countries participation in anger management courses is compulsory and mediated through their legal systems.

Various psychotherapeutic techniques are used, such as stress management and relaxation strategies, as well as learning to empathise with and forgive others. Overall, a balanced approach to anger is advised, which controls the emotion while simultaneously allowing the emotion to be expressed in a healthy way.

A common component of anger management programmes is to learn assertive communication techniques – that is, appropriately expressing feelings and needs without offending or removing the rights of others.

Anger management has proven very successful in reducing aggression levels, and thus has helped many people not to harm others, to stay out of trouble and to feel better about themselves. Overall, the costs involved in health care and legal services associated with violent crime have been reduced. It has probably helped to save a fair few relationships too.

When evaluating explanations of aggression in exam questions, anger management could be used as an example of a practical application, based on the understanding of aggression, which comes from psychological research.

Supplementary learning

Brain structures

Another way that biology influences aggression is through various brain structures that are associated with aggressive behaviour, with the cortex seen as playing an inhibiting role over the subcortical limbic system to prevent aggression.

The amygdala (part of the limbic system) has been seen as having an important role, especially in facilitating the influence on aggression that testosterone has in response to environmental triggers.

Research into violent criminals has linked abnormalities in their limbic systems to murderous behaviour, and tumours within the limbic system have been seen to elicit aggression.

Research

- Bard (1929) removed the cortex from cats' brains, eliciting anger without emotional content ('sham' rage), suggesting that the cortex plays an inhibitory role over the limbic system, regulating aggression.
- Egger and Flynn (1967) found that stimulating one area of the amygdala produced an inhibitory effect, but lesioning it led to increased aggression, suggesting that the amygdala plays a key role in regulating aggression and the cortex has inhibitory control over it (the amygdala being subcortical).
- Raine *et al.* (1997) scanned murderers' brains, finding that they were more at risk of having abnormalities in their limbic systems, which suggests that the limbic system is involved in the control of aggression.

continued ...

...continued

- Sumer *et al.* (2007) reported on a case study of a patient with a tumour in the limbic system exhibiting increased aggressive hyperactivity. When the tumour was treated, the patient returned to normal.

Evaluation

- Stimulating different areas of the amygdala can inhibit or increase aggression, suggesting a complex relationship involving different forms of aggression. For instance, Hernandez-Peon *et al.* (1967) elicited affective rage and flight, but not predatory attack, by applying the neurotransmitter acetylcholine to the amygdala.

- The relationship of the limbic system to aggression is a complex one, with different areas being implicated with different forms of aggression.

- The research linking brain abnormalities to violent crime is only correlational, and although having such abnormalities may increase an individual's vulnerability to being aggressive, other factors may be involved too.

Issues, debates and approaches

- There is a mistaken belief that genes can determine aggressive behaviour on their own, and this has formed the 'natural born killer' defence in murder trials. Stephen Mobley, accused of murder in 1981, pleaded not guilty as he had a gene predisposing him to violence, his argument being that several members of his family were aggressive and he had inherited the tendency. He was executed.

- It may be possible to devise drug treatments for people with the low-level activity version of the MAOA gene to help control aggressive urges. However, Tyrer *et al.* (2008) report that drug treatments have not had success so far in controlling aggression levels, suggesting that other non-biological factors may be involved.

Strengthen your learning

1. Outline what psychologists have learned about the role of testosterone in determining levels of aggression.
2. Evaluate the role of testosterone in determining aggression by compiling a list of points for and against.
3. Outline the possible influence of the MAOA gene on aggression levels.
4. Does research tend to indicate that the MAOA gene is a key player in determining aggression levels? Use evidence to support your answer.

Assessment Check ▶

1. Outline the role of neural and hormonal mechanisms in aggression. (8 marks)

2. Evaluate the role of genetic factors in aggressive behaviour. (16 marks)

3. Discuss the role of neural and hormonal mechanisms in aggression. (24 marks)

4. Compare social psychological and biological explanations of aggression. (24 marks)

Examination guidance

In question 1 only descriptive material, such as the role of testosterone, will get credit, while the reverse is true in question 2, with only evaluative material attracting credit, such as the degree of research support and methodological points that are specific to the topic.

The term 'discuss' in question 3 means to describe and evaluate, remembering that the description only gains a maximum of 8 marks. In essence, it is identical to question 2, so most efforts should be directed at the evaluation, where 16 marks are up for offer. You should be spending around 10 minutes on a description and around 20 minutes on your evaluation.

Question 4 combines two elements from different parts of the specification topic, which is perfectly legitimate, so be prepared for this type of question. At least one social psychological and one biological explanation would need to be outlined and evaluated to gain access to all the marks available.

Evolution and human aggression

The evolutionary approach to explaining aggression sees aggression in terms of its ability to contribute to increasing survival chances and, ultimately, to enhancing reproductive potential. Aggression is thus perceived as having developed through the process of natural selection via our ancestral predecessors and can still be seen in the phenomena of infidelity and jealousy, and also in the actions of group displays, such as at sports events.

It is important when answering questions on evolutionary explanations of aggression that material is shaped to these requirements, in other words that the answer is actually focused upon evolutionary theory and aggression. It is all too easy in this area, especially when dealing with infidelity and jealousy, to create an answer more suited to sexual selection. Infidelity and jealousy are not in themselves forms of aggression, but instead act as possible triggers for aggressive behaviour. Candidates should additionally be careful when selecting and using research studies to ensure that these are focused upon aggression too.

Evolutionary theory

Within each species of animal, there is variation in individual appearance and behaviour. Part of the variation is caused by differences in individuals' genetic make-up (*genetic variation*), 50 per cent inherited from each parent. Genes (strands of DNA) are not always 'switched on'; some are expressed only if combined with other genes and some may undergo *mutation*, a random change affecting an animal's anatomy and, hence, some aspects of its behaviour.

Most mutations are harmful and the individuals concerned are unlikely to reproduce and pass mutated genes on to their offspring. However, on some occasions mutations are beneficial. Individuals compete over limited resources and those that survive may do so because they have benefited from a mutated gene that allowed them to adapt to their environment.

Such individuals stand more chance of surviving into adulthood and reproducing offspring with the mutated gene. Over a long period of time, the characteristic determined by that mutation, if sufficiently distinctive, becomes a permanent feature of particular groups of animals and marks the emergence of a new species. Evolution is the process of *natural selection* by which new species arise from gradual changes to the genetic make-up of existing species over long periods of time.

Evolutionary explanations of human aggression

The evolutionary explanation suggests that aggression serves an important function in terms of both individual survival and procreation potential. In essence, competition arises when resources are limited; therefore animals/ species must compete in order to increase their own 'fitness'. So aggression is advantageous at both individual and genetic levels.

A simple explanation for aggression is that human beings are 'programmed' for violence by their basic nature, and humans have an in-built tendency for violence. Lorenz (1966) suggested that aggression emanates from an inherited fighting instinct that human beings share with other species. In the past, males seeking desirable mates found it necessary to compete with other males. One way of eliminating competition was through aggression, to drive rivals away or eliminate them through fatal conflict. Aggression thus serves an adaptive purpose, one that has evolved as a natural element in the behavioural repertoire of some species because it aids survival and adaptation to the environment. Because males who were skilled at such behaviour were more successful in securing mates and in transmitting their genes to offspring, this would have led to the development of a genetically influenced tendency for males to 'aggress' against other males. Denisiuk (2004) believed that males would not be expected to aggress against females, because females view males who engage in such behaviour as too dangerous to themselves and potential future children, resulting in rejection of them as potential mates. For this reason, males have weaker tendencies to aggress against females than against other males.

In our evolutionary past, some male hunters were more successful than others. Those men who combined the traits of strength, stamina and cunning began to outperform and bring back more resources than others. As a result, their stature grew, while that of others withered. This male dominance in hunting led to battles for dominance in territory and the selection of females, who are essential elements in gene transference.

Females tend to be much more choosy in selecting a mate, as they have a greater investment in their offspring. Women select men who are able to provide for potential offspring through the resources they can bring to a relationship. Men are therefore more competitive with each other through *intrasexual* competition for access to women. This created a demand for men able to provide valuable resources, resulting in the male characteristics of assertiveness, aggressiveness and sensitivity to hierarchy.

Figure 4.10 Men who combined the traits of strength, stamina and cunning brought back more resources than others, and their stature grew as a result

Sadalla *et al.* (1987) reported that dominant behaviour in males increases their attractiveness to females. Although male dominance enhanced their sexual attractiveness, it did not improve their likeability. However, this dominant trait may have arisen as a result of social coercion. For example, a woman who chose a dominant aggressor for a sexual partner may have chosen him in order to stay alive, rather than expressing a personal preference for dominant men.

Infidelity and jealousy

Jealousy occurs through fear of losing affection or status and is a potent cause of aggression, defined as an emotional state aroused by a perceived threat to a relationship or position that motivates behaviour to counter the threat. Jealousy is a reaction related to fear and rage, to protect, maintain and prolong romantic associations.

Infidelity involves a sexual partner being unfaithful. Infidelity can be sexual, emotional or both. *Sexual infidelity* is any behaviour involving sexual contact, like kissing, intimate touching or sexual intercourse. *Emotional infidelity* involves the formation of affectionate attachments to or for another person, and can involve flirting, intimate conversations or falling in love. Ninety-nine per cent of married people expect spouses to be faithful, but 11 per cent of females and 21 per cent of males admit to extramarital sex. Interestingly, when partners are unfaithful, most anger focuses on the partner rather than the rival.

The evolutionary explanation for infidelity and jealousy is related to the evolutionary approach to mating behaviour, with intersexual selection indicating that there are gender differences in what men and women look for in potential partners. Females select on males' ability to provide resources, such as financial status, while males select on females' apparent signs of fertility, such as youthful looks.

Buss (1995) argues that men and women differ in responses to infidelity in ways that have resulted from different adaptations to different reproductive problems. The evolutionary perspective perceives both forms of infidelity, emotional and sexual, as disturbing to both sexes, but believes that the cues triggering sexual jealousy are weighted differently in men and women. Men are more distressed about sexual infidelity because of the adaptive problem of uncertain paternity and the risk of investing resources in a child who is not their own. Therefore, if a man suspects that his partner is being sexually unfaithful, it evokes sexual jealousy and possible aggression.

Women are always certain of maternity, but a woman's adaptive problem is finding a mate willing and able to invest resources in her and her children in the long term.

If a woman suspects that the father of her child is emotionally involved with another woman, there is the potential that he will invest his resources in the other woman. This loss of resources could affect her children's survival chances, and her own future reproductive potential, and therefore evokes emotional jealousy. Jealousy can also be initiated by the presence of younger, more attractive women.

There is much evidence to back up these claims, coming mainly from studies using forced-choice, hypothetical scenarios.

Material from Chapter 3: Relationships, on sibling rivalry (see page 105) could also legitimately be used to answer questions on jealousy as an evolutionary explanation of aggression.

You are the researcher

Design a questionnaire to investigate whether there is a difference in the types of and amount of jealousy experienced between males and females whose partners have had affairs.

How would you design questions that assess the amount of jealousy experienced?

How would you ensure that your questionnaire is ethical?

In what ways would this method be superior to the usual 'imagined scenario' type of study? (See 'Contemporary research: Schutzwohl (2004)' on page 151.)

Research: infidelity and jealousy

- Daly and Wilson (1988) reported, that men who have just been left, or are about to be left, by their partners commit a high proportion of homicides of their partners, possibly due to the jealousy of potentially losing them to another male.

- Buss and Dedden (1990) found that females criticise the appearance and sexual promiscuity of other females, suggesting that they are reducing their potential rivals' attractiveness, and thus raising their own, in line with evolutionary theory.

- Harris (2003) conducted a meta-analysis of 32 studies on sex differences in emotional responses to infidelity, finding that men were more distressed by sexual infidelity, while women were more distressed by emotional infidelity, supporting the predictions of evolutionary theory.

- Buunk *et al.* (1996) found that women become jealous when partners become interested in other women, resulting in loss of commitment to her and her children, essential to survival.

- Looy (2001) found that jealousy in women is triggered by the presence of younger, more attractive women, in line with evolutionary predictions.

- DeSteno and Salovey (1996) found that emotional infidelity is doubly distressing, as it also implies sexual infidelity.

- Goetz *et al.* (2008) looked at men's violence against intimate partners and found that violence functions to punish and deter female sexual infidelity and acts as an anti-cuckoldry tactic, its frequency related to suspicions of sexual infidelity.

- Daly *et al.* (1982) found that men are violent when partners are sexually unfaithful, supporting evolutionary theory.

- Buss *et al.* (1992) measured stress levels in US students, finding that males had higher levels when viewing pictures of sexual infidelity, while females had higher levels when viewing pictures of emotional infidelity, suggesting that different environmental cues trigger aggression in males and females.

- Buss *et al.* (1999) set up scenarios of infidelity that were mutually exclusive – that is, partner engaged in sexual or emotional infidelity but not both – finding that 61 per cent of men, but only 13 per cent of women, reported greater distress due to sexual infidelity, while 39 per cent of men and 87 per cent of women were more distressed by emotional infidelity, supporting evolutionary predictions.

Evaluation

Infidelity and jealousy

- Harris (2003) found the results from forced-choice studies about males being more stressed by sexual infidelity and females by emotional infidelity to be true of imagined scenarios, but in real instances both males and females felt threatened by emotional fidelity. The results from the imagined scenarios might be explained as males being aroused by images of sexual infidelity rather than feeling threatened.

- Cultural differences in murder rates of wives by husbands and in the degree of anxiety felt in response to sexual infidelity by males suggest that factors other than those determined by evolution play a part.

- Some critics feel that evolutionary explanations justify violence by men against women as natural and inevitable.

continued ...

...continued

- Dreznick (2004) suggested that there may be an alternative explanation to evolutionary theory, such as a difference in beliefs of what constitutes infidelity. If men do not perceive emotional infidelity as infidelity, then they would not be particularly jealous in response to a partner's emotional infidelity.

- The forced-choice methodology does not allow participants to specify the level or quantity of their agreement. In Buss *et al.*'s (1992) original study, although more men were distressed than women by sexual infidelity (49 per cent compared to 19 per cent), 51 per cent of men were distressed by emotional infidelity, compared to women's 81 per cent – that is, more men were distressed by emotional than sexual jealousy, which goes against evolutionary theory.

- The evolutionary perspective offers an explanation of how aggressive behaviour due to suspicions of infidelity may arise via natural selection.

Issues, debates and approaches

- Evolutionary explanations account for male and female differences in their experiences of infidelity and jealousy as due to different selective pressures, and therefore are not gender biased.

- Evolutionary theory brings explanations of infidelity and jealousy down to the level of genes and therefore can be perceived as being reductionist. It is also determinist, as it disregards any role for free will in behaviour relating to infidelity and jealousy.

To read a fuller account of Goetz *et al.*'s (2008) study, which contains a wealth of useful information concerning evolutionary explanations of human aggression, go to www. farnaz-kaighobadi.com/uploads/Goetz-et-al-AVB-2008.pdf

Contemporary research

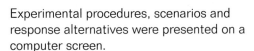

Schutzwohl (2004)

Which infidelity type makes you more jealous?

Previous research had indicated men to be more jealous of sexual infidelity and women to be more jealous of emotional jealousy. This study tested the assertion by examining male and female decision times in deciding jealousy choice.

Aim

To replicate and extend the scenario used by Buss *et al.* (1992), examining whether emotional or sexual infidelity by a partner would upset them more.

Procedure

An opportunity sample of 100 male and 100 female German university students formed the sample.

Experimental procedures, scenarios and response alternatives were presented on a computer screen.

Participants were presented with four scenarios involving social situations and a choice of two alternative responses. Only the responses to scenario four were of interest to the study.

Participants were asked to vividly imagine the scenarios before responding. Participants were told that the scenarios referred to romantic relationships they had been in, were currently in or would like to be in.

continued ...

...continued

Scenario four read as follows:

Imagine that you discover that your partner formed both a deep emotional and a passionate sexual relationship with another person. Which aspect of your partner's involvement would make you more jealous?

(A) The deep emotional relationship

(B) The passionate sexual relationship

The description of the infidelities – that is, sexual and emotional – was counterbalanced across participants.

Choices were recorded, along with the times taken to make a decision after scenario presentation.

Findings

Both sexes reported more jealousy concerning the partner's emotional involvement, but more males (37 per cent) than females (20 per cent) selected their partner's sexual involvement as making them more jealous.

Women who selected emotional infidelity reached their decision faster than women selecting sexual infidelity.

Men who selected sexual infidelity reached their decision faster than men selecting emotional infidelity.

Conclusions

Men who are more jealous of sexual infidelity employ less elaborate decision strategies than men who are more jealous of emotional infidelity, while women who are more jealous of emotional infidelity employ less elaborate decision strategies than women who are more jealous of sexual infidelity.

Men and women who choose their adaptively primary infidelity type – that is, sexual for men, emotional for women – rely on their initial response tendency suggested by their respective jealousy mechanism, whereas men and women selecting their adaptively secondary infidelity type engage in additional considerations that lead them to override their initial response tendency.

Evaluation

Previous results from similar research, suggesting that women who select the emotional infidelity option engage in a more elaborate decision-making process than women selecting sexual infidelity, are refuted by this study.

The study does not identify the exact nature of the decision processes undertaken, especially by men, when selecting their adaptively secondary infidelity type.

Research in focus

Schutzwohl (2004) found a significant difference between male and female jealousy and would thus have been able to accept her experimental hypothesis. However, in doing so there would be a chance of making a type I error.

What is a type I error and under what circumstances would it occur?

Explain how a type II error differs from a type I error and under what circumstances it would occur.

Evolutionary explanations of group displays in humans

Group displays are ritualised displays of aggression by and between groups of people, which serve the functions of determining dominance hierarchies in relation to ownership of territory and intimidation of other groups. The evolutionary significance of this would be to increase survival rates and increase chances of reproductive success. Sports events include a number of features demonstrating group displays; indeed, many aspects of sporting competitions serve as a vehicle for group display, both on and off the pitch.

Lynch mobs are another example of group display, where temporary groups of people come together to be involved in the common pursuit or undertaking of some violent act.

Group displays and sports events

Group displays at sporting occasions can occur as phenomena among and between fans, as well as between sporting teams themselves. The aggressive posturing and ritualised displays that occur are not seen as especially violent in themselves, though there is a degree of discussion as to whether they can act as a catalyst for serious acts of aggression to take place.

The group displays that occur at and around sporting occasions tend to be heavily policed, with other security measures apparent too, such as the segregation of fans, which means that there are actually very few, if any, opportunities for violent behaviour.

There is a body of opinion that sees sports events more in psychodynamic terms, as being ceremonies of catharsis in terms of aggression, where both fans and competitors use the sporting occasion as a safe means of releasing aggressive tendencies through the use of group displays.

Sports events have always been associated with violence, and modern sporting events are often sanitised versions of their former selves. For instance, football started life all over Britain as mob football – occasional competitions between adjoining communities that took place without rules, refereeing or even territorial boundaries. Such matches could last for days, were associated with heavy alcohol consumption, the settling of vendettas and excessive use of violence. Indeed, mob football matches became generally banned due to associated criminal behaviour and the deaths and serious injuries that occurred to players. One annual match still occurs in Ashbourne, but continues to attract calls for it to be banned. Such events are explained in evolutionary terms, through their incorporation of ritualized and actual aggression, towards increasing survival and reproductive success.

In the late 1800s, the movement of 'muscular Christianity' associated with Dr Arnold, headmaster of Rugby School, 'cleaned up' traditional sports, introducing rules, officials and playing territories, and turned sporting events into a vehicle for promoting healthy and moralistic principles, with the emphasis on teamwork, personal endeavour and fair play. Many of our modern sports emanate from this time, but can still be seen as being based upon evolutionary principles.

The phenomena of football hooliganism attracts much debate. 'Firms' of hooligans, such as the 'Ultras' in Italy, are highly organised structures with strict codes of conduct, who use violence in heavily ritualised ways, often prearranging fights between rival firms.

So, in one respect group displays in sport can be seen as having replaced tribal warfare, where one identifiable tribal team goes into ritualized battle against another identifiable tribal team. Sport involves displays and trials of strength and skill, behaviours attractive to females who will select winning males for reproductive success on the basis of their displays of genetic fitness. With its highly ritualized nature, sport allows such competition between males without incurring much risk of serious injury (though sport can often involve hostile aggression too). Victory in sport brings increased status and thus reproductive fitness to supporters of teams, as well as players and thus evolutionary theory can explain the passion and dedication that many fans display to their team and sporting heroes. This also explains the behaviour of hooligan fans, as being part of their team's battle for dominance against rival fans. This particular aspect is backed up by the fact that the keenest, hardest fought rivalries in sport usually involve 'derby' matches, between local teams, such as Celtic and Rangers in Glasgow and Stoke City and Port Vale in Stoke-on-Trent. Victory in such encounters is especially important, as the battle for dominance includes that for local resources, such as females and territory.

Group displays at sporting events take several forms, including:

- *War dances/supporter displays* – these are rituals performed before and during battle by warriors, to intimidate the enemy and to motivate their own members. They are incorporated into sporting occasions to serve the same purpose – for example, the New Zealand haka, performed before kick-off by the national rugby league and union sides. Other sports developed specialist dance troupes to rouse the crowd's emotional support and intimidate the opposition – for example, the Dallas Cowboys cheerleaders. Football clubs use mascots to the same end and there have been examples of mascots coming to blows (see 'In the news' on page 122). Elements of war dances have been incorporated into supporter displays, like the wearing of club colours, face painting and club anthems – for example, Liverpool supporters singing 'You'll never walk alone'. Such displays are motivating and increase social identity. In the 1980s, there was a very strange phenomenon of fans flourishing various inflatable objects to indicate sporting allegiance – for example, Grimsby fans went to matches carrying giant inflatable fish, while Stoke City fans, for no discernible reason, would not leave home without an inflatable Pink Panther.

Figure 4.11 Cheerleaders rouse the crowd's emotional support

- *Territorial behaviour* – group displays serve to mark out and defend territories – for example, football team supporters congregating in traditional areas and violently resisting attempts by opposition fans to occupy the same territory. A common feature of the football hooligan days of the 1970s was for away fans to arrive early at a ground and try to 'take' the opposition fans' traditional area. In the ensuing, predictable brawls, it was a common occurrence for people to get seriously hurt. In most sports there is a noticeable home advantage, due in some part to territorial behaviour.

- *Ritual behaviour* – a lot of aggressive behaviour between rival sports fans is ritualistic, where lots of posturing and verbal abuse occurs, but little actual violence, which suggests that it is a symbolic show of strength designed to limit injuries. This serves to bond and motivate and is linked to territorial behaviour (see above).

Research: Group displays and sports events

- Sua Peter (2007) reported that the Siva Tau, the traditional war dance performed by Samoan rugby players before a match, was to be upgraded to a more aggressive, intimidatory style, reflecting the islanders' warrior traditions.

> The singing of 'You'll never walk alone' by Liverpool fans, their adopted club anthem, is an example of a group display in sport. To view a rendition of this powerful spectacle, go to www.youtube.com/watch?v=Y7xvegPH_Lw&feature=related A good example of a war dance that has been incorporated into sport is the Siva Tau, performed by the Samoan rugby team before games. To view them enacting it, go to www.youtube.com/watch?v=qHTJOStlVqc

- Shwarz and Barkey (1977) believed that sports teams win more games at home due to the social support of the home supporters, suggesting that territorial group displays may be a factor.

- Morris (1981) conducted a non-participant observation of Oxford United fans, home and away, finding their behaviour to be extremely territorial and ritualised, suggesting that such group displays serve a social purpose explainable in evolutionary terms.

- Maynard-Smith and Parker (1976) found that territorial ownership by animals was an evolutionary stable strategy, suggesting that it may have evolved due to its adaptive value.

- Marsh (1982) conducted observations of football fans, finding that most aggression was verbal, symbolic, non-serious and harmless, serving to reduce levels of aggression, and suggesting that group displays act as catharsis, allowing for the safe release of negative emotions, which suggests a more psychodynamic explanation.

- End (2005) found that the environment of sports events encourages aggressive group displays, suggesting that they are a social construction.

- Grieve (2005) believed that identification with sports teams is psychologically important in an increasingly transient and insular society, suggesting that group displays allow individuals to feel a sense of social identity.

Evaluation

Group displays and sports events

- The universal nature of war dances cross-culturally in sport suggests that the behaviour may have an evolutionary component related to ritualised aggression.

- Many sports teams' war dances are artificial, constructed for commercial purposes, and do not reflect traditional practices.

- Marsh (1982) believed that if ritual aggressive practices between fans were curtailed, violence rates would increase, which suggests that group displays allow the formation of dominance hierarchies, but without harm occurring to participants, in line with evolutionary theory.

- Dunning et al. (1988) argued that far from being ritualised and harmless, a lot of aggression at sports matches is violent, resulting in many deaths.

- Although group displays may be a factor in aggression levels related to sports events, there are other explanatory factors too, including biological and cognitive ones.

- Group displays at sports events can be explained as a socialisation process, serving to emphasise social identity.

- There are methodological challenges in studying group displays at sporting occasions. Berk (1974) noted that crowd events happen quickly, often without warning, often simultaneously, over a wide area, and involve processes leaving few traces. It would also be dangerous and difficult to interview people during such displays, and subsequent accounts tend to be unreliable.

- Guttman (1986) believed that no single explanation can cover the behaviour of sports crowds, as they differ so widely.

Football club mascots are an example of a group display in sport. To view the rather odd Club Mascot Grand National, an annually held event, go to www.youtube.com/watch?v=Ki3FXJQoFrla ndfeature=related

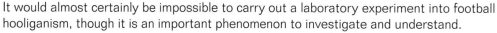

You are the researcher

It would almost certainly be impossible to carry out a laboratory experiment into football hooliganism, though it is an important phenomenon to investigate and understand.

Instead, design a self-report method investigating to what degree the aggression of football hooliganism is ritualistic or consists of actual violence.

What would be the advantages and disadvantages of using this method?

Then design a non-participant observation to investigate the same thing.

After detailing the disadvantages and advantages of this method, decide which method would probably generate more valid findings.

Lynch mobs

Lynch mobs are named after Charles Lynch, a US justice of the peace. They originally occurred when mobs took the law into their own hands to administer aggressive acts resulting in death, usually by hanging, although shooting, beating to death and burning at the stake were also popular. Between 1852 and 1955 there were over 3,000 recorded lynchings of black people by white mobs in the USA, along with 1,300 lynchings of white victims. These events were often witnessed by great gatherings, who would take their entire families, including children, to watch, as they were considered quite joyful social occasions to participate in or witness. Members of lynch mobs often took photographs of what they had done and some of these were published and sold as postcards.

Similar mob killings occurred in South Africa in the 1980s, with mobs of black people killing supposed government collaborators, with the favourite instrument of death being the 'necklace', a tyre filled with petrol placed round the victim's neck and set alight.

In Europe after the Second World War, women who were suspected of dating German soldiers were known as Jerry-bags and tarred and feathered and paraded through the streets as a punishment.

Evolutionary explanations of group displays

Evolutionary theory sees the group behaviour of lynch mobs as having an adaptive purpose, in that it increases status and dominance, access to resources, chances of survival and opportunities for reproductive success. A dominant group, in the first case above the white community, by indulging in aggression against the minority black community counters the threat of black people increasing in status and influence and thus challenging the power base of the dominant whites. Any threat to or reduction of the white community's dominance would be seen as lowering their adaptive fitness, that is, that it would decrease survival chances. Therefore, evolutionary theory explains lynch mob behaviour as allowing one group (white people) status over another group (black people), allowing them greater access to resources, including women (a common factor in lynchings was the perceived threat of black men impregnating white women, thus causing the reproduction of their genes at the expense of white men's). Evolutionary theory also sees the perpetrators of lynch mob aggression as having more reproductive success, thus leading to genes for such behaviour becoming more widespread throughout the population.

Blalock's (1967) Power-Threat hypothesis, argues that as a minority group, such as black people in America, increase in size and status, majority group members of the white community will intensify efforts to retain dominance, including killing black people by lynchings. Thus lynching is seen to be a form of social control.

Dehumanization is also a powerful factor here, whereby debasing black people as 'niggers' allowed them to be perceived by white people in lesser terms, thus 'justifying' and making easier acts of aggression against black people. Such dehumanization occurred by the white community portraying their aggressive,

murderous behaviour as a defence of their people against the threat of dominance by brutal, inferior black people. Therefore, lynching can be seen as an evolved adaptation to perceived threats.

Issues, debates and approaches

- The theoretical nature of explanations of lynch mobs reflect the philosophical nature of the debate. Such actions can be seen either as unconscious and deterministic or motivated and regulated by the individual's own free will.
- Evolutionary theory can be argued to be an incomplete explanation of group displays and having limited practical applications. Theories that are truly scientific should be complete, offering full explanations of phenomena, and should lend themselves to real-world applications.

Strengthen your learning

1. In what ways does evolutionary theory see aggression as being adaptive?
2. Outline the differences in male and female jealousy.
3. Explain in terms of evolutionary theory why such differences exist and may lead to aggression
4. What research evidence is there to support the idea of gender differences in jealousy?
5. What functions might group displays serve at sporting events?
6. Outline evolutionary explanations of lynch mob killings.

Assessment Check

1. Outline infidelity as an explanation of human aggression. (4 marks)

2. Outline one evolutionary explanation of group display in humans. (4 marks)

3. Evaluate the role of jealousy in human aggression. (16 marks)

4. Outline evolutionary explanations of human aggression. (8 marks)

5. Evaluate evolutionary explanations of group display in humans. (16 marks)

6. Compare evolutionary and social psychological theories of aggression. (24 marks)

Examination guidance

Questions 1 and 2 require purely descriptive material, with question 1 worth slightly more credit. Question 3 requires entirely evaluative material that is focused specifically on the role of jealousy.

Question 5 is worthy of more time and effort than question 4, as it earns a lot more credit.

Question 6 combines elements from different parts of the specification topic and there is a need to outline and evaluate at least one evolutionary and one social psychological explanation – for example, social learning theory and infidelity.

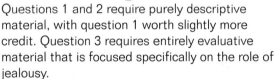

Summing up

- Social psychological theories focus on how individuals and groups elicit aggression.

- Social learning theory (SLT) sees aggression as acquired through observation and imitation.

- There are four component processes to SLT: attention, retention, production and motivation.

- SLT has much research support, especially from Bandura's bobo doll studies.

- The media provides an important source of imitative aggression.

- Deindividuation is the loss of individual identity and the loosening of normal inhibitions.

- Deindividuation sees individuals as more likely to be aggressive when unidentifiable and not accountable for the consequences of their actions.

- Support for deindividuation is mixed – people aren't always aggressive when anonymous.

- The importation model believes prisoners import social histories and traits into prison, and the aggressive behaviour seen in prison environments is the same that they demonstrate in normal society.

- The deprivation model sees the origins of prison subculture emanating from within an institution, with various deprivations leading to increased likelihood of aggression.

- An interaction between the importation and deprivation models provides a more convincing understanding of the impact of imprisonment on inmate violence than either model separately.

- Biological explanations see aggression as resulting from internal physiological causes. Some may have greater genetic dispositions for aggression, but for genes to produce aggressive effects they must express themselves through other biological means, such as hormonal and neural mechanisms.

- Testosterone is mainly a male hormone – it's often associated with aggression, but the relationship between aggression and testosterone levels in humans is far from clear-cut. Indeed, evidence suggests that aggression increases testosterone levels.

- Research sees aggression as influenced by genetic factors, especially a variation of the MAOA gene, which is sensitive to social experiences early in development, indicating that an interaction of genetics and environment is at work in determining human aggression.

- Some brain structures may affect aggression, such as the amygdala and the limbic system.

- The evolutionary approach perceives aggression in terms of its ability to increase survival chances and enhance reproductive potential.

- Jealousy occurs through fear of losing affection or status and is a potent cause of aggression, while infidelity involves sexual partners being unfaithful.

- Group displays are ritualised displays of aggression by and between groups, which serve the functions of determining dominance hierarchies in relation to ownership of territory and intimidating of other groups.

- Group displays at sporting events can take the form of war dances, supporter displays, territorial behaviour and ritual behaviour.

- Lynch mobs are a phenomenon whereby mobs take the law into their own hands to administer aggressive acts resulting in death.

- Several explanations for group displays have been proffered, such as deindividuation, contagion theory, convergence theory, emergent norm theory and social identity theory.

5 Eating behaviour

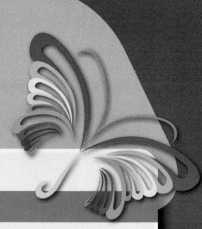

Factors influencing attitudes to food and eating behaviour   **160**

Mood   161

Cultural influences   164

Health concerns   165

The success and failure of dieting   167

Biological explanations of eating behaviour   **172**

Neural mechanisms involved in controlling eating behaviour   172

Evolutionary explanations of food preferences   178

Eating disorders   **185**

Obesity   186

Summing Up   **197**

Decoding the specification

The factors listed as influencing food and eating behaviour are examples, with no specific requirement to study them; they will not feature directly in examination questions. Material on other relevant factors is equally acceptable, though the examples given provide appropriate and detailed sources of material.

Explanations for the success and failure of dieting can be drawn from many sources, and you may be asked to outline explanations and/or evaluate them.

There is a need to understand eating behaviour from a biological perspective. Neural mechanisms are specifically identified and must be studied, as they may feature specifically in examination questions. A knowledge of evolutionary theory and how it can be applied to food preferences is also required. You should be prepared to provide both descriptive and evaluative material on these topics.

The eating disorders listed are examples and could not be referred to directly in examination questions; any relevant eating disorder would be acceptable. Only one eating disorder needs to be studied, but this must include psychological explanations and biological explanations, especially neural and evolutionary explanations, as they are directly referred to and could be directly examined.

Factors influencing attitudes to food and eating behaviour

Eating is essential to survival and to normal healthy development. It is concerned with many psychological areas, such as being a source of comfort and a contributor to self-image, as well as serving important social functions due to the group nature of much eating behaviour.

There are many factors influencing attitudes towards food and eating, like mood, cultural influences, health concerns and socio-economic factors. The sensory qualities of food exert an influence too, through both innate and learned sources. These factors interact to shape attitudes and expectations about food and eating, which shape actual eating behaviour.

IN THE NEWS

Frenchman eats TV dinner

Michel Lotito's nickname of 'Monsieur Mangetout', literally means Mr. Eat-all and is certainly a name the Frenchman lives up to.

He's perhaps best known for eating a whole Cessna airplane (it did take him a year), but has also wolfed down 18 bicycles, alongside ample servings of TV sets, supermarket trolleys and, perhaps the ultimate pudding, a coffin, though it was an empty one.

Michel eats, digests and excretes such exotic foodstuffs without causing himself any harm; his stomach lining is much thicker than an average person's, which might explain his extraordinary talent. His compulsive behaviour began at nine years of age when he began eating bits of metal, glass and toxic substances from TV sets.

Michel also regularly ate light bulbs and razorblades, but although his behaviour was encouraged by the fame and money it brought, ultimately it can be considered an eating disorder, related to compulsive behaviour beginning in childhood. It is

Figure 5.01 Monsieur Mangetout

difficult to see how Michel gained much in the way of nutrition from his consumptions. Eating is necessary for existence and good health, psychological and physical. Eating also fulfils many social functions related to group living. However, there is a worrying increase in the number of individuals being diagnosed as having eating disorders. Michel's particular disorder may not be commonplace, but obesity and other conditions like anorexia and bulimia nervosa are. Psychology can help us to understand eating behaviour and develop therapies to combat eating disorders.

Michel died of natural causes in 2007, aged 57.

Mood

Emotional states affect eating habits, either in small ways or in ways that explain abnormal eating practices, like binge eating. Mood can be affected by stress, either by a *general affect*, where stress changes a person's consumption of food, generally by creating physiological changes, or by *individual differences*, where stress influences eating practices in particular groups of people. This may occur due to differences in childhood experience of food, attitudes towards eating, or variations in biology that cause dissimilarities in vulnerability to the effects of stress. Those exhibiting vulnerability respond to stress by eating more, while those with low vulnerability eat less.

Want to see Monsieur Mangetout in action, including the contents of his stomach? Go to www.youtube.com/watch?v=h6PI2-lx12A and work up an appetite.

Contemporary research

Garg *et al.* (2007)
Sweet home Alabama

Mood influences eating behaviour and negative moods are associated with eating disorders, like bulimia. Advertisers are aware of the power of this factor and attempt to manipulate and associate certain mood states to create favourable images of food products, like chocolate being associated with pleasurable emotions. The researchers here manipulated people's mood states and then measured how this affected food consumption.

Aim/hypothesis

To assess how manipulating happiness and sadness through the content of a movie influences the consumption of hedonistic foods.

It was predicted that sad people would attempt to repair their negative mood by consuming more hedonistic food than happy people.

Procedure

By random selection, participants either watched *Love Story*, to evoke a sad mood, or *Sweet Home Alabama*, to evoke a happy mood. These films were used as they were similar in running length, box office success and content areas.

Participants watched the films in groups. They were given calorie-free drinks and popcorn, which was pre-weighed, each portion containing an average of 180 grams of butter popcorn.

At the end of the film participants indicated their assessment (1 = sad to 9 = happy) and rated their mood.

The popcorn container was weighed and the amount consumed was calculated.

Findings

The films were successful in creating the desired emotions.

Participants consumed 28 per cent more popcorn while watching the sad film than the happy film. The mean popcorn consumed for the sad condition was 124.97 grams against 97.97 grams consumed in the happy condition.

Conclusions

People in a sad mood eat hedonistic food in an attempt to return to a happier state.

Evaluation

- The research used objective measurements and a controlled experimental method, allowing causality to be established.

- The films were familiar and participants may have consumed popcorn due to anticipation/expectation rather than actual mood state.

- The findings have practical applications for advertisers in the marketing of foodstuffs.

Key terms

Mood – emotional states affecting eating practices

Cultural influences – eating practices transmitted to members of cultural groupings

Health concerns – the effects on eating behaviour and attitudes generated by the desire to eat nutritionally

Attitudinal ambivalence – the moderating effect on eating behaviour of holding simultaneous positive and negative attitudes to food and eating

Dieting – restrained eating involving voluntary restriction of food intake

Calories – the energy content of food

Research in focus

In Garg *et al.*'s (2007) study, mean popcorn consumption was used as a measurement of the dependent variable.

Explain how a mean value is calculated.

Give one strength and one weakness of a mean.

Can the mode and the median ever be considered superior to the mean?

Research: mood

- Dye and Blundell (1997) found that women more commonly report food cravings than men, and such cravings occur when premenstrual, during the menopause and during pregnancy, all times of hormonal fluctuations. This suggests that mood alterations related to hormonal fluctuations can affect females' eating behaviour.

- Garg *et al.* (2007) found that happy people treat pleasurable products, like buttered popcorn and sugar-coated nuts, as mood threatening and avoid them, whereas sad people consider them mood uplifting and over-consume them. This suggests that mood affects attitudes and behaviour towards different food types. This was supported by Tice *et al.* (2001), who found that participants responded to distress by eating more fattening, unhealthy snack foods, but the tendency was reversed if they believed that eating would not alter their mood state.

- Antelman *et al.* (1975) induced stress in rats by pinching their tails, and observed significant increases in gnawing, eating and licking food, supporting the idea of stress affecting eating through a general effect. This was supported by Michaud *et al.* (1990), who found that children consumed more fatty foods due to the stress of an upcoming exam.

- Wansink *et al.* (2008) offered popcorn and grapes to participants, finding that those watching a sad film ate more popcorn to cheer themselves up, while those watching a comedy ate more grapes to prolong their mood. This suggests that people use food deliberately to influence mood.

- Wolff *et al.* (2000) found that female binge eaters had more negative moods on binge-eating days than female normal eaters, suggesting that negative moods are related to abnormal eating practices.

- Grundberg and Straub (1992) found that male participants who had not been stressed by watching an unpleasant video consumed more sweet, salty and bland foods than male participants who did watch the video. Females in the stressed condition consumed more sweet foods than those in the unstressed condition, suggesting a gender individual difference in how stress affects eating behaviour.

Evaluation

Mood

- Research support for stress influencing eating behaviour as a general effect is mixed. Bellisle *et al.* (1990) found no difference in the amount and types of food eaten by men when due or not due to undergo surgery. Also, generalising from animals to humans is problematic.

- Research has not identified the relative influences of acute and chronic stressors on eating behaviour, nor the mechanisms by which a general effect would occur.

- The idea that stress affects identifiable groups of people in different ways can explain the differences in eating behaviour between genders in response to stress.

- Research into possible individual differences between the effects of stress on male and female eating patterns is inconclusive. Stone and Brownall (1994) tested married couples, finding that men and women were likely to eat less in response to stress, with women being particularly less likely to increase eating as the severity increased. Connor and Armitage (2002) found that both males and females favour eating sweet foodstuffs in response to stress, suggesting a similarity between genders in response to stress.

- Research on mood states suggests that comfort foods should display nutritional information to stop depressed people eating badly, as such habits can contribute to becoming bulimic.

Supplementary learning

Food preferences during pregnancy

Evidence suggests that food preferences develop in the womb. Foetuses start consuming amniotic fluid, which contains traces of the mother's diet, from 12 weeks. Mennella *et al.* (2006) exposed babies prenatally, through their mother's diet, to carrot juice or water. At 5 months, when starting to eat solids, babies prenatally exposed to carrot juice showed less negative facial expressions to carrot-flavoured cereal than those not prenatally exposed and those given carrot-flavoured breast milk. This suggests that healthy eating is created during pregnancy by exposing unborn children to nutritious foods.

Figure 5.02 Pregnancy food cravings can even include cigarette butts

Pregnant women with unhealthy diets may pass on unhealthy food preferences to unborn children. Bayol *et al.* (2007) found that the resultant offspring of pregnant rats fed on a pre-maternal diet of junk food showed more preference for junk food compared to rats not prenatally exposed. Poor diet also damages children in the womb. Abate *et al.* (2008) performed a meta-analysis of studies controlling for genetic and post-natal environmental factors, finding a link between prenatal alcohol exposure and later alcoholism.

Around 75 per cent of women have food cravings during pregnancy, often for bizarre foodstuffs, or even ones they loathe. (My wife ate pickled eggs in curry sauce with unbridled passion throughout her first pregnancy and has never touched them since.) Cravings for salty foods are common and explanations include hormonal imbalances, but also the idea that unborn children somehow influence mothers' diets to obtain the necessary nutrition. This idea is difficult to test for ethical reasons and many pregnant women have pica cravings – desires for non-nutritious items, like cigarette butts, soap and rubber – that cast doubt on this explanation.

Cultural influences

Eating is influenced by social and cultural circumstances, with cultural and subcultural groups having different eating practices. These are transmitted to group members, usually via reinforcement and social learning, and include the consumption of different foodstuffs and differences in traditions of preparation and eating practices, like extended families eating together and eating practices marking special occasions, like eating pancakes on Shrove Tuesday. Cultural eating practices are also found in local cuisine, such as North Staffordshire oatcakes.

Certain cultural practices can lead to restrictions, like excluding pork. Cultural influences are flexible, however, and newcomers often adopt particular food habits of the local culture.

Minority ethnic groups are disproportionately represented in lower-income areas within Britain, and those with lower incomes often have poorer quality diets.

Cultural attitudes to the health concerns of food and eating vary widely. Culture influences behaviour directly, but usually has a moderating role on other variables to determine individual eating practices.

Figure 5.03 North Staffordshire oatcakes: an example of local cuisine

Research: cultural influences

- Lawrance *et al.* (2007) used nationwide discussion groups to investigate factors affecting the food choices of ethnic minority females. Bangladeshi and Pakistani females learned cooking skills from older family females and took pride in traditional cooking practices, but admitted that they ate western junk food when food preparation time was short. Zimbabwean women noted that the western cultural pressure to be slim, reflected in their eating practices, was not present in Zimbabwe. All women valued healthy eating, but did not necessarily practise it. The findings suggest that eating behaviour is influenced by culture, time, availability, cost, health and price.

- Stead *et al.* (2004) found that the minority ethnic groups studied lived in the poorest socio-economic conditions, and had lower disposable incomes and a poorer quality diet. They also lacked cooking skills, as they were removed from their cultural teaching influences.

- Stefansson (1960) found that Copper Inuits were disgusted at the taste of sugar. They lived in isolation from other people, on a diet of flesh and roots, having no experience of other foodstuffs. This suggests that a cross-cultural preference for sweet-tasting foods may not exist.

Evaluation

Cultural influences

- Culture can influence eating behaviour directly, but more often plays a moderating role on other variables to determine individual eating practices.

- Cultural eating practices often reflect local environmental conditions – for instance, the seasonal or non-availability of certain foods, coupled with the ability to transport and keep foodstuffs in hygienic conditions. For example, it makes good sense not to eat meat in cultures where meat can easily go off and become hazardous to health.

- With the increase in world population mobility, developments in transport systems and modern food hygiene practices, such as the wider availability of refrigeration, eating behaviours are more global and less based on individual cultural locations.

Health concerns

The desire to eat nutritious food and avoid unhealthy diets affects attitudes and behaviour, with differences between individuals and cultural groupings. Education plays a role, as higher-level education is associated with increased health awareness and health-based behaviour. The source of health-based information is important: if the source is perceived as confusing, conflicting or emanating from an untrusted basis, it has less effect.

Although people have knowledge of health and food and a desire to eat healthily, other factors, such as available income, accessibility to healthy foods and social and cultural influences, may result in healthy eating practices not occurring.

Research: health concerns

- Xie *et al.* (2003) found that children and adolescents from higher-income families ate more healthily than those from lower-income households, consuming more polyunsaturated fats, protein, calcium and iron, as well as eating the recommended amount of dairy products. This suggests that income has a regulating effect on healthy eating.

- Monneuse *et al.* (1991) found that people with a preference for high sugar content in dairy products chose items with lower sugar content, suggesting that health concerns affect eating behaviour.

- Dennison *et al.* (2001) found that reduced–fat milk was drunk more in families where parents were college educated, while families with parents who were not college educated drank full-fat milk. This suggests that level of education plays a role in healthy eating.

- Steptoe *et al.* (1995) ranked factors taken into account when selecting food. Sensory qualities were highest, above health concerns, indicating that healthy eating is not the most important factor in determining behaviour.

- De Almeida *et al.* (1997) found that health information disseminated from a source perceived as non-trustworthy or that comes in a confusing or conflicting form, is not acted on, which implies that information on its own is not sufficient to promote healthy eating practices.

- McFarlane and Pliner (1987) found that only people who consider nutrition to be important have preferences for healthy foods, suggesting that there are individual differences in healthy eating practices based on attitude.

Evaluation

Health concerns

- Although health concerns are of importance, other factors are more influential and can override intentions to eat healthily. Tuorila and Pangborn (1988) found that females had intentions of eating healthily, but actual consumption of food was based more on sensory qualities than health values.

- Information promoting healthy eating needs to be clear, consistent and originating from a trusted source in order to be effective. Advertising campaigns should utilise these points and use positive role models to put across messages that will be acted on.

- Knowledge about and intentions to eat healthily do not guarantee the adoption of healthy eating practices, because individuals are unsure how to act on knowledge.

Issues, debates and approaches

- Research into factors influencing attitudes to food and eating behaviour can help to construct beneficial practical applications. Findings from research studies into health concerns can be used to create eating programmes that shape and maintain healthy dietary practices – for instance, in the way that information about healthy eating is presented and which groups are targeted.

- Research into cultural influences is often culturally biased, as attitudes towards food and eating are culturally specific, and what is true for one culture is not necessarily true for another. For instance, western cultural concerns with dieting and problems with obesity are not applicable to cultures where the focus is more on counteracting starvation.

Psychology in action

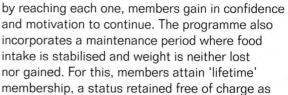

Weight Watchers: the psychology of dieting

Weight Watchers was founded in 1963 and operates in 30 countries. Although a private company (the Heinz food company owned it from 1978 until 1999), independent research suggests that its weight loss programmes are effective. This is due to the well-tested psychological factors at its core.

The most important of these is the social support that members offer to each other. Although online versions exist, most members attend group meetings where positive role models in the form of successful dieters are provided, as well as vicarious reinforcement and the creation of a positive social environment that motivates members to believe they can succeed.

Weight Watchers utilises another psychological tool too, that of goal setting. Members are encouraged to set target weights that are healthy and attainable. The long-term target weight is broken down into achievable short-term goals, and by reaching each one, members gain in confidence and motivation to continue. The programme also incorporates a maintenance period where food intake is stabilised and weight is neither lost nor gained. For this, members attain 'lifetime' membership, a status retained free of charge as long as members stay within 2 pounds of their maintenance weight.

Miller-Kovach et al. (2001) compared the Weight Watchers programme to a self-help programme over a 2-year period, finding the former to be more successful. Lowe et al. (2004) found that 72 per cent of members reaching their target weight maintained it over a 5-year period, having initially lost at least 5 per cent of body weight. This suggests that the programme is successful in terms of losing weight and maintaining weight loss, highlighting the importance of incorporating psychological principles into successful dieting.

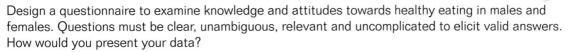

You are the researcher

Design a questionnaire to examine knowledge and attitudes towards healthy eating in males and females. Questions must be clear, unambiguous, relevant and uncomplicated to elicit valid answers. How would you present your data?

Then assess if behaviour actually matches attitudes. This could be achieved by observing which food items males and females choose from the college/school cafeteria. You will need to work out in advance which category – for example, healthy/unhealthy – each available food item fits into.

The success and failure of dieting

Dieting is a form of restrained eating involving voluntary restriction of food intake. It is an ancestral behaviour: the ability to diet had an adaptive value in times of food scarcity. Means of attaining successful dieting are desirable, with obesity currently so widespread. Bartlett (2003) reports that in the USA over 50 per cent of people are obese or overweight, and 300,000 deaths a year are credited to preventable weight-related conditions. However, the downside of dieting is that it is the main consequence of body dissatisfaction and leads to eating disorders like anorexia nervosa.

Wing and Hill (2001) define success as 'successful long-term weight loss maintenance, involving the intentional loss of at least 10 per cent of initial body weight and keeping it off for at least one year'. According to this definition, 20 per cent succeed. Dieters differ in the extent to which eating is restrained and for how long, and these factors also affect success levels. The majority of dieters are women, of whom 87 per cent have dieted at some time.

There are many explanations for the success and failure of dieting, involving varied biological and psychological factors. However, these should be considered in conjunction with each other (*multi-causal*), rather than as individual explanations.

Explanations for failure

Restraint theory

Restraint theory emerged in the 1970s as a means of researching dieting, incorporating self-report scales to measure individuals' dieting behaviour. The theory sees dieters as placing a cognitive boundary on food intake and then indulging in reduced eating. However, rather than such behaviour leading to weight loss and thus dieting success, it can lead instead to episodes of overeating. Research indicates restraint theory to be true and has identified several important factors.

Research: restraint theory

- Ogden (2003) tested restraint theory by giving dieters and non-dieters a pre-load/taste test. Participants were given either a high-calorie 'pre-load', like chocolate, or a low-calorie snack, like crackers. After eating, participants were told that they were going to participate in a taste preference test and given several different foods to taste, like biscuits, snacks and ice cream, with different taste qualities, like saltiness, sweetness, and so on. The participants were left alone to do the test in their own time. The key factor was how much of the taste test food they ate, a factor that participants were not aware of. Non-dieters reduced food intake in response to the high-calorie pre-load food, whereas the dieters who had had the high-calorie pre-load ate more. Dieters did, however, eat less after the low calorie pre-load. The results suggest that although dieters eat less on some occasions, restrained eating is also associated with eating more at other times and this explains why dieters are often unsuccessful.

- Ruderman and Wilson (1979) found that dieters end up eating more food than non–dieters, suggesting that restrained eating leads to weight increase, rather than weight decrease.

- Wardle and Beale (1988) assigned 27 women to one of three groups – a diet group, an exercise group and a control group – for 7 weeks, with food intake regularly assessed under laboratory conditions. Those in the diet condition ate more than those in the exercise and control groups, implying that overeating by dieters is caused by dieting itself.

- Herman and Polivy (1984) found that dieters reported that they could not be bothered to maintain dieting, as it took too much effort, suggesting a cognitive shift in thinking involving a breakdown of self–control or 'motivational collapse'.

- Polivy and Herman (1999) manipulated dieters' moods by telling them that they had either passed or failed a cognitive task, then gave them either unlimited food or food in controlled amounts. Those given unlimited amounts attributed distress to eating rather than task failure. This suggests that dieters overeat to shift responsibility for negative moods onto eating behaviour.

- Ogden (2003) found that the more dieters try to suppress thoughts of 'forbidden foods', the more preoccupied they become with them, suggesting that denial actually creates more pressure to break a diet.

- Keys *et al.* (1950) found that conscientious war objectors given half their normal daily food intake for 12 weeks lost 25 per cent body weight, becoming so obsessed with food that they hoarded or stole it, thinking of little else. This suggests that restrained eating leads to alterations in cognitive state.

Evaluation

Restraint theory

- Research supports the central idea that restrained eating leads to episodes of overeating and, ultimately, dieting failure and, indeed, most diets do fail. However, the theory cannot explain the minority of dieters who succeed in attaining weight loss through restrained eating. Also, anorexics experience huge weight losses without recourse to overeating.

- Herman and Polivy (1984) presented the boundary model to explain how dieting causes overeating. The model suggests that dieters set a 'diet boundary' and try to eat within this self-imposed limit. However, periodically they break their boundary and binge until full, because the physiological set-point boundary (see 'Biological explanations' on page 172) overrides the self-imposed cognitive boundary, leading to overeating.

- Cognitive shifts in thinking lead to overeating as a form of rebellion, where rather than becoming resigned to failing, dieters decide to overeat as an act of defiance against their self-imposed cognitive limit.

- Most dieters indulging in restrained eating fail to lose and maintain weight loss; therefore, it is surprising how many try and try again. Polivy and Herman (1999) explain this as 'false hope syndrome', where making a commitment to diet leads to a temporarily improved mood and self-image, which overrides the memories of past failures.

- Methodological techniques, like the pre-load/taste test, are laboratory based and artificial, having little relevance to real-life behaviour. Studies on dieters using self-monitoring forms find that some dieters often do eat less than unrestrained eaters and do not fall prey to overeating.

Other explanations

Most diets fail, mainly because they are unsustainable, the prime factor being a lack of knowledge and skills necessary to diet sensibly. Dieters set unrealistic targets, like restricting themselves to too few calories per day, which cannot be continued for more than a short period. Also, many dieters, who have generally spent

prolonged periods becoming overweight, expect to lose weight quickly and, again, this is not realistic. Although initial weight loss can be considerable, continued weight loss tends to decline, which is perceived as less reinforcing; therefore, motivation to continue declines and weight is regained, which is even more demotivating.

The more restrictive the diet, the more likely it is that it will fail. Being on a low-calorie diet brings unpleasant side effects, like lack of energy, dizziness and stress, which again leads to loss of motivation and abandonment. Also, dieters perceive dieting as being a temporary regime, and once weight loss targets are achieved they think they can return to old eating habits and regain weight. This results in constant weight fluctuations (yo-yo dieting) through undertaking a repetitive cycle of restrictive eating.

A biological role is played by the hormone ghrelin, which stimulates appetite, making hungry people even hungrier during dieting, as the body tries to address the weight loss by increasing the physiological desire to eat. This increases the chances of abandonment.

Cognitive factors play a role too, with a lessening of concentration associated with diets failing, as well as a change in cognitive style, such as cognitive shifts.

Research: other explanations

- Jeffery (2000) found that obese people start regaining weight after 6 months due to failing to maintain behavioural changes, suggesting that factors like loss of motivation and social pressure have negative influences.

- Cummings *et al.* (2002) found that low-calorie diets stimulate appetite by increasing ghrelin production by 24 per cent, reducing the chances of losing weight, as individuals become more physiologically motivated to eat. This is supported by the success of stomach-reduction surgery being due to shrunken stomachs producing less ghrelin.

- Williams *et al.* (2002) found that individuals lacking concentration are unsuccessful with diets, as they lose focus on targets and strategies, indicating that cognitive factors play a role in abandonment.

- D'Anci *et al.* (2008) found that low-carbohydrate diets have a cognitive effect, reducing glycogen levels, which then leads to a lack of concentration. This suggests that it is certain types of diet that influence cognitive factors and that cognitive processes are affected by biological factors.

Explanations for success

When diets succeed, it is generally due to a combination of strategies that produce weight loss in a realistic and attainable manner and then maintain the loss over an extended period. One means of accomplishing this is *relapse prevention*, which involves achieving a stable energy balance around the new lower weight. Relapse prevention involves learning to identify situations in which 'lapses' could occur, and how to 'refocus' if and when they do, so that dieters do not return to pre-weight-loss eating behaviours and lose the motivation and belief that a lower weight can be sustained.

Motivation and confidence help to determine success, alongside incentives and social support. Operant conditioning is utilised in the form of rewards acting as *positive reinforcements* to condition the desired weight-loss effect. For example, dieters might reward themselves with new clothes that fit their new body shape. The use of social networks is also beneficial – for example, utilising family and friends to provide support during the weight-loss period. Weight Watchers is a dieting organisation that uses group meetings to actively encourage members to provide social support for each other, creating a positive social identity for individual dieters that fosters confidence and motivation to adhere to diets. Social learning theory is also used, by providing successful role models for dieters to observe and model.

These all increase the chances of success, but the process is dependent on setting achievable targets for the amount of weight loss and the time period in which it is to occur. The chances of success are maximised by not setting overly specific goals, and the goal–setting process should consist of a series of short–term goals leading up to the ultimate long–term goal. Advice from health professionals is necessary to achieve this and to avoid setting unrealistic targets. Dieters must set a clear, objectively defined path to success in order to maintain motivation throughout the weight-loss process. If setbacks occur too often, even using relapse prevention will not stop motivation from dropping and the diet will be abandoned. Initial targets are easily achievable, as reaching them increases confidence and motivation. Regular monitoring and feedback occur, with necessary readjustments being made. Although expert opinion is sought, individuals are involved in target setting to create a sense of 'ownership'.

Individuals who diet successfully share common behaviours that promote weight loss and its maintenance, and once weight loss has been maintained for 2 years, the chances of long-term success increase dramatically.

Research: explanations for success

- Thomas and Stern (1995) found that financial incentives did not promote significant weight loss or help to maintain weight loss, going against the idea of such incentives being useful motivational tools. They did find that creating group contracts for weight loss had some success, suggesting that social support does play a motivational role.

- Miller-Kovach *et al.* (2001) reported that the social support methods that Weight Watchers offers were superior to individual dieting regimes over a period of 2 years, suggesting that social network support is a successful motivational device.

- Lowe *et al.* (2004) found that an average of 71.6 per cent of Weight Watchers members maintained a body weight loss of at least 5 per cent. This indicates that social support motivates people not only to lose weight, but to maintain the loss too.

- Bartlett (2003) found that dieting success occurs best with a target of reducing calorific intake of between 500 and 1,000 calories a day, resulting in weight loss of about 1 to 2 pounds a week, supporting the idea that achievable goal setting is a strong motivational force.

- Wing and Hill (2001) reported that common behaviours leading to successful weight loss and its maintenance included a low-fat diet, constant self-monitoring of food intake and weight, and increased physical activity.

Figure 5.04 Successful dieting is difficult to achieve and many will relapse

Evaluation

The success and failure of dieting

- Individual differences contribute to success rates. 'Low-restrainers' find dieting easy, while 'high-restrainers' find it difficult. Mensink *et al.* (2008) think that high-restrainers are hypersensitive to food cues, and thus likely to abandon diets. Stirling *et al.* (2004) found that high-restrainers could not resist forbidden chocolate. However, it is not known whether being a high- or low-restrainer is innate or learned.

- Nolen-Hoeksema (2002) found that females on low-fat diets develop negative moods, which they address by overeating, with 80 per cent of these going on to develop clinical depression within 5 years. This suggests that dieting can lead to a risk of developing mental disorders.

continued ...

...continued

- Due to ethical concerns, the types of research that can be conducted is restricted. For example, setting up experimental designs could be problematic, so self-reports are often used.
- Research findings will hopefully lead to the identification of strategies for successful dieting that can address the growing problem of obesity.

You are the researcher

Design an experiment to test whether goal setting results in fewer diets failing.

What would your IV and DV be? How would you operationalise failure/success?

What experimental design would you use?

How would you go about getting a self-selected sample? (Remember, this a study of dieters.)

Dieting is a sensitive area. How would you address ethical concerns through standardised instructions?

What level of significance would be used, and why?

Issues, debates and approaches

- Research into dieting can be seen as gender biased, because it tends to focus on females and thus research findings cannot be generalised to males. Some dieting behaviour can have negative consequences, like the development of anorexia nervosa; although this is primarily a female complaint, it has about a 15 per cent incidence of male sufferers, so it is important to understand male dieting behaviour too.
- Psychological research has contributed towards the formation of effective diets and weight reduction programmes. Psychological knowledge, when applied properly, can lead to long-term effectiveness in the form of weight stabilisation around an ideal target weight. Such success can be measured in terms of people's heightened psychological well-being, as well as reduced costs to the health services.

Strengthen your learning

1. Outline and evaluate how the following may affect attitudes to eating. Remember to include research evidence in your evaluations.
   i) Mood
   ii) Cultural influences
   iii) Health concerns
2a) Outline restraint theory.
2b) To what degree does research support restraint theory?
2c) What other evaluative points can be made about restraint theory?
3a) What other reasons might lead to dieting failure?
3b) Evaluate these reasons, including the use of research evidence.
4a) For what reasons might diets succeed?
4b) Evaluate these reasons, including the use of research evidence.

Assessment Check

1. Outline and evaluate factors influencing attitudes to food and eating behaviour. (24 marks)

2. Discuss explanations for the success and/or failure of dieting. (24 marks)

3. Outline factors for the success of dieting. (4 marks)

4. Outline and evaluate factors influencing attitudes to food and eating behaviour. (20 marks)

Examination guidance

Question 1 calls for a 'longer' outline of factors, one that could earn all 8 marks. The wording of the question means that at least two factors must be offered to gain access to all the marks on offer. There are 16 marks available for the evaluation, hence more time and effort should be spent here, and this could be achieved in terms of theoretical considerations, research support and methodological considerations.

The term 'discuss' in question 2 means to describe explanations and then evaluate them. A decision needs to be made as to whether to offer explanations of the success or the failure of dieting, or both. If only one type is offered, more detail would be expected.

Question 3 only requires descriptive material, so any evaluation would not be creditworthy.

Question 4 is similar to question 1, but calls for a 'shorter' outline of factors, as this time it is only worth 4 marks. The evaluation has the same rating of 16 marks.

Biological explanations of eating behaviour

Hunger is activated by many different cues, both biological and environmental. All animals have a motivation to eat, and this motivation increases as energy levels decrease. An imbalance occurs when the energy expended exceeds the energy consumed, with this imbalance being signalled to the brain in a number of different ways. Various neural mechanisms have been linked to the control of eating, with the hypothalamus being seen as the hunger centre of the brain. The ventromedial hypothalamus and the lateral hypothalamus have been identified as playing key roles and feature in both *dual control theory* (DCT) and *set point theory* (SPT). Other areas of the limbic system may also have a part to play, indicating the complexity of biological factors in hunger and satiation. More contemporary research has indicated the contributory role that hormonal factors play too.

Neural mechanisms involved in controlling eating behaviour

Stomach contraction theory

Cannon and Washburn's (1912) *stomach contraction theory* suggested that hunger pangs originated from the stomach, stimulating eating, which suggested that motivation to eat did not come from neural mechanisms, but from a peripheral signal in the stomach. Although stomach signals do play a contributory role, subsequent research showed that hunger was not just a reflex action to an empty stomach.

Key terms

Neural mechanisms – influence of brain components in regulating eating behaviour

Ventromedial hypothalamus – brain region associated with the cessation of eating

Lateral hypothalamus – brain region associated with hunger and the onset of eating

Dual control theory – a homeostatic view of eating, whereby hunger motivates eating, which in turn leads to satiety and cessation of eating

Set point theory – that each individual is orientated biologically to a specific body weight

Lesions – damaged brain tissue

Evolution – the process of adaptation through natural selection

Pleistocene era – time when most human evolution occurred (also known as the EEA, or Environment of Evolutionary Adaptiveness)

Dual control theory

Lashley (1938) believed that there must be a brain mechanism involved in the motivation to eat. From experiments involving rats, Lashley identified the vital role the *hypothalamus* brain area plays in regulating food intake. The *lateral hypothalamus* (LH) was seen as the 'hunger centre', initiating eating behaviour; and the *ventromedial hypothalamus* (VMH) was seen as the 'satiety centre', producing a feeling of fullness that caused cessation of eating.

The hypothalamus is the body's control centre, playing a vital role in many physiological functions, such as emotions, as well as food/water intake. In the same way that a thermostat maintains temperature, the hypothalamus maintains the body's homeostasis by receiving messages from different parts of the body and making appropriate responses. This became known as *dual control theory* (DCT), which centred on the idea of a homeostatic perception of hunger and satiety, whereby when the level of *glucose* (blood sugar) is low, the liver sends signals to the lateral hypothalamus, giving rise to the sensation of hunger that motivates a search for food. When eaten, the food releases glucose, which activates the ventromedial hypothalamus, giving rise to the sensation of satiety, which stops any further eating.

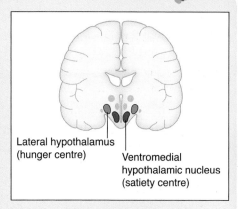

Figure 5.05 The hypothalamic nuclei involved in the regulation of appetite

The hypothalamus thus helps to maintain a constant internal environment. The particular foods consumed in response to low glucose levels depends on numerous factors, such as usual diet, culture, availability, habits, and so on. Although there was initial research support for DCT, problems with the theory were discovered, such as the fact that rats were able to reach satiety, even if their satiety centre was removed (by lesioning the VMH); conversely, rats with their hunger centre removed (by lesioning the LH) were still able to become hungry.

Neuropeptides and hormones

Further research showed the hypothalamus to be an extremely complex brain area, containing many different types of specialised nerve cell and controlling many different physiological functions. Apart from the lateral and ventromedial hypothalamus, the *arcuate nucleus* of the hypothalamus also plays a vital role. This region contains several different types of nerve cells, one of which manufactures the *neuropeptide* NPY, a very potent *orexigen* (appetite stimulator). Neuropeptides are minute proteins encoded by genes, which work as chemical messengers between neurons, or between the fat deposits of the body and the brain. The fat hormone *leptin* is a neuropeptide secreted from fat cells into the blood, which signals to the brain, via the hypothalamus, that calorific storage is high. When people do not eat enough, fat is used up and fat cells cease to secrete leptin, causing leptin levels in the blood to fall. The hypothalamus detects the drop in leptin, interprets low leptin levels as a lack of calories and generates the sensation of hunger.

Several neuropeptides have been identified as playing subtly differing roles in the response to calorific deficiency. *Agouti-gene-related peptide* (AGRP) signals hunger, with food deprivation leading to levels of NPY and AGRP being increased in the brain. However, NPY and AGRP have different effects, with NPY levels increasing rapidly with food deprivation and NPY injections inducing feeding for a few minutes, while AGRP rises slowly during fasting and declines slowly upon refeeding. NPY neurons are also activated by *ghrelin*, a hormone secreted from the stomach, whose concentration in the blood falls after each meal and rises progressively until the next.

Leptin and ghrelin are not the only signals reaching the hypothalamus; cells in the ventromedial nucleus and some in the lateral hypothalamus are directly sensitive to glucose concentrations, some being inhibited when glucose concentrations are high, while others are facilitated. The hypothalamus also contains neurons sensitive to *insulin*, which is secreted in amounts proportional to the size of body fat stores, as another signal the brain can use to evaluate energy reserves. Other hormones are produced by the stomach, pancreas and gastrointestinal tract, including *pancreatic polypeptide* and the products of the gastrointestinal L cells, *glucagon-like peptide 1* (GLP-1), *oxyntomodulin* and *peptide YY* (PYY 3-36), which act as satiety signals.

Satiation

Satiety, the feeling of fullness after eating, is mediated by signals arising from the stomach and gastrointestinal tract. These include signals arising from stretch receptors as the stomach is inflated by food, and chemical signals arising in the stomach as the result of secretion from cells regulating digestion, which activate afferent fibres of the vagus nerve. For example, the gut hormone *cholecystokinin* (CCK) is secreted in the stomach during eating, activating CCK-A receptors on the nerve endings of the gastric vagus nerve. These vagally mediated signals reach the hypothalamus via nuclei in the caudal brainstem, most notably the nucleus of the solitary tract. Noradrenergic neurons in this area play an important role in carrying these signals, projecting to many parts of the hypothalamus.

Eating ceases when satiety signals reaching the hypothalamus are sufficiently strong to activate populations of neurons that make *anorexigenic* (loss of appetite) peptides. There are different anorexigenic peptides, just as there are different *orexigenic* peptides (appetite stimulants), with one of the most important anorexigenic peptides being *alpha melanocyte-stimulating hormone* (alpha-MSH), which is manufactured in another population of neurons in the arcuate nucleus. These neurons project to different parts of the hypothalamus where alpha-MSH is released and act on other neurons via specific *melanocortin receptors*.

Set point theory

A solution to the inability of the dual point theory to explain the long-term effects of lesions to the LH and the VMH was set point theory (SPT). This suggests that everyone has an individual metabolic set point, a certain weight their body is geared towards, determined by the rate at which calories are consumed. Set points can alter depending on several factors, including eating patterns and exercise. When people diet, leptin levels decrease, causing the hypothalamus to trigger hunger pangs. The set point for obese individuals is higher than for healthy individuals, and lower for underweight individuals.

Lipostatic theory

Lipostatic theory perceives the sensations of hunger as arising from lower fat levels within the body, with the hormone *leptin*, which is derived from fat, playing a crucial role as a *chemosensitive* mechanism that helps to maintain a balance of energy levels. The theory therefore sees the cessation of eating occurring from a negative feedback signal (see 'Classic research: Coleman (1973)' on page 176).

Glucose theory

Glucose theory sees hunger arising when blood glucose levels are low, with the brain monitoring blood-glucose levels through *glucoreceptors* located in the VMH. Glucose is supplied from the intestine, which produces CCK in the presence of food and which, in turn, makes the liver produce glucose and sends signals to the brain.

Research: neural mechanisms involved in controlling eating behaviour

- Washburn (1912) found that when he inflated a balloon in his stomach (he swallowed it attached to a pumping tube to achieve this – don't try this at home!) he did not feel hungry. This led to the formation of stomach contraction theory. However, individuals who have their stomachs surgically removed, for medical reasons, still experience hunger, refuting the theory.

- Lashley (1938) and co-workers such as Brobeck (1946) performed a series of experiments where rats were trained to negotiate a maze to gain food. Different parts of hungry rats' brains were lesioned (cut out) to assess the effect on eating behaviour. Lesions to the lateral hypothalamus made animals stop eating spontaneously, while lesions to the ventromedial hypothalamus caused the rats to overeat to excess. This supports the idea of the hypothalamus being the 'eating centre' of the brain, with the lateral hypothalamus being the 'hunger centre' and the ventromedial hypothalamus being the 'satiety centre'.

- Hetherington and Ranson (1940) found that lesions to the VMH lead to hyperphagia (overeating) and weight gain. Anad and Brobeck (1951) found that lesions to the LH lead to aphagia (undereating) and weight loss, suggesting support for DCT.

- Stellar (1954) found that when stimulated the VMH decreases eating, but when lesioned increases eating, while the LH when stimulated and lesioned produces the opposite effects. As predicted by DCT, this indicates that these two brain areas are the feeding and satiety centres.

- Teitalbaum (1957) got rats to push a bar an increasing number of times to get food. Lesioned VMH rats initially work hard, in line with DCT, but became less willing to work hard as more presses were required. It was also found that VMH lesioned rats are fussy eaters and eat less than normal rats if food tastes stale or bitter. These findings do not fit the predictions of DCT.

- Powley and Keesey (1970) found that rats that lose weight by being starved and then have lesions made to their LH do not lose further weight, supporting SPT, as it seems to indicate that the rats had slimmed down to a new set point before the lesions were created.

- Han and Liu (1966) took rats that were obese through having VMH lesions and force-fed them to increase their body weight even more. The rats then fed freely and lost weight, returning to the weight they were before force-feeding – that is, back to their new increased set point, supporting the idea of set point theory.

- Schneider and Tarshis (1995) found that lesioning the LH leads to body weight falling, as stored body fat is released to compensate for the fall in insulin production. As the bloodstream is now energy-rich, brain mechanisms believe that eating is not required. This suggests that that the LH has a role in the control of insulin.

Figure 5.06 Fat rat: lesions to different brain areas will cause rats to either under- or overeat

- Pinel (2000) showed that lesioned VMH rats have increased insulin levels, causing food to be converted to fat. The rats eat more to address the shortage of glucose in their bloodstream, causing weight increase, suggesting that the VMH too plays a role in insulin control.

- Bash (1994) transfused blood from a satiated dog to a starved dog, resulting in the termination of stomach contractions in the starved dog, supporting the glucose theory. However, Le Magnen (1995) suggests that blood glucose levels do not change much under normal conditions, lessening support for the theory.

You are the researcher

Imagine you are to conduct an experiment using rats to investigate brain structures and eating behaviour. Explain the experimental techniques involved in determining the role of:

i) the lateral hypothalamus

ii) the ventromedial hypothalamus.

To accomplish this, you will need two groups of rats for both experiments – one to act as an experimental group and the other as a control group in each instance. Taking into consideration that previous research has already suggested what the functions of these structures are, write suitable experimental hypotheses for both experiments.

Classic research

Coleman (1973)

Effects of parabiosis of obese mice and mice with diabetes with normal mice

Research in the 1950s found that eating was restrained by levels of fat present in food, which suggested that feeding was controlled by a negative feedback signal. This became known as lipostatic theory, which saw sensations of hunger deriving from lower fat levels, with leptin, a hormone derived from fat, playing a crucial role. This was confirmed by Coleman's work with obese mice.

Figure 5.07 Parabiotic mice: parabiosis is a technique that unites separate animals physiologically

Aim

To test lipostatic theory by using different genetic strains of mice.

Procedure

Parabiosis was used, a technique that unites separate animals physiologically, in order to pair up different genetic strains of mice.

Two forms of obese mice that were of different genetic mutations were used, 'ob' mice and 'db' mice.

Findings

When 'ob' mice were paired with normal wild mice, the obese mice lost weight.

When 'db' mice were paired with wild mice, the normal mice starved to death.

When 'db' mice were paired with 'ob' mice, they coexisted well, with the 'ob' mice losing weight.

Conclusions

'db' mice have a circulating factor that stops eating in 'ob' and normal mice, but 'db' mice are resistant to it.

When paired with normal mice, 'ob' mice get the circulating factor from the normal mice and lose weight due to a decrease in hunger.

'db' mice circulate a factor that their satiety centre in the ventromedial hypothalamus does not respond to, while 'ob' mice have a normal satiety centre, but produce inadequate levels of the satiety signal.

Evaluation

● The research provides support for the lipostatic theory and displays the complexity of the mechanisms involved in the regulation of eating.

continued ...

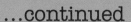

...continued

- The research confirms the key role that leptin plays in the regulation of hunger and appetite.
- The research was conducted on animals, due to the ethical restraints of performing similar research on humans (though many would question the ethics of performing such research on animals too). However, this raises the question of generalisation to humans.

Evaluation

Neural mechanisms involved in controlling eating behaviour

- Perceiving the LH as a 'feeding centre' is an oversimplification: it is possible to recover from LH lesions, and LH lesions also produce disruptions in aggression levels, sexual behaviour and reinforcement behaviour; also, lesions to the *nigrostriatal tract* (NST), a brain structure that passes through the LH, produce aphagia (undereating) and adipsia (under-drinking) on their own.
- Although hypothalamic mechanisms are important in controlling hunger and satiety, they are not fully understood. For example, it isn't clear how ghrelin and leptin reach targets in the brain, as both are large peptides that do not cross the blood–brain barrier readily. Also, the degree to which hypothalamic mechanisms are working independently or in conjunction with each other is not understood.
- The various signals sending information to the hypothalamus are only part of the complex systems regulating eating, as other factors apart from neural mechanisms play a role too, such as biological rhythms. For example, rats become most active and start to eat after darkness descends, due to another area of the hypothalamus, the suprachiasmatic nucleus.
- Much research into neural mechanisms involves animal experimentation, creating problems of generalisation to humans. However, Quaade (1971) found that stimulating the VMH of obese people made them feel hungry, similar to studies on rats. Also, post-mortem studies have tended to lend support to animal studies, suggesting that findings can be generalised to humans.
- Cognitive factors also have a role to play in determining satiety. Individuals are aware that they have eaten and therefore logically assume that they are full.
- The notion of a biologically determined set point for body mass has experimental support and has been used to create practical applications in the form of therapies to treat obese people.
- Research has tended to consist of artificial laboratory experiments, where animals are not allowed to eat freely, suggesting that results may not be ecologically valid.

Issues, debates and approaches

- Much research into neural mechanisms involves animal studies, many of which can be criticised on ethical grounds for the distress they cause, like Coleman's (1973) research that surgically united separate animals by parabiosis. Such experiments would now be difficult to justify on cost-benefit grounds, though it could be argued that this type of research might lead to effective treatment of eating disorders.
- To focus solely on neural mechanisms as responsible for eating behaviour is deterministic, as it disregards the element of free will that individuals have over their eating behaviour.

Research in focus

Coleman's (1973) research into eating behaviour in mice led to the deaths of some animals. How might some justify this by recourse to cost-benefit analysis?

Is this still ethically justifiable by today's standards?

Supplementary learning

Techniques used to study eating and satiation

Researchers have used various techniques that allow them to study the biological mechanisms underpinning eating behaviour.

Central micro-injection

Minute quantities of certain neurotransmitters are injected into specific brain areas of animals, causing them to perform complex behaviours similar to naturally occurring ones. Lee and Stanley (2005) showed that micro-injections of neuropeptide Y into specific areas of the hypothalamus caused animals to over eat and, with chronic stimulation, to develop massive obesity. By determining which neurotransmitters act similarly and which brain areas are involved, specific neurochemicals and brain sites involved in controlling eating behaviour can be identified.

Measurement of neurotransmitter release

Experimental methods are used to manipulate animals' behaviour and then various biochemical techniques are utilised to measure corresponding changes in brain chemistry. Stanley (2008) reported that noradrenaline, another neurotransmitter stimulating eating when injected into a certain brain area, is also released from this same brain area during natural eating behaviour.

Imaging brain activity

This technique exploits the fact that more active brain areas have higher metabolic rates. Using brain-imaging techniques, it is possible to see which brain areas are activated during eating behaviour. This permits the identification of neuronal sites and brain pathways activated by central neurotransmitter injections that produce eating, as well as those activated naturally during eating behaviour.

Evolutionary explanations of food preferences

Key terms

Obesity – the condition of being chronically overweight

Psychodynamic explanation – that obesity results from unresolved childhood conflicts

Behavioural explanation – that obesity results from maladaptive learned overeating behaviour

Cognitive explanation – that obesity results from maladaptive thought processes concerning food and eating

Genetic explanation – that obesity results from an inherited predisposition

Neural explanation – that obesity results from abnormally functioning brain mechanisms

Evolutionary explanation – that obesity results from the evolutionary tendency to store energy as fat for times of food scarcity

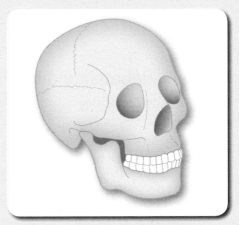

Figure 5.08 Modern skulls house a Stone Age mind (Cosmides and Tooby, 1992)

Evolutionary theory proposes the idea that there is genetic variability within humans, just as there is in any animal species. Specific genes are handed down to an individual by their parents, and if a particular individual's genes suit the environmental conditions they find themselves in, they will have an advantage, in that they will be more able to exploit their environment and thus survive to reproduce themselves into the next generation. By this process of natural selection, such genes would become widespread throughout the population. Therefore, any genetic variability that assisted individuals in finding ample quantities of safe, edible foods would have given them a selective advantage, allowing them to survive and pass on the advantageous genes to their children. In this way, according to evolutionary theory, human eating behaviours were shaped and modified.

Most human evolution is regarded as having occurred during the Pleistocene era, a time period stretching between 10,000 and 2 million years ago, also referred to as the Environment of Evolutionary Adaptiveness (EEA). Evolutionary theory sees the eating behaviour of humans as being shaped in these ancestral times, but still apparent in the dietary habits exhibited today. The Pleistocene era was a time of nomadic hunter-gatherers, who lived in small, tightly knit, closely related groups. Life would have been much harsher and shorter than it is now, with the risk of death ever present. Indeed, humans faced a battle every day, just to find enough food to survive. The end of this era was marked by human populations becoming less nomadic and more static, and food being cultivated through agricultural practices. Before this radical change occurred, however, food was something often available only periodically and which required a great deal of skill and application to obtain. Therefore, energy-rich, nutritious foods were at a premium, and humans evolved preferences for such foodstuffs, while simultaneously evolving methods of detecting which foods were toxic and should be avoided. These preferences are still apparent today; indeed, the evolutionary desire to eat as much calorie-rich food as possible, and store the excess as fat to see people through times of food scarcity, is offered up as an explanation of the modern phenomenon of obesity.

Sweet taste preferences

Evolutionary theory sees a preference for sweet-tasting foods having become widespread, because sweetness is associated with high-energy and non-toxic content, and therefore sweet foods would have aided survival. This would have been acted on by natural selection to become a universal food preference throughout human populations.

Research: sweet taste preferences

- Meiselman (1977) found that people of all ages prefer sweet foods to other tastes. This was supported by Capaldi *et al.* (1989), who found this to be equally true for many other species, such as horses, bears and ants.

- Zhao *et al.* (2008) found that the genetic component of sweetness preference is due to the influence of two genes, T1r2 and T1r3, which are code for the two proteins that combine to form the sweetness taste receptor. T1r3 is also activated on its own in the presence of high sugar concentrations, but not by low concentrations of artificial sweeteners. This may explain why artificial sweeteners are not perceived as being as sweet as sugar. A genetic component to sweetness preference implies that human variation in sweetness preference may be explained by variability within the T1r2 and T1r3 genes rather than culture differences, lending support to the evolutionary explanation of food preferences. Research has indicated that a preference for sweet foods is innate.

- Using choice preferences and facial expressions, Desor *et al.* (1973) and Steiner (1979) both found that neonates prefer sweet foods to bitter ones, implying the preference to be innate. This is supported by Grill and Norgren (1978), who reported that neonates show an acceptance of sweet tastes the first time they come across them. This acceptance response appears to be an innate, reflexive response.

- Logue (1991) found that the human tongue has specific receptors for detecting sweetness. This is not the case with other tastes, which are detected by non-specific receptors. There are also more receptors for detecting sweetness than for other tastes, which implies that sweet tastes are more important and that the preference has a genetic component shaped by evolution.

Figure 5.09 Sweet tastes are indicative of high energy and low toxin risk

Evaluation

Sweet taste preferences

- The idea of a preference for sweet tastes determined by evolution has a wide range of research support, including cross-cultural evidence. However, Stefansson (1960) reported that Copper Inuits were disgusted at their first taste of sugar. This goes against the notion of sweetness being a universal preference.

- A fondness for sweetness is found throughout the animal kingdom. Indeed, animals will go to great trouble to procure sweet-tasting foods – for example, bears being stung extensively by bees to get at the honey inside their hives – lending support to it being an evolutionary preference.

- Neonate studies suggest an innate sweetness preference, but interpreting neonates' facial expressions is somewhat subjective and may not produce reliable results.

- Read and McDaniel (2008) point out that genes alone are not thought to be responsible for the variations in sweetness reception in humans. The protein hormone leptin has an inhibitory effect on taste reception cells, reducing the amount of sweetness signals transmitted to the brain. During times of food scarcity, less leptin is produced, making sweet foods appear less attractive.

Salty taste preferences

'Some seek not gold, but there lives not a man who does not need salt' (Cassiodorus).

Salt is necessary for the body to function properly, being essential for maintaining neural and muscular activity and water balance. Salt contains sodium chloride, essential for keeping hydrated, though too much salt is injurious to health. The concentration of salt in the blood must be kept at a specific level and regularly needs topping up, as small amounts are lost through sweat and the action of the kidneys. Salt deprivation can cause intense salt cravings, and animals will travel huge distances to find deposits of salt. There are even African elephants near Mount Elgon in Kenya that travel far underground through cave systems just to obtain access to salt deposits. In human populations, salt was a valuable commodity that was exchanged for other goods, with huge industries arising out of salt mining and trading.

Research: salty taste preferences

- Beauchamp (1983) found that people with sodium deficiency (salt-starved) have an innate response to ingest salt and find it more palatable, less aversive at high concentrations, and eat more of it than related family members. This appears to be an evolutionary determined mechanism that helps to maintain sodium levels in the body, which has a high adaptive survival value.

- Denton (1982) found that an innate preference for salt is found in many, varying animal species, which suggests that the preference has a survival value and is determined by evolution.

- Dudley *et al.* (2008) found that ants in inland areas in salt–poor environments prefer salty solutions to sugary ones, seemingly an adaptive response to maintain their evolutionary fitness. This was supported by the fact that carnivorous ants did not have such a preference, presumably because they get ample salt supplies from the prey they consume. This difference in preference is exhibited in other animals too – for example, deer in the Scottish Highlands wander onto roads in winter to lick the salt they are gritted with, even though many are killed by cars. However, other animals, such as tigers, do not seek salt licks, as they gain sufficient salt from their kills.

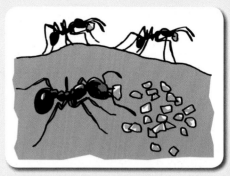

Figure 5.10 Ants in salt-poor environments prefer salty tastes to sugary ones

Evaluation

Salty taste preferences

- Humans are not born with an apparent innate preference for salt and cannot taste salt very well until about 4 months, at which time they do show a marked preference for salty foods over non-salty foods. At 2 years of age, children will reject foods that do not contain an expected amount of saltiness; this preference for salt is universal and is not restricted to cultural experiences. This suggests that a liking for salty tastes may be a maturational preference, with taste buds developing to be able to detect salt in time for weaning.

- It is difficult to test for salt preference in neonates, as from an ethical point of view it would not be possible to feed them salty foods in any meaningful concentrations. Care must be taken when researching with neonates not to cause harm, and in experimental conditions babies are not directly fed salt, but instead exposed to small stimuli on the tongue. From a practical point of view, it is also difficult to read young infants' facial expressions to see whether they like/dislike salty tastes.

- Although a preference for salt was adaptive in the EEA, it now causes problems for people who consume too much. Critics argue that food companies exploit our evolutionary inheritance by producing over-salty food, which has serious health implications in the long term.

- There are wide individual differences in salt preference, which is puzzling, as evolution would predict a standard universal preference. There may, however, be a genetic basis to liking salty tastes. Zinner (2002) found that 23 per cent of neonates had a salt preference; they also had higher blood pressure than other babies and at least one grandparent with hypertension (indicative of high salt consumption). This could explain individual differences in salt preferences.

Bitter and sour taste preferences

An ability to be able to detect and reject bitter and sour tastes makes evolutionary sense, as such tastes indicate the presence of poisons. Plants produce toxins to discourage being eaten, and therefore it is evolutionarily beneficial to develop an ability to dislike bitter and sour tastes. Herbivorous animals, whose diet consists solely of plants, have evolved high tolerance levels to the toxins contained within such foodstuffs, by having livers that can break down and neutralise poisonous compounds.

Humans have an innate ability to detect bitter tastes, possessing around 30 genes that code for bitter taste receptors; as each receptor is able to interact with several compounds, this means that humans can detect a wide variety of bitter-tasting substances. Children are especially sensitive to bitter tastes and this makes evolutionary sense, as such young children would not yet have had sufficient environmental experiences to develop learned and culturally acquired taste preferences.

Research: bitter and sour tastes preferences

- Merrit *et al.* (2008) tested human ability to detect bitter tastes by using a bitter, synthetic compound called phenylthiocarbamide (PTC). PTC is not found in nature, but the ability to taste it correlates strongly with the ability to taste other bitter substances that do occur naturally, especially toxins. Soon after the discovery of PTC, geneticists determined that there is an inherited component that has been preserved by natural selection. The existence of PTC can be explained by evolutionary pressure to avoid the toxins that plants produce to defend themselves against herbivores. People with the PTC taster gene can taste a wider range of toxic, bitter compounds, giving them an evolutionary survival advantage. As individuals have two copies of all their genes, combinations of the bitter taste gene variants determine whether someone finds PTC intensely bitter, somewhat bitter or without taste at all.

- Go *et al.* (2005) looked at the prevalence of the bitter taste receptor gene T2R in humans and 12 other primate species, to test for an evolutionary ability to detect bitter tastes. The results showed that humans have accumulated more pseudogenes (dead genes) than other primates, indicating that humans' bitter tasting capabilities have deteriorated more rapidly. T2R molecules play a key role in the avoidance of bitter, toxic substances, so the modification of the T2R gene repertoire may reflect different responses to changes in the environment resulting from species–specific food preferences during evolution. Perhaps due to environmental changes, natural selection is acting to reduce humans' ability to detect bitter tastes.

- Liem and Mennella (2003) investigated children's and adults' preferences for sour tastes, using 5- to 9-year-old children and their mothers. All mothers and 92 per cent of the children placed the sour tastes in rank order. However, 35 per cent of the children (but hardly any of the adults) had a preference for extreme sour tastes, indicating that sour taste preferences are heightened during childhood, possibly because such children are less food neophobic and more willing to try new foods. They also tended to eat a greater variety of fruits. The results suggest that sour taste preferences indicate a greater interest in trying new foods, which would have a selective advantage.

Figure 5.11 Children often cannot swallow bitter-tasting things as they suggest the presence of poisons

Evaluation

Bitter and sour taste preferences

- Many medicines are naturally bitter-tasting and thus unpalatable to children, who are especially sensitive to bitter tastes. Children given such medicines will vomit them straight back up, as their body is rejecting the poison it believes it has ingested. Therefore, many children's medicines are sweetened in order for them to be successfully swallowed and ingested. This suggests that there is an evolutionary ability to detect, and reject, bitter-tasting compounds.

- If the ability to taste bitter compounds does bring a selective advantage, then non-PTC tasters should have died out. Although PTC tasters are found worldwide, the ratio is roughly 75:25 between PTC tasters and non-tasters. It is thought non-PTC tasters may possibly have the ability to taste another bitter compound.

- The fact there are only two taste receptors for sweet tastes, but 27 for bitter tastes, suggests an evolutionarily determined need to discriminate between sweet-tasting, energy-rich foods and bitter-tasting, toxic foods. This implies that the need to avoid poisonous foods is more important to survival than finding edible foods – that is, being hungry is preferable to being dead.

continued ...

...continued

- It makes evolutionary sense for humans to have different levels of bitter/sour food preferences. As bitter/sour tastes are indicative of toxins, most humans will have evolved the ability to detect and reject such tastes. However, it is also beneficial to have some humans who do not have such evolutionary reluctances, so that new foodstuffs would be tested and adopted by the general population if proven to be safe and nutritious.

Meat

Humans do not appear to have an innate tendency to eat meat. It is introduced into children's diets at a relatively late stage of development, and there are many children who are reluctant to eat it. Children from cultures that practise vegetarianism do not suffer any apparent ill-health effects, nor do they exhibit a later preference for meat.

Humans are omnivores, capable of digesting both plant and flesh foodstuffs. Some meat eating does occur among other primates, such as chimpanzees, while others, like gorillas, are vegetarians. The evidence for when and how meat eating in humans occurred is sketchy and leads to much debate, due to theoretical links to the development of intelligence. Evidence from prehistoric sites suggests that meat eating did occur up to 1.5 million years ago, though how much of this was from hunted or scavenged meat is unclear. The use of fires to cook meat probably led to the eating of it becoming more widespread, and safer, and by smoking meat it could be preserved for later use. The tendency towards eating meat would, through natural selection, have seen an emerging predominance of humans more able to digest meat and have resistance to harmful pathogens contained within it.

The advantages of meat were that it is rich in fat and thus high in energy, and as it was available all year round it had an advantage over seasonal plant foods. Some see meat eating as directly leading to advances in intelligence, through providing the energy to allow brain growth, while others see it as a more indirect effect, due to the development of intelligence for hunting skills and inter-group living. However, the disadvantages of a meat diet are the dangers associated with hunting it, the toxins that can be contained within it and the dangers of diseases transmissible across species. There is a popular viewpoint that the HIV virus was transmitted to humans from monkeys by the consumption of 'bush meat'.

Research: meat eating

- Dunn (1990) reported that in common with other primates, humans evolved to thrive on plants that were abundant in the EEA; human dental structures, digestive systems and other physiological traits are more similar to herbivores than carnivores. This suggests that consuming plants is more natural for human bodies and that humans do not have an innate preference for meat.

- Goudsblom (1992) found archaeological evidence that controlled fires allowed greater meat eating, as cooking meat made it more edible for humans and smoking meat preserved it for later eating.

- Foley and Lee (1991) compared primate feeding strategies with brain size, finding evidence that meat eating led directly to a growth in human intelligence, suggesting that meat eating was evolutionarily favoured.

Figure 5.12 Meat eating can be dangerous as it can contain toxins

- Finch and Standford (2004) believed that humans adapted to eat diverse foods, including meat, as it allowed them to exploit new environments, especially harsh ones devoid of abundant plant foods, suggesting an adaptive advantage to meat eating.

Evaluation

Meat eating

- Kendrick (1980) studied cultural groups around the world noted for their longevity, finding that a common factor was their vegetarianism, which suggests there is a price to pay for meat eating, that of having a shorter lifespan.
- Environmental changes in the EEA, such as more long-term food scarcities, may have led to a change to meat eating. This is supported by the fact that meat, unlike other human foodstuffs, is not naturally palatable. Dunn (1990) pointed out that real carnivores eat meat raw, guts and all, and it is only humans who have to cook it and smear it in spices and sauces to make it palatable.
- The American Academy of Paediatrics (1998) reports that neonates can only ingest one food type: milk; and there is evidence for an innate preference for sweet tastes and a distaste for bitter tastes. However, meat has to be introduced into youngsters' diets, suggesting that there is no evolutionarily determined preference for meat eating.
- The fact that meat eating can be dangerous, but has been adopted by most human cultures, suggests that the benefits of consuming meat override the disadvantages. This suggests that the tendency has been shaped by evolutionary forces, due to its survival value.

Issues, debates and approaches

- Critics of evolutionary theory argue that it is an explanation of how things came to be and thus is not falsifiable, as it cannot be tested like a truly scientific theory should be able to be tested. However, this is not so, because the basic idea behind food preferences is that they indicate which foods aid survival and reproduction, and which should be avoided. Therefore, such preferences and dislikes should be innate and this is testable. In other words, evolutionary theory predicts how behaviour should be, and such predictions can be examined to see whether they are valid and give support to the theory.
- The evolutionary approach can be considered part of the nature side of the nature versus nurture debate, as it sees food preferences as being biologically determined by genetic means. This neglects the nurture side of the debate, like the influence of environmental learning and cultural factors in eating behaviour.

Strengthen your learning

1. Explain how the following may affect eating behaviour, and for each one provide research evidence that illustrates its action:
   i) stomach contraction theory
   ii) dual control theory
   iii) neuropeptides and hormones
   iv) set point theory
   v) lipostatic theory
   vi) glucose theory.
2. Why might eating preferences have evolved?
3. Outline and evaluate the following, including the use of research evidence:
   i) sweet taste preference
   ii) salty taste preference
   iii) bitter/sour taste preference
   iv) meat eating preference.

Assessment Check

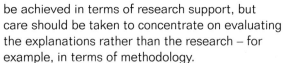

1. Outline the role of neural mechanisms involved in controlling eating behaviour. (8 marks)

2. Evaluate evolutionary explanations of food preference. (16 marks)

3. Discuss evolutionary explanations of food preference. (24 marks)

4. Outline an evolutionary explanation of one food preference. (4 marks)

5. Outline and evaluate the role of neural mechanisms involved in controlling eating behaviour. (20 marks)

Examination guidance

Question 1 only requires descriptive material, so offering evaluative material is not creditworthy and wastes valuable examination time best spent answering another question. Question 2 is similar in having a specific focus; this time only evaluation of evolutionary explanations is required. This could be achieved in terms of research support, but care should be taken to concentrate on evaluating the explanations rather than the research – for example, in terms of methodology.

The term 'discuss' in question 3 means both describe and evaluate evolutionary explanations. As the evaluation scores more credit, 16 marks as opposed to 8, more time and effort should be spent on this element.

Care should be taken in question 4 to only offer one food preference – for example, the salty food preference. If more than one was offered, all would be marked, but only the best one credited. Question 5 calls for a brief outline, as only 4 marks are on offer. It would be best to move on quickly to the evaluation, where there are 16 marks to be earned. Material on neurotransmitters, hormones and so on, must be explicitly linked to neural mechanisms to gain credit. The same is true in question 1.

Eating disorders

Anorexia and bulimia nervosa are two fairly common eating disorders that have attracted a lot of press in recent years and that have become more predominant in the population. However, this book concentrates on obesity, which is arguably more problematic, having reached epidemic proportions and causing huge health implications. There are several psychological explanations for obesity, which divide broadly into psychological and biological models. Only through rigorously conducted research can a full understanding of the condition be reached and effective treatments be created and applied.

Obesity

When fat accumulates to an extent that body mass index (BMI) is 30 kg/m², then a person is defined as clinically obese. Although clearly an eating disorder with a devastating impact on both physical and psychological health, obesity, unlike anorexia and bulimia nervosa, is not classed as a mental disorder. In Britain in 2008, 24 per cent of people were obese, with levels increasing worldwide. In the USA it is the second biggest cause of preventable death, being linked to cardiovascular diseases and diabetes, with 9 per cent of total health costs being attributed to the condition. Various factors contribute to obesity, and only by gaining insight into the condition will it be successfully addressed.

> For a video presentation of what obesity is, how to determine it and what the consequences are, go to www.youtube.com/watch?v=8HSqE1U_m_0 and www.youtube.com/watch?v=TyUu0EUjD-s&feature=channel

Psychology in action

Therapies for eating disorders

Practical applications are created from psychological explanations and theories. These should be of positive benefit to society, because the knowledge on which they are based is generated from a rigorous process of carefully conducted research. A main area of such practical applications is that of therapies for all sorts of mental disorders, and as psychologists have learned more about the motivations and attitudes underpinning eating behaviour, this knowledge has helped to form effective ways to combat eating disorders. The work performed at Rhodes Farm displays this perfectly.

Rhodes Farm is a residential centre, more like a boarding school, near London, for children with eating disorders. Started by Dr Dee Dawson in 1991 when it was her family home, the centre has places for 32 children, where treatment is received while a family style of life is maintained. Treatment is based on the philosophy that those with eating disorders need specialist care and that hospitals are more suited to the physically rather than the psychologically sick. A therapeutic environment is created where children are cared for in a nurturing way, with clear goals and plans, a predictable, structured programme, and continual help and support. Ultimately, though, nothing is imposed; it is the children who make their own healthy choices, with expert guidance.

Negotiations help to set attainable target weights, and treatment goals that are broken down into small, achievable units, alongside a full educational and activities programme. Antisocial and ritualistic eating behaviours are gradually broken down, and parents are also empowered to help their children regain and maintain health. Motivational reinforcements are used to reward progress – for instance, children move on to using an unsupervised kitchen as they improve. Each child also receives individual therapy at least once a week, with an integrated approach using tailored therapies, such as cognitive behavioural therapy and psychoanalytical psychotherapy. Group and family therapy sessions also occur, and each child has a key nurse.

Not surprisingly, 90 per cent of patients are on track towards weight targets at any given time, and the success of Rhodes Farm can be seen as being due to the dedication and skill of its staff, coupled with the solid, tested psychological knowledge that forms its core.

Psychological explanations

The psychodynamic explanation

The psychodynamic explanation of human behaviour emanates from the work of Freud; it sees adult problem behaviours as being due to unresolved conflicts occurring during childhood development through psychosexual stages.

The psychodynamic explanation sees obesity particularly as arising from unresolved conflicts, such as emotional deprivation or overindulgence, during the oral stage, where the libido is focused on the mouth. An adult personality characterised by oral gratification develops and manifests itself through overeating. It is also possible that obesity may be linked in some cases to other factors, such as depression or low self-esteem, with these factors being explicable by psychodynamic means.

You can view life at Rhodes Farm in a video documentary by following these links:

www.youtube.com/watch?v=uonpD6cXtO4
www.youtube.com/watch?v=hRY2acESlAs
www.youtube.com/watch?v=vyzjhRfBuFk
www.youtube.com/watch?v=nur3WXRKjzU
www.youtube.com/watch?v=LpiKBvYCmqk

The psychodynamic explanation can be tested by seeing whether psychotherapy reveals underlying, common, childhood–based traumas, and whether psychodynamic therapies help to alleviate the condition.

Classic research

Felliti (2001)

Sleep-eating and the dynamics of morbid obesity, weight loss and regain of weight in five patients

It is difficult to imagine that all cases of obesity can be explained in terms of one psychological model; indeed, it is a strong possibility that obesity has many different causes. In this instance, the researcher reports on five cases of sleep-eating, a condition where people consume food while asleep, all of which suggest a psychodynamic explanation.

Aim

To report and assess five cases of sleep-eating in morbidly obese participants with a history of up and down fluctuations.

Procedure

A case study method was used, where five participants being treated for morbid obesity and sleep-eating self-reported on their condition.

Findings

Case 1: 25-year-old female nurse weighing 410 pounds. Dieted to 132 pounds 1 year later. Returned to 400 pounds faster than she had lost the weight, generally as a result of sleep-eating. She was sexually molested from the age of 5 years.

Case 2: 47-year-old female probation officer who was sexually molested by her father. Raped at age 20. At 27 years weighed 140 pounds and married the first of four husbands. Her weight fluctuated widely with marriage and divorce cycles.

Case 3: 55-year-old housewife who was molested by family members and neighbours as a child. Became obese during a traumatic marriage. Had episodes of losing and regaining 150 pounds of weight in short periods. Was unaware of her sleep-eating.

Case 4: 57-year-old morbidly obese female who had been lean as a child. Continually molested from age 10. Gained 150 pounds through sleep-eating.

Case 5: 31-year-old from a troubled family. Became obese at high school. Highly promiscuous from an early age and heavy drug taker. Became celibate and lost 200 pounds. Became promiscuous again, started sleep-eating and put on 100 pounds.

continued ...

...continued

Conclusions

There is a relationship between childhood abuse/sexual behaviour, sleep-eating and obesity, which can be understood by interpreting such behaviour as an unconscious protective device and anxiety reducer, with eating being seen as a de-stressor and obesity reducing sexual attractiveness.

Evaluation

- Other factors may have played a role too – for example, case 1 had a mother over 400 pounds and siblings of similar weight, suggesting a genetic component.
- The findings come from self-reports, which are reliant on accurate, full and honest recall. However, some evidence, such as sleep-eating, was verified by witnesses.

Research in focus

Before Felliti's (2001) research could be published, it had to be subjected to peer review.

Outline the process of peer review and explain why it needs to occur.

What criticisms are there of peer review?

Evaluation

The psychodynamic explanation

- This explanation may only be true for a few people, as the vast majority of obese people have not suffered such abuse, nor do they indulge in sleep-eating.
- Obesity has grown to epidemic proportions, but there is no evidence of a parallel rise in unresolved childhood conflicts, casting doubt on the explanation.
- Cases of depression, and so on, linked to obesity, may actually be an effect of obesity rather than a cause.

Behaviourist explanations

Behaviourism sees obesity occurring through maladaptive overeating behaviours, though if this is true, it should be possible to use learning experiences to eradicate the maladaptive eating behaviours, replacing them with adaptive ones. Behaviourism suggests three means by which obesity could arise:

1. **Classical conditioning** – obesity is seen as arising through food cues becoming associated with the natural pleasure response that eating food brings – for example, coming to associate eating with watching TV.

2. **Operant conditioning** – obesity is seen as arising through food being used to reinforce (reward) desirable behaviour and for not exhibiting undesirable behaviour – for example, being given a takeaway meal for getting good marks at school.

3. **Social learning theory** – obesity is seen as being caused by the observation and imitation of obese role models. If parents are obese, children may copy their eating behaviours, and if obese people are portrayed in a positive manner in the media – for example, that fat people are jolly – then overeating and being sedentary may be imitated to try to achieve parity with the role models.

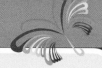

Behaviourist explanations can be tested by seeing whether therapies based on the approach are effective in addressing obesity.

Research: behaviourist explanations

- Foster (2006) found that treatments based on classical conditioning are successful, as they help patients to identify cues triggering inappropriate eating and to learn new responses to them. Therefore, causes may be due to classical conditioning too.

- Wing *et al.* (2002) found that treatments based on learning new responses to inappropriate cues led to average weight loss of 15.6 kg in 18 months, lending support to the explanation.

- Jackson (2008) found that using food to reinforce good behaviour in children creates a compulsion that leads to obesity, which suggests that operant conditioning in childhood is to blame.

- Devlin and Yanovski (1995) reported that operant conditioning techniques were successful in reinforcing healthy eating practices, resulting in an average weight loss after 5 months of between 15 and 20 pounds. This supports the idea of operant conditioning being a cause.

- Hardeman *et al.* (2000) reported that treating obesity by role models encouraging healthy lifestyles led to significant weight loss, lending support to the social learning explanation.

Evaluation

Behaviourist explanations

- Treatments based on classical conditioning have the benefit of creating specific goals that can be easily measured and identify clearly what is required. By examining cues leading to overeating, it is possible to identify areas where behaviour modifications can be made to prevent future overeating.

- The fact that treatments based on the behaviourist explanation help to treat obesity does not necessarily support the explanation. The concept of treatment aetiology fallacy believes that it is a mistaken notion that the success of a treatment reveals the cause of a disorder.

- Food is a prime reinforcer and presents many opportunities to be used as reinforcement for desirable behaviour, which lends strength to the idea of operant conditioning being involved in obesity.

- Variations in rates of obesity in different cultures, subcultures and genders may be explicable by reference to using food as a reinforcement differently between separate groups of people.

- Therapies to address obesity based on social learning have only short-term success, suggesting that underlying biological and cognitive factors are more important. Also, it is difficult to explain the huge rise in obesity as being due to learning factors.

You are the researcher

Design a study that compares the psychodynamic and behaviourist explanations of obesity. Remember that this study will have to be both practical and ethical.

You will need to consider how both approaches explain the onset of the condition in order to make a comparison.

In what way(s) would your study generate data and how will this be analysed?

Cognitive explanations

Cognitive explanations go beyond behaviourism, which only relates to observable behaviour, and instead focuses on the faulty thought processes that direct the maladaptive behaviours leading to obesity – for example, 'I need to eat a lot to maintain the energy to work'. Food and food-related materials are seen as becoming predominant in information processing, with a strong emotional component also at play that sees individuals constantly thinking about food and seeking opportunities to eat. Cognitive explanations can be tested by seeing whether faulty thought processes are related to overeating, and whether therapies based on the cognitive approach are successful in treating obesity.

Research: cognitive explanations

- Braet and Crombez (2001) found that obese children were hypersensitive to food-related words, suggesting an information-processing bias for food stimuli, leading to obesity.

- Cserjesi *et al.* (2007) examined cognitive profiles of obese boys, finding them deficient in attention capabilities, suggesting that childhood obesity involves cognitive deficits.

- O'Rourke *et al.* (2008) reviewed several methods of treating obesity, finding that cognitive behavioural therapy significantly improved weight loss, which suggests that cognitive factors may be involved in the development of obesity.

Evaluation

Cognitive explanations

- Attention deficits may be an effect of being obese. Elias (2003) found that early-onset long-term obesity leads to a decline in cognitive functioning, weakening the cognitive explanation as a cause of obesity.
- The success of therapies based on the cognitive approach suggests that cognitive factors may be involved in developing obesity. However, as with behavioural therapies, the concept of *treatment aetiology fallacy* believes that the success of a treatment doesn't necessarily reveal the cause of a disorder.

Contemporary research

Sullivan *et al.* (2007)

Personality characteristics in obesity and their relationship with successful weight loss

One proposed explanation for obesity is that obese individuals share common personality characteristics; it has been suggested that the trait of novelty seeking may be involved in obesity and difficulties in losing weight, because high novelty seeking indicates a strong appetite drive. This team of researchers decided to test this notion by conducting personality tests and looking for common characteristics in those who found weight loss difficult.

Aims

To see whether personality characteristics differ between lean and obese persons and between obese persons who were successful and unsuccessful in achieving behavioural therapy-induced weight loss.

Procedure

The Temperament and Character Inventory (TCI) personality measurement test was given to 264 lean participants and 239 obese participants enrolled in weekly group behavioural therapy and diet education sessions for 22 weeks.

Findings

Compared with lean participants, obese participants scored higher in novelty seeking, lower in persistence and lower in self-directedness.

continued ...

...continued

Obese participants who were successful in losing at least 10 per cent of body weight after 22 weeks of behavioural therapy scored lower in novelty seeking than those who were unsuccessful.

Conclusions

Personality traits differ between lean and obese persons.

High scores in novelty seeking are associated with decreased success in achieving behavioural therapy-induced weight loss.

Evaluation

- Obese people who seek weight reduction therapy differ in personality characteristics from obese people in the general population, so the findings may not be generalisable to obese people as a whole.

- There is evidence to suggest that individual variations in novelty seeking are mediated by genetic variability in dopamine transmission, putting the explanation into the biological arena. Wiesbeck *et al.* (1995) found that novelty seeking was related to dopaminergic activity, though in brain areas not directly associated with personality traits.

- One practical application of this research is that weight loss programmes should be designed to take personality traits into consideration.

Issues, debates and approaches

- The development of psychological explanations for obesity has led to the introduction of practical applications in the form of treatments for the condition, with the most successful being cognitive behavioural therapy. Behavioural treatments are successful too, but more as a short-term than a long-term remedy.

- Psychological explanations and research studies of obesity are applicable only to cultures where obesity exists. It is culturally biased, therefore, to apply such theoretical models and findings to cultural groupings where obesity is not found and where, indeed, starvation may be an everyday issue.

Biological explanations

Genetic factors

There may be an inherited genetic basis to obesity, with some individuals being more genetically predisposed to become obese, and those with multiple genes towards obesity having an increased risk of developing the condition. The genetic explanation in combination with the evolutionary explanation offers a reason as to why only certain people become obese (see 'Evolutionary explanations' on page 194). The genetic explanation can be tested by seeing whether obese people share genetic similarity.

Research: genetic factors

- Frayling *et al.* (2007) found that people with two copies of the fat mass and obesity gene FTO had a 70 per cent increased risk of becoming obese, while people with only one copy had only a 30 per cent increased risk, supporting a genetic explanation.

- Wardle *et al.* (2008) assessed twins on BMI and body fat deposits, finding a heritability figure of 77 per cent, suggesting that genetic factors have a major influence on obesity.

- Sorensen and Stunkard (1994) compared the degree of obesity of adopted participants with their adoptive and biological parents, finding that an individual's weight was more correlated with biological relatives, lending support to the genetic explanation.

- Willer *et al.* (2008) located six new genes associated with obesity. These variant genes increase the chances of being obese by up to 25 per cent, suggesting that genetics does play a role in creating a predisposition to obesity.

Evaluation

Genetic factors

- Musani *et al.* (2008) suggested that obese people may be more fertile, reproduce more and ultimately increase genes favouring obesity in the population.
- Most cases of obesity are not explained by genetics alone. Genes do not determine obesity; they need an environment in which to express themselves.
- Genes cannot explain the upsurge in obesity. Genes have not changed, but environmental factors, like the availability of food have, suggesting that environment plays the larger role.
- The discovery of genes related to obesity may lead to effective gene therapies for the treatment of the condition.

Neurological factors

The hypothalamus is the brain structure that has been identified as playing the central role in the regulation of eating. Therefore, neurological explanations focus on the idea that faulty functioning of the hypothalamus is associated with the development of obesity. Attention has focused on the workings of the VMH, which in a normally functioning person acts as the satiety centre, informing an individual when they are full so that eating can cease. Research has also been directed at specific mechanisms. For example, the action of *leptin*, a hormone produced by fat cells in the stomach in proportion to the amount of body fat, on the *proopiomelanocortin* (POMC) and NPY neurones is seen as especially important. The amount of leptin influences these neurones, which regulate appetite.

Neurological factors are investigated by studying animals, and the faulty-functioning brain structures and neurological mechanisms of obese individuals.

Research: neurological factors

- Reeves and Plum (1969) conducted a post-mortem on an obese female, finding that her VMH had been destroyed, which suggests that the hypothalamus is associated with the development of obesity.

- Friedman (2005) reports that obese people do produce leptin, but its ability to suppress the neuron POMC is blocked, so their appetite stays high and they gain weight up to a point thought to be genetically determined, demonstrating the role of neurological factors in combination with genetics.

- Stice *et al.* (2008) found that obese people have a poorly functioning dorsal striatum, which leads to lessened dopamine signalling in the brain, causing them to overeat. This demonstrates the role of the neurotransmitter dopamine in determining obesity.

Evaluation

Neurological factors

- The evidence linking dopamine to obesity tends to be correlational, so it is not clear whether dopamine is a cause or an effect of being obese.
- It was hoped that leptin injections would prove an effective treatment for obesity, but they only work for a few people, casting doubt on the importance of leptin's role.
- Much research into leptin was carried out on mice, so the results may not be generalisable to humans.

Hormonal factors

Several hormones have been associated with having possible effects on the development of obesity. Aside from leptin and its relationship to the NPY and POMC neurones, three hormones in particular have attracted research interest:

1. **Insulin** – a hormone associated with the storage and use of energy. It has attracted attention due to the link between insulin resistance and obesity. There is a link here to the genetic explanation, as insulin resistance mainly occurs due to genetic factors.

2. **Cortisol** – a *glucocorticoid* hormone exerting a strong metabolic effect. Individuals with high cortisol levels tend to overeat, leading to weight increase and eventual obesity.

3. **Ghrelin** – a growth hormone found in the stomach that is associated with slowing down metabolism and decreasing the body's ability to burn fat.

Research: hormonal factors

- Kahn and Flier (2000) found that individuals with insulin resistance who eat large amounts of junk food, which has a high glycaemic value, tend to become obese. This indicates that insulin is involved in the development of obesity.

- Epel *et al.* (2001) found that overeating of sweet foods occurred in females with high cortisol levels, suggesting that cortisol is linked to the causality of obesity.

- Yildiz *et al.* (2004) found that ghrelin levels increase during the day in thinner people, suggesting a flaw in the circadian system of obese individuals.

Evaluation

Hormonal factors

- Insulin is not regarded as a direct cause of obesity, nor is its influence on obesity fully understood.
- Although cortisol is linked to obesity, it is not known whether cortisol is a cause or an effect of obesity.
- Sun *et al.* (2006) reported that ghrelin antagonists, drugs designed to combat obesity, may actually be effective against diabetes rather than obesity, casting doubt on ghrelin being a causative agent for obesity.

Evolutionary explanations

Obesity may be an evolutionary hangover. In the Pleistocene era, humans existed in a harsh world in which survival was dependent on expending a lot of physical effort to find food, and food was not always plentiful or constantly available. Therefore, selective pressure favoured those who were able to store excess energy as fat to see themselves through times of famine. Nowadays humans live in a world of constant, plentiful, easily available food, but evolution causes bodies to behave as if they were still living in the ancestral past, and because the gene pool has not altered substantially, genes that once favoured survival now favour obesity.

> A clear, comprehensive account of the thrifty gene hypothesis, and its counterpart the fertile plain hypothesis, can be found at www.independent.co.uk/news/science/scientists-link-obesity-to-thrifty-gene-of-our-ancestors-596874.html This explains the innate biology underpinning why some become obese, while others remain lean.

Fatty foods are preferred, as they are so energy-rich, and humans overeat in order to lay down fat stores that in ancient times would see them through the regular periods of food scarcity. Evolution also sees humans as preferring sedentary lifestyles, as in the EEA conserving energy was essential to survival. Modern humans continue to behave as if food supplies are irregular, resulting in dysfunctional overeating. Humans may also be vulnerable to overeating foods that were not part of their evolutionary past, such as liquid calories, because they do not trigger neural mechanisms that control appetite.

Evolution explains why some individuals seem more vulnerable to dramatic weight increases, by reference to the *thrifty gene model*, which believes that in the EEA there was a selective advantage for people with insulin resistance, as they would have been able to metabolise food more efficiently. This was advantageous in times of food scarcity, but now that food is constantly available in certain parts of the world, it leads to obesity.

Research: evolutionary explanations

- DiMeglio and Mates (2000) found that participants given liquid calories, rather than an equal amount of solid calories, put on more weight, implying that liquid calories have caused the huge increase in obesity, because humans are not shaped by evolution to cope with them.

- Bray *et al*. (2004) believed that high-fructose corn syrup (HFCS) causes obesity. Used as a drinks sweetener, its consumption in the USA increased by 1,000 per cent between 1970 and 1990, a time of increased obesity. Not a foodstuff familiar to our evolutionary ancestors, it is seen as not stimulating leptin and insulin production that normally act to regulate eating, leading to weight gain.

- Friedman *et al*. (1994) found heightened evidence of the thrifty gene in the Pacific islanders of Kosrae, where only a small minority, who remain lean but possess the same eating habits, are seen as not possessing the gene.

- Rowe *et al*. (2007) found Pima Indians who have high levels of obesity from a thrifty metabolism that allows them to metabolise food more efficiently. Once an advantage in times of food scarcity, it now leads to obesity, supporting the evolutionary thrifty gene hypothesis.

Figure 5.13 Heightened obesity rates among Pacific islanders may be due to a high incidence of the thrifty gene

Evaluation

Evolutionary explanations

- The idea that foodstuffs not present in the EEA cause obesity can be criticised on the grounds that obesity levels have also risen in countries where HFCS is not commonly used.
- The thrifty gene hypothesis is able to explain not just why people tend to overeat to prepare for times of food scarcity, but why only people with the gene would become obese.
- The thrifty gene hypothesis explains why identifiable groups of people who do not have the gene are able to eat lots and not put on weight, such as the people of the Nile delta, where historically there were no food shortages.

Issues, debates and approaches

- By understanding the adaptive significance of obesity, it may be possible to develop practical applications to treat the condition successfully. Such applications would need to be directed against sedentary lifestyles, which contribute greatly to an increase in bodily fat deposits, as these were not lifestyles found in the EEA. Genetic profiling could help to identify those most at risk, like those carrying the thrifty gene, so that treatments could be more focused on individuals with the greatest need.
- Biological explanations of obesity can be seen as reductionist in only concentrating on physiological factors of the condition. A more holistic approach is necessary, which focuses on a combination of biological and psychological factors.

Strengthen your learning

1a. What does the psychodynamic explanation see as the cause of obesity?
1b. What evidence is there to support this view?
1c. What limitations are there of this explanation?
4a. How does the behaviourist explanation see obesity arising in terms of:
    i)   classical conditioning?
    ii) operant conditioning?
    iii) social learning theory?
4b. What evidence is there to support these explanations?
4c. What are the strengths and weaknesses of behaviourist explanations?
5a. What does the cognitive explanation see as the cause of obesity?
5b. What evidence is there to support this view?
5c. What criticisms are there of the cognitive explanation?
6a. Why might personality factors be involved in the onset of obesity?
6b. To what extent is this viewpoint supported?
7. For the following:
   • genetic factors
   • neurological factors
   • hormonal factors

   explain:
   a) how they may be involved in the onset of obesity
   b) to what extent they are supported by research evidence
   c) what other strengths and weaknesses these explanations have.
8. Why might obesity be an evolutionary hangover?
9. How can the thrifty gene hypotheses explain differences in vulnerability to obesity?
10. To what extent are evolutionary explanations supported by research?

Assessment Check

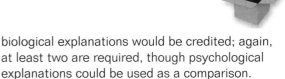

1. Outline psychological explanations of one eating disorder. (8 marks)

2. Evaluate biological explanations of one eating disorder. (16 marks)

3. Compare psychological and biological explanations of one eating disorder. (24 marks)

4. Outline one biological explanation of one eating disorder. (4 marks)

5. Outline and evaluate one psychological explanation of one eating disorder. (20 marks)

Examination guidance

In question 1, only descriptive material will be considered in relation to psychological explanations, of which there must be at least two. If more than two explanations were offered, less detail would be expected. Describing biological explanations would not be creditworthy. In question 2, only evaluative material that is centred on biological explanations would be credited; again, at least two are required, though psychological explanations could be used as a comparison.

Question 3 requires both psychological and biological explanations to be outlined, with a reasonable balance necessary to access the top band of marks. The evaluation could assess both approaches in terms of individual weaknesses and strengths, as well as the relative strengths and weaknesses in comparison to each other.

If more than one biological explanation was offered in response to question 4, all would be marked, but only the best one credited. The requirement for an outline in question 5 is the same as for question 4, but this time in terms of a psychological explanation, for 4 marks. The evaluation could use other explanations, both psychological and biological, as a form of comparison.

Summing up

- Eating is essential to survival and to normal healthy development and relates to many psychological areas.

- Mood can affect eating behaviour, either as a general effect or by individual differences relating to stress influences.

- Different eating practices are transmitted through social and cultural influences.

- Health concerns can mediate attitudes to food, with differences apparent between individuals and groups.

- Dieting is a form of restrained eating involving voluntary restriction of food intake.

- Restraint theory sees most diets failing due to episodes of overeating.

- There are other reasons for failure, such as setting unrealistic targets, cognitive shifts and loss of motivation.

- Dieting succeeds when weight is lost in an attainable fashion and strategies utilised to prevent relapse, such as reinforcements and social support.

- Goal setting is important in establishing and attaining targets and maintaining confidence and motivation.

- Dual control theory sees the hypothalamus as the feeding centre of the brain, with the LH as the feeding centre and the VMH as the satiety centre.

- Set point theory sees body weight as determined by individual metabolisms, which can be influenced by eating patterns, exercise, and so on.

- Evolutionary theories see taste preferences as arising from their survival values, with sweet and salty taste preferences being favoured, plus the ability to detect and avoid bitter-tasting foods, as they are indicative of toxins.

- Meat eating does not seem to be an innate tendency, but may have arisen for various reasons, such as being energy-rich and constantly available.

- Obesity is a serious disorder, with negative physical and psychological consequences.

- Psychological theories include the psychodynamic explanation that sees the condition as arising from unresolved childhood trauma; the behavioural explanation that sees the condition as being learned; and the cognitive explanation that sees obesity resulting from irrational thought processes.

- Biological explanations include perceiving a genetic link to the condition or that faulty neurological mechanisms may be to blame, with hormonal factors also seen as playing a role.

- Obesity may be an evolutionary hangover, with individuals overeating fatty foods to lay down fat deposits for times of food scarcity.

- The thrifty gene hypothesis sees some individuals as more vulnerable to becoming obese through overeating than others.

6 Gender

**Psychological explanations of
gender development**   **199**
  Cognitive developmental theory   200
  Gender schema theory   203
Biological influences on gender   **206**
  The role of hormones and genes in
  gender development   206
  Evolutionary explanations of
  gender roles   211
  The biosocial approach to gender
  development   214
  Gender dysphoria   216
Social influences on gender   **221**
  Cultural influences on gender role   230
Summing up   **234**

Decoding the specification

The specification outlines what must be studied to enable you to answer any examination question you might face. As Kohlberg's cognitive developmental theory is specifically named, you should have sufficient knowledge to describe and evaluate the theory. A similar requirement is necessary for gender schema theory, or you might be asked to compare the two theories.

Three biological influences on gender are specified, the role of hormones and genes in gender development, evolutionary explanations of gender and the biosocial approach, including gender dysphoria. Each of these is a separate sub-topic in itself, and questions could focus on one specific sub-topic or several.

When studying social influences, the influences named of parents, peers, schools and media are only examples, so would not be specifically stated in examination questions. Therefore, any other relevant influences would be equally creditworthy.

There is also an explicit requirement to have a working knowledge of cultural influences on gender.

Psychological explanations of gender development

According to Bussey and Bandura (2004):

'Gender development is a fundamental issue, because some of the most important aspects of people's lives, like the talents they cultivate, the conceptions they hold of themselves, and others, the social opportunities and constraints they encounter, and the social life and occupational paths they pursue, are heavily prescribed by societal gender typing. It's the primary basis on which people get differentiated, with pervasive effects on their daily lives.'

IN THE NEWS

Caster Semenya has male sex organs and no womb or ovaries

Figure 6.01

Eighteen-year-old South African athlete Caster Semenya caused controversy after her stunning victory in the World Championship 800 metres in Berlin recently. Rumours abounded that she was a hermaphrodite – a person with both male and female characteristics – with medical tests reported to have found she has no womb or ovaries and possesses three times the usual amount of testosterone for a female. Indeed scans indicated the existence of internal testes, male organs that produce testosterone.

Establishing gender is not easy; indeed, the female gender verification test for Olympic sports was dropped in 1999 for being 'scientifically complicated', and the International Amateur Athletics Federation's (IAAF) threshold for when a female is considered ineligible to compete as a female is unclear. There have been several cases of hermaphrodites in sport, like Mary Weston, the English shot-putter; and controversy reigned in 1975, when Richard Raskind, a father, underwent sex reassignment surgery, changed his name to Renee Richards, and was denied entry to the US tennis open for 'not being born a woman' and refusing to take chromosomal testing. This was successfully challenged in 1977 and she won the right to play as a woman without being tested. Renee was ranked as high as 20th in the world and reached the finals of the US ladies doubles before retiring in 1981. Caster Semenya was cleared to run as a woman in July 2010, though it is believed she has had prolonged treatment with female hormones.

How easy is it to determine the gender of female athletes? For a history of gender testing in sport, a background explanation of what gender is and an interactive challenge to determine whether an athlete is eligible as a female to take part in the United Earth Games, go to www.hhmi.org/biointeractive/gendertest/gendertest.html

Key terms

Sex – whether an individual is biologically female or male

Gender – the social and psychological characteristics of males and females

Gender role – culturally determined male and female behaviours

Gender schema – a means of understanding gender knowledge that changes with environmental experience

Cognitive developmental theory

The focus is on how children's thinking develops, with thinking occurring in qualitatively different stages. Gender identity is perceived as the outcome of children actively structuring their own experiences, and not as a passive outcome of social learning. Cognitive developmental theory regards thinking and understanding as the basis behind gender identity and gender role behaviour. Kohlberg perceives children as developing an understanding of gender in three distinct stages, with gender role behaviour only apparent after an understanding that gender is fixed and constant. Gender schema theory shares the same cognitive view of gender understanding, but perceives children as having schemas for gender at an earlier stage than Kohlberg.

An important difference between the two theories is that schema theory believes that children only need gender identity to develop gender-consistent behaviours, while Kohlberg sees the acquisition of gender constancy as necessary first.

Kohlberg's (1966) theory of gender constancy

Other theories of gender role development, like social learning theory (SLT), assume that children know which gender they are and proceed to learn appropriate roles. Kohlberg sees such knowledge arising from children actively constructing an understanding of the world through interacting with it.

Kohlberg's theory was influenced by earlier theories of cognitive development that saw children progressing through stages of understanding. Gender concepts are seen as occurring through environmental interactions, restricted by cognitive capabilities at a given time.

Children's discovery that they are male or female causes them to identify with members of their own gender, not the other way round, as SLT and psychoanalytic theories suggest. Kohlberg sees children as acquiring an understanding of the concepts 'male' and 'female' in three stages, attaining increasingly more sophisticated gender concepts, with a new stage only appearing after thinking has matured to a certain point. Consequently, children understand gender differently at different ages, with gender concepts developing as children actively structure their social experiences. It is not, therefore, a passive social learning process occurring through observation and imitation.

It is only after gender consistency is reached, at about 7 years, that children start to develop gender concepts to suit their own gender.

Stages in the development of gender identity

Stage 1: Gender labelling or basic gender identity – this occurs between 1.5 and 3 years, and refers to children's recognition of being male or female. Kohlberg perceives knowing one's gender as a realisation that allows individuals to understand and categorise the world. This knowledge is fragile, with 'man', 'woman', 'boy' and 'girl' little more than labels, equivalent to personal names. Children sometimes choose incorrect labels and do not realise that boys become men and girls become women.

Stage 2: Gender stability – by the age of 3 to 5 years, most children recognise that people retain gender for life, but rely on superficial, physical signs to

determine gender. If someone is superficially transformed – for example, a woman having long hair cut short – children infer that the person has changed gender.

Stage 3: Gender constancy or consistency – at around the age of 6 to 7, children realise that gender is permanent; if a woman has her head shaved, her gender remains female. Gender constancy represents a kind of *conservation*, an understanding that things remain the same despite changing appearance. Gender understanding is complete only when children appreciate that gender is constant over time and situations.

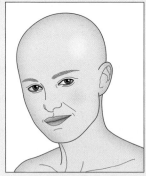

Once children acquire gender constancy, they value the behaviours and attitudes associated with their gender. They then identify with adult figures possessing the qualities seen as relevant to their concept of themselves as male or female. This entails imitating same–sex models and following sex-appropriate activities. Maccoby and Jacklin (1974) called this 'self-socialisation', because it does not depend directly on external reinforcement.

Figure 6.02 With gender constancy, children realise that a woman with a shaved head remains female

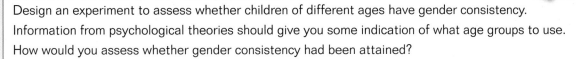

You are the researcher

Design an experiment to assess whether children of different ages have gender consistency.

Information from psychological theories should give you some indication of what age groups to use.

How would you assess whether gender consistency had been attained?

Classic research

Slaby and Frey (1975)

Gender constancy and selective attention to same-sex models

SLT saw gender development as based on observation and imitation of same-sex models, while Kohlberg's cognitive development theory saw children's understanding of gender as a permanent attribute. The researchers wanted to see whether children's attention to same-sex models was influenced by level of gender constancy.

Aim

To see whether children with higher levels of gender constancy show more selective attention to same-sex models.

Procedure

Fifty-five children aged between 2 and 5 years had their level of gender constancy assessed by a series of 14 questions and counter-questions.

Some questions tested gender labelling. For example:

- Is this a girl or a boy? (showing boy/girl doll)
- Are you a girl or a boy?

Some questions tested gender stability. For example:

- When you were a little baby, were you a little girl or a little boy?
- When you grow up, will you be a mummy or a daddy?

continued ...

...continued

Some questions tested gender consistency: For example:

- If you wore [opposite of child's sex] clothes, would you be a girl or a boy?
- Could you be a [opposite of child's sex] if you wanted to be?

Children were classified as low on gender constancy if they answered wrongly on gender labelling or gender stability items, and high otherwise. Several weeks later, the children watched a short film of a man and a woman performing gender-stereotypical activities on different sides of the screen.

The amount of time that children's eyes were fixated on each side of the screen was measured.

Findings

High gender-constancy boys watched the male model more than the female model, but this was less so for low gender-constancy boys. The opposite was true for girls.

The selective attention to the same-sex model was stronger among the high-constancy boys than among the high-constancy girls; indeed, both boys and girls spent more total time watching the male model than the female model.

Table 6.01 Mean percentage of time spent watching the male rather than the female model

SEX OF PARTICIPANT	LOW GENDER CONSTANCY	HIGH GENDER CONSTANCY
Boys	47.9%	61.4%
Girls	57.8%	50.8%

Conclusions

Children with higher levels of gender constancy show more selective attention to same-sex models than those with low levels of gender constancy.

Evaluation

- The results indicate that children at this stage watch their own gender in order to acquire information about gender-appropriate behaviour, backing up Kohlberg's notion that gender development is an active process.
- The results support Kohlberg's claim that gender constancy is a cause of the imitation of same-sex models, rather than an effect.
- The results indicate the influence of both cognitive and social factors in gender development.
- The results can be considered evidence for self-socialisation, where children actively construct gender-role knowledge through purposeful monitoring of the social environment.

Research: Kohlberg's theory

- McConaghy (1979) found that if a doll was dressed in transparent clothing so its genitals were visible, children of 3 to 5 years judged its gender by its clothes, not its genitals, supporting the idea of children of this age using superficial physical indicators to determine gender.

- Rabban (1950) found, by asking questions about gender, that children's thinking changes as they age. By 3 years of age most children demonstrated gender identity, but did not have an understanding of what gender they would grow into. By 5 years of age, 97 per cent demonstrated gender stability, supporting the stages of Kohlberg's theory.

- Thompson (1975) found that by 2 years, children given pictures of boys and girls could select same-sex pictures, demonstrating that children could self-label and identify the gender of others. By 3 years, 90 per cent showed gender identity, compared to only 76 per cent of 2-year-olds, showing the developmental nature of the concept.

- Frey and Ruble (1992) informed children that certain toys were either 'boy' or 'girl' toys. Boys who had achieved gender constancy chose 'boy' toys, even when they were uninteresting. Girls of the same stage exhibited similar tendencies to a lesser degree.

Evaluation

Kohlberg's theory

- Research evidence suggests that the concepts of gender identity, stability and constancy occur in that order across many cultures, lending support to Kohlberg's theory and suggesting a biological mechanism.

- A problem for Kohlberg's theory is that it predicts little or no gender-specific behaviour before children acquire gender constancy. But even in infancy, boys and girls show preferences for stereotypical male and female toys. Children generally demonstrate gender-appropriate behaviours and reward gender-appropriate behaviours in peers, before they have reached gender constancy, casting doubt on Kohlberg's idea of universal stages of development.

- Kohlberg may have underestimated the age at which gender cognition occurs. Bem (1981) believes that children have an awareness of gender and gender-specific behaviours from around 2 years, due to the development of *gender schemas*.

- The theory concentrates on cognitive factors and may overlook important cultural and social influences, like parents and friends.

Gender schema theory: Martin and Halverson (1981)/Bem (1981)

Gender schema theory sees gender identity alone as providing children with motivation to assume sex-typed behaviour patterns.

The difference between this approach and Kohlberg's is that for initial understanding of gender to develop, children need not understand that gender is permanent. Like SLT, this approach sees children as learning 'appropriate' patterns of behaviour by observation. But, consistent with Kohlberg, children's active cognitive processing of information also contributes to sex-typing.

Gender schema, an organised grouping of related concepts, begins to develop at 2 to 3 years, and once children have gender identity, they accumulate knowledge about the sexes, organising this into gender schemas. Such schemas provide a basis for interpreting the environment and selecting appropriate forms of behaviour, and thus children's self-perceptions become sex-typed. *In-group schemas* are formed concerning attitudes and expectations about one's own gender, and *out-group schemas* about the other gender. Toys, games and even objects become categorised as 'for boys' or 'for girls'.

Maccoby (1998) believed that because gender is clearly an either/or category, children understand very early that this is a key distinction and it serves as a 'magnet' for new information. Alternatively, adults and other children emphasise gender differences in countless small ways.

Figure 6.03 Gender schema theory see toys becoming categorised as either 'for boys' or 'for girls'

Whatever the origin of early schema, once established, many experiences are assimilated and children show preference for same-sex playmates and for gender-stereotyped activities, actively ignoring the other gender. However, gender schema undergoes change as the children's general cognitive abilities develop.

Developmental changes in children's gender schema

- Preschoolers learn distinctions about what kinds of activities and behaviour go with each gender, by observing other children and through reinforcements received from parents – for example, 'men have short hair' and 'girls play with dolls'. They also learn gender 'scripts', sequences of events that go with each gender, like 'cooking dinner' (female) and 'building with tools' (male).

- From the age of 4 to 6 years, children learn subtle and complex sets of associations for their own gender: what children of the same gender like and do not like, how they play, how they talk, what kinds of people they spend time with. Not until age 8 to 10 do children develop schemas of the opposite gender matching the complexity of the same-gender schema.

- When gender constancy develops at 5 to 6 years, children's understanding of 'what people like me do' becomes more elaborated. This 'rule' is treated as absolute.

- By late childhood and early adolescence, it is understood that 'rules' are just social conventions, and gender-role schemas become more flexible. Teenagers abandon the automatic assumption that what their own gender does is preferable, and a significant minority of teenagers define themselves as *androgynous*.

Research: gender schema theory

- Rathus (1990) found that children learn that strength is linked to the male role stereotype and weakness to the female role stereotype, and that some dimensions, including strength–weakness, are more relevant to males. This supports the idea that gender schemas provide a basis for interpreting the environment and selecting appropriate forms of behaviour, and for children's self-perceptions to become sex-typed.

- Bauer (1993) found that boys, but not girls, are aware of, and more willing to imitate, gender-matched scripts as early as 2 years old, suggesting a gender difference in when gender schemas are established.

- Martin and Little (1990) found that preschool children have gender stereotypes about what is appropriate for boys and girls, before they develop much understanding about gender, supporting the idea of the formation of gender schemas.

- Masters *et al.* (1979) found that children aged between 4 and 5 years selected toys by their gender label (boy toy/girl toy), rather than which gender was seen playing with the toy, again indicating the formation of gender schemas.

- Campbell (2000) tested infants aged between 3 and 18 months, finding that even the youngest ones had a preference for watching same-sex babies. By 9 months, boys showed an increasing tendency to pay attention to 'boy toys'. This shows that children from an early age pay more attention to their same-sex group, supporting the idea of gender schemas forming early on. This trend is more noticeable in boys.

- Poulin-Dubois *et al.* (2002) asked 2- to 3-year-olds to choose a doll to carry out stereotypical male or female jobs. Two-year-old girls could select the gender-appropriate doll, suggesting a schema for gender-appropriate tasks. By 2.5 years, boys were demonstrating the behaviour too, showing that young children learn from models on the basis of their own sex.

- Martin and Halverson (1983) asked children to recall pictures of people, finding that children under the age of 6 years recalled more gender-consistent ones – for example, a male footballer – than gender non-consistent ones – for example, a male nurse. This is in line with gender schema theory predictions.

- Aubry *et al.* (1999) performed a longitudinal study into preferences for gender-related articles. It was found that once a belief had taken hold that an item was for the opposite sex, a reduced preference for that item developed, implying that gender schemas affect behaviour.

Figure 6.04 When asked to recall pictures of people, boys recall more gender-consistent ones – for example, footballers, not nurses

Evaluation

Gender schema theory

- There is a wealth of research evidence supporting the theory, but some studies show that children act in a gender-typical way before they have developed gender schema. Eisenberg et al. (1982) found that 3- to 4-year-olds justified their gender-specific choice of toys without reference to gender stereotypes. Schaffer (1996) thinks the influence might be in the opposite direction: children's monitoring of their own and others' behaviour leading to the development of gender schemas.

- The theory explains why children's attitudes and behaviour concerning gender are rigid and lasting. They only focus on anything that confirms and strengthens their schemas, ignoring behavioural examples that contradict the theory.

- The theory predicts that as a gender schema develops, a child should exhibit behaviour consistent with perception of its own gender. Some research shows this, but there is contradictory evidence too. Campbell et al. (2002) found that 2-year-old boys and girls who possessed high levels of gender knowledge did not display preferences to play with gender-specific toys.

- When children perform activities not normally stereotypical of their gender, like a boy cooking, they adjust their thinking so the activity becomes acceptable. This implies that thinking is affected by behaviour, while cognitive schema theory predicts the opposite, therefore weakening support for the theory.

Issues, debates and approaches

- Kohlberg's theory of gender development is more of a holistic than a reductionist theory, as it combines social learning and biological developmental factors to explain how gender development occurs.

- Gender schema theory can be regarded as somewhat reductionist, as although it offers a plausible compromise between SLT and cognitive developmental theories, the theory neglects the influence of biological factors, assuming that all gender-orientated behaviour is created through cognitive means.

Strengthen your learning

1. Summarise the main points of:
   i) Kohlberg's theory of gender constancy (including his three stages)
   ii) Gender schema theory (including developmental changes).
2. In what ways are the two theories similar and in what ways are they dissimilar?
3. Use research evidence to evaluate the main strengths and weaknesses of both theories.

Assessment Check

1. Outline Kohlberg's cognitive developmental theory. (4 marks)

2. Outline and evaluate Kohlberg's cognitive developmental theory (24 marks)

3. Outline gender schema theory (8 marks)

4. Discuss gender schema theory. (20 marks)

Examination guidance

Question 1 is worth 4 marks, so provide a 'shorter' description of Kohlberg's theory, rather than a 'longer', 8-mark description. Question 2 however, has 8 marks on offer for Kohlberg's theory, so a 'longer' description is required. There's also 16 marks on offer for the evaluation, which could centre around the degree of research support for the theory, as well as pertinent, embedded IDA points, rather than low-scoring generic points tagged on at the end. Question 3 requires descriptive material only, therefore any evaluation will not be creditworthy. As 8 marks are on offer, a more substantial amount of detail would be expected.

The term 'discuss' in question 4 means to describe and evaluate. A 'short' description is needed, as that element is only worth 4 marks. More time and effort should be spent on the evaluation part, as it is worth 16 marks.

Biological influences on gender

The role of hormones and genes in gender development

Many of the physical and behavioural differences between males and females are biological. Biological sex is determined by the sex chromosomes X and Y, with an XX combination for a female and an XY combination for a male. Sex chromosomes contain genetic material that controls development as a male or female. During this process, sex hormones are produced that direct the majority of sexual development.

Gonadal hormones and sexual differentiation

The influence of hormones on sexual differentiation begins early in pregnancy and involves internal and external genitalia, as well as the brain and behaviour. According to Hines (2004), 'Infants enter the world with some predispositions to masculinity and femininity, and these predispositions appear to result largely from hormones to which they were exposed before birth.'

The gonads are originally identical in both XY and XX embryos. However, in XY individuals, genetic information on the Y chromosome causes the gonads to become testes, and by week 8 of gestation they are producing hormones, particularly the primary androgen, testosterone. If the gonads do not become testes, they become ovaries, which do not appear to produce significant amounts of hormones prenatally. The SRY gene on the Y chromosome controls whether gonads become ovaries or testes.

Consequently, XY foetuses have higher levels of testosterone than XX foetuses, particularly between 8 and 24 weeks of gestation. Between then and birth, gonadal hormone levels are low in both sexes, but a surge of testicular hormones after birth makes testosterone once again higher in boys than in girls, for about the first 6 months. When released, testosterone causes the development of male sex organs, but also acts on the hypothalamus; without this, the brain would develop as a female type. Testosterone has been associated with masculinisation of the brain, such as the development of brain areas linked to spatial skills. Similarly, the female hormone oestrogen plays a role in feminising the brain.

There are differences in the hypothalamus of males and females, with the *sexual dimorphic nucleus* considerably bigger in males; it is believed that these differences may occur through the action of sex hormones, though this is not a universal view.

During puberty, testes and ovaries play an important part in determining the secondary sexual characteristics that distinguish men from women.

Gonadal hormones, intersex conditions

Hormones influence human genitalia, but hormonal influences on behaviour are harder to establish, partly because behaviour is subject to social and other influences after birth. In addition, it is unethical to manipulate hormones experimentally in humans during early life. For this reason, natural experiments represented by cases of intersex individuals are of particular importance. For instance, congenital adrenal hyperplasia (CAH) is an inherited disorder, present at birth, which affects a baby's adrenal glands and therefore the ability to produce certain steroid hormones. Girls with CAH usually have normal internal reproductive organs, but also have male external genitalia.

Play behaviour

Interviews and observations show that CAH girls display increased preferences for male-type toys, like cars, and reduced preferences for female-type toys, like dolls. This male-typical behaviour occurs despite the girls having been surgically feminised and raised as girls.

Core gender identity

Despite Money's claim (see 'Supplementary research: the case of the penectomised twin' on page 210) that sex of rearing is more important than chromosomal or hormonal sex, evidence suggests a greater influence of biology.

Although for most CAH individuals, and other intersex conditions, core gender identity is consistent with the sex of rearing, some do experience gender dysphoria and a desire to change sex. Although dysphoria is rare among intersex individuals, it is more frequent than in the general population.

(see 'Supplementary research: the case of the penectomised twin' on page 210)

Key terms

Hormones – chemical messengers released into the bloodstream from glands

Genes – a region of DNA that controls hereditary characteristics

Evolutionary explanations – theories perceiving gender roles as serving an adaptive purpose related to survival

Biosocial approach – an explanation perceiving gender identity as arising from the interaction of environmental and biological influences

Gender dysphoria – unhappiness with one's physical sex

Sexual orientation

Although females with CAH tend to be heterosexual, they are more likely than sisters, or demographically matched controls, to report bisexual or homosexual interests. Women with CAH also report reduced erotic interest in general. These outcomes for adult sexuality could be influenced by problems related to ambiguous genitalia and surgery. Feminising surgery does not usually produce genitalia that are identical to those of normal females, and surgery can make intercourse problematic. Individuals with CAIS, an inherited inter-sex condition where babies with male sex chromosomes develop as girls because their bodies cannot respond to androgens, almost always report a heterosexual orientation towards men, and are as likely as other women to form long-term heterosexual relationships or to marry. This suggests that their inability to respond to androgens, or their feminine appearance and socialisation, is more important than the Y chromosome in determining sexual orientation.

Research: the role of hormones and genes in gender development

- Hines and Kaufman (1994) found that girls with CAH choose boys and girls equally as favourite playmates, whereas normal girls choose other girls 80–90 per cent of the time, supporting the idea that CAH girls have increased male preferences, despite feminising surgery and being raised as girls, suggesting a biological influence. This was supported by Berenbaum and Hines (1992), who found CAH girls to be more interested in male activities than sisters without the condition, which implies that male hormones have a masculinising effect on the brain during pregnancy. However, such support was undermined by Hines (1994), finding that girls with CAH, although seeming to prefer playing with boys, did not show significant differences in the amount of rough-and-tumble play to girls without the condition.

- The fact that CAH girls are more likely to have bisexual and homosexual preferences than normal girls has been shown in studies in the USA, the UK, Germany and Canada, suggesting that it is cross-cultural and therefore biologically based.

- Money and Ehrhardt (1972) found that a sample of girls whose mothers had taken drugs containing androgen during pregnancy exhibited male-type behaviours, like playing energetic sports, and an absence of female-type behaviours, like playing with dolls. This suggests that male hormones have an influence on gender behaviour.

- Koopman *et al.* (1991) found that genetically female mice lacking the SRY gene developed into male mice if the gene was implanted into them, demonstrating the important role the SRY gene plays in determining gender.

- Young (1966) gave male hormones to female mice and female hormones to male mice. The effect was a reversal of usual gender-related behaviours, suggesting that hormones have a key role in determining gender behaviour.

A good site for information about and examples of intersex conditions, run by the American Psychological Association, can be found at www.apa.org/topics/sexuality/intersex.pdf

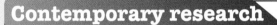

Contemporary research

Deady *et al.* (2006)

Reproductive ambition and salivary testosterone levels

Previous research linked testosterone levels with sex-specific personality traits in women. The researchers here were interested in examining the relationship between maternal personality – that is, the importance of having children – and levels of the male hormone testosterone.

Aim

To assess a possible relationship between degree of maternal personality and salivary testosterone levels in healthy adult women.

Procedure

Twenty-seven women aged between 25 and 30 years completed the Bem Sex Role Inventory (BSRI), which measures levels of masculinity, femininity and androgeny.

Additional questions were asked about maternal personality, like the importance of having children, self-rated maternal broodiness, reproductive ambition (ideal number of children, ideal own age at first child) and the importance of having a career.

Testosterone levels were measured from saliva samples.

Findings

Higher circulating testosterone levels were associated with lower scores on measures of maternal personality and reproductive ambition.

Career orientation (the importance of having a career) was not significantly associated with testosterone levels.

Participants with high scores for masculinity had higher levels of testosterone than low scorers.

Femininity scores were not significantly associated with testosterone levels.

Conclusions

Females' maternal drive is negatively linked to levels of testosterone.

Evaluation

- The results show some indication of maternal tendencies being androgen driven.
- The results are correlational and therefore do not show a causal relationship.
- Testosterone levels are known to fluctuate over the course of a menstrual cycle and therefore may not be a valid measurement.
- The results are orientated to self-reports of maternal ambitions, which may reflect socially desirable answers, rather than actual maternal desires. Young women in career-structured employment may feel a need to express low maternal desire.

Research in focus

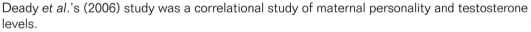

Deady *et al.*'s (2006) study was a correlational study of maternal personality and testosterone levels.

What is meant by a correlational study?

The results indicated a negative correlation. Explain in the context of this study what a positive correlation would mean.

Why can a correlation not show causality?

The study was reliant somewhat on a question-and-answer technique. What disadvantages are there to this method? What other method could have been used to overcome these disadvantages?

Evaluation

The role of hormones and genes in gender development

- Research evidence consistently shows biological factors to be important in gender development, though the influence of social factors is crucial too.

- Research indicates associations between hormones and gender-related behaviour. However, this does not show causality and other factors may be involved. Davies and Wilkinson (2006) found evidence that genes may also be involved in producing the masculinisation and feminisation of the brain.

- If biological factors were responsible for sex differences, these would be apparent from an early age. However, there is little evidence of early behavioural differences between males and females. Therefore, differences that appear later on may be explicable to some extent by social factors.

- Ethical concerns must be considered when performing research on people with abnormal conditions, like CAH. Such participants are especially vulnerable to distress and psychological harm. A cost-benefit analysis may help to decide whether such research is beneficial.

Supplementary learning

The case of the penectomised twin

The unusual, and ultimately tragic, tale of Bruce Reimer highlights some important points in the topic of gender and shows how the biased views of investigators can influence conclusions drawn from research findings.

John Money was an expert in the field of sexual identity and gender, and coined the phrase 'gender identity'. It was his belief that gender identity is fluid up to a certain age, after which gender becomes consolidated and set for life.

In 1972, Money and Ehrhardt reported on 'Bruce', a male twin who accidentally had his penis burned off at 8 months of age. Partially on Money's recommendation, the boy was given female hormones, sexual reassignment surgery

Figure 6.05 Bruce Reimer

and raised as a girl called Joan, without any knowledge of his/her early history. Money published a series of papers stating that the reassignment was successful, accentuating how Joan conformed to a stereotypical female gender role. However, the reality was that Joan behaved in a masculine way as a child and endured rejection and teasing at school, having few friendships. By age 14, the female hormones she was taking were competing with her male hormonal system and Joan was so distressed at Money's insistence that she needed further genital reconstruction surgery that her parents revealed her previous history to her. She immediately returned to a male gender role, adopting the name John, later having several sex reassignment operations. Eventually, he married and seemed happy, but in a series of misfortunes lost his job, was the victim of a financial scam, endured his twin brother dying of a drug overdose and was separated from his wife. He committed suicide in 2004, aged 38.

Subsequently, arguments raged, with accusations that Money falsified research and sexually abused the twins. Money strongly denied this and counterclaimed that the boy's parents had lied to his laboratory staff about Joan's progress. Whatever the truth, a strong point is how quickly a male gender identity and gender role was assumed when returning to being a male after so many years being raised as a female. This suggests that biological influences are stronger than was first thought, and the case also emphasises the influence that researcher bias can have on the implications of research. It is estimated that thousands of infants had sexual reassignment surgery based on views such as those held by Money.

Diamond and Sigmundson (1997) suggest that future cases be managed in view of what occurred, to prevent a repeat of such distress.

A BBC *Horizon* programme was made about the story of Bruce Reimer, which included a consideration of what it indicated about gender roles and their acquisition, plus the issue of possible researcher bias. This can be viewed in several parts by going to:

www.youtube.com/watch?v=6mbKXLu9qT4
www.youtube.com/watch?v=noqRhuE8_XAandfeature=related
www.youtube.com?v=5ctg3poxT9gandfeature=related
www.youtube.com?v=Fnb3EwJtsDsandfeature=related
www.youtube.com?v=2OelTsQgKnsandfeature=related

Research in focus

Research into intersex individuals has attracted much controversy, especially the work of John Money.

Explain the ethical issues associated with such research. From a cost-benefit point of view, should such research be conducted?

What is meant by researcher bias? How might this have occurred in research into intersex individuals? What important implications might this have?

Psychology in action

The therapeutic value of help groups

One way in which psychology makes a positive contribution is the subject's input into help groups for all manner of conditions, both physical and psychological.

One example is the Intersex Society of North America, formed in 1993, somewhat in response to negative experiences people had had with the health care system.

The organisation uses health professionals, including psychologists, to ensure that people receive support and advice based on scientifically established facts, so they can make informed decisions about their lives. Such guidance, based on solid knowledge, is extremely reassuring to people who may be feeling confused, outcast and depressive to the point of suicide.

Such organisations also attract finance and act as a forum for discussion and research into often sensitive areas that ultimately promote more understanding and tolerance.

Evolutionary explanations of gender roles

Evolutionary theory

Evolution sees changes in behaviour and physical appearance occurring through mutations. Most mutations are not beneficial and die out, but some are beneficial in terms of helping individuals to maximise resources and survive to sexual maturity, and thus produce offspring bearing the mutated gene. Through the adaptive process of natural selection, the mutation becomes more widespread in the population and can, over time, become sufficiently distinctive to be a permanent feature of particular species.

Evolution therefore sees gender roles as having occurred due to different selective pressures on males and females. In other words, gender differences have evolved because they are advantageous to each sex.

Mating strategies

Differences between male and female sexual behaviour arose as they were subject to different selective pressures. These occurred due to *anisogamy*, differences between the nature and amount of *gametes* (sperm and eggs) produced. Males produce lots of small, highly mobile sperm and can fertilise many females at little cost to reproductive potential. Males cannot be sure of paternity, so natural selection favours male behaviours maximising the number of potential pregnancies, with a male's best strategy to enhance his chances of reproducing genes into the next generation being to have as much sex as possible with as many fertile females as possible. Various male strategies have arisen, like males seeking females displaying signs of fertility, like health, youth and childbearing hips, as mating with fertile females enhances the chances of successful reproduction. Physical aggressiveness is seen between competing males, which is why males have evolved to be bigger and stronger.

Females produce a few, relatively large eggs, each one representing a sizeable reproductive investment, though females are always sure of maternity. Females ovulate one egg each month, meaning they only have about 300 opportunities in a lifetime to reproduce. Males, in theory, can reproduce about three times a day, and remain fertile for a longer period. It follows, therefore, that females must be more selective about who they mate with, as each mating involves a relatively sizeable part of reproduction potential compared to males.

Figure 6.06 Courtship encourages males to invest time and resources in relationships

Natural selection therefore favours female behaviours maximising the chances of successful reproduction through various strategies, like careful mate selection, monogamy and high parental investment. Females seek males displaying genetic fitness, like strength, status and resources. Females indulge in *intersexual* competition, where females choose males from those available. Females also utilise practices like courtship, which help to select the best male from those available, and also serve to make males invest time, effort and resources in them and any resulting offspring, thus increasing the chances that the male will not desert and will offer more protection and resources to the female and her offspring. Females also compete to be seen as more attractive. Gender roles are therefore centred on these differences in mating strategies – for instance, males being more competitive and aggressive, and females being nurturing and protective.

Adaptive advantage of sex roles

The development of sex roles in humans bestowed an adaptive advantage. Men hunted, and women, with child-caring duties, farmed and prepared food. This led to the creation of bigger social groups and an ability to avoid starvation. Neanderthals became extinct, possibly because they did not have such sex roles.

Gender roles

Differences in behaviour between the sexes may be due to evolution. Most societies/cultures divide activities between the sexes, and as women are restrained by child-caring duties and men possess greater physical strength; women conduct behaviours consistent with nurturing children and men conduct behaviours requiring mobility and power, like hunting and warfare.

If gender roles are indeed evolutionarily determined, they should be cross-cultural – that is, found in all cultures, with the different genders being socialised to the gender roles they are best adapted to. On the other hand, if gender roles are cultural constructions, then a degree of variability should be expected across cultures. Research suggests that the former is true, with men and women appearing mainly to perform the gender roles that evolutionary theory predicts for them. Men appear to have attained higher status too, as they are not as constrained by childbearing and child-rearing as females, and thus are free to engage in trade, competition and travel, and assume more powerful public positions. Females are only able to perform activities they can do simultaneously with childcare, like preparing and cooking food and gathering fuel.

Interpersonal sex roles

Females are more nurturing and this has an evolutionary advantage in threatening situations, where female responsibility lies in caring for children. For males, as the hunters, the better response is one of flight or fight.

Figure 6.07 Females are often restricted to occupations they can do while caring for children

Research: evolutionary explanations of gender

- Daly and Wilson (1988) found that all cases of female-female murders in Denmark between 1933 and 1961 were of infanticide – mothers killing children. Hardy (1999) argued that this shows, contrary to the belief that women are always warm and nurturing, that mothers have to respond to environmental conditions in ways that enhance the chances of their own survival, as well as that of their offspring. Therefore, sometimes – for example, due to poverty – female gender roles involve favouring one child over another, abandoning infants or even murdering them.

- Kenrick et al. (2004) cited the example of the Xavante hunter-gatherer people, where the average number of offspring for males and females was 3.6. However, the variance was 3.9 for women and 12.1 for men. In other words, some Xavante men had many offspring and others had few. Only one of 195 women was childless at age 20, but 6 per cent of men were still childless at age 40. One man fathered 23 children, whereas for a woman the highest number of children was 8. This pattern holds for most species: females, compared to males, tend to have fewer offspring and have a greater investment in them, supporting the mating strategies predicted by evolutionary theory.

- Wood and Eagly (2002) conducted a cross-cultural study comparing gender behaviours in different societies. Characteristic of non-industrial societies was men hunting and killing animals and manufacturing tools, and women looking after children and collecting and cooking food, suggesting that gender behaviours have their origins in evolution.

- Zeller (1987) found that although some activities were perceived as being exclusively male or female, there were many other activities that were seen as being applicable to either sex, like milking, manufacturing and harvesting food. This weakens the evolutionary explanation somewhat.

Figure 6.08 Evolutionary theory sees men as attracted to youthful, healthy females, signs of fertility

- Tamres et al. (2002) found that in times of threat and stress, women seek the company of others much more than men, supporting the idea that interpersonal sex roles have been naturally selected by evolution.

- Buss (1989) gathered information about mate preferences from 37 cultural groups. Females tended to seek males with resources and ambition, while males sought physical attractiveness much more than females, and also desired younger partners, supporting the idea that mating strategies have evolved differently between the sexes due to different environmental demands. The idea that men would place more importance on chastity was only supported to a small extent, lowering support for the explanation.

- Holloway *et al.* (2002) investigated the idea of males being larger in order to compete for females (and impress choosy females). It was found that human males tend to be 1.1 times bigger than females, but in chimpanzees, where pressures for male competition are more intense, males tend to be 1.3 times bigger, strongly supporting the idea of gender size differences being due to evolutionary pressures.

Evaluation

Evolutionary explanations of gender

- The evolutionary approach is criticised by some as being deterministic in seeing gender differences as biologically inevitable.
- Evolutionary theory provides a plausible explanation for physical differences between males and females, and also for why men tend to be more promiscuous and women more choosy in their sexual behaviour.
- One problem with cross-cultural studies, often used to judge predictions based on evolutionary theory, is that samples are very different in composition, which casts doubts on the validity of the results.
- Even if gender roles have evolved, it does not necessarily mean they have produced positive outcomes. For example, men can be negatively affected by feelings of jealousy and rejection.
- Although, as predicted by evolutionary theory, many traditional male activities require strength, so do some typically female activities, like carrying water and food. However, evolution may have shaped women to perform activities that could be carried out in conjunction with child-rearing.

Issues, debates and approaches

- The evolutionary approach to gender is criticised by some as being deterministic in seeing gender differences as biologically inevitable and allowing no scope for less determinist factors, like cultural influences.
- Evolutionary explanations of gender could be argued to involve socially sensitive issues, because the fact that they see males and females as unable to escape from biologically ordained roles creates social and political issues concerning women in the workplace and male involvement in childcare.

The biosocial approach to gender development

Biosocial theory sees gender as determined by both biological and social factors, working in conjunction with each other to produce masculine and feminine behaviours and identities. It sees the interaction between biological and social factors as important, rather than biology's direct influence. Therefore, gender cannot be explained by biology alone – for instance gender dysphoria (see page 216) indicates that biological sex does not necessarily reflect gender.

From birth, the way adults respond to children is influenced by a child's sex: to them, a baby's sex is just as important as its temperament. Adults bring sexual stereotypes into their interactions with children, but are

these expectations responsible for creating differences in children, or do adults react to differences already present? Biosocial theory believes that it is the perceptions of biological sex that lead to gender identity and gender role behaviour. A newborn baby is labelled as male or female and this labelling has consequences for how the child will be perceived and treated, with boys and girls being treated differently – for example, how they are handled. So gender is seen as socially constructed and therefore differing across cultures and over time.

Various research studies presented babies live or on videotape, with participants tending to label babies' behaviour differently and in gender-stereotyped ways, according to whether they were told that a baby was a girl or a boy. This suggests that adults respond to the child's sex.

Money and Ehrhardt (1972) believed that 'anatomy is destiny': how an infant is labelled sexually determines how it is raised or socialised. In turn, this determines a child's gender identity, and from this emerges its gender role identity and sexual orientation. Psychologically, gender identity is not determined at birth; it becomes determined as masculine or feminine in the course of the various experiences of growing up. While biological explanations see gender behaviours as being exclusively due to biology and therefore fixed and constant, the biosocial model sees them as much less rigid. This means it should be possible for a person to change and develop in ways that are not confined by traditional views of male and female behaviour and identity.

Much of the evidence for biosocial theory comes from studies of people with intersex conditions, like individuals with CAH, whose gender of rearing is 'out of synch' with their chromosomal/hormonal/anatomical status, allowing an assessment of the relative influence of environmental and biological factors on gender identity. Much research was performed by, or inspired by, John Money, and in his view it was possible to harmlessly change a child's gender of rearing, provided it was done within a 'critical' or 'sensitive' period of between 2.5 to 3 years, suggesting that gender of rearing was more important than biological sex. However, Money's research and interpretations of data have proven controversial (see 'Supplementary research: the case of the penectomised twin' on page 210).

Research in focus

Research into people with intersex conditions is an example of *natural experiments*, where the relative contributions of environmental and biological factors are assessed and compared.

What are natural experiments and how do they differ from field experiments?

What advantages and disadvantages do natural experiments have over laboratory experiments?

Why do some critics not regard natural experiments as true experiments, but refer to them as *quasi-experiments*?

Research: biosocial theory

- Money and Ehrhardt studied ten people with CAIS. They showed a strong preference for the female role, suggesting that gender of rearing is more important than biological sex.

- Bradley *et al.* (1998) reported on a case of a biological male who, after accidental damage to his penis, had reassignment surgery and was raised as a female. This individual exhibited some male behaviours as a child, but preferred female company, and, as an adult, perceived himself as female and was happy that way. This particular case study suggests that biological sex does not determine gender identity.

- Smith and Lloyd (1978) dressed babies in non-specific gender clothes, then labelled them with a boy's or a girl's name. It was found that people would play with them in different ways according to their gender label, with 'boys' being treated in a more physical manner. This is in line with biosocial theory, which explains that the gender label would direct how the child would be perceived and treated.

- Wetherell and Edley (1999) offered support for the biosocial view that gender behaviour is flexible. They found several different styles of adult masculinity being exhibited by men, like 'unconventional', 'sporty' and 'new man', indicating that gender role is not fixed exclusively by biology.

- Schaffer (2004) showed a sample of over 200 adults, male and female, a video of a 9-month-old baby, either called David or Dana, playing with toys and responding to stimuli. The adults labelled the baby's behaviour and emotions in gender-typical ways according to whether they believed it to be a boy or a girl, supporting the idea that adults respond to gender labels in predetermined ways.

Evaluation

Biosocial theory

- Studies of individuals given reassignment surgery and raised as opposite gender to their biological sex produced contradictory results and were prone on occasion to researcher bias. For instance, Reiner and Gearhart (2003) reported on 16 biological males born without a penis, given reassignment surgery and raised as females. All exhibited male tendencies and ten decided to become male again by 16 years of age. Money (1991), however, reported on 250 cases of people being happy with gender reassignment. Clear conclusions, therefore, have not been made.

- Controversy has arisen over Money's insistence, often despite blatant evidence to the contrary, that gender identity and gender role are learned. Diamond and Sigmundsson (1997) subsequently challenged two basic assumptions of Money and Ehrhardt's biosocial theory, that individuals are psychosexually neutral at birth and that healthy psychosexual development is intimately related to the appearance of the genitals. There are, however, other documented cases of sex reassignment cases where gender dysphoria has not occurred (see Bradley *et al.* (1998) in 'Research: biosocial theory' on page 215), which offer a degree of support for the theory.

- Intersex individuals are not a typical sample of people and there is no evidence that people in general are as flexible in their psychosexual development. Perhaps intersex individuals are just making the best of a bad situation.

- Early gender-related behaviours appear to be more biologically directed. Kujawski and Bower (1993) found that 1-year-olds prefer to watch same-gender children, suggesting that initially innate factors dominate.

- There is some evidence that ideas about gender differ cross-culturally, therefore suggesting that gender roles and behaviours are a social construction.

Gender dysphoria

The wording of the specification allows for separate questions to be asked on gender dysphoria and the biosocial approach. However, gender dysphoria can also be regarded as part of the biosocial approach, thus the material detailed here could be shaped to answer questions on both gender dysphoria itself and the biosocial approach too.

Gender dysphoria is a psychiatric disorder, occurring when an individual feels uncomfortable with their biological sex and wishes to change it. Prejudice and negative feelings of anxiety and distress can be experienced, leading to depression, self-harm and even suicide. It affects males more than females, and it is estimated that 1 in 11,000 people have the condition. Indications of the condition may occur fairly early, with children being unhappy wearing clothes of their biological gender or playing gender-stereotypical games. Most gender dysphoria occurs in childhood, and for the majority of such children it does not persist after puberty. However, those for whom it does persist tend to have stronger gender dysphoric symptoms in childhood. Often, because of the distress and disgust with the bodily signs of their 'wrong' sex, gender dysphorics may assume the gender role of the desired sex, wearing gender-typical clothes and adopt gender-stereotyped behaviours. This helps them to feel better about themselves. Masculinising or feminising hormones can be taken to alter physical features, with the ultimate remedy being gender reassignment surgery.

Early explanations centred on psychological factors, like maladaptive learning experiences, maladaptive cognitive processes and psychodynamic fixations occurring in childhood development. However, biological explanations have become increasingly favoured and supported by research evidence.

Genetics

Evidence suggests a role for genetics in gender dysphoria. Attention has centred on gene variants of the androgen receptor that influence the action of testosterone and is involved in the masculinisation of the brain. More research is needed, especially to identify what types of environmental factors are required to elicit an influence, and the biological processes through which genetic effects may be mediated.

Hormones

Genetic effects may be mediated through hormones. Many gender dysphorics take opposite-sex hormones as part of their treatment, but little is known about the long-term effects of this process. What evidence there is does not indicate any substantial difference in hormone levels in individuals with gender dysphoria.

There is some evidence from case studies of children suggesting that hormones determine gender identity, but there are problems in generalising from such samples to the general population, and there is also the possibility that it is the gender of rearing that is crucial in determining gender identity, and not genetic/chromosomal sex.

Conditioning

Parents of gender dysphorics often report that they encouraged and gave attention to their children when they cross-dressed, particularly boys. Such family reactions could contribute to the conflict between anatomical sex and acquired gender identity.

Conditioning experiences may explain why more children than adults are identified as gender dysphoric: early life experiences are dominated by the family, but as the individual grows up, others outside the family exert an influence, making it more likely that an individual will be punished for behaving in 'inappropriate' ways.

Social learning could also play a part, with an absence of or inappropriate role models to imitate.

Research: gender dysphoria

- Hare *et al.* (2009) examined gene samples from male gender dysphorics and non-dysphorics. A significant correlation was found between gender dysphoria and variants of the androgen receptor gene, implying the gene to be involved in a failure to masculinise the brain during development in the womb, again supporting a biological explanation.

- Kula and Slowikowska-Hilczer (2000) performed a meta-analysis of studies, finding that animal studies indicated that sex hormones present during pregnancy influence sexual behaviour in adulthood, suggesting that hormones affect masculinisation and feminisation of a child's brain in the womb. This was backed up by another finding; that in individuals with abnormal genitals caused by hormone imbalances, their biological sex and gender identity did not match, again suggesting that hormones may play a key role in the development of the condition.

- Gladue (1985) reported that there were few, if any, hormonal differences between gender dysphoric men, heterosexual men and homosexual men, evidence against the influence of hormones on gender dysphoria. Similar results are found with women.

- Rekers (1995) reported that of 70 gender dysphoric boys, none had evidence of biological causes, but there was a common factor of a lack of stereotypical male role models, suggesting that social learning factors play a role in the condition.

- Wallien and Cohen–Kettenis (2008) performed a longitudinal study that studied a group of gender dysphoric children. At around 19 years of age, about 40 per cent of those followed up were still gender dysphoric, and these were the individuals who exhibited more extreme symptoms. These individuals also tended to have a homosexual or bisexual orientation, indicating that the majority of children exhibiting gender dysphoria only do so in the short term, and that there is an association between being homosexual/bisexual and having childhood gender dysphoria.

- Zucker *et al.* (2008) performed a longitudinal study on gender dysphoric females between 2 and 3 years of age who had been referred to a clinic. Only 12 per cent were still gender dysphoric at age 18. A study on equivalent males found that 20 per cent were still gender dysphoric as adults, again suggesting that the majority of people exhibiting gender dysphoria do so only in the short term.

Classic research

Blanchard *et al.* (1987)

Heterosexual and homosexual gender dysphoria

The researchers were interested in looking for differences between homosexual and heterosexual gender dysphorics that might offer some insight into the condition. They were especially interested in investigating the different prevalence rates of gender dysphoria between males and females.

Aims

To investigate why more males than females report dissatisfaction with their biological sex (gender dysphoria).

Procedure

New referrals to a gender identity clinic in Toronto, Canada were classified as either heterosexual or homosexual.

Males divided into 73 heterosexual and 52 homosexual gender dysphorics, while females divided into 1 heterosexual and 71 homosexual gender dysphorics.

Personal data was collected by questionnaire and participants were also individually interviewed.

Findings

Heterosexual males reported their first cross-gender desires occurred at the same time they first cross-dressed; while homosexual males reported that cross-gender desires occurred around 3-4 years before first cross-dressing.

80 per cent of heterosexual men acknowledged a history of fetishistic arousal (sexual arousal through an inanimate object e.g. clothing or body parts), compared to less than 10 per cent of homosexual men and 0 per cent of homosexual women.

Conclusions

The findings suggest that males are not more at risk of developing gender dysphoria than females, but that they are more susceptible to a predisposing condition of gender transvestism (arousal through dressing up as or pretending to be a member of the opposite sex).

Evaluation

- The findings are dependent upon the honesty of participants' answers. It may be that heterosexual men are more inclined to own up to fetishistic arousal.

- The participants may be atypical in that they voluntarily attended a gender identity clinic. Gender dysphorics, both heterosexual and homosexual, who are unwilling to report/acknowledge their condition may have a different profile, suggesting that the results cannot be generalised to all gender dysphorics.

Evaluation

Gender dysphoria

- Bennett (2006) reported that 2 per cent of more than 300 monozygotic twins showed some evidence of gender dysphoria based on self-report measures. Applying statistical modelling techniques to their data, Coolidge *et al.* (2002) found that 62 per cent of the variance in reported symptoms could be attributed to biological factors, and 38 per cent to environmental factors, implying that the causes of the disorder are primarily biological, not psychological.

- Hines (2004) stated: 'The strong, persistent desire to change sex, and the willingness to undergo surgery and hormone treatment despite formidable obstacles, including, in some cases, social stigmatisation and job loss, suggests a biological imperative.'.

- Individuals with the condition often do not perceive it as a disorder, but believe that gender characteristics are a social construction with no relation to biological sex.

- Although gender confusion in childhood can indicate gender dysphoria, only a minority will exhibit the condition into adulthood.

- Increasingly, evidence suggests that the influence of hormones and genetics are responsible for gender dysphoria. However, this is somewhat simplistic, and because research studies have not shown distinct result patterns, it is probable that many other interacting factors contribute to the condition.

- Bennett (2006) pointed out that while SLT can explain the development of non-gender-typical behaviours, it cannot explain the strength of such beliefs about one's gender and resistance to any form of psychological therapy. This suggests that biology is a stronger factor.

An excellent site containing a wealth of information about gender dysphoria is run by the Gender Identity Research and Education Society [GIRES] and can be found at http://gires. org.uk/dysphoria.php?gclid=COGI_JHbtacCFYEc4QodcHqHAQ

You are the researcher

Designing questionnaires is not straightforward. Design a questionnaire into gender dysphoria, by devising 6 to 10 questions assessing the level of the condition in males and females. Take care to make questions concise, clear and unambiguous. Compile suitable standardised instructions.

How would each question be scored?

How would the data be interpreted to make sense of them?

What steps would be taken to ensure that the questionnaire was ethical?

Why might there be a risk that the data generated would be invalid?

Issues, debates and approaches

- The biosocial theory combines biological and social factors to explain gender development and is therefore an example of a more holistic theory, demonstrating how different approaches can work in unison. Explanations do not necessarily involve a reduction to single, exclusive accounts of human behaviour.

- The biosocial theory can also be seen to involve elements of nature, through its biological component, and elements of nurture, through its social component, and thus can be regarded as an interactionist approach.

- An ethical issue when researching individuals with gender dysphoria is that care must be taken not to cause psychological distress to people who may, by the very nature of their condition, already be distressed and vulnerable.

- A socially sensitive issue when researching gender dysphoria is that identification of genes possibly associated with the condition cause concern about foetal gene screening, with a view to aborting 'at-risk' pregnancies.

Strengthen your learning

1. How is biological sex determined?
2. Summarise the effect of gonadal hormones on sexual characteristics.
3. Why have psychologists been interested in studying intersex individuals?
4. Does evidence concerning the effects of hormones and genes on gender development tend to favour a biological or an environmental explanation? Give details.
5a. What does evolutionary theory predict about differences in gender roles between males and females?
5b. How does evolutionary theory explain such differences as having occurred?
6. What degree of support is there for evolutionary explanations? Give details.
7. How does the biosocial approach explain the development of gender?
8a. Is the biosocial approach supported by evidence? Give details.
8b. Why is it difficult to draw clear conclusions in this area?
9. What is meant by gender dysphoria?
10a. What explanations have been given for gender dysphoria?
10b. Evaluate each of these explanations, including references to research evidence.

Assessment Check ▶

1. Outline the role of hormones and genes in gender development. (8 marks)

2. Evaluate evolutionary explanations of gender. (16 marks)

3. Discuss the biosocial approach to gender development. (24 marks)

4. Outline the biosocial approach to gender development. (4 marks)

5. Outline and evaluate the role of hormones and genes in gender development. (20 marks)

6. Outline and evaluate explanations of gender dysphoria. (24 marks)

continued ...

... continued

Examination guidance

Question 1 calls solely for descriptive material; offer any evaluation and it will not gain credit. As 8 marks are on offer, a more substantial amount of detail is expected. Conversely, question 2 only requires evaluative material, so providing descriptions of evolutionary explanations will not score marks.

In question 3 the term 'discuss' means to describe and evaluate, with more time and effort dedicated to the evaluation, as it is worth 16 marks compared to 8 marks for the outline.

Question 4 also requires an outline of the biosocial approach, but this time it is a 'shorter' version that is needed, as it is only worth 4 marks, not 8. The outline in question 5 is only worth 4 marks (compared to the 8 marks on offer for a longer version in question 1), so do not overdo it; it is better to dedicate the majority of time to the evaluation, where 16 marks are available. Question 6 is a standard essay question, so 8 marks are gained by outlining explanations of gender dysphoria and 16 marks from evaluating the explanations, possibly by focusing on their degree of research support.

Social influences on gender

Social learning theory

Social learning theory (SLT) perceives gender roles as learned through observation and imitation of *socialising agents*, like parents, teachers, peers and the media, who convey repetitive messages about the importance of gender role-appropriate behaviour.

Based on learning theory principles of operant conditioning, children are seen as being positively reinforced (rewarded) for behaving in gender-appropriate ways and punished for behaving in gender-inappropriate ways.

Socialising agents model examples of appropriate and inappropriate behaviour, and also the consequences of conforming or not conforming to gender norms. Through observational learning, children acquire knowledge regarding gender roles without actually 'doing' anything; children observe models being reinforced or punished for gender-appropriate or gender-inappropriate behaviour and will subsequently imitate behaviours that they saw being reinforced and not imitate those they saw being punished. SLT therefore explains the acquisition of gender role stereotypes in this manner.

The influence of parents

SLT believes that girls and boys learn dissimilar gender roles because parents and others treat them differently. For example, studies show that adults react in different ways to babies according to their gender role stereotypes, which depend on whether they believe the baby to be a boy or a girl (see 'Research: biosocial theory' on page 215). Therefore, when a son or daughter demonstrates what is perceived as gender-appropriate behaviour, it will be reinforced by rewards of praise and attention. Thus girls and boys are given different toys, have their rooms decorated differently and are even spoken to in different terms. Some research identifies a gender difference in the way parents behave, fathers seeming to reinforce sex-typed behaviours more than mothers, especially in sons. SLT also perceives same-sex models as more influential in being more likely to be imitated.

Children may also, by a gradual process of immersion, take on parents' gender schemas.

Key terms

Reinforcement – an outcome of a behaviour that strengthens the chances of the behaviour recurring

Peers – individuals of equal status

Media – formats of conveying public information, such as newspapers

Cross-cultural studies – research studies comparing people from different cultures

Research: the influence of parents

- Block (1979) found that boys are positively reinforced more for behaviours reflecting independence, self-reliance and emotional control, while girls are reinforced for dependence, nurturance, empathy and emotional expression. This suggests that SLT can explain why males and females acquire different gender roles.

- Quiery (1998) found that fathers interact in a more instrumental and achievement-orientated way and give more attention to their sons, while mothers attend equally to their sons and daughters. This suggests that fathers reinforce sex-typing more than mothers. However, Karraker *et al.* (1995) found that this had declined, and that there were no differences between mothers and fathers.

- Huston (1983) found that although parents believe they respond in the same way to aggressive acts committed by sons and daughters, they actually intervene more frequently and quickly when girls behave aggressively, demonstrating how parents treat children in gender-biased ways.

- Eccles *et al.* (1990) reported that children were encouraged by their parents to play with gender-stereotypical toys, supporting the idea that parents reinforce gender roles.

Figure 6.09 Fathers tend to reinforce sex-typing more than mothers

- Lytton and Romney (1991) found that parents reinforced with praise and attention stereotypical gender behaviours in both boys and girls – for example, what activities they participated in – suggesting that social environmental factors are important in determining gender behaviour. However, children were also raised similarly in many ways, suggesting that reinforcement alone cannot account for the development of gender behaviours.

Evaluation

The influence of parents

- Findings from studies in different cultures demonstrate the universality of influence that SLT provides. For instance, Bandura and Walters (1963) pointed out that parents in different cultures present offspring with direct examples and instruction (modelling) in appropriate gender role behaviours, and also provide children with toys and play materials that are stereotypically male or female.

- Maccoby and Jacklin (1974) found no consistent differences in the extent to which boys and girls are reinforced for aggressiveness or autonomy; indeed, there appears to be remarkable uniformity in how genders are socialised. This is supported by Lytton and Romney (1991), who found few gender differences in terms of parental warmth, overall amount of interaction, encouragement of achievement or dependency, restrictiveness and discipline, or clarity of communication. Such findings refute the influence of SLT in establishing male and female gender roles.

- Some studies fail to find children as more likely to imitate same-gender than opposite-gender models. Barkley *et al.* (1977) reviewed 81 studies testing the prediction that children will imitate same-gender models; only 18 supported the prediction. Indeed, Maccoby *et al.* (1979) found that children prefer imitating behaviour appropriate to their own gender, regardless of the model's gender.

- A problem with explaining how boys acquire 'traditional' gender roles by reference to SLT principles comes from Smith and Daglish (1977), who found that children were more likely to imitate the parent they have most contact with, usually the mother.

- Fagot and Leinbach (1995) compared children raised in 'traditional' families, where dad went to work and mum cared for the children, with 'alternative' families, where mum and dad shared child care. At age 4, children were given gender-labelling tasks as a means of testing gender schemas. The 'traditional' family children displayed more gender role stereotyping and used gender labels earlier, suggesting that parents do act as gender role models for their children.

The influence of the media

Media forms, such as television, cinema, magazines and pop music are seen as an important social influence on the acquisition, shaping and maintenance of gender roles. Males are more represented in most types of TV programmes – even more so in children's programmes. Males are also portrayed in a wider range of and higher-status roles than females.

Across all forms of media, males and females are portrayed in gender stereotypical ways, like men being dominant, aggressive and independent, while women are seen in submissive, nurturing and dependent roles. Even within shared formats, gender roles are apparent – for example, in the composition of pop groups, with females seen as singers, while males are portrayed as musicians.

SLT perceives media influences as being invasive and persistent, providing children especially with a constant source of information as to which behaviours are and are not appropriate to each gender. Research shows that children who 'consume' the most media influences – for example, watch a lot of television – develop stronger and more polarised (extreme) gender role views. However, this view is seen as simplistic, and evidence exists to counter these claims.

Research: media influences

- Huston and Wright (1998) found that in US TV programmes males outnumber females by two or three to one on almost every kind of programme; and in children's programmes it is more like five to one, demonstrating the dominance of males in TV programming.

- Durkin (1986) found that males are shown in more dominant roles, with higher occupational status, while women are often presented in a narrow range of traditional feminine occupations, like housewife, secretary and nurse, or in more subordinate roles, illustrating the differences in gender role presentations.

- Huston and Wright (1998) found that men on TV are shown solving problems and being more active, aggressive, powerful and independent, while women are portrayed as submissive, passive, attractive, sensual, nurturing, emotional and less able to deal with difficult situations. Such portrayals illustrate and reinforce gender role stereotypes.

- Bee (2000) cited research showing that commercials for boys' and girls' toys are produced differently: those for boys are 'action-packed', being fast, sharp and loud, while those for girls are gradual, soft and fuzzy. Even 6-year-olds notice these differences in style, suggesting that such gender role portrayals are influential for young children at an age when gender roles are being developed.

- Bee (2000) found that books, including picture books and early reading books, are stereotyped. As in TV commercials, the leading characters are more likely to be male, demonstrating the wide range of media influences on gender roles.

- Gunter (1986) found that children categorised as 'heavy' viewers of television hold stronger stereotyped beliefs than 'lighter' viewers, a fact Huston (1990) did not find surprising, as the average American child has already been exposed to thousands of hours of TV. By the age of 18, the average child has spent more time in front of the TV than in a classroom, demonstrating the potential strength of media influences on gender concepts.

- Peirce (1993) conducted a content analysis of teenage girls' magazines. Girls tended to be portrayed as weak and reliant on others, with a focus on being in a relationship rather than having independent aspirations, demonstrating the influence of the media in establishing gender attitudes and behaviours.

Figure 6.10 Even in shared formats, gender roles are apparent

Evaluation

Media influences

- The fact that 'heavy' TV watchers hold stronger gender-stereotyped beliefs is merely correlational evidence, not necessarily indicating TV to be the cause of holding such attitudes. All it shows is that the greater the exposure to TV, the stronger the stereotypes. A factor not controlled for is that highly gender-typed children may like to watch lots of TV, because it confirms their limited world view. Also, while 'heavy' TV viewers might hold stronger stereotyped beliefs than 'lighter' viewers, no precise measures have been taken of the programmes they actually watch.

- Correlations also tend to be generally weak, and often minimal or non-existent. Durkin (1995) found that 'heavy' viewers actually scored lower on a test of gender stereotype acceptance.

- The view that TV impacts on a passively receptive child audience with messages about gender role stereotyping and moulds young children's conceptions of gender is oversimplistic. Gunter and McAleer (1997) maintained that children respond selectively to particular characters and events; and their perceptions, memories and understanding of what they have seen may often be mediated by the dispositions they bring with them to the viewing situation.

- If media influences do exert a negative influence in establishing and reinforcing traditional gender stereotypes, they should equally be able to promote, create and maintain positive non-gender role stereotypes through pro-social media influences, like portraying female scientists and sports stars. To test this, Johnston and Ettema (1982) showed 12-year-olds episodes of a television programme designed to counter gender stereotypes, and both boys and girls exhibited reduced stereotyping.

- Media influences on gender development may have been exaggerated, because a lot of gender development occurs before 4 years of age when media influences are not very great. In later years, media influences probably reinforce existing gender beliefs rather than create them.

Contemporary research

Steinke *et al.* (2008)

Gender stereotypes of scientist characters in television programmes popular among middle school-aged children

Figure 6.11

Gender stereotyping is found among many types of television programmes, especially those designed for children's viewing, like animated cartoons. As more opportunities now exist for females to become scientists, the researchers were interested to see whether there was a gender difference in the way in which scientists were portrayed in children's TV programmes.

Aims/hypotheses

To examine gender stereotyping in portrayals of scientist characters in television programmes popular with middle school-aged children.

It was predicted that:

- There would be a greater frequency of male scientists.

- Male scientist characters would be of higher status than female ones.

- Female scientists would be more likely to be married.

- Female scientists would be more likely to have children.

- The portrayal of scientists would be gender stereotyped.

Procedure

Fourteen popular television programmes with a scientific element to them were identified from ratings listings of shows watched by 12- to 17-year-olds.

Eight episodes of each programme broadcast between April and May 2006 were randomly selected for analysis – in all, 112 episodes.

Criteria for identifying scientist characters were constructed – for example, conducting experiments – and inter-rater reliability was established by using two raters.

A total of 196 scientist characters were identified and the following characteristics listed: sex, race, age group, scientific status, marital status and parental status.

Each character's behaviour was coded for gender stereotypical and non-gender stereotypical behaviour.

Findings

- Of 196 scientist characters, 113 (58 per cent) were male, 83 (42 per cent) were female.

- Of these, 72 per cent were white, 13 per cent black, 7 per cent Hispanic, 6 per cent Asian, 1 per cent Native American and 1 per cent not determined.

- Of the total scientist characters, 56 per cent were adults, 25 per cent young adults/students and 19 per cent children.

- Male scientists were no more likely than females to be portrayed as high status.

- Of the 42 scientist characters determined to be married, slightly more were male.

- Of the 13 scientist characters determined to be parents, slightly more were male.

- Female scientist characters were not more likely than males to be portrayed with feminine qualities of dependence and being caring and romantic.

- Male scientists characters were more likely to be portrayed than females with masculine qualities of independence and dominance, but not athleticism.

Conclusions

Popular children's TV programmes portray more male than female scientist characters.

continued ...

...continued

Male scientist characters are more likely to be portrayed with stereotypically masculine characteristics.

Evaluation

- Progress seems to have been made in presenting scientific characters in children's TV programmes in a non-biased way – for instance, earlier studies, such as Steinke and Long (1996), found that females were more likely to be portrayed as assistants.

- Most programmes featuring female scientist characters were educational science programmes funded by the National Science Foundation, implying that major network media providers are more to blame for gender-stereotyping portrayals.

- Although results suggest a reduction in gender stereotyping in areas like marital and parental status, these findings should be treated with caution, as sample numbers were small, making generalisation difficult.

You are the researcher

Use sports reports from newspapers/magazines to see whether there is a gender-based difference in how male and female sportspeople/teams are portrayed.

A content analysis will be required of the language used to describe sportspeople/teams, by recording the frequency of certain words/phrases used. Coding units need to be created to achieve this.

At least two coders (raters) will be needed to establish inter-rater reliability. Explain how to achieve this.

Supplementary learning

The colour pink

The colour pink is named after flowers called pinks, referring to their frilled flowers, and is regarded as the universal colour of love. It is also associated with homosexuality, because the Nazis forced homosexuals to wear a pink triangle as a badge of shame – it is now worn with pride by gay people.

Figure 6.12
Stephanie: positive role model or negative gender stereotype?

However, the most interesting debate around the colour pink is its association with gender stereotypes. Pink is seen as a female colour, with blue for boys. Indeed, in Italy either blue or pink ribbons are placed on a front door to indicate whether a boy or a girl has just been born. The association of pink with girls attracts a lot of criticism in feminist circles, especially the fashion for manufacturing myriad girls' articles in vibrant pink, as this is seen as pandering to negative gender stereotypes of girls being frivolous, weak and submissive. One fictional girl who has attracted storms of wrath is Stephanie, erstwhile heroine of hit children's TV show *Lazy Town*. This Icelandic-produced show features the superhero Sportacus, who, along with sidekick Stephanie, is actually a positive role model for an active, healthy lifestyle; but it is Stephanie's pink hair and pink outfits that have attracted criticism, for the colour's associations with weak female gender roles. Some feminist groups, such as the Swedish radical feminist party Feminist Initiative, have even sought to reclaim the colour as a sign of female strength, not weakness.

The strange but true fact is that pink was not always seen as having feminine associations. It is only since the 1940s that pink has been a 'girly' colour; before that, blue was the colour associated with girls and pink was a masculine colour. Indeed, Westminster School, one of Britain's leading public schools, has a long tradition of boys wearing pink ties. It is not really clear why the change occurred, but it does show that there is nothing inherent in girls been associated with pink, nor in it being a sign of negative female sex-typing.

The influence of peers

Peers have a strong social influence by acting as role models, with children more likely to imitate same-sex models. Children's play is sex-typed from an early age, usually around 2 years. Children seek like-minded peers with similar resources, and such peers are likely to possess strong gender role stereotypes themselves.

Gender differences emerge primarily in social situations like peer settings, rather than in individual settings, and children soon show preferences for same-gender playmates and segregate into predominantly same-gender groups, where they resist adult interventions aimed at encouraging them to be nice to the opposite gender. The influence of peers as role models is strong and they help to reinforce gender stereotypes – for example, by praising gender-appropriate clothes and ridiculing non-appropriate ones.

Peers are also intolerant of others' cross-gender behaviour. As Durkin (1995) says, 'From early childhood, gender is not just another thing to learn about, but a vital social category that determines whom one mixes with and how one behaves'.

Young children's gender identity and gender role stereotypes are rigid and inflexible compared with older children, adolescents and adults. Once these develop, the critical variable is not *vertical reinforcement* from parents and other adults, but rather *horizontal social engagement* in the form of interaction and play with peers.

Research: the influence of peers

- Langlois and Downs (1980) compared peer and maternal reactions to preschoolers' play with opposite-gender toys. When boys played with girls' toys, mothers accepted this, but their male peers ridiculed and even hit them, demonstrating the intolerance of peers to cross-gender behaviour, and thus the strength of their influence on establishing gender roles.

- Archer and Lloyd (1982) reported that 3-year-old children who played the opposite sex's games were ridiculed by their peers and ostracised, supporting the idea that peers police gender roles.

- Lamb and Roopnarine (1979) found evidence of peers rewarding sex-appropriate play in preschool children and ridiculing sex-inappropriate play, demonstrating the strong influence that peers have in reinforcing gender behaviour.

- Maccoby (1990) reported how children quickly associate with playmates of the same sex, congregate and divide themselves into same-gender groupings and are resistant to attempts to get them to associate with and be nice to opposite-gender members, demonstrating how gender differences emerge mainly in social situations involving peers.

Interested in challenging the colour pink as a negative influence for girls? Then check out the 'pinkstinks' website, home page of the group that promotes and campaigns for positive gender roles for girls: www.pinkstinks.co.uk

Evaluation

The influence of peers

- Peers may have a stronger role in reinforcing gender roles than parents, because peers police gender behaviours – for instance, by ostracising those who indulge in non-stereotypical behaviour.

- Parents have more influence over children's gender concepts and behaviour when they are young, but peers become more important as gender role models in later childhood.

You are the researcher

Design a correlational study to test the strength of relationship between individual children's degree of gender stereotyping and that of their peer groups. You will need two co-variables.

How would the degree of gender stereotyping be measured?

How many participants are needed for assessment?

What statistical test would be used to analyse the data? What kind of graph would be used to plot the data?

The influence of schools

Schools can exert social influences in several ways. First, teachers moderate parent and peer influences by reinforcing fewer gender-stereotypical attitudes and behaviour, but they also enforce gender stereotypes – for example, through separate dress codes for boys and girls and by praising and scolding pupils for gender-appropriate/inappropriate behaviour.

Another way in which sex-type behaviour is reinforced is through the curriculum – for instance, promoting and making it easier for girls to do 'girl-type' subjects, like home economics, and for boys to do 'boy-type' subjects, like metalwork.

Teaching materials can also exert an influence – for instance, books portraying males and females in gender-stereotypical ways. Apart from influencing gender roles, such materials can also impact on children's perceptions of what roles are available for them in adult life, perceptions that will shape their learning and lives. For instance, if scientists are portrayed as male figures and in scientific positions of higher status relative to females, this influences female perceptions of and motivation to be scientists (see 'Contemporary research: Steinke *et al.* (2008)' on page 225).

In recent years, girls have outshone boys academically, with one explanation for why boys do comparatively worse being that primary school teachers tend to be female, so, from an early age, boys perceive learning as for girls.

Figure 6.13 Primary school teachers tend to be female, with boys perceiving that learning is for girls

In secondary education, there is a tendency for men and women teachers to teach gender-stereotypical subjects – for instance, men teaching maths – and pupils regard subjects as being either 'girl subjects' or 'boy subjects'. Again, these influences are reinforced and policed by parents, peers and teachers.

Research: the influence of schools

- Renzetti and Curran (1992) found that teachers gave reinforcement in the form of praise to boys for instances of 'cleverness', while girls received praise for 'neatness', supporting the view that teachers enforce gender stereotypes.

- Colley (1994) found that in secondary schools pupils had a tendency to view individual subjects as either masculine or feminine, demonstrating that social influences on attitudes and beliefs about gender are apparent in schools.

- Huston (1983) found that girls in primary school education are less likely to be to be told off than boys for equally disruptive behaviour, suggesting that expectations of gender-typed behaviour are reinforced by teachers.

- Stanworth (1981) found that high school boys became known by name to teachers more quickly than girls did, and it also took longer for teachers to identify female students as individuals, implying that boys were seen as more important than girls.

- Meece (1987) found that going to school not only represented a more formal structuring of children's lives, but also raised prospects of the future – that is, what children were going to be when they grew up. This was also shown through schools maintaining gender-biased practices in terms of opportunities and advice, like career counselling, that they offered.

Evaluation

The influence of schools

- The fact that children respond in a selective manner to reinforcement suggests that cognitive factors are important too in influencing gender behaviour. Fagot (1995) found that teachers try to reinforce female behaviours in boys and girls, but only girls learn them.

- Although sex discrimination laws have been passed so that all subjects are available to boys and girls, the curriculum can be argued to quickly become seen as gendered in pupils' eyes, with subjects like computing and physics perceived as for boys, while psychology and nursing are seen as for girls.

- The fact that boys become known by name faster than girls, and are more quickly identifiable as individuals, may not be due to teachers seeing them as more important, but because their behaviour causes them to stand out more, implying that it is not teachers reacting to them in a gender-stereotypical way. This is supported by Sabar and Levin (1987), who found that boys dominated discussions, but that girls performed equally well academically.

- The fact that girls outshine boys academically may not be due entirely to boys perceiving education as 'for girls', but because the element of coursework in many subjects has increased, something regarded as being more attractive to girls, who often work in more organised and studious ways. However, this assumption may reflect a gender stereotype in itself.

- Girls tend to perform better academically in single-sex schools, which suggests that boys dominate more and/or are treated as more important in mixed-sex environments. However, single-sex schools tend to be comprised of girls from higher socio-economic backgrounds, so therefore cannot be compared equally with mixed-school intakes of female students.

Issues, debates and approaches

- Research into the influence of schools on the social context of gender roles can be regarded as culturally biased, as most of the research was conducted on schools in a western cultural setting; therefore, it would be inappropriate to apply findings to other cultures with very different educational systems.
- Studies of the social contexts of gender roles, demonstrating the influences of parents, peers, schools and so on, can be seen not to be gender biased, as research has outlined the effects of such influences on both boys and girls.

Research in focus

In Steinke *et al.*'s (2008) study, the criteria for identifying scientist characters were constructed and inter-rater reliability was established by using two raters.

Explain in the context of this study the purpose of establishing behavioural criteria.

What is inter-rater reliability and how would it be established using two raters?

Cultural influences on gender role

The majority of data on gender and gender differences comes from studies of western, primarily US, samples – representing a small portion of the world's population – that fails to consider the entire range of variation in human behaviour. Cross-cultural research helps to correct this imbalance by examining gender-related behaviours within the context of numerous cultural variations. The thinking behind cross-cultural studies is that if similarities are found in gender roles across cultures, it suggests that they are biological in nature, while if differences are found it suggests that they are socially constructed.

Cultural relativism represents the most direct challenge to the biological approach. If gender differences reflect biological differences, then the same differences should occur in different cultures. If differences in gender roles are found between cultures, that would support the view that gender role is culturally determined – that is, that it is not biological.

Conducting research into and interpreting results from cross-cultural sources is problematic in several ways. There is the problem of an *imposed etic*, where researchers use research methods and tools relevant and applicable in their own culture, but alien and non-applicable to other cultures, which can result in flawed conclusions being drawn. Many attempts to replicate US studies in other parts of the world have involved an imposed etic.

Researchers also tend to assume that males are naturally more aggressive and females naturally more nurturing, without first actually gaining evidence to see whether this is true cross-culturally. Consequently, such researchers defined nurturing in ways that excluded altruistic, caring activities of men – for example, men nurturing their families by providing food for mother and child, and sacrificing their own lives if necessary to save family members. Similar misclassifications occurred over definitions of aggression in females.

Sex categorisation represents a more fundamental cultural construction. In contemporary western societies, biological sex and sex category are confused with each other. The agreed criterion for classification as a member of one or the other sex is male or female genitalia. But genitals are not usually available for public inspection; instead, inferences are made about people's genital sex based on viewable aspects of their appearance, based on the assumption that the latter are reliable indicators of the former. However, social constructionists have challenged the common-sense idea that there can be only two sexes, as determined by sexual dimorphism (bodily differences between males and females). Many older, non-western cultures have recognised a third, and even fourth, sex for a very long time.

Some examples of a third and fourth sex

- Among the Sakalavas in Madagascar, boys perceived as pretty are raised as girls and adopt female gender roles. Similarly, Alentian islanders in Alaska raise handsome boys as girls; their beards are plucked and they are later married to rich men. They too adapt readily to their assigned gender role.

- Studies of certain Native American peoples reveal more than two basic gender roles. The *berdache*, a biological male of the Crow tribe, is someone who chooses not to follow the role of a warrior. Instead, he might become the 'wife' of a warrior, but is not scorned or ridiculed by fellow Crows.

- Some *hijras* in India are physical hermaphrodites, others have male genitalia, while some were born with male genitalia, but opted to undergo castration. *Hijras* adopt female names and wear women's clothing, but do not try to pass as women. Their heavy make-up, long, unbound hair and sexualised gestures set them apart from women in general.

- In Thailand, *kathoeys* have male genitalia but dress in women's clothing. However, *kathoeys* are not men who wish to be women; nor do they believe they have a 'woman's mind' trapped inside the 'wrong body', in the way that many transsexuals in western countries describe themselves. Rather, they take some pride in their male genitals and do not wish to pass as women; they act in dramatic, loud, brash ways that violate the norms of femininity in Thai culture.

- The Mohave Indians recognise *four* distinct gender roles: traditional male, traditional female, *alyha* and *hwame*. The *alyha* are males who choose to live as women, mimicking menstruation by cutting their upper thighs and undergoing a ritualistic pregnancy. The *hwame* are females who choose to become men.

You are the researcher

Design a study comparing gender roles in four different cultures. Try to choose cultures that are very different from each other.

How would gender roles be defined and evaluated? What method(s) would be used to collect data?

Explain what is meant by an imposed etic and what measures would be taken to ensure that your research was not affected in this way.

Research: cultural influences on gender role

- Hargreaves (1986) observed that in some cultures men weave and women make pots, whereas in others these roles are reversed; in some parts of the world women are the major agricultural producers, and in others they are prohibited from agricultural activity. This suggests that although biological factors play a part in the sexual division of labour, the content of this work varies enormously between cultures.

- Mead (1935) conducted research into gender differences between various tribes in Papua New Guinea. In one tribe, the *Arapesh*, both males and females exhibited gentle, caring personas. In another, the *Tchambuli*, the men exhibited what would be regarded in western culture as female behaviours, while women exhibited traditional (western) male behaviours. A third tribe, the *Mundugumor*, both exhibited aggressive personalities. This seems to indicate that gender roles are socially constructed rather than being biological in nature. There is the possibility of researcher bias in interpreting the behaviours exhibited, and Mead did subsequently change her views, believing instead that gender behaviours can be biological in nature.

- Whiting and Edwards (1988) researched the gender attitudes and behaviours of various cultures and found that it was fairly universal for girls to be encouraged into domestic and child-caring roles, while boys were assigned tasks involving responsibility outside the home, such as looking after animals. This suggests that it is the activities males and females are given to do that are responsible for the differences in gender roles.

- Williams and Best (1990) looked at attitudes to gender roles in different cultures. It was found that there was universal agreement across cultures about which characteristics were masculine and which feminine, with men being perceived as dominant and independent, and women as caring and sociable. The researchers also found that children from these cultures exhibited the same attitudes. The implication is that attitudes to gender roles are universal and therefore biological in nature.

- Barry *et al.* (1957) performed research across many non-westernised cultures, looking at which qualities were deemed important for males and females. Nurturing was seen as a dominantly feminine characteristic, while self-reliance was seen in the same way for males. These findings reflect those from western cultures and therefore suggest a biological basis to gender roles.

Evaluation

Cultural influences on gender role

- Globalisation may contribute to the lessening of cultural differences, and there has been a reduction in the differences between masculine and feminine gender roles, implying that social influences are stronger than biological ones.

- Many attempts to replicate US studies in other parts of the world involve an imposed etic: they assume that the situation being studied has the same meaning for members of the alien culture as it does for members of the researcher's own culture.

- A methodological problem with cross-cultural studies is that it is difficult to obtain identical samples, and there can be problems with researchers being biased in terms of their own cultural viewpoints.

- Collectivist cultures seem to hold much clearer views than individualistic cultures about which gender roles are male and which are female.

- Margaret Mead's initial research conclusions that gender roles were cultural constructions were influential. However, she changed her views to believe that gender roles were predominantly biological in nature. This dramatic conversion is argued by Booth (1975) to have come about due to Mead falling in love with and getting married to a man with very 'traditional' views on the roles of men and women, and to her having her own child. This suggests that the personal viewpoints investigators bring to their research can have strong effects on the conclusions they ultimately draw.

Issues, debates and approaches

- Cultural influences on gender can be related to the nature versus nurture debate. If gender roles, behaviours and attitudes are universal, this suggests that they are innate and therefore due to nature, while if cultural differences in gender roles are found, this is more indicative of nurture influences.

- Methodologies and measuring scales designed for use in specific cultures should not be used in cultural groups for which they were not intended, an example of an imposed etic. For instance, Kaschak and Sharratt (1983) reported the failure of researchers who translated masculinity–femininity scales developed in the USA into other languages and administered and scored them using US scoring systems. These translated scales were used in an attempt to develop a sex role inventory with Costa Rican university students. Using Spanish translations of 200 items, they found that only two of the 55 PAQ items and half of the 60 BSRI items discriminated between men and women, suggesting that many items representing masculinity–femininity in the USA do not have the same representation in Costa Rica. Similar failures have occurred with BSRI items used in South India, Malaysia and Mexico.

Strengthen your learning

1. How can social learning theory explain the acquisition of gender roles in terms of:
   i) parents
   ii) the media
   iii) schools
   iv) peers.
2. Compile a list of evaluative points for and against SLT being able to explain the acquisition and maintenance of gender roles. Include research evidence.
3. Why might psychologists wish to perform cross-cultural studies of gender roles? Consider *cultural relativism* when answering this question.
4. What problems are there in conducting cross-cultural research into gender roles?
5. Outline how cross-cultural evidence suggests the existence of more than just two sexes.
6. What conclusions can be drawn from cross-cultural studies of gender roles? Give details.

Assessment Check

1. Discuss social influences on gender – for example, the influence of parents, peers, schools and the media. (24 marks)

2. Outline one social influence on gender. (4 marks)

3. Outline and evaluate cultural influences on gender role. (20 marks)

4. Outline cultural influences on gender role. (8 marks)

Examination guidance

The term 'discuss' in question 1 means to describe and evaluate. The examples given are there to guide you, with no requirement to include them.

Any relevant material on social influences on gender would be creditworthy.

Question 2 calls for only one social influence; provide several and all would be marked, but only the best one would be credited.

Question 3 needs both an outline and an evaluation of cultural influences on gender role, but as the outline is only worth 4 marks a 'short' version is required, while most time and effort should be directed at the evaluation, where 16 marks are on offer.

Question 4 also calls for an outline of cultural influences on gender role, but this time a 'longer' version is needed, as it's worth 8 marks.

Summing up

- Kohlberg's cognitive developmental theory perceives children as developing an understanding of gender in three distinct stages: *gender labelling, gender stability* and *gender constancy*, with gender role behaviour apparent only after an understanding that gender is fixed and constant.

- Children understand gender differently at different ages, with gender concepts developing as children actively structure their social experiences.

- After gender constancy is reached, at about 7 years, children start to develop gender concepts suiting their own gender, and to value the behaviours and attitudes associated with their gender.

- A major problem for cognitive developmental theory is its inability to account for gender-specific behaviour occurring before children have acquired gender constancy.

- Gender schema theory sees gender identity alone as providing children with motivation to assume sex-typed behaviour patterns.

- Gender schemas provide a basis for interpreting the environment and selecting appropriate forms of behaviour; in this way, children's self-perceptions become sex-typed.

- The evidence for gender schema theory is mixed, and much supporting evidence is correlational.

- Many of the physical and behavioural differences between males and females are biological ones, with sex hormones, like testosterone, seen as directing the majority of sexual development, though hormonal influences on behaviour are harder to determine.

- Evolutionary explanations of gender focus on the different selective pressures on males and females, leading to differences in mating strategies and the establishment of gender-based behaviours.

- Biosocial theory sees gender as being determined by both biological and social factors working in conjunction with each other to produce masculine and feminine behaviours and identities.

- Much of the evidence for biosocial theory comes from studies of people with intersex conditions, but this has proved a controversial area, difficult to draw clear conclusions from.

- Gender dysphoria is a psychiatric disorder where individuals feel uncomfortable with their biological sex and may wish to change it.

- Evidence suggests a role for genetics, with attention centring on gene variants of the androgen receptor, which influences the action of testosterone and is involved in the masculinisation of the brain.

- Hormonal factors, conditioning and various other psychological factors are also suggested as playing a role in gender dysphoria.

- Social influences on gender centre around the influence of social learning theory, with the major influences being parents, peers, the media and schooling.

- There is a wealth of evidence to back up the idea of gender roles being acquired through social learning, though the theory is not without criticism.

- Most research on gender roles is based on western culture. Cross-cultural studies help to determine whether gender role acquisition is fundamentally biological or social in nature.

- A major problem is that of an *imposed etic*, where researchers use methods and tools relevant and applicable in their own culture, but alien and non-applicable to other cultures.

- Sex categorisation also varies between cultures, with some societies perceiving the existence of a third and even fourth sex.

7 Intelligence

Theories of intelligence	**236**
Psychometric theories	237
Information-processing theories	241
Animal learning and intelligence	**249**
Simple learning (classical and operant conditioning)	249
The role of simple learning in the behaviour of non-human animals	251
Intelligence in non-human animals	254
Human intelligence	**261**
Evolutionary factors in the development of human intelligence	261
Genetic and environmental factors associated with intelligence test performance	267
Cultural influences on intelligence test performance	274
Summing up	**277**

Decoding the specification

The specification outlines what you must study in order to answer any examination question you might face. Psychometric and information-processing theories must be studied, as the wording of the specification is such that specific questions could be asked about them. However, the theories listed (Spearman, Cattell, Thurstone, Sternberg and Gardner), are merely examples, so questions cannot specifically refer to them and any relevant alternative theories are equally creditworthy. Simple learning, in the form of classical and operant conditioning and their role in the behaviour of non-human animals, must also be studied as they are explicitly referred to. However, the examples listed of intelligence in non-humans (self-recognition, social learning and Machiavellian intelligence) cannot feature specifically in exam questions, any alternative relevant examples being acceptable.

The specification demands an understanding of evolutionary factors in the development of human intelligence and again the factors listed are examples and cannot feature explicitly in the wording of exam questions. Any relevant material is equally acceptable. However, when studying the role of genetic and environmental factors associated with intelligence test performance, the influence of culture must be included as it is specifically named.

Theories of intelligence

Intelligence concerns an individual's ability to have knowledge of their world and use that knowledge in an effective manner. An early approach to psychology concentrated on trying to measure human mental qualities, such as intelligence, with a view to developing practical applications from these measurements. However, psychologists notoriously cannot agree on a common definition of intelligence, let alone if it should be measured. The topic area is also affected by widely varying political and philosophical viewpoints that makes unbiased study difficult.

Theories of intelligence break down into two broad types. First, *psychometric theories*, which focus on measuring intellectual abilities to show the differences between individuals; and second, the later *information-processing theories*, which study the processes that people employ when solving problems.

IN THE NEWS

Adapted from an exhibition by the Royal Institute of British Architects

The mud masons of Mali

Djenne, a UNESCO world heritage site, is the oldest city in sub-Saharan Africa and an important centre of Islamic learning and pilgrimage. Among its many mud-built architectural treasures is the Great Mosque, which holds 3,000 worshippers. Built of sun-dried mud bricks held together by mud mortar and re-plastered with fresh mud every spring, the great Mosque has walls 61 cm thick, to bear the weight of the huge structure and to insulate it from the fierce sun. Each of its three massive towers is topped with an ostrich egg to symbolise fertility and purity. Eighty senior masons, who teach a vast army of apprentices the necessary skills to repair and enhance the city's mud buildings, oversee their maintenance.

In 2001, Dr Trevor Marchand, a senior lecturer at the University of London, signed on as an apprentice, and returned over several years, in order to learn the construction skills himself and observe the teaching methods. You would imagine that buildings of such elaborate construction would need an education system involving reading, writing and formal examinations. However, the transferral of knowledge is entirely practice-based,

Figure 7.01

with skills being communicated, understood and negotiated between practitioners without words and by physical repetition.

In psychological terms, this is a bodily kinaesthetic form of intelligence, one of several types of intelligence proposed by Howard Gardner in his theory of multiple intelligences. Of course, such an intelligence type, by its very nature, cannot be tested for by traditional IQ tests.

If you would like to find out more about Dr Trevor Marchand's work on the mud masons of Mali, go to his web page at www.soas.ac.uk/staff/staff31381.php

Psychometric theories

Psychometric psychologists create tests that attempt to measure human abilities and characteristics. Psychometricists assume that intelligence consists of component parts that can be determined by *factor analysis*, a statistical method analysing the relationships among a set of variables in order to reduce them to their basic factors.

Psychometric theories differ from each other by the number of separate factors seen as comprising intelligence.

Spearman's two-factor model (1904)

Early psychologists were keen for the subject to be accepted as a serious scientific discipline. Therefore psychology had to show that it could use scientific principles and practices, and produce applications of use to society. Spearman was a pioneer in devising and applying scientific measuring techniques to the study of intelligence. He believed that his theory would allow psychology to become a real scientific discipline. Spearman noticed that individuals tend to achieve similar scores on different mental tests and therefore believed that there must be a common intelligence factor shared by everyone. He used factor analysis to find two basic factors of intelligence:

1. 'g' – a *general intelligence* factor underpinning all intelligent behaviour and abilities. This form of intelligence is innate and is not affected by learning.

2. 's' – *specific intelligence* factors, such as mathematical ability, which relate to particular tasks. This form of intelligence is learned.

Spearman believed that intelligent behaviour consists of general and specific factors, with general intelligence being more important, because differences between individuals were largely differences in 'g'. In effect, his belief was that 'g' is what is meant by the term 'intelligence'. Spearman believed that 'g' was innate and a form of mental energy related to the efficiency of the nervous system.

Psychometric tests of intelligence are generally composed of questions like these:

1. Which of the following is the odd one out?

   (a) robin (b) sparrow (c) chicken (d) blue jay

2. What number comes next?

   3, 6, 10, 15, 21, ?

Research: Spearman's two-factor model

- Spearman (1927) estimated the intelligence levels of 24 village children using his factor analysis method, finding a 'perfect' correlation, inferring 'g' to be real and not a mathematical abstraction.

- Johnson and Bouchard (2005) used factor analysis to find a single, higher-order intelligence factor, suggesting that there is a general intelligence factor underpinning intelligence.

Key terms

Intelligence – understanding the essentials of a situation and responding to them appropriately

Psychometrics – a branch of psychology seeking to measure mental abilities by the formation of tests

Factor analysis – a statistical technique used by psychometricists, which attempts to reduce large amounts of data to a basic number of factors

Information processing – an approach perceiving the mind as using logical rules and strategies to process and make sense of incoming sensory data

Multiple intelligences – the idea that several, independent forms of human intelligence exist

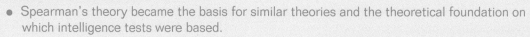

Evaluation

Spearman's two-factor model

- Spearman's theory became the basis for similar theories and the theoretical foundation on which intelligence tests were based.

- There are arguments about whether 'g' actually exists, and therefore suspicions about the validity of theories based on Spearman's assumptions and the value of intelligence tests.

- Spearman's theory was not widely accepted and became replaced by multi-factor theories, such as Gardner's theory of multiple intelligences (see page 244).

- Some psychologists still work in a psychometric fashion, but Kitcher (1985) said that most psychologists do not believe there to be a single, general measure of intelligence. Indeed, Thorndike, a contemporary of Spearman, argued for a completely different theory that sorted intellectual abilities into three different classes: abstract or verbal intelligence (involving the ability to manipulate symbols), practical or mechanical intelligence (involving the ability to manipulate objects), and social intelligence (involving the ability to deal with other people).

Thurstone's primary mental abilities (1938)

Thurstone devised a set of 56 tests given to 240 college students. Using factor analysis techniques that he developed himself, the results were analysed and led to a new theory of intelligence, challenging Spearman's idea of a two-factor theory. Thurstone believed that Spearman's idea of 'g' was an artificial product of the mathematical procedures he used. Instead, Thurstone found that intelligent behaviour arose from seven independent factors called *primary abilities*:

- *word fluency* – speed with verbal material, as when making rhymes

- *verbal comprehension* – the ability to understand word meanings

- *spatial visualisation* – the ability to mentally visualise and manipulate objects in three dimensions

- *number facility* – an ability with numbers, like mental arithmetic

- *associative memory* – the ability to remember words, letters, numbers and images

- *reasoning* – obtaining general ideas and rules from information

- *perceptual speed* – the ability to swiftly distinguish visual details and perceive similarities and differences between pictured objects.

Research: Thurstone's primary mental abilities

- Thurstone (1938) performed research on 14-year-olds and college students and did not find, as Spearman did, that mental tests of ability correlated equally. When Thurstone analysed the data sampled from people with similar overall IQ scores, he found different profiles of primary mental abilities, lending support to his theory and weakening that of Spearman.

- Blewett (1954) used Thurstone's *primary mental abilities* tests to assess the intelligence levels of 52 same-sex twins aged between 12 and 15, finding correlations that supported the theory.

Thurstone's primary mental abilities

- When Thurstone administered his tests to children with very different intellects, he failed to find his seven primary abilities separate from each other, uncovering evidence instead of the existence of 'g', supporting Spearman's two-factor theory.

- Thurstone produced a mathematical solution resolving his contradictory results and produced an updated version of his theory, accounting for the existence of both a general factor of intelligence and his seven primary mental abilities. This ingenious compromise led to the formation by other researchers of hierarchical theories and multiple intelligences.

Guildford's structure of intellect model (1967)

Spearman argued for two factors of intelligence, Guildford believed there were 120 (by 1984 he was arguing for 150). Guildford also rejects the notion of a general intelligence factor. Guildford believed that intellect could be divided into five types of *operation* (type of thinking being performed), four types of *contents* (what an individual must think about) and six kinds of *products* (type of answer required). These multiply together to produce 120 separate abilities, and Guildford set out to devise tests to measure each one.

Guildford's theory was used to construct the structure of intellect (SOI) teaching programme, which provides individual assessments based on identification of strengths and weaknesses, followed by a personalised learning programme.

Research: Guildford's structure of intellect model

- Guildford (1985) devised 70 tests measuring separate mental abilities, but the scores gained on these tests often correlated with each other, suggesting that there are possibly fewer than the 120 separate abilities he originally proposed.

- Assessing SOI, Manning (1975) found it effective in helping gifted children to think more creatively. This suggests that Guildford's theory, on which it was based, has solid foundations.

Guildford's structure of intellect model

- Guildford's theory illustrates the desire by society for easily applicable, objective tests that had a biased interpretation of intelligence, comprising only the ability to read, compute mathematically and perform other similar subjects. However, Guildford's theory has a wider scope, as it also encompasses creative elements.

- Guilford's theory allows for newly discovered categories to be added in terms of operations, contents and products, with the model also suggesting where new abilities might be discovered based on existing abilities.

- Guildford showed intelligence to be incredibly complex. After his input intelligence was no longer considered a monolithic global trait that was innate and absolute.

Evaluation

Psychometric theories

- Psychometric theories have made an important contribution to the study of intelligence and have provided practical applications, like IQ tests.

- Factor analysis produces widely ranging numbers of basic factors, from Spearman's two factors to Guildford's 150, suggesting that the process is not as objective and scientific as first claimed. This occurs because there are several ways to factor-analyse data, each producing different patterns of factors.

- A methodological issue is that different researchers use different types of participants. British theorists like Spearman used schoolchildren, who have more diverse levels of intelligence than the college students used by US theorists like Guildford and Thurstone. This may have contributed to the differing results and conclusions reached.

- The interpretation of the factors produced by factor analysis is open to criticism. Researchers decide which factors are uncorrelated and separate; they do not come ready labelled. Thus the process is open to researcher bias: researchers interpreting data in a way that matches their beliefs about the nature of intelligence.

- Psychometric theories explain little about the processes underlying intelligence. The information-processing approach proposed a solution, to directly study the mental processes underlying intelligence and relate them to the factors of intelligence proposed by the psychometric approach.

- Duncan *et al.* (2000) found biological support for the existence of 'g'. The use of PET scans while participants completed diverse intelligence tests showed that the lateral prefrontal cortex area of the brain was activated, but not when other non-intellectual activities were performed.

Issues, debates and approaches

- Psychometric theories of intelligence are by their nature reductionist, as they seek to reduce intelligence, by the statistical technique of factor analysis, to its basic factors in order to measure them. Also, as psychometric theories see 'g' as being innate, such theories are biologically determined, with intelligence levels being determined by hereditary factors.

- Psychometric theories can be considered socially sensitive, as they seek to create tests to measure intelligence, and such tests can have far-reaching educational and occupational consequences for individuals.

- Psychometric theories have practical applications. Bradfield and Slocumb (1997) found that Guildford's SOI teaching programme made students better critical thinkers, and it is used in schools and learning clinics in the USA to diagnose and help students with learning disabilities, as well as for the enrichment of gifted students.

Supplementary learning

Uses and misuses of psychometric theories

There was a desire in the early days of psychology to prove not only that the subject was a serious scientific discipline, but also that it could benefit society. The main aim of psychometric theories was to measure intelligence. This was a noble aim, as intelligence test scores could be used to appropriately select people for different educational, occupational and military purposes. However, the history

continued ...

of intelligence testing is one of controversy, with accusations of racial bias and cultural bigotry. Intelligence tests were even used to screen potential immigrants to the USA, and as a justification for sterilising women of low intelligence. Many supporters of such tests were advocates of *eugenics*, which championed the idea of selectively breeding humans to improve the genetic stock. The Nazis took this to the extreme of exterminating those, like the Jews, whom they saw as of 'inferior' genetic quality. Over time, due to the wealth of criticisms, intelligence tests fell out of favour. However, intelligence tests still have their supporters and are still in use – for example, testing for learning disabilities and for academic selection. Yet the main criticism still remains unanswered: how is it possible measure something for which there is no agreed definition?

Information-processing theories

While psychometric theories focus on the content of intelligence, information–processing theories concentrate on the cognitive processes utilised to solve problems.

Classic research

Hunt *et al.* (1973)
Individual differences in cognition
Aim

To measure the time taken to perform the individual steps involved in solving a problem, and to see if these correlate with psychometric test scores of intelligence.

Procedure

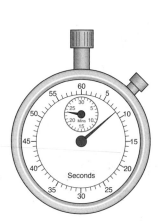

Figure 7.02 Is intelligence linked to speed of thought?

Participants were presented with pairs of letters like AA, Aa or Ab, and asked to answer as quickly as possible one of two questions: 'Are the letters the same physically?' or 'Are the two letters the same only in name?'

The researchers were interested in the question about letter names, as they believed that a critical ability underlying intelligence is the speed of retrieval of information from memory. By subtracting the time taken to react to the first question about physical similarity from the time taken to react to the question about name similarity, they isolated the speed taken to read the questions and push buttons on a computer. Participants also completed an IQ test.

Findings

There was a positive correlation between speed of retrieval of information from memory and score on an intelligence test.

Conclusions

Intelligent people, especially those who are verbally fluent, are able to absorb and then retrieve quickly from memory lots of information.

Evaluation

Sternberg believed that a relatively weak correlation was found between psychometric test scores and cognitive tasks, because only low-level cognitive abilities were tested, and although such processes are involved in intelligence, they are not processes central to it. He suggested that research should be focused on identifying the mental processes that individuals use to perform the tasks found in intelligence tests.

Research in focus

Hunt's (1973) study is an example of a correlational study.

Can you think of one strength and one limitation of correlational studies?

What do correlations test for?

What is meant by a correlation coefficient?

In what way does a positive correlation differ from a negative one?

Select an appropriate graph to display correlational data.

How could you assess the reliability of Hunt's findings?

Sternberg's theory of intelligence (1977)

Sternberg saw intelligence in terms of how successfully individuals deal with their environment. He believed that psychometric theories focused only on measurable mental abilities and 'school-smart' people. Sternberg was more interested in 'street-smart' people, those who could adapt and shape their environment, but who did not do well on IQ tests.

His theory is regarded as the first cognitive theory and challenges more established psychometric theories.

Sternberg's triarchic theory is made up of three facets (sub-theories): *analytical*, *creative* and *practical*.

Analytical intelligence

This is similar to the psychometric viewpoint, of a type of intelligence measured through academic problems and involving a series of three components: *metacomponents*, *performance components* and *knowledge-acquisition components* (see Table 7.01).

Table 7.01 Components of analytical intelligence

METACOMPONENTS	Executive, higher-order control processes, involved in planning, problem solving and decision making
	Oversee *performance components* when carrying out desired actions
	For example, selecting the best strategy to solve a problem and then overseeing the performance components in carrying out the necessary actions
PERFORMANCE COMPONENTS	Processes that undertake actions dictated by *metacomponents*
	Uses long-term memory to permit perception of problems and relationships between objects and applies these relationships to decision making and problem solving
	For example, calculating numbers to aim at in a game of darts
KNOWLEDGE ACQUISITION COMPONENTS	Processes used to acquire new knowledge
	Selectively combines new information from diverse sources to complete tasks
	For example, using 'chunking', where a common meaning is found to join several items together in memory

Creative intelligence

This deals with the relationship between intelligence and experience. It involves how well a task is performed with regard to a person's level of experience. Experience has two parts: *novelty* and *automation* (see Table 7.02).

Table 7.02 Types of creative intelligence

NOVELTY	Situations not experienced before
	Gifted individuals can transfer skills from familiar experiences to unfamiliar (novel) experiences
	For example, transferring skills and strategies learned from playing a familiar sport, like basketball, to an unfamiliar one, like netball
AUTOMATION	Situations experienced many times before, therefore allowing other processes to be performed simultaneously (*parallel processing*)
	For example, an experienced driver driving a car safely, while being able to take part in a conversation at the same time

Individuals may be gifted in one type of creative intelligence, but not necessarily both. Creative intelligence is also associated with *synthetic giftedness*, the ability to create new ideas and solve novel problems – for example, using old plastic bottles to make flowerpots. Such individuals do not necessarily score highly on IQ tests, as such tests do not measure this talent.

Practical intelligence

This deals with the relationship between intelligence and an individual's external world. It involves the use of three processes to create a 'fit' between oneself and the environment: *adaptation*, *shaping* and *selection*. Such individuals are 'street-smart'.

Figure 7.03 Gifted individuals can transfer skills from familiar situations to unfamiliar ones

Table 7.03 The processes of practical intelligence

ADAPTATION	Involves a person changing within themselves in order to adjust to a changing environment
	For example, wearing warmer clothes as the temperature drops
SHAPING	Involves changing an environment to suit a person's needs
	For example, only speaking when spoken to in an interview
SELECTION	Involves choosing a new environment in preference to an existing, inferior one, to fit a person's needs
	For example, buying a camper van when the cost of holidaying rises

Practical intelligence is also associated with *practical giftedness*, an ability to apply new ideas and analytical skills to practical situations – for example, an accomplished athlete using experience to devise coaching schedules for younger athletes.

Sternberg argued that individuals are not necessarily restricted to being intelligent in just one of the three sub-components, but can have a high degree of intelligence across all the sub-components.

Research: Sternberg's theory of intelligence

- Merrick (1992) factor-analysed data from the Cognitive Abilities Self-Evaluative Questionnaire (CASE-Q) given to 268 Dutch high school girls and found individuals with all three types of intelligence detailed by Sternberg, therefore supporting the components of his theory.

- Grigorenko *et al.* (2003) provided support for Sternberg's theory by finding that teaching methods based on his theory, stressing analytical, creative and practical thinking, were superior in improving reading ability to more conventional methods.

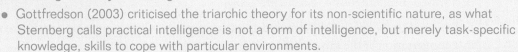

Evaluation

Sternberg's theory of intelligence

- Gottfredson (2003) criticised the triarchic theory for its non-scientific nature, as what Sternberg calls practical intelligence is not a form of intelligence, but merely task-specific knowledge, skills to cope with particular environments.
- Gottfredson (2003) also believes that IQ tests do measure 'street-smartness', as they can predict a high scorer's ability to live longer, have a good job, stay out of jail, etc.
- Sternberg's model can be perceived as having a broader scope, as it measures synthetic and practical skills in addition to analytical skills and thus can be seen as more inclusive by accounting for 'street-smart' as well as 'school-smart' individuals.

Gardner's theory of multiple intelligences

Gardner (1983) argued that traditional theories of intelligence did not include the wide-ranging types of human ability. He argued that a child weak in language abilities might actually be able in other intellectual areas.

Gardner saw individuals as possessing a *cognitive profile*, involving different amounts of various kinds of intelligence. The theory is an educational theory, as Gardner believes that schools should offer individual teaching programmes fitting each person's cognitive profile and improving their intellectual weaknesses. Gardner also thought there was a danger, by not acknowledging certain types of intelligence, of devaluing individuals who possess high levels of ability in those areas.

Each person's cognitive profile is based on eight core types of intelligence, as set out in Table 7.04.

Table 7.04 Eight core types of intelligence

BODILY KINAESTHETIC	Concerns bodily movements
	Learning occurs by physical interaction – for example, sports players
	Such individuals tend to have strong muscle memories, remembering things through physical actions and fine motor movements rather than visual or verbal memory
INTERPERSONAL	Concerns interactions with others
	Learning occurs through group discussion – for example, managers
	Such individuals are sensitive to others' moods and emotions and communicate well

INTRAPERSONAL	Concerns self-awareness
	Learning occurs via introspection – for example, scientists
	Such individuals learn best by concentrating on a subject alone and seek perfection in their work
LINGUISTIC	Concerns the use of language
	Learning occurs by reading and note-making – for example, writers
	Such individuals have an advanced linguistic memory and communicate persuasively through language
LOGICAL-MATHEMATICAL	Concerns logic
	Learning occurs by reasoning and the use of numbers – for example, engineers
	Such individuals are skilled in using scientific principles and practices
MUSICAL	Concerns sensitivity to sound and music
	Learning occurs by auditory means – for example, musicians
	Such individuals can use song forms to memorise information and work well with background music playing
SPATIAL	Concerns vision and spatial judgement
	Learning occurs by visualisation and mental manipulation – for example, architects
	Such individuals have strong visual memories and artistic talents involving hand–eye coordination and directional sense
NATURALISTIC	Concerns the natural world
	Learning occurs by sensitivity to nature – for example, farmers
	Such individuals collect and analyse information relating to the natural world and are skilled at growing plants and caring for and interacting with animals

Although not dependent on each other, these intelligence types rarely operate in isolation and everyone has varying degrees of each type.

Several criteria were used to provide evidence for the existence of each type of intelligence – for instance, finding gifted individuals who are talented in one area, but not another, neurological evidence indicating specialised brain areas and the existence of unique, step-by-step developmental trends for each type of intelligence.

Other types of multiple intelligences have been suggested, such as *existential*, the ability to think in a philosophical manner and *moral* intelligence, wisdom of character. However, moral intelligence does not meet the criteria for a separate type, and existential intelligence has not been linked to a specific brain area.

Figure 7.04 Individuals with naturalistic intelligence have a sensitivity to nature

Research: Gardner's theory of multiple intelligences

- Marchand (2008) found that mud masons in Mali communicated building skills without using words, but by physical repetition, supporting the idea of a separate bodily kinaesthetic intelligence. This could have practical applications in the teaching of apprentices.

- Traub (1999) reported on neuroscientific evidence supporting the idea of different intelligence types having localised function in the brain. Brain imaging and studies of brain-damaged individuals showed different mental activities associated with different brain areas, supporting the theory.

- Turner (2008) provided evidence for the existence of a separate musical intelligence. Teachers used memorable tunes to successfully fit in lyrics that represented material being learned, with students exhibiting advanced levels of musical intelligence remembering more of the content.

Evaluation

Gardner's theory of multiple intelligences

- Naturalistic intelligence may exist as a form of intelligence in cultures where people live close to nature.
- Musical and bodily kinaesthetic intelligences have been criticised as being talents rather than types of intelligence.
- Gardner's intelligence types may simply be types of personality, rather than forms of intelligence, as there are no tests that can identify and measure them.

Issues, debates and approaches

- Gardner's theory can be argued to be reductionist, as it breaks intelligence up into its separate, constituent types.

- Gardner's theory has many practical applications for education – for example, the development of bodily kinaesthetic intelligence among apprentice mud masons in Mali – while Kornhaber (2001) reports that Gardner's theory permits the creation of new teaching methods that meet the wide range of learning styles that students exhibit. Lazear (1992) showed that teaching methods incorporating individually tailored projects lead to increased SAT scores and better student discipline and motivation.

You are the researcher

Go to www.bgfl.org/bgfl/custom/resources_ftp/client_ftp/ks3/ict/multiple_int/index.htm where you will find a test to measure multiple intelligences (you can have a go yourself and print off your cognitive profile).

Using the test as your measuring device, design a study to test for a difference in cognitive profiles between two distinct groups of people – for example, science and drama students.

What experimental design would you use?

What would be your IV and DV?

Draw up an appropriate table for your findings. What would an appropriate measure of central tendency be? Justify this decision.

How many participants are required to form a representative sample?

Evaluation

Information-processing theories

- Information-processing theories can be seen as superior, because psychometric theories merely describe intelligence, while information-processing theories explain how problems are solved by identifying the cognitive processes involved.
- Information-processing theories identify a much broader scope of abilities than those offered by the narrow focus of psychometric theories.
- Information-processing theories neglect the influence of perceived intelligence, levels of which create specific forms and degrees of motivation, directly affecting how information is processed.

Issues, debates and approaches

- Information-processing theories concentrate on the mental processes that underpin intelligent behaviour, like identifying the steps taken to identify and solve problems. In this way, they can be considered part of the cognitive approach.
- Sternberg's theory considers the interaction of several components, such as analytical skills, creativity and practical skills. In this way, it can be considered a holistic theory, as opposed to psychometric theories that are more reductionist in nature.
- Information-processing theories have practical applications, especially in education.

Strengthen your learning

1. Why were early psychologists interested in measuring intelligence?
2. What is factor analysis?
3a. Describe the two intelligence factors proposed by Spearman.
3b. Give one positive and one negative criticism of Spearman's theory.
4. Describe Thurstone's seven primary abilities of intelligence.
5. Outline Guildford's theory of intelligence and give two evaluative points for it.
6. What main practical application have psychometric theories provided?
7a. Outline the three facets (sub-theories) of Sternberg's triarchic theory.
7b. Give one positive and one negative criticism of Sternberg's theory.
8. Why may information-processing theories be considered superior to psychometric ones?
9a. Outline Gardner's eight core types of intelligence. For each type, give an example and describe the qualities such a person may have.
9b. What three criteria have been used to provide evidence for the existence of separate types of intelligence?
9c. Give one positive and one negative criticism of Gardner's theory.

Assessment Check

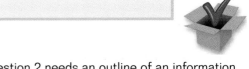

1. Outline and evaluate two psychometric theories of intelligence. (24 marks)

2. Outline one information processing theory of multiple intelligences. (8 marks)

3. Evaluate information-processing theories of intelligence. (16 marks)

4. 'There is a body of evidence that suggests that several independent forms of human intelligence exist.' Critically discuss one information theory of multiple intelligences. (24 marks)

5. Compare and contrast psychometric theories of intelligence with information-processing theories of intelligence. (24 marks)

Examination guidance

Question 1 calls for a description and evaluation of two psychometric theories. You will not gain extra marks by doing a third, and you will lose access to several marks by only covering one, however well it is done. Non-psychometric theories could be utilised as part of the evaluation.

Question 2 needs an outline of an information processing theory, such as Sternberg's or Gardner's, and providing evaluation will not gain credit and wastes valuable time. Question 3 calls for an evaluation of information-processing theories, so any description will not gain credit. There are 16 marks available, compared to only 8 in question 2, so more attention should be focused on question 3.

Question 4 requires a description and an evaluation of one information processing theory, with most marks available for the evaluation. Suitable evaluation could include the degree of support from research studies and relevant practical applications.

Question 5 requires a comparison of psychometric and information-processing theories, involving outlining both types of theories (either generally and/or by reference to specific theories) and then evaluating them. This could be achieved by focusing on strengths and weaknesses.

Animal learning and intelligence

Simple learning (classical and operant conditioning)

Classical and operant conditioning form the basis of behaviourism, which sees learning occurring from experience via the process of association. In classical conditioning a *stimulus* becomes associated with a *response*, while operant conditioning involves learning behaviour due to its consequences.

Classical conditioning is associated with behaviour not under conscious control, while operant conditioning is associated with voluntary behaviour.

Classical conditioning

While researching the salivation reflex of dogs, Pavlov (1927) noticed that the dogs salivated before food was presented, as they could predict its arrival due to other environmental features becoming associated with their feeding – for example, the sight of their food bowl. Therefore the dogs learned to produce a natural reflex (salivation) to a stimulus not normally associated with that response. Pavlov found that by pairing the presentation of food with the sound of a bell, he could very quickly get the dogs to salivate to the sound of the bell alone. This process of classical conditioning is as follows:

> **Key terms**
>
> **Classical conditioning** – learning occurring through association of a neutral stimulus with an involuntary unconditioned stimulus
> **Operant conditioning** – learning occurring via reinforcement of behaviour, thus increasing the chances of behaviour occurring again
> **Social learning** – learning occurring by the observation and imitation of others
> **Self-recognition** – the ability to identify one's own self-image, suggesting the possession of a self-concept
> **Theory of mind** – the ability to attribute mental states to oneself and others
> **Machiavellian intelligence** – the ability to serve one's own interests by manipulation of or cooperation with others, which does not upset the social cohesion of a group

- Before learning: FOOD (unconditioned stimulus: UCS) → SALIVATION (unconditioned response: UCR)

- During learning: FOOD (UCS) + BELL (neutral stimulus: NS) → SALIVATION (UCR)

- After learning: BELL (conditioned stimulus: CS) → SALIVATION (conditioned response: CR)

Pavlov then performed a series of experiments that highlighted various features of classical conditioning. These are illustrated in Table 7.05.

Table 7.05 Features of classical conditioning

ONE-TRIAL LEARNING	A form of classical conditioning where just one pairing of a UCS and a CS produces a CR
	For example, being thrown into a swimming pool as a child leads to a lifetime fear of water
FIRST- AND SECOND-ORDER CONDITIONING	First-order conditioning involves pairing a CS (e.g. bell) with an UCS that directly satisfies a biological urge (e.g. food)
	Second-order conditioning pairs a CS (e.g. bell) with a UCS that indirectly satisfies the biological urge by its motivational value (e.g. a light)
GENERALISATION	The conditioning process can be generalised by slightly varying the CS to produce weaker forms of the CR (e.g. bells with increasingly different tones produce an increasingly weaker CR)

DISCRIMINATION	Discrimination occurs when the UCS is paired with one specific CS and the CR occurs to this pairing only
	For example, feeding dogs only when a bell of a certain tone is rung
EXTINCTION	If the CS is continually given without the presentation of the UCS, the CR grows weaker and then ceases
	For example, if the bell is continually rung without food being given
SPONTANEOUS RECOVERY	After apparent extinction, if a rest period is given followed by re-presentation of the CS, the CR is revived
	For example, ringing the bell again after a break will re-produce the salivation reflex

Operant conditioning

Operant conditioning is based on Thorndike's (1911) *law of effect*, which found that behaviours resulting in pleasant outcomes are likely to be repeated in similar circumstances, while behaviours resulting in unpleasant outcomes are unlikely to be repeated.

Under controlled laboratory conditions, Skinner (1938) built on Thorndike's work. He used a *Skinner box*, where animals were rewarded with food pellets for producing desired behaviours. By an accidental process of trial and error, an animal would produce a behaviour, like pressing a lever, causing a food pellet to be released. Gradually, the animal learns to associate the behaviour with the reward and produce the behaviour every time.

The food pellet (or any form of reward) is a *reinforcement*, because it strengthens the chances of the behaviour recurring.

There are four possible outcomes of any behaviour:

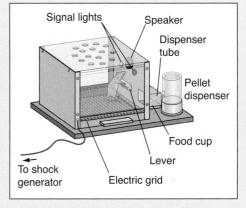

Figure 7.05 A Skinner box

- Positive reinforcement: receiving something pleasant – for example, a food pellet

- Negative reinforcement: not receiving something unpleasant – for example, not having to do chores

- Positive punishment: receiving something unpleasant – for example, being grounded

- Negative punishment: not receiving something pleasant – for example, not receiving a promised treat

Reinforcements increase the chances of behaviour recurring, while punishments decrease the chances. However, punishments do not teach desired behaviours.

Reinforcements can be *primary reinforcements*, directly satisfying biological needs – for example, food – or *secondary reinforcements*, which are motivational and require learning and indirectly satisfy biological needs – for example, money.

Behaviour shaping

This is a means of achieving target behaviour by reinforcing behaviours that gradually resemble the desired one, like training dolphins to take tools to deep-sea divers. The routine is broken down into its constituent parts, with the first part being reinforced and the second part added on to gain the reinforcement, and so on, until only the whole routine is reinforced.

Reinforcement schedules

This involves varying the frequency at which reinforcements are given and affects the rate at which animals will respond. For instance, a *variable ratio reinforcement schedule*, where reinforcements are given after an average number of responses, leads to animals responding steadily and frequently; when the reinforcements stop, extinction is slow to occur.

The role of simple learning in the behaviour of non-human animals

Classical conditioning

Animals use classical and operant conditioning to learn about their environment and adapt to changing environments. Research in laboratory and natural settings demonstrates classical conditioning being used by animals to learn whether food sources are safe.

One-trial learning is a form of classical conditioning where one pairing of a CS with a UCS is enough to produce a CR.

Seligman (1970) proposed the idea of *biological preparedness*, where some associations are learned more readily, as an animal is biologically predisposed to do so. Such behaviours are adaptive and bestow a survival value.

Research: classical conditioning

- Sahley *et al.* (1981) exposed slugs just once to a highly attractive food odour of potato or carrot and a saturated solution of guanidine sulphate, a bitter-tasting plant substance. The slugs subsequently displayed reduced preference for that specific food odour, demonstrating one-trial learning in non-human animals.

- Garcia and Koelling (1966) illustrated biological preparedness in non-human animals by pairing a sweet-tasting liquid attractive to rats with an injection containing lithium chloride, which made them ill. The rats quickly learned to associate the sweet-tasting liquid with being ill and declined to drink it, because they were biologically predisposed to do so – that is, it is a natural adaptive behaviour. However, when the sweet-tasting liquid was paired with an electric shock, the rats continued to drink the sweet-tasting liquid. They had not developed a taste aversion, as rats have no natural biological predisposition to avoid things paired with electric shocks.

- Garcia *et al.* (1990) found that taste aversions occur naturally, as wolves and coyotes made ill by being fed mutton laced with lithium chloride refused to approach live sheep and instead displayed submissive behaviour, rolling onto their backs to expose their stomachs.

- Armstrong *et al.* (2006) demonstrated one-trial learning in 3-day-old mice. The mice were deprived of their mothers for 2 hours and then conditioned to associate a certain odour when returned to their mothers and given access to suckling. The mice were again deprived of their mothers and demonstrated a preference for the conditioned odour over other novel odours.

- Curtis *et al.* (1999) created squirrel-proof birdseed. Birdseed was coated in chilli pepper, which is unpleasant to squirrels in taste and smell and they quickly learned to avoid it, but birds, having no capsaicin receptors, cannot be conditioned to avoid the birdseed and continued to eat it.

Operant conditioning

Operant conditioning allows animals to interact with their environment, and, by trial-and-error learning, shape behaviour via reinforcement and punishment processes – for example, to find food and avoid danger. So if animals exhibit behaviour with no pleasurable outcome, such as a bear continually jumping into a river, but failing to catch fish, this reduces the chances that the behaviour will be exhibited again. However, exhibited behaviours with a pleasurable outcome, such as a bear putting its head, open-mouthed, under water to catch fish successfully, increases the chances of the behaviour being exhibited again. Thus new behaviours are acquired that are adaptive and bestow a survival value. It is also much easier for animals to learn behaviours similar to innate ones than acquiring behaviours dissimilar to natural ones.

Research: operant conditioning

- Wehner *et al.* (1996) reported how desert ants learn by trial and error to use landmarks when navigating within a familiar area, demonstrating the importance of operant conditioning in the behaviour of non-human animals.

- Lukas *et al.* (2010) reported how behaviour shaping successfully taught Roger, a rhinoceros hornbill, to move to four different locations in his cage in response to hand direction cues. Trainers used a target on a stick, placing it in various positions within the cage. When Roger touched a target he was reinforced with grapes; then subsequent desired target behaviours were added on similarly, allowing keepers to relocate Roger more efficiently, illustrating the use of operant conditioning in non-human animals.

- Breland and Breland (1961) demonstrated *instinctive drift*, where pigs were taught to put wooden tokens into a piggy bank in order to earn a reinforcement. However, the pigs kept using the tokens to root around in the ground, as such behaviour is more natural to pigs, demonstrating how it is easier for animals to learn behaviours similar to innate ones.

- Fisher and Hinde (1949) reported how blue tits pecked holes in the foil tops of milk bottles to consume the cream. It seemed that the birds learned this purely by imitation, backed up by the fact that the behaviour spread through blue tit populations since it was first observed in Southampton in 1921. However, blue tits probably found it easier to acquire this behaviour, it being similar to their natural tendency to strip tree bark to find grubs to eat, demonstrating how it is easier for animals to learn behaviours similar to innate ones.

- Lipp *et al.* (2009) analysed 216 experienced pigeons' flights over distances of 30 miles. Birds followed highways and a railway track 50 per cent of the time, using these even when they deviated from their destination. Such behaviour can be explained by trial-and-error learning, but more probably occurs because it resembles pigeons' innate tendency to navigate using rivers and coastlines.

Research in focus

Research into simple learning often involves animals in laboratory and naturalistic settings. However, such research is not without criticisms.

By reference to *cost-benefit analysis*, do you think animal experimentation can be justified?

Much laboratory research takes place with animals like rats. What is the potential problem with findings generated by such research?

Explain one advantage and one disadvantage of conducting naturalistic research with wild animals.

Psychology in action

The National Parks of the USA attract millions of visitors each year, many to see the bears living there. However, people tend to feed the bears, which become food-conditioned and ransack bins, cars and tents, and attack humans in their search for easy pickings. However, in Sequoia National Park conditioning techniques are used to stop the bears scavenging and attacking humans. Mazur (2010) evaluated the effectiveness of aversive conditioning in stopping wild black bear attacks. Pepper sprays, low-impact projectiles and rubber slugs were fired at the bears. There was a marked decrease in attacks from food-conditioned bears and the action proved effective in preventing non-food conditioned bears from becoming food-conditioned, demonstrating a practical application of operant conditioning with wild animals.

Figure 7.06 Conditioning can be used to stop bears scavenging

Evaluation

Animal learning

- Research shows that both classical and operant conditioning play important and powerful roles in animal learning, such as in foraging and navigation.

- Classical conditioning associates new stimuli with existing responses, but animals often learn new responses in response to their environment, so classical conditioning cannot fully explain how animals learn. Operant conditioning can explain new behaviours as learned by their consequences.

- Behaviourist explanations of learning ignore the role of thought processes (cognitions). Kohler (1925) reported how chimpanzees used insight learning to eat bananas. A banana some distance outside the cage was reached by use of a stick found inside the cage, a behaviour not taught to or previously witnessed by the chimp. Solving the problem of reaching the banana required no conditioning, but instead insight into the problem and its solution.

- As well as classical and operant conditioning, animals use social learning, via observation and imitation, to learn about and interact with their environment.

- Behaviourism cannot explain latent learning, where learning occurs without reinforcement. Tolman (1930) found that rats learned to navigate a maze without being rewarded, but only showed this learning when given the motivation of a reward.

- Behaviourism cannot account for innate influences, like biological preparedness and instinctive drift.

You are the researcher

On the Mckenzie River in Canada, grizzly bears gather annually to catch salmon in order to put on sufficient fat deposits to see them through their winter hibernation. By trial and error the bears learn the best strategies.

Design an observational study to test the efficiency of the strategies bears may use. You will need to create observational categories of fishing strategies (there are lots of videos of bears fishing on www.youtube.com that will demonstrate this). How would you ensure you had *inter-observer reliability*? Continuous observation may not be possible, so consider using *event sampling* and *time sampling*.

Issues, debates and approaches

- The emphasis in behaviourism of the environment's role in shaping behaviour can be considered reductionist, as only stimuli, responses and consequences of responses are considered. Behaviourism sees no role for unseen mental process and does not consider biological influences, which research indicates to be important, like biological preparedness and instinctive drift.

- Much research into simple animals is performed on animals and this incurs ethical considerations, like the health and welfare of animals being tested and the justification of such research in cost-benefit terms.

- Some uses of conditioning may be unethical, like training animals for warfare.

- Findings from research into classical and operant conditioning suggest practical applications for domestic and wild animals, like the training of dogs.

Strengthen your learning

1. Outline the key characteristics of both classical and operant conditioning.
2. Explain the relationship between extinction and spontaneous recovery.
3. Explain how you would use behaviour shaping to get a poodle to ride a bike.
4. Outline what psychologists have discovered about the role of classical and operant conditioning in the behaviour of non-human animals.
5. Outline two research studies that make reference to the role of classical conditioning and operant conditioning in the behaviour of non-human animals.

Intelligence in non-human animals

Intelligence in animals can be regarded as a hierarchy of learning processes, with species differing in the degree of their behaviour that is learned. Alternatively, intelligence can be regarded as the capacity to learn and process information. Ultimately, animal intelligence is closely associated with the ability to survive and reproduce.

Social learning

Social learning refers to behavioural processes allowing social interactions to affect what animals learn. Social animals live permanently, or temporarily, in groups, and use social learning to assist group interactions, by observation and imitation of each other, thus avoiding the problems associated with trial-and-error learning, like personal safety. Research focuses on social learning that facilitates the solving of social problems, indicating intelligence through the use of mental representations and conceptual thinking.

Table 7.06 Types of social learning

IMITATION	Behaviour is observed and directly copied to solve a problem
ENHANCEMENT	Attention is directed to particular features of the environment to solve a problem
EMULATION	The consequences of a behaviour are reproduced, rather than direct imitation of behaviour
TUTORING	Animals act as models to encourage, punish or provide behavioural examples to others to acquire certain skills, usually at a price to the model

Research: social learning

- Whiten (1999) examined chimpanzees' ability to use twigs and blades of grass to obtain food sources, such as ants. Differences in chimp populations were found between how probing tools were used and the types of foodstuffs obtained. Chimps in Tanzania hold long sticks in one hand, using their free hand to scoop ants into their mouths, while chimps in the Ivory Coast use short sticks to get one ant at a time, which they nibble directly off the stick. This suggests that population-specific behaviours are learned by one individual directly *imitating* the behaviour of another individual.

- Nagell (1993) criticised the conclusions reached by Kawai (1965), who reported that Japanese snow monkeys observed and directly imitated the potato-washing behaviour of a troop member. Nagell believed the behaviour was actually due to attention being focused on the potatoes and the water, *enhancing* the chances of the skill being learned by trial and error.

- Tomasello *et al.* (1987) found that chimpanzees *emulated* a model demonstrating using a rake to get food. The chimpanzees did not imitate specific actions, but developed their own techniques, implying that they were trying to reproduce the consequences of the action.

- Rendell and Whitehead (2001) found that adult orcas act as tutors by delaying the killing and eating of seals, so that juveniles can practise hunting skills. Adults pulled seals off the shoreline and released them near juveniles, so that capture techniques could be practised and perfected.

You are the researcher

Design a study using chimpanzees from a zoo (or similar social animals) to establish what forms of social learning, if any, they use. The study will involve playing a video of wild chimpanzee behaviour, where they demonstrate some form of tool use.

Why will you need a control group that does not see the video?

Could a group of chimps watch the video collectively, or would you need to study them individually?

What would be your IV and DV, and how would you analyse your data?

Evaluation

Social learning

- Due to subjective interpretation, *inter-rater reliability* may not be established, creating difficulties in understanding how behaviours arise. For instance, researchers may disagree about whether imitation or enhancement is occurring, as with the different interpretations of Japanese snow monkeys washing potatoes. *continued ...*

...continued

- Dugatkin (2000) proposes that social learning of one form or another is essential for animals to maximise mate selection, for the avoidance of predators, and so on. Social learning plays a role in mate choices of guppies and quail, and in predator avoidance among blackbirds and monkeys. However, such claims of a major role for social learning in the evolution of behaviour are recent and, as yet, lack convincing evidence.

- Examples of tutoring are rare and disputed. Adult orcas may not be delaying killing for youngsters to learn hunting skills; they may simply be amusing themselves by playing with their food.

- Social learning may show the origins of culture. McGrew (1992) says chimps showing population-specific behaviours, a demonstration of culture in human terms. However, Galef (1992) says this can only be true if animals transmit behaviours across generations by direct learning involving imitation and tutoring. Tutoring by animals lacks convincing evidence and true imitation is rarely found. In human cultures, behaviour becomes increasingly complex over generations because social transmission involves learning directly about behaviour using imitation or tutoring, and not by altering attention to environmental stimuli, as in enhancement and emulation.

Self-recognition

Humans are self-aware and recognise that they are separate from others. Research suggests that nine animal species have this ability to self-recognise, implying that such animals have intelligence. Self-awareness indicates the possession of a self-concept necessary for high-level cognitive functioning associated with human intelligence. The main research tool is Gallup's (1971) mirror test, where an odourless red spot is painted onto an animal's forehead while it is unconscious, and the degree of touching of the spot is recorded when the animal looks into a mirror. Research suggests that many species have this ability, including some not normally associated with high intelligence – for instance, the great apes, dolphins, orcas, elephants, pigs, magpies and pigeons.

Research in focus

In 2008, Prior *et al.* found that magpies could self-recognise. Before his study was published it had to be subjected to *peer review* (see 'Validating new knowledge and the role of peer review' in Chapter 13, page 485). Explain what is meant by peer review and evaluate the process in terms of the negative criticisms directed at it. How can these criticisms be addressed?

Research: self-recognition

- Gallup (1970) used his mirror test to find that after prolonged exposure to their reflected images in mirrors, chimpanzees marked with red dye on their foreheads showed evidence of being able to recognise their own reflections. Monkeys, however, did not have this capacity.

- De Veer *et al.* (2003) performed an 8-year longitudinal study on 92 chimpanzees, finding that chimpanzees can self-recognise and that mirror self-recognition is a stable trait, but subject to decline with age.

Figure 7.07 A dolphin examining its reflection in Marten and Psarakos's (1995) study

- Marten and Psarakos (1995) adapted the mirror test for dolphins, using self-view television, finding that dolphins engage in twisting manoeuvres that bring the painted dot into view, implying that dolphins have self-recognition, though results from some dolphins were clearer than from others.

- Prior *et al.* (2008) marked magpies' feathers with a bright or a non-noticeable colour, finding that mark–directed behaviour occurred when a mirror was present and feathers were marked with a bright colour. This suggests that magpies can self-recognise.

Evaluation

Self-recognition

- The fact that pigeons seem to self-recognise casts doubts on the mirror test being a valid measurement of the ability. Pigeons are not generally credited with higher cognitive skills. Pigeons could only detect spots on their own body after they had been trained to do so, and untrained pigeons never pass the mirror test.

- Some bird species, like magpies, need higher intelligence to recognise and recall which birds observed them storing food, to prevent stealing. It may be, therefore, that some bird species are capable of self-recognition.

- Some species use senses other than sight, suggesting that the mirror test is not a valid measure of self-awareness. Bekoff (2005) designed a smell test, using urine, for testing self-awareness in dogs, finding that canines recognise their own scent.

- Criticism of the mirror test falls into two camps: those who see the methodology as flawed, and those who believe that interpretation of the test results is flawed.

- Mirror test experiments generally use small samples in environments not rigorously controlled, where test subjects have frequent contact with humans and observers who may unintentionally influence the animals' behaviour.

- The mirror test may not be a valid measure of self-recognition, as autistic children pass the test, even though they have severely impaired self-awareness, while prosopagnosics (see 'Explanations of prosopagnosia' in Chapter 2, page 72), with self-awareness, fail the test.

Contemporary research

Plotnik (2006)

Self-recognition in an Asian elephant

Earlier studies with small mirrors suggested that elephants have the ability to self-recognise. However, no studies were done with large mirrors allowing elephants to see their whole body.

Aim

To test elephants' ability to self-recognise using a giant, durable mirror.

Procedure

A mirror measuring 2.5 metres square was placed in the elephant pen at the Bronx Zoo, New York. The elephants' behaviour with and without the mirror was recorded. The three resident elephants had, independently, had a white cross painted on one cheek and a non-coloured spot on the other cheek. The degree of trunk touching of each spot when looking in the mirror was recorded.

Findings

All three elephants showed self-directed behaviour, like bringing and eating food in front of the mirror and inspecting themselves by moving their trunks to see inside their mouths, a part of their body they usually cannot see. Further, they did not mistake their reflection for another elephant. One elephant, Happy, when she went to the mirror, repeatedly touched the visible mark, but not the invisible mark. However, the other two elephants did not pass this test.

continued ...

...continued

Conclusions

Elephants have a degree of self-awareness and their self-recognition behaviour is similar to other animals demonstrating the behaviour, exhibiting exploratory and mirror-testing behaviour before more explicitly self-directed activities.

Evaluation

- Only one elephant out of three passing the test is not inconsistent with other species that self-recognise – only about 50 per cent of chimpanzees exhibit the behaviour.

- In an unpublished experiment similar to Plotnik's, Nissani found that elephants failed the mark test, casting doubt on the findings. Nissani (2006) says that Happy may have been exploring the unfamiliar mark on her head, but not making the connection between the mirror image and her body, suggesting that she cannot self-recognise.

- More work is needed, with more elephants, different approaches and alternative designs before it is concluded that elephants are capable of self-referential behaviour in front of mirrors.

Figure 7.08 Evidence suggests that some elephants can self-recognise

Theory of mind

Theory of mind (TOM) was proposed by Premack and Woodruff (1978). Beings that have a theory of mind can attribute mental states – beliefs, intents, desires, pretending, knowledge, and so on– onto themselves and others. Having a TOM involves understanding that others have beliefs, desires and intentions different to one's own. Such beings can explain and predict others' behaviour. TOM is integral to human intelligence – for example, it is involved in skilful social interactions and language usage.

Classic research

Premack and Woodruff (1978)

Does a chimp have a theory of mind?

A debate occurs over whether, and to what extent, animals have a TOM. This is contentious, involving inferring from animal behaviour the existence of thinking and the existence of self-awareness.

Aim

To see if chimps could work out the nature of problems and recognise potential solutions, indicating a TOM.

continued ...

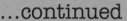

...continued

Procedure and findings

Premack and Woodruff (1978) showed Sarah, an adult chimpanzee, videotaped scenes of a human actor struggling with one of eight problems and then showed her two photographs, one displaying an action or object that could form a solution to the problem. On seven of the eight problems, the chimp chose the correct photograph.

The researchers then tested if animals that apparently understood the behaviour of others could give false information in order to deceive. Four young chimps were shown which of two containers held food, but they could not reach the containers. Two trainers entered who had access to the containers, but did not know which held food. One trainer was a 'good guy', who shared food when he found it; the other trainer was a 'bad guy', who would not share food. The two trainers were distinguishable by different face masks. The rule was that the trainers could only select a container when signalled by the chimp, either by glancing or pointing at a container. All four chimps when dealing with the 'good guy' indicated which container held the food. However, with the 'bad guy' they did not indicate the correct container, but refused to look or point at it. The experiment lasted over a year and the 'bad guy' always eventually got the three youngest chimps to look at the container holding the food, thus identifying it. However, the oldest chimp increasingly glanced and pointed at the wrong container. When she fooled the 'bad guy' into choosing the wrong container her gaze darted instantly to the correct container.

Conclusions

Chimps have a TOM, as they can work out the nature of problems and recognise potential solutions.

Evaluation

- Because it took a long time before evidence of deception was exhibited, the results may be due to operant conditioning, with the chimps learning the correct responses to display to different trainers.

- It is probable that animals do not display false positives very often, because to fool a recipient by looking or pointing at the wrong place, the animal must resist the overpowering desire to look in the right place.

Research: theory of mind

- Cheney and Seyfarth (1988) investigated how animals communicate danger. Vervet monkeys have distinct alarm calls for different predators. A vervet monkey detecting a predator gives the appropriate alarm call and other monkeys exhibit the correct response. When a 'leopard alert' call is given, monkeys scan the horizon and run up nearby trees for safety. The researchers repeatedly played a tape of a particular monkey's leopard alarm call when there was no leopards around. The other monkeys learned to ignore these calls, but reacted to other monkeys' leopard alarm calls, indicating that vervet monkeys have the ability to understand and predict others' behaviour – a prerequisite for TOM.

- Povinelli *et al.* (1990) introduced a new test for TOM involving four food containers, each with a handle a chimp could pull to get food. At the beginning of each trial, the containers were behind a screen and a chimp watched as the experimenter put food in one, witnessed by a confederate called 'the knower', though the chimp cannot see which container is selected. A second confederate, 'the guesser', enters the room and they and the 'knower' each get a separate choice of one container. If the chimp has TOM, it understands that the knower has the correct knowledge and follows that person's selection when given a choice itself. All four chimps tested did this, suggesting that they do have TOM. However, there were 300 trials, so they had many opportunities to learn by conditioned discrimination by being rewarded for selecting the person in the room when food was put into a container.

Machiavellian intelligence

Machiavellian intelligence, proposed by Whiten and Byrne (1988), sees the ability to solve problems associated with social living as the main constituent of intelligence. An intelligent animal can manipulate others, but without upsetting the social cohesion of a group, by the use of deception and the formation of coalitions.

Research: Machiavellian intelligence

- Maestripieri (2007) found that female macaques use Machiavellian intelligence by having sex with a dominant male so he will protect their newborn infants, while having sex without his knowledge with other males, so they will offer similar protection if the dominant male dies.

- Nishida *et al.* (1992) reported that alpha males do not share food with rivals, but will share with non-rivals so that they will assist in power struggles that may arise.

- Kummer (1967) demonstrated that female Hamadryas baboons successfully threaten rivals by sitting in front of the harem male, so any threat against her is seen as directed at him.

- Whiten and Byrne (1988) showed how young baboons act dishonestly by screaming, to get their mothers to chase adults away from foodstuffs so they may eat them.

Evaluation

Machiavellian intelligence

- Machiavellian intelligence seems to exist in primates, especially those in large social groups with high social complexity and ability to memorise socially relevant information.
- The evolution of advanced cognitive abilities necessary for Machiavellian intelligence has not been adequately explained as yet.
- Some examples of Machiavellian intelligence, such as that provided by Whiten and Byrne (1988), might be conditioned responses occurring through experience via reinforcement which are exhibited again in similar circumstances.

Issues, debates and approaches

- Research into intelligence in non-human animals focuses on wild animals, especially social animals. Such research is considered ethical as long as the fitness of such animals is not lowered in any way – for instance, affecting their ability to forage or reproduce.

- Research into animal intelligence focuses on behaviour that enhances survival and reproduction and, as such, can be placed within the evolutionary approach, seeing intelligence as an adaptive feature shaped by natural selection.

Strengthen your learning

1. What are social animals and how do they use social learning?
2. Explain what is meant by *imitation*, *enhancement*, *emulation* and *tutoring*, and for each of these give details of a relevant research study.
3. What evidence is there for social learning showing the origins of culture?
4. Outline Gallup's mirror test.
5. Compile a list of evaluative points concerning self-recognition in animals.
6. Outline what is meant by TOM.
7. What evidence is there that some animals have a TOM?
8. What is Machiavellian intelligence?
9. What evidence is there that animals can use Machiavellian intelligence?

Assessment Check ▶

1. Outline and evaluate evidence for intelligence in non-human animals. (24 marks)

2. Discuss the nature of simple learning (classical and operant conditioning) and its role in the behaviour of non-human animals. (24 marks)

3. Outline the nature of simple learning (classical and operant conditioning). (8 marks)

4. Evaluate evidence for intelligence in non-human animals (for example, self-recognition, social learning, Machiavellian intelligence). (16 marks)

Examination guidance

Question 1 requires an outline and an evaluation of evidence for intelligence in non-human animals. Only 8 marks are available for the outline, but 16 for the evaluation, so concentrate more fully on the evaluation, as most credit is gained there.

For question 2, you are required to outline the nature of classical and operant conditioning, but then to concentrate on an evaluation of this specifically in relation to the behaviour of non-human animals.

Question 3 again calls for an outline of classical and operant conditioning, but in question 4 there is a need to focus solely on evaluating evidence for intelligence in non-human animals. Some examples are given in the question, but they are purely for guidance; any relevant material is equally creditworthy.

Human intelligence

Evolutionary factors in the development of human intelligence

Human intelligence is presumed to have evolved, as fossil evidence indicates that early humanoids did not have the brain capacity and functions of modern-day humans. The evolutionary approach believes that human intelligence evolved due to the demands of an ever-changing environment creating selective pressure for increased intellect. Humans needed to contend with the ecological challenges of foraging for food, dealing with increasing social complexity and the need to develop a more advanced brain.

Key terms

Evolution – the process by which the genetic composition of a population changes over successive generations through the process of natural selection
Ecological demands – the features of an animal's environment providing a survival value
Social complexity – the amount of organisation and order among animal social groupings
Genetic factors – developmental influences passed through heredity
Heritability – the degree to which a quality or behaviour is genetically determined
Environmental factors – developmental influences acquired through experience
Cultural influences – developmental factors originating from a cultural grouping

Ecological demands

Intelligence is perceived as prospering within a given environment, especially by demonstrating foraging abilities. Humans adapted to global cooling in Palaeolithic times by finding food and exploiting new environments, due to the development of higher mental skills, like cooperative hunting and tool use. With plants only available periodically, hunting meat became a necessity, as meat is calorie-rich and hunting was less labour-intensive than foraging for other foodstuffs. Being a good forager required higher levels of intelligence, which increased survival rates, leading to individuals being naturally selected.

Foraging hypotheses

Milton (1988) argued that increased intellect occurred due to the demands of foraging. Fruits grow seasonally and are distributed unpredictably over large areas. The development of mental maps helped *frugivores* (fruit-eaters) to know when and where to look for food, and monitoring the availability of different fruits helped to develop this ability. This was achieved by natural selection acting to create advanced memory skills and foraging techniques, attained by the development of more advanced brains.

Gibson (1987) proposed the *food extraction hypothesis*, seeing the need to find hidden (embedded) foods as driving the evolution of intelligence. Hidden foods, like roots, are difficult to locate and extract, but provide rich nutrition, especially during times of scarcity. The need for cognitive processing, manual dexterity and tool use created selective pressure for a larger cortex, which allowed juvenile animals to develop advanced imitative abilities.

Parker (1996) proposed an extension to the food extraction hypothesis, *apprenticeship*, where co-evolution of a set of interrelated cognitive abilities – such as imitation, intelligent tool use, self-awareness and demonstration teaching – enabled immature hominid apes to learn tool-based extractive foraging skills and ease maternal pressures by boosting an offspring's ability to learn these talents.

Research: foraging hypotheses

- Milton (1988) found that frugivore spiders have greater relative brain size, larger home ranges and a more protracted learning/dependency period, supporting the idea of greater intelligence evolving in frugivores.

- Barton (1996) found that fruit eating correlates positively with brain size in haplorhines (higher primates), again supporting the idea of increased intelligence in frugivores.

- Boesche *et al.* (1992) tested Gibson's hypothesis, finding that chimps' use of tools to open nuts closely matched archaeological evidence of early nomadic humans noted for their foraging skills, thus supporting the hypothesis.

Figure 7.09 Fruit-eating spiders have greater relative brain size, supporting the idea of greater intelligence having evolved in frugivores

- Mitchell (1994) found that the set of social and cognitive abilities required for extractive foraging developed as a cluster of simultaneous skills in great apes, supporting the idea of apprenticeship.

- Dunbar (1992) tested Milton's hypothesis, examining the amount of fruit in an animal's diet and the size of its neocortex. No significant relationship was found. However, only small amounts of fruit may be needed to supply necessary nutrition, casting doubts on Dunbar's conclusion.

Evaluation

Foraging hypotheses

- Extractive foraging may be a cause or an effect of intelligence. However, animals who extract one food type all the time tend to use tools in a less intelligent way, while those who extract many types display more intelligent tool use. Therefore, tool use may be a consequence of intelligence.

- Foraging skills involve different brain areas. Monitoring food supplies and extraction skills involve the neocortex, while the hippocampus, prefrontal and parietal lobes are associated with the construction of mental maps.

- Milton's foraging hypothesis does not explain why fruit eaters need a high-quality diet. Did they need more energy to fuel a larger brain, or did their brains grow to develop the skills to find fruit?

- Many animal species have mental maps for stored food items; therefore, it seems unlikely that developing mental maps produces cognitive evolution.

- With the food extraction hypothesis, the levels of difficulty in extracting foodstuffs are not well explained, meaning that the hypothesis is difficult to test.

You are the researcher

Design a study investigating whether the amounts of fruit different species eat is related to the size of their brains.

What type of research method would you employ? Clue: what would your two co-variables be?

Draw an appropriate graph to plot your data. Make sure that it is properly titled and labelled.

Name a suitable statistical test to analyse your data.

Research in focus

Much research into the intelligence of animals involves observational studies to see whether behaviour matches evolutionary theory.

What is meant by *inter-observer reliability*? How can it be achieved?

What are the main strengths and limitations of observational studies?

Why might observational studies be an ethical way of studying wild animals?

What is meant by event sampling and time sampling?

Social complexity

Human brains are larger than metabolic needs predict. It may be that intelligence evolved more in species facing demanding challenges, like using tools to extract hidden foods. Another explanation is the *social complexity hypothesis* (SCH), which sees high levels of intelligence as advantageous to animals living in complex social groups. The hypothesis believes that increased intelligence evolved in such animals due to the need to predict, react to and influence the social behaviour of other group members. Such animals have larger brains, reflecting the cognitive demands of social living. The frontal cortex of the brain is linked to social decision making, and thus the SCH believes that the demands of social living led to the evolution of a large frontal cortex in human brains. Early research focused on primates, but recent research has highlighted other social animals, like hyenas and some bird species. SCH proposes that mammals living in large complex groupings should display enhanced social cognition skills like those found in humans.

Contemporary research

Paz-y-Miño *et al.* (2004)

Pinyon jays use transitive inference to predict social dominance

Some birds are social and the researchers were interested in seeing whether such creatures would display higher intelligence.

Aim

To see whether social birds solve transitive inference tasks in a social setting to predict dominance hierarchies.

Procedure and findings

Four jays were placed in each of two cages (A, B, C, D + 1, 2, 3, 4) and allowed to form dominance hierarchies, the two cages being separate from each other so the birds were not familiar with each other.

The relative dominance hierarchies of the two cages containing pinyon jays was shown as follows:

- Cage 1: A >B >C >D
- Cage 2: 1 >2 >3 >4

Bird 3 was removed from its group and allowed to witness two paired encounters. In the first encounter, bird A dominated bird B. Then bird B dominated bird 2. It should be noted that only bird 2 was familiar to bird 3. Bird 3 was then placed in a cage with bird B and in all cases deferred to bird B. Bird 3 made the transitive inference that 'B is subordinate to A, but is clearly dominant to 2. Given that 2 is dominant over me, I shall be submissive to B'.

Conclusions

Living in large social groups favours the evolution of enhanced cognitive abilities. Social birds make calculations about status by recognising the relative ranks existing among other birds, supporting the SCH.

The evidence suggests that social complexity is linked to the ability to store information concerning relative ranks, lending support to the SCH.

Evaluation

As the number of possible interactions increases rapidly with group size, individual members benefit by making judgements about relationships on the basis of indirect evidence. Transitive reasoning helps social individuals assess relationships from observations of interactions among others.

Research: social complexity

- Grosenick *et al.* (2007) studied African cichlids, fish living in complex hierarchical groups, finding that males calculate their status within a group by observing fights between rival males and using *transitive inference*, where unknown relationships are inferred from known relationships. This suggests that reasoning is used, because the fish inferred the hierarchies not through direct experience, but through observation. The findings support the social complexity hypothesis, which proposes that social complexity is a driving force in the evolution of intelligence.

> A full account of Guillermo Paz-y-Miño's fascinating research with Pinyon jays, including diagrams and references, can be found at www.biosci.unl.edu/avcog/research/articles/SocCog04.pdf

- Holekamp and Engh (2003) (2004) studied spotted hyenas, which live in complex groupings, comparing brain structures to other social carnivores, and finding a positive correlation between size of brain structures and complexity of social living. Subsequently, the researchers used data relating to which group members individuals formed alliances with, to find that the hyenas could calculate other group members' status, implying that cognitive abilities are shaped by the demands of life in complex societies, supporting the SCH.

- Ehmer *et al.* (2001) studied species without a cortex. Larger antennal lobes and collars were found in female paper wasps living socially in colonies than in solitary females. The increased sociability of paper wasps living in colonies creates a need to discriminate between familiar and unfamiliar individuals and to monitor other females' dominance and breeding status. This suggests that increased social complexity leads to higher intelligence.

Figure 7.10 African cichlids use transitive inference to calculate their status

Figure 7.11 A group of spotted hyenas feeding communally – animals in complex social groups have large brains

Evaluation

Social complexity

- The predictions of the social complexity hypothesis of advanced social cognition abilities and larger brain structures are supported by research.
- Evidence suggests that neocortical increases occur as group size increases, lending support to the social complexity hypothesis.
- Much research into social complexity involves the use of animals, creating generalisation problems, as animal species may not be representative of human evolution patterns.
- Evidence from observations of animals involves subjective interpretation that may be subject to researcher bias.

Kay Holekamp continues to research the behaviour of spotted hyenas, maintaining two websites detailing her findings: www.hyaenidae.org www.hyenas.zoology.msu.edu

Brain size

Larger brains may have evolved to allow individuals to cope with the demands of social living, like Machiavellian intelligence, transitive reasoning, and so on, and environmental pressures, like ecological demands, such as foraging.

Having a large brain incurs costs – for example, it is not easy for females to give birth to babies with large brains. Also, larger brains consume much energy and require more nutrition. A human brain consists of 2 per cent of body weight, but consumes 35 per cent of calorific intake. The fact that large brains have evolved suggests that the adaptive advantages outweigh the disadvantages.

Having a large brain does not correlate with higher levels of intelligence; elephants have larger brains than humans, but are not considered more intelligent. If brain size is considered relative to body size, humans have the largest ratio of all large mammals, at 2 per cent of body weight, though smaller mammals, like the shrew, seem superior, with a brain-to-body ratio of 10 per cent.

It is only when *encephalisation quotient* (EQ) is used, where actual brain mass of a species is divided by expected brain size for that body size, that humans emerge superior. The standard rating for mammals is cats, with an EQ score of 1.0, while humans have the highest rating of 7.6, followed by dolphins at 5.0. This form of measurement is problematic too, as capuchin monkeys outscore seemingly more intelligent animals like chimps and gorillas.

Another method of measuring brain size considers absolute and relative brain size, especially of the prefrontal cortex, associated with higher cognitive abilities. Humans do not possess the largest cortex, but have the largest amount of cortical neurons, about 11.5 billion. However, this is only about half a billion more than whales and does not account for the gap in intellectual ability. The method of measurement correlating best with intelligence and showing the dominance of humans comes by combining the number of cortical neurons with the speed of neural conductivity. Information travels faster along human nerve pathways, as the myelin sheaths, which insulate nerve fibres, are thicker than in other species. Also, neural signals travel further in large animals like elephants. Overall, it seems that the superior information-processing speed of human brains may account for human intellectual superiority.

Human language ability is superior. Many species demonstrate language abilities, but even highly trained animals cannot develop verbal skills more advanced than 3-year-old children. The absence of an intricately wired language region in the brains of other species may explain why humans alone have complex grammatical language abilities. The development of grammar and syntax is dated to between 80,000 and 100,000 years ago, fairly recent in evolutionary terms, and perhaps explains the highly advanced intelligence in humans.

Table 7.07 Brain weight, EQ and amount of cortical neurons in selected mammals

TYPE OF ANIMAL	BRAIN WEIGHT (GRAMS)	EQ	NUMBER OF CORTICAL NEURONS (MILLIONS)
Human	1,250–1,450	7.4–7.8	11,500
African elephant	4,200	1.3	11,000
Bottlenose dolphin	1,350	5.3	5,800
Gorilla	430–570	1.5–1.8	4,300
Chimpanzee	330–430	2.2–2.5	6,200
Dog	64	1.2	160
Cat	25	1.0	300
Rat	2	0.4	15

Research: brain size

- Lynn (1989) showed from fossil evidence that brain size grew by 300 per cent during the evolution of hominids, bestowing on humans the adaptive advantages of increased intelligence.

- Roth and Dicke (2008) explain that at age 3 years, grammar and vocabulary become advanced in humans and this corresponds with the development of Broca's speech area in the left frontal lobe, which may be unique to humans.

- Byrne (1995) proposes that neocortical enlargement in the brain correlates better with social than environmental complexity – for example, social group size and the complexity of social relationships – and that this accounts for the superiority of human intelligence.

- Willerman *et al.* (1991) performed a meta-analysis of the relationship between brain volume and IQ. A positive correlation was found, suggesting that brain size and intelligence are related.

- Narr *et al.* (2006) found a positive relationship between cortical thickness and IQ, suggesting that brain size is related to intelligence.

Evaluation

Brain size

- Sassaman and Zartler (1982) studied children with abnormally small brains: 40 per cent were not retarded, suggesting that brain size does not reflect intelligence.
- Crows show intelligent tool use, planning and cognitive flexibility, but have small brains. This seems contradictory, but crows have a relatively large cortex, which may be the source of their intelligence.
- Humphrey (1999) believes that if big brains are not related to general intelligence, they contribute to other evolutionary specialisms, like language abilities.

Issues, debates and approaches

- Evolutionary explanations of human intelligence have been accused of being reductionist, as they reduce complex behaviours to one explanation of adaptiveness and therefore do not consider other important factors, like cultural influences.

- Explanations of human intelligence based on evolutionary theory can be argued to be deterministic in that they see intelligence as caused by past environments coded into humans in the form of innate genetic structures. Therefore, the approach sees no role for free will through other psychological influences.

Strengthen your learning

1. Why may foraging have contributed to the evolution of intelligence?
2. What research support is there for foraging hypotheses?
3. Construct a concise, evaluation of foraging hypotheses.
4. Explain the social complexity hypothesis.
5. Outline two research studies into social complexity.
6. Write an evaluation of social complexity in about 300 words.
7. Why may humans have evolved larger brains?
8. Do research studies suggest that brain size is related to intelligence? Give details.

Genetic and environmental factors associated with intelligence test performance

The concept and history of intelligence testing is controversial. The idea that intelligence is an objective entity, existing in a measurable form, comes from the psychometric tradition, which attempts to show differences in intelligence between people, so tests could be used to select for educational and employment purposes. This depends on the existence of general intelligence ('g'), an innate level of intellect unaffected by environmental influences, found in varying levels in everyone. However, many argue that the existence of 'g' is not proven, and IQ tests are actually tests of school attainment rather than tests of natural talent.

The first IQ test was designed by Binet (1905), to identify French children needing educational support, but the test was adopted as a test of general intelligence, something it was never intended for.

Research revolved around the idea that if differences in IQ are genetic, closely related people should have similar IQ scores, and IQ scores should not be affected by environmental influences, like the quality of education received, with IQ levels staying constant throughout life.

Twin studies

If IQ levels of identical (monozygotic: MZ) twins correlate more closely than non-identical (dizygotic: DZ) twins, this indicates that intelligence is genetically determined, as MZ twins are genetically identical, while DZ twins only share 50 per cent genetic similarity. A problem with twin studies is that not only do twins share genetic similarity, they also tend to share environmental similarity. Therefore, research concentrated on MZ twins reared apart – that is, with genetic, but not environmental similarity.

Research: twin studies

- Newman *et al.* (1937) conducted a 10-year study of 100 pairs of twins reared together and 19 pairs of MZ twins reared apart. Not only did MZ twins reared together have a closer IQ correlation (91 per cent) than DZ twins reared together (64 per cent), but MZ twins reared apart had a closer correlation too (67 per cent), suggesting that intelligence is more genetic in nature.

- Burt (1955, 1958, 1966) performed research into twin studies, finding that MZ twins reared together had an IQ correlation of 94.4 per cent, MZ twins reared apart 77.1 per cent, and DZ twins reared together only 55.2 per cent. This seemingly backs up Newman *et al.*'s findings.

- Bouchard and McGue (1981) performed a meta-analysis of 111 family studies of IQ correlations, finding that MZ twins reared together had an IQ correlation of 86 per cent, MZ twins reared apart 72 per cent, and DZ twins reared together only 60 per cent. They also found that as the degree of genetic relationship between family members declined, so did the degree of IQ correlation, suggesting that intelligence is mainly genetic in origin.

- Thompson *et al.* (2001) used MRI scans, finding that MZ twins had similar structures in brain areas associated with intellect and in test scores of 17 different intellectual activities, suggesting that intelligence has a genetic basis.

Evaluation

Twin studies

- 'Separated twins' often have similar environments – for example, they may be raised by similar families. Shields (1962) found that separated MZ twins raised in dissimilar families only had an IQ correlation of 51 per cent, throwing doubt on the genetic argument.

- Burt, an influential figure who believed that intelligence is inherited, is accused of fabricating results. However, he added many more twin pairs to his data and the overall IQ correlations remained the same – almost a statistical impossibility. Also, little proof was found of his co-researchers' existence, weakening the genetic argument and calling into doubt the findings of researchers influenced by Burt.(See p.483.)

- There is debate over how identical some twins are, and how similar shared environments were in research. This makes analysis of results difficult.

- If intelligence were entirely genetic, concordance rates for MZ twins would be 100 per cent. As they are not, environment must play a role; indeed, all genes need an environment in which to express themselves.

Adoption studies

The idea behind adoption studies is that if intelligence is genetic, adopted children should have IQ levels more similar to their biological parents than their adoptive ones. Adoption studies theoretically separate out the influences of genetics and environment, as adoptive children live with adoptive families, with whom they share environmental, but not genetic similarities, and not with their biological families, with whom they share genetic, but not environmental similarities.

Another feature of adoption studies is that it is possible to see whether over time IQ levels of adoptive children move away from or towards those of adoptive families, which would indicate whether heredity or environmental factors are at work.

> The debate over whether Burt falsified data is an important one, as he greatly influenced educational policy. It is difficult to ascertain the truth, but a reasonably unbiased account of the debate can be found at http://pubs.socialistreviewindex.org.uk/sr196/parrington.htm

Research: adoption studies

- Skodak and Skeels (1949) found a positive correlation between adopted children and their biological mothers' levels of IQ. This increased into adolescence. At age 4, the correlation was 28 per cent, while at age 13 it had risen to 44 per cent, supporting the genetic viewpoint.

- Capron and Duyme (1989) examined the socio-economic status (SES) of biological and adoptive parents where children were adopted before the age of 6 months, finding that children raised by high-SES adoptive parents had higher IQs than those raised by low-SES adoptive parents. The intelligence level of adopted children can be raised by nearly 16 IQ points when adoptive parents are of high SES. This difference is enough to determine whether an individual will study to degree level, and suggests that environment is important in determining IQ levels.

- Scarr and Weinberg (1983) found that black children adopted by white families scored above average on IQ and higher than black non-adopted children. The transracially adopted children also had IQ levels higher than those of their biological parents, emphasising the importance of environmental factors.

Evaluation

Adoption studies

- Rose et al. (1984) criticised Skodak and Skeels' (1949) study on methodological grounds. The control group of biological parents and biological children used as a comparison was not matched with the adoptive parents and adopted children – for instance, the adoptive parents were older.

- McGue (1989) believes that Capron and Duyme's (1989) study does not explain why or how high-SES adoptive homes create children with higher IQ levels, and suggests that the SES effect may be related to good-quality education or intellectual stimulation at home, or to adoptive parents' emphasis on educational success. McGue believes that encouragement offered by adoptive parents leads to confidence and subsequent elevated IQ test performances.

- Levin (1994) disagrees with Scarr and Weinberg (1983), stating that their data support the hereditarian viewpoint, as adopted children with two biological black parents scored less well than adopted children with one black and one white parent, who in turn scored less well than adopted children with two white biological parents. Waldman (1994) responded to this, pointing out that pre-adoption factors were not controlled, forming a confounding variable, which prevents an unambiguous interpretation of the results.

Gene mapping

Due to technological advances, research has concentrated on identifying genes associated with heritability of intelligence and found that many genes may be involved. The identification of such genes may permit the development of practical applications to combat things like learning difficulties and intellectual decay in old age.

Research: gene mapping

- Plomin *et al.* (1998) compared the DNA of children with high IQ and average IQ, finding a variant of the IGF2 receptor gene more common in the high–IQ children, accounting for an intellectual difference of about four IQ points.

- Lahn *et al.* (2004) identified a gene, ASPM, linked to higher intelligence. ASPM appears to affect the expansion of the cerebral cortex, possibly explaining how genes influence intelligence.

- Gosso *et al.* (2007) used IQ scores from Dutch adults and children, along with expression levels of the CHRM2 gene in participants' brains, to find that specific variants of the gene correlated to high intelligence, suggesting that intelligence has genetic origins.

Evaluation

Gene mapping

- Plomin's (1998) study is criticised, as only half of the high-IQ children had the intelligence-promoting form of the gene. On its own, this gene cannot explain where the superior intelligence came from. Plomin believed that slight genetic influences come from individual genes, as intelligence may be influenced by up to 50 genes, including one at least from all 23 pairs of chromosomes. Collectively, these would exert a large influence, meaning that intelligent individuals would possess favourable versions of these genes.

- Genetics may influence intelligence in an *indirect* manner. Genetically determined personality factors help to shape children's *micro-environments*, which then influence the development of intelligence. A naturally sociable child has many friends, and the increase in social contacts could help to promote intellectual growth.

- Another indirect genetic influence could be parents with high intelligence levels creating more intellectually stimulating environments at home.

Environmental factors

Research has identified several environmental factors that influence intelligence, like social stimulation, birth order and diet.

Research: environmental factors

- Saltz (1973) investigated the influence of a foster grandparent programme (FGP) on children's intellectual development. Elderly people were paired with children from institutional care to provide social stimulation for at least 4 years. FGP children outscored similar children not on the programme, suggesting that social stimulation achieves intellectual development.

- Zajonc and Marcus (1975) developed the *conference model*, a mathematical model of the effect of birth order and family size on IQ scores. As families grew, the average IQ levels of family members dropped, though only by three IQ points, supporting the idea that birth order and family size affect intelligence. As families grow, parental attention and resources may decrease.

- Lynn (2006) believed that the main environmental influence on IQ is diet. He believed that people in colder climates developed larger, more intelligent brains than people in warmer climates, as surviving cold winters required hunting meat, as no plant foods were available. Meat would provide the proteins, minerals and vitamins necessary for brain development.

- Mortensen *et al.* (2002) tested the relationship between breastfeeding and intelligence. A positive correlation was found between duration of breastfeeding and IQ scores, suggesting that nutrition, especially during early development, is important to establishing intelligence.

- Isaacs *et al.* (2008) tested adolescents born prematurely, finding that premature babies who were fed enriched formula milk outscored on IQ premature babies not given the supplementary diet. MRI scans also showed that the *caudate nucleus*, a brain structure associated with IQ, was larger in those receiving the supplementary diet. This suggests that brain structures important for the development of IQ are influenced by nutrition in infancy.

Figure 7.12 Some evidence has suggested that nutrition in infancy is linked to intelligence

Psychology in action

Although there is heated debate over whether improved nutrition boosts intellect, research indicates that diet can help to develop the intellectual potential of disadvantaged children, like those born prematurely (see, for example, Isaacs *et al.* (2008)). Some health and educational authorities have introduced nutritional supplements for disadvantaged children. If this proves successful, benefits to society would occur at a trivial cost – for example, the reduction of unemployment, prison populations and welfare costs are all associated with low levels of intelligence.

Evaluation

Environmental factors

- The decline in US high school intelligence levels since the Second World War may be due to larger, closer-spaced families, as detailed in the conference model.

- Contrary to Lynn's (2006) ideas about meat eating and intelligence, Gale (2002) found that vegetarians have higher IQs than meat eaters, though possibly because brighter children make a moral choice not to eat meat.

- Environmental factors, like improved nutrition, boost intellectual capabilities more in deprived children who lack an adequate diet, social stimulation, and so on, than in non-deprived children.

Enrichment

A basic testable premise is that if intelligence were genetically determined, any attempts to improve it by enrichment would not work. Various interventionist programmes have tried to boost intelligence levels by providing stimulating environments. *Operation Headstart* (1965) was a US enrichment programme that attempted to elevate disadvantaged children's preschool IQ levels by enhancing social and cognitive development through the provision of educational, health, nutritional, social and other services to enrolled children and families. By 2005, 22 million children had participated in the programme (see 'Research: enrichment' below).

Another large-scale enrichment programme was the *Milwaukee project* (see 'Classic research: Heber *et al.* (1972) on page 273).

Research: enrichment

- Barnett (1995) reported that for participants of Operation Headstart, although IQ was boosted in the short term, it was short-lived, a phenomenon known as 'Headstart fade', with participants falling behind non-participant peers as early as the second grade.

- Lazar and Darlington (1982) found that Operation Headstart had long-term positive outcomes, with individuals years later showing better reading and mathematical skills, more competence and being increasingly likely to continue into higher education. There was also less involvement with crime and a reduced level of teenage pregnancies.

- Hunt (1972) believed that Operation Headstart was inappropriate, as it did not provide the skills that middle-class children develop in preschool life.

- Atkinson (1990) reviewed several enrichment programmes, finding that parental involvement leading to stimulation at home raised IQ levels and social skills.

Evaluation

Enrichment

- The benefits of enrichment programmes may only be short-lived, with a loss of improvements in the long term.

- Drawing conclusions from such research is problematic, due to methodological considerations – for instance, Operation Headstart provision varies widely between locations, in terms of content, ages served, duration of time and student:teacher ratios, and such variation makes studies of Headstart's effectiveness difficult to interpret. Bias in interpretation of findings, due to political and philosophical leanings, makes drawing conclusions difficult.

- Positive outcomes of enrichment may not be limited to direct improvements in IQ scores; there may also be indirect improvements, like the boosting of motivational and confidence levels.

Classic research

Heber *et al.* (1972)

The Milwaukee project

Aim

To study how intellectual stimulation affects children from deprived environments.

Procedure

Forty newborn black children from a disadvantaged area of Milwaukee, with mothers with IQ scores below 80, were selected as participants. Twenty of the mothers received education, job training, homemaking and child-care tuition, while their children received regular personalised enrichment in their own homes. The other 20 children received no such enrichment and acted as the control group.

Findings

The children were tested at age 6, with the enrichment-project children gaining superior scores in all measurements, including problem-solving ability and language skills. The enriched children had an average IQ score of 121, compared to the non-enriched children's score of 87. However, by age 10, the enriched children's average IQ fell to 105, compared to 85 for the non-enriched children.

Conclusions

Enrichment programmes boost intellectual performance, but improvements decline once enrichment ceases.

Evaluation

- The reason for a decline in enriched children's IQ once the enrichment stopped may be due to their local school only catering for children with lower IQs and not stimulating the enriched children.
- Another reason for the decline could be that once the children attended school they did not get the nutritious diet that was part of the enrichment programme.
- The key factors to enrichment success seem to be diet, parental involvement and the boosting of confidence and motivation.

Issues, debates and approaches

- Gene-mapping studies are socially sensitive, as they could lead to the development of therapies seeking to alter the genetic make-up of individuals towards being more intelligent, or even to demands for the abortion of unborn children identified as having 'low-intelligence genetic profiles' and the sterilisation of low-intelligence adults to prevent them reproducing.
- The discussion of whether intelligence is more genetic or environmental in nature is central to the nature versus nurture debate, though the evidence indicates that an interactionist viewpoint is more suitable, where intelligence is seen as determined by an interaction of genetic and environmental factors.
- People often misunderstand genetic research, believing that genes alone determine intelligence. Environment plays a role too, but gene-mapping studies show little about the relative contributions of genetics and environmental factors to actual levels of intelligence.
- Foster grandparent programmes (see 'Research: environmental factors' on page 270) suggest a credible practical application to help raise the IQ levels of socially impoverished children.

Cultural influences on intelligence test performance

Some believe that intelligence is different things in different cultures, and people from non-western cultural backgrounds do badly on IQ tests, because the tests are designed by and standardised on people from western cultures. Supporters of the tests claim that they assess aptitude (natural general ability), are not affected by environmental factors and are culture-fair tests. However, critics argue that the knowledge assessed in IQ tests is school-learned knowledge based on dominant western culture and is culture-biased. Gross (1992) says: 'The IQ test can be regarded as an ideological weapon, used by a white-dominated society to oppress minority groups'.

Attempts were made to design culture-free tests, where questions, usually non-verbal, were not culturally based to allow a fair comparison of people. The best known example is Raven's Progressive Matrices (1936), which comprises multiple-choice questions of abstract reasoning that become increasingly more difficult to solve.

Controversy over race and intelligence has raged since the earliest days of psychology, dragging the discipline into disrepute. *Eugenicists* believe that intelligence is inherited, occurring in different amounts in different races, and ranking black people lower than white people in terms of IQ. However, IQ tests are culturally determined and biased towards the culture devising them.

IQ tests were devised early in psychology's existence, when the discipline was eager to prove itself of scientific merit and useful to society. IQ testing became a way of providing an apparently scientifically valid method of assessing intellectual levels, and was a means of selection – for example, for the military. However, such tests were founded on the notion that intelligence was inherited and they were poorly applied, with the result that black recruits, who received lesser educations, attained scores below those of white recruits. These results were used to 'scientifically' validate eugenic beliefs seeing black people as intellectually inferior.

Eugenicists believed that people of lower intellectual ability threatened the fabric of society because they bred quickly, and as intelligence was thought to be inherited, they were seen as dragging average IQ scores down. The data was used to justify forced sterilisations, the majority on black people. From 1907 to 1960, more than 100,000 Americans were sterilised in more than 30 states. Eugenicist policies led to the mass exterminations in Nazi Germany, after which the *pseudoscience* fell from grace. Immigration policies were formed on the basis of such data. It is estimated that the quota systems introduced led to 6 million people being barred entry to the USA between 1924 and 1939. Many were in danger of persecution in their European homelands, and subsequently perished during the war years.

The idea of separate races is debatable; often people of seemingly similar biological origins come from different cultural and subcultural backgrounds. Indeed, there is more genetic variation within any so-called racial group than between racial groups.

Research: cultural influences on intelligence test performance

- Heather (1976) points out that before 1937 women scored on average ten IQ points less than men, evidence seemingly for men being more intelligent. However, when the tests were re-standardised to include women, average scores became the same, suggesting that IQ tests are culturally biased.

- Mackintosh (1986) found that white and West Indian children in England, matched in terms of environment, had a difference of 2.6 IQ points, in favour of the white children, but this extended to 9 points when the children were not matched, with the West Indian children having poorer family backgrounds, and so on, suggesting that poor IQ test performance is explained by environmental means.

- Jensen (1969) sparked controversy by claiming that because black people have an average IQ score of 15 points less than white people, this showed that their racial grouping was of inferior natural intellect.

- Hermstein and Murray (1994) produced the *bell curve hypothesis*, proposing that hereditary factors are the determining factor in explaining race and class differences in IQ levels. Eugenic policies were again proposed, like voluntary sterilisation for low–scoring intelligence groups.

Supplementary learning

The BITCH test: Williams (1972)

The Black Intelligence Test for Cultural Homogeneity (BITCH) was devised by Williams in 1972 as an attempt to give black people an advantage, in contrast to the usual intelligence tests that privileged the experience of white people. The BITCH included 100 multiple-choice questions, most requiring the test-taker to select the right words and expressions from black culture, the idea being that black people, who normally score poorly on IQ tests, would do well, and that people from the white culture would score poorly. This proved to be true. Butler-Omololu (1983) found that black people scored higher on the BITCH-100, while white people scored higher on more traditional IQ tests, suggesting that IQ tests are culturally biased.

The following are examples of questions from the BITCH test:

1. In the famous blues legend, whom did 'Stagger Lee' kill?

    His brother

    Frankie

    Johnny

    His girlfriend

2. What is a 'yard'?

    A measuring stick

    $100

    A playground

    Some drugs

3. 'I ain't got no dust' means 'I have no':

    Money

    Women

    Clothes

    Drugs

Evaluation

Cultural influences on intelligence test performance

- IQ tests are biased towards white culture and do not test 'white' against 'black' intelligence, but only how well black people do on tests of white culture.
- Culture-free tests may still be culturally biased, as a culturally based familiarity with the concept of testing is required to perform well.
- Vernon (1969) believed that intelligence is not something that people of all cultures have in varying amounts, determining aptitude (potential).
- Gould (1994), in his book *The Mismeasure of Man*, stated that the bell curve held no new arguments or compelling data, but was cashing in on a depressing temper of the time.
- Critics deride the bell curve hypothesis as a right-wing ideology interpreting data in a biased manner. Indeed, Fischer *et al.* (1996) noted that the original data did not fit the theory and had to be reshaped in order to do so – an example of the theory driving the data.

Issues, debates and approaches

- The whole debate over the influence of culture and race on intelligence levels is socially sensitive, due to the misuses of IQ tests for eugenic purposes, like forced sterilisations and the idea of using IQ to select people for various purposes on racial and cultural grounds.
- Research into whether IQ is more affected by environment or hereditary factors can be considered as culturally specific, as nearly all research is based on western cultures and therefore cannot be applied to other cultures.
- The fact that women used to score on average less than men on IQ tests is an example of gender bias. Such scores were used to 'prove' the lesser intellectual quality of females. However, when tests were re-standardised to include women, females performed as well as males.

Strengthen your learning

1. What predictions can be made and tested if intelligence is genetic?
2. Summarise what twin studies inform us about the inheritance of intelligence.
3. What criticisms of twin studies can be made that question the idea of intelligence being mainly genetic in origin?
4. Explain two weaknesses of adoption studies.
5. What practical applications may arise from identifying genes associated with intelligence?
6. What evidence is there that diet influences IQ?
7. What evaluation can be made of enrichment programmes?
8. Why might it be difficult to construct culture-free tests?

Assessment Check ▶

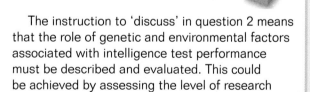

1. Outline and evaluate the role of culture in intelligence test performance. (24 marks)

2. Discuss the role of genetic and environmental factors associated with intelligence test performance. (24 marks)

3. Outline the role of genetic factors associated with intelligence test performance. (8 marks)

4. Evaluate the role of evolutionary factors in the development of human intelligence. (24 marks)

5. Discuss the role of evolutionary factors in the development of human intelligence – for example, self-recognition, social learning, Machiavellian intelligence. (24 marks)

Exam guidance

Question 1 offers 8 marks for an outline, but 16 for an evaluation, so ensure that you focus more on the evaluation than the outline.

The instruction to 'discuss' in question 2 means that the role of genetic and environmental factors associated with intelligence test performance must be described and evaluated. This could be achieved by assessing the level of research support.

Question 3 requires an outline of genetic factors associated with intelligence test performance, with any description of environmental factors not creditworthy. Question 4 requires an evaluation of evolutionary factors in the development of human intelligence, with any descriptive material not gaining credit.

In question 5, evolutionary factors must be described and evaluated, but the examples listed are purely for guidance. Any relevant material would be equally acceptable.

Summing up

- Intelligence concerns an individual's ability to have knowledge of their world and to use that knowledge in an effective manner.

- Psychometric theories attempt to measure intelligence by reducing it to its component parts using factor analysis, and differ from each other by the number of separate factors seen as comprising intelligence.

- Spearman introduced the concept of innate general intelligence, 'g', which underpins all intelligent abilities.

- Thurstone saw intelligence instead arising from primary abilities.

- Guildford also rejected 'g', seeing intelligence as comprised of 120 separate factors.

- Sternberg's triarchic theory is made up of three facets: analytical, creative and practical. He was more interested in 'street-smart' people, those who adapt and shape their environment, but do not do well on IQ tests.

- Gardner perceived each individual as having a cognitive profile based on eight core types of intelligence.

- Classical conditioning sees learning occurring involuntarily by a stimulus becoming associated with a response.

- Operant conditioning sees learning as being shaped voluntarily by reinforcements.

- One-trial learning is a form of classical conditioning where one pairing of a conditioned stimulus with an unconditioned stimulus produces a conditioned response.

- Biological preparedness involves animals learning behaviours rapidly when they are biologically predisposed to when do so.

- Simple learning can explain many animal behaviours, like foraging and navigation.

- Social learning involves learning by social interactions, such as by imitation, enhancement, emulation and tutoring.

- Several species of animals can self-recognise, which suggests they have a self-concept.

- Several species of animals have demonstrated a theory of mind, where they understand that the intentions and mental processes of others are different to their own.

- Machiavellian intelligence is the ability to solve problems associated with social living, without upsetting social cohesion.

- Human intelligence evolved due to the demands of an ever-changing environment creating selective pressure for increased intellect.

- Foraging hypotheses see intelligence as having evolved in order to find and exploit foodstuffs.

- The social complexity hypothesis sees intelligence as evolving in social animals due to the need to predict, react to and influence the social behaviour of other group members.

- Larger brains may have evolved to allow individuals to cope with the demands of social living.

- Intelligence testing is controversial due to political and philosophical arguments about the nature of intelligence.

- Research supporting the inheritance of intelligence comes from twin, adoption and gene-mapping studies.

- Environmental factors are also argued to play a part, like social stimulation, diet and birth order.

- Enrichment programmes try to boost IQ levels by providing stimulating environments.

- IQ tests are argued to be culturally determined and biased towards the culture they are based on.

8 Cognition and development

Development of thinking   **279**

    Theories of cognitive
development   279

    Application of theories to
education   288

**Development of moral
understanding**   **292**

    Kohlberg's theory of moral
development   292

Development of social cognition   **298**

    Development of the child's sense
of self   298

    Development of children's
understanding of others   304

    Biological explanations of social
cognition   308

Summing up   **312**

Decoding the specification

The specification outlines what you must study in order to answer any examination question you might face. As Piaget's and Vygotsky's theories are explicitly named, they could figure in the wording of examination questions, so you should be able to fully describe and evaluate both theories. A similar approach is required to how they can be applied to education, with candidates being able to describe and evaluate the applications.

Kohlberg's theory of moral understanding is explicitly listed and so must be learned, as it could feature directly in the wording of examination questions.

Finally, the specification centres on explaining how individuals develop social cognition. Theory of mind is explicitly listed and so must be studied as part of the development of a child's sense of self, similarly perspective taking must be included too as part of the development of children's understanding of others and as the mirror neuron system is also explicitly named it also must form part of your studies of biological explanations of social cognition. It is likely that these elements will be directly required in examination questions, either singularly or in conjunction with each other. Selman is merely listed as an example of perspective taking, so couldn't feature directly in the wording of examination questions.

Development of thinking

Theories of cognitive development

Theories of cognitive development attempt to explain the growth of mental abilities. Some theories see thought processes as undergoing qualitative changes as children age, with biological processes directing these changes. Other theorists believe that learning experiences are the major influence. Therefore, the relative influence of innate and environmental factors are a key issue.

IN THE NEWS

Robber goes free after £6,000 raid to pay for wife's cancer treatment

Figure 8.01

A man who robbed a building society to raise money for his wife's cancer treatment was released on a suspended sentence yesterday by a sympathetic judge. John Dawson, 48, raided the Scarborough Building Society in Bridlington after being told the National Health Service would not pay for specialist treatment for his wife. Dawson of Sheffield, South Yorkshire, frightened building society staff into handing over £6,000 by grabbing a customer by the hair, pointing an imitation gun at her head and threatening to shoot.

Sentencing him to 2 years' imprisonment, suspended for 2 years, Mr Ken Gillance, the assistant recorder, said he was taking an exceptional view of Dawson's actions. 'It is clear to me at the time you committed this offence your wife, to whom you're devoted, was gravely ill'.

As the sentence was read, Dawson broke down in tears, thanking the judge for his compassion.

This story is similar to one of Kohlberg's moral dilemmas, where he offered participants a choice between two alternatives to assess their level of moral reasoning. By raiding the building society, John Dawson broke the law of the land, but his actions may have saved his wife's life. Kohlberg was not interested in whether people thought such actions were right or wrong, but rather in the reasoning behind their choice. From his dilemmas, Kohlberg constructed his theory of moral reasoning (see page 292). Ultimately, this story illustrates that moral decisions are not always simple right or wrong choices.

see page 292

Key terms

Schemas – ways of understanding the world

Operations – strings of schemas assembled in a logical order

Assimilation – fitting new environmental experiences into existing schemas

Accommodation – altering existing schemas to fit in new experiences

Equilibrium – a pleasant state of balance

Disequilibrium – unpleasant state of imbalance that motivates a return to equilibrium

Zone of proximal development – the distance between current and potential intellectual ability

Scaffolding – tuition given by more knowledgeable others

Discovery learning – learning that occurs through active exploration

Piaget's theory of cognitive development

Piaget was interested in intelligence, helping Binet form his intelligence test at the turn of the twentieth century. As his children grew, he became interested in how their intelligence changed, a process he called *genetic epistemology*.

Piaget performed a series of experiments, concluding that cognitive development occurs through the interaction of innate capacities and environmental events that proceed through a series of stages of intellectual development. Piaget therefore saw intelligence as a process, with individuals learning about the world around them and how to interact with it.

> *'Intelligence is a state of balance or equilibrium achieved by the person when he is able to deal adequately with the data before him. But it is not a static state, it is dynamic in that it continually adapts itself to new environmental stimuli.'*

Humans therefore adapt to their environment, constructing an understanding of reality by interacting with the environment. Knowledge is actively discovered by using mental structures known as:

1. Functional invariants – structures remaining the same throughout the developmental process, which assist in the discovery and understanding of knowledge. There are two of these:

    i.   *the process of adaption* – involves *accommodation* and *assimilation*

    ii. *the process of equilibration* – involves swinging between equilibrium and disequilibrium.

2. Variant structures – structures that change and develop as knowledge is discovered. There are two of these:

    i.   *schemas* – units of intelligence/ways of understanding the world

    ii. *operations* – strings of schemas assembled in a logical order.

A baby's earliest schemas are inborn reflexes, such as sucking. These give babies something by which to interact with the environment and thus to discover knowledge with.

Early schemas are external and physical, with later schemas more internal and cognitive (mental). These are the earliest forms of thinking. They become less reflex and more deliberate, and under the baby's control.

Cognitive development can be seen through the example of the innate schema of sucking. At first, babies will suck everything they come into contact with in the same unlearned manner. This is called *assimilation* (part of the process of adaption) and involves fitting new environmental experiences into existing schemas. If this is possible, infants are in a state of *equilibrium* (part of the process of equilibration), a pleasant state of balance.

When infants experience something new that they cannot suck in the usual way, like drinking from a cup, they experience *disequilibrium* (the other part of the process of equilibration), an unpleasant state of imbalance. Children are naturally motivated to return to the balanced state of equilibrium, achieved by *accommodation* of the new experience (the other part of the process of adaption). This involves altering existing schemas to accommodate (fit in) new experiences, like using new lip shapes to drink/suck out of different things.

Therefore, cognitive development involves a constant swinging between equilibrium and disequilibrium, involving continuous series of assimilation (fitting knowledge into new schemas) and accommodation (altering schemas to fit in new knowledge). When new schemas are formed, assimilation allows for the practice of the new experiences until they are automatic.

This process continues through life, but is most apparent in the first 15 years.

Stages of cognitive development

Piaget noticed that children give similar wrong answers at similar ages, demonstrating that they go through different stages of cognitive development. He saw these stages as invariant and cross-cultural – that is, all children go through the same stages, in the same order, at roughly the same age, all over the world. This indicates that the stages and development of intellect occurring with them are genetically controlled.

There are also transitional periods, in which children's thinking is a mixture of two stages.

Sensorimotor stage (birth to 2 years)

In this stage, babies only 'think' when perceiving or acting on objects. They have no internal representation of objects or events that adults would recognise as thinking. Therefore, when an object is not being perceived or acted on, it does not exist – that is, the baby has no *object permanence*.

Between 1 and 4 months, babies will look at where objects disappear for a few moments, but will not search for them. Then babies start to reach for partially hidden objects, suggesting that they realise that the rest of the object is attached to the visible part. At 1 year of age, babies will search for hidden objects, but only where they were last seen. Object permanence is not fully formed until 2 years of age.

The other development in the sensorimotor stage is the establishment of the *general symbolic function* (GSF). This occurs in the final part of the stage, involving the development of mental images to represent objects that children have experienced. Children are no longer dependent on physical manipulation of objects to 'think' about them; they can 'think' inside their heads, marking a transition of schemas to being internal rather than external.

Pre-operational stage (2 to 7 years)

The GSF continues to develop, but children are still influenced by how things seem rather than by logical principles or operations, hence, 'pre-operational'. Piaget subdivided the stage into the *pre-conceptual* and *intuitive* sub-stages.

1. **Pre-conceptual** (2 to 4 years)

   Several developments occur here:

   - *Centration* – children cannot classify things in a logical manner.
   - *Transductive reasoning* – relationships between two objects are based on a single attribute – for example, a dog has four legs, a cat has four legs, hence a cat is a dog.
   - *Animistic thinking* – there is a belief that inanimate objects are alive.
   - *Seriation* – children find it hard to put items in order – for example, of size; they can only perceive biggest or smallest.

2. **Intuitive** (4 to 7 years)

   Intuitive children can think in relative terms, but find it difficult to think logically, like understanding the relationship between the whole of something and its parts. Children are *egocentric*, meaning that they can only see things from their point of view and not from the viewpoint of others. For example (to a boy):

   Question: Do you have a brother?

   Answer: Yes.

   Question: Does your brother have a brother?

   Answer: No.

Children in this stage cannot *conserve*; they fail to recognise that things remain the same in amount even if they change their appearance. For instance, intuitive children believe a stretched–out row of seven objects has more objects in it than a more compact row of seven objects.

Concrete operational stage (7 to 11 years)

In this stage, children develop a mental structure known as an *operation*, an action performed mentally. At this stage, this can only be done if objects are physically present, hence 'concrete'. Conservation is an example of an operation, and concrete operational children can understand the relationship between the whole of something and its parts.

Egocentrism declines, with children increasingly able to see things from the perspective of others. This process is called *decentring*.

Formal operational stage (11+ years)

Manipulating objects concerns *first-order operations*, but children can now manipulate ideas, *second-order operations*.

Hypothetical situations are thought about – that is, possibilities, not actualities.

Abstract reasoning of concepts and ideas with no physical presence now occur.

This stage is not as uniform. Some reach it by age 15, others by age 20, and individuals acquire formal operations in different areas of aptitude and experience. Perhaps, therefore, this stage is not as genetically controlled as the others. Some estimates claim that as few as a third of people reach this stage.

Supplementary learning

Horizontal and vertical decalage

Some types of conservation are mastered earlier than others and their order is invariant.

- *Liquid quantity* – develops by age 6 to 7, *substance/quantity* and *length* by 7 to 8 years, *weight* by 8 to 10 years, and *volume* by 11 to 12 years.
- This step-by-step acquisition of new operations is called *decalage*.
- In conservation, decalage is *horizontal*: there are inconsistencies *within* the same kind of ability or operation – for example, a 7-year-old can conserve number but not weight.
- *Vertical decalage* refers to inconsistencies *between* different abilities or operations – for example, children may master all kinds of classification, but not all kinds of conservation.

Table 8.01 Piaget's stages of cognitive development

SENSORIMOTOR STAGE (BIRTH TO 2 YEARS)	New schemas arise from matching sensory to motor experiences Object permanence occurs
PRE-OPERATIONAL STAGE (2 TO 7 YEARS)	Internal images, symbols and language develop Child is influenced by how things seem, not logic
CONCRETE OPERATIONAL STAGE (7 TO 11 YEARS)	Development of *conservation* (use of logical rules), but only if situations are concrete, not abstract Decline of egocentrism
FORMAL OPERATIONAL STAGE (11+ YEARS)	Abstract manipulation of ideas (concepts without physical presence) Not achieved by all

Classic research

Piaget and Inhelder (1956)

The Swiss mountain scene study

Pre-operational children, aged between 2 and 7, show errors in logic, as they are egocentric (they can only see the world from their own point of view). This was demonstrated by children in this study only being able to select pictures of a view they could see themselves. The study, however, is not without its criticisms.

Aim

To see whether children below 7 years are only able to see the mountain scene model from their own perspective.

Figure 8.02

Procedure

Children aged between 4 and 8 years were presented with three papier-mâché mountains of differing colours, each with something different on the top: a red cross, a covering of snow or a chalet. Children walked round the model, exploring it, then sat on one side while a doll was placed on one of the other sides. Children were then shown ten pictures of different views of the model, including the doll's and their own. They were asked to select the picture representing the doll's view.

Findings

Four-year-olds chose the picture matching their own view. Six-year-olds showed some awareness of other perspectives, but often selected the wrong picture. Seven- and 8-year-olds consistently chose the picture representing the doll's view.

Conclusions

Four-year-olds are unaware that there are perspectives other than their own.

Children under 7 years are subject to the *egocentric illusion*, failing to understand that what they see is relative to their position. Instead, they believe that their own view represents 'the world as it really is'.

Evaluation

- Swiss mountains are outside of young children's experience; therefore, what Piaget may have witnessed was not egocentrism, but a lack of understanding – that is, use of poor methodology. Hughes (1975) found that 90 per cent of children aged between 3.5 and 5 years could hide a doll in a 3D model of intersecting walls where a police doll could not see it, but they could see it, suggesting that young children are not egocentric. They accomplished this because they were using knowledge of playing hide-and-seek. Similarly, Gelman (1979) showed that 4-year-olds adjust explanations of things to make them clearer to a blindfolded listener, and use simpler forms of speech when talking to 2-year-olds. This would not be expected if they were egocentric. Siegal (2003) sums it up thus: 'A reasonable conclusion is young children are not egocentric all the time, but their perspective-taking skills clearly improve during childhood'.

- The study is not an experiment, as many books claim, (it has no IV) but a 'clinical observation'.

Research: Piaget's theory of cognitive development

- Bower and Wishart (1972) found that 1-month-old babies show surprise when toys disappear, suggesting that Piaget witnessed immature motor skills, not a lack of object permanence.

- Piaget (1952) used three beakers, A, B and C, to demonstrate that 7-year-olds cannot conserve liquid (see Figure 8.03). Children of this age agree that A and B contain equal amounts, then witness A being poured into C and state that C contains more. Donaldson (1978) believed that because the same question is asked twice, young children think a different answer is required, suggesting that Piaget's methodology was not suitable for such young children.

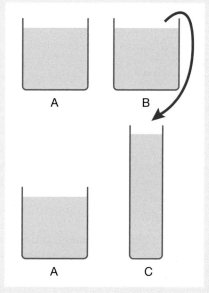

Figure 8.03

- Piaget (1960) performed another conservation task of number. Two equally spaced rows of counters are laid out and pre-operational children agree that there is the same number in both. One of the rows, in sight of the child, is compressed and the child states that the longer line has more. McGarrigle and Donaldson (1974) repeated the study and children again initially agree that the two rows contain the same number. Then 'naughty teddy', a glove puppet, 'secretly' pushes one of the rows together and children state that they still contain the same number. Children believe, from experience, that adults are always changing things, so a different answer is needed when adults meddle with the counters. Berko (1960) also believed that children misinterpret the words 'more' and 'less' as meaning 'taller' and 'shorter'.

Research in focus

A criticism of Piaget concerns his methodology.

In what ways can Piaget's methodology be considered to be inadequate?

What effects may this have had?

Evaluation

Piaget's theory of cognitive development

- Dasen (1977) believed that as formal operational thinking is not found in all cultures, this stage is not genetically determined.
- Cross-cultural evidence implies that the sequence of development is invariant and universal (except for formal operations), suggesting that it is a biological process of maturation.
- Piaget overemphasised cognitive aspects at the expense of emotional and social factors.
- Piaget saw language ability as reflecting the level of cognitive development, while Bruner saw language development as preceding cognitive development.
- Piaget's theory functioned as a starting point for many subsequent theories and research, stimulating interest in the area. According to Schaffer (2004), it is the most comprehensive account of how children come to understand the world. However, Piagetian theory has declined in importance in recent years.
- Piaget believed that the rate of development could not be accelerated, but Meadows (1988) found that direct tuition speeded up development.
- Meadows (1995) maintained that Piaget saw children as independent and isolated in their construction of knowledge and understanding of the physical world, excluding the contribution of others to cognitive development. The exclusion from Piaget's theory of the social nature of knowledge is a basic feature of Vygotsky's theory.
- Piaget's poor methodology led him to underestimate what children of different ages could accomplish.

Vygotsky's theory

Vygotsky did not produce a fully formed theory, probably because he died young, at age 38.

Vygotsky and Piaget agreed that knowledge is constructed as a result of a child's active interaction with the environment, but Vygotsky essentially saw cognitive development as a *cultural construct* – that is, affected by the socialisation of whichever culture learning occurs in.

For Vygotsky, cognitive development is a social process. He aimed to explain how higher mental functions – reasoning, understanding, and so on – arise out of children's social experiences by considering development mainly in terms of *cultural* and *interpersonal* levels.

The cultural level

Children benefit from the wisdom of previous generations, which they gain through interactions with caregivers, taking the culture from one generation to another, developing it further, then handing it on to the next generation. Each child 'inherits' a number of *cultural tools*, which can be:

- technological (clocks, bicycles and other physical devices)
- psychological (concepts and symbols, like language, theories and maths)
- values (like speed, efficiency and power).

Through cultural tools, children learn to live in socially effective and acceptable ways and understand how the world works. Computers are a recent example of a cultural tool.

For Vygotsky, the most essential cultural tool is language.

The interpersonal level

At the interpersonal level, culture and the individual meet. It is the level at which Vygotsky made his major contribution.

Internalisation and the social nature of thinking

The ability to think and reason by and for oneself is called *inner speech* or *verbal thought*. At birth, infants are social beings capable of interacting with others, but able to do little practically or intellectually by themselves. Gradually, children become more self-sufficient and independent, and by participating in social activities their abilities become transformed.

For Vygotsky, cognitive development involves active *internalisation* of problem-solving processes, taking place as a result of mutual interaction between children and those they have social contact with. This replaces Piaget's *child as a scientist* with the *child as an apprentice*, where cultural skills and knowledge are gained through collaboration with those who possess them.

Scaffolding and the zone of proximal development

The zone of proximal development (ZPD) is the distance between current and potential ability. Cultural influences and experts push children through the ZPD and on to tasks beyond their current ability.

Mentors with understanding of an area encourage and help children to promote learning. In this way, their role in regulating children's performance is gradually reduced, with children being given more opportunities to perform the task independently.

The concept of sensitive guidance for development is called *scaffolding*, involving being given clues rather than answers. At first, learning involves shared social activities, but eventually individuals self-scaffold and learning becomes an individual, self-regulated activity.

Semiotics

Semiotics help cognitive development through the use of language and other cultural symbols. These act as a medium for knowledge to be transmitted, turning elementary mental functions into higher ones.

At first, children use *pre-intellectual language* for social and emotional purposes, and *pre-linguistic thinking* occurs without language. From 2 years of age, language and thought combine.

- *Social speech* (birth to 3 years) – pre-intellectual language
- *Egocentric speech* (3 to 7 years) – self-talk/thinking aloud
- *Inner speech* (7+ years) – self-talk becomes silent and internal, and language is used for social communications.

From research, Vygotsky proposed four stages of *concept formation*, as set out in Table 8.02.

Table 8.02 The four stages of concept formation

VAGUE SYNCRETIC	Trial-and-error formation without comprehension. Similar to Piaget's pre-operational stage
COMPLEX	Use of some strategies, but not very systematic
POTENTIAL CONCEPT	More systematic, with one attribute being focused on at a time – for example, weight
MATURE CONCEPT	Several attributes can be dealt with systematically – for example, weight and colour Similar to Piaget's formal operations

Research: Vygotsky's theory

- Woods *et al.* (1976) conducted a study examining tutoring support that mothers gave to 4- and 5-year-olds, ranging from simple encouragement, through verbal instruction, to a full demonstration of how to do the task – fitting wooden blocks together to make a pyramid. A full demonstration frustrated the children due to the adult imposition of a solution, and verbal instructions that were too difficult were also ineffective. Children learned best with 'sensitive guidance', mothers providing assistance when children got stuck so they were not overwhelmed. This supports Vygotsky's idea of the ZPD, that knowledgeable mentors can assist children on to levels beyond their current competence.

- Vygotsky (1934) gave children blocks with nonsense symbols on them and they had to work out what the symbols meant. Four different approaches were observed, from which he devised stages of concept formation.

- Gredler (1992) reported that in New Guinea the symbolic use of fingers and arms when counting among natives limited learning, supporting the idea of cultural influence influencing cognitive development.

Figure 8.04 According to Vygotsky, children learn best with 'sensitive guidance', where tutors give guidance only when it is needed

- McNaughton and Leyland (1990) observed mothers giving increasingly explicit help to children assembling progressively harder jigsaws, supporting the idea of scaffolding and suggesting sensitivity to a child's ZPD.

- Wertsch *et al.* (1980) found that the amount of time children under 5 years of age spent looking at their mothers when assembling jigsaws decreased with age, supporting the idea of increased self-regulation.

- Berk (1994) found that children talked to themselves more when doing difficult tasks, supporting the idea of egocentric speech. This decreased with age.

To view a video presentation of the life and work of Vygotsky, narrated by the man himself (sort of), go to www.youtube.com/watch?v=7J195Qmny_4

You are the researcher

Devise a study testing the impact on learning of various levels of support that parents could provide to children building model aeroplanes.

You will have to describe quite clearly what the levels of support will be and decide how you will measure the impact on learning.

Evaluation

Vygotsky's theory

- Piaget's stage theory has overshadowed the stage aspects of Vygotsky's theory, acknowledged more for its emphasis on the social, language-driven nature of children's cognitive development. While emphasising the cultural and interpersonal levels, at the individual level Vygotsky identified several stages, derived from experimental work on the sorting of blocks of various colours and shapes (see Table 8.02 on page 286).
- Vygotsky's theory explains (which Piaget's theory does not) the influence of the social environment, through culture and language, on cognitive development.
- Vygotsky's theory stimulated a lot of interest and research – for example, scaffolding and peer tutoring. His ideas were extended by others and applied to education.
- Schaffer (2004) believes that Vygotsky's neglect of emotional factors is a serious omission, with no reference to the frustrations of failure, the joys of success or what motivates children to achieve particular goals.
- There is a lack of research support for the theory, but as it focuses on processes rather than outcomes, it is harder to test.
- The theory overemphasises the role of social factors at the expense of biological and individual ones. Learning would be faster if development only depended on social factors.
- The theory is more suited to collectivist cultures with more stress on social learning.
- There are strong central similarities between Piaget's and Vygotsky's theories, and an integration of the two may be feasible and instructive.

Issues, debates and approaches

- Piaget's theory is a good example of how science works, because since the theory was proposed, it has been subjected to research and evaluation, as other psychologists have scrutinised and commented on it. The theory has therefore been amended considerably – for instance, in later versions Piaget talked of spirals of overlapping development, rather than set stages. In this way, psychology can be seen as a search for verisimilitude, or closeness to the truth.
- Vygotsky's theory can be seen as one that fits the collectivist culture that he was part of and, as such, can be regarded as culturally biased. The theory therefore becomes less appropriate when applied to cultures of a less collectivist nature.

To learn more about Lev Vygotsky, access his archive at www.marxists.org/archive/vygotsky

Application of theories to education

Piaget's contribution to education

Piaget wrote little about the educational implications of his theory. However, it has three main implications: the concept of *readiness*, the *curriculum* and *teaching methods*.

1. Readiness – relates to limits set on learning by children's current stage of development. According to Schaffer (2004), Piaget's biggest contribution to education, especially the teaching of maths and science, is recognising the role of individual children's capacity for handling particular experiences. A *child-centred approach* is required, where tasks set by teachers are adapted to children's cognitive levels.

2. The curriculum – Piaget suggested that certain things should be taught at certain ages. However, a too rigid age-based curriculum holds back gifted children and is too swift a progression for less able ones. The idea of a curriculum works best with the teaching of mathematics and science.

3. Teaching methods – *discovery learning* emphasises child-centred learning, where children learn about themselves and the world around them through interaction with the environment. This provides the momentum to push children through the process of adaption via the process of equilibration. Children construct knowledge for themselves and this active learning leads to deeper understanding. Discovery learning is at the core of primary school education, while more formal or rote learning occurs in secondary education.

Figure 8.05 Teaching methods based on Piaget's theory emphasised discovery learning

The role of the teacher in the Piagetian classroom

- Teachers assess individual children's current stage of cognitive development to determine levels of readiness. Children are set tasks tailored to their needs, therefore motivating them.

- Teachers provide children with learning opportunities to enable them to advance to the next developmental step. This is achieved by pushing them into disequilibrium, so that they have to accommodate new learning experiences, thus learning and progressing. Teachers create appropriate learning activities for this to occur.

- Children are encouraged to ask questions, experiment and explore.

- Teachers encourage children to learn from each other. Hearing other views helps to break down egocentrism, and working in pairs promotes long-lasting perspective taking.

Research: Piaget's contribution to education

- Modgil *et al.* (1983) found that discovery learning leads to poor reading and writing skills in children who need assistance.

- Danner and Day (1977) found that coaching 10- and 13-year-olds had no effect, supporting Piaget's concept of readiness. However, it did assist 17-year-olds, suggesting that tuition helps at a later stage of development.

- Meadows (1988) found that direct tuition speeded up development, contradicting other findings, and suggesting that researcher bias plays a part in this contentious area.

- Driscoll (1994) found that a number of instructional strategies have been derived from Piaget's theory, including provision of a supportive environment, utilising social interactions and peer teaching, as well as guiding children to see errors and inconsistencies in their thinking.

Evaluation

Piaget's contribution to education

- Vygotsky proposes a more dynamic policy of educational intervention, advocating an active intervention in the form of *scaffolding* and the *zone of proximal development*.
- Piaget never intended his theory as an educational tool; others put it to this use.
- Piaget's theory influenced education. The Plowden report recommended that primary education move from being teacher-led to child-centred.
- The Piagetian idea of manipulating concrete materials when learning about abstract principles formed the basis of the Nuffield secondary science project and the Montessori approach to teaching, with reported success.
- Piaget's research sample was small and consisted of children of well-educated professionals, suggesting that his findings do not suit the educational needs of other children.

Vygotsky's contribution to education

Because he emphasises the social nature of development, much of Vygotsky's theory is directly or indirectly concerned with formal schooling.

Zone of proximal development (ZPD)

The idea of the ZPD is intrinsically linked to education through its capacity for teachers, as knowledgeable others, to guide students from what they are currently able to do, on to what they can do with help and thus will be able to do by themselves in the near future.

Collaborative learning

With collaborative learning, children at similar levels of competence work together, either in pairs or in groups. Collaborative learning and peer tutoring offer an effective environment for guiding children through their ZPD, because such settings encourage children to use language, provide explanations and work cooperatively or competitively, all of which produce cognitive change. Therefore, knowledge is socially constructed by learners working collectively on common tasks, where all individuals depend on and are accountable to each other, assisting individuals to then work better on their own.

The role of the teacher

Vygotsky defined intelligence as the capacity to learn from instruction. Rather than teachers playing an enabling role, Vygotsky believed that they guide pupils in paying attention, concentrating and learning effectively. By doing this, teachers scaffold children to competence, and experienced people assist development, providing general and specific tutoring, enabling individuals to achieve more. Eventually, scaffolding becomes self-instruction. Expert tutoring is an effective teaching tool if the boundaries of a child's ZPD are taken into account.

Research: Vygotsky's contribution to education

- Slavin's (1990) Student Teams Achievement Divisions (STAD) involves small groups of varying ability, gender and ethnic background working on a topic. These groups show greater achievement than controls taught by more conventional methods, supporting the teaching methods based on Vygotsky's theory.

- Bennett and Dunne (1991) found that children who worked in cooperative groups displayed more logical thinking and were less competitive or interested in status, supporting Vygotsky's concept of collaborative thinking.

- Cloward (1967) found that peer tutoring had more learning benefit for the tutor than the designated learner, demonstrating the benefit of the method.

- Gokhale (1995) tested students on critical thinking, finding that those undertaking collaborative learning outscored those who studied alone, supporting the idea of cooperative learning.

- Wood *et al.* (1976) found that scaffolding worked best when general encouragement was given if children were working well, and specific instructions are given when learners are struggling, demonstrating the flexibility of scaffolding practices.

Evaluation

Vygotsky's contribution to education

- Vygotsky's teaching methods are dependent on teachers being expert in recognising the boundaries of ZPDs as well as knowing how and when to give tuition. This may be unrealistic in real terms.
- Some children do not benefit from collaborative thinking, learning best alone, suggesting that individual differences are a factor.
- Learning via cooperative groups needs careful monitoring or some individuals will dominate, while others have little involvement.
- Vygotsky's approach may work less well in individualistic settings, where the emphasis is on competitiveness and being autonomous. Vygotsky lived in a strongly collectivist society – Soviet Russia; therefore, his theory, and its applications to education, favour that type of society as that is what it was based on.

Issues, debates and approaches

- The applications of Piaget's theory to education create an issue of bias, as a criticism exists that those of a left-wing political and philosophical persuasion used his theory to provide support for the education system they desired. For example, Walkerdine (1984) believed that educationalists used Piaget's theory as a convenient vehicle to justify changes they wished to make.
- The concepts of sensitive guidance, scaffolding and ZPD are easily applied to different cultures where particular skills and learning goals will differ, suggesting the concepts to be 'culture-fair'.

Psychology in action

Applications to education

The material on the contributions to education made by Piaget and Vygotsky can be used not just in response to questions on applications to education, but also as general evaluation when answering questions on these cognitive theorists.

It might be of use here to reference material in Chapter 7: Intelligence and learning namely Gardner's (1983) theory of multiple intelligences (see page 244), which is also based on cognitive development theories.

Strengthen your learning

1. Outline the main principles of Piaget and Vygotsky's theories, highlighting their similarities and differences.
2. For Piaget and Vygotsky's theories, compile a list of evaluative points for and against that assesses the degree of support each theory has.
3. Describe the ways in which Piaget and Vygotsky's theories can be applied to education and evaluate each one in terms of research evidence.

Assessment Check ▶

1. Outline and evaluate two theories of cognitive development. (24 marks)

2. Outline Piaget's theory of cognitive development. (8 marks)

3. Evaluate Vygotsky's theory in terms of its application to education. (16 marks)

4. Outline one or more applications of Piaget's theory of cognitive development to education. (4 marks)

5. Outline and evaluate Vygotsky's theory of cognitive development. (20 marks)

Examination guidance

In question 1, when outlining two theories (Piaget and Vygotsky would be popular choices), a reasonable balance needs to be achieved to access the top band of marks. With the evaluation, research support could be utilised, as well as the applications of the theories to education. Comparison of the two theories would also be creditworthy.

Question 2 requires an outline of Piaget's theory; any material on other theories would not be creditworthy and neither would evaluation of Piaget's theory. Question 3 calls solely for evaluation of Vygotsky's theory in terms of its application to education; therefore, any descriptive material would not attract credit, nor would general evaluative material.

Question 4 requires an outline of one or more applications of Piaget's theory to education; any evaluation of these applications would not gain marks. Question 5 is a more general question, based around Vygotsky's theory. There are only 4 marks available for the outline, so the majority of time and effort should be spent on the evaluation, possibly in terms of research support, applications to education and comparisons with other theories.

Development of moral understanding

Morality concerns the rules by which a society judges what kinds of behaviour, beliefs and attitudes are acceptable. Psychologists are more interested in *moral reasoning*, the thinking behind moral behaviour and how this develops over time.

Kohlberg's theory of moral development

Kohlberg believed that morality develops gradually during childhood and adolescence. He was interested in reasons for moral judgements rather than judgements themselves – for example, people's beliefs about upholding the law, as well as views about whether there are circumstances in which breaking the law can be justified. He was also interested in how views change as individuals develop.

Kohlberg's theory is based on cognitive development, seeing morality developing in a number of innate stages in a set order. Morality develops when biological maturation is sufficiently advanced, but disequilibrium plays a part, as experiences not fitting existing schemas challenge current ways of thinking about morality. Women are seen as less morally developed than men, as they are restricted to a domestic life.

Stages of morality are separate, as they involve different kinds of thinking to reach moral decisions, the focus being on how moral thinking occurs, rather than what is thought about a particular moral issue. The theory asserts that moral behaviour is a direct result of moral thinking, and Kohlberg perceived cognitive development as necessary for, and setting a limit on, the maturity of moral reasoning, with the latter lagging behind.

Kohlberg assessed moral reasoning through the use of *moral dilemmas*, scenarios involving a choice between two alternatives, both of which are socially unacceptable – for example, the *Heinz dilemma*.

The Heinz dilemma

A woman was close to death from cancer. There was one drug that the doctors thought might save her that a chemist had recently discovered. The chemist was charging $4,000 for a small dose, ten times what it cost him to make the drug.

The sick woman's husband, Heinz, tried to borrow the money, but could only amass $2,000, half of what the drug cost. He told the chemist that his wife was dying and asked him to sell it cheaper or let him pay later. The chemist refused, stating that it was his discovery and he wanted to make money from it.

Heinz was desperate and considered breaking into the chemist's store to steal the drug.

1. Should Heinz steal the drug? (Why, or why not?)

2. If Heinz did not love his wife, should he steal the drug for her? (Why, or why not?)

3. Suppose the person dying was not his wife, but a stranger. Should Heinz steal the drug for the stranger? (Why, or why not?)

4. (*If you favoured stealing the drug for a stranger*) Suppose it is a pet animal he loves. Should Heinz steal to save the pet animal? (Why, or why not?)

5. Is it important for people to do everything they can to save another's life? (Why, or why not?)

6. Is it against the law for Heinz to steal? Does that make it morally wrong? (Why, or why not?)

7. Should people try to do everything they can to obey the law? (Why, or why not?)

8. How does this apply to what Heinz should do?

Using his moral dilemmas, Kohlberg performed a longitudinal study on a group of 72 boys from Chicago, lasting for 20 years. From this research, Kohlberg identified six qualitatively different stages of moral development, differing in complexity, with more complex types being used by older individuals. The six stages span three levels of moral reasoning (each level having two stages):

1. Pre-conventional level – individuals do not have personal codes of morality; instead, they are shaped by the standards of adults and the consequences of following or breaking their rules.

2. Conventional level – individuals begin to internalise moral standards of valued adult role models.

3. Post-conventional level – society's values, the need for democratically agreed rules and mutual interactions are affirmed, and at the higher stage individuals are guided by universal ethical principles, in which they do what their conscience dictates, even if this conflicts with society's rules.

Kohlberg's three levels and six stages of moral development, and their application to the Heinz dilemma

Based on Crooks and Stein (1991), Rest (1983)

Level 1: Pre-conventional morality

Stage 1 (punishment and obedience orientation): right and wrong are determined by what is and is not punishable. If stealing is wrong, it is because authority figures say so and punish such behaviour. Moral behaviour is essentially the avoidance of punishment.

- Heinz *should* steal the drug. If he lets his wife die, he would get into trouble.

- Heinz *should not* steal the drug. He would get caught and be sent to prison.

Stage 2 (instrumental relativist orientation): right and wrong are determined by what brings rewards and what people want. Other people's needs and wants are important, but only in a reciprocal sense ('If you scratch my back, I will scratch yours').

- Heinz *should* steal the drug. His wife needs to live and he needs her companionship.

- Heinz *should not* steal the drug. He might get caught and his wife would probably die before he got out of prison, so it would not do much good.

Level 2: Conventional morality

Stage 3 (interpersonal concordance or 'good boy–nice girl' orientation): moral behaviour is whatever pleases and helps others, and doing what they approve of. Being moral is 'being a good person in your own eyes and the eyes of others' – in other words, what the majority thinks is right.

- Heinz *should* steal the drug. Society expects a loving husband to help his wife, regardless of the consequences.

- Heinz *should not* steal the drug. He would bring dishonour on his family and they would be ashamed of him.

Stage 4 (maintaining the social order orientation): being good means doing one's duty, showing respect for authority and maintaining social order for its own sake. Concern for the common good goes beyond stage 3 concern for the family: society protects the rights of individuals, so the individual must protect society. Laws are accepted and obeyed unquestioningly.

- Heinz *should* steal the drug. If people like the chemist are allowed to get away with being greedy and selfish, society would break down.

- Heinz *should not* steal the drug. If people are allowed to take the law into their own hands, regardless of how justified an act might be, social order would break down.

Level 3: Post-conventional morality

Stage 5 (social contract-legalistic orientation): because laws are established by mutual agreement, similar democratic processes can change them. Although laws should be respected, as they protect individual rights

as well as society, individual rights sometimes override these laws if they become destructive or restrictive. Life is more 'sacred' than legal principles, thus the law should not be obeyed at all costs.

- Heinz *should* steal the drug. The law is not set up to deal with circumstances in which obeying it would cost a human life.

- Heinz *should not* steal the drug. Although we could understand why he would want to steal it, even such extreme circumstances do not justify a person taking the law into their own hands. The ends do not always justify the means.

Stage 6 (universal ethical principles orientation): the ultimate judge of what is moral is a person's own conscience operating in accordance with universal principles. Society's rules are arbitrary and may be broken when they conflict with universal moral principles.

- Heinz *should* steal the drug. When a choice is made between disobeying laws and saving a life, one must act in accordance with the higher principle of preserving and respecting life.

- Heinz *should not* steal the drug. He must consider others who need it as much as his wife. By stealing the drug, he would be acting in accordance with his own particular feelings, disregarding the values of all the lives involved.

You are the researcher

Create your own moral dilemma with more of a modern theme to it – for example, one involving mobile phones.

Create example pairs of should/should not answers that fit each of Kohlberg's three levels.

Research: Kohlberg's theory of moral understanding

- Kohlberg (1969) tested the moral reasoning of participants in several cultures, like Mexico and Taiwan, finding the same sequence of moral development, suggesting that transition through the stages occurs as an innate biological process.

- Fodor (1972) compared delinquents' and non-delinquents' levels of morality, finding non-delinquents at a higher level of morality, supporting the notion that moral thinking reflects actual moral behaviour.

- Kohlberg (1975) gave students a chance to cheat on a test and observed that only 15 per cent of participants with post-conventional morality cheated, while 70 per cent of those with pre-conventional morality did, supporting the idea that moral reasoning reflects moral behaviour.

- Colby *et al.* (1983) tested Kohlberg's original sample for 26 years, finding that at age 10 the majority showed stage 2 moral reasoning, with a few instances of stages 1 and 3. By age 22, the majority were in stages 3 and 4, with no one in stage 1. By the age of 36, the majority, 65 per cent, were in stage 4, with only 5 per cent progressing to stage 5.

- Rest (1983) performed a longitudinal study over 20 years, following a sample of men from early adolescence to their mid-thirties, finding that the stages of development followed the set order proposed by Kohlberg, but that change occurs very gradually, with most participants changing fewer than two stages, suggesting a degree of support for Kohlberg.

- Colby *et al.* (1983) reported that the moral dilemmas and interviews used to assess people's levels of morality made it impossible to differentiate between stages 5 and 6. Therefore, stage 6 may not be part of the normal developmental sequence.

- Berkowitz and Gibbs (1983) found that development through the stages was assisted by *transactive interactions*, where discussions are held about moral possibilities, supporting Kohlberg's idea that creating disequilibrium in an individual's way of thinking develops moral growth, but only if biological maturation allows.

- Walker *et al.* (1987) found that most children demonstrate stage 2 moral reasoning at age 10, and stage 3 by age 16, demonstrating a progression in line with Kohlberg's theory. However, nine rather than six stages were proposed, to cater for the fact that children often seem to be between stages.

Figure 8.06 Only 15 per cent of students with post-conventional morality cheat, while 70 per cent with pre-conventional morality do

Evaluation

Kohlberg's theory of moral understanding

- Kohlberg's theory has research support from his own longitudinal study and a wealth of other studies, suggesting that stages 1 to 5 are universal and occur in an invariant sequence. This suggests that they are under genetic control.

- As he found no evidence of stage 6 reasoning in normal participants, and little evidence of stage 5, Kohlberg (1978) decided that stage 6 might not exist.

- As only 12 per cent of adults reach post-conventional morality, Atkinson *et al.* (1990) argued that it is more of a philosophical ideal than part of a normal developmental sequence.

- Hartshorne and May (1928) gave students opportunities to lie, cheat, steal and spend money on themselves or others, finding that moral behaviour was situation-specific and not universal across all situations, casting doubt on Kohlberg's belief that moral behaviour is a reflection of moral thought.

- Moral dilemmas are not real-life scenarios, and people may behave differently to their moral reasoning if actually placed in such situations. Gilligan (1982) questioned women deciding whether to have abortions, finding a different pattern of moral thought to Kohlberg, though this may be due to using females rather than males.

Supplementary learning

Piaget's theory of morality

Piaget's theory influenced Kohlberg. Piaget saw morality developing gradually during childhood and adolescence through two different types of *moral orientation*, with the emphasis on effects and emotions rather than cognition.

To discover how moral knowledge and understanding changes with age, Piaget studied the rules that children use when playing marbles (a game relatively free from adult influence). Children aged 5 to 10 years saw the rules as having always existed and that they could not be changed, even though they broke them themselves. Older children saw rules as changeable if everyone agreed to the change.

Piaget also told children pairs of stories where someone breaks/steals something or lies. For example, John accidentally breaks 15 cups, or Henry breaks one cup while trying to steal some jam. Children aged 5 to 10 years base their judgement of who is naughtiest on the amount of damage done – that is, 1 cup or 15 – while older children base their judgements on intentions.

continued ...

... continued

Piaget called the morality of younger children *heteronomous* (subject to another's laws), while older children's morality he called *autonomous* (subject to one's own laws). Piaget saw the shift from heteronomous to autonomous morality occurring due to the development of operational thinking – that is, a movement away from egocentrism. This suggests that moral development is dependent on cognitive factors, but as morality lags 2 years behind, other factors must be involved.

Another important development is the move away from *unilateral* respect, an unconditional obedience of parents/adults, to *mutual* respect, where disagreements between peers have to be negotiated and resolved.

Evaluation

• Piaget's theory, like Kohlberg's, is gender biased. For instance, he saw girls' games, like hopscotch, as simpler than boys' games, and not worthy of investigation.

• Piaget underestimated younger children's understanding of intention. Armsby (1971) found that 60 per cent of 6-year-olds (compared to 90 per cent of 10-year-olds) thought that someone who deliberately breaks a cup is guiltier than someone accidentally breaking a TV, suggesting that the majority of 6-year-olds can judge intentions.

Issues, debates and approaches

• Kohlberg's theory is accused of gender bias. He saw morality as based on principles of justice, while Gilligan argues that women operate differently on principles of care. Kohlberg's negative rating of female morality is a result of being assessed by male-created standards and methodological shortcomings, whereby he used only male participants.

• Although evidence suggests that Kohlberg's stages of moral development are cross-cultural, this may be because people of non-western cultures cannot understand dilemmas drawn from western cultural experiences, where individual needs are greater than those of others. Snarey *et al.* (1985) believed that the morality of collectivist cultures is centred on obeying elders and aiding society, yet these are assessed at low levels by Kohlberg, suggesting that the theory may not be cross-cultural, as it is making cultural judgements about morality.

• There are ethical considerations with Kohlberg's theory, especially of harm, when researching young children and exposing them to potential distress.

Strengthen your learning

1. Outline how Kohlberg explains the development of morality.
2. What are moral dilemmas and how did Kohlberg use them to form his theory?
3. Outline Kohlberg's three levels of morality.
4. What positive and negative criticisms can be made of Kohlberg's theory? (You may wish to use research evidence to help with this.)

Assessment Check

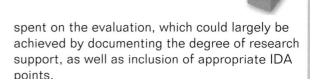

1. Outline and evaluate Kohlberg's theory of moral understanding (24 marks)

2a. Outline and evaluate one theory of cognitive development (12 marks)

2b. Outline and evaluate Kohlberg's theory of moral understanding. (12 marks)

3. Outline Kohlberg's theory of moral understanding. (8 marks)

4. Evaluate Kohlberg's theory of moral understanding. (16 marks)

Examination guidance

Question 1 has 8 marks available for outlining the theory, but 16 marks for evaluating it, therefore most time and effort should be spent on the evaluation, which could largely be achieved by documenting the degree of research support, as well as inclusion of appropriate IDA points.

Question 2 cuts across two sub-areas of this topic. Four marks would be available for outlining a theory of cognitive development, such as Piaget or Vygotsky's, with 8 marks available for the evaluation. 4 marks are then available for outlining Kohlberg's theory of moral understanding, with again 8 marks on offer for the evaluation.

Questions 3 and 4 are basically question one, but seperated out into two individual parts. Therefore, care must be taken here to only include descriptive material in question 3 and evaluative material in question 4.

Development of social cognition

Social cognition relates to the mental processes by which information concerning ourselves and others is processed and understood, and by which social behaviour is conducted. Social cognition is involved with explaining how individuals develop the ability to make sense of their social world, like developing a sense of self, the growth of perspective taking and the biological role of mirror neurons.

Development of the child's sense of self

Development of self-recognition

Developing a sense of 'self' is an important factor in social interactions, the ability to self-recognise being found in only a few species and associated with the intelligence necessary for social living.

Self-recognition is tested with the *mirror test*, where a coloured mark is made on the face and participants placed in front of a mirror. If participants touch the mark, they can self-recognise. Some infants do this by 15 months of age, and the majority by 2 years. The thinking behind the test is that for an individual to understand whom the mirror image is of, there must be a mental representation of self.

Figure 8.07 Some children can recognise their mirror image by 15 months of age, and most by 2 years of age

Research: self-recognition

- Amsterdam (1972) tested 88 children aged between 3 and 24 months on the standard mirror test, finding that 42 per cent of participants aged between 18 and 20 months, and 63 per cent of those aged between 21 and 24 months, could self-recognise.

- Bertenthal and Fischer (1978) examined self-recognition from a Piagetian perspective, noting the sensorimotor operations performed by children of different ages when regarding their own reflections. From this they devised five stages of self-recognition that an infant should progress through in its first 2 years of life, culminating in being able to name the image. The results supported the predicted developmental sequence of mirror-image responses. However, some criteria used are criticised as not relating to self-recognition, like touching a hat on your head when regarding your image.

- Lewis and Brooks-Gunn (1979) observed children between 9 and 12 months of age smiling at their own image, but not touching the mark on their face. By 21 months of age, 70 per cent were touching the dot. The fact that children of 18 months identified with their own image in a photograph suggests that self-recognition is possible from still images too.

- Mans *et al.* (1978) showed that self-recognition in Down's syndrome children was delayed, but by 4 years of age 89 per cent could do it, suggesting that recognition of self, and thus self-awareness, is related to cognitive development.

Gender concept

Developing gender identity is crucial in attaining a self-concept, with most children developing *gender identity*, where they realise that they are male or female, between 2 and 3 years of age. Between 3 and 7 years, *gender stability* is attained, where children realise that gender is permanent, and by 12 years of age, *gender consistency* is reached, where it is understood that changes in looks or behaviour do not change gender (see Chapter 6: Gender).

The distinction between the physical and the psychological self

Being able to distinguish between physical and psychological selves is a vital part of self-awareness, signifying comprehension of a personal, invisible self. Children between 3 and 4 years of age are aware of the difference, but mainly describe themselves in physical terms.

Self-referential emotions

Certain emotions, like embarrassment, convey a sense of self-awareness, involving thinking about oneself in relation to others.

Self-esteem

The ability to self-evaluate is dependent on assessing the difference between the actual and the ideal self. It differs between individuals and across situations.

You are the researcher

Design an experiment examining for a difference between younger and older children in terms of whether they describe themselves more in physical or psychological terms.

What age categories would you use?

What type of experimental design would this be and what would be your IV?

How would you determine your data?

Using children from one school, how would you create a random sample and a systematic sample?

Research: development of the child's sense of self

- Eder (1990) found that 3- to 4-year-olds can describe how they behave in various situations, implying an awareness of a psychological self.

- Selman (1980) believed that children under the age of 6 years could not distinguish between physical and psychological selves. By the age of 8 years, most children had developed the ability.

- Lewis *et al.* (1989) found that children who are asked to dance in front of adults display embarrassment around the same age that they demonstrate self-recognition, supporting the idea that they use self-referential emotions to convey a sense of self-awareness.

- Harter (1987) found that a child's self-esteem is dependent on levels of perceived competence, decreasing in mid-childhood due to input from others.

- Vershueren *et al.* (2001) found that children between 4 and 5 years have a sense of self-esteem that is related to attachment patterns, with securely attached individuals having higher levels.

Evaluation

Development of a child's sense of self

- Some studies of self-recognition – for example, Dickie and Strader (1974), who put red tape on children's faces – may provide tactile clues and thus lack validity.

- Some studies of self-recognition accept image naming as evidence for recognition of one's own image. However, this may be a learned response and not demonstrate the ability.

- A methodological difficulty in researching the development of social cognition is the lack of language skills in small children, making conclusions difficult to arrive at.

- Both visual self-recognition and self-referential emotions demonstrate the development of self-awareness.

- A child's sense of self may be affected by different factors. Case (1991) reported that 'I' comes from learning how behaviour affects others, while 'me' occurs as a result of watching one's own movements.

- As children age, there is a gradual shift from describing the self in terms of activities to psychological characteristics. Hart *et al.* (1993) found that this change was most noticeable between 6 and 8 years of age.

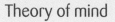

Theory of mind

Comprehension of another's thoughts and emotions is found in few animal species and is perceived as indicating higher intelligence. Indeed, the term 'theory of mind' (TOM) was originally coined by Premack and Woodruff (1978) to understand the cognitive abilities of chimpanzees. They defined TOM as the ability to attribute mental states, knowledge, wishes, feelings and beliefs to oneself and others. Indications of TOM in humans are found in everyday use of language, such as, 'I think she was upset'.

An important aspect of understanding the mind is the realisation that other people have feelings, desires, beliefs – that is, that they have a mind too. Equally important is the realisation that others' beliefs and so on differ from our own. Research into TOM indicates that this ability is not present at birth, but develops over time.

TOM is investigated by presenting children with *false belief tasks*, where a scene is witnessed with one character leaving the room; while they are absent, something is moved from being concealed in one container to another. When the character returns, researchers record whether children witnessing the scene realise that the character will not look for the object in it is new placing, but where it was originally. If they do, they have a TOM. If they believe the character will look for the object in its new placing, then they are egocentric, seeing it from their own point of view, and cannot have a TOM. Research findings show that children of 4 years of age give egocentric answers (have a false belief), while 6-year-olds get it right – that is, they have a TOM. Interestingly, autistic children find it difficult, which may explain their difficulty in conducting social relationships.

TOM is akin to Piaget's idea of egocentrism, with TOM not developing until cognitive development does, at around 4 years of age. A more recent view emphasises modularity, where specific brain areas, like the amygdala and basal ganglia, are associated with TOM processing, with a set sequence of development and with TOM reasoning being inferred from other knowledge. With the development of TOM comes the ability to manipulate and deceive by hiding one's emotions and intentions. This occurs from 3 years of age. It is possible that there is a more primitive precursor to TOM, called shared attention mechanism (SAM), developing between 9 and 18 months of age, allowing two people to realise that they are attending to the same thing.

Research: theory of mind

- Wimmer and Perner (1983) used models to act out a story, to 4-, 6- and 8-year-olds, about a boy called Maxi who put some chocolate in a blue cupboard. While Maxi is absent, the children saw his mother transfer the chocolate to a green cupboard. The children were asked where Maxi would look for the chocolate. Most 6- and 8-year-olds gave the correct blue cupboard answer, while most 4-year-olds said that he would look in the green cupboard. They think he will act on the basis of his false belief, implying that they have not developed a TOM.

- Shatz *et al.* (1983) believed that children under 4 years of age can differentiate between different mental states. At 2 years of age, they can name emotional states, and by 3 years of age, they can demonstrate knowledge of what thinking is, suggesting that acquisition of a TOM is a developmental process.

- Harris (1989) reported that at around 4 years of age, children become aware of their emotions and use them to pretend to be someone else, permitting them to be aware of others' thinking, suggesting that this is a pivotal age in realising that others think differently.

- Flavell *et al.* (1986) found that 3-year-olds who handled a sponge looking like a rock, called it a rock, while 4-year-olds called it a sponge, suggesting that the development of a TOM requires an appreciation of what is false, suggesting that a lack of TOM is a cognitive deficit.

- Bartsch and Wellman (1995) found that TOM acquisition follows a common developmental pattern in both US and Chinese children, suggesting that the ability is biologically controlled.

- Avis and Harris (1991) found that children in developed and non-developed countries realise at 4 years of age that people can have false beliefs, supporting the idea of biological maturation.

- Frith and Frith (1999) found that the amygdala, basal ganglia, temporal cortex and frontal cortex show heightened rates of activity when participants had to consider others' mental states, suggesting that these brain areas are associated with TOM.

Classic research

Baron-Cohen *et al.* (1985)

The Sally-Anne experiment

The idea of a theory of mind is that children develop the ability to realise that others have a mind whose viewpoint may be different to theirs. The researchers wanted to see whether autistic children had a theory of mind by using a false belief study.

Aim

To see whether a lack of a TOM was at the core of autism.

Procedure

The participants were:

- 20 autistic children of average age of 12 years and an average verbal mental age of 5.5 years
- 14 Down's syndrome children of average age 11 years and average verbal mental age of 3 years
- 27 normal children of average age 4.5 years and average verbal mental age 4.5 years.

The normal and Down's syndrome children served as control groups, with the autistic children as the experimental group.

Each child witnesses a scenario played out with the Sally and Anne dolls.

The naming question: each child was checked to ensure that they knew which doll was Sally and which was Anne.

Sally places a marble in her basket and leaves the scene, and Anne transfers the marble and hides it in her box. When Sally returns, children are given the Sally-Anne test: success or failure depends specifically on their response to the third of three questions:

1. Where is the marble really? (*reality question*)
2. Where was the marble in the beginning? (*memory question*)
3. Where will Sally look for her marble? (*belief question*)

The *correct answer* requires a child to attribute a *false belief* to Sally (she will look in the *wrong place*). The first two questions act as *control* questions to ensure that the child has attended to and knows the current location of the marble, and also that they remember where it was before.

Findings

All children passed the naming question, as well as the reality and memory questions.

Twenty per cent of autistic children passed the false belief question, compared to 85 per cent of normal children and 86 per cent of Down's syndrome children.

Conclusions

Autistic children do not have a TOM and therefore cannot attribute beliefs to others.

These findings support the TOM hypothesis: autistic children are unable to attribute beliefs to others, disadvantaging them when predicting others' behaviour.

continued ...

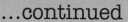

...continued

Evaluation

- The study was based on Wimmer and Perner's (1983) study of false beliefs (see page 301), but was shorter, simpler and more appropriate for older children.
- The failure of autistic children to attribute beliefs to others is a specific deficit, as it cannot be explained in terms of the general effects of mental retardation, as the more severely retarded Down's syndrome children performed slightly better than even the normal children.
- The fact that a sizeable minority of autistic children pass the test suggests that lack of TOM is not the core deficit in autism.
- The Sally-Anne test is more of a 'probe' to examine cognitive skills of 4- to 6-year-olds; it cannot be used to test whether adults have a TOM.

Evaluation

Theory of mind

- TOM appears in childhood, though there is disagreement as to whether this occurs suddenly at age 4, or more gradually.
- A lack of TOM is similar to Piaget's idea of egocentrism, coinciding at similar ages, and suggesting that the two concepts are linked.
- A false belief task involves a *first-order belief* – for example, 'I think Sally believes the marble is in the basket'. A *second-order belief* involves understanding that someone else can have beliefs about a third person: 'I think Anne believes that Sally believes the marble is in the basket'. Baron-Cohen (1989) found that all the autistic children failed the second-order belief task. However, many adults with Asperger's syndrome, an autistic disorder not associated with retarded language development, pass second-order TOM tests, contradicting Baron-Cohen's claim that lack of TOM is the core cognitive deficit in autism.
- Younger children may fail to understand false belief tasks, not because they do not have a TOM, but because the language of the questions is too complex. For instance, 'Where will he look for the chocolate?' could be taken to mean 'Where is the chocolate?' Therefore, results may be due to poor methodology.

Issues, debates and approaches

- Research into the development of children's sense of self was initially culturally inapplicable, because inappropriate and non-standardised methodologies were used. Indeed, cross-cultural studies of TOM initially gained mixed results due to the use of different methodologies. When a standard methodology was applied, results showed that TOM develops by 5 years of age in children of all cultures, suggesting that a biological mechanism is at work.
- There are ethical considerations to take into account when conducting research with children, especially those of informed consent and harm. This is even more the case when using autistic and Down's syndrome children, as when conducting TOM research.

Development of children's understanding of others

Theories of and research into cognitive development explain how children develop the ability to see from another's perspective. A major element is the ability to empathise, understanding others' feelings and motives. The ability to self-recognise occurs simultaneously to acquiring empathy, at around 18 months of age.

Perspective taking

Perspective taking concerns the ability to assume another's perspective and understand their thoughts and feelings. Being able to differentiate between other people's perspectives and one's own enhances the understanding of others and oneself.

Selman (1980) proposed *role-taking theory* to explain the development of perspective taking, where adopting the perspective of others allows for comprehension of their feelings, thoughts and intentions. The theory was developed through research involving *interpersonal dilemmas*, like whether expert tree-climber Holly, who promised her father she would not climb trees anymore, should climb a tree to save a kitten. The theory has five levels, developed from children's answers to questions about the dilemmas. As children mature, they take more information into account, coming to realise that people can react differently to the same situation. They develop the ability to analyse various people's perspectives from the viewpoint of an objective, neutral bystander, and have a realisation of how different cultural and societal values affect the perception of the bystander.

Selman's stages of social role taking (1976)

Stage 0: Egocentric viewpoint (3 to 6 years)

Children have a sense of differentiation of self and other, but fail to distinguish between the social perspective (thoughts, feelings) of others and self. Children can label others' overt feelings, but do not see the cause-and-effect relationship between reasons and social actions.

Stage 1: Social informational role taking (6 to 8 years)

Children are aware that others have social perspectives based on their own reasoning, which may or may not be similar to theirs. However, children tend to focus on one perspective rather than integrating different viewpoints.

Stage 2: Self-reflective role taking (8 to 10 years)

Children are conscious that each individual is aware of the other's perspective, and that this awareness influences self and the other's views of each other. Putting the self in the other's place is a way of judging their intentions, purposes and actions. Children can form a coordinated chain of perspectives, but cannot yet abstract from this process to the level of simultaneous mutuality.

Stage 3: Mutual role taking: (10 to 12 years)

Children realise that both self and others can view each other mutually and simultaneously. Children can view the interaction from a third-person perspective.

Stage 4: Social and conventional system role taking (12 to 15 years and over)

People realise that mutual perspective taking does not always lead to complete understanding. Social conventions are seen as necessary, because they are understood by all members of the group (the *generalised other*), regardless of their position, role or experience.

Contemporary research

Epley *et al.* (2004)

Perspective taking in children and adults

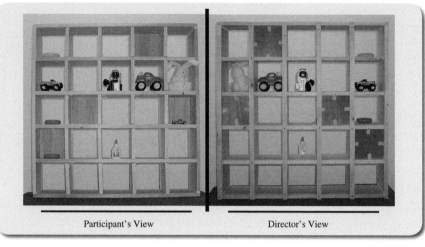

Participant's View | Director's View

Figure 8.08

Perspective taking concerns the ability to adopt the outlook of another and understand their thoughts and feelings. This involves being able to differentiate between one's own and others' perspectives. Accurate perspective taking is not a skill humans are born with, but one that develops.

The researchers wanted to see whether adults, rather than processing information less egocentrically than children, are actually better able to correct initial egocentric interpretations.

Aim

To examine why egocentric bias (interpreting perceptions from one's own viewpoint) is less common in adults.

Procedure

The participants were 33 children aged between 4 and 12 years and 32 adults (parents of the children), who were visitors to the Children's Museum of Boston in the USA.

Participants moved objects around a 5 x 5 upright arrangement of 25 boxes (four boxes of which were hidden from the director's sight by wooden slats – see Figure 8.08), as instructed by the director on the opposite side of the arrangement of boxes.

At the beginning of each trial, objects would be placed in the arrangements of boxes and the director given a picture with some of the objects in different positions.

The director instructed participants to move objects from their initial positions to the positions in his picture.

Each participant took part in four trials, each trial consisting of four separate instructions to move an object.

Participants' eye movements were recorded on video.

Within each trial, one critical instruction could refer only to one object from the director's view, but to two objects from the participant's view. For example, the critical instruction in Figure 8.08 was 'Move the small truck above the glue'. The smallest of the three trucks in the participant's view was hidden from the director's sight, so what he appeared to be referring to was the medium-sized truck.

The other three instructions in each trial referred to mutually observable items.

Different forms of ambiguous objects were used in different trials.

continued ...

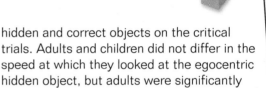

...continued

Two raters who were unaware of the hypotheses coded the eye movements.

The speed with which participants looked for and reached for objects were averaged.

The 'trick' for each participant is to disregard their initial egocentric choice and perceive the scene from the director's point of view by realising that he cannot see what is behind the four slatted boxes.

Findings

Adults made significantly fewer egocentric reaching errors than children.

Egocentric reaching errors with children were correlated with age, older children making fewer errors than younger children.

To test the prediction that differences between adults and children were produced by a difference in the ability to correct, rather than make egocentric interpretations, participants' eye movements were analysed to reveal the processing that went before their hand movements. Adults were found to be faster than children at looking at target objects, with older children faster than younger children.

The researchers' main interest was in the relative speed with which participants looked at the hidden and correct objects on the critical trials. Adults and children did not differ in the speed at which they looked at the egocentric hidden object, but adults were significantly quicker to look at the mutually observable target object.

Conclusions

Adults are no less likely than children to consider events from an egocentric viewpoint, but are more likely to correct this and consider events from another's perspective.

Egocentrism is not something that is outgrown; instead, experience teaches us that we can only see something from another's perspective after realising not to consider it from our own perspective. There is therefore no radical change in how we process information.

Evaluation

The findings do not identify why adults are better at correcting egocentric interpretations, though common sense suggests that constant experience in altering such interpretations to accommodate different perspectives makes the process more efficient with age.

The results provide an important insight into the process and development of perspective taking.

Research in focus

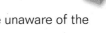

In Epley *et al.*'s (2004) experiment into perspective taking, two raters who were unaware of the hypotheses coded the eye movements.

Why was it important that the raters were unaware of the hypotheses?

Why was it considered necessary to have two observers coding the eye movements?

Research: perspective taking

- Kravetz *et al.* (1999) used Selman's methodology to compare 22 normal children and 22 children with learning disabilities, on levels of interpersonal understanding, finding that severity of learning disability was positively correlated with difficulties in interpersonal relationships.

- Underwood and Moore (1982) found that the ability to perspective take correlated positively with pro–social behaviour, suggesting that perspective taking enhances social relationships.

- Schultz and Selman (1990) found that the transition from self–centred perspectives to an ability to perceive from others' perspectives is related to the development of enhanced interpersonal negotiation skills and concern for others, suggesting that perspective taking plays a key role in social maturation.

- Wentzel (1993) reports that perspective taking increases pro–social behaviour, in turn enhancing academic motivation and success.

Evaluation

Perspective taking

- Durkin (1995) believed that the extent to which children engage in perspective taking is correlated with success in resolving social problems and gaining from interactions with others. Therefore, viewing it as a multifaceted process helps to perceive perspective taking not as the 'driving force' of social cognition and social behaviour, but as a set of skills that grow out of what children know about social interactions.

- Research supports the developmental claims of Selman's model: individuals progress gradually to higher stages over time, with little evidence of regression to lower stages.

- Much research into perspective taking is correlational and does not show causality. Other mediating factors may be involved.

- Selman's stage theory and use of dilemmas provides researchers with an objective means of assessing social competence.

- Selman's research is used to ascertain when children can take part in competitive sports, as competition becomes meaningful when children can conceptualise competition from others' viewpoints.

Issues, debates and approaches

- Perspective taking has practical applications as a means of conflict resolution. Walker and Selman (1998) used perspective taking to reduce violence levels by getting individuals to empathise with other people's feelings and viewpoints.

- Research into perspective taking can be considered culturally biased, as research was carried out on children of a western culture and therefore findings may not be applicable to children of other cultures. Quintana et al. (1999) criticised Selman's work as disregarding the development of perspective taking in ethnic subcultural groupings.

You are the researcher

Construct a naturalistic observation assessing whether 6-year-old girls have a greater degree of empathy than 6-year-old boys.

What behavioural categories would you use?

How would you ensure that you had inter-observer reliability?

Psychology in action

Perspective taking and bullying

Figure 8.09

Bullying happens. However much people speak against it, whatever practices are put into place, it continues. As well as the fear and violence, it inhibits learning, creates interpersonal problems and is positively correlated with adult criminality. Children commit suicide each year through being bullied.

Most anti-bullying programmes concentrate on perpetrators and victims, and their success rate is not great. More effective are programmes based on developing empathy in all children by encouraging perspective taking. It is important to note that in 85 per cent of bullying episodes, there are onlookers. Teaching perspective-taking skills enables students to gain insight into how others feel and to develop a sense of social responsibility. Developing empathy through perspective taking means that children are empowered to challenge cruelty, bullying and meanness.

At the heart of the Roots of Empathy programme running in Canadian schools are regular visits from an instructor with a parent and baby. Students observe the infant's development and label its feelings, and this helps children to identify and reflect on their own feelings and those of others. This development of empathy decreases instances of physical, emotional and psychological bullying, and children are taught to challenge cruelty and injustice.

Assessments have shown that children who take part in such programmes demonstrate:

- *an increase* in social and emotional knowledge
- *a decrease* in aggression
- *an increase* in pro-social behaviour – for example, sharing, helping and including
- *an increase* in perceptions among Roots of Empathy students of the classroom as a caring environment.

In the words of a holocaust survivor, 'Pay attention, get involved, and never, ever look away.'

Biological explanations of social cognition

It is thought that biological factors, like genes and brain processes, interact with environmental variables, producing individual differences in social competence. Humans are social animals and social interactive success is dependent on the development of brain systems geared to processing social information. Although learning experiences are necessary for normal development, without innate neural systems processing social stimuli it is hard to explain the universality and speed of social learning. Brain abnormalities impair social interactions in different ways, suggesting that social skills are directed by brain systems. Brain-imaging studies indicate that a network of brain areas linking the medial prefrontal and temporal cortex form the neural substrate of mentalising, allowing for representation of one's own and others' mental states.

> To learn more about the Roots of Empathy programme and the work the organisation does in developing empathy through perspective taking, go to www.rootsofempathy.org

The role of the mirror neuron system

Mirror neurons are nerves in the brain, active when specific actions are performed or observed in others, allowing observers to experience the action as if it were their own. They allow individuals to share in the feelings and thoughts of others by empathising with and imitating others, and to have a TOM.

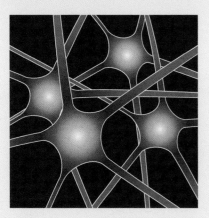

Research shows that when individuals experience an emotion themselves, like disgust, and view an expression of disgust on another's face, the same motor neurons are activated. This allows observers and the observed to have direct experiential understanding of each other, which could explain how we empathise with others.

Mirror neurons are found in brain areas involved in social cognition, especially motor-related areas. Mirror neurons may be the key to understanding the mental states of others, and defective mirror neuron systems could explain conditions of social communication and interaction deficiencies, like autism.

Figure 8.10 Mirror neurons allow people to experience others' actions as if they were their own

Contemporary research

Dapretto *et al.* (2006)
Understanding emotions in others

Mirror neurons allow observers to experience the actions of others. This is important, as it allows humans to empathise. The researchers were interested in seeing whether specific brain areas were related to mirror neuron ability, by comparing normal children with autistic children, who are believed to lack this ability.

Aim

To examine mirror neuron ability in autistic and normal children using fMRI scanning.

Procedure

Participants were ten high-functioning autistic children and ten normally functioning children aged between 10 and 14 years.

Participants and their parents gave informed consent in line with the Ethics Review Board of the University of California.

Eighty faces representing five different emotions – anger, fear, happiness, neutrality and sadness – were presented for 2 seconds each in a random sequence.

fMRI scans were used as participants either observed or imitated the faces presented (counterbalanced within each group).

Findings

Both groups of children observed the stimuli and imitated the facial expressions.

However, children with autism showed no mirror neuron activity in the inferior frontal gyrus (pars opercularis) brain region.

The relationship between activity in mirror neuron brain areas and symptom severity of the autistic children was examined, using scores on the Autism Diagnostic Interview-Revised scale. A negative correlation was found between activity in the pars opercularis and the autistic children's scores.

Activity in the insula and limbic structures, brain areas underlying emotional understanding, were also negatively correlated with symptom severity.

Conclusions

The neural strategies adopted by typically developing and autistic children are different. Typically, developing children rely on a right hemisphere mirror neuron mechanism, which interfaces with the limbic system via the insula brain area, whereby the meaning of an observed emotion is directly understood. In autistic children this mirroring mechanism is not engaged, thus the emotional significance of observed emotions is not understood.

Mirror neurons underlie the ability to read others' emotional states from facial expressions.

Evaluation

- The lack of mirror neuron activity during the observation and imitation of emotional expressions in autistic children provides support for the idea that early dysfunction in the mirror neuron system is a key factor of the social deficits seen in autism.

- The research suggests a biological foundation to autism.

Research in focus

In Dapretto *et al.*'s (2006) study, the order of presentation of the 80 faces was done in a random sequence.

What does this mean in this context?

Why was it considered important to randomise the sequence?

The study was conducted with the permission of the Ethics Review Board of the University of California.

Explain what ethical boards/committees are and what their purpose is.

Research: the role of the mirror neuron system

- Rizzolato *et al.* (1996) found evidence of mirror neurons in the frontal and parietal lobes of macaque monkeys. These neurons behaved in the same manner when observing other monkeys pick up food, as when the monkey did it itself.

- Rizzolato and Craighero (2004) used brain scanning on human participants, finding a network of neurons in the frontal and parietal brain areas appearing to work as mirror neurons.

- Gallese (2001) used fMRI scanning to find that the anterior cingulate cortex and inferior frontal cortex are active when individuals experience emotion or observe another person experiencing the same emotion, suggesting mirror neuron-type activity.

- Wicker *et al.* (2003) found that smelling an unpleasant aroma activated the anterior cingulate and insula brain areas, but observing another's facial expression of disgust also activated these brain areas, suggesting that mirror neuron activity allows empathy with others' emotions.

- Keysers *et al.* (2004) found that within the cortical region there is a localised neural network, activated when an individual is touched or when another person is observed to be touched, indicating possible mirror neuron activity.

- Stuss *et al.* (2001) reported that individuals with damage to their frontal lobes often had an inability to empathise with and read other people's intentions and were easy to deceive, suggesting a biological link to social cognition.

Evaluation

The role of the mirror neuron system

- There is a methodological problem in studying mirror neurons in humans, as it is not possible to study the actions of single neurons.
- Social cognition seems to only exist in some higher animals, suggesting a biological basis that has evolved due to its survival value.
- Research indicates that it is the sensory motor system that facilitates imitation of others, allowing empathy of observed emotions through simulation of the related body state.
- Dysfunction within the mirror neuron system may explain the inability of autistics to empathise with others.
- Jacob and Jeannerod (2004) have pointed out that a mirror neuron system is too simplistic an explanation, as it cannot explain how the same actions performed in others can be interpreted differently by an observer in different contexts.

Issues, debates and approaches

- Biological explanations of social cognition are reductionist, perceiving only influences like mirror neurons at work, and thus ignoring the role of important non-biological factors, such as cognitive processes.

- Research into mirror neurons has indicated a possible biological explanation for autism, and greater understanding may pave the way for developing methods of counteracting the social deficits associated with the disorder.

Strengthen your learning

1. Describe the factors that contribute to children's development of a sense of self.
2. Explain how false belief tasks are used to assess whether an individual has a theory of mind.
3. What have research studies revealed about theory of mind?
4. What is meant by perspective taking?
5. Outline Selman's stages of social role taking.
6. Compile an evaluation of what psychologists have learned about perspective taking in no more than 300 words.
7. Explain why mirror neurons may indicate social cognition to have a biological basis.
8. Does research evidence indicate that social cognition actually has a biological basis?

Assessment Check

1. Describe and evaluate research studies into the development of the child's sense of self. (24 marks)

2. Outline the theory of mind. (4 marks)

3. Evaluate biological explanations of social cognition. (20 marks)

4. Discuss children's understanding of others. (24 marks)

Examination guidance

Care must be taken with question 1 to focus on research studies, as this is specific in the question; 8 marks are available for outlining them, possibly in terms of aims, procedures, findings and conclusions drawn, and 16 marks are available for evaluating them, possibly in terms of research support, methodological considerations, ethical issues and practical applications. Care should be

taken to use and shape research studies that focus explicitly on the development of the child's sense of self.

Question 2 requires descriptive material of the theory of mind; description of anything else, or any evaluation, will not gain credit and wastes valuable examination time.

Question 3 calls for an evaluation of explanations, perhaps in terms of research support. The wording of the question calls for at least two explanations to be presented.

The term 'discuss' in question 4 means to describe and evaluate, in this particular instance children's understanding of others, possibly focusing on perspective taking, as it is a compulsory part of the specification and has to be studied, so you might as well use the material here where it gains maximum credit.

Summing up

- Theories of cognitive development attempt to explain the growth of mental abilities.

- Piaget saw intelligence as a process, involving stages of intellectual development.

- Knowledge is actively discovered through functional invariants, like the process of adaptation and the process of equilibrium, and variant structures, like schemas and operations.

- Cognitive development involves swinging between equilibrium and disequilibrium, in a continuous series of assimilations and accommodations.

- Vygotsky saw cognitive development as a cultural construct, affected by the culture learning occurs in.

- Cognitive development involves an active internalisation of problem-solving processes taking place as a result of mutual interaction between children and those they have social contact with.

- Scaffolding – tuition given by more knowledgeable others – allows children to perform tasks independently, this occurring within their zone of proximal development.

- Vygotsky's theory sees teachers as mentors, with a role in education for collaborative learning involving children of equal competence.

- Both Piaget and Vygotsky's theories have implications for education.

- Morality concerns how society judges which behaviours, beliefs and attitudes are acceptable, with psychologists interested in the development of moral reasoning – the thinking behind moral behaviour.

- Kohlberg sees morality developing in a number of innate stages in a set order. He developed a theory of three levels: pre-conventional, conventional and post-conventional, each level has two stages.

- Kohlberg assessed people's moral reasoning through the use of moral dilemmas, scenarios involving choice between two alternatives.

- Social cognition relates to the mental processes by which information concerning ourselves and others is processed and understood, and by which social behaviour is conducted.

- Developing a sense of self has several components, like self-recognition, gender concept, the distinction between physical and psychological selves, self-referential emotions and self-esteem.

- Theory of mind (TOM) is the ability to attribute mental states, knowledge, wishes, feelings and beliefs to oneself and others. Research indicates that the ability develops over time.

- TOM is investigated through false belief tasks, assessing whether individuals can perceive another's point of view.

- Perspective taking concerns the ability to assume another's perspective and understand their thoughts and feelings.

- Role taking theory explains the development of perspective taking, where adopting the perspective of others allows comprehension of their feelings, thoughts and intentions.

- Selman saw social role taking as having five stages: egocentric viewpoint, social informational role taking, self-reflective role taking, mutual role taking and social and conventional system role taking.

- It is thought that biological factors, like genes and brain processes, interact with environmental variables, producing individual differences in social competence.

- Mirror neurons are nerves in the brain, active when specific actions are performed or observed in others, allowing observers to experience actions as if their own.

- Mirror neurons are found in motor-related brain areas involved in social cognition.

9 Psychopathology

Psychopathology	**314**
Classification and diagnosis	**315**
DSM-IV	315
Reliability of diagnosis	316
Validity of diagnosis	316
Schizophrenia	**318**
Depression	**335**
Anxiety disorders	**351**
Summing up	**374**

Decoding the specification

You only need to study one mental disorder: either schizophrenia, depression, or one of two anxiety disorders – phobic disorders or obsessive-compulsive disorder. In the examination there will be one question each on schizophrenia, depression and anxiety disorders (which can be answered by reference to either phobic disorders or obsessive-compulsive disorder). For your chosen disorder, you should know its clinical characteristics and relevant issues of classification and diagnosis, including reliability and validity, as these are specifically listed. You must be able to describe and evaluate psychological and biological explanations of your chosen disorder. The explanations listed are examples and would not feature directly in the wording of examination questions; therefore, any relevant explanations would be equally creditworthy. You will also be required to describe and evaluate psychological and biological therapies relating to your chosen disorder. Again, those listed are examples and would not feature directly in examination questions. Any relevant therapies would be equally creditworthy.

Psychopathology

Psychopathology is the branch of psychology concerned with abnormal behaviour that advances theoretical explanations of the origins, development and manifestations of mental and behavioural disorders. Psychopathology utilises both biological and psychological approaches, on which many varied therapies for the treatment of abnormal conditions have been developed.

You are required to study one mental disorder from the four on which this chapter concentrates. However, there is a degree of general material that all students should acquaint themselves with before focusing on your chosen specific disorder. This will be useful in providing descriptive and evaluative content to exam questions on any disorder.

IN THE NEWS

Closing in on schizophrenia

Brian Charnley had suffered from schizophrenia for 23 years since the age of 18. He fought a daily battle against the illness and yet despite his loneliness Bryan made one last triumphant effort. In a remarkable 3-month experiment he used his skills as an artist to convey to outsiders the experiences he and his fellow sufferers endure. In a series of paintings called Self Portrait he showed what it is like to live at the edge of human experience. In order to record his journey through madness he altered the mixture and dosage of the drugs on which he depended for relative stability. As he became overwhelmed by his inner torment, he still retained his insight to search for rational symbols to express his tortured, irrational thoughts.

He set out to inform the world of his experiences, not as therapy for himself, but to help others at the expense of considerable personal suffering.

'My paintings stand as an attempt to penetrate this wall of silence'.

One in three of us will be treated at some point in life for a mental disorder. Yet the horrors of mental afflictions are hard to understand, even from descriptions by those afflicted. But we must comprehend in order to offer the understanding and compassion required. Bryan Charnley set out to paint what it feels like to be mad by coming off his medication in order to experience his schizophrenia in an unadulterated form. This he communicated to the world in 17 paintings documenting the pain and horror of going insane.

The final portrait was found on the easel in his studio where he committed suicide in 1991.

Figure 9.01 Painting number 1

Figure 9.02 Painting number 9

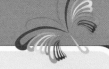

Classification and diagnosis

As with physical conditions, mental disorders first have to be diagnosed; in order to do this, clinicians use *classification systems*. These are based on the idea that certain groups of symptoms can be classed together as a *syndrome*, which has an underlying cause and is separate from other syndromes. In this way, mental disorders are perceived in a similar way to physical disorders, as mental illnesses, which can be identified (diagnosed), treated and cured.

DSM-IV

The Diagnostic and Statistical Manual of Mental Disorders, 4th edition (DSM-IV) is the official classification system of the American Psychiatric Association, but is used worldwide. It consists of five *axes* on which disorders can be assessed:

- Axis I: Clinical disorders

- Axis II: Personality disorders and mental retardation

- Axis III: General medical conditions connected to mental disorders

- Axis IV: Psychosocial and environmental problems, such as limited social support

- Axis V: Global assessment of functioning (psychological, social and job-related functions are evaluated on a continuum between mental health and extreme mental disorder).

The classification system then places disorders into categories, such as anxiety disorders, schizophrenia and other psychotic disorders, mood disorders, and so on.

DSM-IV does acknowledge that 'there is no assumption that each category of mental disorder is a completely discrete entity with absolute boundaries dividing it from other mental disorders or from no mental disorder.'

A video presentation of the 17 paintings accompanied by entries from Bryan's diary can be found at www.youtube.com/watch?v=ArqUt5dllG8 There are also details of how to go and see some of his work at the Bethlem hospital in London at www.visitlondon.com/events/detail/5056576

Key terms

Diagnosis – identification of the nature and cause of illness

DSM-IV – Diagnostic classification system produced in the USA

ICD-10 – Diagnostic classification system produced by the World Health Organization

Reliability – consistency of diagnosis

Validity – accuracy of diagnosis

Genetic explanation – transmission of abnormality by hereditary means

Biochemical explanations – determination of abnormality by neurotransmitters and hormones

Evolutionary explanations – abnormality perceived as having an adaptive purpose

Cognitive explanation – determination of abnormality through maladaptive thought processes

Sociocultural explanation – determination of abnormality through family and social environments

Behaviourist explanations – determination of abnormality through learning processes

ECT – treatment of abnormality by applying electrical voltages across the brain

Drug therapy – chemical treatment of abnormality through tablets and intravenous means

Psychosurgery – treatment of abnormality by irreversible destruction of brain tissue

Behavioural therapies – treatments of abnormality that modify maladaptive behaviour by substituting new responses

Cognitive behavioural therapy – treatment of abnormality that modifies thought patterns to alter behavioural and emotional states

Reliability of diagnosis

Reliability refers to the *consistency* of symptom measurement and affects classification and diagnosis in two ways:

- **Test–retest reliability** – occurs when a practitioner makes the same consistent diagnosis on separate occasions from the same information.

- **Inter-rater reliability** – occurs when several practitioners make identical, independent diagnoses of the same patient.

Evaluation

Reliability of diagnosis

- Making reliable diagnoses is problematic, as practitioners have no physical signs, but only symptoms (what the patient reports) to base decisions on.
- Practitioners have to make subjective decisions due to the wording of DSM-IV – for example, comparing patients to 'average people'.
- Also, DSM-IV states that arbitrary numbers of symptoms must be evident for diagnosis to occur – for example, depressed mood and four other symptoms for major depression. Again, this does not seem objective.

Validity of diagnosis

Validity concerns how accurate, meaningful and useful diagnosis is. There are several ways in which validity can be assessed:

- **Reliability** – a valid diagnosis has first to be reliable, though reliability itself is no guarantee of validity.

- **Predictive validity** – if diagnosis leads to successful treatment, the diagnosis is seen as valid.

- **Descriptive validity** – to be valid, patients diagnosed with different disorders should differ from each other.

- **Aetiological validity** – to be valid, all patients with the same disorder should have the same cause.

Evaluation

Validity of diagnosis

- However much reliability of diagnosis is improved, there is no guarantee that validity is established.
- Descriptive validity is reduced by *comorbidity*, where patients have two or more disorders simultaneously, suggesting that such disorders are not actually separate.
- Predictive validity is difficult to attain, as practitioners assign treatments from biased viewpoints.
- Winter (1999) argues that 'diagnostic systems are only aids to understanding, not descriptions of real disease entities'.

Supplementary learning

Culture and gender bias in assessment and treatment

The reliability and validity of classification systems reflects western culture and therefore cannot necessarily assess people of other cultures. Such cultural bias occurs in several ways:

1. British black people are more likely to be diagnosed as schizophrenic, more likely to be committed to a mental hospital and more likely to be given major tranquillisers and ECT. Black people are also less likely to be diagnosed with depression. *continued ...*

...continued

2. Ethnic minority and working-class people are less likely to be referred for psychotherapy than middle-class people.

3. Women are more likely to be diagnosed as psychiatrically ill.

Such bias occurs because clinicians are predominantly white, middle-class males, ignorant of the cultural and social situations of black, working-class and female patients. More attention is now given to how symptoms of disorders differ depending on the culture in which they appear.

Culture-bound syndromes (CBSs) are disorders associated with particular cultures. DSM-IV is just coming round to recognising this, defining them as 'locally specific patterns of aberrant behaviour and troubling experience that may or may not be linked to a persistent DSM-IV diagnostic category'. For instance, *ghost sickness*, a disorder specific to Native Americans, is caused by funeral rituals not being adhered to. However, CBSs are perceived as 'outside' the classification systems of mainstream western psychiatry, and only western mental disorders are perceived as *culturally neutral* and defined and diagnosed objectively. This is culturally biased in itself, as only CBSs are perceived as being culturally influenced and this affects reliability and validity of diagnosis.

Supplementary learning

ICD-10

The International Classification of Diseases, 10th revision (ICD-10) is a classification system of illnesses and health complaints, including abnormal conditions, created by the World Health Organization.

Similar to DSM-IV, signs and symptoms are used to categorise diagnoses, and it is regularly updated to reflect changes in knowledge. ICD-10 recognises 11 general categories of mental disorder, such as schizophrenia, schizotypal and delusional disorders, as well as mood disorders and neurotic, stress-related and somatoform disorders. Work is ongoing to merge the categories of DSM-IV and ICD-10 to create better consistency. The USA will officially use ICD-10 from 2013.

Psychology in action

Self-help groups

Self-help support groups are encounter or personal growth associations that provide a setting in which people who share similar experiences come together to offer practical and emotional support in a non-critical, reciprocal and mutually beneficial manner. They are based on humanistic psychology, an approach perceiving humans as inherently good and motivated to improve themselves. There are self-help groups for most mental disorders, such as the National Schizophrenia Fellowship, the Black Dog Institute for depression and Daily Strength for anxiety disorders.

Such groups have benefited from the growth of the internet, where vulnerable people can now discuss their problems, support one another and get advice in a virtual environment without having to meet physically, though internet groups are often a first step to joining a physical group.

Some believe that self-help support groups actually perpetuate and even precipitate mental disorders – for example, they accuse pro-anorexia groups of being 'academies for eating disorders'. However, many groups have provided the route by which people have sought and obtained psychological help, and without them the mental health of the nation would be a lot bleaker.

Figure 9.03 The Black Dog Institute is a well-regarded self-help group for people suffering from depression

Psychology in action

Psychosurgery

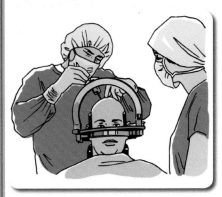

Figure 9.04 Psychosurgery is a 'last-chance' treatment for a variety of disorders

Psychosurgery is a biological therapy used as a treatment for schizophrenia, depression and anxiety disorders (see 'Anxiety disorders' on page 351). Devised by Moniz in 1935, it involves the destruction of brain tissue and is irreversible. Most early operations were lobotomies, where the nerves connecting the frontal lobes to the rest of the brain were severed in the mistaken belief that they would regenerate. In the UK, about 10,000 operations were carried out between 1942 and 1952, 65 per cent on people with schizophrenia and 25 per cent on people with depression. With the advent of anti-schizophrenic drugs in the 1950s, it became only rarely used as a treatment for schizophrenia, though countries such as China still operate on individuals with schizophrenia.

The use of psychosurgery nowadays is much improved and more sophisticated, with specific and small amounts of brain tissue targeted, usually in the limbic system, an area associated with the regulation of emotion. *Bimedial leucotomies* are used with depressive and obsessive patients, and *orbital leucotomies* with depressive and obsessive patients, and patients with extreme anxiety.

The treatment tends to be used as a 'last chance', when all other therapies have failed, quality of life is much reduced and, often, where there is a heightened risk of suicide. There is no guarantee of success, with symptom reduction being seen in about 50 to 80 per cent of patients, dependent on the specific treatment. Some patients incur a worsening of symptoms and side effects can be experienced, such as personality changes. Recently there has been a shift towards deep-brain stimulation, a less invasive and destructive treatment involving electrodes planted in the brain.

Schizophrenia

Clinical characteristics

'Schizophrenia is a generic name for a group of disorders, characterised by a progressive disintegration of emotional stability, judgement, contact with and appreciation of reality, producing considerable secondary impairment of personality relationships and intellectual functioning.' (Stafford–Clarke, 1964)

People from all sections of society and cultures can develop schizophrenia. Overall 1 per cent of people suffer worldwide, but with differences in prevalence rates of between 0.33 per cent and 15 per cent.

Schizophrenia is the world's most common mental disorder, accounting for 40 to 50 per cent of all mental patients. It is difficult to compile accurate statistics, due to inadequately agreed criteria for diagnosis, but there are between 24 and 55 million people with schizophrenia worldwide.

Schizophrenia is a serious mental disorder affecting thought processes and the ability to determine reality. Degree of severity varies between sufferers: some only encounter one episode, some have persistent episodes, but live relatively normal lives through taking medication, while others have persistent episodes, are non-responsive to medication and remain severely disturbed. Schizophrenia may be a group of disorders, with different causes and explanations. Clinicians refer to Type I schizophrenia, an acute type characterised by positive symptoms and better prospects of recovery, and Type II schizophrenia, a chronic type characterised by negative symptoms and poorer prospects for recovery.

To be diagnosed with schizophrenia, two or more symptoms must be apparent for more than 1 month, as well as reduced social functioning. Positive symptoms are additional features to everyday experience, involving an excess or distortion of perceptual functioning. These generally occur in acute episodes, with more normal periods in between, and respond favourably to medication. Negative symptoms consist of a lessening or loss of normal functioning, are chronic, as they last beyond acute episodes, and are resistant to medication.

Other differentiations are *chronic onset schizophrenia*, where sufferers become increasingly disturbed through gradual withdrawal and motivational loss over a prolonged period; and *acute onset schizophrenia*, where symptoms appear suddenly, after a stressful incident.

> ## Key terms
>
> **Schizophrenia** – mental disorder characterised by withdrawal from reality
> **Type I schizophrenia** – acute form characterised by positive symptoms and responsive to medication
> **Type II schizophrenia** – chronic type characterised by negative symptoms and unresponsive to medication
> **Schizophrenogenic explanation** – determination of schizophrenia through emotionally cold, controlling mothers
> **Psychodynamic therapies** – treatments based on psychoanalytic theory that explore unconscious motives to highlight the roots of emotional distress

Schizophrenia commonly occurs between 15 and 45 years of age, with an equal incidence rate between males and females, though males generally show onset at an earlier age.

Symptoms

Schneider (1959) detailed *first-rank symptoms* of schizophrenia, subjective experiences based on patients' verbal reports. Most are positive symptoms.

1. Passivity experiences and thought disorders: thoughts and actions are perceived as under external control – for example, by aliens. Sufferers may also believe that thoughts are being inserted, withdrawn or broadcast to others.

2. Auditory hallucinations: sufferers experience voices inside their head, often derogatory and obscene, which form running commentaries, or discuss the sufferer's behaviour, anticipate their thoughts or repeat their thoughts out loud. These often occur with concurrent delusions.

3. Primary delusions: sufferers usually experience *delusions of grandeur*, believing they are someone important – for example, Jesus Christ reincarnated. Later, delusions become *delusions of persecution*, where sufferers believe someone is out to get them. Some sufferers may experience only one type of delusions.

Figure 9.05 People with schizophrenia often hear voices that accuse them of terrible acts

Slater and Roth (1969) added four additional symptoms, directly observable from patients' behaviour. Most are negative symptoms consisting of behavioural deficits, enduring beyond acute episodes and resistant to treatment.

1. Thought process disorders: sufferers wander off the point, invent new words and phrases, stop mid-sentence, muddle their words and interpret language literally – for example, proverbs.

2. Disturbances of effect: sufferers appear indifferent to others, exhibit inappropriate emotional responses – for example, giggling at bad news – or display sudden mood swings.

3. Psychomotor disturbances: sufferers adopt frozen, 'statue–like' poses, exhibit tics and twitches and repetitive behaviours – for example, pacing up and down.

4. Lack of volition: sufferers display an inability to make decisions, have no enthusiasm or energy, lose interest in personal hygiene and lack sociability and affection.

Subtypes of schizophrenia

There is no such thing as a 'normal' schizophrenic person exhibiting 'usual' symptoms. Therefore, several subtypes have been proposed The ICD-10 classification system lists seven subtypes, while DSM-IV has five.

1. Paranoid: characterised by delusions of grandeur and/or persecution. There is less noticeable disturbance than with other subtypes.

2. Catatonic: sufferers are excitable and occasionally aggressive. Sometimes they may be mute and adopt statue-like poses or alternate between these two states. Negativism is apparent, where sufferers do the opposite of what they are told. Hallucinations and delusions are less obvious.

3. Disorganised (hebephrenic): onset occurs in early to mid-twenties, with sufferers experiencing auditory hallucinations, delusions, thought process disorders and disturbances of effect. Behaviour appears bizarre.

4. Residual: sufferers exhibited symptoms previously, but not presently, though negative symptoms are experienced during the past year. Sufferers display mild positive symptoms.

5. Undifferentiated: a category for schizophrenics not fitting other subtypes, or having symptoms of several subtypes.

6. Simple (only found in ICD-10): appears in late adolescence, with a slow, gradual onset. An increase in apathy and social deterioration occurs, with a decline in academic or occupational performance.

7. Post-schizophrenic depression (only found in ICD-10): a subtype for people with schizophrenia meeting criteria for the disorder in the last year, though not at present, who exhibit severe and prolonged depressive symptoms.

Issues surrounding classification and diagnosis

(Refer to pages 315–16 for an explanation of classification systems and the reliability and validity of diagnosis.)

Research: reliability

- Beck *et al.* (1962) reported a 54 per cent concordance rate between experienced practitioners' diagnoses when assessing 153 patients, while Söderberg *et al.* (2005) reported a concordance rate of 81 per cent using DSM-IV-TR, the most up-to-date form of the DSM classification system. This suggests that classification systems have become more reliable over time.

- Nilsson *et al.* (2000) found a 60 per cent concordance rate between practitioners using the ICD classification system, implying that the DSM system is more reliable.

- Read *et al.* (2004) reported test-retest reliability of schizophrenia diagnosis to have only a 37 per cent concordance rate, and noted a 1970 study where 194 British and 134 US psychiatrists provided a diagnosis on the basis of a case description; 69 per cent of the Americans diagnosed schizophrenia, but only 2 per cent of the British. This suggests that the diagnosis of schizophrenia has never been reliable.

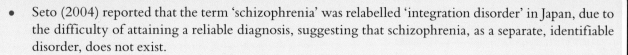

- Seto (2004) reported that the term 'schizophrenia' was relabelled 'integration disorder' in Japan, due to the difficulty of attaining a reliable diagnosis, suggesting that schizophrenia, as a separate, identifiable disorder, does not exist.

- Jakobsen *et al.* (2005) tested the reliability of the ICD-10 classification system in diagnosing schizophrenia. A hundred Danish patients with a history of psychosis were assessed using operational criteria, finding a concordance rate of 98 per cent, demonstrating the high reliability of clinical diagnosis of schizophrenia using up-to-date classifications.

Evaluation

Reliability

- The DSM classification system is regarded as more reliable than the ICD, because of the amount of specificity in the symptoms outlined for each category.
- The reliability of schizophrenia diagnosis, assessed at 81 per cent, is superior to that for anxiety disorders, at 63 per cent. The reliability of schizophrenia diagnosis is also generally considered superior to the validity of schizophrenia diagnosis.
- Even if reliability of diagnosis based on classification systems is not perfect, they do provide practitioners with a common language, permitting communication of research ideas and findings, which may ultimately lead to a better understanding of the disorder and the development of effective treatments.
- Evidence generally suggests that reliability of diagnoses has improved as classification systems have been updated.

Research: validity

- Heather (1976) argued that few causes of mental disorders are known and there is only a 50 per cent chance of predicting what treatment patients will receive based on diagnosis, suggesting that diagnosis of schizophrenia is not valid.

- Hollis (2000) studied 93 cases of early onset schizophrenia, applying DSM classification diagnoses to patient case notes. The findings indicated that the diagnosis of schizophrenia had a high level of stability, suggesting that diagnoses are to a large extent valid.

- Allardyce *et al.* (2006) reported that the symptoms used to characterise schizophrenia do not define a specific syndrome, but rather the concept allows a number of different combinations, so that many permutations of the defining symptoms are possible, suggesting that schizophrenia is not a separate disorder and therefore that diagnosis of the disorder is invalid.

- Dikeos *et al.* (2006) used factor analysis to correlate symptoms, and found that diagnostic entities are similar with regard to the key symptom dimensions, thus suggesting that diagnosis of the disorder does have validity.

- Bottas (2009) reported that the incidence of schizophrenia is about 1 per cent, and about 3 per cent for obsessive-compulsive disorder (OCD). However, the incidence of schizophrenia with OCD is much higher than probability would suggest. Genetic and neurobiological evidence now indicates that there may be a separate schizo-obsessive disorder, which in turn suggests that separate types of schizophrenia may indeed exist.

- Jansson and Parnas (2007) reviewed 92 polydiagnostic studies, which apply different definitions of the disorder to the same patient samples, to assess the reliability and validity of schizophrenia diagnoses. Both ICD-10 and DSM-IV showed moderate reliability, but both were weak on all measures of validity, again casting doubt on whether the disorder exists as a separate condition.

Classic research

Rosenhan (1973)

On being sane in insane places

It would be expected that psychiatrists make valid diagnoses – that is, correctly identify the mental disorders people suffer from. However, this famous study casts doubts on this expectation.

Aims

To test the validity of schizophrenia diagnosis using the DSM-II classification system.

Procedure

Eight volunteers presented themselves to different mental hospitals, claiming to hear voices. All were admitted and acted normally. Time taken to be released and reactions to them were recorded.

Subsequently, a hospital was informed that an unspecified number of pseudo-patients would attempt entry over a 3-month period. The number of suspected impostors was recorded.

Findings

The eight volunteers took between 7 and 52 days to be released, diagnosed as schizophrenics in remission. Normal behaviours were interpreted as signs of schizophrenia. However, 35 out of 118 actual patients suspected they were sane.

During the subsequent 3-month period, 193 patients were admitted, of whom 83 aroused suspicions of being false patients.

No actual pseudo-patients attempted admission.

Conclusions

The diagnosis of schizophrenia lacks validity, as psychiatrists cannot distinguish between real and pseudo-patients.

Evaluation

- It is not usual for people to fake insanity to gain admission to mental hospitals, and clinicians are there to help people, not turn them away. This explains the admission of the original eight pseudo-patients.

- The original results can also be explained by an expectation effect: the doctors expected them to be ill and looked for evidence to verify this. Their nervousness contributed to this.

Being diagnosed as schizophrenic is a stigmatic, 'sticky label' – difficult to remove, with serious consequences, and yet manufactured by psychiatrists with low degrees of accuracy.

Evaluation

Validity

- Kraeplin (1898) saw schizophrenia as a chronic deteriorating condition in all cases. This is not true, with many outcomes possible, from complete recovery to chronic suffering, suggesting that schizophrenia may not be a unitary, separate disorder.

- Cochrane (1977) reported the incidence of schizophrenia in the West Indies and Britain to be similar, at around 1 per cent, but that people of Afro-Caribbean origin are seven times more likely to be diagnosed with schizophrenia when living in Britain. This suggests that Afro-Caribbean people living in Britain either have more stressors leading to schizophrenia, or that invalid diagnoses are being made due to cultural bias. *continued ...*

...continued

- Bentall (2003) claimed that the diagnosis of schizophrenia says nothing about its cause, implying diagnosis to be invalid. Diagnosis also says nothing about prevalence rates, which differ widely from rural to urban environments, again suggesting diagnosis to be invalid.

- Whaley (2004) believed the main reason for the incidence of schizophrenia among black Americans being greater than among white Americans is cultural bias, where ethnic differences in symptom expression are overlooked or misinterpreted by practitioners. This suggests a lack of validity in diagnosing schizophrenia cross-culturally.

- The diagnosis of schizophrenia bestows a stigma on sufferers that incurs a major and long-lasting negative impact. Once gained, the label is hard to remove, yet such diagnoses are being made with little evidence of validity that the condition exists as a separate condition.

- In response to the claim that schizophrenia should be abolished as a concept for being scientifically meaningless, Kendell and Jablensky (2007) stated that diagnostic categories are justifiable concepts, as they provide a useful framework for organising and explaining the complexity of clinical experience, allowing clinicians to derive inferences about outcomes and to guide decisions about treatment.

Research in focus

Rosenhan's study concerns the validity of schizophrenia diagnosis, but why do such diagnoses have to be reliable before they can be valid?

Does a reliable diagnosis guarantee a valid diagnosis?

Why is it that the diagnosis of schizophrenia in terms of reliability and validity is so problematic? What has research into the reliability and validity of schizophrenia diagnosis revealed?

Biological explanations

Biological explanations have focused on several areas, including genetics and evolution. Although causes of schizophrenia are not fully understood, and indications are that several contributory factors combine to cause the onset of the disorder, evidence does suggest that biological factors play a major contributory role.

Genetics

Research traditionally uses twin, family and adoption studies to assess what role genetics plays in the causation of schizophrenia, by examining concordance rates of schizophrenia between people with different degrees of genetic relationship. Research has indicated a genetic component, though separating out environmental influences is problematic.

More recently, gene–mapping studies have compared genetic material from families with high incidence and low incidence of schizophrenia. Results indicate that several genes are involved and that genes make some individuals more vulnerable than others in developing the disorder.

Research: genetics

- Torrey *et al.* (1994) reviewed evidence from twin studies, finding that if one MZ twin develops schizophrenia, there is a 28 per cent chance that the other twin will too.

- Gottesman and Shields (1976) reviewed five twin studies and reported a concordance rate of between 75 and 91 per cent for MZ twins with severe forms of schizophrenia, suggesting that genetics plays a larger role with chronic forms of the disorder.

- Kety and Ingraham (1992) found that prevalence rates of schizophrenia were ten times higher among genetic than adoptive relatives of adopted schizophrenics, suggesting that genetics plays a greater role than environmental factors.

- Sorri *et al.* (2004) performed a longitudinal study over 21 years on Finnish adoptees with biological mothers with schizophrenia, comparing them with adoptees whose biological mothers did not have schizophrenia, but also considered family rearing styles among adoptive families. Adoptees with a high genetic risk of developing schizophrenia were more sensitive to non–healthy rearing patterns, suggesting that environmental factors are important too.

- Varma and Sharma (1993) found a concordance rate of 35 per cent for first–degree relatives of individuals with schizophrenia, compared to 9 per cent in first–degree relatives of non–schizophrenics, indicating a role for genetic factors.

- Parmas *et al.* (1993) conducted a longitudinal family study of schizophrenia, finding that 16 per cent of children whose mothers have schizophrenia developed the disorder, compared to 2 per cent of children whose mothers did not have schizophrenia, suggesting that schizophrenia is more genetic in nature.

- Gurling *et al.* (2006) used evidence from family studies indicating that schizophrenia was associated with chromosome 8p21-22, to identify a high-risk sample. Using gene mapping, the PCM1 gene was implicated in susceptibility to schizophrenia, providing more evidence for genetics.

- Using gene mapping, Benzel *et al.* (2007) found evidence suggesting that NRG3 gene variants interact with both NRG1 and ERBB4 gene variants to create a susceptibility to developing schizophrenia, suggesting an interaction of genetic factors.

Evaluation

Genetics

- Twin studies suggest a genetic factor in the onset of schizophrenia, but do not consider the influence of social class and socio-psychological factors between twins. Twin studies and familial studies also fail to consider shared environmental influences.

- If genes caused schizophrenia on their own, concordance rates between MZ twins would be 100 per cent, which they are not. Twin studies also produce conflicting evidence, with heritability estimates ranging from 58 per cent down to as low as 11 per cent for MZ twins.

- Leo (2006) argued that Kety's adoption study evidence is not as convincing as it first appears. Sample sizes were very small, making generalisation difficult, and many of the biological relatives found to have schizophrenia were quite distant relatives, such as half-siblings, with low biological similarity.

- Hedgecoe (2001) believed that scientists have attempted to construct schizophrenia as a genetic disease by using evidence from twin and adoption studies in a biased way to 'produce a narrative about schizophrenia which subtly prioritises genetic explanations'.

- Findings from genetic studies provide evidence for the diathesis-stress model, where individuals are seen as inheriting different levels of genetic predisposition to developing schizophrenia, with ultimately environmental triggers determining if individuals go on to develop schizophrenia.

- Gene mapping offers the possibility of developing tests to identify high-risk individuals, though this raises socially sensitive and ethical concerns. *continued ...*

...continued

- Tosato *et al.* (2005) conducted a review of gene mapping and similar studies, concluding that there are several genes indicating susceptibility to schizophrenia, suggesting that schizophrenia does not have a singular genetic cause.

Biochemical explanation

The biochemical explanation centres on the idea that the neurotransmitter dopamine is connected to the onset of the disorder. Neurotransmitters are chemicals acting on the biology of the body associated with the transmission of signals along the nervous system, especially signals sent across gaps between nerve fibres during synapses.

Snyder (1976) proposed that during synapses too much dopamine is released, leading to the onset of schizophrenia, with sufferers showing high levels of D-2 receptors on receiving neurons, which creates increased dopamine binding and more neurons firing. The theory developed after it was discovered that phenothiazines, antipsychotic drugs that lessen the symptoms of schizophrenia, inhibit dopamine activity. Also, the dopamine-releasing drug L-dopa creates schizophrenic-like behaviour in non-psychotic people. Other drugs influencing the dopaminergic system, like LSD, a hallucinogenic, also create schizophrenic-like behaviour in non-psychotics and aggravate symptoms in those susceptible to the disorder. It is possible that genetic factors may also be involved in creating faulty dopaminergic systems in those with schizophrenia.

Davis *et al.* (1991) updated the original theory, because high levels of dopamine are not found in all individuals with schizophrenia, and the modern anti-schizophrenic drug clozapine, with very little dopamine-blocking activity, works effectively against the disorder. Davis suggested that high levels of dopamine in the mesolimbic dopamine system are associated with positive symptoms, while high levels in the mesocortical dopamine system are associated with negative symptoms.

Interest has also focused on the neurotransmitter *glutamate*, as there is reduced function of the NMDA glutamate receptor in people with schizophrenia. Abnormal glutamate functioning may be more associated with the onset of schizophrenia, with dopamine involved too, as dopamine receptors inhibit the release of glutamate.

Research: biochemical explanations

- Randrup and Munkvad (1966) created schizophrenic-like behaviour in rats by giving them amphetamines, which activate dopamine production, and then reversed the effects by giving them neuroleptic drugs, which inhibit the release of dopamine.

- Iversen (1979) reported that post-mortems on people who had had schizophrenia found excess dopamine in the limbic system, suggesting that the neurotransmitter is involved in the disorder.

- Kessler *et al.* (2003) used PET and MRI scans to compare people with schizophrenia with non-sufferers, finding that the former had elevated dopamine receptor levels in the basal forebrain and substantia nigra/ventral tegmental brain areas. Differences in cortical dopamine levels were also found, suggesting that dopamine is important in the onset of schizophrenia.

- Javitt *et al.* (2000) found that glycine, a glutamate receptor agonist, reverses phencyclidine hydrochloride-induced psychosis (which closely resembles schizophrenia) in rats, and brought about improvements in people with schizophrenia, lending support to the glutamate theory.

Evaluation

Biochemical explanations

- Overall, the evidence is inconclusive. There is no consistent difference in dopamine levels between drug-free schizophrenics and non-sufferers; nor is there evidence of higher levels of other metabolites indicating greater dopamine activity.

- Several neurotransmitters may be involved in the development of schizophrenia. Along with dopamine and glutamate, newer anti-schizophrenic drugs implicate serotonin's involvement too.

- Healy (2000) believed that pharmaceutical companies were keen to see the dopamine theory promoted, as they would make huge profits from manufacturing anti-schizophrenic drugs that inhibited dopamine production.

- The theory cannot explain why sufferers recover only slowly when given neuroleptic drugs, when the medication has an instant effect on dopamine levels.

- Lloyd *et al.* (1984) believed that even if dopamine is a causative factor, it may be indirect, because abnormal family circumstances may lead to high levels of dopamine that in turn trigger the symptoms.

- Differences in the biochemistry of schizophrenics could just as easily be an effect rather than a cause of the condition.

Psychological explanations

Cognitive explanations

The cognitive explanation sees maladaptive (faulty) thinking linked to many schizophrenic symptoms, such as hallucinations and disordered thinking, which suggests a cognitive input. This can occur directly or indirectly – for example, brain abnormalities could lead to the experience of hallucinations.

Interest has centred on the role of attention, the possibility being that people with schizophrenia cannot filter out irrelevant sensory information and thus become overwhelmed with data they cannot interpret meaningfully and experience a sensory world different to that experienced by others.

Hemsley (1993) perceived a breakdown occurring between information stored in memory and new, incoming data. Stored information is used to create schemas permitting individuals to interpret and deal with current situations, but in people with schizophrenia, due to the breakdown in cognitive processing, these schemas are not activated, sensory overload occurs and sufferers cannot determine what to attend to and what to ignore, leading to delusional thinking, and because thoughts seem not to originate from memory, they are interpreted as arising externally.

Frith (1992) explained schizophrenia similarly, in terms of problems with information processing, focusing especially on *meta-representation*, the ability to reflect on thoughts and experience, and *central control*, the ability to suspend automatic responses and perform actions based instead on conscious intent. Positive symptoms of schizophrenia, like delusions, are perceived as problems of meta-representation, where there is an inability to distinguish external speech from internal thoughts, while negative symptoms, like disorganised thinking, are seen as problems of central control, where there is a failure to distinguish between behaviour of conscious intent and that of automatic response.

Research: cognitive explanations

- Liddle and Morris (1991) found that people with schizophrenia perform poorly on the Stroop test, where the desire to read out the colour a word is written in is suppressed in order to read out the actual word. This suggests that positive symptoms of schizophrenia are a failure of willed action, with

schizophrenic behaviour determined by irrelevant stimuli.

- Robinson and Becker (1986) reported that neuronal circuits involving the limbic system are involved in the inability of people with schizophrenia to integrate moment-to-moment sensory inputs with stored memories, as per Hemsley's theory. Resulting distress leads to increased dopamine production, which then influences the functioning of these brain areas, suggesting a link between biological and cognitive factors.

- Frith (1970) gave schizophrenic and non-schizophrenic individuals a two-choice task, where they had to guess whether the next playing card in a pack was either red (R) or black (B). People with schizophrenia produced stereotypical choices, like R R R R R R or R BR BR B, while non-schizophrenics produced more random choices, suggesting that people with schizophrenia have problems generating spontaneous actions, thus supporting the idea of negative symptoms resulting from a lack of central control.

- Bentall *et al.* (1991) found that schizophrenics struggled to identify words belonging to a certain category, such as birds, that they had read earlier, created themselves or had not seen before, supporting Frith's theory that people with schizophrenia have metarepresentation problems.

Evaluation

Cognitive explanations

- Hemsley (1996) believed that cognitive models allow schizophrenia to be linked to neural bases, creating opportunities for useful therapies to be constructed.
- Garety *et al.* (2001) believed that schizophrenia is best understood by linking together different explanations, both biological and psychological, with cognitive explanations being a vital link in the chain.
- Camozzato and Chaves (2002) believed that cognitive impairments do not occur in a uniform fashion among people with schizophrenia, supporting the possibility of the existence of different subtypes of the disorder.
- Kane and Lencz (2008) proposed that the inclusion of cognitive impairment in the diagnostic criteria for schizophrenia would greatly improve the validity of diagnosis and improve treatment by targeting cognitive enhancement as a primary goal.

Socio-cultural explanations

Socio-cultural explanations focus on social and cultural factors, like the family and social environments. For instance, labelling theory sees being identified as schizophrenic as a social phenomenon, where significant others, such as family, psychiatrists, and so on, label individuals as schizophrenic. Labelling creates a social role, a kind of *self-fulfilling prophecy*, where individuals behave in a stereotypically expected way. The label also affects how others interpret and react to their behaviour (see 'Classic research: Rosenhan (1973)' on page 322).

The degree of *expressed emotion* within a family (hostility, over-concern and so on) is seen as an indicator of relapse in people with schizophrenia, and acts as a social factor contributing to the maintenance of the disorder.

Another socio-cultural factor is the *double-bind theory,* where schizophrenia is seen as a learned response to conflicting messages and mutually exclusive demands during childhood. Over time, this leads to disorganised thinking and communication.

A further aspect is *social causation*, where the lower social classes, who are subject to more stressors, have heightened levels of schizophrenia, suggesting that this may be a causal factor.

Research: socio-cultural factors

- Bateson *et al.* (1956) found that schizophrenia occurred in families using pathological communication, especially contradictory messages, implying a social cause.

- Leff (1976) reported a relapse rate of 51 per cent for people with schizophrenia returning to homes with high rates of expressed emotion, compared to only 13 per cent for those returning to homes with low rates of expressed emotion.

- Haley (1981) found unclear, confusing and conflicting communication patterns in families of individuals with schizophrenia, suggesting that these expressed emotions contributed to the development and persistence of schizophrenia.

- Using data from a national cohort study in Sweden, Hjern *et al.* (2004) found that social adversity in childhood was associated with an increased risk of developing schizophrenia, lending support to the social causation viewpoint.

- Cooper (2005) found that the Afro-Caribbean population in Britain have many social handicaps in their lives, like urban living, unemployment and separation from family, suggesting that it is these social factors that explain the heightened vulnerability to schizophrenia for the British Afro-Caribbean population.

Evaluation

Socio-cultural explanations

- Davison and Neale (2001) reported that most people who have worked in a psychiatric setting have witnessed abuses of the diagnostic process, where patients are sometimes given unjustified labels.

- Miller and Morley (1986) argued that being schizophrenic is not just a label, as there is a reality behind it. They believed that the terms 'labelling' and 'mental illness' are both wrong, creating a false dichotomy.

- MacLeod (1998) saw labelling theory as especially applicable to the involuntary hospital admissions of the 1960s, when the theory was devised. At that time, 90 per cent of psychiatric admissions were involuntary, but by 1979 the figure was only 18 per cent. This suggests that the theory was a product of its time.

- An alternative explanation to social causation is that of downward drift, where schizophrenia results in reduced social status, and sufferers drift down through society into the lower classes.

- Socio-cultural factors may be effects rather than causes of schizophrenia – for instance, expressed emotions may occur within a family due to the stresses and conflicts associated with living with someone with schizophrenia, rather than contributing to the condition's onset.

- If high rates of expressed emotion within families is a contributory factor in developing schizophrenia, this suggests that treatments should be targeted at changing this element within families, rather than targeting individuals with schizophrenia.

- After reviewing evidence from research into the double-bind theory, Haller (1989) concluded that it was extremely difficult to evaluate its worth as an explanation, due to methodological constraints.

Biological therapies

Drugs

The prime treatment for schizophrenia is the use of antipsychotic drugs, the first being chlorpromazine, introduced in 1952, which quickly had a major effect by enabling many people with schizophrenia to live relatively normal lives outside of mental institutions. Antipsychotics do not cure schizophrenia, but they dampen symptoms down so that a degree of normal functioning can occur.

Antipsychotics can be taken in tablet form, as a syrup or by injection, and are divided into first-generation (typical) and second-generation (atypical) varieties. Typical varieties, like chlorpromazine, work by arresting dopamine production through blocking the receptors in synapses that absorb dopamine, thus reducing positive symptoms of the disorder, like auditory hallucinations.

Atypical antipsychotics introduced in the 1990s, such as clozapine, work by acting on serotonin as well as dopamine production systems, affecting negative symptoms of the disorder, like reduced emotional expression. Although atypical drugs have fewer side effects, it is not known specifically how they alleviate symptoms.

Some sufferers only have to take a course of antipsychotics once, while others have to take regular doses in order to prevent schizophrenic symptoms reappearing. There is also a sizeable minority of patients who do not respond to drug treatment.

Figure 9.06 The prime treatment for schizophrenia is antipsychotic medication

Research: drugs

- Davis *et al.* (1989) performed a meta-analysis of over 100 studies that compared antipsychotics with placebos, finding drugs to be more effective, with over 70 per cent of sufferers treated with antipsychotics improving in condition after 6 weeks, while fewer than 25 per cent improved with placebos, suggesting that antipsychotics have a beneficial medical effect.

- Lieberman *et al.* (2005) examined the effectiveness of first- and second-generation antipsychotics in treating 1,432 individuals with chronic schizophrenia, finding that 74 per cent of patients discontinued their treatment within 18 months due to intolerable side effects. Discontinuation rates and time to discontinuation were similar between first- and second-generation antipsychotics, though for different reasons, with discontinuation of first-generation drugs being more associated with muscular disorders, and discontinuation from second-generation drugs more associated with weight gain and metabolic effects.

- Schooler *et al.* (2005), comparing the effectiveness of first- and second-generation antipsychotics, found both effective in treating schizophrenia, with 75 per cent of patients experiencing at least a 20 per cent reduction in symptoms. However, 55 per cent of those receiving first-generation antipsychotics suffered relapses, compared to only 42 per cent for second-generation treatment, with relapses occurring earlier in those taking first-generation drug treatment. Side effects were fewer with second-generation antipsychotics. This implies that second-generation drugs are superior, but other studies have produced conflicting results.

- Kahn *et al.* (2008) compared first-generation with second-generation antipsychotics in their effectiveness of treating first-instance schizophrenia, finding that antipsychotics are effective for at least 1 year, but that second-generation drugs were not necessarily any more effective than first-generation ones.

Evaluation

Drugs

- Antipsychotics are effective, as they are relatively cheap to produce, easy to administer and have positive effects on many sufferers, allowing them to live relatively normal lives outside of mental institutions. Less than 3 per cent of people with schizophrenia in the UK live permanently in hospital.

- One problem with antipsychotics is the high relapse rate – around 40 per cent in the first year after treatment, and 15 per cent in subsequent years – generally due to stopping medication because of side effects.

- Antipsychotics have serious side effects, like muscle tremors associated with first-generation drugs, and even neurological symptoms leading to coma and death. Second-generation antipsychotics were introduced to reduce such problems; however, there is evidence suggesting that they also incur serious side effects, like a reduction in the number of white blood cells.

- Although the use of antipsychotics can produce relatively minor side effects, such as constipation and weight gain, some sufferers can incur serious neurological symptoms (see above).

- Second-generation drugs, like clozapine, reduce negative symptoms and incur a lower dropout rate.

You are the researcher

Design an experiment to test the effectiveness of a new anti-schizophrenic drug.

How could a placebo condition be utilised?

What would be the IV and the DV?

What experimental design would you use? Justify your decision.

How many participants would be required to generate representative data?

Explain how you would use a systematic sample for your study.

Compose a suitable two-tailed hypothesis and justify its use.

Electroconvulsive therapy

The 1930s was a period when the warehousing of patients in mental hospitals, combined with a shortage of trained staff, created a climate that allowed experimentation with radical biological interventions; one such was electroconvulsive therapy (ECT), first used as a treatment for schizophrenia by Cerletti in 1938, on the spurious basis that inducing an epileptic fit would remove schizophrenia, as the two conditions cannot exist together. This did not prove effective, but ECT has been reintroduced as a treatment for schizophrenia in some instances and is more effective than placebos, though not as effective as drug therapies.

ECT works best when applied bilaterally (to both sides of the head). Treatments are given in conjunction with an anaesthetic and a muscle relaxant, and involve applying an electrical shock across the brain for a fraction of a second, which produces a seizure similar to that of epilepsy, lasting up to a minute. A course of ECT generally consists of two to three treatments a week for a total of up to 12 treatments.

Research: electroconvulsive therapy

- Tharyan and Adams (2005) reviewed 26 studies of ECT treatment for schizophrenia, concluding it to be fairly effective in the short term, being better than no treatment, but not as good as antipsychotic drugs.

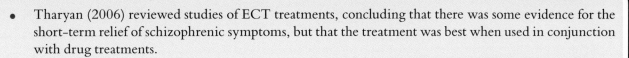

- Tharyan (2006) reviewed studies of ECT treatments, concluding that there was some evidence for the short-term relief of schizophrenic symptoms, but that the treatment was best when used in conjunction with drug treatments.

- Tang *et al.* (2002) found ECT to be effective in treating people with schizophrenia who did not respond positively to treatment with antipsychotic drugs, suggesting that the treatment provides some relief to such patients.

- Fisk (1997), reviewing clinical literature, concluded that ECT had a success rate of between 60 and 80 per cent, but is only effective against certain categories of schizophrenia, and more treatments (20 to 30) are needed than with other disorders.

Evaluation

Electroconvulsive therapy

- Between 20 and 50 per cent of people with schizophrenia who respond positively to ECT relapse within 6 months, suggesting that it does not offer a long-term solution to treating the condition.

- Unilateral ECT treatment produces fewer side effects, like short-term memory loss, but is not as effective in treating schizophrenia. Memory generally returns to normal, but 1 per cent suffer severe memory loss, and such loss is cumulative – the more treatments a patient has, the worse the memory loss becomes.

- ECT has a bad image to shake off, as its usage can seem brutal and be perceived by patients as a punishment for their condition. Its negative image has a lot to do with previous poor applications performed by untrained practitioners.

- ECT is no more dangerous than minor surgery under general anaesthetic, with a death rate of approximately 1 in 10,000.

Psychological therapies

Cognitive behavioural therapy

Cognitive behavioural therapy (CBT) is the main psychological treatment used to combat schizophrenia, and works by modifying hallucinations and delusional beliefs. The idea is that beliefs, expectations and cognitive assessments of self, the environment and the nature of personal problems affect how individuals perceive themselves and others, how problems are approached, and how successful people are in coping and attaining goals. People with schizophrenia have maladaptive thinking and distorted perceptions, including those about the self, so CBT can help reduce symptoms, if antipsychotics are used to reduce psychotic thought processes that interfere with psychological treatments. CBT is administered around once every 10 days, for about 12 sessions, to identify and alter irrational thinking. Drawings are used to display links between sufferers' thoughts, actions and emotions. Comprehending where symptoms originate from is useful in alleviating sufferers' anxiety levels.

One CBT approach is *personal therapy* (PT), involving detailed evaluation of problems and experiences, their triggers and consequences, and strategies being used to cope. Cognitive techniques are developed between patient and therapist, such as:

- distractions from intrusive thoughts
- challenging the meanings of intrusive thoughts
- increasing/decreasing social activity to distract from low moods
- using relaxation strategies.

PT is also used to counteract problems faced by people with schizophrenia who are discharged, taking place in small groups or as a one-to-one therapy. Patients are taught to recognise small signs of relapse, which can build up to produce cognitive distortions and unsuitable social behaviour.

Rational emotive therapy is incorporated to teach sufferers that emotional volatility is a predisposition of schizophrenia (biological diathesis) that they must live with. Patients use muscle relaxation techniques to detect gradual anger build-ups and then apply relaxation skills to control emotions.

Research: cognitive behavioural therapy

- McGorry *et al*. (2002) compared individuals at high risk of having a first episode of schizophrenia, who received different treatment interventions. After 6 months of treatment, 36 per cent of those receiving supportive psychotherapy developed schizophrenia, compared to 10 per cent of those receiving combined CBT and drugs, suggesting CBT to be effective in preventing first-episode psychosis.

- Tarrier (2005) reviewed 20 controlled trials of CBT using 739 patients, finding persistent evidence of reduced symptoms, especially positive ones, lower relapse rates and a speedier recovery rate of acutely ill patients. These were short-term benefits, with follow-ups needed to assess CBT's long-term benefits.

- Tarrier *et al*. (2000) found that people with schizophrenia receiving 20 sessions of PT in 10 weeks, coupled with drug therapy, followed by four booster sessions during the following year, did better than sufferers receiving drug therapy alone or supportive counselling. One-third of patients receiving PT achieved a 50 per cent reduction in psychotic experiences, with 15 per cent free of all positive symptoms, compared to 15 per cent in the counselling group, with 7 per cent free of all positive symptoms. No patients in the drugs-only group were symptom-free. One year later, similar differences still existed, though at a 2-year follow-up the PT group's advantage over the counselling group had vanished, though both groups still outscored the drugs-only group.

- Trower *et al*. (2004) conducted a controlled trial of CBT, finding that it did not reduce the intensity of hallucinations, but made them seem less of a threat by persuading sufferers that they 'outranked' the voices. Patients receiving CBT had reduced positive and negative symptoms and a better quality of life, implying that CBT is not a replacement for medication, nor suitable for everyone, but is an effective treatment.

Evaluation

Cognitive behavioural therapy

- There is considerable evidence suggesting that CBT plus antipsychotics is effective in treating schizophrenia.

- Rathod *et al*. (2005) found that non-Afro-Caribbean therapists had less success using CBT with Afro-Caribbean than white ethnic patients, suggesting that the degree of empathy between clinicians and sufferers is important in determining the effectiveness of CBT.

- For CBT to be effective, training is essential, successful treatment being dependent on developing empathy, respect, unconditional positive regard and honesty between patient and practitioner.

- CBT is not suitable for all patients, especially those refusing medication or thought too disorientated, agitated or paranoid to form trusting alliances with practitioners.

Psychodynamic therapy

Psychodynamic explanations of schizophrenia perceive the causes of schizophrenia as developed in early relationships, with treatments providing insight into links between symptoms and early experiences. Poor early relationships are seen as leading to a poor sense of self, which leads to people with schizophrenia having faulty meta-representations, and an inability to distinguish between personal thoughts and external sources. Therapists provide a surrogate parenting role to facilitate normal personality development, allowing proper meta-representation, so that patients can distinguish personal thoughts from others.

Sullivan (1923) pioneered the use of psychoanalysis with schizophrenics, using it to help sufferers avoid unnecessary anxiety that created barriers to communication. Patients are taught adult forms of communication to achieve insight into the role the past played in current problems, and individual life histories are examined to identify the roots and consequences of sufferers' maladaptive interpersonal patterns, as displayed in the relationship with the therapist and in everyday life. Over many sessions, sufferers develop trust in their therapist, which gives them confidence to examine their interpersonal relationships.

More recent psychosocial interventions, such as *social skills training* (SST), *family therapy* (FT) and *reducing expressed emotion* (REE), take a more active, present-focused and reality-orientated approach, where therapists help patients and families to deal directly in coping with the consequences of schizophrenia, especially the social pressures faced when sufferers leave hospital.

Research: psychodynamic therapy

- Normand and Bluestone (1986) found combination treatments of antipsychotics and psychotherapy useful, but only for patients with advanced verbal skills, able to express themselves fully, suggesting that psychotherapy is not a universal treatment.

- Stein and Test (1980) found fewer symptoms, better social functioning and more patient satisfaction when home treatment psychotherapy was used rather than hospital-based treatment, suggesting that institutionalisation may contribute to difficulties in treating schizophrenia.

- Knapp *et al.* (1994) found problem-orientated, home-based psychotherapy cost-effective, producing 'mildly encouraging' results over a 20-month period, suggesting some support for psychotherapy.

- Malmberg and Fenton (2009) conducted a review of psychodynamic therapies, finding that such regimes have little, if any, benefit unless used with drug treatments, suggesting that only with the use of antipsychotics can patients benefit from talking therapies.

- Kopelowicz *et al.* (2002) reported SST to be effective in teaching severely disturbed patients new social behaviours. Sufferers had fewer relapses, better social functioning and better quality of life.

Evaluation

Psychodynamic therapy

- Apart from several studies in the 1970s and 1980s, the use of psychodynamic therapies as a sole treatment for schizophrenia has rarely been evaluated, suggesting that it is difficult to make firm conclusions about such treatments.

- There is evidence that rather than being helpful, psychotherapy can have adverse effects. Stone (1986) reported a high suicide rate among people with schizophrenia treated with psychotherapy, while Gunderson *et al.* (1984) found that those receiving such treatment spent longer in hospital than those receiving other forms of treatment.

- Barton (1976) believed that psychotherapy has an advantage over other treatments as it can be administered outside a hospital, thus reducing the risk of institutionalisation.

- The theoretical basis for using psychodynamic therapies with schizophrenia is weak, and with little supporting evidence for its use, other than as a combination therapy with drug treatment therapy, there is no strong case for its use as a sole treatment.

- Roth and Fonagy (2005) concluded that the effectiveness of insight-orientated psychotherapy is largely negative, and the emotional intensity of psychodynamic treatments may harm some patients, being too intensive and intrusive for some to handle.

- Evidence for the long-term benefits of SST is mixed, implying modest improvements at best, becoming more effective when combined with drug therapy.

An almost inexhaustible source of information on anything you want to know about schizophrenia, including news, explanations, treatments and discussion forums, can be found at www.schizophrenia.com

Strengthen your learning

1. Outline the clinical characteristics of schizophrenia.
2. Outline the symptoms of schizophrenia, explaining the differences between first-rank and additional symptoms.
3. With reference to research evidence, is the diagnosis of schizophrenia
   i) reliable?
   ii) valid?
4a. What evidence is there for schizophrenia being genetic?
4b. Aside from research evidence, what other evaluative points can be made about the genetic explanation?
5a. Outline the biochemical explanation of schizophrenia.
5b. To what extent can the biochemical explanation be supported?
6a. Outline the cognitive explanation of schizophrenia.
6b. What degree of research support is there for the cognitive explanation?
7a. Outline the socio-cultural explanation of schizophrenia.
7b. Construct an evaluation of the socio-cultural explanation of schizophrenia, including reference to research evidence.
8a. What effects do drugs have on schizophrenia?
8b. Explain the strengths and weakness of drug treatments.
9. Is ECT an effective treatment for schizophrenia? Give details.
10a. Describe CBT as a treatment for schizophrenia.
10b. Evaluate CBT's effectiveness.
11. Is psychotherapy an effective treatment of schizophrenia? Give details.

Assessment Check

1. Outline one or more psychological explanations of schizophrenia. (8 marks)

2. Evaluate biological therapies for schizophrenia. (16 marks)

3. Outline clinical characteristics of schizophrenia. (4 marks)

4. Evaluate issues associated with classification and diagnosis of schizophrenia. (16 marks)

5. Outline and evaluate one psychological therapy for schizophrenia. (20 marks)

6. Outline and evaluate biological explanations of schizophrenia – for example, genetics, biochemistry. (24 marks)

Examination guidance

There is a breadth/depth trade-off with question 1, in that if you offer one explanation, you would be expected to present more depth/detail in your answer than if you were offering more than one explanation. Care should be taken with question 2 not to outline biological therapies, as such description would not be creditworthy. Psychological therapies could be legitimately used as comparison.

In question 3, a 'short version' is required, as only 4 marks are up for grabs. In question 4, issues should only be evaluated and not described to gain credit. This could be achieved by reference to relevant issues of reliability and/or validity. More time and effort should be spent on question 5, in evaluating a psychological therapy, as 16 marks are available, as opposed to only 4 marks for the outline.

In question 6, 8 marks are available for outlining biological explanations, of which there must be at least two. This leaves 16 marks for the evaluation, which could be achieved through the degree of research support. The examples are only for guidance and do not necessarily have to be referred to.

Depression

Depression is a mood disorder involving prolonged and fundamental disturbance of emotions. There are two main types, *unipolar* and *bipolar* (also known as manic depression), and depression can also be broken down into *endogenous* depression, related to internal biochemical and hormonal factors, and *exogenous* (reactive) depression, related to stressful experiences, though sufferers can have elements of exogenous and endogenous depression combined.

Twenty per cent of people suffer from depression, with women twice as vulnerable. Depression can occur in cycles, with symptoms coming and going over time and generally lasting between 4 and 6 months. There is also a high suicide rate associated with the condition: 10 per cent of severely depressed people commit suicide, with 60 per cent of all suicides associated with mood disorders.

Depressed people experience a loss of energy and enthusiasm. Depression can begin any time from adolescence onwards, with average age of onset being the late twenties, though age of onset has decreased over the past 50 years as prevalence rates have increased. With treatment, episodes last from 2 to 3 months, but 6 months or longer if untreated.

Unipolar depression

This form of depression, also known as *major depression*, is differentiated from bipolar depression by its manifestation as pure depression, without the manic

Key terms

Depression – mood disorder characterised by feelings of despondency and hopelessness

Unipolar depression (major depression) – form of depression occurring without alternating periods of mania

Bipolar depression (manic depression) – mood disorder characterised by alternating periods of depression and mania

episodes that sufferers of bipolar depression experience. Unipolar depression is characterised by clinical symptoms, usually occurring in cycles. Delusions sometimes accompany unipolar depression, and patients who experience such delusions do not respond well to antidepressants, but do respond favourably to a combination of antidepressants and antipsychotics. This is more severe than depression without delusions, involving more social impairment and less time between episodes.

Bipolar depression

Also known as *manic depression*, this form of depression is less common, with about 1 per cent of people suffering from it. It usually appears in one's twenties and before the age of 50. Mixed episodes of mania and depression are more common than mania alone.

DSM-IV lists the clinical characteristics of depression, and at least five symptoms must be apparent every day for 2 weeks for depression to be diagnosed, with an impairment in general functioning also evident, that cannot be accounted for by other medical conditions or events – for example, mourning a loved one. Symptoms affect many areas of functioning, including behavioural, motivation, somatic and emotional aspects. One of the five symptoms must be a constant depressed mood or lessened interest in daily activities.

Clinical symptoms of depression

1. Constant depressed mood – feelings of sadness either reported by the sufferer or observed by others.

2. Lessened interest – diminished concern with and/or lack of pleasure in daily activities, either reported by the sufferer or observed by others.

3. Weight loss – significant decrease (or increase) in weight and/or appetite.

4. Sleep pattern disturbance – constant insomnia or oversleeping.

5. Fatigue – loss of energy and displacement of energy levels – for example, becoming lethargic or agitated.

6. Reduced concentration – difficulty in paying attention and/or slowed-down thinking, indecisiveness, either reported by the sufferer or observed by others.

7. Worthlessness – constant feelings of reduced worth and/or inappropriate guilt.

8. Focus on death – constant thoughts of death and/or suicide.

A distinction is made between *major depression* (clinical depression) and *dysthymic disorder* (chronic depression), the difference being in the duration, type and number of symptoms. Patients meeting DSM-IV-TR criteria for dysthymic disorder have three or more symptoms, instead of the five required for major depression, including depressed mood, but not suicidal thoughts, and cannot be without these symptoms for more than 2 months. People with the same diagnosis can vary greatly from one another. Some bipolar patients experience a full range of symptoms of mania and depression almost every day, while others have symptoms of only one or the other during an episode.

Issues surrounding classification and diagnosis

(Refer to pages 315–16 for an explanation of classification systems and the reliability and validity of diagnosis.)

A major problem is that moods vary over time in most people, so reliably diagnosing depression is difficult, though the modern requirement for symptoms to be present for some time has aided the diagnostic process. Another problem is taking into consideration the degree to which people are depressed.

Diagnosis was performed mainly by clinical interviews, but increasing use has been made of depression inventories.

Research: reliability

- Sato *et al.* (1996) assessed the test–retest reliability of the Inventory to Diagnose Depression, Lifetime version (IDDL), finding a concordance rate of 77 per cent, which implies that the use of inventories to diagnose depression is highly reliable.

- Einfeld *et al.* (2002) assessed the degree of inter-rater reliability between skilled clinicians in diagnosing depression, finding a high level of agreement that implies a high degree of inter-rater reliability.

- Moca (2007) found an 88 per cent concordance rate for inter-rater reliability in the diagnosis of depression, and a 78 per cent concordance rate for test-retest reliability, lending support to diagnosis of depression being reliable, though these figures are lower than for the reliability of schizophrenia diagnosis.

- Baca-Garcia *et al.* (2007) reviewed the reliability of diagnosis of over 2,300 patients, assessed at least ten times each, finding a concordance rate of only 55 per cent, suggesting that the reliability of diagnosis over time is relatively poor.

Evaluation

Reliability

- Beck (1972) evaluated the use of depression inventories, an alternative to psychiatric assessment by clinical interview, where a standard list of descriptive items is used in a uniform manner to facilitate diagnosis. This method of assessment is not subject to the inconsistencies and biases often found with psychiatric evaluations occurring through interview, and therefore it is effective as a criterion measure. However, it is often difficult for patients to discriminate between alternative descriptive statements, reducing the efficiency of the diagnostic technique.

- A drawback in assessing the reliability of diagnosing depression over time is that patients may have improved in condition between diagnoses.

- Chao-Cheng *et al.* (2002) proposed the possibility of self-diagnosis of depression through the use of internet-based self-assessments. The researchers reviewed the test-retest reliability of such a programme, finding a concordance rate of 75 per cent, suggesting that it is a reliable method of diagnosis.

- Jürges (2008) reported that one problem with the use of self-assessment inventories to diagnose depression is that changes in self-ratings of health are underestimated by patients, reducing the reliability of such a diagnostic method.

Research: validity

- Zigler and Phillips (1961) reported that symptoms of depression were equally to be found in patients assessed as neurotic as in those assessed as having bipolar disorder, as well as in 25 per cent of people diagnosed with schizophrenia, implying a low diagnostic validity of depression.

- Almeida and Almeida (1999) assessed the validity of the Geriatric Depression Scale (GDS), with both the ICD-10 and DSM-IV classification systems, in diagnosing depression among 64 elderly Australians, finding the GDS to be highly valid, though not useful in assessing the severity of depressive episodes.

- Van Weel-Baumgarten (2000) assessed the validity of diagnosis of depression among doctors in general practice in the Netherlands, using DSM-IV criteria. There were 99 participants, of whom 33 were depressed, 33 had chronic nervous functional complaints and 33 had no mental disorders; 28 of the depressed participants were correctly diagnosed as depressed, along with 7 of the participants with chronic nervous functional complaints, suggesting that the validity of diagnosis, though not perfect, is high.

- Sanchez–Villegas *et al.* (2008) assessed the validity of the Structured Clinical Interview to diagnose depression, finding that 74.2 per cent of those originally diagnosed as depressed had been accurately diagnosed, suggesting this diagnostic method to be valid

Evaluation

Validity

- A significant obstacle to the treatment of depression is the failure to diagnose symptoms. Burrows *et al.* (1995) found that health care providers under-diagnose depression in as much as 56 per cent of nursing home residents.
- Although the classification and diagnosis of depression is not without its criticisms, it is probably the most effective method of assessment and diagnostic criteria, and allows clinicians to communicate using a common language.
- Not all diagnostic scales in clinical use have been found to be valid. Anderson *et al.* (2003) used the GDS, which had previously been proven valid, to assess the value of the Minimum Data Set Depression Rating Scale, finding it to be of low validity and therefore of little clinical use.
- Validation of diagnostic scales is important not only in proving such criteria as valid in themselves, but because such diagnostic scales can then be used to further assess the validity of other diagnostic measures.

Biological explanations

There are a variety of indicators suggesting that biology underpins depression, including hereditary factors, the uniformity of symptoms across genders, age and cultural groups, the physical aspects of symptoms, such as weight fluctuations and fatigue, and the fact that biological therapies such as drug treatments are successful in addressing the symptoms of depression. Overall, evidence indicates a major role for biological factors, though environmental factors play a role too.

Genetics

Research has used twin, family and adoption studies by examining concordance rates of depression between people with different degrees of genetic relationship, to assess what role genetics plays in the causation of depression. Results indicate depression to have a genetic component, especially with early onset depression.

More recently, gene-mapping studies have compared genetic material from families with a high incidence and low incidence of depression. Results indicate that several genes are involved and that genes make some individuals more vulnerable than others to developing the disorder.

Research: genetics

- Sevey *et al.* (2000) reviewed twin studies of bipolar disorder, finding a concordance rate of 69.3 per cent in MZ twins, but only 20 per cent in DZ twins. As MZ twins share 100 per cent genetic similarity, compared to 50 per cent in DZ twins, this suggests a genetic influence in bipolar disorder.
- Mendlewicz and Rainer (1977) focused on adoptees with bipolar disorder, finding that the rate of the disorder was 7 per cent in biological parents, compared to 0 per cent in adoptive parents, suggesting a stronger genetic influence.
- Wender *et al.* (1986) found that adopted children who develop depression were more likely to have a biological parent with depression, even though adopted children are raised in different environments, implying that biological factors are more important than environment.

- Taylor *et al.* (1995) reviewed family studies of depression, finding that the prevalence of the disorder in the general population was 1 per cent, while in first-degree relatives of individuals with bipolar depression it was between 5 and 10 per cent, implying a genetic pathway to bipolar disorder.

- Oruc *et al.* (1998) found that depression occurs across generations in families, and that the chances of developing depression increase the closer the genetic relationship. First-degree relatives of people with depression are three times more likely to develop the disorder than those without first-degree relatives with the disorder.

- Caspi *et al.* (2005) used gene mapping to find a relationship between depression and abnormalities in the 5-HTT gene, suggesting a genetic link. 5-HTT is associated with the manufacture of serotonin and therefore implies a link between genetics and biochemical factors.

- Wilhelm *et al.* (2006) found that individuals experiencing negative life events and possessing the short-short variation of the serotonin transporter gene were more likely to become depressed, suggesting that this variation of the transporter gene creates vulnerability to developing depression in the presence of negative life events.

Evaluation

Genetic explanations

- There is a possibility with twin studies of diagnostic unreliability – that is, if researchers are aware that one twin suffers from depression, then this clouds their judgement in assessing whether the other twin also has the disorder.

- Twin and family studies suggest a genetic factor in the onset of depression, but do not consider the role played by social class and socio-psychological factors between family members. Although such studies support the genetic viewpoint, they do not consider shared environmental influences, weakening the genetic viewpoint. If genes caused depression on their own, the concordance rate between MZ twins would be 100 per cent, which is clearly not the case.

- Sullivan *et al.* (2000) reported that the few adoption studies of depression that have been carried out are negatively affected by methodological flaws, like small sample sizes and indirect methods of clinical diagnosis, making it difficult to draw clear conclusions.

- Gene mapping offers the possibility of developing tests to identify individuals with a high risk of developing depression, though this raises many socially sensitive and ethical concerns.

- Findings from studies involving genetics support the *diathesis-stress* model, which sees individuals inheriting different levels of genetic predisposition to developing depression, but that ultimately it is environmental triggers that determine if individuals go on to develop depression.

Biochemical explanations

Biochemical explanations centre on the idea that abnormal levels of neurotransmitters and hormones cause depression. Focus has been on a group of neurotransmitters called monoamines, like serotonin, noradrenaline and dopamine, low levels of which are found in the brains of individuals with depression. The importance of monoamines is supported by the fact that antidepressant drugs work by increasing the production of monoamines. For instance, *selective serotonin reuptake inhibitors* (SSRIs) raise levels of serotonin, producing an antidepressant effect. Because SSRIs are effective in treating unipolar depressive disorder, a stronger link has been established between low levels of serotonin and depression.

Certain forms of depression, like premenstrual syndrome, seasonal affective disorder and postnatal depression, are also associated with hormonal changes.

Research: biochemical explanations

- Teuting *et al.* (1981) found abnormally low amounts of by-products associated with noradrenaline levels in urine samples from individuals with depression, implying a biochemical cause for the disorder.

- McNeal and Cimbolic (1986) found low amounts of the chemical 5-H1AA, which is created when serotonin is broken down, in the cerebrospinal fluid of individuals with depression, supporting the biochemical explanation.

- Mann *et al.* (1996) found that major depression results from a deficiency of serotonin, or insufficient serotonin receptors, suggesting a biochemical cause of depression.

- Delack *et al.* (1995) found that fluoxetine, an SSRI, was effective in addressing depressive symptoms, supporting the biochemical explanation.

- Mann *et al.* (1996) found that the reduction in depressive symptoms achieved by increasing monoamine levels through using antidepressants is reversed when serotonin levels are decreased by dietary manipulation, further supporting the biochemical explanation.

- Klimek *et al.* (1997) performed post-mortems on individuals with depression and those without the disorder, finding differences in the structure of the locus coeruleus, a brain area associated with the production of noradrenaline, suggesting that abnormal brain structures may affect neurotransmitter levels, which leads to depression.

- Zhou *et al.* (2005) found that SSRIs work by increasing dopamine levels in people with depression, suggesting a role for the neurotransmitter in the causation of depression.

- Kalynchuck *et al.* (2005) reported that patients with Cushing's syndrome are often depressed and have high levels of the stress hormone cortisol, suggesting that depression stems from chronic overstimulation of the hypothalamic-pituitary-adrenal axis, which produces the hormone.

- Chen *et al.* (2006) suggested that a decline in the level of the hormone insulin following childbirth was responsible for postnatal depression. Insulin affects the secretion of serotonin in the brain; therefore, decreased insulin may be influencing depression.

Contemporary research

Kendler *et al.* (2006)

A Swedish national twin study of lifetime major depression

One way of assessing the role of genetics in the causation of depression is to conduct twin studies. If there is a higher correlation between identical (MZ) twins than lesser related people, it is seen as evidence for a genetic component. This particular Swedish study tested for a gender difference in genetic risk factors for depression.

Aim

To replicate findings of previous studies that the heritability of major depression is moderate, at between 35 and 40 per cent.

To assess whether genetic influences in major depression are more important in women or men.

Figure 9.07 Twin studies have been performed to assess the degree to which depression is genetic

continued ...

...continued

To assess whether the heritability of major depression changes over time.

Procedure

A meta-analysis of five previous studies was conducted.

Lifetime major depression was assessed by interview using the DSM-IV classification system in 42,161 twins, including 15,493 complete pairs from the Swedish national twin registry. Birth dates ranged from 1900 to 1958.

Findings

A moderate level of heritability of 38 per cent was found.

Heritability of depression was higher in females, at 42 per cent, than in males, at 29 per cent.

Levels of depression were constant over time.

Conclusions

Genetic risk factors for depression are higher for women.

Depression is moderately heritable.

The heritability of depression is constant.

Evaluation

- The high number of participants used from five different studies increases the reliability and validity of the results.

- The study provides support to previous estimates of moderate heritability to depression.

- The study was not able to assess the similarity of environment between male and female MZ twins.

- The findings support those of Bierut *et al*. (1999), who found similar gender differences in Australian twins.

Research in focus

Twin studies like Kendler *et al*.'s (2006) have historically been a popular way of investigating the role of genetics in psychology.

How do twin studies work?

Why do some twin studies use MZ twins who have been reared separately?

Twin studies generally use correlation coefficients. What does this term mean?

How do adoption studies perform the same role as twin studies?

What criticisms can be made of twin and adoption studies can you discover?

Evaluation

Biochemical explanations

- The biochemical explanation is the longest-standing and most persistent biological theory of depression, demonstrating its worth.

- Claridge and Davis (2003) found that when people who do not suffer from depression are given drugs that reduce levels of serotonin and noradrenaline in the brain, they do not become depressive, weakening support for the explanation.

- A problem with the biochemical explanation is whether fluctuations in neurotransmitter and hormonal levels are a cause or effect of depression.

- The fact that monoamine neurotransmitters are involved in arousal and mood levels indicates that they are involved in depression, which itself is a mood disorder.

continued ...

...continued

- Antidepressant drugs do not produce identical effects in all people with depression, suggesting that causes may be different for different individuals.
- Neurotransmitter levels are affected immediately by taking antidepressants, but symptoms often take weeks to improve, weakening support for the biochemical viewpoint.
- The fact that women are more subject to fluctuating hormone levels – for example, with menstruation, pregnancy and the menopause – may explain why they are three times more likely to suffer from depression.
- As reduced insulin levels are associated with postnatal depression, it may be possible to prevent the disorder by increasing the amount of carbohydrates eaten, as carbohydrates stimulate the production of insulin.

Psychological explanations

Although biological factors play an important role in the onset of depression, it is generally accepted that psychological factors are involved too.

Behaviourist explanations

Behaviourism perceives depression as a learned condition, and not as a mental illness with a physical cause.

Lewinsohn (1974) proposed that depression occurs due to a decline in positive reinforcement. For example, after a romance ends there are reduced opportunities for experiencing enjoyable outcomes and therefore fewer positive reinforcements, resulting in depression. Individuals can then become trapped in a cycle of social withdrawal, prolonging the depression.

Operant conditioning sees depressive behaviour as being rewarding due to the attention and sympathy it brings, reinforcing such behaviours as a secondary gain.

Behaviourism also explains the high incidence of depression in some families in social learning terms – that is, from observing and imitating affected family members.

An informative and wide-ranging source of information about depression, including symptoms, explanations, therapies and useful links to other sites can be found at www.rcpsych.ac.uk/mentalhealthinfoforall/problems/depression/depression.aspx

Behaviourism also explains depression occurring through *learned helplessness*, where individuals learn through experience that seemingly they cannot influence events – for instance, being unemployed and applying for lots of jobs, but not getting any interviews, leads to a chronic loss of motivation and eventually depression.

Research: behaviourist explanations

- Alloy *et al.* (1979) compared the ability of 144 clinically depressed and 144 non-depressed participants to estimate the relationship between pressing a button and various outcomes. Non-depressed participants overestimated the relationship for desirable outcomes and underestimated it for non-desirable outcomes, while depressed participants were accurate throughout. Therefore, the depressed individuals were more realistic and pessimistic in their estimates, probably due to negative learning experiences, supporting the concept of learned helplessness.

- Maier and Seligman (1976) found that participants placed in a situation from which escape from noise or shocks was impossible did not try to escape from future similar situations where escape was possible, lending support to the concept of learned helplessness.

- Rehm (1977) found that depressed individuals had deficits in self-regulatory monitoring and proposed a behavioural model for the self-control of depression that focused on an individual's maladaptive self-regulatory processes in coping with stress.

- Coleman (1986) found that individuals receiving low rates of positive reinforcement for social behaviours become increasingly passive and non-responsive, leading to depressive moods, providing support for Lewinsohn's learning theory.

- Rice and McLaughin (2001) found that depressive individuals focus on negative events, set overly stringent criteria for evaluating their performance and administer little reinforcement to themselves, supporting Lewinsohn's model, as it focuses on the idea that reduced activity and lack of reinforcement are correlated with helplessness and depression.

Evaluation

Behavioural explanations

- Although behaviourism explains depression in terms of being a secondary gain – for example, the sympathetic attention of others following a negative event – it cannot explain why depression continues after such attention declines.
- Kanter *et al.* (2004) state that behaviourism has yet to offer an account of depression that addresses its complexity satisfactorily.
- Ferster (1973) demonstrated that reinforcement schedules and environmental influences were important factors in depressive behaviour, creating opportunities to develop specific behavioural techniques for treatment of the disorder.
- Learned helplessness has not proven to be a universal occurrence: in some cases where individuals were placed in situations of helplessness, the experience actually led to improved performance.

Cognitive explanations

Beck (1967, 1987) believes that individuals become depressed because negative schemas, where the world is perceived negatively, dominate thinking and are triggered whenever situations are encountered resembling those in which negative schemas were learned.

These negative schemas fuel and are fuelled by cognitive biases, causing individuals to misperceive reality:

- *Ineptness schemas* make people with depression expect to fail.

- *Self-blame schemas* make people with depression feel responsible for all misfortunes.

- *Negative self-evaluation schemas* constantly remind people with depression of their worthlessness.

Cognitive biases

- **Arbitrary inference** conclusions drawn in the absence of sufficient evidence, for example, a man concluding that he is worthless because it is raining on the day he hosts an outdoor party.

- **Selective abstraction** conclusions drawn on the basis of one element of a situation, for example, a worker feeling worthless when a product does not work, even though several people made it.

- **Overgeneralisation** sweeping conclusions drawn on the basis of a single event, for example, a student regarding poor performance in a single class as proof of his or her worthlessness.

- **Magnification and minimisation** exaggerations in evaluation of performance, for example, a man believing that he has ruined his car due to a small scratch (maximisation), or a woman believing herself to be worthless despite much praise (minimisation).

Negative schemas, together with cognitive biases/distortions, maintain the *negative triad*, which regards negative thoughts as being about:

- **the self** – where individuals regard themselves as being helpless, worthless and inadequate

- **the world** – where obstacles are perceived within one's environment that cannot be dealt with

- **the future** – where personal worthlessness is seen as hindering any improvements.

Overall, depression is seen as resulting from cognitive vulnerabilities.

Figure 9.08 People with depression often feel helpless, worthless and inadequate

Abramson *et al.* (1978) proposed another cognitive explanation by revising learned helplessness in terms of *depressed attributional style*, based on three dimensions:

- internal/external locus – whether the cause concerns the individual or not

- stable/unstable – whether the cause is a permanent or temporary feature

- global/specific – whether the cause relates to the whole person or just one feature.

Therefore, people with depression believe that failure is due to internal, global, stable factors.

Research: cognitive explanations

- Boury *et al.* (2001) monitored students' negative thoughts with the Beck Depression Inventory, finding that people with depression misinterpret facts and experiences in a negative fashion and feel hopeless about the future, giving support to Beck's cognitive explanation.

- Saisto *et al.* (2001) studied expectant mothers, finding that those who did not adjust personal goals to match the specific demands of the transition to motherhood, but indulged instead in negative thinking patterns, showed increased depressive symptoms, supporting Beck's cognitive theory.

- McIntosh and Fischer (2000) tested the negative cognitive triad to see whether it contains three distinct types of negative thought, but found no clear separation of negative thoughts, but instead a single, one-dimensional negative perception of the self, suggesting that retention of all three areas of the triad as separate dimensions is unnecessary for representing the structure of depressive cognition.

- Seligman (1974) reported that students making global, stable attributions remained depressed for longer after examinations, supporting the cognitive explanation of attributional style.

- Peterson and Seligman (1984) found that people identified by the Attributional Style Questionnaire as being prone to depression explained negative life events as being due to internal, global, stable factors and were more likely to develop depression when experiencing stressors, demonstrating support for the concept of depressed attributional style.

Evaluation

Cognitive explanations

- There is a wealth of research evidence supporting the idea of cognitive vulnerability being linked to the onset of depression, with individuals with depression selectively attending to negative stimuli.

- The cognitive explanation of depression lends itself readily to scientific research, allowing for refinement of cognitive models that allow greater understanding of the disorder.

- A relatively high degree of success has been achieved in treating depression with therapies based on cognitive explanations, thus providing support for such explanations.

- The majority of evidence linking negative thinking to depression is correlational and does not indicate that negative thoughts cause depression. Beck came to believe that it was a *bidirectional relationship*, where depressed individuals' thoughts cause depression and vice versa.

- Beck's theory led to the formation of cognitive behavioural therapy (CBT), which has proved very effective in treating depression, which suggests that the theory on which it is based has validity.

You are the researcher

Design a correlational study to assess the relationship between socio-economic status and risk of developing depression. What would be your co-variables? They must include how socio-economic status and risk of depression would be measured. (You might want to incorporate a questionnaire.)

Compose and justify the use of a suitable directional correlational hypothesis.

If the data was of at least ordinal status, what statistical test could be used?

Identify one confounding variable that could occur in this study.

Biological therapies

The most common treatment for depression is antidepressant drugs, which stimulate the production of monoamine neurotransmitters in the brain, leading to increased physical arousal. In Britain, more than £291 million was spent on antidepressants in 2006. There are three types of drug used to treat depression:

- monoamine oxidase inhibitors (MAOIs)

- tricyclics

- selective serotonin reuptake inhibitors (SSRIs).

All three increase serotonin production; the main difference is their side effects rather than effectiveness or speed of action. Most are given once per day and 'kick in' after 10 to 14 days. They are withdrawn slowly: sudden cessation causes restlessness, insomnia, anxiety and nausea.

First–generation antidepressants like MAOIs stop serotonin, noradrenaline and dopamine being broken down, so that levels are increased, while tricyclics stop dopamine and noradrenaline being reabsorbed, and some also block the reuptake of serotonin, so that levels are increased, though some have no known effects on any of these systems. Although effective in treating the symptoms of depression, these antidepressants can incur side effects, like drowsiness and constipation.

More modern antidepressants tend to affect only the level of one monoamine – for instance, SSRIs, like Prozac, prevent serotonin being reabsorbed or broken down, thus making it more available. There is no best drug, as patients respond differently to different drugs, and drug choice is also affected by symptoms displayed and side effects exhibited.

Research: drug therapies

- Bennett (2006) found that MAOIs are less effective than tricyclics in treating severe depression and mild depression, with a success rate of about 50 per cent.

- Hirschfield (1999) reported that tricyclics are effective in the treatment of mild and severe depression and are the first choice of treatment in the latter. Of patients taking tricyclics, 60 to 65 per cent experience improvement in symptoms.

- Olfson *et al.* (2006) found that antidepressant drug treatment for depression was related to a high incidence of suicide attempts in children and adolescents between 6 and 18 years of age. Therefore, clinical monitoring is essential during antidepressant drug treatment of severely depressed young people.

- David *et al.* (2009) performed research with rodents, finding that SSRIs reverse changes in the hippocampus caused by depression. The researchers identified candidate genes whose expression was decreased in the hypothalamus and normalised by Prozac. Mice deficient in the gene beta-arrestin 2 displayed a reduced response to Prozac, indicating that beta-arrestin 2 signalling is necessary for the antidepressant effects of Prozac.

- Kirsch (2008) found that second-generation antidepressants, like SSRIs, work no better than placebos for most patients with mild and even severe depression, and accused drug companies of suppressing research evidence that cast doubt on their effectiveness.

- Furukawa *et al.* (2003) reviewed 35 studies, finding antidepressants superior to placebos, implying that antidepressants are an effective treatment.

Evaluation

Drug therapies

- MAOIs are not favoured because of side effects, including cerebral haemorrhage, triggered by eating certain foodstuffs containing tyramine, like cheese and red wine, or taking other drugs like decongestants. More recent *reversible selective* MAOIs are designed to avoid these problems.

- Tricyclics have side effects, including toxic effects on the cardiovascular system, and they are lethal in overdose, presenting dangers to suicidal patients. Beneficial effects are not felt for two to three weeks, making it difficult to persuade patients to keep taking them, and medication must continue after improvements in mood are achieved, as 50 per cent relapse if they stop taking them. Modified tricyclics, like *lofepramine*, cause fewer side effects.

- Prozac produces fewer side effects, but is linked to violent acts and suicide. Victims and families of killers have sued the manufacturer in 200 court cases. 250,000 people taking Prozac have attempted suicide, with 25,000 succeeding.

- Another SSRI, Seroxat, is also controversial. It is taken by between 600,000 and 800,000 people in Britain, but in 2003 was banned for under-18s because of an increased suicide risk. The ban applies to all SSRIs except Prozac. Townsend (2004) reported that it is still being prescribed to under-18s, despite the ban.

- Depressed people selected for clinical trials are usually only moderately depressed, not suicidal and free from other disorders, making accurate evaluation of antidepressants difficult. Assigning depressives to placebo conditions and therefore depriving them of possibly effective treatments is ethically problematic.

continued ...

...continued

- Research indicates that the placebo effects of drug treatment is high, suggesting a psychological rather than biological effect.
- Antidepressant drugs are cost-effective, occur in tablet form, are a familiar and trusted form of treatment and have the added benefit of being self-administered.
- Research indicates that psychological treatments are more effective than antidepressants, but such treatments are not favoured as they are more costly.

Electroconvulsive therapy

Electroconvulsive therapy (ECT) was originally introduced as a treatment for schizophrenia by Cerletti (1938), but quickly became a standard treatment for depression. ECT involves administering a shock, lasting about 1 second, of 70 to 150 volts, through electrodes on the temples, producing a seizure lasting up to 1 minute. Bilateral shocks, to both sides of the head, are more effective than unilateral shocks, to one side of the head, but produce more side effects. Modern forms of ECT use mild shocks for very brief periods, about two to three times a week for around eight treatments, along with an anaesthetic and a muscle relaxant to prevent bone fractures. Sometimes ECT treatments continue every 2 to 4 weeks for another 6 months, to prevent relapse.

ECT usage declined in the 1950s with the introduction of psychotropic drugs, but is regarded as a useful treatment for cases of depression non-responsive to other treatments, which incur poor quality of life and/or a heightened risk of suicide.

ECT is a controversial treatment; it seems brutal and has side effects, such as temporary memory loss, which become more severe as treatments continue. It is not clear how ECT works, but modern forms are more humane and are deemed to be an appropriate treatment when other treatments have failed, or when a patient is perceived as a high suicide risk.

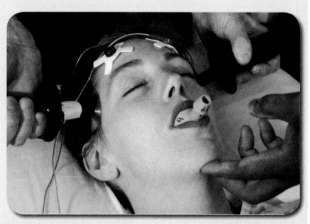

Figure 9.09 ECT is often used when other treatments for depression have failed

Research: electroconvulsive therapy

- Sackheim (1989) reviewed studies of ECT, finding real treatments to be more effective than simulated ones, bilateral treatments more effective than unilateral ones, ECT more effective than medication and the most effective treatment for severe depression, though medication is required post-treatment to prevent relapse.

- Paguin *et al.* (2008) performed a meta-analysis of ECT, comparing studies of ECT, placebos and antidepressant drugs, finding ECT to be superior, suggesting that it is a valid therapy for depression, including severe and resistant forms.

- Levy (1968) compared bilateral with unilateral forms of ECT, finding that unilateral treatments incurred less memory loss, but bilateral treatments produced slightly better relief of depressive symptoms.

- Antunes *et al.* (2009) reviewed studies on the effectiveness of ECT, symptom remission, patients' perceptions, cognitive impairments and quality of life, finding ECT to be more effective than antidepressants, with remission rates between 50 and 80 per cent, quality of life improved and patients having positive perceptions of the treatment, implying that ECT is an appropriate treatment, especially since improvements in its procedure were introduced.

- Taylor (2007) found that ECT produces a response rate of 55 per cent in people with depression, and a response rate of 80 to 90 per cent when it is used as an initial treatment for severe depression.

Evaluation

Electroconvulsive therapy

- The side effects of ECT are more severe with children, adolescents, the elderly and pregnant women, and should not be used as a treatment for these categories of people, unless as a last resort.

- Use of ECT declined in the USA between 1975 and 1986, from 58,667 to 36,558 patients, due to the introduction of new-generation antidepressants and negative media reports. However, from 1987 to 1992, the use of ECT rose from 4.2 to 5.1 per 10,000 individuals, suggesting that the treatment is seen more favourably and that new-generation antidepressants are not as effective as was originally hoped.

- Coffey (1998) argued that patients should be evaluated to a set criteria before ECT is prescribed, including a review of previous psychiatric history, a medical evaluation to define risk factors, gaining of informed consent, appropriate diagnostic tests and a review of any previous ECT treatments.

- Aside from side effects like memory loss, ECT also has high relapse rates. Sackheim *et al.* (2001) reported that 84 per cent of patients relapsed within 6 months, implying that the treatment is not effective in the long term. Bregin (1997) found that the benefits of ECT only lasted 4 weeks, with high relapse rates.

Psychological therapies

Cognitive behavioural therapy

Cognitive behavioural therapy (CBT) is the main psychological treatment used with individuals suffering from depression. The idea behind CBT is that beliefs, expectations and cognitive assessments of self, the environment and the nature of personal problems affect how individuals perceive themselves and others, how problems are approached, and how successful individuals are in coping and attaining goals. Therefore, CBT assists patients in identifying irrational and maladaptive thoughts and altering them. As behaviour is perceived as being generated by thinking, the most logical and effective way of changing maladaptive behaviour is to change the maladaptive thinking underlying it. Thoughts are perceived as affecting emotions and behaviour, so are modified to reduce depressive symptoms. Drawings are employed, illustrating links between thoughts, actions and emotions, with understanding where symptoms originate from being useful in reducing anxiety. Treatment entails one or two sessions of CBT every 2 weeks for around 15 sessions.

With CBT, therapists and patients work together to verify reality. If a patient makes the negative statement, 'I'm a bad parent, because my children misbehave', the therapist encourages the patient to assess its truth and examine the idea that someone is a bad parent because children are sometimes naughty. Patients therefore become more objective, more able to distinguish fact from fiction, and do not perceive things in extreme terms.

After an initial *education phase*, where individuals learn about the relationships between, thoughts, emotions and behaviour, *behavioural activation* and *pleasant event scheduling* is introduced, aimed at increasing

physiological activity and engagement in social and other rewarding activities – for instance, socialising with others. Cognitive factors are then addressed, after patients have experienced improvement in mood or energy, by being taught to identify faulty thinking responsible for low mood and to challenge these thoughts. Between sessions, patients are given goals to boost self-esteem. These involve *hypothesis testing* of negative thoughts through behavioural coping skills – for instance, testing the belief that they are incapable of being included in conversations by talking to strangers in social situations. Therapists only set tasks they are confident patients can succeed at; failure reinforces the ineptness patients believe in. To prevent relapse, a few 'booster' sessions are given in the subsequent year.

Research: cognitive behavioural therapy

- Whitfield and Williams (2003) found that CBT had the strongest research base for effectiveness, but recognised that there is a problem in the National Health Service being able to deliver weekly face-to-face sessions for patients. They suggested that this could be addressed by introducing self-help versions of the treatment, like the SPIRIT course, which teaches core cognitive behavioural skills using structured self-help materials.

- The Department of Health (2001) reviewed research papers of treatments for depression, including behavioural, cognitive, humanistic and psychotherapeutic ones, finding CBT to be the most effective, but did not endorse the use of CBT alone, as other treatments, like behavioural therapy, were effective too.

- The National Institute for Mental Health (1994) found CBT to be less effective than antidepressant drugs and other psychological therapies in treating depression, though there is a problem in using assessment methods with CBT that were specifically designed to investigate the worth of biologically based drug treatments.

- Flannaghan *et al.* (1997) used a questionnaire to identify stroke victims who had developed clinical depression. Nineteen patients were then given CBT sessions for 4 months, resulting in reduced symptoms, suggesting CBT to be a suitable treatment for specific groups of depressed people.

Evaluation

Cognitive behavioural therapy

- CBT is the most effective psychological treatment for moderate and severe depression, and one of the most effective treatments where depression is the main problem. It also has few side effects.

- For patients with difficulty concentrating – often problematic for people with depression – CBT can be unsuitable, leading to feelings of being overwhelmed and disappointed, which strengthens depressive symptoms rather than reducing them.

- CBT, as with all 'talking therapies', is not suitable for patients who have difficulties talking about inner feelings, or for those without the verbal skills to do so.

- Although evidence finds CBT effective, there is little research assessing its cost-effectiveness against other treatments.

Behavioural therapies

Behavioural therapies are based on the idea that depression is acquired through environmental experience and can be modified through learning theory principles, such as operant conditioning and social learning. Reinforcements, in the form of rewards for desirable behaviour, are used to elevate mood and encourage participation in positive behaviours, while social reinforcements, in the form of family members and social networks, are utilised to provide support for depressed individuals. Use is also made of social models, who demonstrate desirable behaviours to be imitated.

Behavioural activation therapy (BAT) is a powerful and progressive therapy that steers away from the idea that depression is an illness or weakness, instead perceiving the disorder as an indication of the things in an individual's life that need to change. Exercises are used that help people with depression to concentrate on activities delivering feelings of joy and mastery. A schedule of activities is built up that sufferers need to participate in to create normal and satisfying lives. BAT offers quick relief from depression, connecting patients with simple, naturally occurring reinforcements that seek to change how they approach day-to-day activities, make life choices and deal with crises.

Social skills training (SST) is a form of behaviour therapy that helps those who have difficulties in relating to others, a frequent feature of patients suffering from depression. Individuals lacking social skills can have difficulties in building networks of supportive friends and become increasingly socially isolated, increasing the risk of becoming depressive. SST operates on the principle that when patients improve their social skills, levels of self-esteem increase and others respond more favourably to them. A key goal is to improve the ability to function in everyday social situations. Patients are taught to alter behaviour patterns by practising selected behaviours in individual or group therapy sessions.

Research: behavioural therapies

- Houghton *et al.* (2008) evaluated the effectiveness of BAT on 42 patients with self-reported depression, finding the treatment effective, tolerable and possessing a low dropout rate.

- De Jong-Meyer and Hautzinger (1996) assessed Coping with Depression, a course of group therapy treatment based on BAT, finding that it achieved comparable acute outcome and better long-term outcome than antidepressant medication, indicating that the therapy provides clinicians with a convenient, cost-effective treatment that can be tailored to the individual needs of patients.

- Herson *et al.* (1984) reported that social skills treatments are equal in effectiveness to traditional psychotherapies in addressing the symptoms of depression.

- La Fromboise and Rowe (1983) found that structured learning therapy, a treatment based on SST, is more readily employable for different groups of patients than traditional psychotherapies, and improves the psychosocial functioning of people of varying ages and ethnic backgrounds, as well as proving useful in treating those who have difficulties with traditional psychotherapy.

Evaluation

Behavioural therapies

- BAT is a useful treatment for depression, as it can be successfully modified for use with different groups of patients with very different needs, such as the elderly or adolescents.
- BAT compares favourably with cognitive behavioural therapy, producing a similar success level of 50 per cent immediately after treatment, reducing to 25 per cent after 2 years. As BAT is a simpler method of treatment, it is arguably more effective than CBT.
- Therapists using SST should progress slowly, so patients are not overwhelmed by attempting to change too many behaviours at once, which may intensify feelings of social incompetence and deepen depression rather than reducing it.
- One problem with SST is the difficulty in generalising newly learned social skills to real-life situations. Generalisation occurs more readily when SST has a clear focus and patients are highly motivated to reach realistic goals, with skills taught being suitable for specific patients.

Strengthen your learning

1. Outline the clinical characteristics of depression.
2. Outline the symptoms of depression, explaining the differences between clinical and chronic depression.
3. With reference to research evidence, is the diagnosis of depression:
   i) reliable?
   ii) valid?
4a. What evidence is there for depression being genetic?
4b. Aside from research evidence, what other evaluative points can be made about the genetic explanation?
5a. Outline the biochemical explanation of depression.
5b. To what extent can the biochemical explanation be supported?
6a. Outline the behaviourist explanation of depression.
6b. What degree of research support is there for the behaviourist explanation?
7a. Outline the cognitive explanation of depression.
7b. Construct an evaluation of the cognitive explanation, including reference to research evidence.
8a. What effects do drugs have on depression?
8b. Explain the strengths and weakness of drug treatments.
9. Is ECT an effective treatment for depression? Give details.
10a. Describe CBT as a treatment for depression.
10b. Evaluate CBT's effectiveness.
11. Is psychotherapy an effective treatment of depression? Give details.

Assessment Check

1. Outline one biological and one psychological explanation for depression. (8 marks)

2. Evaluate issues surrounding the classification and diagnosis of depression. (16 marks)

3. Outline the clinical characteristics of depression. (8 marks)

4. Evaluate one psychological and one biological therapy for depression. (16 marks)

5. Discuss biological explanations for depression. (24 marks)

Examination guidance

To access the top band of marks in question 1, a reasonable balance must be achieved between the two explanations.

In question 2, only evaluative material will be creditworthy, with reference to the degree of support from research evidence into reliability and validity being a good way to achieve this.

Question 3 requires a 'longer version' outline of clinical characteristics, as 8 marks are available.

The evaluation in question 4 could be achieved by reference to research evidence, as well as comparing the two therapies in terms of strengths and weaknesses.

The term 'discuss' in question 5 means to describe and evaluate. At least two biological explanations must be presented; less depth will be expected if more than two are covered.

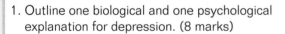
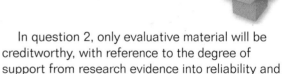

Anxiety disorders

(Phobias and obsessive-compulsive disorder (OCD) are both covered here, but only one needs to be studied to guarantee being able to answer the unit 4 examination question on anxiety disorders. Both can be studied if desired, of course. For each explanation and therapy, both biological and psychological, material is offered first on phobic disorders and then on OCD.)

Clinical characteristics

Anxiety disorders have the shared characteristic of fear. Although sometimes it is healthy to be anxious – for example, in threatening situations – one in five people will at some time experience anxiety levels so high that they become maladaptive, their anxiety negatively affecting day-to-day functioning.

Phobic disorders are characterised by uncontrollable, extreme, irrational and enduring fears, involving anxiety levels beyond any actual risk. Many sufferers attempt to deal with the condition themselves, so it is difficult to estimate what the occurrence rate of phobic disorders is. Phobic disorders are twice as common among females, and around 10 per cent of the population suffer from a specific phobia at some point, with most phobias originating in childhood and diminishing in strength during adulthood. Agoraphobia, a fear of open spaces, is common, often occurring with panic disorder, where sufferers endure panic first, with the anxiety generated making them feel vulnerable about being in open spaces. Social phobias are also widespread, involving overanxiety about being in social environments, like talking in public or eating in restaurants. Simple phobias occur where sufferers have fears of specific things and environments, like astraphobia, an extreme fear of thunderstorms, or pediophobia, a severe fear of dolls.

Animal phobias have the earliest onset, followed by other simple phobias, social phobias and then agoraphobia.

> ## Key terms
>
> **Anxiety disorders** – abnormal conditions characterised by extreme worry, fear and nervousness
> **Phobias** – anxiety disorders characterised by extreme irrational fears
> **Obsessive-compulsive disorder** – anxiety disorder characterised by persistent, recurrent, unpleasant thoughts and repetitive, ritualistic behaviours

Figure 9.10 Pediophobia is a severe fear of dolls

Obsessive-compulsive disorder (OCD) occurs in about 2 per cent of the population, with sufferers enduring persistent and intrusive thoughts occurring as obsessions, compulsions or a combination of both.

Obsessions consist of forbidden or inappropriate ideas and visual images, leading to feelings of extreme anxiety, whereas compulsions consist of intense, uncontrollable urges to repetitively perform tasks and behaviours, like constantly cleaning door handles. Most OCD sufferers understand that their compulsions are inappropriate, but cannot exert conscious control over them, resulting in even greater levels of anxiety.

Both phobias and OCD are exaggerated versions of normal behaviour and are perceived as mental disorders when they become detrimental to everyday functioning – for instance, when an agoraphobic's fear of open spaces means they cannot leave home to go to work.

Symptoms

Phobic disorders

- Persistent, excessive fear – high levels of anxiety due to the presence or anticipation of the feared object or situation.

- Fear from exposure to phobic stimulus – immediate fear response, even panic attack, due to presentation of the phobic object or situation.

- Recognition of exaggerated anxiety – sufferers are aware that levels of anxiety are overstated.

- Avoidant/anxiety response – feared objects and situations are avoided or lead to high-anxiety responses.

- Disruption of functioning – anxiety/avoidance responses are so extreme that they severely interfere with the ability to conduct everyday working and social functioning.

Subtypes

Phobias are divisible into simple phobias, social phobias and agoraphobia. Simple phobias are also divisible into subtypes:

1. **Animal phobias** – for example, arachnophobia (fear of spiders)

2. **Injury phobias** – for example, haematophobia (fear of blood)

3. **Situational phobias** – for example, aerophobia (fear of flying)

4. **Natural environment phobias** – for example, hydrophobia (fear of water).

Obsessive-compulsive disorder

Obsessions

- Recurrent and persistent – recurrently experienced thoughts, impulses and images that are inappropriate and intrusive, leading to high levels of anxiety and distress.

- Irrelevant to real life – thoughts, impulses and images experienced are not relevant to real-life situations.

- Suppressed – sufferers attempt to suppress thoughts, impulses and images with alternative thoughts or actions.

- Recognised as self-generated – sufferers understand that their obsessional thoughts, impulses and images are self-invented and not inserted externally.

Compulsions

- Repetitive – sufferers feel compelled to repeat behaviours and mental acts in response to obsessional thoughts, impulses and images.

- Aimed at reducing distress – behaviours and mental acts are an attempt to reduce distress or prevent feared events, even though there is little chance of doing so.

Other symptoms

- Recognised as excessive – sufferers realise that obsessions/compulsions are excessive.

- Time-consuming – obsessions/compulsions are time-consuming, cause distress and interfere with the ability to conduct everyday working and social functioning.

- Not related to substance abuse – disorder is not related to substance abuse or other medical condition.

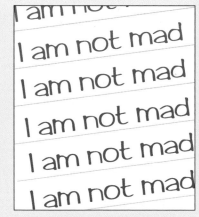

Figure 9.11 OCD is characterised by repetitive behaviours

Issues surrounding classification and diagnosis

(Refer to pages 315–16 for an explanation of classification systems and the reliability and validity of diagnosis.)

Research: reliability

Phobias

- Silverman *et al.* (2001) examined the test-retest reliability of phobic disorders in 62 children aged between 7 and 16 years. The Anxiety Disorders Interview Schedule (ADIS) for DSM IV was administered twice, with an interval of 7 to 14 days, with results indicating reliability for simple and social phobias.

- Mataix-Cols *et al.* (2005) studied the reliability of the Work and Social Adjustment Scale (WSAS), finding internal consistency high, with WSAS consistently measuring work and social adjustment, though simple phobics had less consistent ratings across WSAS items, suggesting that some items were less relevant to their disorder.

- Alstrom *et al.* (2009) assessed the inter-rater reliability of phobic disorder diagnosis in Swedish patients, finding that inter-rater reliability had around a 90 per cent concurrence rate.

Obsessive-compulsive disorder

- Geller *et al.* (2006) assessed the reliability of the Child Behaviour Checklist in the diagnosis of OCD in children, finding it reliable and possessing psychometric properties that identified children with OCD.

- Di Nardo and Barlow (1987) found that diagnosis of OCD had an excellent 80 per cent diagnostic reliability, second only to simple phobias among anxiety and mood disorders.

- Using Likert scales, Foa *et al.* (1987) obtained large correlations among patients', therapists' and independent observers' ratings of OCD features, including avoidance and compulsion severity, suggesting good inter-rater reliability.

Evaluation

Reliability

Phobias

- Silverman and Saavedra (1998) believed that the use of diagnostic interview procedures greatly enhances the inter-rater reliability of diagnoses.

- Assessment of inter-rater reliability generally involves one rater interviewing and another observing the same interview either live or on video. Therefore, both diagnoses are based on identical information and, not surprisingly, generate high levels of reliability. A better method would be for one rater to perform an interview and the second rater to perform a separate independent interview on the same patient.

- Research studies differ in the assessment of reliability even when identical measuring scales are used. Early assessments of ADIS found low levels of reliability for phobic disorders, while later studies found high levels, suggesting that it was the revision of measuring scales that led to improved reliability of diagnosis.

Obsessive-compulsive disorder

- The high prevalence of OCD in young people and the secretive nature of the disorder, which leads to its under-recognition, as well as the lack of specialised child psychiatry services in many areas, suggests the acute need for a simple, quick, reliable diagnostic tool to identify cases.

- The American Psychiatric Association (1987) reported that, compared to other anxiety disorders, the diagnostic reliability of OCD was relatively favourable.

- OCD has easily observable symptoms, which assist in clear diagnosis of the disorder and thus contribute to high levels of reliability (the same can be argued for the diagnosis of phobias).

Research: validity

Phobias

- Herbert *et al.* (1992) assessed the descriptive validity of social phobias, comparing them with avoidant personality disorder (APD) on a number of variables, including anxiety levels and social skills. They found that social phobias and APD represented quantitatively but not qualitatively distinct disorders, suggesting that social phobias are not a separate disorder.

- Eysenck (1997) found poor descriptive validity, reporting that 65 per cent of patients with an anxiety disorder also had other anxiety disorders, implying that subtypes of anxiety disorders are not independent of each other.

- Vasey and Dadds (2001) tested the predictive validity of anxiety disorder diagnoses, finding few differences in treatment outcomes for the different subgroups, suggesting low predictive validity.

Obsessive-compulsive disorder

- Assessing the validity of diagnosis of OCD, Leckman and Chittenden (1990) found that up to 50 per cent of Tourette's syndrome patients also had OCD, suggesting that OCD is not a separate disorder.

- Scahill *et al.* (1997) assessed the validity of the Children's Yale-Brown Obsessive Compulsive Scale, applying it to 65 children and adolescents with OCD. They found that validity was influenced by age and the difficulties involved with integrating data from parental and patient sources.

- Deacon and Abramovitz (2004) tested the validity of the Yale-Brown Obsessive Compulsive Scale [Y-BOCS], the gold-standard measure of OCD, by applying it to 100 patients with a diagnosis of OCD. They found problems with the Y-BOCS sub-scales' ability to accurately measure the components of OCD, suggesting that the scales need revision.

Evaluation

Validity

Phobias

- The predictive validity of diagnostic systems relating to children's anxiety disorders has not been subjected to much research, and those studies carried out indicate little evidence of childhood anxiety disorders predicting different outcomes, suggesting low predictive validity.

- Validation of diagnostic scales is important not only in proving the criteria valid in themselves, but because the diagnostic scales can then be used to further assess the validity of other diagnostic measures.

- Rabung *et al.* (2009) believed that self-rating instruments are valid measuring tools of phobic anxiety, as they are sensitive to change, suitable for clinical use and cost-effective, because they can be downloaded free from the internet.

Obsessive-compulsive disorder

- Diagnoses of OCD have long-term negative effects on sufferers' lives, yet such diagnoses are made with little evidence of the disorder existing as a separate condition.

- Although evidence indicates that many measuring scales used to assess OCD are not valid, they are still regarded as the most effective assessment tool in determining diagnostic and treatment outcomes.

- Thordarson *et al.* (2003) reported that the revision of measuring scales for OCD will lead to more valid diagnoses, which is desirable if it leads to a better understanding of the disorder.

Biological explanations

Genetics

Historically, research has used twin and family studies to assess what role genetics plays in the causation of anxiety disorders. Results indicate some genetic influence, though one problem with such studies is separating out environmental influences.

Technology now allows gene-mapping studies to be undertaken. This involves comparing genetic material from families with high and low incidences of anxiety disorders. Results from gene mapping indicate particular genes to be involved, making some individuals more vulnerable than others in developing such disorders. Therefore, genes probably do not cause anxiety disorders on their own; indeed, if they did, the concordance rate between MZ twins would be 100 per cent, which it is not.

Research: genetics

Phobias

- Reich and Yates (1988) interviewed social phobics attending an anxiety treatment clinic and used information on first-degree relatives to assess the inheritance of the disorder, finding the rate of social phobia to be higher in relatives of social phobics (6.6 per cent) than in relatives of non-social phobic controls (2.2 per cent), suggesting some genetic influence.

- Kendler *et al.* (1992) examined 2,163 female twin pairs, finding a 24.4 per cent concordance rate for social phobia in MZ twins, compared to only 15.3 per cent for DZ twins, suggesting a genetic influence.

- Gelertner *et al.* (2004) conducted a gene-mapping study on sufferers of social phobias, finding a link to social phobias for various markers of chromosome 16, with additional interest also centred on chromosomes 9, 14 and 18, suggesting evidence of a genetic component to the disorder.

- Ost (1992) found that 64 per cent of blood/injection phobics had a first-degree relative who also had the disorder, compared to a 3 per cent rate in the general population, suggesting a genetic component to the disorder.

Figure 9.12 Some people may have a genetic fear of snakes, while others plainly experience no such fear

Obsessive-compulsive disorder

- Lenane *et al.* (1990) performed a study into the prevalence of OCD among related family members, finding evidence for the existence of heritable contributions to the onset of the disorder, lending support to the genetic viewpoint.

- Grootheest *et al.* (2005) reviewed 70 years of twin studies into OCD, finding a heritability rate of between 45 and 65 per cent for OCD in children, and between 27 and 47 per cent in adults, suggesting a genetic contribution.

- Samuels *et al.* (2007) used gene mapping to compare OCD sufferers who exhibited compulsive hoarding behaviour with those who did not, finding a link to chromosome 14 marker D14S588, implying a genetic influence to compulsive hoarding behaviour, which may also indicate the existence of separate OCD subtypes.

- Stewart *et al.* (2007) performed gene mapping on OCD patients and family members, finding that a variant of the OLIG-2 gene commonly occurred, which suggests a genetic link to the condition.

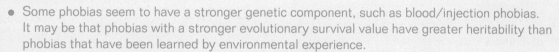

Evaluation

Genetics

Phobias

- Some phobias seem to have a stronger genetic component, such as blood/injection phobias. It may be that phobias with a stronger evolutionary survival value have greater heritability than phobias that have been learned by environmental experience.

- Although research indicates some genetic involvement in the onset of phobic disorders, the evidence is stronger for other mental disorders, such as schizophrenia.

- A case can be made for the onset of phobic disorders as involving the *diathesis-stress model*, where individuals can be seen as inheriting different degrees of vulnerability, but with environmental triggers ultimately determining whether an individual goes on to develop the disorder.

- Although evidence from twin and family studies suggests a genetic influence, it may be that related individuals acquire phobias through similar environmental experiences, or through imitation.

Obsessive-compulsive disorder

- Pato *et al.* (2001) reported that a substantial amount of evidence suggests that OCD is a heritable condition, but that few details are understood about actual genetic mechanisms underpinning the disorder. It is hoped that ongoing molecular genetic analyses might yield details.

- Weissman (1985) noted that the tendency for anxiety disorders, such as OCD, to run in families was first observed over a century ago; therefore, such an idea is not new and has greatly influenced subsequent research.

- Evidence from family and twin studies indicates that genetic factors are at work in the expression of some forms of OCD, especially obsessions about contamination, aggression and religion, and compulsions involving washing, ordering and arranging.

- The fact that family members often display dissimilar OCD symptoms – for example, a child arranging dolls and an adult constantly washing dishes – weakens support for the genetic viewpoint; if the disorder was inherited, then exhibited behaviours could be expected to be the same.

Evolutionary explanations

Historical evidence indicates that anxiety disorders have been around for a very long time. The fact that they continue to be apparent in the population suggests that anxiety disorders have an adaptive value and therefore an evolutionary basis. If the disorder had no useful purpose, natural selection would have selected it out and the condition would no longer exist. So rather than perceiving anxiety disorders in maladaptive terms, evolution views the disorder as fulfilling a beneficial purpose.

Biological preparedness is a concept introduced by Seligman (1971), which sees animals possessing an innate ability to display certain fears because they possess an adaptive value linked to survival and reproduction abilities. Thus animals develop some conditioned fears more readily – for example, a dread of snakes – as they would have constituted a serious threat in the Pleistocene era when most evolution occurred. Such fears have genetic and environmental components, as phobias have to be learned from environmental experience, with the predisposition to learn the fear being the inherited component.

Phobias serve several adaptive functions – for example, the fear element of phobias can result in cessation of movement, immobilising individuals and aiding concealment from predators, just as a flight response would help individuals to outrun predators. Alternatively, fear could make individuals submit to dominant

aggressors, saving them from harm. Fear responses even cause the release of hormones aiding the clotting of blood, helping to heal wounds, as well as stimulating the liver to release glucose to provide energy, important in facilitating flight or fight.

OCD involves repetitive behaviours, like washing and grooming, and these would have protected against infection. Other similar behaviours may have increased vigilance and alertness, again incurring a survival value. Thus behaviours like continually cleaning door handles can be regarded as exaggerations of prehistoric adaptations.

Research: evolutionary explanations

Phobias

- Garcia and Koelling (1966) found that rats quickly learned not to drink a sweet-tasting liquid paired with an injection that made them sick, as this is a natural adaptive response, but did not develop such a taste aversion when the sweet-tasting liquid was paired with an electric shock, as this would not be an adaptive response – electric shocks not being apparent in the EEA – thus supporting the idea of biological preparedness.

- Cook and Mineka (1989) demonstrated to laboratory-raised monkeys the fear response of a wild monkey to a snake and a rabbit. Subsequently, the laboratory-raised monkeys showed a similar fear response to a toy snake, but not a toy rabbit, suggesting an evolutionary readiness to fear snakes, but not rabbits.

- Rakison (2009) found that 11-month-old girls learned more quickly than boys to associate negative facial emotions with snakes and spiders. There was no gender difference for fear-irrelevant objects like mushrooms, suggesting an evolutionary basis to the fact that four times as many females have snake and spider phobias, as they are more likely to encounter snakes and spiders while foraging.

Obsessive-compulsive disorder

- Polimeni (2005) reported that OCD tendencies like counting and checking carry the potential to benefit society, suggesting an ancient form of behavioural specialisation with evolutionary origins.

- Abed and Pauw (1998) believed that OCD is an exaggerated form of an evolved ability to foresee situations and predict the outcome of one's own thoughts and behaviour, so that dangerous scenarios can be coped with before they happen, suggesting that OCD helps in the avoidance of harm.

- Marks and Nesse (1984) believed that lacking concern for others incurs a risk of ostracism from social groups, so because many OCD sufferers have concern for the welfare of others, this risk is reduced, suggesting an adaptive value.

- Chepko-Sade et al. (1989) found that rhesus monkeys who performed the most grooming of others were retained within a group following group in-fighting, suggesting that OCD tendencies have an adaptive value, as continued group membership is crucial to survival.

Evaluation

Evolutionary explanations

Phobias

- Learned helplessness explains why it is harder to develop fears of dangerous, modern-day objects and situations, like guns, because they were not around in the EEA and thus are not coded into human genes.

- Some phobias are so bizarre and individual that they are best explained as purely conditioned responses, rather than having an evolved component.

- Evolutionary explanations of phobias can be regarded as deterministic, as they tend not to account for individual and cultural differences.

- Davey (2004) did not believe that humans have an evolutionary fear of snakes and spiders, but instead an evolutionary disgust of them as they are linked in many cultures to disease.

Obsessive-compulsive disorder

- Behavioural features of OCD, like precision and hoarding, would be beneficial in hunting and foraging, and therefore useful in the EEA; they remain now due to genome lag, where genes take time to evolve and fit current environments.

- Evolutionary explanations of OCD may help clinicians and patients to gain a better understanding of causes and symptoms that lead to effective therapies.

- There is a common-sense value to OCD having occurred through the process of evolution and thus having a genetic basis, leading to neuroanatomical and biochemical influences.

- Saad (2006) believed that OCD may be overactivation of warning systems of evolutionary importance. Therefore, gender differences in OCD reflect the evolutionary differences in male/female priorities like mating and parenting.

Figure 9.13 Behavioural features of OCD, like hoarding, would have had an adaptive advantage in the EEA

Classic research

Bennett-Levy and Marteau (1984)

Fear of animals. What is prepared?

Evolutionary explanations see phobias as having a survival value; if they did not, natural selection would have selected them out long ago. So instead of being maladaptive, the evolutionary view sees phobias as of benefit. The researchers here tested this idea by rating human fear responses to various animals.

Aim

To investigate biological 'preparedness' for fear and its relationship to specific characteristics of different animals.

To investigate whether people are more afraid of and avoid animals that move quickly or abruptly and differ in form to humans.

Procedure

One hundred and thirteen mixed gender participants were randomly assigned to one of two self-report groups.

Sixty-four participants completed a questionnaire, rating questions related to fear and avoidance of 29 small harmless animals using the following scales:

- Fear scale: 1–3 (1 = not afraid, 3 = very afraid)
- Nearness: 1–5 rating of closeness of contact they would accept (1 = enjoy picking it up, 5 = move further away than 6 feet).

Forty-nine participants completed a different questionnaire, rating the same 29 animals on four perceptual dimensions of ugliness, sliminess, speed and sudden movement, using a 3-point rating (1 = not, 2 = quite, 3 = very).

Findings

- Females were less likely to pick up or approach ten of the species, including jellyfish, cockroaches, spiders and slugs.
- There were no gender differences in ratings of ugliness, sliminess, speediness or suddenness of movement.
- Rats were the most feared animal.

The four perceptual dimensions correlated with fear and nearness ratings:

- Ugly animals were less likely to be approached closely.
- The more ugly an animal, the more fear it elicited.
- Slimy animals were less likely to be approached closely.
- The slimier an animal, the more fear it elicited.
- Speedy and sudden-moving animals were less likely to be approached closely and elicited greater fear, but this was less important than ugliness or sliminess.

Conclusions

Humans have innate preparedness in relation to perceptual properties of animals, rather than fear of specific animals.

The less that animals resemble humans, the more feared they are.

Phobias may develop as humans have an adaptive readiness to fear certain things more than others.

Evaluation

- Only imagined scenarios were used; actual behaviour was not investigated, lowering the validity of the findings.   *continued ...*

...continued

- Fear ratings were not supposed to be related to actual dangerousness – for example, the snake was a harmless grass snake. But subsequent questioning revealed that some ratings were rated by perceived harmfulness.
- Different perceptual characteristics suggest different desensitisation applications. People fear slugs as they are slimy, therefore therapy should involve slimy inanimate substances like porridge.

You are the researcher

Design a questionnaire that determines whether there is a gender difference in types of phobias experienced. You will need to think carefully about how to phrase questions so that you determine what phobias people suffer from.

Ensure that your questions also measure the intensity of phobias that people experience.

Compile a suitable results table and draw relevant conclusions from it.

Research in focus

Bennett-Levy and Marteau's (1984) study used questionnaires to measure animal phobias. Why is it a good idea to test questions with a pilot study?

Why do questionnaires often use 'filler' questions? Why is it considered good practice to start questionnaires with easy questions, saving more probing questions until later on? What are the strengths and weaknesses of questionnaires? How might quantitative and qualitative data be generated by questionnaires?

Psychological explanations

Although evidence indicates that biological factors are important in the onset of anxiety disorders, it is generally accepted that psychological factors are involved too.

Behavioural explanations

Classical conditioning sees phobias occurring through association of traumatic events with neutral stimuli, and resulting phobias becoming resistant to extinction because of avoidance responses made to evade feared objects or situations.

Operant conditioning then explains how phobias are maintained, as when avoidance responses are made; the fear element is reduced, reinforcing the avoidance responses, making them more likely to recur. If an individual has a phobia of the dark, due to a night-time traumatic event, then the person is likely to sleep with the lights on, reducing the fear element and increasing chances that the sufferer will again make the avoidance response and sleep with the lights on.

Operant conditioning can also explain the maintenance of OCD; when sufferers experience anxiety, for instance, about dirt and infection, washing door handles is reinforcing, as it reduces anxiety, making the behaviour likely to recur.

Skinner's (1948) *superstition hypothesis* explains OCD as bodily actions becoming associated with reinforcers and thus being repeated – for example, not stepping on the cracks in the pavement becomes associated with anxiety reduction.

Social learning theory (SLT) explains phobias as occurring through observation and imitation, as watching others experience traumatic events can cause observers to subsequently experience the fear response in the presence of the same stimulus.

Research: behaviourist explanations

Phobias

- Watson and Rayner (1920) conditioned 'Little Albert' to fear white furry objects, pairing the neutral stimulus of a white rat with the unconditioned stimulus of a sudden loud noise to produce an innate fear response, demonstrating how phobias can be learned by classical conditioning.

- Gray (1975) used the *two-process theory* to explain how operant conditioning strengthens phobias acquired through classical conditioning. A phobia is learned by a specific event being paired with the fear response; then an avoidance response is learned that reduces the fear element, thus strengthening the avoidance response.

- Ost and Hugdahl (1981) reported the case of a boy who witnessed his grandfather vomit while dying and subsequently developed a persistent vomiting phobia, and even contemplated suicide when feeling nauseous, supporting the idea that phobias can be acquired vicariously through social learning.

Obsessive-compulsive disorder

- Meyer and Cheeser (1970) demonstrated how compulsions are learned responses, reducing the heightened anxiety levels brought on by obsessions, thus providing a behaviourist explanation for elements of the disorder.

- Einstein and Menzies (2003) gave 60 OCD patients the Magical Ideation Scale, which measures beliefs in magical thinking (see anomalistic psychology, p.466) and found a significant correlation between magical thinking and OCD symptoms, suggesting a link between superstition and OCD, in line with Skinner's superstition hypothesis.

- Carr (1974) found that ritualised behaviours are demonstrated when activity in a sufferer's autonomic nervous system (ANS) was heightened, such behaviour then leading to a reduction of arousal in the ANS, suggesting that such compulsive behaviours are reinforcing as they reduce anxiety levels associated with OCD.

Evaluation

Behaviourist explanations

Phobias

- The success of behaviourist treatments, like systematic desensitisation, in addressing phobic symptoms lends support to behaviourist explanations of phobias.

- The behaviourist viewpoint is weakened by the fact that not everyone experiencing traumatic events, like car accidents, goes on to develop a phobia.

- One strength of behaviourist explanations is that they can be combined with biological ones to give a better understanding of phobias. For instance, the idea of genetic vulnerability shows how some individuals are more susceptible to developing phobias through environmental experiences.

Obsessive-compulsive disorder

- Schwartz et al. (1996) reported behavioural therapies to be effective in reducing OCD symptoms, and also that they incur changes in biochemical activity, lending support to the behaviourist explanation.

continued ...

- The avoidance behaviours often characterising OCD, performed to reduce anxiety, like persistent washing, actually create more anxiety. Therefore, it is difficult to view such behaviours as reinforced responses, weakening the behaviourist viewpoint.
- Although certain OCD features are explained by behaviourism, intrusive thoughts, often a key feature, cannot be explained, again weakening the explanation.

Cognitive explanations

The cognitive viewpoint sees some people as being more vulnerable to developing anxiety disorders because of an attentional bias, where perception is focused more on anxiety-generating stimuli. For instance, phobics will concentrate more on threatening stimuli than non-phobics. People with anxiety disorders also tend to have maladaptive beliefs and thoughts about stimuli, like an overfull bath generating a belief that open taps are associated with flooding, which turns into a fear of open taps, which generalises to other scenarios of running water. Therefore, the maladaptive thinking is a reaction to an anxiety-generating situation, which then becomes a phobia. Once acquired, phobias can be maintained through cognitively rehearsing fear reactions, like thinking about phobic stimuli and their possible awful consequences, so that when stimuli are encountered, fear reactions are exaggerated.

The cognitive viewpoint of OCD sees sufferers having impaired, persistent thought processes, like the risk of infection in a given environment being much higher than in reality. Sufferers find it difficult to dismiss intrusive thoughts, leading to self-blame, depression and heightened anxiety, which in turn makes it even more difficult to dismiss such thoughts, and obsessions then occur as sufferers exaggerate the significance of intrusive thoughts. Behaviours that lessen impaired, obsessive thoughts become compulsive because of their anxiety-reducing qualities, and therefore they become difficult to control.

Research: cognitive explanations

Phobias

- Stopa and Clarke (1993) compared videotaped conversations with a confederate of social phobics, anxious controls and non-patient controls, finding that social phobics had more negative self-evaluative thoughts and systematically underestimated their performance, suggesting that they do not monitor other people's responses in social situations and their thoughts are not based on reality. This implies a cognitive bias to social phobias.

- Tomarken *et al.* (1989) investigated the role that distorted thinking plays in phobias. People with snake phobias were presented with slides of snakes and neutral objects such as trees and asked how many snakes, trees, and so on they had seen. Snake phobics overestimated the number of snakes compared to a control group, lending support to the cognitive explanation.

- Kindt and Brosschot (1997) found that arachnophobics took longer to name the ink colour of spider-related words when performing a Stroop test, lending support to the cognitive theory.

Figure 9.14 Snake phobics overestimate the number of snakes in a picture, suggesting a cognitive explanation

- Thorpe and Salkovskis (2000) assessed conscious beliefs related to exposure to phobic stimuli, finding a major role in specific phobics for cognitions (thinking) related to harm, suggesting the nature of specific phobias to be cognitive in origin.

Obsessive-compulsive disorder

- Barrett and Healey (2002) compared children with OCD with anxious children and non–clinic children, finding that OCD children had higher ratings of cognitive appraisals, such as probability and severity of events, and the fusion of thoughts with actions. This suggests that the cognitive conceptualisation of OCD occurs in childhood.

- Rachman and Hodges (1987) reported that some individuals are more susceptible to obsessional thinking because of increased vulnerability due to genetic factors, depression or poor socialisation experiences, which links cognitive factors with other explanations.

- Davison and Neale (1994) found that OCD patients cannot distinguish between fantasy and reality, lending support to the idea of faulty thinking processes being linked to OCD.

- Clark (1992) reported that intrusive thinking is significantly more common in OCD sufferers than in the normal population, again supporting the cognitive argument.

Evaluation

Cognitive explanations

Phobias

- Cognitive explanations can be regarded as superior to behaviourist ones, as they detail the thought processes underpinning phobias. However, phobias are still dependent in many instances on the role of direct conditioning experiences.

- One problem with the cognitive viewpoint is that it is not clear whether distorted and negative thinking cause a phobia, or are merely the effect of the phobia.

- The cognitive explanation is deterministic in that it perceives phobias as caused by psychological factors over which the sufferer has no control.

- The cognitive viewpoint can explain how a phobia is maintained, but not why it originated in the first place. For example, a phobia could be caused by conditioning or genetics and then is perpetuated by faulty thinking.

Obsessive-compulsive disorder

- As with phobias, it is not clear if maladaptive thinking is a cause or an effect of OCD.

- Cognitive treatments of OCD have proven effective by correcting cognitive bias and helping sufferers to become less vigilant, implying support for the cognitive model.

- The cognitive explanation does not really explain the emotional aspect of irrational beliefs, weakening support for the viewpoint.

- Conscious cognitive processing is not required for phobic responses. Ohman and Soares (1994) found that snake and spider phobics showed heightened physiological activity, indicative of anxiety, when shown pictures of phobic objects for periods so brief that participants could not consciously recognise them.

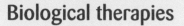

Biological therapies

Drug treatments

Although phobias tend to be treated mainly by psychological means, drug treatments that reduce symptoms of anxiety have proved useful. Anxiolytics are one group of drugs achieving this, such as the benzodiazepines (BZs), like Valium and Librium, which work by increasing the effect of the neurotransmitter GABA. BZs can have side effects though, like drowsiness and addiction.

Phobias can also be treated with antidepressants. Selective serotonin reuptake inhibitors (SSRIs) have a beneficial effect by elevating serotonin levels, while monoamine oxidase inhibitors (MAIOs) increase serotonin and noradrenaline levels.

Antidepressants such as SSRIs are also used to treat OCD, elevating levels of serotonin. Just as with phobias, anxiolytic drugs are used to treat OCD, due to their anxiety-lowering properties. Antipsychotic drugs that have a dopamine-lowering effect have also proved useful in treating OCD, though antidepressants affecting neurotransmitters other than serotonin have not proved effective.

Beta blockers have also had some success in reducing the physical symptoms of anxiety disorders. They work by countering the rise in blood pressure and heart rate often associated with anxiety, by lowering adrenaline and noradrenaline production.

Research: drug treatments

Phobias
- Slaap *et al.* (1996) treated 30 social phobics with the antidepressant SSRIs brofaromine and fluvoxamine, finding that 72 per cent of patients had reduced heart rate and blood pressure, suggesting that drug treatments are effective in lowering the physical symptoms of the disorder.

- Tyrer and Sternberg (1975) followed up for 1 year 26 agoraphobic and social phobic patients treated with the BZ drug phenelzine, during which time the patients either received further drug treatment or behaviour therapy. Drug treatment was effective, but acted mainly by suppressing symptoms, indicating some support for the use of drugs.

- Den Boer *et al.* (1994) reported considerable evidence indicating that MAOI inhibitors, like moclobemide, are effective in reducing social anxiety and social avoidance, though there is an increased risk of hypertension with their usage.

Obsessive-compulsive disorder
- Piccinelli *et al.* (1995) performed a meta-analysis of 36 studies, assessing the worth of antidepressants as a treatment for OCD, finding them effective in the short term, with 61 per cent showing improved symptoms with the tricyclic antidepressant clomipramine, and 28 per cent with newer SSRI medications, both treatments proving more beneficial than non-serotonergic drugs.

- Beroqvist *et al.* (1999) investigated the effect of low doses of the antipsychotic drug risperidone in treating OCD, finding treatment effective due to the drug's dopamine-lowering effect.

- Flament *et al.* (1985) tested the ability of the antidepressant drug clomipramine to address the symptoms of childhood OCD in 19 patients, finding the drug superior over a 5-week period to placebo treatment, lending support to the use of drug treatments.

Evaluation

Drug treatments

Phobias

- BZs should only be used as a short-term treatment to reduce symptoms while longer-term treatments take effect, because long-term BZ use can lead to tolerance effects and addiction.
- Aside from their addictive qualities, another problem with BZs is that once a patient stops taking them, they can experience a sharp rise in anxiety levels.
- Drug treatments have proved effective in reducing the physical symptoms of phobias so that psychological treatments can then be effectively applied.
- There are those within the psychiatric community who see the widespread use of drug treatments as being fuelled by the powerful influence of the drug-producing companies who stand to make huge profits from their application.

Obsessive-compulsive disorder

- It is not certain whether drug treatments effective in treating OCD reduce obsessive symptoms or lessen the depressive symptoms that often accompany the condition.
- Drug treatments cannot be regarded as a cure for OCD, as once drug taking stops, symptoms tend to reappear.
- Drug treatments are widely used to treat the symptoms of OCD, as they are a cost-effective and user-friendly form of treatment.
- Because of the risk of side effects and the tendency of antidepressants to produce heightened levels of suicidal thinking, plus the effectiveness of psychological treatments, it can be argued that drug treatments should not be used to treat OCD.

Psychosurgery

Psychosurgery (see also 'Psychology in Action' on page 318) is occasionally used for severe cases of anxiety disorders that are non-responsive to other forms of treatment, and where there is greatly reduced quality of life and/or risk of suicide. Psychosurgery is a last resort, reluctantly used, as it entails the usual risks associated with invasive surgery and involves irreversible destruction of brain tissue, without guarantees of success, and it can incur serious side effects, such as apathy and reduced intellect.

When used with OCD sufferers, psychosurgery involves destroying brain tissue to disrupt the cortico-striatal circuit by the use of radio frequency waves. This has an effect on the orbital-frontal cortex, the thalamus and the caudate nucleus brain areas, and is associated with a reduction in symptoms.

There has been a recent movement towards using deep-brain stimulation, which is more reversible, to treat severe cases of OCD. This generally involves the use of magnetic pulses on the supplementary motor area of the brain, which is associated with blocking out irrelevant thoughts and obsessions.

There are certain criteria that must be met before psychosurgery will be considered:

1. A clinical diagnosis of an anxiety disorder must have been made.

2. Severe symptoms that obstruct purposeful everyday living must be present.

3. Other treatments must have failed.

4. The patient must have given fully informed consent, with full knowledge of the procedure and the risks involved.

Various forms of psychosurgery are used, generally involving drilling holes in the skull so that heated probes can be inserted to burn away specific, small areas of brain tissue.

Research: psychosurgery

Phobias

- Marks *et al.* (1966) compared 22 severe agoraphobics who had modified frontal leucotomies, with matched cases who had other forms of treatment, finding that 5 years after treatment the leucotomies were superior in lessening symptoms than other treatments, and that personality changes were only mild, supporting the use of psychosurgery for such patients.

- Ruck *et al.* (2003) reported that patients who had capsulotomies performed for anxiety disorders, including severe social phobias, generally had large reductions in anxiety levels, demonstrating the technique to be effective, though some patients suffered severe side effects.

- Balon (2003) reported that thermocapsulotomy can be an effective treatment for selected cases of acute non-obsessive anxiety disorders, including phobias, but is an extreme option, as it carries a significant risk of severe side effects.

Obsessive-compulsive disorder

- Liu *et al.* (2008) followed up 35 OCD patients non-responsive to medications or psychological and behavioural treatments, who underwent stereotactic bilateral anterior capsulotomy psychosurgery. PET scans and questionnaires were used to find that 20 patients (57 per cent) became symptom-free, 10 (29 per cent) experienced significant improvements, while 5 (14 per cent) showed no improvements, suggesting the treatment to be safe and effective in treating OCD.

- Mallett *et al.* (2008) evaluated deep-brain stimulation of the subthalamic nucleus in 16 individuals with treatment-resistant OCD, comparing it with sham stimulation, and found significant symptom reduction, which suggests the treatment to be effective. This was supported by Greenberg *et al.* (2008), who found symptom reduction and functional improvement in 18 out of 26 OCD patients undergoing stimulation of the ventral internal capsule/ventral striatum brain area.

- Kelly and Cobb (1985) reported that 78 per cent of 49 patients suffering from OCD displayed improved symptoms 20 months after limbic leucotomies were performed, suggesting a good level of support for the treatment.

- Hindus *et al.* (1985) followed up gamma capsulotomy surgical cases 3 and 7 years after treatment, finding that only a few OCD patients showed improvements in their condition, suggesting that different forms of psychosurgery have vastly different success rates.

- Richter *et al.* (2004) reported that 30 per cent of OCD patients had a 35 per cent or greater reduction in symptoms on the Yale-Brown Obsessive-Compulsive Scale, but there were infrequent complications, such as urinary incontinence and seizures, demonstrating that although psychosurgery can be effective, it is not without its dangers.

Evaluation

Psychosurgery

Phobias

- Psychosurgery was a more common treatment before the advent of effective behavioural therapies. For most cases, it would not be prescribed nowadays, unless resistance is shown to other treatments and life outcome prospects are poor.

- It seems improbable that different mental symptoms can be relieved by one single form of operation on the brain, and that therefore only operations suitable for precise psychiatric diagnoses should be used.

- More modern-day forms of psychosurgery are targeted on localised, specific brain areas, which therefore avoid large-scale brain destruction, reducing the risks of irreversible side effects such as personality changes.

- The poor response rates to biological treatments, especially psychosurgery, suggest that most phobias do not have a strong biological component.

Obsessive-compulsive disorder

- Psychosurgery should only be used after patients have given fully informed consent. However, it is debatable whether patients with severe OCD can give fully informed consent, suggesting that there may be ethical problems in administering the treatment.

- Whether psychosurgery should be used generally involves a cost-benefit analysis, where the possible costs, such as irreversible side effects, should be compared against the possible benefits, like the lessening of symptoms detrimental to everyday functioning.

- Psychosurgery cannot be considered to be a cure for OCD, and patients who undergo neurosurgery will probably continue to need psychiatric support following the procedure, even if it is considered to be a success.

- OCD responds more positively to psychosurgery techniques, and the added success of deep brain stimulation in alleviating the condition supports the use of treating OCD by these means.

Psychological therapies

Behavioural therapies

Behavioural therapies aim to replace maladaptive behaviours with adaptive ones by using conditioning techniques.

Systematic desensitisation (SD) is the main behaviourist treatment for phobias. Developed by Wolpe (1958), SD is based on classical conditioning, with patients learning in stages to associate fear responses with feelings of calm, rather than previous associations between phobic objects/situations and fear. The two opposing emotions of anxiety and relaxation are perceived as incapable of coexisting simultaneously (*reciprocal inhibition*). SD uses a progressive, step-by-step approach to feared objects or situations and takes about a month to advance through the entire desensitisation hierarchy.

The hierarchy is constructed before treatment commences, going from least to most feared types of contact with phobic objects/situations, and patients are taught relaxation strategies for each stage of contact. Contact is normally achieved by imagining scenarios (*covert desensitisation*), but sometimes involves actual contact (*in vivo desensitisation*). Snake phobics may begin SD treatment by looking at a picture of snakes in a sealed tank, and progressively work through to actually holding one.

Another behaviourist therapy is *implosion* (*flooding*), where instead of a step-by-step approach, patients go straight to the top of the hierarchy and imagine, or have direct contact with, their most feared scenarios. Patients cannot make the usual avoidance responses and anxiety peaks at such high levels that it cannot be maintained and eventually subsides.

SD is also used to treat OCD, with sufferers first taught relaxation strategies and then introduced to objects/situations prompting their obsessions, and using relaxation strategies to lower their anxiety levels.

Exposure and response prevention (ERP) is another behaviourist treatment for OCD, where sufferers are introduced to objects/situations prompting their obsessions, but are not allowed to make the usual obsessive responses. The idea is that because OCD occurred through reinforcement, if anxiety-creating scenarios are avoided, reinforcement is prevented and relearning can occur. If OCD sufferers are prevented from obsessively sweeping up, they realise that the obsession which stimulated feelings of anxiety no longer does so.

Research: behavioural therapies

Phobias

- Jones (1924) used SD to eradicate 'Little Peter's' phobia of white fluffy animals and objects such as rabbits and cotton wool. The rabbit was presented to the patient at closer distances each time his anxiety levels subsided to permit movement to the next stage, and Peter was rewarded with food to develop a positive association towards the rabbit. Eventually he developed affection for the rabbit, which generalised onto similar animals and objects.

- Rothbaum *et al.* (1998) reported on virtual-reality exposure therapy, where patients are active participants within a computer-generated three-dimensional world that changes naturally with head movements. The advantage of this over normal SD and implosion is that treatment occurs without ever leaving the therapist's office, more control is gained over phobic stimuli and there is less exposure of patients to harm and embarrassment.

Figure 9.15 Mary Jones (1924) used systematic desensitisation to remove Little Peter's fear of white fluffy animals and objects

- Wolpe (1960) used implosion to remove a girl's phobia of driving in cars. The girl was forced into a car and driven around for 4 hours until her hysteria was eradicated, demonstrating the effectiveness of the treatment.

Obsessive-compulsive disorder

- Gertz (1966) reported that *in vivo* SD worked well with OCD patients, finding that 66 per cent of sufferers responded to treatment, suggesting that the treatment is effective.

- Lindsay *et al.* (1997) randomly assigned 18 OCD patients to either ERP or anxiety management programmes. After 3 weeks there was a significant reduction in symptoms for the ERP patients, but not for the control group, implying that symptom reduction results from the specific techniques of exposure and response prevention.

- Baer (1991) introduced a self-directed, step-by-step form of ERP that is equally as effective for mild forms of OCD as seeing a therapist, and can therefore be considered cost-effective.

Evaluation

Behavioural therapies

Phobias

- SD is mainly suitable for patients who are able to learn and use relaxation strategies, and who have imaginations vivid enough to conjure up images of feared objects/situations.

- Although patients can gradually confront phobias in an imaginary sense, there is no guarantee that this will work with actual objects/situations, suggesting *in vivo* treatment to be superior to covert desensitisation.

- There are ethical considerations with both SD and implosion, as they can both be psychologically harmful, though cost-benefit analyses may regard the long-term benefits of eradicating the phobia outweighing the short-term costs of distress.

Obsessive-compulsive disorder

- ERP can incur large dropout rates due to the high levels of anxiety it creates; therefore it is usually combined with drug treatment so anxiety levels are controllable.

- ERP is more effective than drug treatments as relapse rates are lower, suggesting that ERP brings long-term, lasting benefits.

- Even patients with long-lasting and severe OCD symptoms benefit from ERP treatment, as long as they are suitably motivated to improve. However, the treatment is less effective for patients who do not exhibit overt compulsions and those with moderate to severe depression.

Cognitive behavioural therapy

Cognitive behavioural therapy (CBT) is the most frequently used treatment for phobias and OCD, a testament to its effectiveness in itself. Treatments generally occur once every 7 to 14 days for about 15 sessions in total.

The aim of CBT is to help patients identify irrational and maladaptive thinking patterns and change them to rational, adaptive ones. Thinking is seen as underpinning feelings and behaviour, so by modifying modes of thought, feelings and behaviour should also change for the better. Sometimes the drawing of diagrams illustrating connections between thinking, emotions and behaviour are used to facilitate the process.

For snake phobias, for example, therapists would encourage phobics to express their beliefs about snakes and then challenge them with rational arguments. Patients would be encouraged to successfully interact with snakes and record details of their experiences that can be referred to if sufferers return to their irrational beliefs.

One specific form of CBT used with people suffering from phobias is cognitive behavioural group therapy (CBGT), where other group members offer support as a hierarchy of fears is worked through, using relaxation strategies at each step. The cognitive element of the treatment involves replacing irrational beliefs that generate anxiety with rational ones. Phobic situations are enacted, with group members challenging each other's irrational beliefs.

With OCD, CBT is directed at changing obsessional thinking, as with *habituation training*, where sufferers relive obsessional thoughts repeatedly to reduce the anxiety created. All types of maladaptive thoughts associated with OCD can be successfully addressed with CBT; *intrusive thoughts* are shown to be normal, and patients come to understand that thinking about a behaviour is not the same as actually doing it. Sufferers are taught to focus on their estimations of potential risks and realistically assess the likelihood of them occurring. Sufferers are encouraged to practise their new adaptive beliefs and to disregard their former maladaptive ones.

Research: cognitive behavioural therapy

Phobias

- Spence *et al.* (2000) assessed the value of CBT in treating 50 children with social phobias aged between 7 and 14 years. Child-focused CBT and CBT plus parental involvement were found to be effective in reducing social and general anxiety levels, and these improvements were retained at a 1-year follow-up, suggesting that CBT has a long-term effectiveness with phobic children.

- Kvale *et al.* (2004) conducted a meta-analysis of 38 treatment studies for people with dental phobias, finding that CBT resulted in 77 per cent of patients regularly visiting a dentist 4 years after treatment.

- Holmberg *et al.* (2006) assessed the value of CBT in treating patients with phobic postural vertigo, where sufferers become anxious and dizzy when standing or walking, a condition seriously hampering normal everyday functioning. They found CBT to have a limited long-term effect, but that the condition was harder to treat than other phobias, suggesting that CBT is more appropriate with certain phobic disorders than others.

Obsessive-compulsive disorder

- Cordioli (2008) reviewed randomised clinical trials and meta-analyses of CBT, finding it effective in reducing OCD symptoms in 70 per cent of patients who complied with treatment, suggesting that the therapy has useful therapeutic value, though the reasons why many sufferers are non-responsive were not identifiable.

- Vogel *et al.* (1992) investigated the effectiveness of habituation training in treating OCD patients, finding declines in obsessional thinking within sessions, but not between sessions, implying that the technique is of little value in the real world.

- O'Kearney *et al.* (2006) assessed the ability of CBT to treat children and adolescents under the age of 18 years with OCD, finding it effective, but more so when combined with drug treatments.

Evaluation

Cognitive behavioural therapy

Phobias

- There may be long-term benefits to CBT, as techniques used to combat phobias can be used repeatedly to help prevent symptoms recurring.

- For CBT to be effective, training is essential, successful treatment being dependent on developing empathy, respect, unconditional positive regard and honesty between patient and practitioner.

- One of the advantages of CBT compared to other forms of treatment is that it produces little in the way of side effects.

Obsessive-compulsive disorder

- The chances of CBT being successful are strongly correlated with the strength of the working relationship created between therapist and client, indicating the pivotal role that the therapist plays in the administering of the treatment.

- Suitably trained nurses have proven as effective as psychiatrists and psychologists in treating clients with OCD, demonstrating the simplicity of the treatment and its cost-effectiveness.

- One problem with CBT, as with all 'talking therapies', is that it is not suitable for patients who have difficulties talking about inner feelings, or for those who do not possess verbal skills to do so.

Contemporary research

Sousa *et al.* (2006)

Cognitive behavioural group therapy and sertraline in the treatment of OCD

CBGT and SSRIs have both proved effective in treating OCD, but the only way to assess which is superior is to compare their relative efficacy directly.

Aim

To compare CBGT with the SSRI antidepressant sertraline, to assess their relative worth in reducing OCD symptoms.

Procedure

Fifty-six OCD outpatients were randomly allocated either CBGT for 12 weeks or 100 mg/day of sertraline.

Efficacy was measured by reduction in scores on the Yale-Brown Obsessive-Compulsive Scale.

Findings

Both treatments were effective.

Patients receiving CBGT showed symptoms reduced by 44 per cent, while those receiving sertraline showed symptoms reduced by 28 per cent.

CBGT was more effective in reducing OCD symptoms.

Eight patients (32 per cent) receiving CBGT had complete remission of OCD symptoms, compared to one patient (4 per cent) receiving sertraline.

Conclusions

Both CBGT and drug therapy are effective in treating OCD.

CBGT is more effective than drug therapy in treating OCD in terms of symptom reduction and symptom eradication.

Evaluation

- It is not known how long-term the symptom reduction/eradication was with both treatments. Follow-up studies would be needed to assess this.

- A further benefit of CBGT is that it produces fewer side effects.

- In terms of cost-effectiveness, drug treatment is superior, as there are fewer costs in its production and administration.

- There may be an additional benefit to combining the two treatments.

A good site to find wide-ranging information about phobias, including a descriptive list of phobias and links to other sites that focus more specifically on types and treatments, can be found at http://phobialist.com
For OCD, a good site that basically acts as a directory for other websites that focus on specific aspects of the condition is at www.ocdtodayuk.org

Research in focus

Sousa *et al.* (2006) knew that both CBGT and drug therapy had proved effective in treating OCD, but there was no indication which was superior. Devise a suitable experimental hypothesis and justify its use.

The study was looking for a difference, so what research method was being used? What type of design was used?

Participants were randomly allocated to conditions. What is random sampling? How would this be achieved? Why does random sampling not guarantee a representative sample?

You are the researcher

Design a twin study to assess the heritability of OCD. What kind of experimental design would you be using? What would be the IV and the DV? Identify one important confounding variable.

Your study should produce a heritability estimate. What does this mean?

Explain two other research methods that could be used to check your results.

Strengthen your learning

1. Outline the clinical characteristics of phobias/OCD.
2. Outline the symptoms of phobias/OCD.
3. With reference to research evidence, is the diagnosis of phobias/OCD reliable?
4a. What evidence is there for phobias/OCD being genetic?
4b. Aside from research evidence, what other evaluative points can be made about the genetic explanation?
5a. Outline the evolutionary explanation of phobias/OCD.
5b. To what extent can the evolutionary explanation be supported?
6a. Outline the behaviourist explanation of phobias/OCD.
6b. What degree of research support is there for the behaviourist explanation?
7a. Outline the cognitive explanation of phobias/OCD.
7b. Construct an evaluation of the cognitive explanation, including reference to research evidence.
8a. What effects do drugs have on phobias/OCD?
8b. Explain the strengths and weakness of drug treatments.
9. Is ECT an effective treatment for phobias/OCD? Give details.
10. Are behavioural therapies an effective treatment of phobias/OCD?
11a. Describe CBT as a treatment for phobias/OCD.
11b. Evaluate CBT's effectiveness as a treatment for phobias/OCD?

Assessment Check

1. Outline the clinical characteristics of one anxiety disorder. (4 marks)

2. Outline one biological explanation for one anxiety disorder. (4 marks)

3. Evaluate the psychological therapies for one anxiety disorder. (16 marks)

4. Outline issues surrounding the reliability of classification and diagnosis of one anxiety disorder. (4 marks)

5. Outline and evaluate one biological therapy for one anxiety disorder. (20 marks)

6. Outline and evaluate two psychological explanations of one anxiety disorder. (24 marks)

Examination guidance

Care should be taken not to overdescribe the answer to question 1, as only 4 marks are on offer. A similar 'short version' answer should be given for question 2 and its tally of 4 marks. If more than one explanation were offered, both would be marked, but only the best one credited. Only evaluative material should be offered in question 3, and at least two psychological therapies should be covered.

Question 4 could be answered by reference to relevant issues of reliability and validity. A 'shorter version' answer is required, as only 4 marks are on offer. The answer in question 5 should be focused on the evaluation, as it is worth 16 marks, compared to only 4 marks for the outline. Psychological therapies could legitimately be used as an evaluative comparison.

The outline in question 6 is worth 8 marks, and a balance needs to be achieved between the descriptions of the two explanations in order to access the top band of marks. The evaluation, worth 16 marks, could make reference to the degree of research support, as well as comparing the two explanations in terms of strengths and weaknesses.

Summing up

- Schizophrenia affects thought processes and the ability to determine reality. It is diagnosed by first-rank symptoms, based on verbal reports, and additional symptoms observed from behaviour.

- Reliability of schizophrenia diagnosis is relatively high, though there are validity issues.

- Research suggests schizophrenia has a genetic component, with the neurotransmitter dopamine also being connected to the disorder.

- The cognitive explanation links maladaptive thinking and information processing to schizophrenia, while sociocultural explanations focus on family and social environmental factors.

- The prime treatment for schizophrenia is antipsychotic drugs. ECT is also suitable as a treatment in some instances.

- CBT can combat schizophrenia, working by modifying hallucinations and delusional beliefs, while psychotherapy benefits some, working best when combined with antipsychotic drugs.

- Depression is a mood disorder, in unipolar and bipolar forms, of prolonged and fundamental disturbance of emotion, with diagnosis performed by clinical interviews and depression inventories.

- The reliability and validity of depression diagnosis is regarded as relatively favourable.

- Research indicates a genetic vulnerability to depression, while biochemical explanations focus on abnormal levels of monoamine neurotransmitters.

- Behaviourism sees depression as a learned condition, occurring due to reduced opportunities for positive reinforcements creating a cycle of social withdrawal.

- Cognitive explanations see depression occurring through negative schemas, where cognitive biases cause reality to be misperceived.

- The most common treatment for depression is antidepressant drugs, stimulating the production of monoamine neurotransmitters to increase serotonin levels. Serious side-effects can occur, like suicide.

- ECT is used against non-responding forms of depression.

- CBT is the main psychological treatment, identifying and modifying irrational and maladaptive thoughts.

- Behavioural therapies use learning techniques to reinforce desirable behaviours and moods.

- Phobias incur uncontrollable, extreme, irrational and enduring fears, involving anxiety levels beyond actual risk, and are divisible into simple phobias, social phobias and agoraphobia.

- OCD sufferers endure persistent and intrusive thoughts, occurring as obsessions, compulsions or a combination of both.

- Reliability and validity of diagnosis of anxiety disorders has improved as diagnostic criteria have developed.

- Genetics are involved in phobias and OCD, individual genes being increasingly identified. Evolutionary theories see anxiety disorders as having adaptive purposes.

- Behavioural explanations see anxiety disorders as caused and maintained by learning experiences, while cognitive explanations see anxiety disorders resulting from maladaptive thought processes.

- Drugs combat anxiety disorders in the short term, while psychosurgery treats unresponsive cases, but is irreversible. Deep-brain stimulation produces favourable results, especially with OCD.

- Behavioural treatments are successful and cost-effective, with CBT also effective.

10 Media psychology

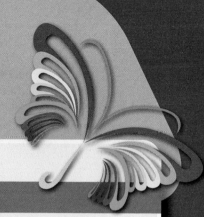

Media influences on social behaviour	**376**
Explanations of media influences on pro-social and antisocial behaviour	377
The positive and negative effects of video games and computers on behaviour	382
Media and persuasion	**388**
Hovland-Yale model	388
Elaboration likelihood model	390
Explanations for the persuasiveness of television advertising	392
The psychology of celebrity	**396**
Social psychological explanations	396
Evolutionary explanations	398
Research into intense fandom	400
Summing up	**408**

Decoding the specification

The specification outlines what you must study in order to answer any examination question you might face. It begins by focusing on explanations of media influences on pro-social and antisocial behaviour, as well as the positive and negative effects of video games and computers on behaviour. There is no direction to concentrate on specific topic areas, so any relevant material is equally creditworthy.

The focus then switches to media and persuasion, and as the Hovland-Yale and Elaboration Likelihood models are specifically listed, they must be studied, as they could be referred to explicitly in examination questions.

No explicit explanations are listed for the persuasiveness of television advertising, therefore, any relevant explanations would be equally creditworthy. There is, however, an explicit requirement to include social psychological and evolutionary explanations when studying the attraction of celebrity. Other explanations can be studied, but those listed may be referred to directly in examination questions.

Finally, for research into intense fandom, celebrity worship and celebrity stalking are explicit requirements for study, as they could be directly referred to in examination questions. The term 'research' refers not just to research studies, but to theories and explanations too.

Media influences on social behaviour

IN THE NEWS

From ABC News, 16 November 2010

Stars who have been stalked

Figure 10.01

Jennifer Aniston has been granted a restraining order against alleged stalker Jason Peyton. On July 15, police found 24-year-old Peyton 'lying-in-wait in a location he believes she frequents, with a sharp object, a bag, a roll of duct tape and written messages about her', and arrested him. Court records described Peyton as 'an obsessed, mentally ill and delusional stalker – with a history of violence and criminal stalking – who drove cross-country in his delusional "mission" to locate and marry Aniston, with whom he believes he is in a relationship.' Peyton has been ordered to stay at least 100 yards away from Aniston's home and place of work.

This is not an unusual story. Research has suggested that one-third of people suffer from 'celebrity worship syndrome', a fascination with the rich and famous, and for some this develops into delusional beliefs about and persistent following, harassing, and so on, of celebrities. Most stalking, though, is not of the famous, but of people we know, usually ex-intimate partners, with a much higher risk of violence in these instances. Not that celebrity stalking is harmless, as was shown in 1993, when Gunter Parche leapt out of the crowd at the Hamburg tennis open and stabbed tennis star Monica Seles. Parche was obsessed with her rival Steffi Graf, whom Seles had replaced as world number one player. Seles did not play again for 2 years and never regained her top ranking. Stalkers can be divided into different types, with recent explanations centring on disturbed childhood attachment patterns and personal loss preceding stalking behaviour.

Explanations of media influences on pro-social and antisocial behaviour

Social learning theory

Social learning theory (SLT) perceives learning via the media as occurring by *indirect reinforcement*, where observed behaviours that are reinforced (rewarded) are imitated (*vicarious learning*). The media is also seen as teaching its audience the negative and positive consequences of violence within a given situation.

Bandura (1965) outlined four steps of modelling:

1. **Attention** – attention is paid to attractive, high-status and perceived similar models (those identified with).

2. **Retention** – observed behaviours are memorised.

3. **Reproduction** – imitation occurs if a person has the skills to reproduce observed behaviour.

4. **Motivation** – direct and indirect reinforcements (both negative and positive), as well as punishments, influence the motivation to imitate.

A model is necessary for imitation, but good levels of *self-efficacy* (situation-specific confidence to perform the behaviour) are also required.

Media influences form the basis of much research, finding that if observers identify with perpetrators of aggressive acts, and/or the more realistic or believable acts of aggression are, the more likely it is that they will be imitated. If perpetrators of aggressive acts are punished for their behaviour, it decreases the chances of behaviour being imitated.

SLT argues that media portrayals of pro-social acts have an equal impact. For instance, watching people help others, like in television charity events, arouses others to do the same. Research suggests that this idea has validity.

If individuals empathise with media characters, by having insight into their feelings, they identify and develop relationships with them, meaning that they are more likely to imitate their antisocial/pro-social behaviours.

Research: social learning theory

- Paik and Comstock (1994) found that the effect of TV violence on antisocial behaviour was greater if actors were rewarded for their actions, suggesting that violence is observed and imitated in line with SLT.

- Bandura *et al.* (1963) showed children a short film in which a model abuses an inflatable bobo doll. The model was either rewarded with sweets and praised, punished by being told off or no consequences occurred. The children were then frustrated by being shown toys they could not touch. Subsequently, when playing, those who had seen the model punished committed fewer aggressive acts than those in the other two conditions. All children were then offered a reward to imitate the observed behaviour and all children were equally aggressive. This suggests that children learn aggression from media portrayals, but expectancy of reinforcement is essential for aggression to be imitated, supporting the concepts of SLT.

- Leyens *et al.* (1975) divided juvenile delinquents into two groups of aggressive and non-aggressive boys. Half of each group watched violent films and half non-violent films. There was an increase in aggression among those watching violent films, suggesting that social learning was an effect, and not personality factors.

- Rushton (1975) found that children developed more positive attitudes to pro-social behaviour after watching pro-social TV. However, although pro-social acts were seen in behaviour, the effect only lasted about 2 weeks, suggesting that pro-social media effects are short-lived.

- Sprafkin *et al.* (1975) found that children taking part in a competition, who had previously watched an episode of *Lassie* where puppies were rescued, spent more time trying to help some distressed puppies than other children, even though doing so reduced their chances of winning. This suggests that they imitated the modelled pro-social behaviour in line with SLT.

- Hearold (1986) performed a meta-analysis of more than 1,000 studies of the effect of TV on social behaviour, finding that pro-social TV affected pro-social behaviour more than antisocial TV affected antisocial behaviour. This suggests that the power of TV to influence pro-social behaviour through social learning is strong.

- Duck (1990) found that adolescents formed close attachments and identified with media figures they would like to emulate, who had characteristics similar to how they perceived themselves, suggesting that empathy can occur through media influences.

Classic research

Huesmann *et al.* (1984)

Intervening variables in TV violence

There have been concerns over the effects of TV violence on behaviour since television began, but evidence was mainly anecdotal and unscientific. Research was difficult to conduct, as experiments are generally unethical and rather artificial. The researchers here performed a longitudinal study that correlated the amount of violent TV watched with the degree of later aggressive behaviour.

Figure 10.02

Aim

To assess the relationship between the amount of violent television watched and aggressive behaviour.

Procedure

A longitudinal design was used where 758 US and 220 Finnish children from school grades 1 to 5 were interviewed and tested annually for 3 years. Efforts were made to also interview at least one parent of each child, and data were collected from the children's peers and schools.

Self-ratings and ratings of others were used to determine levels of aggression. TV viewing habits were recorded and scored for levels of aggression. Parents' levels of aggression were measured by questionnaire.

Findings

For American girls and for boys from both countries, violent TV viewing was related to concurrent aggression and predicted future levels of aggression.

continued ...

...continued

Boys were more aggressive than girls and watched more TV violence than girls.

The strength of the relationship was dependent on the frequency of violence watched as much as the intensity of the violence.

For boys, the effect was enhanced by the degree to which they identified with violent TV characters.

No evidence was found that children predisposed to violence or children with violent parents were more affected by TV violence.

Conclusions

Boys watch more violent TV and identify more with violent characters.

The amount and degree of TV violence viewed correlates positively with later aggressive behaviour.

TV violence produces attitude changes towards the acceptability of aggression.

Evaluation

- The US children had several channels to watch, while the Finns had only two, and the programmes watched were often more familiar to American culture. Therefore, the results from the two countries are not directly comparable.

- Some children's parents were reluctant to be interviewed and these may have been of a particular 'type', making the data unrepresentative.

- The findings suggest a multi-process model, where viewing violence and being aggressive mutually encourage each other.

Cognitive priming

Aggressive ideas or 'cues' presented in the media are seen as affecting both pro-social and antisocial behaviour, with people memorising violent and pro-social acts experienced in the media as scripts for later behaviour. Being in comparable scenarios 'triggers' these scripts into action, activating similar thoughts sharing memory pathways.

Therefore, viewing antisocial/pro-social media increases the chances of individuals acting in antisocial/ pro-social ways when they find themselves in similar contexts to those in which they experienced the media. However, the behaviour is not an exact imitation of what is observed, as with SLT, but just general pro-social or antisocial behaviour inspired (primed) by what was observed.

Research: cognitive priming

- Josephson (1987) found that boys who watched a violent programme involving communicating via walkie-talkies, and subsequently received instructions via walkie-talkies when playing ice hockey, were more aggressive than those who watched a non-violent film, suggesting that the walkie-talkies acted as cues to cognitively prime aggression.

- Murray *et al.* (2007) took fMRI brain scans of children watching violent and non-violent films, finding that those watching violence had active brain areas associated with emotion and arousal, and areas linked to episodic memory, suggesting the storing of aggressive scripts for later use.

- Holloway *et al.* (1977) found that participants who 'overheard' a pro-social message on a radio in the waiting room before participating in a study involving bargaining, were more cooperative in their bargaining than participants who did not hear the bulletin. This suggests a pro-social effect of the cognitive priming of good news.

- In a similar study, Blackman and Hornstein (1977) found that participants hearing a good-news radio bulletin rated human nature, in terms of people's cooperativeness, honesty and decency, as higher than those not hearing the bulletin, again suggesting a pro-social effect of cognitive priming. This was especially so as the 'good news' effect generalised itself beyond the content of the news bulletin, implying that related pro-social concepts in memory were primed (activated) by the original bulletin.

- Moriarity and McCabe (1977) found that children exposed to media models of sportspeople behaving pro-socially performed more pro-social acts than those who were not. These were pro-social acts different from those exhibited by the sportspeople, suggesting that the media models acted as cognitive primers for participants' behaviour.

Figure 10.03 Boys playing ice hockey who received instructions via walkie-talkies after watching a violent film involving walkie-talkies played more aggressively

Desensitisation

Desensitisation involves the reduction or elimination of cognitive, emotional and behavioural responses to a stimulus, suggesting that repeated exposure to violence in the media reduces its impact, as people become habituated (used) to it, increasing the chances of them being violent, as they are divorced from the consequences of their behaviour. Constant exposure to media violence makes people 'comfortably numb' to real-life violence.

Overexposure to pro-social media similarly reduces its impact, creating 'compassion fatigue', where people become numb to 'do-gooders' and the troubles of others – for instance, watching too many television charity events.

Research: desensitisation

- Drabman and Thomas (1974) found that children viewing violent films showed less emotional response and more tolerance of subsequent violence, suggesting a desensitisation effect.

- Bushman and Anderson (2007) found that exposure to violent media produces physiological desensitisation when viewing later scenes of real violence.

- Bushman (2009) found that participants playing violent video games for 20 minutes took longer to respond to someone injured in a staged fight than those viewing non-violent games, suggesting a desensitisation effect.

- Belson (1978) conducted a study of 1,500 teenage boys, finding no evidence that high exposure to television violence desensitised them into becoming more violent, and no evidence that watching television violence reduced consideration for others or respect for authority, lessening support for desensitisation.

- Moeller (1999) reported how after media appeals for donations of help for victims of a natural disaster, donations to similar media appeals would decrease, illustrating the desensitisation effect of compassion fatigue on pro-social behaviour.

Figure 10.04 Children who watch violent films become desensitised to real-life violence

Evaluation

Media influences on pro-social and antisocial behaviour

- Research suggests that pro-social acts are learned via the media, but the fact that there is far more research into antisocial effects suggests a general stereotypical view of TV being a force for antisocial behaviour. Cumberbatch (1989) argued that antisocial acts are more obvious and easier to count, whereas pro-social acts are more subtle and based on value judgements, therefore leading to under-counting of pro-social acts.

- Much research into pro-social effects examines the positive effects of media made explicitly for 'pro-social' purposes. However, pro-social acts also occur in more mainstream media, but few researchers ever investigate the positive effects of media where the primary aim is entertainment rather than promotion of pro-social messages.

- Research in this area is flawed by political desires to label the media as a simplistic cause of rising violence levels. Methodologies are oversimplistic too, relying on crude totalling up of aggressive acts and amount of media consumed. Individuals consume media in different ways and motivation is a more powerful determinant of behaviour than media acts observed. Gauntlett (1995) claims that 'the content analysis approach and method is severely flawed by its inability to recognise the content or meaning of acts'.

- Although there is a correlation between amount of aggressive/pro-social TV watched and degree of aggressive behaviour/pro-social behaviour, causality is not demonstrated; it may be that aggressive/pro-social people choose to watch more violent/helpful programmes.

- Cognitive priming may affect most those with a disposition for aggression and pro-social behaviour, suggesting that the effect is regulated by personality factors.

- Increased rates of aggression may be due to the high level of violent media acts witnessed, providing violent scripts for actual behaviour, suggesting a cognitive priming effect.

- Research does not indicate that desensitisation makes people more aggressive (though they may be less pro-social). Indeed, it may be that desensitised individuals are less aroused and more disinterested by aggression and therefore not provoked by real-life violence. However, desensitisation does suggest that they are less appalled at and more indifferent to the violence or misfortune of others.

You are the researcher

Do soap operas tend to show more antisocial acts than pro-social acts? Choose a popular soap opera and compose a 'tick-box' score sheet to record the number of pro-social and antisocial acts recorded in the episodes broadcast in one week. You will need to classify in advance with a partner what constitutes pro-social and antisocial acts. Watch the shows and record the number of pro- and antisocial acts. Get your partner to watch and score the same shows, but independently. If you have established inter-rater reliability, what should be true of the data? Perform a content analysis of the data and put the results on an appropriate graph.

What conclusions did you reach?

Research in focus

Before research can be published it must be subjected to peer review, with the peer review system regarded as the 'gatekeeper' of scientific validity. Explain what this means and outline how the peer review system works. There are those who argue that peer review is not objective and unbiased. Outline the criticisms on which this argument is based.

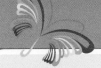

The positive and negative effects of video games and computers on behaviour

Video games

Since the 1970s, video games have had a major impact on young people's leisure time, and due to the fact that they give players active roles and incorporate repetitive learning features, they are perceived as having a greater impact than other media forms, which has given rise to a number of concerns:

- Playing video games may cause addiction problems.

- Giving players active roles in video games, encouraging and rewarding aggression, may lead to the repetition of violence in real life.

- Desensitisation to violence may occur through repeated exposure to video game aggression, with emotional desensitisation causing a numbing of arousal reactions to events that should produce emotional responses.

- Excessive game playing could create cognitive desensitisation, where the belief that violence is unusual is replaced with a belief that it is commonplace.

- Desensitisation might disrupt moral evaluation, causing actions to be taken without consideration of ethical implications.

- Playing video games may retard development – for example, in emotion regulation skills – leading to desensitisation to cues that normally trigger empathetic responses, which increases the likelihood of violent behaviour.

However, other researchers emphasise the positive aspects of playing video games, with creative and pro-social games seen as having educational value, while other games help to release stress and aggression in a non-harmful manner, as well as raising self-esteem.

Effects are not uniform; as research has identified individual differences in video game usage and in the effects they have on players.

Research: video games

(For research into the positive effects of video games, see 'Psychology in action' on page 383.)

- Ballard (1999) reported that the tactile stimulation of games – for example, reality vests allowing players to experience victims' death struggles – enhances sensory experience beyond usual media sources, elevating concerns over their potential for encouraging violent behaviour.

- Matthews *et al.* (2006) found that adolescents randomly assigned to play a violent video game had increased activity in the amygdala, a brain area associated with emotions, and decreased activity in the prefrontal lobe, which regulates inhibition, self-control and concentration, compared to those randomly assigned to a stimulating, non-violent game. This illustrates a specific physical effect on brain functioning, seemingly indicating desensitisation and less control over aggressive tendencies.

- Anderson and Bushman (2001) conducted a meta-analysis of studies measuring the effects of exposure to violent video games, through aggressive behaviour, aggressive thoughts, cooperation, aggressive mood and physiological arousal, finding that short-term exposure to video game violence was associated with temporary increases in aggression among all participants. This suggests a relationship between exposure to violent video games and aggressive behaviour.

- Strasburger and Wilson (2002) found that playing video games desensitises the user to the consequences of violence, brings increased pro-violence attitudes and alters cognitive processing, suggesting that video games have negative consequences, with a key role identified for desensitisation.

- Silvern and Williamson (1987) found that children playing a violent video game exhibited more verbal and physical aggression compared to children who watched a violent cartoon, suggesting that video games have a more powerful negative effect than other forms of media.

- Grusser *et al.* (2007) surveyed 7,000 gamers, finding that 12 per cent were addicted according to World Health Organization criteria. Shotton (1989), however, found that those addicted for 5 years did well educationally and secured high-ranking jobs, suggesting that gaming is a harmless addiction.

- Dunn and Hughes (2001) found that 'difficult' preschoolers who played video games were more likely to engage in violent fantasy play than children without behavioural difficulties, suggesting that there are individual differences to consider.

- Sopes and Millar (1983) found that children playing video games exhibit addictive tendencies, due to the compulsive behavioural involvement, and exhibit withdrawal symptoms, like the shakes, when attempting to stop playing. They also turn to crime to fund their habit.

Psychology in action

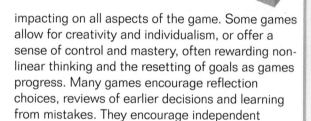

Positive effects of video games

Figure 10.05 The Sims 3 images © 2011 Electronic Arts Inc. All Rights Reserved. Used With Permission

The stereotypical view of video games is negative, with a common portrayal of them as encouraging violence, detracting from children taking physical exercise or socialising with others, and generally creating antisocial, intellectually challenged individuals. However, perhaps they should be better regarded as having psychologically beneficial practical applications that help to foster a wide range of desirable abilities.

Gee (2003) sees benefits from games that empower learners, develop problem solving and help understanding. For example, games with interactive components encourage players to actively create and customise, with their decisions impacting on all aspects of the game. Some games allow for creativity and individualism, or offer a sense of control and mastery, often rewarding non-linear thinking and the resetting of goals as games progress. Many games encourage reflection choices, reviews of earlier decisions and learning from mistakes. They encourage independent thinking, perseverance and commitment.

Kestenbaum and Weinstein (1985) assessed heavy computer game use in adolescent male participants, finding that computer games had a calming effect in helping to manage conflict and discharged aggression by allowing open expression of competition.

Durkin and Barber (2002) found evidence of positive outcomes in 16-year-olds playing computer games. Measures of family closeness, activity involvement, school engagement, mental health, substance misuse and friendship networks were superior in game players than non-playing peers, suggesting that computers can be a positive feature of a healthy adolescence.

Meanwhile, Lieberman (2001) reported that virtual-reality and video games are effective in teaching children about diabetes and asthma management, and in moderating phobias, again illustrating their beneficial uses.

continued ...

... continued

Perhaps the impoverished view of computer games is the domain of anxious parents, with the reality being that their positives far outweigh their negatives.

Evaluation

Video games

- Bias can affect research findings in this area. For instance, Harris (2001) reported that research performed by the gaming industry found no causal relationship between video game violence and aggression. This suggests that an objective view of the topic is difficult to form.

- Much research performed in this area is correlational and does not show a causal relationship between video game use and antisocial behaviour. It may be that individuals with aggressive personalities are attracted to violent video games.

- Research finding negative effects indicates that these are short-term, and as much evidence suggests positive benefits, concern may be misplaced.

- Younger children may be more at risk, as they are still constructing their moral scaffolding, suggesting that the values operating in violent video games have a greater impact than for older individuals with established value systems.

- Desensitisation to violence is difficult to measure objectively; instead, researchers measure related characteristics that they expect to be affected, so these measures may not be completely valid.

- There may be a difference in how video game playing affects desensitisation, with emotional desensitisation blunting empathetic responding, while cognitive desensitisation produces stronger pro-violent attitudes.

- Research has not identified which types of individual are most at risk of negative impact when playing video games and under what conditions negative impacts are more likely.

You are the researcher

Is there a difference in how aggressive video games affect males and females? Design a questionnaire to assess participants' emotions. This should have some kind of scale on it so you can measure the degree of emotion being experienced. Ask an equal number of males and females (you will need about ten of each) to fill in your questionnaire, and then ask them to play a fairly aggressive video game. Then ask them to complete the questionnaire again. How would you analyse your data to see whether one gender is affected more than the other?

For those students who want to read more widely into the effects of video games, including studies on their effects on aggression, self-esteem, academic achievement and crime, as well as an overall appraisal of their positive and negative effects, there is an online government document, produced by the Home Office, available at http://rds.homeoffice.gov.uk/rds/pdfs/occ72-compgames.pdf

Computers

Computer-based media is a constantly growing source of media influence – for example, the internet, emails, blogs, websites, social network sites and games. In Britain, it is estimated that people spend on average 45 per cent of their waking hours using electronic media, with an increase in wireless computers and the advent of mobile phones that access the internet contributing to this growth. Use of computers is also multiplying in other cultures, though there are restrictions on what can be accessed in some societies. There has been an increased use of computers in education, with e-based learning fast becoming a part of most students' lives. Computer usage, for many people, is now an integral part of their lives, whether at work or at school, for practical purposes like shopping and for recreational and social purposes.

Research interest has focused on relationships lacking face-to-face communication, ranging from relationships based on similar interests through to romantic ones, with other research concentrating on the strengths and weaknesses of computers as educational tools. Computers are seen to be a positive tool for communicating, learning and developing social relationships in those lacking social skills and confidence and those living in remote communities, though deception can be difficult to detect. However, computers also have negative attributes, with the possibility of deindividuation leading to disinhibition, causing individuals to act in non-typical ways, as well as a risk of developing technology dependency

Figure 10.06 British people spend 45 per cent of their waking hours using electronic media

(addiction to computers). Critics of computer usage also point to their potential for reducing the development of face-to-face communication skills in the young, though others believe that computers actually enhance social skills and help build relationships.

Research: computers

- Valkenburg and Peter (2009) report that social network sites encourage and permit communication and relationship building. Also, the relative anonymity of such forms of communication encourages self-disclosure in traditionally shy adolescents, suggesting such use of computers to be beneficial in developing sociability and relationship skills.

- Durkin and Barber (2002) found evidence of positive outcomes in 16-year-olds playing computer games. Measures of family closeness, activity involvement, school engagement, mental health, substance misuse and friendship networks were superior in game players than non-playing peers, implying that computers are a positive feature of a healthy adolescence.

- Pearce (2007) presented the same information to students via printed paper (group A), a film of the printed paper (group B) and displayed on a computer screen (group C). Group A recalled 85 per cent of the information, group B 27 per cent, and group C 4 per cent, suggesting that computers are a poor medium for such learning; this may be to do with the way in which individuals cognitively interact with material they are reading.

- Daft et al. (1987) found that computer-mediated communications (CMCs) negatively affect feedback levels, communication cues, language variety and personal focus. As these are important factors in communicating and negotiating, it suggests that computers hinder such processes. This was supported by McGrath and Hollingshead (1995), who found that CMCs incur lower levels of cooperation than visual and audio forms, suggesting that emailing hinders cooperative negotiations.

- Rao and Lim (2000) found deception common in CMCs, because cues to deception, like posture shifts, are not transmitted, suggesting that they are harder to detect, while Caspi and Gorsky (2006) found that Israeli participants believed online deception to be common, but only one-third reported using deception, with frequent users, younger users and more competent users being the main culprits. Those using deception felt that it created a sense of harmless enjoyment, suggesting that CMCs are changing personal moral standards.

Evaluation

Computers

- Although computers have undoubted benefits for young people, there is also a high risk of exposure to computer-mediated material that is inappropriate and potentially harmful. This suggests a need for agreed and policed codes of practice for websites, especially social network sites, which tend to be heavily used by young people. There is also an argument for computers to be manufactured with parental control software, and for sites, games, and so on, to have standardised ratings similar to those on films and videos.

- Differences in research findings concerning the effects of computers on communication and negotiation may be due to differences in the types of CMCs used – for example, emailing and instant messaging. Different systems have varying amounts of time between receiving and sending messages, creating differences in amounts of reasoning, affecting messages sent. Zhou *et al.* (2001) found significant cues in CMCs indicating the use of deception, and believe that these could be incorporated into an automated tool that would detect deception and protect young people from those with negative intentions.

- Research into deception within CMC is based on online questionnaires, which could be prone to idealised and socially desirable answers, suggesting that findings may not be valid.

- It would be simplistic to view computers as either agents for good or bad. They have their beneficial sides, like helping those with social inhibitions to communicate across social and psychological boundaries, and their negative aspects, like creating disinhibition that makes users become more selfish, self-concerned and lacking in feelings for the welfare of others.

Research in focus

Science is supposedly objective, as it is conducted in an unbiased fashion. However, there are many examples of how bias can occur in psychological research.

Explain what is meant by researcher bias. How might this occur in studies of the effect of videos and computer games on young people? What measures can psychologists use to reduce the effects of researcher bias?

Bias can also occur on the part of participants. Outline ways in which participants may be biased when taking part in studies (not just experiments) of the effects of videos and computer games on young people? How can these be reduced?

Strengthen your learning

1. Outline how SLT can be used to explain how the media affects pro-social and antisocial behaviour.
2. In what way does cognitive priming differ from SLT? Use research evidence to illustrate this difference.
3. What is desensitisation?
4. Outline one research study illustrating the effect of desensitisation on antisocial behaviour and on pro-social behaviour.
5. Construct an elaborated evaluation of media effects on pro-social and antisocial behaviour – that is, an evaluation where points build on each other to form an effective commentary.
6. Outline the arguments concerning video games and computers being harmful or beneficial. Refer to research evidence to illustrate your points.
7. Evaluate the argument concerning video games and computers being harmful in terms of strengths and weaknesses.

Assessment Check

1. Outline one explanation of media influences on antisocial behaviour. (4 marks)

2. Evaluate the effects of video games and computers on behaviour. (20 marks)

3. Discuss explanations of media influences on pro-social and antisocial behaviour. (24 marks)

4. Outline and evaluate the effects of video games and computers on behaviour. (24 marks)

Examination guidance

Question 1 requires purely descriptive material, and only that which relates to one explanation of antisocial behaviour. Therefore, any description of pro-social behaviour or evaluative material of any kind would not be creditworthy, and if two valid explanations were offered, both would be marked, but only the best one credited. Question 2, on the other hand, requires only evaluative material, and this could be achieved by reference to the degree of support that research indicates for positive and negative effects, as well as commentary concerning the usefulness and implications of video games and computers.

In question 3, the term 'discuss' means to describe and evaluate. The description must include explanations of both pro-social and antisocial behaviour, with a balance between the two necessary to access marks in the top band. The evaluation could centre on the degree of research support for explanations, as well as comparisons of explanations in terms of their strengths and weaknesses.

In question 4, the outline should include material on the effects of both video games and computers. However, as only 8 marks are available for the outline, more effort and focus should be concentrated on the evaluation, for which 16 marks are on offer.

Media and persuasion

An attitude is a disposition towards an object or situation, prompting individuals to behave in certain ways, while persuasion is the process of changing attitudes. Psychologists became interested in attitudes and persuasion after the Second World War, as the mass media became increasingly influential.

Hovland-Yale model

Hovland's work centred on the role of persuasion, perceiving attitude change as a response to communication. Research done at Yale University identified four important factors:

1. **Communicator** – the person seeking to persuade
2. **Message** – the content of the message
3. **Channel** – how the message is conveyed
4. **Audience** – to whom the message is directed.

Key terms

Attitude – a predisposition towards an object or situation

Hovland-Yale model – an explanation of attitude change as a sequence of stages in response to communication

Elaboration likelihood model – an explanation of how persuasive messages are processed through cognitive evaluation

Cognitive dissonance – a negative mental state from holding two simultaneous conflicting attitudes

Self-perception theory – an explanation perceiving attitudes, emotions and internal states as inferred from observing one's own behaviour

The communicator

Experts are perceived as knowledgeable and therefore more persuasive than non-experts. This is why advertisements are often endorsed by experts, such as top sportspeople, or dressed up in seemingly scientific terms.

The message

There are key message characteristics that influence persuasion:

1. Messages that present a *two-sided, balanced message* are persuasive to undecided audiences, making them resistant to later information contradicting the original message.

2. Proposing weak arguments against the original message 'inoculates' the original message against future stronger arguments.

3. Associating emotions with messages makes them more persuasive – for instance, using 'feel-good' tactics in adverts, like smiling and happy music.

4. Use of fear is especially effective (e.g. 'HIV kills'), if the message also provides a simple way of coping with the fear (practise safe sex) and if the message relates to the audience ('you will get HIV' if you do not practise safe sex).

5. Messages affect the extent to which individuals are affected, with messages associated with positive moods being more persuasive.

6. Repetitive messages are particularly persuasive, with continual exposure to a message sufficient to create a favourable impression of familiarity to something never actually experienced. However, repetition of negative stimuli does not persuade people to be positive and can create more negativity. Repetition can also be overdone and create a backlash.

The channel

Different channels of communication are persuasive in different circumstances. For instance, face-to-face communication is persuasive with individuals, while mass media is persuasive to lots of people simultaneously.

The audience

The type of audience affects the persuasiveness of messages, with people of moderate intelligence and moderate self-esteem more easily persuadable. Other types are less persuadable – for instance, intelligent people comprehend messages, but are more able to spot flaws.

Overall, attitude change is perceived as a sequential process comprising stages of *attention* (the target attends to the message), *comprehension* (the target understands the message), *reactance* (the target reacts to the message either positively or negatively), and *acceptance* (the message is accepted if perceived as credible).

Research: Hovland-Yale model

- Hovland and Weiss (1951) found that more attitude change was produced in participants reading an article about building a nuclear submarine supposedly written by an expert, than those reading the same article supposedly by a low-credibility source. This suggests that experts are more credible and persuasive than non-experts.

- McGuire and Papageorgis (1961) found that participants given a balanced, two-sided argument about teeth-brushing were more resistant to an argument attacking the original message than participants originally given a one-sided argument, demonstrating how balanced messages 'inoculate' against future conflicting arguments.

- Gorn (1982) found that participants preferred a pen presented in an advert with a likeable song to an identical pen presented in an identical advert, but with a dislikeable song, demonstrating how associating emotions with messages makes them persuasive.

- Sinclair *et al.* (1991) found that students supported a message about the need for exams if it was given on a sunny rather than a cloudy day, regardless of whether the message was weak or strong. This suggests that the persuasiveness of messages are dependent on the context of mood.

- Zajonc (1968) found that unfamiliar stimuli, such as Turkish words, that were shown frequently were rated as having 'better meaning' than ones shown less frequently, even though participants did not understand them. This illustrates how mere repeated exposure to messages makes them persuasive.

- Lippa (1994) found printed media more persuasive than visual media with complicated messages, as people pay attention and can recap, demonstrating that different channels of communication are more persuasive in different situations.

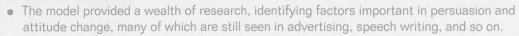

Evaluation

Hovland-Yale model

- The model provided a wealth of research, identifying factors important in persuasion and attitude change, many of which are still seen in advertising, speech writing, and so on.
- The model does not identify which of the factors are most important, with subsequent research questioning the validity of many of them.
- The model does not identify how persuasion occurs, simply assuming that attitude change emanates from message comprehension. This is not always the case, and the model was superseded by cognitively orientated models like the elaboration likelihood model.
- Hovland believed that persuasive messages changed attitudes permanently, but subsequently he discovered the *sleeper effect*, where messages, even from low-credibility sources, could, over time, become equally persuasive.
- Most research was laboratory-based, creating problems of ecological validity. Also, participants gave self-ratings, which are subject to validity issues, like giving socially desirable answers, as well as identical ratings having different meanings for different participants.

You are the researcher

Devise a leaflet to promote healthy eating based on the principles of the Hovland-Yale model. Then design a self-report to test its effectiveness. You will need to assess attitudes before and after your campaign. What form will your data take and how will you analyse them?

Elaboration likelihood model

Petty and Cacioppo's (1981) model explains how persuasive messages are processed through the *central* and *peripheral* routes, with attitude change occurring through cognitive evaluation, and persuasion dependent on the degree of elaboration of messages. Therefore, the model concentrates on cognitions rather than message content.

Central route

The central route (CR) occurs when receivers have both motivation and ability to think about messages. Therefore, the CR is used when listeners care about messages and can listen to and comprehend them, with centrally processed messages more persuasive and resistant to subsequent counter–arguments.

Centrally processed messages have certain characteristics:

- **Persuasive communication** – messages are credible, grab the receiver's attention and convince them they are beneficial.

- **Motivation to process** – messages are relevant, best achieved if messages focus on something that receivers are familiar with.

- **Ability to process** – messages are pitched at the correct level to be comprehended. Elaboration will not occur if messages are too complicated. Receivers need time and opportunity to process messages, which is not easy if there are competing demands.

- **Nature of argument** – messages are strong, clearly argued and convincing. If messages reflect pre-existing attitudes and beliefs, they will have long-lasting effects. If messages engage receivers this far, but are weak, a 'boomerang' effect occurs, whereby receivers reject messages totally.

Peripheral route

When messages fail to impact through the CR, often because listeners cannot fully engage due to simultaneous conflicting demands, they may still be processed via the peripheral route (PR). The PR is used when receivers are uninterested or distracted, with little engagement or consideration of messages occurring. However, persuasion and attitude change can still occur if peripheral cues are present, though in a more passive way than with central processing. The PR also occurs when messages have many or complicated aspects to them and receivers lack ability, time or motivation to think about them sufficiently.

Messages using the PR persuade people by using devices not directly related to the subject matter – for example, using sports stars to advertise shaving foam, with sports stars being a peripheral cue, as there is no obvious link between sporting prowess and shaving foam.

Peripherally processed messages have characteristic cues, none of which refer to the content of the message:

- **Consistency** – evaluation of the persuasiveness of messages is dependent on past thoughts receivers have had concerning the message topic.

- **Likeability** – messages presented from attractive sources are more persuasive.

Figure 10.07 The use of sportspeople to endorse products can be explained by reference to both the Hovland-Yale and elaboration likelihood models

- **Expertise and authority** – receivers are more persuaded by messages emanating from communicators with perceived knowledge and respect.

- **Scarcity** – messages are more persuasive if receivers believe something is available only for a limited time, as they do not wish to lose out.

If there are no peripheral cues, messages are not persuasive and attitude change does not result.

Research: Elaboration Likelihood model

- Petty and Cacioppo (1986) found that central processing leads to longer-lasting attitude change than peripheral processing, as it involves more time and cognitive effort, implying the CR to be a more dominant source of persuasion.

- Chaiken (1980) found that participants were more likely to retain new attitudes achieved via persuasion if attitude changes were acquired by the CR, suggesting that attitude change is greater through the CR.

- Berscheid and Walster (1974) found that physically attractive sources, like sports stars, make messages persuasive, especially if messages concern less involving topics, demonstrating the importance of likeability in peripherally processed messages.

- Miller (2005) found that peripheral route processing relies on environmental conditions, such as perceived credibility of the source, quality of its presentation, attractiveness of the source and catchy slogans, supporting the model.

- Benoit (2008) found that receivers can think deeply about messages, while also perceiving the communicator as a likeable expert, suggesting that the CR and the PR can be used simultaneously as well as independently of each other.

- Petty *et al.* (1981) found that students were most influenced by persuasive messages when personally motivated, and by peripheral cues when not personally motivated, suggesting that different processing routes are used in different circumstances.

Evaluation

Elaboration Likelihood model

- Advertisers are aware that persuasion via the CR is problematic, as people cannot fully engage with messages, due to conflicting demands for their attention. Therefore, peripheral routes are often used to sell products.
- The model is the most influential theory of persuasion, recognising that similar messages can be processed through different cognitive routes, dependent on whether or not people have motivation and ability to use active or passive processing methods.
- The PR suggests there is a lack of thought about messages. Though there is less than with the CR, thoughtful processing does occur, but in a more indirect manner – for example, how knowledgeable is this communicator?
- Much research into the model has been of unfamiliar topics about which participants have no pre-existing attitudes. Therefore, research tends to measure attitude change, rather than attitude formation. Evidence suggests that attitude changes realised by peripheral processing are temporary, and as attitudes are perceived as enduring predispositions, this implies that research measures attitude change, not attitude formation.

Explanations for the persuasiveness of television advertising

(Material on the Hovland-Yale and elaboration likelihood models could also be utilised to answer questions on this topic. See also 'Psychology in action' on page 395.)

Television means different things to different people. Some people watch a lot and are very influenced by its content, including advertisements, while others are occasional viewers only moderately affected, and of course there are those who do not even possess a television.

The most persuasive form of television is public broadcasting campaigns, their effectiveness plain to see by the amount of money that they raise. For instance, Sports Relief raised £40.6 million in 2010, while Red Nose Day, also broadcast on the BBC, raised £67.7 million in 2007.

Most would assume television advertising to be persuasive, due to its ever-present nature and the public popularity of some campaigns, but definitive data are difficult to obtain, and suggestions are that advertising is not as successful as most would assume.

The hypodermic effect

This explanation sees television advertising as a powerful medium that injects its message into a precisely targeted audience, incurring subsequent effects. It suggests that the makers of television advertisements can make their audience do whatever they wish. It assumes that audiences are passive recipients and easily manipulated by advertisement makers.

Two-step flow theory: Katz and Lazarsfeld (1960)

This explanation suggests that the messages within television advertisements are filtered through *opinion leaders*, people who are influential and sensitive to television messages, who pass on the information to other people in society. Thus the audience is active in the process of persuasion, in that interpersonal communication occurs after perception of the message, and this is an important factor in determining which advertisements are persuasive and which are not.

Uses and gratification theory

This explanation sees people as active processors who use television advertisements to fulfil needs. Therefore, the theory does not see television advertisements as affecting audiences on their own, but rather that television advertisements and their audience interact to produce an effect.

There are five areas of gratification:

1. **Escape** – advertisements allow viewers to escape the reality of their lives.

2. **Social interaction** – people can create personal relationships with characters seen in advertisements. This is potentially dysfunctional, but for many it merely helps to create common ground for everyday conversation.

3. **Identification** – people can identify with characters in advertisements, such as adopting products endorsed by a favourite personality.

4. **Inform and educate** – advertisements allow people to gain knowledge of the world around them and how it operates.

5. **Entertain** – advertisements allow people to watch purely for entertainment value.

Classic research

Coon *et al.* (2000)

Relationships between children's use of television during meals and children's food consumption patterns

Television is the biggest media source of messages about food and the majority of money spent on food advertising is from branded manufacturers and fast food chains, specialising in mainly unhealthy food products, while healthy foodstuffs are rarely advertised. The researchers were therefore interested in examining whether having an unhealthy diet was linked to television usage in children.

Aim

To assess the relationship between the presence of television during meals and children's food consumption patterns, including foods not advertised.

Procedure

Ninety-one child-parent pairs were gained through advertisements, with children aged between 8–10 years.

Data on socio-economic background and television usage was collected in interviews. Food consumption for three non-consecutive 24-hour periods was collected for each child.

Data was compared of 41 families where the television was on during mealtimes and 50 families who rarely or never had the television on at mealtimes.

Findings

Children from high television usage families ate significantly more pizza, salty snacks and fizzy, sugary drinks than those from low television usage families. They also derived substantially less of their total energy consumption from carbohydrates and drank substantially more caffeine.

Conclusions

Children where television viewing is a usual part of mealtimes, consume fewer fruit and vegetables and more unhealthy foods and drinks than children from families where eating and watching television are two separate activities.

continued ...

...continued

Evaluation

- As advertisements are a regular feature of television programming and many such adverts are for fast-food based products, television advertising can be seen to have a persuasive effect on children's dietary habits, but to a negative extent.

- The results suggests a practical application, in that public money should be spent on television advertising that promotes healthy food stuffs to improve the public's health. There is also a case for banning the promotion of unhealthy foodstuffs, or at least placing an embargo on them until after children's bedtimes. Parents should be advised not to allow television viewing during mealtimes, due to its negatively persuasive influence on children's lifestyles and health.

Research in focus

The title of Coon's study indicates that it is a correlation. But what feature of the study suggests that it is an experiment? Give two strengths and two weaknesses of this method.

What were the IV and DV in the study?

Were qualitative or quantitative data generated? Justify your answer.

Give one strength and one weakness of both qualitative and quantitative data.

Research: explanations for the persuasiveness of television advertising

- Belch (1982) studied the cognitive effects of advertising repetition by considering the impact of television commercials within a one-hour programme, finding attitudes and purchase intentions weren't affected by message repetition and that cognitive responses became more negative as exposure frequency increased. This suggests that advertisements are not persuasive and can actually create negative mind–sets towards products.

- Oates *et al.* (2006) investigated children's responses to television advertising, testing children aged between 6-10 on their recall, recognition and understanding of television advertisements. Scenes from adverts were recalled after just one exposure, but recall of brand names was poor for the younger children, even after three exposures. Recall of advertising content did generally increase with age and amount of exposure, but only 0 per cent of 6-year olds, 25 per cent of 8-year-olds and 33 per cent of 10-year olds discussed the adverts in terms of persuasion. This suggests that although children do recall television advertisements, their purpose is not fully understood by them.

- Judd & Alexander (1983) investigated the persuasiveness of using sexually suggestive advertisements, showing adverts containing suggestive content to male and female college students. Recall of brand names and product information was lower than for non-suggestive advertisements, suggesting support for the attention-distraction hypothesis, which perceives the suggestive content as decreasing time to concentrate on the product and advertising message.

Evaluation

Explanations for the persuasiveness of television advertising

- The hypodermic model can be seen at work in forms of advertising where viewers are less conscious of being manipulated, and it is for this reason that subliminal advertising, where messages are broadcast so swiftly that they are not consciously acknowledged, but have an unconscious effect, are banned. This demonstrates that there are instances where television is persuasive without conscious awareness.

- Pavlou and Stewart (2000) believed that the growth of internet advertising has created opportunities for interactive advertising, where consumers have a heightened role in determining the effects and persuasiveness of advertising. This suggests that traditional assumptions about how television advertising works are being challenged, for instance by the potential of the internet to allow advertisements to be targeted at an individual's specific needs and interests.

- Huge sums are spent on advertising, but it is difficult to find objective evidence as to their effectiveness, because companies are keen to keep advertising budgets and sales data private. Cashmore (1994) suggested that companies use television advertising not because of its effectiveness, but because they have no other way of raising brand awareness. Gauntlett (1995) estimated that television advertising fails 90 to 99 per cent of the time.

Psychology in action

Public safety campaigns

One practical application of the media's persuasiveness through television is that of public safety campaigns. Vast sums of money are spent to persuade people to change their behaviour in terms of health and safety issues, such as discouraging drink-driving. Whether such campaigns can be judged effective is measurable in several ways, such as overall impact, cost-effectiveness or dramatic changes in a minority of people.

Dwyer *et al.* (1986) reported on an predominantly television-based Australian anti-smoking campaign, costing £250,000: 87 per cent of people recalled seeing it; 50,000 calls were made to the 'Quit Line'; and there was a 1.25 per cent greater decrease in smoking than in areas where the campaign was not aired. This can be deemed cost-effective in terms of medical costs saved from the reduced amounts of smokers.

Palmgreen *et al.* (2001) assessed the effectiveness of a television campaign targeted at high-sensation-seeking adolescents, by comparing marijuana usage in adolescents where the campaign was shown and not shown for 32 months after the campaign aired. Low-sensation seekers reported unchanging low-level usage, while high-sensation seekers reported lower usage than before, suggesting that such campaigns are effective when focused on a target population.

Public communication campaigns seem effective only at great cost and with specific audiences. They perhaps work best when directed at the 2 to 3 per cent of people seen as opinion leaders and agents of social change, as changing their attitudes and behaviour may have a knock-on effect on other people.

Figure 10.08 Targeting high-sensation seekers proved successful in reducing marijuana usage

Strengthen your learning

1a. Outline the following features of the Hovland-Yale model:
    i)   the communicator
    ii) the message
    iii) the channel
    iv) the audience.
1b. To what degree are these features supported by research evidence? Give details.
1c. Aside from research evidence, what other evaluative points can be made about the model?
2a. Explain how the Elaboration Likelihood model sees messages as being centrally processed and peripherally processed.
2b. Use research evidence to decide which processing route is more dominant.
2c. Aside from research evidence, what other evaluative points can be made about the model?
3a. Outline ways in which television advertising may be persuasive.
3b. What evidence is there that public broadcasting campaigns are effective?

Assessment Check

1. Compare the Hovland-Yale and Elaboration Likelihood models in explaining the persuasive effects of media. (24 marks)

2. Outline two explanations for the persuasiveness of television advertising. (8 marks)

3. Outline the Hovland-Yale model of persuasion and attitude change. (4 marks)

4. Evaluate explanations for the persuasiveness of television advertising. (16 marks)

Examination guidance

To answer question 1, an outline of both models is required, with a balance between the two necessary to gain access to the higher band of marks. For this, 8 marks are available. The evaluation, worth 16 marks, would then require the models to be compared in terms of their strengths and weaknesses, possibly in terms of theoretical rigour, degree of research support and practical applications.

In question 2, to gain access to the higher band of marks, a balance should be achieved between the two explanations offered. If more than two explanations are given, all would be marked, but only the best two credited.

Question 3 requires an outline of the Hovland-Yale model, so describing other models or offering any evaluation does not accrue credit.

The evaluation in question 4 must cover at least two explanations to gain access to all 16 marks. If more than two are evaluated, less depth is required.

The psychology of celebrity

The term 'celebrity' means 'well known' and as a concept is a twentieth-century media invention. Several explanations have been devised to explain the public's fascination with celebrities, two of which are the social psychological and evolutionary explanations.

Social psychological explanations

Celebrities are attractive due to their popularity, enviable lifestyle, wealth and glamour, with many aspiring to be like them. This suggests a social learning effect, with celebrities acting as role models to observe and imitate, in the belief that doing so brings similar attractiveness and success. These are *parasocial* or one-sided relationships, which occur with individuals outside of a person's real social network, though they are perceived as real relationships, with celebrity gossip, for instance, treated as actual fact.

Key terms

Celebrity – person of public fame
Evolutionary explanation – perceiving the attractiveness of celebrity as serving an adaptive function
Fandom – the collective supporters of a particular celebrity interest
Stalking – to follow or watch a person persistently out of obsession

Zajonc (1968) saw the popularity of celebrities as due to the *mere exposure effect*, which believes that repeated exposure to a stimulus is sufficient for the enhancement of an individual's attitude towards it. In other words, repeated exposure to celebrities causes people to find them attractive, comforting and trustful.

Personality factors may contribute to an attraction to celebrity, with certain personalities having a greater need for fame and thus a greater need to be associated with those already renowned.

Research has identified many celebrities as coming from impoverished and downtrodden backgrounds, suggesting that some are attracted to celebrity because they feel isolated and rejected by the culture in which they live. Becoming famous helps them to feel wanted and accepted.

Research: social psychological explanations

- De Backer *et al.* (2007) believed that celebrities are viewed as higher-status members of society and thus used for behaviour modelling. Mass media audiences gossip about celebrities to learn about them and thus emulate them, with the motivation that imitation will raise an individual's status, supporting the idea of a social learning effect.

- Aron *et al.* (1991) asked participants to generate visual images of particular individuals, finding that participants had more vivid images of the actress and singer Cher than they did of their own mothers. This illustrates how influential parasocial relationships are, as portrayed by the popularity explanation, giving it increased validity.

- DeBacker *et al.* (2007) conducted a survey of 838 participants and 103 interviews, finding that the younger a person, the more they 'learn' from celebrities, and the greater the media exposure, the more celebrities are interpreted in terms of belonging to people's social networks. Also, the type of influence celebrities have changes as people age, from being a teacher when young, to being a friend when older, again illustrating the different influences that parasocial relationships can have.

- Freedman *et al.* (1978) found that participants given repeated exposure to celebrities with interests, personalities and opinions very different to their own disliked them even more, suggesting that the 'mere exposure' effect only works with agreeable stimuli and therefore acts more to confirm attraction than actually form it.

- Simonton (1994) found that specific personalities had a greater need for recognition, with Type A personalities most likely to have the drive to succeed and a tendency to take risks to do so, supporting the idea that personality factors contribute to finding celebrities attractive.

- Giles (2000) argued there are an abnormally high number of Jewish Nobel Prize winners and black pop musicians and sports people, areas associated with academic and popular fame respectively. This supports the idea that people from oppressed cultural backgrounds are attracted to celebrity as a means of gaining self-esteem and respect. Simonton (1994) backed this up by listing the many homosexuals who achieve fame, especially in the arts, suggesting that 'unconventional people' become obsessively involved in their work as a means of achieving success in cultures in which they feel estranged.

Evaluation

Social psychological explanations

- Studies into personality types and attraction to celebrity lack credibility, as they involve retrospective analysis, relying on identifying famous people and attempting to determine their personality characteristics. They tend to be descriptive, therefore, and lacking in scientific rigour.

- The majority of research into the attraction of celebrity is performed in western cultures and findings may be culturally specific.

- An obsession with celebrity culture may create several problems through people indulging in social comparison with celebrities, something that is encouraged by the media – for instance, materialism, where people come to believe, and pursue, the idea that only through fame and its trappings can happiness be achieved. Such pursuit may actually prevent people from realising true personal growth and happiness. Another problem is caused by media impressions of female celebrities as very slender and 'body perfect', an effect often achieved by doctoring pictures of celebrities. Impressionable people try to emulate celebrity body types, often encouraged by media presentations of 'celebrity diets', leading to eating disorders.

- Social psychological explanations ignore the important role of biological factors in determining attraction to celebrity (see 'Evolutionary explanations' below), and a combination of both types of explanation may lead to a better understanding of the phenomenon. For instance, repeated exposure to celebrities may cause them to seem comforting and trustworthy, for which people have a biological predisposition, as it has an adaptive survival value.

Evolutionary explanations

Evolutionary theory perceives behaviours aiding survival and reproduction as being favoured by natural selection. Therefore, individuals who have qualities suiting their environment benefit from them by having an increased chance of survival and being able to reproduce and pass on those beneficial qualities, through their genes, into the next generation. Through natural selection, such qualities become more widespread throughout the population.

Thus evolutionary theory perceives the widespread attractiveness of celebrity as serving an adaptive function and bestowing a survival value. As most human evolution occurred in the Pleistocene era, also known as the Environment of Evolutionary Adaptiveness (EEA), behaviours linked to the attractiveness of celebrities are seen as adaptive to that environment, rather than to the present.

Evolutionary theory also sees people as becoming celebrities because of their attractive qualities, which gives them an adaptive advantage in giving better access to resources.

Gossip

Language is seen as having evolved to fulfil several functions, one of which was the communication of social information within a group. Dunbar (1997) believes that during the EEA, groups grew so large that gossip became the most effective manner of communicating information about social relationships and hierarchies. Gossiping increased knowledge of events within a group, so good gossipers were better at surviving, because they could keep up to date with the rivalries and affairs of others and pick up vital information about the availability and whereabouts of resources before others did.

This explains the unending appeal of celebrity journalism, as celebrities are seen as alpha males and females, those with attractive qualities important to survival and reproduction. Therefore, keeping up to date with these people, what habits they have, what characteristics they display, is seen as beneficial information to shaping personal behaviour, hence the popularity of celebrity gossip magazines. So just as humans are hard-wired by evolution to consume as much food as possible, evolution similarly compels people to consume as much celebrity gossip as possible.

Gossiping about celebrities is also beneficial, as being in possession of such 'important' information helps to elevate status and cement social relationships, again improving survival chances.

Attractiveness

Evolutionary theory sees attractiveness as adaptive, incurring better reproduction opportunities and therefore having a survival value. Interest in celebrities often focuses on their enhanced attractiveness, explaining their lofty status. For instance, many celebrity females are young, healthy-looking, slender and firm-breasted – all characteristics associated with fertility and which are attractive to males. Male celebrities often possess attractive features beneficial to reproduction, like muscularity, symmetrical features and resource richness. Indeed, interest in celebrity tends to be more female-orientated, which evolution explains as allowing females to compare and focus on desirable males as a means of selection. Female interest in female celebrities is perceived as females competing in levels of attractiveness, as well as learning attractiveness skills from dominant alpha females.

Prestige

Evolutionary theory sees individuals desiring to be celebrities, as enhanced status and resources bestow a survival value and present better opportunities for successful reproduction. There is also a benefit in imitating celebrities, as such imitation may bring more resources, protection and reproductive opportunities, again bestowing an adaptive value.

Research: evolutionary explanations

- Dunbar (1997) reports that two-thirds of conversation is spent on social topics, supporting the idea that language evolved for social purposes.

- De Backer *et al.* (2005) found that interest in celebrity gossip is a by-product of an evolved mechanism useful for acquiring fitness-relevant survival information.

- Fieldman (2008) found that females find male celebrities attractive because of qualities advertising toughness, stamina and high levels of testosterone, all indicators of good genetic quality and an ability to provide resources.

- Morin *et al.* (2008) found that females are more influenced by celebrities endorsing products, supporting the idea of interest in celebrity being a more female-orientated feature.

- Reynolds (2009) believed that evolution programmes humans to find certain individuals attractive, because they share similar genes and thus have the same perception of beauty, explaining why celebrities are universally popular.

Evolutionary explanations

- Giles (2000) saw an evolutionary significance in celebrity as a means of preserving one's identity to guide future generations – as famous Romans were immortalised as statues, celebrities nowadays are immortalised on film, and so on. This places evolution on a cultural, rather than a purely biological level.

- Evolutionary theory sees celebrity as something people have aspired to. However, many are reluctant celebrities, thrust into the limelight without personal desire – for example, the parents of missing toddler Madeleine McCann.

- Celebrity journalism often focuses on attractiveness, romantic liaisons and reproductive success, supporting the idea that attraction to celebrity has an evolutionary basis.

- Evolutionary theory is accused of being reductionist, as it reduces behaviour to the single explanation of adaptive fitness, thus ignoring other explanations. It is also accused of being deterministic in seeing behaviour as driven by biological factors, with no input for free will.

Research into intense fandom

Celebrity worship

Celebrity worship occurs in all age groups, but is seen as peaking between 11 and 17 years, and then declining slowly afterwards. Level of education is also associated with celebrity worship – the less education, the greater the amount of celebrity worship. This may be because educational high-achievers perceive the majority of celebrities as less educated than themselves and thus less worthy of adulation. Males are generally more interested in sports stars, while females are more interested in the entertainment world.

Figure 10.09 Celebrity worship peaks between 11 and 17 years of age

Researchers have attempted to create reliable measurements of celebrity interest, like the Celebrity Attitude Scale, which indicates that some people's interest in celebrities is so high that it can be considered as *celebrity worship syndrome*, a condition characterised by an obsessive enthralment with celebrities (see 'Contemporary research: McCutcheon and Houran (2003)' on page 402). Research also suggests that most people's interest is based on the entertainment value of celebrities, but a minority have an almost pathological interest, characterised by delusions and fantasies.

Research: intense fandom

- McCutcheon *et al.* (2002) found a negative correlation of −0.4 between amount of education and amount of celebrity worship, suggesting that those with less education have a more intense interest in celebrity.

- McCutcheon *et al.* (2002) conducted research on 262 participants from Florida and developed the Celebrity Attitude Scale, measuring items on three categories of celebrity worship:

  1. **Entertainment sub-scale** – measures social aspects of celebrity worship, like discussions with friends.

  2. **Intense personal sub-scale** – measures strength of feelings and levels of obsession.

  3. **Borderline pathological sub-scale** – measures levels of uncontrollable feelings and behaviour.

It was concluded that celebrity worship has a single dimension, with lower-scoring individuals showing an avid interest in celebrities, like reading about them, while high-scoring individuals tend to overidentify and become obsessive about them.

- Maltby *et al.* (2003) amassed data from over 1,700 British participants, aged between 14 and 62, finding three dimensions of fandom:

  1. **Entertainment social** – people who are attracted to celebrities for their entertainment value.

  2. **Intense–personal** – people who develop obsessive tendencies towards celebrities.

  3. **Borderline pathological** – people who develop uncontrollable fantasies and behaviour patterns.

- Maltby *et al.* (2004) found that those in the entertainment social category were mentally healthy, but those in higher categories were prone to poor mental and physical health.

- Maltby's (2002) entertainment social dimension of fandom is consistent with Stever's (1991) observation that fans are attracted to celebrity due to their perceived ability to entertain and capture attention.

- Gabriel (2008) gave 348 students an 11-item questionnaire measuring self-esteem and then asked them to write an essay about their favourite celebrity, followed by the same questionnaire. Participants who initially scored low on self-esteem scored much higher after writing the essay, suggesting that they assimilated the celebrities' characteristics in themselves and thus boosted self-esteem, possibly something they could not do in real relationships, as the fear of rejection stops them getting close to people.

- Maltby *et al.* (2005) found an interaction between intense personal celebrity worship and body image in female adolescents aged between 14 and 16 years, suggesting that parasocial relationships with celebrities seen as having positive body images lead to negative body images in female adolescents and possible eating disorders. However, this was short-lasting, generally disappearing with the onset of adulthood.

- McCutcheon (2006) found no relationship between childhood attachment patterns and mild forms of celebrity worship, suggesting that such interests are not formed by childhood tendencies.

Evaluation

Intense fandom

- McCutcheon *et al.* (2004) believed that low levels of education are associated with high levels of fandom, because education is related to intelligence, and thus more intelligent people are better able to see through the cult of celebrity.

- Much research into celebrity worship uses questionnaires, which although allowing lots of information to be collected relatively quickly, can be affected by socially desirable and idealised answers, and can therefore lack validity. Findings also tend to be in the form of correlations, which do not show causal relationships and may be affected by other variables. For instance, the relationship between low levels of education and high-levels of fandom may actually concern levels of intelligence.

- Mild forms of celebrity worship are potentially beneficial. Larsen (1995) found that intense attachments to celebrities provided young people with attitudinal and behavioural exemplars.

- West and Sweeting (2002) recommended media training in schools to illustrate the dangers of celebrity worship and eating disorders, especially in adolescent girls.

- MacDougal (2005) believed the veneration given to dead celebrities by some fans is like that found in charismatic religions, suggesting that religious and celebrity worship may fulfil similar needs in some individuals.

The world's most obsessive fan (not necessarily a title to be proud of) is possibly Beatle Bob, who, as the name suggests, looks like a Beatle circa the 1960s, and who since Christmas Day 1996 has graced a live show every single day with his 'Beatle Bob' dance, turning up all over the USA to do so. This is even more remarkable when you learn that he does not drive. If you are ever in St Louis on the third Thursday of a month, check out his 'Beatle Bob presents live show', or to access the Beatle Bob story, go to www.beatlebob.com
Beatle Bob has never married.

Contemporary research

McCutcheon and Houran (2003)

Celebrity worship syndrome

Celebrity worship syndrome (CWS) is a fascination with the lives of the rich and famous that can become addictive and cross the border from harmless fun to dysfunctional obsession. Evolutionary explanations have been developed to explain human interest in celebrities, which suggests that such behaviour has an adaptive value, but at its extremes CWS can develop into mentally disordered behaviour, involving delusions and stalking. The researchers here were interested in assessing how common CWS is within the general population, and for what reasons individuals develop such a fascination.

Aim

To assess whether the conventional view that interest in celebrities divides into pathological and non-pathological cases is true.

Procedure

Six hundred participants completed a personality test and were interviewed about their own degree of interest in celebrities.

Participants were asked to rate statements, such as, 'If he/she asked me to do something illegal as a favour, I would probably do it.'

Findings

One-third of the participants suffered from CWS:

- Twenty per cent followed celebrities in the media for entertainment social reasons, with such people tending to have extrovert personalities.

- Ten per cent had developed an intense personal attitude towards celebrities, bordering on an addiction, and often believing they had a special bond with a star. Their personalities tended to be neurotic, tense, emotional and moody.

- One per cent of participants were classed as borderline pathological, exhibiting impulsive, antisocial, egocentric behaviour indicative of psychosis. This group included celebrity stalkers and people willing to hurt themselves or others in the name of their idol.

Conclusions

The findings cast doubt on the conventional view that celebrity worship is categorised into pathological and non-pathological cases (harmless fun and obsession). Instead, they indicate a 'sliding scale', in which celebrity devotees become progressively more fascinated with their idols.

Individuals with intense attitudes towards celebrities are significantly more likely to suffer from anxiety, depression and social dysfunction.

Worshipping celebrities does not appear to make people dysfunctional, but it increases the chances of them becoming so.

Evaluation

- The three types of individuals with CWS correspond to Eysenck's three personality dimensions of extroversion, neuroticism and psychosis, though in unequal amounts.

- The research also indicated that people tend to become interested in celebrities at times when they are looking for direction in life, such as in their teenage years, and that such an interest can develop into addiction at a time of crisis, such as the loss of a loved one. This indicates an area for further research.

- The research does not indicate whether certain personality types develop different forms and intensities of CWS, or whether being obsessed with celebrities causes self-esteem to diminish, which then develops into depression, anxiety and even psychosis.

Research in focus

McCutcheon and Maltby's (2003) study interviewed 600 participants about their degree of interest in celebrities. A big problem with interviews is interviewer effects. Explain what these are and what measures psychologists can take to reduce them. Give two strengths and two weaknesses (other than interviewer effects) of the interview method as it relates to this study.

What ethical issues are raised by interviews and how can these be dealt with?

Such is the obsession with celebrity that some make a living from being lookalikes. Victoria Beckham lookalike Camilla Shadbolt, who spent £70,000 achieving her look, teamed up with David Beckham lookalike Andy Harmer, who spent countless hours perfecting football skills, to form a celebrity lookalike couple. To see a video of the mayhem of interest they cause, go to www.youtube.com/watch?v=zuN85Au2wMg and to www.youtube.com/watch?v=Tmg6zIPf9Kk to see Camilla arriving in Sydney.

You are the researcher

Assess the degree of celebrity worship and the proportion of people who have different levels of it by asking participants the following questions.

First, they need to select their favourite celebrity (FC).

All questions require yes/no answers.

1. I like to discuss my FC.
2. I like to listen to/watch my FC.
3. I keep up to date with news of my FC.
4. My FC is my soul mate.
5. I have a bond/identify with my FC.
6. I have frequent thoughts about my FC.
7. If I had a lot of money, I would spend it on a personal possession of my FC.
8. If my FC asked me to do something illegal, I would.
9. I would be upset if my FC got married.

If participants answer yes to questions 1 to 3, they have a mild degree of celebrity worship. If they also answer yes to questions 4 to 6, they have a moderate level of celebrity worship. If they also answer yes to questions 7 to 9, they have a high level of celebrity worship.

Work out the percentages of those with CWS and of the different levels.

Celebrity stalking

Some individuals form such an interest in celebrities that this becomes a parasocial relationship, where individuals believe they really do have connections with celebrities. Such intense fandom can occur at several levels, from a fairly harmless, even quite healthy form of celebrity worship, to more sinister, intense levels, such as stalking, defined as 'the wilful, malicious and repeated following or harassing of another person that threatens his or her safety'. Stalking lies at the far end of the continuum of celebrity worship or intense fandom, although most stalking does not involve victims who are celebrities.

Stalking has a serious negative impact on its victims and is a more common phenomenon than most people realise.

Research into stalking has attempted to create a typical profile, but although most stalkers are male and most victims female, with a high incidence among stalkers of criminality, mental illness and drug use, there is no single type of stalker. Indeed, research indicates several forms, performed for different reasons, with celebrity stalking being just one subtype. Generally, stalkers are not violent, with some stalking for reasons of care and concern, though a minority of cases have ended in murder.

Research has been aided by the development of measurement scales, like the Obsessive Relational Intrusion and Celebrity Stalking Scale, which is perceived as being reliable and valid. More recently, research has indicated a link between insecure attachment patterns and stalking, as well as personal loss preceding stalking behaviour.

Research: stalking

- Meloy (1998) reported that stalkers, of both celebrities and non-celebrities, often have a history of failed sexual relationships, with stalkers usually not in sexual relationships at the time of the stalking. Stalking in such cases is a reaction to social incompetence, social isolation and loneliness.

- Purcell *et al.* (2002) found a tendency for criminal activity and drug abuse in male stalkers and a wide range of reasons for stalking, whereas females were of a nurturing disposition, were searching for intimacy and stalked people they knew, suggesting a gender difference in stalking behaviour that indicates celebrity stalking to be more of a male pursuit.

- Kienlen *et al.* (1997) found that 63 per cent of stalkers had experienced a change or loss of primary caregiver during childhood, usually due to parental separation, while over 50 per cent reported childhood emotional, physical or sexual abuse by their primary caregivers. Eighty per cent had also experienced severe loss, like death or relationship breakdown, in the 7 months prior to the start of their stalking behaviour. This supports the idea that disturbed attachment patterns and recent personal loss is related to stalking behaviour, with stalkers attempting to compensate for their losses by pursuing their victims.

- McCutcheon *et al.* (2006) measured attraction to celebrities, finding that adults with insecure attachment types had positive attitudes towards obsessive behaviours and stalking, and also that pathological attachment types have a tendency to stalk, implying that stalking behaviour is related to childhood attachment patterns.

- Morris (2002) found that stalking was mainly conducted by males, with most victims not celebrities, but ex-intimate partners, though some offenders indulged in serial stalking. Ten per cent of women and 4 per cent of men have been stalked, rising to 17 per cent of women and 7 per cent of men if the definition is widened to 'persistent and unwanted attention', demonstrating that stalking victims are not just the rich and famous. Most victims suffered deterioration in health and serious psychological impact, and had to make significant changes to their lives, like moving house or changing jobs, suggesting that stalking is a common problem with serious consequences.

- McCutcheon *et al.* (2006) developed the Obsessive Relational Intrusion and Celebrity Stalking Scale as a measurement of celebrity stalking. Using factor analysis, the scale was found to have two sub-scales labelled 'persistent pursuit' and 'threat'. The scale has proven reliability and validity, and because it uses indirect measurements it is perceived as being free from social desirability bias.

- Mullen (2008) scrutinised 20,000 incidents of stalking the British royal family, finding that 80 per cent were by persons with psychotic disorders, like schizophrenia, and were very different from people who stalk non-famous people, suggesting that celebrity stalking is a separate phenomenon to other forms of stalking.

Contemporary research

Kamphuis and Emmelkamp (2000)

Stalking – a contemporary challenge for forensic and clinical psychiatry

Figure 10.10

Stalking is more common that most would suppose and causes intense personal distress, with evidence suggesting between that 12 to 32 per cent of females and 4 to 17 per cent of males have been stalked. The researchers here were interested in assessing whether stalking was limited to celebrities, or whether there were different types of stalkers with different motivations.

Aim

To review demographic and clinical characteristics of stalkers, as well as the psychological consequences for victims of stalking.

Procedure

A meta-analysis was conducted of peer-reviewed articles on stalking published by MEDLINE and PsychLIT.

Findings

Twenty-five per cent of stalking cases resulted in violence, with 2 per cent resulting in murder, though celebrity stalking was not generally associated with risk of violence.

There were differences in types of stalkers:

1. The *erotomanic* stalker, usually female, with a delusional belief that an older man of status is in love with her.

2. The *obsessional* stalker, who generally stalks ex-partners after relationships have soured.

3. The *resentful* stalker, who stalks to frighten and scare.

4. The *predatory* stalker, who may precipitate sexual attacks.

5. The *psychotic* stalker, who targets celebrities.

Conclusions

The general label of 'stalker' is too wide, as there appear to be several types of stalker, with different profiles, who indulge in stalking for different reasons, including psychosis and severe personality disorders.

Evaluation

- For research and treatment purposes, there is a need to arrive at a consensus on types of stalkers and associated diagnostic criteria.

- Due to the dangers associated with the condition, treatment may need to be supplemented with incentives provided by the legal system, such as restraining orders.

- Research is required to identify underlying reasons for stalking; early indications highlight disturbed childhood attachments and recent personal loss.

Evaluation

Celebrity stalking

- Research into celebrity stalking may help to understand the behaviour, leading to the formation of effective therapies. Suggested treatments include psychotherapy to address underlying causes, with a role also for drug treatments, to reduce obsessive tendencies.

- Some instances of celebrity stalking may be preventable by utilising counselling to promote more satisfactory relationship conclusions, preventing subsequent resentment developing into stalking.

- Research into stalking is problematic, as definitions and methods of assessment vary, meaning that conclusions drawn lack reliability, and even estimating stalking frequency is difficult. This suggests a need for agreed diagnostic criteria of classification, in order for meaningful research to progress towards forming effective treatments.

- Obsessive, rejected stalkers respond favourably to psychotherapy, but psychopathic stalkers who prey on celebrities are highly resistant to treatment, implying that stalking is not a unitary behaviour that varies by degree, but instead consists of separate behaviours.

- Legal interventions, like trespassing orders, are the most effective way of dealing with celebrity stalkers, but can make stalkers even more obsessive, malicious and persecutory towards their targets.

Although most are not dangerous, stalkers can pose serious risks to celebrities and to those close to them. Indeed, an obsessive stalker of film star Jodie Foster, to prove his devotion, in 1981 attempted to assassinate US President Ronald Reagan. For a video presentation of some famous stalking incidents, go to http://youtube.com/watch?v=D2YLLMI5L5E

Strengthen your learning

1a. What social psychological explanations are there to account for the attraction of celebrity?

1b. To what degree does research support these explanations?

1c. Aside from research evidence, what other evaluative points can be made about social psychological explanations?

2a. Outline how gossip, attractiveness and prestige can be seen to explain the attraction of celebrity in evolutionary terms.

2b. Construct an elaborated evaluation of evolutionary explanations, including reference to research – that is, an evaluation where points build on each other to form an effective commentary.

3a. Outline what research has suggested about celebrity worship and stalking.

3b. Construct an evaluation of studies into intense fandom in terms of their methodologies, practical applications and implications.

Assessment Check

1. Outline the social psychological explanation of celebrity. (4 marks)

2. Outline and evaluate evolutionary explanations for the attraction of celebrity. (20 marks)

3. Outline and evaluate research studies into intense fandom. (24 marks)

4. Discuss the social psychological explanation of celebrity. (24 marks)

Examination guidance

The outline in question 1 should be sufficient to gain the 4 marks on offer, so do not over-produce it, as extra credit would not be earned and valuable examination time would be wasted.

In question 2, most effort should be spent on evaluating the evolutionary explanation, as it is worth 16 marks, compared to only 4 marks for the outline.

Question 3 requires a discussion of relevant research studies. Description of these is required, though the mark allocation is more heavily in favour of the evaluation, 16 marks as opposed to 8. Research studies into celebrity worship and stalking would be appropriate, with evaluation possibly centring on what research tells us about fandom and appropriate methodological considerations.

With question 4, there are a number of social psychological explanations, such as SLT, social identity theory, positive active model, so a good way to construct an answer would be to outline at least two of these and then create an evaluation based on comparing the strengths and weaknesses of the different explanations.

Summing up

- SLT sees the learning of pro-social and antisocial behaviours occurring through the media, by observation and imitation of role models.

- Research suggests that pro-social and antisocial behaviours are learned via SLT.

- Cognitive priming sees media cues in memory being used as scripts for later similar scenarios.

- Desensitisation through repeated exposure to media reduces responses to stimuli, creating indifference to violence and compassion fatigue.

- Although there's concern over harmful effects, research suggests that video games have positive aspects too.

- Computers are associated with negative concerns, like deindividuation, disinhibition, addiction and retarded development. However, they also have positive functions as educational tools, teaching social skills and building relationships.

- The Hovland-Yale model centres on the role of persuasion, perceiving attitude change as a response to communication and a sequential process, comprising stages of attention, comprehension, reactance and acceptance.

- The elaboration likelihood model explains how persuasive messages are processed through central and peripheral routes, with attitude change occurring through cognitive evaluation and persuasion, dependent on the degree of elaboration of messages.

- The persuasiveness of television is dependent on individual differences in viewing habits and influence.

- The most persuasive form of television is public broadcasting campaigns, while advertising is relatively non-cost-effective.

- The hypodermic effect sees television as manipulating carefully targeted audiences.

- The two-step flow theory sees television filtering messages through opinion leaders.

- The uses and gratification theory sees people as active processors, using television to fulfil their needs, with television and its audience interacting to produce an effect.

- The SLT explanation of celebrity suggests that celebrities act as role models, who people observe and imitate, in the belief that doing so brings similar attractiveness and success.

- The mere exposure effect believes that repeated exposure to celebrities causes people to find them attractive, comforting and trustworthy.

- Evolutionary theory perceives the widespread attractiveness of celebrity as serving an adaptive function and bestowing a survival value by giving better access to resources.

- Celebrity gossip reflects an adaptive advantage of communicating information beneficial to increased survival.

- Evolutionary theory sees individuals as desiring to be celebrities because enhanced status and resources bestow a survival value, presenting better opportunities for successful reproduction.

- Celebrity worship ranges from those attracted to celebrities for their entertainment value, to those who are borderline pathological with delusional fantasies.

- Stalking lies at the far end of the continuum of celebrity worship, involving wilful, malicious and repeated following or harassing of another person that threatens their safety.

- There are several forms of stalking, of which celebrity stalking is just one type.

- Research sees a link between stalking and insecure attachment types and recent personal loss.

11 The psychology of addictive behaviour

Models of addictive behaviour	**410**
The biological model	411
The cognitive model	414
Learning models	415
Explanations for specific addictions	418
Vulnerability to addiction	**426**
Media influences on addictive behaviour	431
Reducing addictive behaviour	**434**
Models of prevention	434
Types of intervention	436
Summing up	**445**

Decoding the specification

The specification outlines what you must study in order to answer any examination question you might face. It focuses first on biological, cognitive and learning approaches to explaining initiation, maintenance and relapse of addiction and their applications to smoking and gambling. These are explicitly listed and could be referred to in the wording of examination questions.

When studying vulnerability to addiction, the risk factors of stress, peers, age and personality must be covered, as direct questions could be asked about them.

There is a general requirement to understand media influences in addictive behaviour, so studying any relevant material would be appropriate.

When learning about ways of reducing addictive behaviour, the theory of planned behaviour must be covered as a model of prevention, as it is specifically named and therefore could be directly examined. Similarly, the types of intervention listed, psychological, biological and public health interventions must be studied, including their effectiveness, as they too could be specifically tested.

Models of addictive behaviour

IN THE NEWS

Adapted from the *Daily Telegraph*, 19 August 2010, © Telegraph Media Group Limited 2010

Britons spend half their waking hours using technology, finds Ofcom

The average Briton spends 45 per cent of their waking hours using technology, the media regulator Ofcom found.

Listening to the radio, viewing television, surfing the web or communicating using other gadgets at work and at home contribute to the total.

Rising use of 'smartphones', which allow access to the internet while on the move, and social networking websites like Facebook are partly responsible for the high figure.

Some 13.5 million people surfed the internet on their mobile phone this year, up from 5.7 million 2 years ago.

Facebook was the most popular site for people on the move, accounting for 45 per cent of mobile internet use, compared with 8 per cent for Google.

People are also using several different forms of media at the same time, surfing the internet while watching television, or listening to the radio as they write emails.

That allows the average person to cram 8 hours and 48 minutes of media time into a 7-hour period during the day.

Figure 11.01

The use of technology is definitely a key part of many people's lives, and there are indisputable benefits for both work and leisure. However, the downside is the rapidly increasing number of people exhibiting clinical signs of dependence on technology usage; indeed, the Capio Nightingale mental hospital in London is now providing a dedicated treatment service for 'young person technology addiction'. Traditionally, people think of addiction as involving dependency on physical substances, like those found in alcohol, drugs or cigarettes. But addiction to technology, just like addiction to gambling, is just as much a dependency, bringing all the associated problems of addiction with it. So if you find you cannot go 10 minutes without checking your emails, or feel sensations of panic if deprived of your mobile phone, then maybe your use of technology is going beyond being a benefit to your life and starting to become dysfunctional.

The biological model

The biological model perceives addiction as a physiologically controlled pattern of behaviour, with initiation of addiction occurring by genetic vulnerability, triggered by environmental stressors, while maintenance is regulated through the activation of dopamine, which some drugs, like cocaine, have a direct effect on. Relapse is explained as due to physiological cravings.

On a neurobiological basis, the model perceives brain circuitry regulating survival behaviours as underlying the development and maintenance of substance abuse. For instance, the *mesocorticolimbic dopamine pathway* (MDP) involved in reinforcements associated with natural reward states, such as eating, and with less basic needs, such as social interaction, is similarly activated with drug cravings.

The prefrontal cortex (PFC) is seen as having an executive function in decision making and controlling behaviour, inhibiting the drive to respond to urges for immediate reinforcement, if the long-term consequences result in negative outcomes. Therefore, addicts are perceived as having impairments in the workings of their PFC, overriding inhibitions to not seek long-term damaging reinforcements.

When the brain is activated excessively, neurochemical changes occur, leading to changes in brain function. Chronic drug use increases dopamine production, leading to *desensitisation*, the neural mechanism underlying tolerance, whereby dopamine receptors become less sensitive and individuals require higher/more frequent doses to achieve the behavioural effect. This also reduces PFC activity, reducing addicts' ability to resist cravings.

Initial research relied on animal experimentation, with many species showing intense preference for self-administering drugs. Such findings are backed up by more recent brain–imaging techniques.

Research: the biological model

- Small *et al.* (2001) used brain imaging to find that eating chocolate was associated with increased blood flow in the MDP, and that motivation to eat more chocolate activated the same parts of the pathway as did drug cravings, suggesting that brain circuitry involved in reinforcing survival behaviours is similarly involved with addiction.

- Ginovart *et al.* (1999) used PET scanning to find reduced dopamine D2 receptor density after animals were chronically exposed to amphetamines, suggesting that desensitisation had occurred through biochemical changes, an alteration in brain function seen as affecting tolerance levels.

- Overstreet *et al.* (1993) found that different genetic strains of rats demonstrated differences in levels of liking for alcohol, suggesting that preference for alcohol is under genetic control.

- Van den Bree *et al.* (1998) studied 188 twin pairs, finding that dependency was influenced by genetic factors, especially so for males. In females, genetic influences accounted for 47 per cent of differences between identical and fraternal twins, rising to 79 per cent in males, suggesting a gender difference in dependency vulnerability.

Are you addicted to technology? Take the following online test to check your dependency levels, but remember it is only a bit of fun, not a proper diagnostic test. Go to http://mygaming.co.za/forum/archive/index.php/t-4604.html

Key terms

Addiction – dependency on something psychologically or physically habit-forming

Biological model – addiction occurring as a physiologically controlled pattern of behaviour

Cognitive model – addiction occurring as distorted thinking relating to dysfunctional beliefs

Learning models – addiction occurring by environmental interactions producing euphoric outcomes.

- Nielsen *et al.* (2008) compared DNA from former heroin addicts and non-addicts, finding a relationship between addiction and certain gene variants. Some genes also seemed to act against becoming addicted, these differences in behaviour patterns indicating a genetic basis to addiction.

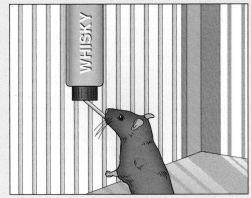

Figure 11.02 Research with rats indicates that the degree of preference for alcohol is genetically controlled

Classic research

Kendler and Prescott (1998)

Drug abuse among female twins

Some people who take drugs become addicts, causing serious problems in their own and others' lives. However, some individuals can take drugs on an occasional basis without ever becoming dependent. By studying patterns of drug use in twins, the researchers hoped to clarify the role that genes play in predisposing individuals to drug addiction. MZ twins share identical genes and similar environments, while DZ twins also share similar environments, but a much lesser genetic relationship (50 per cent compared to 100 per cent). Therefore, if the concordance rate for drug abuse were higher among MZ twins it would indicate a genetic link.

Aim

To compare concordance levels among MZ (identical) and DZ (non-identical) twins of drug abuse.

Procedure

Interviews were conducted with 1,934 female twins aged 22 to 62 years, about their usage of drugs, including cocaine.

Drug use was defined as at least one instance of taking a particular narcotic drug.

Drug abuse was defined, as per the DSM-IV classification system definition, as demonstrating symptoms such as recurrent social or interpersonal problems caused by effects of the drug.

Drug dependence was defined, again as per DSM-IV, as displaying symptoms such as taking larger amounts of the drug.

Findings

Concordance rates for using, abusing or being dependent on drugs were higher for MZ than for DZ twins.

For cocaine use, concordance was 54 per cent for MZ twins against 42 per cent for DZ twins.

For cocaine abuse, concordance was 47 per cent in MZ twins against 8 per cent for DZ twins.

For cocaine dependence, concordance was 35 per cent in MZ twins against 0 per cent in DZ twins.

Conclusions

There is a genetic link to drug usage.

Genetic factors play a major role in the progression from drug use to abuse and dependence.

continued ...

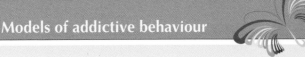

...continued

Evaluation

- Abuse and dependence seem highly heritable; the investigators estimate that for cocaine usage genetic factors are responsible for between 60 and 80 per cent of the differences in abuse and dependence between fraternal and identical twin pairs.

- Family and social environmental factors are also influential in determining whether individuals use drugs; otherwise, concordance rates would be 100 per cent for MZ twins.

- As only female twins were used, results cannot be generalised to males. Van den Bree *et al.* (1998), researching into twins, found that genetic factors for drug abuse are even higher in males than in females.

Research in focus

Twin studies compare concordance rates. What is meant by this term?

Explain how twin studies can help to explore the nature versus nurture debate?

In what way might adoption studies be considered a better research method?

An alternative to genetic or environmental determination of behaviour is the interactionist viewpoint. Explain why this alternative is a better way of understanding the nature versus nurture debate.

Evaluation

The biological model

- It is unclear whether impairments in the workings of the PFC cause addictive behaviour, or occur because drug-taking damages reward circuitry, leading to maintenance of dependent behaviour. In other words, does addiction cause brain changes, or are addicts' brains like this before addiction occurs.

- The model relies heavily on evidence from animal studies, which may not be generalisable to humans. There is also the problem of subjectively interpreting animal behaviour, as they are unable to relate their feelings/motivations. Animal experimentation raises ethical issues for some, with justification occurring through use of cost-benefit analyses, like the possibility that such research may lead to effective therapies to treat addictions.

- Biological explanations do not consider the role that psychological factors play. Explaining addiction by reference to brain structure and function implies that once identified, addiction is fully explained. But identical brain activity is also triggered when addicts are not directly involved in addictive behaviour, suggesting that psychological factors, like conditioned responses and cognitive processes, are also involved. These can be seen as complementing biological factors, but neurobiological approaches are reductionist, as they exclude non-biological factors.

- There is a wealth of evidence from research into genetics, twin and family studies, supporting the biological model, indicating the existence of biological predispositions towards addiction.

- The model is more able to explain physical addictions, like drugs, though other addictions like gambling can be explained by biological means too.

- Addiction to one drug can produce cross-tolerance to other related drugs – for example, opiates – and withdrawal symptoms from abstaining from an addicted drug can be addressed by taking a similar drug – for example, methadone for heroin. This suggests that similar drugs act on the nervous system in the same way, supporting the biological model.

The cognitive model

The cognitive model sees addiction as due to distorted thinking relating to dysfunctional beliefs, like social functioning being dependent on drug use. These maladaptive cognitive processes relate to mood, causing addicts to believe that happiness is impossible without drugs. Such dysfunctional beliefs are self-fulfilling, leading to a perception of personal incapability in controlling drug usage, in turn leading to an inability to direct attention away from addictive behaviour.

Faulty thinking also leads addicts to focus on positive features of drug use and minimise negative ones, again strengthening dependency. Another cognitive feature is impaired decision-making abilities; addicts classically focus on strategies of immediate pleasure, even with the knowledge that such choices will be harmful in the long term.

The *relapse prevention model* (RP) explains initiation of dependency, by perceiving *discriminative stimuli*, contexts in which positive outcomes are expected, as triggering motivation to take drugs. If addicts believe that heroin is rewarding when they are unhappy, they are motivated to take it when unhappy. The model also sees cognitive factors influencing whether relapses occur after periods of abstinence – for example, by the strength of motivation not to take drugs, knowledge/belief in coping strategies and an individual's belief in their capacity to resist. Therefore, the model views prevention of relapse as due not just to possessing adequate cognitive strategies, but also having sufficient personal resources to use such strategies. The fewer alternatives an individual has for dealing with a situation, the higher that positive outcome expectancies for drug use become and the increasingly likely relapse is. If drug use is successfully resisted and attributed to personal ability, confidence in handling future threats is raised.

Cognitive dissonance explains addiction as due to the conflict between two opposing beliefs – for example, 'I am a drug addict' and 'I want to be drug-free'. Individuals are motivated to reach consistency between their dissonant beliefs, for instance by creating irrational support for one of the beliefs, such that some inherent personal quality means they cannot give up – that is, 'It is no use even trying' – and they relapse. This is an easier option than changing the other belief by giving up drugs.

Cognitive explanations can be applied to all forms of dependency.

Research: the cognitive model

- Miller *et al.* (1996) found that among alcoholics being treated as outpatients a strong predictor of relapse was a lack of coping skills, illustrating the cognitive nature of addiction.

- Cummings *et al.* (1980) found that alcoholics, smokers, opiate addicts, gamblers and overeaters lapsed due to negative emotional states: 35 per cent of lapses were preceded by negative mood; another 16 per cent followed interpersonal conflict; and a further 20 per cent was attributed to social pressure. This suggests that addictive behaviour is engaged in because of its stress-reducing qualities, and stressful situations are particularly risky to recent 'quitters'.

- Koski-Jannes (1992) found that addictions form from short-sighted means of dealing with stressful situations, giving initially positive, but later negative consequences, leading to a self-perpetuating cycle of addiction regulated by self-serving thoughts. This suggests that the cognitive model explains how addictions are initiated.

- Using brain scans, Grant *et al.* (1996) found increased activity in areas of the frontal cortex associated with decision making during periods of craving, suggesting that the cognitive and biological models can be linked.

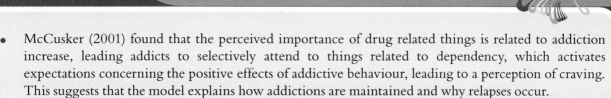

- McCusker (2001) found that the perceived importance of drug related things is related to addiction increase, leading addicts to selectively attend to things related to dependency, which activates expectations concerning the positive effects of addictive behaviour, leading to a perception of craving. This suggests that the model explains how addictions are maintained and why relapses occur.

- Using a questionnaire, Ratelle *et al.* (2004) found that gambling addicts had persistent thoughts about gambling and poorer concentration on daily tasks, indicating a cognitive element to addiction.

- Hester and Garavan (2005) found that as thoughts of drug use are in working memory, attention remains focused on relevant environmental features, which maintains thoughts relating to drug use within working memory, suggesting that addictive behaviours and cravings become self-perpetuating.

Evaluation

The cognitive model

- The RP model has elements in common with health behaviour models that have considerable research support. RP's link to cognitive dissonance also gives it strength, as cognitive dissonance is well supported too.
- The biological model is a better explanation of the initiation of dependency, but the cognitive model accounts more ably for maintenance and relapses.
- Cognitive models offer incomplete explanations, being based on expectations and beliefs, thus ignoring important biological factors.
- The relative success of cognitive behavioural treatments suggests that addiction must have a cognitive component.
- Ryle (1990) believed that 'dilemmas' in which alternatives are seen in too limited a manner – for example, 'Without drugs I would have no friends' – and 'snags', where appropriate aims are abandoned due to perceiving them as dissatisfactory – for example, 'I would abstain but …' – create mental obstacles to changing addictive behaviour, illustrating the cognitive nature of the problem.

Learning models

Classical conditioning

This sees addiction occurring through two stimuli becoming associated with each other. One of these, the *unconditioned stimulus* (UCS), produces a certain response naturally. The other, the *conditioned stimulus* (CS), produces the same response, but through association with the first, as below.

Operant conditioning

This sees dependency behaviours, like drug taking, as being positively reinforcing, through the euphoria that drugs provide, and negatively reinforcing, due to the anxiety they reduce. Such reinforcements strengthen the drug-taking behaviour, increasing the likelihood of the behaviour recurring and the individual becoming addicted. Increased drug usage can be perceived as an attempt to increase the reinforcements. The neurotransmitter dopamine is especially seen as a reinforcer within the *brain reward system*, as many drugs act on dopamine synapses to produce euphoria.

One schedule of reinforcement is the *variable ratio* schedule (VR), where reinforcement occurs every so often on average, so that the number of responses required on any particular occasion is unpredictable. This produces a high, steady rate of response, just like that seen in gambling. The gambler knows a win will happen eventually, but not exactly when. Therefore, as long as they win occasionally, gamblers will continue gambling, whatever their losses.

Social learning theory

Social learning theory (SLT) sees addiction resulting from vicarious learning, where dependent behaviour is observed and imitated if the model is seen to receive some form of reinforcing reward. The media is seen as a powerful source of social learning.

Social learning theorists also believe there are influential *cognitive mediating variables* between stimuli and responses influencing behaviour, including *self-concept*, *self-monitoring* and *self-efficacy* (the belief that individuals can act effectively and exercise control over events influencing their lives). These factors especially influence abstinence from addictive behaviour, by the degree to which individuals see themselves as capable of affecting their own behaviour.

Research: learning models

- Meyer *et al.* (1995) found that the sight of a hypodermic needle created positive feelings in addicts, demonstrating the role of classical conditioning in addictive behaviour.

- White and Hiroi (1993) found that rats preferred locations where they had previously received injections of amphetamines, suggesting that 'place preference' had been learned by a process of association.

- Claridge and Davis (2003) noted that burst-firing of dopamine reward neurons occurs not just during rewarding activities, but before they begin – for example, cocaine addicts' reward systems respond when offered a line of cocaine.

- Olds (1958) found that rats with an electrode placed into certain brain areas, especially the *nucleus accumbens*, press a lever in a Skinner box up to 2,000 times a minute until collapsing, suggesting a link between biological and learning factors.

- Farber *et al.* (1980) found an important difference between alcohol use through negative reinforcement (escape drinking) and positive reinforcement (social drinking), suggesting that particular learning factors may be more linked to addiction.

Figure 11.03 The sight of drugs paraphernalia creates positive emotions in addicts, emphasising the role of classical conditioning in dependency behaviours

- Bahr *et al.* (2005) found from research on over 4,000 US teenagers that drug taking by peers was a big influence in initiating drug use, suggesting an important role for SLT.

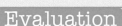

Evaluation

Learning models

- Classical conditioning explains how stimuli associated with addictions, such as drug paraphernalia, produce similar responses to dependent behaviours, but cannot explain why dependent behaviours are initiated, as classical conditioning only accounts for involuntary behaviour.

- Sharpe (2002) claimed that although VR reinforcement schedules explain social gambling, they do not explain pathological gambling, where consistent and significant losses do not stop gambling behaviour. Possibly large wins early in a gambler's 'career' establish and sustain pathological gambling, distorting expectations of the outcomes of gambling and supporting big losses in the expectation of future big wins.

- The fact that many abstaining addicts do not experience withdrawal symptoms and cravings suggests that biological factors are not as important as learning ones.

- Many forms of addiction respond favourably to behavioural treatments, indicating a learning component. However, such treatments only produce short-term benefits, suggesting that symptoms are addressed, but not causes, implying that others factors are involved too.

- SLT explains initiation of addiction. Exposure to a model, observed to be reinforced for their behaviour, is sufficient for imitation of the model to occur. For instance, seeing someone win a bet might inspire an individual to bet too.

- When researching addictive behaviour, care must be taken with ethical concerns – for instance, addicts cannot always give informed consent, with the potential for harm also greatly enhanced.

- Redish (2004) produced a computational learning model of addiction based on the idea that drug taking increases dopamine production as part of a learning-reward system. This model allows predictions to be made and tested, building a better understanding of addiction that may lead to the development of effective treatments.

Supplementary learning

The addicted brain

Drugs provide a high by boosting the activity of the brain's reward system: a complex circuit of neurons that, when stimulated, produce feelings of euphoria, encouraging repetition of whatever induced the pleasure. Chronic drug use induces changes in the structure and function of the reward system's neurons, lasting for weeks, months or years. These changes contribute to the tolerance, dependence and craving, fuelling repeated use, and lead to relapses after periods of abstinence.

The ventral tegmentum midbrain area (VTA) is rich in dopamine neurons, sending projections through the medial forebrain bundle to a set of limbic brain regions, including the nucleus accumbens (NA) and amygdala, and to the prefrontal cortex.

Together, these and related structures are known as the 'common reward pathway', with activation experienced as pleasurable and reinforcing. There are pathways linking these to other brain areas, making addicts sensitive to reminders of past highs, such as drugs paraphernalia and experiencing compulsions to take drugs again. The VTA-NA pathway informs other brain centres how rewarding activities are. The more rewarding they are, the more likely it is that they will be remembered and repeated – for instance, fMRI

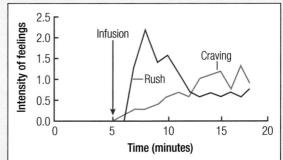

Figure 11.04

continued ...

...continued

and PET scans show that the NA in cocaine addicts' brains 'light up' when offered a line or even shown a photograph of cocaine.

These brain areas influence highs experienced and drug cravings, which increase as effects wear off. Indeed, the NA is known as the 'universal addiction site', as all drugs/addictive behaviours stimulate dopamine production in this area, which plays a pivotal role in providing stimuli with the incentives needed to increase addictive behaviour. The same regions even react in compulsive gamblers when they are shown images of slot machines.

Explanations for specific addictions

Smoking

Over 20 per cent of British people over the age of 16 smoke, with smoking perceived as a substance-related disorder by the DSM-IV classification system. Smoking produces a physical addiction to nicotine, influencing dopamine production and the brain reward system. Smokers are aware of health risks, two-thirds want to quit, and there are wide differences in how much and how often people smoke and how difficult it is to quit. Smoking is best understood by combining biological and psychological explanations. For instance, biology explains increased tolerance and maintenance of smoking, while SLT better explains initiation of smoking. Most smokers start in adolescence, few after the age of 20, with research indicating that addiction occurs quickly.

Figure 11.05 Most adult smokers started in their teens

Biological explanations

Smoking affects the production of the neurotransmitters dopamine and acetylcholine through stimulation of nicotine receptors in the brain. The neural pathways activated stimulate dopamine neurons in the mesolimbic brain area, producing a pleasurable effect in the brain reward system. Neurochemical changes in brain function lead to desensitisation and increased tolerance and maintenance of smoking behaviour, as dopamine receptors become less sensitive and individuals require increased consumption to achieve reward effects. Abstinence creates physiological cravings due to non-stimulation of nicotine receptors. Gene-mapping studies suggest a genetic link to dependency, with some more genetically vulnerable than others.

Psychological explanations

Initiation of smoking is perceived as occurring through the vicarious reinforcement of social learning, via observation and imitation of role models, especially among adolescents, which is when most first experience smoking. Smoking is often a shared social activity, presenting many opportunities for social learning experiences, including peer pressure.

Operant conditioning explains the maintenance of smoking, due to the positive reinforcement that the pleasant effect of nicotine inhalation produces. As nicotine is rapidly removed from the body, frequent reinforcements via smoking are required.

Cognitive factors also play a part, with smokers seen as possessing irrational thoughts, like believing that smoking improves concentration. Dysfunctional ideas become self-fulfilling – for instance, not smoking produces anxiety in individuals, making them believe they cannot quit, leading to a 'vicious circle' of continually giving in to cravings.

Research: explanations for smoking

- DiFranza (2008) found that 10 per cent of teenage smokers who went on to be addicts had strong cravings for smoking 2 days after first inhaling and 35 per cent within 1 month, suggesting that nicotine is strongly addictive, with long-term use not necessary for addiction. The fact that those who had cravings early on were 200 times more likely to become daily smokers suggests a genetic vulnerability.

- The US National Institute on Drug Abuse (NIDA) (2005) found that 90 per cent of US smokers started smoking as adolescents, mainly due to observation and imitation of peers, suggesting that initiation of smoking is due to SLT. Brynner (1969) found that media images of smoking create perceptions of it being attractive and tough, lending support to SLT.

- Goldberg *et al.* (1981) found that monkeys press a lever in a Skinner box to receive nicotine at similar rates as for cocaine, suggesting that smoking is maintained through its reinforcing effect, lending support to operant conditioning as an explanation.

- Pergadia *et al.* (2006) found a heritability factor in the experience of nicotine withdrawal symptoms, suggesting a genetic link and thus supporting a biological explanation.

- Calvert (2009) reported that smokers shown cigarette packets experienced strong activation in the ventral striatum and nucleus accumbens brain areas, suggesting a biological explanation of craving behaviour.

Contemporary research

deCODE genetics

New genetic factors behind nicotine dependence and lung cancer

Smoking is a leading cause of preventable death, associated with 5 million premature deaths each year. Evidence for a genetic influence on nicotine dependence prompted a search for susceptibility genes. deCODE, an organisation based in Iceland, conducting research into the human genome, has helped discover key genetic risk factors for many physical and psychological conditions. In this research, they discovered evidence for a genetic link to nicotine addiction.

Aims

To investigate the link between specific gene variants and smoking behaviour.

Procedure

A smoking history questionnaire was distributed to some 50,000 Icelanders, asking respondents whether they had ever smoked, were still smokers, and, if so, how many cigarettes they smoked per day.

Over 300,000 single-letter variations of the human genome were then analysed in a subset of more than 10,000 smokers.

Findings

A common variant in the nicotinic acetylcholine receptor gene cluster on chromosome 15q24 was discovered that was associated with the number of cigarettes smoked a day and with nicotine dependency.

Each copy of the risk variant brings a 30 per cent increase in risk of lung cancer and a 20 per cent increase in risk of peripheral arterial disease (PAD). Roughly half of all people of European descent carry at least one copy of the variant, accounting for some 18 per cent of lung cancers and 10 per cent of cases of PAD.

Conclusions

There is a genetic link to smoking dependency.

Nicotine addiction is related to the onset of serious illnesses.

continued ...

...continued

Evaluation

- The results do not explain how increased risk is conferred. It may be that those for whom nicotine is more addictive are driven to smoke more, thus increasing their exposure to environmental harm and increasing their chances of becoming seriously ill.

- The results suggest that it may be possible to develop a DNA-based test, to identify those most at risk of nicotine dependency and serious illness, so that smoking cessation efforts can be targeted at those people.

- The variant is less common among smokers who smoke fewer than 10 cigarettes per day than among non-smokers, suggesting that the variant does not influence smoking initiation, but instead incurs the risk of nicotine dependence among those who start.

Research in focus

Aside from using gene-mapping data, deCODE also gave a questionnaire on smoking habits to 50,000 Icelanders. Why are questionnaires referred to as 'self-reports'?

Give one strength and one weakness of questionnaires compared to interviews.

For what reasons might the data from the deCODE questionnaire not be valid?

What is the difference between questionnaires with 'open' questions and those with 'closed' questions?

What purpose do 'filler' questions fulfil?

Evaluation

Explanations for smoking

- Ogden (2004) reported that researchers often polarise explanations, some arguing that smoking is entirely due to biology, while others rely implicitly on SLT. However, explanations contain elements of each other – for instance, SLT explains initiation and biology explains increased tolerance.

- Shiffman (2009) reported that two-thirds of smokers only indulge occasionally in certain situations and have little desire to quit. Most research has concentrated on heavy smokers and may have led to invalid conclusions about smoking addiction; indeed, occasional smokers are not true addicts and thus challenge the idea that smoking is universally addictive.

- Personality may also be involved in smoking behaviour. Furnham and Heaven (1999) report that smokers score higher on extroversion, impulsiveness and sensation-seeking, as well as neuroticism. However, personality could be a direct causal factor, mediate other causal factors or influence behaviours detrimental to health. Interestingly, Ogden (2004) reported smokers to be problem-prone, low academic achievers, low in self-esteem and high risk takers, as well as being popular types high in self-esteem, seen as leaders of academic and social activities, illustrating the wide range of personality factors associated with smoking. This suggests that smoking can have several explanations and be performed for a range of reasons, like social acceptance and stress release.

- A better understanding of smoking has led to treatments helping people quit. Biological and psychological therapies have proven effective, suggesting that both types of explanation are valid. For instance, the success of nicotine patches implies a biological explanation, while the fact that many quit without nicotine replacement or cravings suggests a role for social and cognitive factors.

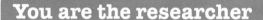

You are the researcher

Design a questionnaire of ten questions that measures attitudes and behaviour of 16- to 19-year-olds in relation to smoking. Use five open and five closed questions, plus some additional filler questions. Questions should be clear, unambiguous and simple. Your questionnaire should generate quantitative and qualitative data.

How will these two forms of data be analysed?

What steps are necessary to ensure that your questionnaire is ethical?

Gambling

Although a gambling addiction does not involve dependency on physical substances, its symptoms and effects make it as much an addiction as that to drugs. As with smoking, not all gamblers are addicts, and 30 per cent have alcohol-related problems, indicating that some may have addictive personalities. Gambling, like smoking, is best understood by combining biological and psychological explanations. For instance, biology explains the increased maintenance of and increased gambling, while SLT better explains initiation.

Biological explanations

Just like physical addictions, neurobiological mechanisms are involved in gambling dependency, with gambling increasing dopamine and other neurotransmitter production, creating pleasurable sensations in the brain reward system. Cortisol levels are also raised. Research indicates that genetic factors are at work, with some individuals more genetically vulnerable to becoming addicts, or even developing multiple addictions. Indeed, personality factors associated with gambling dependency may be under genetic influence too.

Psychological explanations

Socio-cultural factors, like increased exposure and encouragements to gamble, can explain initiation of gambling behaviour – for example, 65 per cent of the eligible British population played the National Lottery when it was introduced in 1994. SLT also explains gambling initiation through observation and imitation of gambling role models seen to gain some form of reinforcement, like monetary gain or the approval of others. Operant conditioning provides a plausible explanation for maintenance of gambling behaviour, due to the unpredictable reinforcement of periodic wins (see discussion of the variable ratio schedule under 'Operant conditioning' on page 415).

Personality also plays a part, with research indicating that pathological gamblers are impulsive, high sensation seekers, susceptible to boredom. Other important traits are sensitivity to punishment and reward orientation, qualities enabling gambling successes to have strong positive effects, which may explain continuation into dependency. Personality factors may have a genetic influence.

From a cognitive point of view, dependent gamblers have irrational thoughts and distorted beliefs about levels of skill and luck, such as successes being perceived as due to skill and losing as due to bad luck or not paying attention (see 'Classic research: Griffiths (1994)' on page 423). Superstitious beliefs often develop to account for winning and losing, leading to greater risk taking and increased persistence.

Research: explanations for gambling

- Bennett (2006) reported that twin studies indicate that genetic factors are more involved with pathological gambling than environmental factors, and a variant of the AD2 dopamine receptor, DA21, is more prevalent in pathological gamblers, supporting the biological explanation.

- Shinohara *et al.* (1995) found that raised levels of dopamine and noradrenaline occur in social gamblers only when they are gambling, but occur in anticipation of gambling and in response to gambling paraphernalia in pathological gamblers, suggesting that learning processes and biology are involved in gambling dependency.

- Roy *et al.* (2004) found higher noradrenaline levels in chronic blackjack gamblers and higher dopamine levels in chronic casino gamblers, showing pronounced activation of the HPA axis and sympathoadrenergic system, suggesting that biological neuroendocrine disturbances account for dependency.

Figure 11.06 Gamblers distort beliefs about winning and losing, seeing successes as due to skill

- Meyer *et al.* (2004) found that salivary cortisol levels rose in regular blackjack gamblers while playing, continuing long afterwards, suggesting that this reinforces future gambling.

- Clark *et al.* (2009) found that gambling near misses were misperceived as special events, encouraging gambling to continue. Brain activity was heightened in the striatum and insula cortex, areas receiving dopamine input, which have been linked to other forms of addiction, suggesting that cognitive distortions, reinforcements and biological factors are involved in gambling dependency.

- Loxton *et al.* (2008) found that chronic gamblers score higher on impulsiveness and reward orientation than non-gamblers, while Bonnaire *et al.* (2007) found that chronic gamblers score higher on sensation seeking and boredom susceptibility than non-dependent gamblers, suggesting that personality explains why some gamblers become dependent.

- Anholt *et al.* (2003) found that problem gamblers had obsessive-compulsive thinking, suggesting that dependency can be explained by cognitive factors.

Evaluation

Explanations for gambling

- The fact that pathological gamblers experience physiological withdrawal symptoms similar to those for substance addictions suggests that the same neurological brain mechanisms are involved, supporting a biological explanation.

- Care must be taken when conducting research with dependent gamblers, indeed any form of addicts, as ethical concerns of harm are heightened, and it is debatable whether people with such pathological conditions can give informed consent.

- Kim and Grant (2001) found that the drug naltrexone, which acts on dopamine production, was successful in reducing compulsions to gamble, lending support for a biological explanation, but also demonstrating how such explanations can lead to effective practical applications.

- The fact that dopamine is linked to dependency may lead to the manufacture of drugs acting on dopamine production, which could reduce not only gambling dependency, but other forms of addictive behaviour too.

- Grosset *et al.* (2009) found that dopamine agonists used to treat Parkinson's disease turn 10 per cent of patients into pathological gamblers, suggesting that dopamine is linked to gambling dependency, supporting the biological explanation.

- Paul (2008) reports that 20 per cent of teenage gambling addicts contemplate suicide, demonstrating the need for valid explanations in order that effective treatments can be developed.

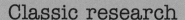

Classic research

Griffiths (1994)

The role of skill and cognitive bias in fruit machine gambling

Although gambling does not involve dependency on a physical substance, it is as much an addiction as that to drugs. Several explanations have been put forward, but in this instance a possible cognitive link to gambling dependency was investigated, which instead of using a self-report method examined actual gambling behaviour as it occurred.

Aim

To test the idea that gamblers think and behave differently to non-gamblers due to cognitive bias.

Procedure

A natural experiment was conducted where 30 regular gamblers, playing at least once a week, were compared with 30 non-regular gamblers, playing less than once a month.

A volunteer sample was used of people responding to a poster.

Each participant was given £3 to gamble on a machine that gave 30 free gambles.

The objective was to stay on the machine for 60 gambles and win back the £3.

If 60 gambles were achieved, they kept the money or carried on gambling.

Cognitive activity was measured as verbalisations uttered while participants played a fruit machine.

Perception of skill was measured by post-experimental semi-structured interview.

Findings

- Regular gamblers made comments indicating themselves to be more skilful than they actually were.
- Regular gamblers made more irrational verbalisations while playing, such as 'putting only a quid in at a time bluffs the machine'.
- Regular gamblers made verbalisations that indicated that they thought the machine to have a personality, such as 'this machine is not in a good mood'.
- Regular gamblers explained losses occurring as near misses as actually being near wins.
- Fourteen regular gamblers 'broke even' (achieved 60 gambles): ten of them stayed on until they lost all the money.
- Seven non-regular gamblers 'broke even': two of them stayed on until they lost all their money.

Table 11.01 Analysis of gamblers' and non-gamblers' verbalisations during play

CONTENT ANALYSIS OF VERBALISATIONS	NON-REGULAR PLAYERS	REGULAR PLAYERS
Machine personification	1.14	7.54
Explaining losses as near wins	0.41	3.12
Talking to the machine	0.90	2.64
Referring to personal skill	1.47	5.34

continued ...

...continued

Table 11.02 Analysis of gamblers' and non-gamblers' belief in skill or luck during play

BELIEF THAT SKILL WAS INVOLVED	NON-REGULAR PLAYERS	REGULAR PLAYERS
Mostly chance	19	10
Equal chance/skill	7	18
Skill	0	8

Conclusions

Regular gamblers believe they are more skilful than they actually are.

Regular gamblers have irrational beliefs indicating cognitive bias.

Gambling behaviour is maintained because of cognitive distortions.

Evaluation

- The criteria used to indicate regular/irregular gamblers was somewhat subjective and arbitrary, and not indicative of gambling dependency, casting doubt on the validity of the results.
- The results indicate that due to the cognitive element to gambling dependency, cognitive behavioural therapy could help gamblers to recognise and modify their irrational thinking.
- The cognitive model explains why only certain people – that is, those with cognitive biases, are at risk of becoming gambling dependent.

Research in focus

Griffiths' (1994) study was a natural experiment. Why is this research method sometimes called 'quasi-experimental'?

In what way does a natural experiment differ from a field experiment?

Under what circumstances is a natural experiment used?

Explain why in Griffiths' study participants could not be allocated randomly to the experimental conditions and why this might affect the validity of the results.

You are the researcher

Design a natural experiment to test for differences in behaviour between problem drinkers and social drinkers.

What problems are there in determining criteria to decide what classification of drinkers people are?

Explain how you would get a self-selected sample.

You will need to collect several measurements. What would they be and how would these be analysed and the results presented?

How could you also use an interview to examine cognitive activity associated with addictive behaviour?

Supplementary learning

An evolutionary perspective

Motivational systems evolved in the EEA to support responses aiding survival and reproduction. Therefore, activities found pleasurable today are rooted in behaviour increasing survival chances in the past.

Most people find gambling pleasurable, but as the odds of winning are relatively poor, why is such behaviour rewarding? The answer lies in prehistoric times, when those hunter-gatherer ancestors who were prepared to take risks and explore new areas, try new foods, and so on, were more likely to out-compete more conservative, risk-reluctant peers. If the risk taking proved to be beneficial, they were more likely to survive and pass their genes on to future generations. Hence, humans still have risk-taking genes and therefore enjoy a gamble, but usually in non-life-threatening ways.

Figure 11.07 Risk taking by young males bestows an evolutionary advantage

If gambling does aid survival and reproduction, then it should be more associated with males approaching sexual maturity, a time when they would become involved in hunting and exploration, and by doing so attract potential mates. Females at this time are likely to take fewer risks as part of their preparation for child-rearing.

Strengthen your learning

1. Outline how neurobiology may be involved in addiction.
2. Is there a genetic link to dependency? Give details.
3. Compose an evaluation of the biological model in terms of its strengths and weaknesses.
4a. Outline the cognitive model of addiction.
4b. Is the model supported by evidence?
5a. Explain the different ways in which learning experiences can lead to addiction.
5b. To what extent can learning explanations be supported? Use some research evidence in your answer.
6a. Compare biological and psychological explanations for smoking dependency and gambling dependency in terms of support from research evidence.
6b. Compose an evaluation of explanations for smoking dependency and gambling dependency, without direct reference to research studies.

One 'new' addiction featured in the media is sex addiction. It does really exist and can be as destructive as any other addiction. To learn more about the condition, go to www.bbc.co.uk/health/emotional_health/addictions/sex_addiction.shtml There are also links to lots of other addictions.

Assessment Check

1. Discuss explanations for smoking and gambling addictions. (24 marks)

2. Outline the cognitive and learning models of addiction. (8 marks)

3. Outline and evaluate the biological model of addiction to explaining initiation, maintenance and relapse. (20 marks)

4. Outline one explanation for smoking. (4 marks)

5. Outline and evaluate explanations for gambling. (20 marks)

Examination guidance

The term 'discuss' in question 1 means to outline and evaluate. The wording of the question means that explanations for both addictions must be provided. The more explanations that are provided, the less detail would be expected.

Questions 2 and 3 concern models of addiction, but in question 2 the two named models only need to be described, with a reasonable balance between the two necessary to access the top band of marks. Any evaluative material provided here would not be creditworthy. Question 3 needs an outline of the biological model, but as only 4 marks are available for this, most time and effort should be centred on the evaluation, as it accrues 16 marks. The elements of initiation, maintenance and relapse must be covered within the answer.

Question 4 requires just one explanation of smoking; offer more and all would be marked, but only the best one credited. However, question 5 requires at least two explanations, this time of gambling, though only 4 marks are available for this, so do not over-produce material. Most focus should be on the evaluation, where 16 marks are on offer. It is worth remembering that the evaluations should be primarily centred on the explanations and not on more peripheral issues, like the methodologies of associated research studies.

Vulnerability to addiction

Individuals have different levels of vulnerability to becoming dependent on different types of substance and behaviour. Factors influencing individual vulnerability can be internal, like genetic vulnerability, or external, like stress levels.

Personality

Originally it was believed that addiction led to personality defects, however research indicated that defective personality characteristics precede addiction. Indeed, it was found that neurotic and psychopathic personality types were more vulnerable to addiction, due to the attraction of substance abuse in helping to escape the everyday stresses of life that didn't bother psychologically fit people. Therefore, addiction can be seen as being related to pathological personalities, rather than addiction causing such pathology.

Various theorists have proposed the existence of an addictive personality. Eysenck (1997) outlined the psychological resource model, which proposes that dependencies arise as addictive behaviours fulfil needs related to personality type. Individuals with high levels of neuroticism [N], characterised by moodiness, irritability and anxiety, and high levels of psychotism [P], characterised by aggressiveness, emotional coldness and impulsivity, are seen as more vulnerable to addiction.

Overall, evidence suggests that personality predisposes certain individuals to vulnerability, though the concept of a distinct addictive personality type has not been supported. Common traits include: not valuing achievement, a desire for immediate gratification and high-levels of reported stress.

Key terms

Vulnerability – degree of susceptibility to addiction
Personality – the relatively enduring characteristics of a person
Peers – persons of equal status
Stress – a state of emotional strain
Media – the influence of formats of public communication on addictive behaviour

Research: personality

Chein *et al.* (1964) found that low self-esteem, learned incompetence, passivity, negative outlook and a background of dependent relationships characterised ghetto adolescent addicts, which suggests that individuals with personalities tending towards a negative outlook on life are more vulnerable to addiction.

Limson *et al.* (1991) compared alcoholics and non-alcoholics on levels of personality and assessed the relationship between personality and neurological mechanisms, by recording measures of cerebrospinal fluid concentrations. Alcoholics demonstrated significantly different personality profiles and a negative correlation between aggression and levels of cerebrospinal fluid, indicating some support for the idea that addiction is related to personality, which in turn is regulated by underlying neurobiology.

Gossop & Eysenck (1980) administered the Eysenck Personality Questionnaire to 221 addicts and 310 non-addicts, finding a large number of personality items differentiated between the two groups. An addiction scale [A-Scale] was constructed from the 32 items on which the groups differed most, most of these being drawn from the neuroticism [N] scale and associated with anxiety and depression. This suggests that [N] is related to vulnerability to addiction, though the neurotic component was found to play a lesser role in differentiating between female addicts and non-addicts.

Evaluation

Personality

- The idea of an addictive personality is supported by the fact that certain individuals can become dependent on many things, either simultaneously or over time. For example, a drug addict overcomes their dependency and then subsequently becomes addicted to alcohol

- The idea that addiction is linked to personality is also supported by the fact that many recovered addicts develop equally strong compulsions towards other activities not seen as harmfully addictive, for interest long-distance running or religious fervour.

- Traditionally, individuals with certain personality defects have been linked to dependency, due to the effects of addictions on personality, or that they are more liable to self-medicate their symptoms with addictive substances/behaviours. However, it's possible that other mediating factors are at play, such as genetics or childhood trauma. This suggests that vulnerability to addiction is more complex than first thought.

Peers

Peer pressure is very influential and can affect an individual's behaviour, especially during childhood and most especially during adolescence, where peer groupings are a prime influence on attitudes and behaviour. If peer groupings have positive attitudes towards addictive behaviours, thrill seeking and experimentation, then individuals within such peer groupings will have an increased vulnerability to dependency, indeed many individuals with addiction problems often blame the initiation and maintenance of dependency on peer pressure.

Adherence to peer pressure can be seen as a form of conformity involving normative social influence, where individuals are influenced by peer pressure due to a desire to be accepted and avoid ridicule and rejection. When a peer group adopts addictive behaviours as part of their 'norms of behaviour', then such behaviours can quickly become part of an individual's 'in-group' repertoire, used not only to show allegiance to the group, but also to identify the group as separate from other 'out-groups', that is, ones without positive attitudes to dependency behaviours.

Peer pressure can also be seen as a form of operant conditioning, where the group reinforces participation in and positive attitudes towards addictive behaviours, by rewards of praise and increased status within the group. Peers also act as a form of social learning, modelling addictive behaviours so that other individuals will observe and imitate such behaviours, as a form of vicarious reinforcement (where behaviour is imitated to gain rewards seen as occurring to those modelling the behaviour).

Peers can also be seen as influencing recovering addicts to relapse. Many addicts, after treatment, often return to their old social influences, including peer groups, where pressure may be experienced to return to dependency behaviours.

Research: peers

- Sussman and Ames (2001) found that friend and peer use of drugs is a strong predictor of drug use among teenagers, with deviant peer groupings role-modelling and offering drugs, demonstrating the influence of social networks in determining levels of individual vulnerability.

- Sussman and Ames (2001) reported that family conflict, poor supervision or drug-use tolerance by parents, family modelling of drug-using behaviour, and deviant peer group association all influence initiation of drugs, which suggests that peers are just one of several social influences relating to addiction vulnerability.

- Wagner and Anthony (2002) found that cannabis smokers were more likely to progress to cocaine usage, due to being in peer groupings where there are opportunities for new drug experiences, showing how peers can act as a social context 'gateway' to other dependencies.

- Thombs *et al.* (1997) used a questionnaire with 2,213 high school and college students, finding alcohol consumption linked to social context, especially in the form of perceived norms, with drinking consumption linked to close friends' drinking consumption, demonstrating the strength of peer group influence on addictive behaviours.

Evaluation

Peers

- It is possible that instead of peer groups influencing dependency behaviours, individuals who are already dependent, or attracted to dependency, tend to select peer groups that conform to their own dependency behaviour patterns – that is, social selection as opposed to social influence. Bullers *et al.* (2001) performed a longitudinal study of over 1,200 adults, which found that people's peer groups predicted individual drinking, but individual drinking also predicted subsequent peer group drinking. This suggests that social selection is a stronger influence than social influence. Similar results have been found in studies of adolescents.

- Leshner (1998) believed treatment strategies must include social context elements, such as peer groups, as well as biological and behavioural ones if they are to be successful, as recovered addicts may relapse when leaving a clinic, due to the original social context still being in place.

- Peer group influences are just one of many social context effects. Others include such factors as economic and social deprivation and all should be considered when assessing levels of vulnerability to dependency, as dependency is rarely related to just one factor.

Age

The prime time for initiation of dependency behaviours, such as smoking, is during adolescence and there is a positive correlation between early onset of dependency behaviours and reduced probability of abstaining. Indeed 17.3 per cent of adolescents from 132 countries were classed as smokers in 2006. Those who commence their addictions early are also more likely to relapse when trying to quit. Early onset of dependency behaviour is also related to increased likelihood of other dependency behaviours and as such early onset dependency behaviours can be regarded as 'gateway' behaviours, paving the way to other dependencies.

Although early experience of addictive substances and behaviours is highly correlated with later dependency, failure to quit and relapses after quitting, there is also an increased vulnerability in old age to addiction. About a third of alcoholics develop their dependency after retirement, which suggests the change in lifestyle and/or status may be linked to this phenomenon, though another possible reason is the increased stresses of older age, such as boredom and the death of loved ones. Tranquilliser and sleeping tablet abuse have also been found to be problematic among elderly females.

Research: age

- Shram (2008) measured age differences in neural responses to acute nicotine administration and to the rewarding and aversive effects of nicotine in adolescent and adult rats self-administering nicotine intravenously. Age differences in nicotine withdrawal were also assessed. Nicotine was found to have a greater activating effect on the neural structures of adolescents, who were also more sensitive to the rewarding qualities of nicotine, but less sensitive to its aversive effects. Adults were more resistant to extinction and showed more aversive effects to nicotine withdrawal. The results suggest that the rewarding effects of nicotine are highest in adolescence, demonstrating why this is a prime time for initiation of smoking, but why quitting is more difficult for adults.

- Data from a Health Canada Youth Smoking Survey (2006) compared smokers who initiated dependency between 12-15 years of age with non-smokers, finding early onset smokers were more likely to drink alcohol (91 per cent compared to 52 per cent), binge drink (58 per cent compared to 23 per cent)) and smoke cannabis (50 per cent compared to 5 per cent). This implies that adolescent cigarette smoking is a 'gateway', facilitating progression to other legal and illegal drug use.

- Fidler *et al.* (2006) studied 5,863 adolescents from ages 11 through to 16, assessing their smoking habits, including taking saliva samples to measure nicotine levels. Adolescents, who had smoked just one cigarette by age 11, were twice as likely to be a regular smoker at 14 as those who hadn't smoked at 11. The data also showed that those who became smoking addicts in later years were far more likely to have tried smoking at an early age than those who did not become dependent. This suggests there is a 'sleeper effect', where early experience of smoking creates a dormant vulnerability that can take years to express itself. This may be due to biological factors, such as early onset smoking affecting brain structures associated with reward and addiction, or because of social factors, such as individuals identifying themselves as smokers from an early age. Alternatively, it could be a combination of several factors.

- Helfer (2006) found 17 per cent of Swiss women over 75 years of age use painkillers or sleeping tablets everyday and 6 per cent also take tranquillisers. A huge increase in painkiller and tranquilliser usage was also noted between those of 55-64 years of age. As for alcohol, 46 per cent of men over 75 drank every day, compared to 6 per cent of 25-34 year olds. This suggests that the older a person is, the more likely they are to use certain addictive substances.

Evaluation

Age

- Research indicates that public health initiatives would be more effective if targeted at specific age groups (for instance, in opposing experimentation with tobacco by young adolescents, an age that has been associated with increased vulnerability to dependency, both immediately and in the future).

- Dependency in old age is a somewhat taboo area, with older people reluctant to admit to or talk about their addictions, and dependency problems may be a lot less evident, for instance the taking of addictive medication by old ladies is far less visible than public drinking by the young. This has implications for treatment, as younger people may feel more able to admit to dependency problems and seek help than the elderly, and having less visible problems reduces the chances of friends and family intervening. *continued ...*

...continued

- It may well be that addiction problems in the young are more highlighted by society and the media, who promote and maintain a stereotypical view of dependency being a problem among younger age groups. Until recently, most attention and resources have been targeted at younger age groups, but evidence suggests that late middle-age and senescence are at least equal times of vulnerability and with people living increasingly longer, it is essential that dependency problems in older people become better documented and catered for.

Stress

Stress has for a long time been seen as increasing vulnerability to addiction. The basic idea is that increased stress levels are positively correlated with an increased vulnerability to developing dependency habits, often as a maladaptive way of dealing with stress. Such stressors can include things like neighbourhood disorganisation, where there is a lack of centralised authority and increased social stressors, such as poor housing and economic deprivation. These types of stressors tend to be found more in dense urban environments, which are also associated with heightened levels of addictive behaviours. However, such a relationship may not be so clear cut, for instance it may be that certain individuals are more negatively affected by everyday stressors, which others find easy to cope with and therefore it may be that those who are more easily stressed are more vulnerable to addiction. The increased stresses, both biological and psychological, experienced when attempting to quit dependency behaviours and maintain quitting behaviour may also be responsible for individuals relapsing back into dependency.

There is some evidence of molecular and cellular changes associated with chronic stress and addiction, drawn from brain-imaging studies and research into stress, cravings and their relationship to specific brain areas associated with reward and addiction risk. A critical role has been identified for prefrontal brain areas involved in adaptive learning that help to control distress and desires.

Furthermore, those who develop a dependency may experience heightened stress due to having a dependency, for example strained relationships, financial cost of maintaining the dependency, maintaining work performance and so on. Therefore, heightened stress levels may well be a consequence of addiction rather than its cause.

Research: stress

- Piazza *et al.* (1989) investigated how stress affected vulnerability to addiction in rats, by demonstrating how previous repeated exposure to stressful tail-pinching and amphetamines increased activity in the dopamine neural system through behavioural sensitisation, making the rats more disposed to self-administer amphetamines. This suggests that stress affects drug taking via the action of neurobiology.

- Kosten *et al.* (2000) found that neonate rats who were subjected to isolation stress for 1 hour a day on their second to ninth days of life, had a greater tendency to cocaine administration when adults, than rats who did not suffer isolation stress when neonates. Although this affect was specific to cocaine, the results have important implications for the role of early childhood stress in vulnerability to addiction.

- Cleck and Blendy (2008) reported that people with stress-related psychiatric disorders – such as depression and anxiety often involved with addictive drug usage and exposure to chronic stressful life events, like sexual abuse – is linked to increases in nicotine, alcohol and cocaine usage. Also the greater and longer an individual endures childhood abuse, is positively correlated with an increased likelihood of developing dependencies in later life. Stress exposure is also related to increases in current drug use and precipitates relapse back into dependency. The findings strongly suggest a leading role for stress in determining vulnerability levels to addiction.

Stress

- A practical application of research into stress and addiction is that it may be possible to construct a stress index that would predict the level of risk of developing addictions. Such an index could prove to be an effective tool in counteracting addictive behaviours and help form part of an early warning system, with early interventions against dependencies seen as much more effective than trying to break dependencies later on.

- Much evidence of neurobiological changes associated with chronic stress and addiction is correlational and as such does not indicate causality. Such neurobiological changes could just as easily be effects of stress and addiction as causes.

- Heightened levels of dependency behaviours, such as drug usage, are associated with poor urban environments where there are high levels of stress. However, it may well be that the elevated levels of dependency in such areas is more to do with the high availability of and easy access to addictive substances like drugs in these neighbourhoods than any elevated stress levels.

- Much research into stress has involved animal studies, which presents an issue of extrapolation to humans. Studies are on done on animals due to the perception that such research would be unethical to perform on humans and is justified by a cost-benefit analysis, where the benefit of the knowledge gained is seen to outweigh the harm caused to the animals. However, increasingly more people challenge this assumption and perceive such studies as inherently unethical.

Media influences on addictive behaviour

The media communicates information about dependencies through public formats, which affects people's perceptions and behaviour towards them, as well as their conceptions of addiction risks, often in an invalid manner. The advent and popularity of the internet has increased the capacity for spreading information rapidly and affecting large groups, with an ever-growing international cultural impact.

Addictive behaviours are also portrayed through exposure to role models who promote dependency behaviours through media sources like film and music – for instance, drug-taking musicians. Such media sources are increasingly experienced cross-culturally, multiplying their impact.

Research has examined the extent to which the media affects dependency behaviours. Media sources have various influences on different age groups, with the focus mainly on social learning effects of media influences, many of which are seen as presenting enhanced opportunities for dependency behaviours.

Another aspect is that of addictions to media itself, where a psychological dependence on social media and user-generated content develops, with research indicating it to be a growing problem, due to the ever-increasing provision of media formats into people's lives, such as the internet and expanding television channels. The media, through its content, can also affect people's conceptions of addiction risks, often in an invalid manner.

Gambling and the media

The gambling industry consistently uses techniques based on appeals to expressive needs and the manipulation of situational factors to attract new custom. One such marketing method is the use of situational characteristics to get people to commence gambling. These are primarily features of the environment, including advertising locations of gambling outlets, the number of outlets in a specified area and the use of advertising inducing people to gamble. These variables are important in initiating gambling behaviour and help to explain why some forms of gambling are more attractive to particular socio-economic groups. For instance, the success of the National Lottery is due to being heavily advertised on billboards, on television and in national newspapers, with accessibility so widespread that it is difficult to avoid in many shops. TV programmes that feature lottery draws and interactive gambling via the internet and telephone generate the impression that gambling is normal, acceptable, even socially expected behaviour. *The National Lottery Live* programme is watched by 12 million viewers and contributes to the lottery's success by highlighting the simplicity of winning, while simultaneously hiding the huge number of viewing losers.

Research: the role of the media

- Sussman and Ames (2001) reported that commercials associating smoking with excitement-seeking cues and social popularity are important influences on the initiation of smoking, demonstrating how the media influences choice of behaviour.

- Griffiths (1997) reviewed studies of national lotteries from around the world, concluding that people from lower-class backgrounds were over-represented and those from middle-class backgrounds under-represented as being involved. As television viewing is greater among the lower classes, this implies that the impact of television-based marketing of lottery gambling is greater for this social group.

- Charlton (1986) found that viewing cigarette advertisements made children associate smoking with looking grown-up and having confidence, showing how the media promotes addictive behaviours.

- Gunsekera et al. (2005) found that drug taking in films was portrayed in a positive fashion, with little reference to possible negative consequences, suggesting that the media promotes dependency behaviour.

- Roberts et al. (2002) found that drug taking in music videos was fairly uncommon, portraying the behaviour in a neutral manner. However, such portrayals could increase drug usage, by depicting it as commonplace.

- Walther (1999) reported on the increase in communication addiction disorder (CAD), where the disinhibition of the internet makes it attractive to potential addicts who have problems in establishing and maintaining normal social relationships. CAD creates serious disturbances in psychosocial functioning and people's ability to maintain positive work practices, illustrating the negative influence of the media on vulnerable individuals.

- Kimberley (2006) found that social medias are addictive in themselves, leading to increased usage to sustain 'highs' and increased anxiety without periodic access. Even minor exposure can create physical and psychological dependence, suggesting social media addiction (SMA) is a real and problematic condition.

Evaluation

The role of media

- The Centre for Addiction Recovery has developed the Internet Addiction Test so that people can assess whether they are at risk of developing SMA, demonstrating how psychological methodology can be used in a practical manner.

- Farber (2007) reported that SMA is an increasing problem at work, with many employees feeling persistent needs to access social media sites, suggesting that such behaviour seriously affects performance.

- The media has both positive influences on addictive behaviours, like the use of positive role models and education, as well as negative ones, like negative role models, misinformation and addictions to media formats themselves.

- There is a danger that addicts are demonised through media-created moral panics, negatively affecting the chances of addicts receiving adequate social support to help them abstain, or even of seeking treatment at all.

- Media sources are especially influential with young children, who tend not to question their credibility, which suggests that there should be bans on programmes with content pertaining to addictive practices being broadcast until after children's bedtime.

Research in focus

When gathering data on people's drug-taking habits, questionnaires are often used, but what problems, both ethical and practical, are there with using this method?

What would be the disadvantages of using the following alternative methods?

1. Experiment

2. Correlation

3. Observation

4. Case study

5. Interview

Overall, which would be the best method to use? Explain your decision

Addictions can occur to many different things, and even those that seem bizarre to the majority are genuine dependency conditions, exhibiting all the features of more mainstream addictions. For a review of several of these, including addictions to tanning and ice-eating, with explanations and links to further details, go to www.oddee.com/item_96496.aspx

Strengthen your learning

1a. Outline how the following can affect addictive behaviour:
   i)   Personality (including self-esteem)
   ii) Peers
   iii) Age
   iv) Stress
1b. For each of the above factors, give details of three pieces of research evidence that illustrate their effects on addictive behaviour.
1c. For each of the above factors, compose an evaluation without direct reference to research studies.
2a. Describe ways in which the media influences dependency behaviours.
2b. Evaluate the media's role in dependency behaviours. Make some reference to research evidence in doing this.

Assessment Check ▶

1. Discuss risk factors in the development of addiction. (24 marks)

2. Outline how personality and age can affect vulnerability to addiction. (8 marks)

3. Evaluate media influences on addictive behaviour. (16 marks)

4. Outline and evaluate media influences on addictive behaviour. (24 marks)

Examination guidance

The term 'discuss' in question 1 means to outline and evaluate, and as no specific factors are given, any relevant material would be acceptable, with most candidates probably drawing on material relating to stress, age, personality and peers. At least two of these need to be covered, with an expectation of less detail if more than two are included.

Question 2 is more direct, focusing specifically on the role of personality and age. Outlining other factors would not gain credit, and neither would offering evaluative material. A reasonable balance between the two factors needs to be achieved to access the top band of marks.

Question 3 requires only evaluative material, which could be achieved by focusing on the strengths and weaknesses of methodologies employed to research this area.

Question 4 is similar to question 3, but with the added requirement to outline media influences on addictive behaviour. This possibly offers more scope to create an evaluation formed around the degree of research support.

Reducing addictive behaviour

Models of prevention

A fundamental question for health psychologists is why people adopt, or do not adopt, particular health-related behaviours. Models of health behaviour try to answer this question by assuming that decisions between different courses of action are based on two types of cognition:

1. **Subjective probabilities** – that a given action will produce a set of expected outcomes.

2. **Evaluation** – an assessment of action outcomes.

Individuals choose from alternative courses of action the one most likely to produce positive results and avoid negative ones. The driving idea behind such rational reasoning is that individuals think consciously about the likely consequences of behavioural alternatives available to them before engaging in an action.

Theory of planned behaviour: Ajzen (1988)

The theory of planned behaviour (TPB) is an adaptation of the earlier theory of reasoned action, which perceived addictive behaviours and attempts to manage or refrain from them, as due to decision making and factors supporting decision making rather than predisposing factors. A new component was added with the core of this being that addicts must be confident that their current skills and resources will enable them to overcome difficulties and achieve abstention from their dependency behaviours. This is crucial to understanding motivation: if an individual thinks they are unable to quit smoking, they will not even try. Perceived behavioural control has a direct effect on behaviour, bypassing behavioural intentions.

The model has several components:

- **Behavioural beliefs** – these link the behaviour of interest to expected outcomes and comprise the subjective probability that behaviour will produce a given response. Behavioural beliefs determine the prevailing *attitude towards behaviour*, the degree to which performance of such behaviour is positively or negatively valued.

- **Normative beliefs** – these refer to the perceived behavioural expectations of a relevant social group, and combine with an individual's level of motivation to determine prevailing *subjective norms*, the perceived social pressures to be involved or not in the behaviour.

- **Control beliefs** – these involve the perceived presence of factors that help or hinder performance of the behaviour and are seen as determining *perceived behavioural control*, which refers to people's beliefs about their ability to perform a given behaviour. To the extent that it is an accurate measurement of actual behavioural control, perceived behavioural control, along with *intention*, can be used to predict behaviour, intention being a measure of an individual's willingness to perform a behaviour.

TPB allows assessment of an individual's motives for continuing with dependency behaviours and their personal belief in their resolve to quit, with these factors important in resolving to quit and in resisting withdrawal effects and cravings. To succeed, a person's perceived behavioural control must be high enough to convince them that they can conquer all difficulties. For instance, a gambler must be convinced that they will not gamble or go to casinos. The more a person believes they possess behavioural control, the more the

Key terms

Theory of planned behaviour – explanation of factors influencing dependent behaviour

Biological interventions – therapeutic methods of abstention from dependency based on physiological means

Psychological interventions – therapeutic methods of abstention from dependency based on non-physiological means

Public health interventions – communal campaigns to reduce and protect against dependency behaviours

theory predicts success in quitting; and the harder quitting is believed to be, the more persistent they will be in trying to quit.

Research: theory of planned behaviour

- Penny (1996) found that if individuals have failed several times to quit smoking, they are less likely to believe that they will succeed in the future and therefore less likely to try, demonstrating the influence of past behaviour in perceived behavioural control, as predicted by the model.

- McMillan *et al.* (2005) used TPB to investigate factors underlying smoking intentions and later smoking behaviour in schoolchildren. TPB produced good predictions of intentions, attitude, subjective norms and perceived behavioural control, though intentions did not fully predict the subjective norm– behaviour relationship, lending some support to the model.

- Oh and Hsu (2001) used a questionnaire to assess gamblers' previous gambling behaviour, their social norms, attitudes, perceived behavioural control (such as perceived gambling skills and levels of self-control), along with behavioural intentions. A positive correlation was found between attitudes and behavioural intentions and actual behaviour, supporting the model.

- Walsh and White (2007) asked 252 university students to complete two questionnaires about high-level mobile phone use. The first measured TPB constructs of attitude, subjective norms and perceived behavioural control, and the second measured actual mobile phone use the previous week. Support for TSB was found in predictions of intentions and behaviour, though self-identity processes were also an influence.

- Walker *et al.* (2006) used interviews to assess whether TPB could explain gambling behaviour. Although some attitudes and norms were important, controllability was not an important factor for many participants in determining intention. Intention was an important predictive factor, indicating some support for the model.

- Goodie (2005) found that chronic gamblers were overconfident in their wagers compared to social gamblers, indicating that levels of perceived behavioural control differ between addicts and non-addicts.

Evaluation

Theory of planned behaviour

- TPB is currently the most popular and widely used social cognition model in health psychology, testimony to its validity.

- TPB only considers cognitive determinants of attitudes and beliefs; therefore, additional factors need to be considered, especially *anticipated regret*, the strength of emotional disappointment that occurs if the intended behaviour is not achieved.

- TPB has the advantage of including a degree of irrationality, in the form of evaluation, and attempts to address the issue of social and environmental factors (normative beliefs). The extra 'ingredient' of perceived behavioural control also provides a role for past behaviour.

- The model assumes that behaviours are conscious, reasoned and planned, which is not always true with addicts.

- TRB may be reliant on invalid evidence, as research relies on self-reports, which are subject to social desirability, like addicts playing down their degree of dependency, or even because addicts are not aware of the true extent of their dependency.

- The model has practical applications, in that clinicians can use it to tailor treatment processes to individual needs.

- Although contributing to the understanding of addiction, the lack of universal research support suggests that further explanations are required if prevention treatments are to increase their successfulness.

Types of intervention

Biological interventions

The main biological treatment is drug therapy. *Benzodiazepines* (BZs), like valium, are used with detoxifying alcoholics, who reduce alcohol intake gradually and take BZs, which have a relaxing effect, to prevent delirium tremens (the shakes). BZs are then withdrawn gradually. In hospitals, lower doses are used, tailored to the emergence of withdrawal symptoms as rated by nursing staff.

Disulfiram is an *agonistic* drug that interferes with the metabolic degradation of alcohol and is used to prevent relapse by producing an unpleasant reaction, including vomiting, when even a small quantity of alcohol is drunk.

Antagonistic drugs are also used. These lessen or eliminate the effects of neurotransmitters by blocking cellular activity, altering the effects of addictive drugs. For example, *buprenorphine* is an agonist used to reverse morphine addiction, while *acamprosate*, which affects the glutamate and GABA neurotransmitter systems, reduces cravings for alcohol. These drugs are more effective when combined with CBT.

Drug maintenance therapy involves the use of substitute drugs, like *methadone* for heroin addiction. This produces less of a high and is taken orally, so does not involve contextual cues, like needles and pipes (and reduces HIV transmission risks). There is a risk of side effects, like insomnia and reduced sexual functioning, which encourages dropout. Antagonistic and agonistic drugs are used simultaneously.

Agonistic drugs are site-specific drugs triggering cellular activity. As many drugs act on dopamine levels to produce a 'high', dopamine agonists – for example, disulfiram, which reduces cocaine dependency by elevating dopamine level – are used, often also lessening withdrawal symptoms by producing more dopamine in the brain.

A biological treatment for smoking is to present nicotine in alternative ways, such as by patches, inhalers or gum. Treatment by patches usually lasts 10 to 12 weeks, with ever-smaller patches used to reduce the dose. Dependency to these methods can occur, but is much less harmful than ingestion by smoking. Treatment works best when combined with CBT.

Psychology in action

Treating cocaine addiction with viruses

Figure 11.08

We tend to think of viruses in a negative way, but could they be the key to alleviating addictions?

Americans spend more on cocaine than all other illegal drugs combined. About 1.7 million people use cocaine in the USA, with cocaine the leading cause of heart attacks and strokes for people under 35.

But now scientists have designed a potentially valuable tool for treating cocaine addiction by creating a modified phage-virus that soaks up the drug inside the central nervous system, preventing the drug exerting its narcotic effect. The virus is coated with an antibody that binds to molecules of cocaine, helping to clear the drug from the brain, which suppresses the positive reinforcing aspects of the drug by eliminating cocaine's psychoactive properties.

Indeed, the technique of displaying therapeutic proteins or peptides on phage particles could be useful as a general way of delivering therapies into the brain for all sorts of addictive behaviours, illustrating a possibly life-saving practical application based on biopsychological principles.

Research: biological interventions

- Hollander *et al.* (2000) found that fluvoxamine, a selective serotonin reuptake inhibitor (SSRI), brought about a greater reduction in gambling behaviour and gambling urges in pathological gamblers than placebo treatment. However, only 10 out of 15 participants completed the study, making generalisation difficult.

- Gelder *et al.* (1999) found that when BZs are used to help withdrawal from alcohol, they produce a smooth course of withdrawal, and are not likely to be abused, demonstrating their effectiveness.

- Fuller (1988) found that disulfiram did not provide specific benefits in addressing alcohol dependency, with an 80 per cent dropout rate, and Gelder *et al.* (1999) reported side effects such as impotence and confusion, casting doubts on the drug's effectiveness.

- Mason (2001) reviewed double-blind, placebo-controlled clinical trials of acamprosate, finding it to be an effective treatment for alcohol dependency.

- Davison *et al.* (2004) report that 12-month abstinence rates from smoking by using nicotine patches was 28 per cent, compared to 18 per cent for placebo patches, suggesting some effectiveness for the treatment.

- Moore *et al.* (2009) assessed the effectiveness of a range of nicotine replacement therapies, finding them an effective intervention therapy in achieving sustained abstinence for smokers who cannot or will not attempt immediate abstinence.

- Kosten *et al.* (2002) evaluated the ability of dopamine agonists to address addiction. Some indirect agonists, like *selegiline*, proved useful in combating alcohol and cocaine dependence, with an indication that partial agonists and subtypes of dopamine receptors, like D3, may also be useful, suggesting that further research is required to identify which specific agonists combat which specific dependencies.

- Warren *et al.* (2005) assessed the effectiveness of methadone in treating heroin addiction among 900 prisoners. Inmates receiving methadone used heroin on an average of 15.24 days a year, compared to 99.96 days a year for inmates not receiving methadone, showing methadone to be effective.

Evaluation

Biological interventions

- BZs should not be used continuously for longer than 14 days, because patients can develop dependency. Also, Davison *et al.* (2000) question whether substance-abuse problems should be treated by giving another substance to people proved to be looking for chemical solutions to their problems. Also, some therapeutic drugs, like heroin substitutes, are themselves addictive.

- Outpatient alcohol detoxification is equal to hospital-based treatment and is more cost-effective. However, for those with little social support, or living in alcohol-friendly environments, or with additional psychological problems, inpatient treatment is preferable.

- Drugs used to combat addictions can have serious side effects. *Varenicline*, used to treat smoking dependency, can result in depression and suicide, though withdrawal symptoms may contribute too.

- Methadone, an antagonist used to treat heroin addiction, is associated with psychiatric disorders such as depression. Trauer (2008) found those on methadone maintenance to be ten times more likely to have psychiatric disorders than the general population. However, Nunes *et al.* (1991) found that treatment with *imipramine* reduced depression in 53 per cent of such patients.

Psychological interventions

Interventions based on classical conditioning

In *aversion therapy*, an undesirable response to a particular stimulus is removed by associating the stimulus with another, aversive, stimulus. For example, alcohol is paired with an emetic drug, inducing vomiting, so that vomiting becomes a conditioned response to alcohol. Between conditioning trials, patients sip soft drinks to prevent generalisation to all drinking behaviour. Aversion therapy can also be performed with electric shocks, and has been used to treat pathological gambling, though it is not as effective as covert desensitisation.

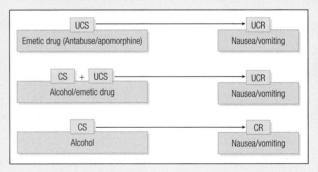

Figure 11.09

Covert desensitisation is a variant of aversion therapy, where the aversive stimulus is imagined alongside the dependency behaviour, so that the two become associated. 'Relief' scenarios are imagined too, where not indulging in the dependency behaviour is associated with pleasant sensations.

Interventions based on operant conditioning

Treatment for alcohol abuse using operant conditioning is called *contingency management* (CM), and is based on the belief that environmental contingencies of reinforcement and punishment play a role in encouraging or discouraging drinking.

Patients and significant others are taught to reinforce behaviours consistent with not drinking, like avoiding situations associated with drinking and staying sober. Reinforcement takes the form of vouchers exchangeable for goods. CM also teaches job-finding and social skills, as well as assertiveness training for refusing drinks. Socially isolated individuals are assisted and encouraged to establish contacts with those not associated with drinking. CM is also used with drug addicts.

Behavioural self-control training is another treatment based on operant conditioning, which emphasises patient control and includes one or more of the following:

- **Stimulus control** – patients narrow the situations in which they are allowed to drink, like only on special occasions.

- **Modification of the topography of drinking** – for example, having only mixed drinks and taking small sips rather than gulps.

- **Reinforcing abstinence** – for example, awarding oneself a non-alcoholic treat for resisting the urge to drink.

Cognitive interventions

Cognitive interventions try to forge trusting relationships with patients, focusing on identifying and deconstructing false beliefs, reducing craving and helping to establish control over addictive behaviours. Triggers are identified and strategies developed that increase willpower, so that self-control becomes greater than the strength of the craving. *Relapse prevention training* involves learning strategies to increase control to cope with and resist cravings, like developing rational explanations to address false beliefs and to prevent perceiving lapses as catastrophic. Patients learn to avoid high-risk situations and develop alternative activities.

Another cognitive-based strategy is cognitive behavioural therapy (CBT), which aims to affect how addicts think about dependency. Behavioural self-control training, which enables addicts to realise when they are at risk, is combined with coping skills, like relaxation techniques and *positive self-talk*, to help resist temptation.

Research: psychological interventions

- Meyer and Chesser (1970) found that 50 per cent of alcoholics abstained for at least a year following treatment and that aversion therapy was better than no treatment, suggesting that the therapy is effective. However, Smith *et al.* (1997) compared matched patients who received electrical aversion as part of their treatment, with inpatients mainly receiving counselling. Although aversion-treated patients had superior abstinence rates at 6 months, the benefit was not sustained at 12 months, suggesting that it is only of short-term benefit.

- Gelder *et al.* (1989) reported that though covert sensitisation is preferable on humanitarian grounds, it is no more effective than aversion therapy, casting doubts on its suitability as a treatment. However, McConaghy *et al.* (1983) compared covert sensitisation as a treatment for gambling dependency against electrical aversion therapy, finding covert desensitisation to be more effective over a 12-month period, with 79 per cent of these patients, compared to 50 per cent of aversion patients, reporting control over, or not indulging in gambling, in a long-term follow-up study between 2 and 9 years after treatment. This suggests that the treatment has long-term effectiveness.

- Petry *et al.* (2000) found CM to be more effective in treating alcoholism than intensive outpatient treatment. Only 26 per cent of CM patients relapsed by the end of the programme, compared to 61 per cent of the controls. This was supported by Smith *et al.* (2001), who reviewed available literature, finding CM consistently effective and cost-effective.

- Williams and Connolly (2006) found that cognitive interventions altered thinking, but not addictive behaviour in chronic gamblers. However, Floyd *et al.* (2006) found that cognitive interventions combined with a behavioural component to form CBT are effective in addressing gambling addiction.

Evaluation

Psychological interventions

- The challenge with therapies based on operant conditioning is to get addicts to use the techniques without constant supervision.
- Although CBT emphasises the development of coping skills, few studies demonstrate whether this is the mechanism through which it works.
- CBT is a relatively brief treatment, and thus suited to the resource capabilities of most clinical programmes; it can be tailored to individual circumstances. Its effects are long-lasting and even address the dependencies of severely addicted individuals.
- Cognitive interventions have proved to be of value, but are often more effective when combined with drug treatments.
- Different treatments work best for different kinds of patients. Carroll *et al.* (1995) found the antidepressant drug *desipramine* effective for patients with low degrees of cocaine dependence, while cognitive treatment was superior for patients with high dependence.

Psychology in action

Addiction therapists signing up to *World of Warcraft*

Figure 11.10

A report by Sweden's Youth Care Foundation describes *World of Warcraft* as "more addictive than crack cocaine". The game, attracting 12 million players every month, is set in a fantasy environment, with users taking on characters and interacting with other players in a virtual world. Dr Richard Graham, a consultant psychiatrist at the Tavistock Centre in London, said that some players were so addicted they play for 16 hours a day, neglecting social lives and education and losing touch with the real world.

Psychologists have come up with a radical practical application to treat such addiction problems by providing online therapy. Clinicians are creating their own 'avatars' in online fantasy games to treat youngsters addicted to virtual worlds, with therapists communicating more easily with at-risk players in their preferred environment. Another planned strategy is that of recruiting existing players to act as 'peer mentors' for users of the game, to help create strategies to prevent players from becoming addicted.

Psychologists have turned to these methods because although the effects are as grave as other forms of dependency, internet addiction is difficult to identify, as the isolation involved means that sufferers are often out of sight and out of mind.

You are the researcher

Design a study to test the effectiveness of a smoking ban in public places about to be introduced into a city. You will need to establish some method of measuring smoking behaviour before and after the ban.

What research method would you use? What form would the data take and how would they be analysed, both numerically and pictorially?

Give one strength and one weakness of your research method as it applies to this study.

Public health interventions

Public health interventions aim to promote behaviour change in whole populations, not just those seeking or needing help, and are often targeted at vulnerable groups. Public health interventions take the form of medical advice, worksite interventions, community-wide approaches and government interventions. Several techniques are used to promote health and dissuade individuals from dependency behaviours:

- *Social inoculation* tries to strengthen people's attempts to resist temptation and persuasion to addictive activities, by providing counterarguments as an inoculation defence against such attempts, and by providing supportive defence statements, reinforcing beliefs that people already hold.

- *Fear arousal* is used in health campaigns to strengthen the persuasiveness of arguments against addictive practices.

- *Targeting risk groups* is based on the idea that health promotion campaigns are more successful if they are specifically directed at vulnerable individuals, making the campaigns more cost–effective.

Medical advice

Seventy per cent of smokers visit a doctor each year. Research suggests that doctors, who are regarded as credible sources of information, are successful in promoting smoking cessation.

Worksite advice

Worksite advice generally takes the form of worksite bans on smoking (which became a legal requirement in 2007) and work-based health promotion programmes.

Worksite interventions reach individuals who would not otherwise receive interventions, and the large numbers involved provide opportunities for group motivation and social support. Smoking bans eliminate passive smoking, a risk factor for coronary heart disease and lung cancer, but only in areas where bans are in force. Smoking bans in public buildings have led to increased smoking in outdoor areas, and historical attempts to ban activities like gambling and drinking led to such activities going underground, increasing criminal activity around their provision.

Figure 11.11 Smoking bans in public buildings lead to increases in smoking in outdoor areas

Community-based programmes

Community-based programmes aim to reach those who would not attend clinics, and use group motivation and social support. Such programmes target populations especially vulnerable to forming dependency behaviours.

Government interventions

Government interventions take the form of restricting/banning advertising. In the UK alcohol cannot be portrayed as improving sexual or social success, while tobacco advertising is banned. Governments also increase taxation on products, with research suggesting a relationship between cost and consumption.

Attempts to influence addictive behaviours through legislation have been attempted and policing bodies utilised to enforce legislation. However, although making drugs illegal prevents some usage, it increases the criminality associated with them, creating health issues, like disease risks and incidents of overdosing/poisoning.

Research: public health interventions

- Russell *et al.* (1979) found that 5.1 per cent of smokers advised by doctors to quit and given advice on how to quit were not smoking 12 months later. This was superior to other groups of smokers not told to quit who were given questionnaires, and even those given questionnaires and advised to quit. This suggests that it is the credibility of advisers and guidance that are important. Gross (2005) reported the effectiveness of doctors' advice increases if they are trained in patient-centred counselling techniques.

- The Irish Office of Tobacco Control (2010) reported that since the 2004 Irish smoking ban in public places, smoking prevalence fell from 26.4 per cent to 23.6 per cent, suggesting the ban was effective. However, after an initial drop in prevalence of 1.45 per cent, the rate actually increased to 27.4 per cent in 2008, so the recent drop may be due to economic reasons – that is, lower incomes. Also, although cigarette sales fell, heavy smokers are smoking more, suggesting that the ban has hardened their attitudes.

- Farquhar *et al.* (1990) found that individuals receiving face–to–face instruction on how to stop smoking, plus a media campaign, as part of the Stanford Five City Project, showed a 13 per cent reduction in smoking rates compared to controls. This suggests that community-based programmes are effective and was supported by Puska *et al.* (1985), finding that males targeted by the North Karelia Project's intensive educational campaign showed a 10 per cent reduction in smoking prevalence compared to controls.

- McGuire (1964) found that *inoculation defence* in the form of counterarguments, and *supportive defence* in the form of strengthening statements, helped resistance to temptation and persuasion to indulge in addictive behaviours.

- Quist-Paulsen and Gallefoss (2007) found that Norwegian cardiac patients subjected to fear arousal were more able to quit smoking and not relapse over a 12–month period, suggesting that the strategy is effective.

Contemporary research

Conrod *et al.* (2004)

School-based intervention successfully lowers drinking rates in at-risk children

Figure 11.12

Many costly public health interventions have been aimed at reducing alcohol abuse in adolescents, often with disappointing results. The researchers here aimed to produce a more focused and cost-effective programme by finding means to identify at-risk individuals and then target resources specifically at them.

Aim

To assess the impact of intervention targeted at adolescents with a high risk of substance abuse.

Procedure

A total of 2,506 adolescents with a mean age of 13.7 were evaluated on the Substance Use Risk Profile Scale, a 23-item questionnaire, assessing personality risk for substance abuse along four dimensions of sensation-seeking, impulsivity, anxiety sensitivity and hopelessness. Of these, 624 identified as being at high risk for substance abuse received intervention consisting of two 90-minute group sessions conducted by a trained educational professional. A matched high-risk group of 384 participants received no intervention.

Findings

A 6-month follow-up found that intervention significantly decreased the likelihood of drinking alcohol, with the control group 1.7 times more likely to have consumed alcohol. Binge drinking was also 55 per cent lower in the intervention group compared to the control group, with fewer alcohol-related problems reported too.

Conclusions

Intervention-based programmes directed at high-risk individuals produce positive outcomes in terms of efficacy and cost-effectiveness.

continued ...

...continued

Evaluation

- The programme is effective in the short term, but was designed to evaluate long term mental health symptoms, academic achievement and substance-use uptake; therefore, longer-term assessments are required.

- Alcohol use was recorded by self-reports, which may be prone to inaccuracy and thus produce flawed findings.

- The results suggest that it may be possible to produce personality-targeted early prevention intervention programmes that would benefit the health prospects, both short- and long-term, of adolescents.

Evaluation

Public health interventions

- It is difficult to evaluate legislative attempts to curb addictive practices, as by criminalising behaviours it is difficult to assess how many users there are.

- Identifying risk groups can be cost-effective as it targets resources at those who might benefit from them most (see 'Contemporary research: Conrod et al. (2004)' on page 442).

- Health campaigns seem to work best when based on models of behaviour change like TPB.

- Although governments introduce programmes targeted at reducing dependency behaviours, such as reduced advertising of products, the success of such programmes is not always in their best interests, as it leads to reduced taxation revenues. Also, the British government introduced the National Lottery in 1994, which was criticised by many as promoting gambling as an acceptable pastime and thus increasing the chances of vulnerable individuals becoming pathological gamblers.

You are the researcher

Two hundred heroin-addicted inmates at a prison have been given a course of CBT to try to stop their drug taking.

How could you evaluate the treatment by:

a. Giving 100 of the prisoners a questionnaire of ten questions. Think carefully about what questions you will ask. Will you use closed, open or a mixture of both types of question?

b. Evaluate the other 100 prisoners with an experiment. What design would you use? What would be your IV and DV? You may need to use non-addicted prisoners too.

Give one strength and one weakness of both types of evaluation as they relate to this scenario.

The best-known British organisation for providing unbiased information and advice on drugs is Release. Set up in 1967, they run a website at www.release.org.uk/about/mission-vision including a database with just about everything you could possibly wish to know about drugs.

Strengthen your learning

1a. Outline TPB, paying particular attention to the concept of perceived control and the model's components.
1b. What level of validity does research evidence suggest for the theory? Give details.
1c. Evaluate TPB in terms of its strengths and weaknesses.
2a. Outline the different ways in which drugs are used to combat dependencies.
2b. To what extent has research found drugs to be effective in combating addiction? Give details.
3a. Outline how interventions based on the following are used to combat dependencies:
    i) classical conditioning
    ii) operant conditioning
    iii) cognitive techniques.
3b. How effective does research evidence suggest psychological interventions are in treating addictions? Give details.
4a. Outline public health interventions in terms of their aims and the forms and techniques they use.
4b. Use research evidence to assess how effective public health interventions are.

Assessment Check

1. Outline the theory of planned behaviour as a model for addiction prevention. (8 marks)

2. Evaluate the effectiveness of public health interventions in reducing addictive behaviour. (16 marks)

3. Outline one type of intervention into reducing addictive behaviour. (4 marks)

4. Outline and evaluate the theory of planned behaviour as a model for addiction prevention. (20 marks)

5. Discuss the effectiveness of biological and psychological means of reducing addictive behaviour. (24 marks)

Examination guidance

In question 1 a 'longer' version description of the theory is required, as 8 marks are available. Evaluative material would not be creditworthy here. However, only evaluative material is required in question 2, so take care not to outline public health interventions. Evaluation should be focused specifically on how effective such interventions are, possibly by reference to the degree of support for research and considerations of the methodologies used.

Question 3 requires an outline of just one type of intervention. Offer more and all will be marked, but only the best one credited. Question 4 needs an outline of TPB, but as it's only for 4 marks a 'shorter' version than that offered in question 1 should be provided. Most of your energies should be centred on compiling the evaluation, where 16 marks can be earned.

The term 'discuss' in question 5 means to outline and evaluate. A balance should be achieved in the description of the effectiveness of biological and psychological means in reducing addictive behaviour if the top band is to be accessed. A useful method of evaluation would be to compare the effectiveness of the two, using the degree of research support as an assessment tool, as well as practical applications.

Summing up

- The biological model perceives addiction as a physiologically controlled pattern of behaviour, related to neurological and genetic factors.

- The cognitive model sees addiction as due to distorted thinking relating to dysfunctional beliefs and impaired decision-making abilities.

- Learning models are based on classical conditioning, which sees addiction occurring through stimuli becoming associated with each other; operant conditioning, which sees dependency behaviours as being reinforcing; and social learning, which sees dependency behaviours as being observed and imitated.

- Biological explanations see smoking as physiologically addictive through stimulation of nicotine receptors in the brain.

- Psychological explanations see smoking initiation occurring through social learning, while maintenance occurs through operant conditioning via reinforcements. Cognitive factors, like irrational beliefs, also play a role.

- Biological explanations perceive neurobiological mechanisms involved in gambling dependency, with gambling activating the brain-reward system.

- Several psychological explanations are seen as influencing gambling dependency, including sociocultural factors, learning factors, personality and cognitive influences.

- Neurotic and psychopathic personality characteristics have been associated with increased vulnerability to addiction.

- Peer pressure is also influential in determining levels of vulnerability in childhood and adolescence, especially if peer groups promote and support dependency behaviours.

- Research indicates a link between initiating dependency behaviours at an early age and subsequently becoming addicted, developing multiple addictions, failure to abstain and relapsing after quitting.

- There is also increased vulnerability to addiction in old age, though such dependencies may be less immediately apparent.

- Stress is strongly related to vulnerability to addiction, with research indicating a link between stress and brain areas associated with reward and addiction risk.

- The media communicates information about dependencies through public formats, affecting people's perceptions and behaviour, especially by means of social learning.

- The theory of planned behaviour (TPB) centres on the influence of perceived control, with abstention resulting from confidence in skills and resources to quit dependency behaviours.

- TPB allows for assessment of motives for continuing with dependency behaviours and personal beliefs in motivation to quit.

- The main biological intervention is drug therapy, which assists in detoxification, relapse prevention and can involve substitute drugs, as part of maintenance therapy.

- Psychological treatments use behavioural therapies based on classical conditioning, like aversion therapy, and operant conditioning techniques that encourage personal management of dependency.

- Cognitive interventions focus on identifying and deconstructing false beliefs and reducing craving, and help to establish control over addictive behaviours.

- Public health interventions promote behaviour change in whole populations and take the form of medical advice, worksite interventions, community-wide approaches and government intervention.

- Research suggests that targeted public health interventions are effective, but some initiatives increase dependency behaviours in some individuals.

12 Anomalistic psychology

The study of anomalous experience 447

Pseudoscience and the scientific
status of parapsychology   448
Methodological issues related to the
study of paranormal cognition   451

**Explanations for anomalous
experience   460**

The role of coincidence and
probability judgements in anomalous
experience   460

Explanations for superstitious
behaviour and magical thinking   464

Personality factors underlying
anomalous experience   468

**Research into and explanations
for exceptional experience   471**

Psychic healing   471

Out-of-body/near-death experiences   474

Psychic mediumship   476

Summing up   479

Decoding the specification

The specification outlines what you must study in order to answer any examination question you might face. There is an initial need to have knowledge of pseudoscience and the scientific status of parapsychology, quite a broad area, with any relevant material equally creditworthy, as examination answers will not require focus on specific aspects. The next part of the specification is more explicit, focusing directly on methodological issues relating to the study of paranormal cognition concerning i) ESP, through Ganzfeld studies, and ii) paranormal cognition, through psychokinesis.

You will also need knowledge of explanations for anamolous experience, specifically the role of coincidence and probability judgements, as well as explanations for superstitious behaviour and magical thinking, along with personality factors that underlie anomalous experience. These elements are specifically listed and therefore can be examined directly.

The specification concentrates finally on research into and explanations of exceptional experience, focusing on three explicit areas: psychic healing, near–death/out-of-body experiences and psychic mediumship and examination questions could be directed at any of these, with the term 'research' not just relating to research studies, but also to theories and explanations.

The study of anomalous experience

'Not our houses but our brains are haunted' (G.M. Beard, 1879)

Anomalistic psychology studies *paranormal* experiences, those beyond immediate scientific explanation. Experimental studies of the paranormal are known as *parapsychology*, while anomalistic psychology has a wider scope, taking in all unexplained phenomena.

IN THE NEWS

Chicken run

Paul Brimble is the owner of Gloucestershire Cricket Club's new mascot, a fish that came back from the dead to eat the previous mascot, a frozen chicken.

While out fishing Paul caught the sea bass, which distinguished itself by the extended plucky fight it put up. Eventually he landed it, rapped it on the head and stored it in his fridge alongside Gloucestershire's lucky chicken, which had seemingly lost its magic powers when Surrey beat the West country team in the 2001 Benson and Hedges Cup final.

The next morning the chicken was missing, evidently consumed by the greedy sea bass and it was immediately decided that the fish would be the new mascot.

So far the sea bass has not disappointed, it made an appearance at the semi-final, which Gloucestershire won and will have pride of place at the final.

In 1977, lowly Gloucestershire County Cricket Club got to the final of the Benson and Hedges Cup, and by teatime were facing defeat. A glum fan dipped his hand into his bag in a search for food and pulled out a plucked chicken his wife had packed by mistake. The bird was promptly held aloft, as other supporters sang, 'He's got the whole chicken in his hands.' Gloucestershire rallied and went on to win their very first title, with the chicken attaining stardom and being stashed away in the deep freeze for the next 20-odd years until Gloucestershire again reached a final. Her subsequent thawing and reappearance at Lord's coincided with a second trophy win, and from then on the increasingly ragged-looking chicken appeared at all cup games, as the club reached and won three successive finals. Luck, however, seemed to run out when reaching the

Figure 12.01

following year's final, when Gloucestershire finally lost to Surrey.

Then Paul Brimble caught his sea bass, which allegedly devoured the frankly inedible chicken, becoming the club's new lucky mascot, to be fervently waved and passed around as Gloucestershire advanced to and won another two Lord's finals.

Superstitions are irrational beliefs that objects, actions or circumstances not logically related to a course of events influence outcomes. As often is the case, the chicken and subsequent fish superstitions emerged from coincidence, the corresponding of two unconnected events – that is, the animals' appearance and the team's successes. The belief in such magical thinking underpins a lot of anomalistic phenomena, and psychologists' attention focuses as much on why people hold such beliefs, as on whether such beliefs have any credence.

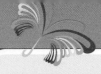

Pseudoscience and the scientific status of parapsychology

Pseudoscience means 'false science' and refers to so-called sciences and scientific practices with little or no scientific basis, like eugenics, which believed in inherited racial differences in levels of intelligence. Practical applications based on pseudoscience are generally doomed to failure, as they have no basis in scientific fact, and can even do a lot of harm. For example, eugenic beliefs resulted in the forced sterilisation of thousands of Americans, most of them black. Pseudoscience is not generally associated with deliberate deception, while scientific fraud is a problem that has at times plagued parapsychology. Scientific fraud is also different from pseudoscience, as fraud is not generally associated with deviant or unorthodox beliefs. James Randi, the US magician, has exposed the trickery of several people claiming to have psychic powers, offering a prize of $1 million to anyone who can show paranormal powers under test conditions. The prize remains unclaimed.

The Chinese pseudoscience debate

In China, after the death of leader Mao Zedong, ancient Chinese superstitions began to become popular. Individuals with 'special powers', who could project qi, the 'power of the universe', gained enormous followings. For example, Honcheng (1993) claimed to be able to make petrol by adding a 'secret' potion to water, while Zhang Yingging, a lecturer at Shandong University in the 1990s, introduced *holographic biology*, which claims that parts of an organism – for example, a finger, mirrors an organism's overall structure, and by looking at such parts the health of the whole body can be deduced.

Such popular claims alarmed the government and were denounced as pseudoscience by the Chinese biological community; Zhang lost his funding and job, while Honcheng was jailed. However, Song (2006) claimed that the refusal of the Chinese scientific community to accept this and other controversial theories is actually due to their conservative attitudes and narrow-mindedness. This was all part of an ongoing debate in China about traditional practices and philosophies labelled as pseudoscience and centred on China's Science Popularisation Law (2003), over which TV debates and lawsuits raged, with the scientific community claiming that because of widespread superstition in Chinese society, the public is easily hoodwinked by false scientific theories. There have even been calls for traditional Chinese medicines to be withdrawn from medical care, as they are not based on scientific principles.

Fang Shimin, a biochemist with a PhD, is known as the head of the 'science police' for his persistent exposure of scientific misconduct. However, many claim that the term 'pseudoscience' is abused by Fang and others to discredit innovative sciences and inventions based on traditional cultures, like holographic biology. They argue that science should not be based solely on repeatable experiments, and advocate instead the use of traditionally accepted beliefs, ones that cannot be tested scientifically. Fang says that no matter how innovative a theory, it must abide by the principles of accepted scientific disciplines, and that the scepticism of the scientific community is not because they are too conservative, but because the theories involved cannot offer persuasive evidence, testable by experiment.

Telepathy and scientific fraud

Telepathy is a belief in non-sensory communication. Soal (1939) tested 160 participants for ESP on 128,000 card guessing trials, finding no evidence of telepathy. He then rechecked his data for *displacement*, the idea that a psychic might be one or two cards behind the guessing due to *temporal distraction*. By this method, Basil Shackleton was identified as a telepath. Shackleton was tested in rigorously controlled experiments in front of academic witnesses, taking part in 40 trials of 50 card guesses each, at which Soal looked at a card and Shackleton reported what the researcher was seeing. Compelling evidence was produced, with Shackleton even able to correctly guess a card two ahead of the target. The odds were estimated at 1,035 against the effect being due to chance. A whole generation of researchers were convinced and influenced by these findings; even Cyril Burt, the famed researcher into intelligence who is widely believed to have falsified data, was convinced. Any accusations of fraud were dismissed as envy and an attack on Soal, and on the integrity of his participants and academic witnesses.

It took over 30 years for Markwick (1978) to show that Soal had cheated. Markwick reanalysed the original results, finding that false data had been added, which, when removed, reduced the findings to within-chance levels. Soal had produced scorecards with large amounts of number ones, which he later changed to fours or fives. This was reported by witnesses, and copies of the scorecards were scrutinised, Soal having claimed the originals were lost. These revelations did intense harm to parapsychology.

> Uri Geller claimed to have psychic powers. For a demonstration of Uri's spoon bending, go to www.youtube.com/watch?v=GRn7d4D7haw
> To see James Randi debunk Geller's claims, go to www.youtube.com/watch?v=M9w7jHYriFo where there are links to more 'demonstrations' and 'exposes'. Make up your own mind.

Figure 12.02 Zenner card symbols were used by Samuel Soal to claim ESP abilities for his subject Basil Shackleton; in 1978, Betty Markwick demonstrated that Soal was a fraud

The scientific status of parapsychology

Parapsychology (PP) is the term introduced in the 1930s to refer to the scientific study of paranormal phenomena. Science considers sensory information to be the only way by which humans can perceive and experience their world. However, some phenomena seem to involve exchanges of information that *exceed* the capacities of the sensory (and motor) systems as they're currently understood. It is these paranormal phenomena that parapsychology seeks to explain by scientific methods.

The history of PP can be divided into three phases:

1. **Spiritualism** – most Victorian scientists were Christians who believed in an immortal soul and so many became interested in spiritualism, a scientific searching for the departed souls of the dead. Research was conducted under laboratory conditions, both by believers and by sceptics who exposed many practitioners (mediums) as frauds, to such an extent that by 1900, scientific focus moved from seances to more plausible aspects of the paranormal.

2. **Psychical research** – this was the era of the 'ghost hunter', scientists pursuing manifestations in haunted houses, poltergeist activity, demonic possession, apparitions and premonitions, with interest also developing in telepathy and precognitive dreams.

3. **Modern parapsychology** – PP was founded by biologists J.B and Louisa Rhine in the 1930s, who sought to dissociate themselves from the often discredited studies of spiritualism and psychical research and establish a truly scientific discipline of PP that was rooted in the unbiased setting of the laboratory.

They established the term 'parapsychology', established a department of PP at Duke University in the USA and developed new experimental methods of strict scientific rigour, defining all areas of research in strictly objective operational terms.

The major centre for studying paranormal psychology in Britain is the Koestler Parapsychology Unit at Edinburgh University, which dates back to 1985, though Dr John Beloff taught parapsychology there as long ago as 1962.

Parapsychology as science

The world of PP is ever-shrinking, because as scientists develop an understanding of phenomena such as hypnosis and hallucinations, they aren't considered part of PP anymore. This suggests that PP should only study phenomena that apparently lie outside the range of normal scientific explanations and investigations and that once 'paranormal' phenomena have been accounted for scientifically, they're no longer 'paranormal'. However, sceptical scientists believe that paranormal phenomena are a scientific impossibility and therefore reject the scientific legitimacy of parapsychological inquiry, especially as so many practitioners of apparent psychic ability have been proven to be frauds.

While strong opposition to PP is understandable, pre-judgements about the impossibility of psychic phenomena are inappropriate in science. Many psychologists who aren't convinced that psychic phenomena have been demonstrated are nevertheless open to the *possibility* that compelling evidence may emerge. Many parapsychologists believe that the case for paranormal phenomena has already been 'proven', or that experimental procedures exist that have the potential for doing so.

Evaluation

Pseudoscience and the scientific status of parapsychology

- Sagan (2010) believed that pseudoscience gets in the way of proper science by providing easy answers, dodging scrutiny and championing desirable, but impossible notions, like astrology. Pseudoscience purports to use the methods and findings of science, but actually is based on insufficient facts, ignores contrary evidence, avoids contact with reality and panders to the gullible. Pseudoscience is popular because it fulfils powerful emotional needs that science leaves unfulfilled; it satisfies spiritual hunger, promises cures for disease and an afterlife, and assures humans of their central importance in the universe.

- Science isolates errors, cutting them out one by one, with hypotheses framed so they can be disproved. A succession of alternative hypotheses is invited and tested to achieve *verisimilitude*, closeness to the truth. Pseudoscience does the opposite, proposing hypotheses unable to be disproved in a scientific manner and opposing sceptical scrutiny.

- It is important to have a demarcation between science and pseudoscience, as the acceptance of pseudoscientific beliefs and practices could lead to inefficient and dangerous practices in health care, environmental policy, science education and courts of law.

- It is misleading to suggest that experimenter fraud is rife in parapsychology, or even that it is more common than in other disciplines. Broad and Wade (1982) show that fraud is more likely when rewards are high and chances of being caught low, and this characterises mainstream science, like medicine, much more than psychic phenomena, which often take place under public scrutiny.

- Instances of fraud with psychic phenomena and the high degree of scepticism have led to the development of modern procedures so controlled that fraud is effectively ruled out. Such controls include random automated target selection, automated result recording, predetermining the number of trials, screening and independent judging. *continued ...*

...continued

- One of the enduring problems with parapsychology is that most significant results are produced by a small number of researchers, usually believers in psychic phenomena, and these are not replicated by more sceptical researchers see 'Extra-sensory perception (ESP) – Ganzfeld studies' below.

- Most studies of psychic ability involve ordinary people with no previous history of paranormal powers. People who make special claims of having strong psychic abilities are rarely tested, as it is assumed that they must be cranks, or because assessing the possibility that they might be fraudulent requires extensive, time-consuming experimental controls to rule out the possibility of cheating.

- Fang Shimin (2006), head of China's 'scientific police', who consistently exposed examples of Chinese pseudoscience, was ruled by a court of law to have libelled an ex-government consultant Liu Zihua, who claimed to have used the 'Eight Diagrams Theory', based on the ancient Chinese philosophy of Bagua, to find a tenth planet in the solar system. This shows how pseudoscience persists if it attracts popular support, has traditional status and legal backing.

- Blackmore (2001) claimed that pseudoscience in psychology exists because of a popular belief in the existence of a consciousness seen as the controlling mechanism of the mind, and because there exists a desire to find the 'power of consciousness'.

- Pseudoscience uses scientific terminology and mirrors scientific practice because it wishes to acquire the high status and acceptability that science holds in society. Mahner (2007) argued that science is our most reliable source of knowledge, and we need to take care to distinguish scientific knowledge from its lookalikes.

Methodological issues related to the study of paranormal cognition

Extra sensory perception – ganzfeld studies

Metzger introduced the ganzfeld (entire field) technique in the 1930s, and ganzfeld experiments have been hailed by many parapsychologists as providing scientific proof of telepathy, where individuals get specific information without using their ordinary senses. The technique uses unpatterned sensory stimulation to produce an effect similar to sensory deprivation. Honorton (1974) developed the technique to assess extrasensory perception (ESP) and it is now the main tool of parapsychological research.

There are three phases to ganzfeld studies:

1. **Preparing the receiver** – a receiver relaxes in a room for half an hour, receiving white or pink noise through headphones (white noise is sound produced of all frequencies, pink noise is without the high frequencies) to eliminate sensory input from sounds. Halved table–tennis balls are placed on the eyes and a red light shone on the face, producing an overall mild sense of sensory deprivation. A relaxation tape is also played and hallucinations are common at this stage.

2. **Sending the target** – a sender is in another soundproof room, not adjacent to the receiver, with opaque packets containing four images each. Each packet is randomly selected, as is the actual image. The experimenter is not aware of the chosen image until after the sender has sent the message and the receiver guessed it. The sender uses mental intention to telepathically relay the message. In later *auto-ganzfeld* studies, selection and showing of images was automated with no human involvement.

> *Fortean Times* is the long-established 'journal of unexplained phenomena, which examines all manner of psychic phenomena and anomalous experience in an unbiased and objective manner. There is a website, complete with a vast database accessible through a search engine. Go to www.forteantimes.com

3. **Judging the outcome** – a session lasts between 15 and 30 minutes, then the receiver is relieved of headphones and eye-covers and presented with four images to rate from the mental imagery received. The order of presentation is randomised each time due to the possibility of senders using a predictable pattern of choice.

Receivers should achieve, by chance factors, a success rate of about 25 per cent, but in the 1970s and 1980s, several studies and meta-analyses seemed to show a significant effect beyond this figure. In a series of experiments, in some senses collaborations at times, Charles Honorton, somewhat a believer in telepathy, found significant results, while Ray Hyman, more of a sceptic, identified possible flaws in the procedure:

- **Security flaws** – accidental sensory leakage by experimenters talking to receivers

- **Statistical flaws** – wrong choice of tests and inappropriate forms of analysis

- **Procedural flaws** – randomisation and documentation problems.

Tighter controls were introduced, including the autoganzfeld technique and the use of psychic entertainers to check for deception. Arguments also centred on the criteria to be used for meta-analyses. Significant findings continued to be found, but debate still exists as to whether the phenomenon is evidence of true psychic phenomena or can be explained by more mundane means.

Classic research

Honorton and Ferrari (1989)

Future telling: a meta-analysis of forced-choice precognition experiments, 1935–87

Ganzfeld studies test whether there is above-average evidence for individuals having ESP through 'psychic energy transfer', in being able to identify targets they cannot see. Many claimed that the studies provided scientific proof of telepathy, while others argued that although no intentional deceit was occurring, the statistically significant results were explicable by reference to flawed methodological procedures. In this study, the researchers, avid supporters of the ganzfeld technique and the notion of people possessing ESP, performed a meta-analysis of previous studies to try to answer these conflicting claims.

Aim

To assess whether by using the ganzfeld technique there is evidence for above-average accurate target identification, and, if so, what the size of the phenomenon is.

To assess whether observed effects are in fact due to variations in methodological quality, which suggest that no psychic phenomenon is occurring.

Procedure

A meta-analysis was conducted of 309 forced-choice pre-recognition experiments (ganzfeld studies) by 62 researchers, published between 1935 and 1987, involving attempts to identify randomly selected stimuli over intervals ranging from several hundred milliseconds to 1 year following participants' responses.

The analysis involved around 2 million trials from 50,000 participants.

Each study was scored for its quality of controls.

Findings

Overall there was a small, but statistically significant, reliable effect.

Of all the studies, by 40 researchers, 30 per cent were statistically significant in themselves.

Effect size remained constant over the survey period, during which time research quality improved substantially.

continued …

...continued

Studies using participants selected on the basis of demonstrating prior testing performance showed larger effects.

Participants tested individually showed larger effects than those tested in groups.

Studies where participants were given feedback after each trial found greater effects.

The shorter the gap between target generation and participants' responses, the bigger the effect.

Seven out of eight studies using selected participants, tested individually and given feedback after each trial, produced significant effects.

Conclusions

Precognition ability to identify forced-recognition targets exists at a significant level.

Such precognition ability is evident in studies using high research control methods.

There are moderating variables affecting performance concerning individual differences in ability, when feedback is given and when participants are being tested individually rather than in groups.

Evaluation

- Since 1975, the parapsychological association has vetoed the practice of only publishing significant studies; since then, 70 per cent of studies published show non-significant results. However, 75 per cent of ganzfeld studies were published before 1975, so selective publication bias may have affected the findings of the meta-analysis.

- The identification of moderating variables suggests areas to concentrate further research on.

- There were problems with many of the studies used, involving *sensory leakage* – for instance, not using soundproof rooms – *randomisation* problems, using *non-peer-referenced* studies and statistical flaws. Even so, when suspect studies were removed, a statistically significant result was still found.

Research: ganzfeld studies

- Honorton (1982) reported a meta-analysis of 42 published ganzfeld studies conducted between 1974 and 1981, of which 55 per cent produced positive results, with a hit rate of 38 per cent (25 per cent is expected by chance). Hyman (1985) performed a meta-analysis on the same data, using different criteria of which studies to exclude. He also found a hit rate of 38 per cent, though only 31 per cent of studies showed positive results. This suggests that some effect was evident beyond chance occurrences. However, Hyman claimed that experimental procedures were not rigorous enough or were not statistically analysed correctly, stating flaws in randomisation of targets and the judging procedure, as well as insufficient documentation.

- Blackmore (1987), after visiting his laboratory, criticised the research practices of Sargent, a leading parapsychologist. Sargent blamed random errors, rather than deliberate fraud, but retired from further research.

- Hyman and Honorton (1986) issued a joint communique agreeing that results were not due to chance or biased reporting, and agreeing on a need for replication performed under more stringent conditions, which were agreed by them both. Honorton then conducted autoganzfeld experiments, performed with computer-controlled tests and the receiver isolated in a soundproof, steel-walled, electromagnetically shielded room.

To read a more detailed account of the ganzfeld phenomenon, including the technique, related studies and an analysis of how it possibly works, go to http://dbem. ws/ganzfeld.html

- Honorton and Bem (1994) reported that autoganzfeld studies conducted between 1983 and 1989 replicated the results of earlier studies, though under much more stringent controls, preventing accidental information transference.

- Milton and Wiseman (1999) carried out a meta-analysis of 30 independent studies, finding no significant result. This was criticised for using non-standard methods, like musical rather than visual targets. Bem and Palmer (2001) redid the meta-analysis on studies using the standard procedure, with ten new additional studies, finding a significant result.

Evaluation

Ganzfeld studies

- There is still a danger with the ganzfeld technique of bias occurring, where believers in paranormal experiences produce seemingly positive findings. Results from ganzfeld studies tend to match researchers' beliefs.

- Findings from meta-analyses depend on which studies are excluded. Therefore, establishing the existence, or not, of ESP cannot be achieved in this manner, illustrating the need for well-designed studies, with procedures agreed by everyone involved in advance.

- The fact that receivers guess above chance levels is indisputable, but arguments rage over whether psychic energy is transferred. Hyman (1995) claimed that results remain meaningless until an explanation of the process behind them is outlined and validated. But as Bem and Honorton (1994) said, if there is an anomalous transfer of information or energy, it does not have to be paranormal.

- The use of the ganzfeld technique has led to the introduction of more rigorously controlled, unbiased research techniques in mainstream psychology.

Paranormal action – psychokinesis

Psychokinesis (PK) is the process of moving or otherwise affecting physical objects by the mind, with no physical contact. Some forms are known as *macro-PK*, where there is a large effect, visible to the naked eye, like the bending of spoons, and *micro-PK*, which involves small effects on systems of probability that need special instruments or statistical analysis to detect them, like dice-throwing effects. Claims are also made for levitation, moving objects and controlling weather patterns.

Bio-PK, or *distant influence on living systems* (DILS) studies, examine the effects of people's intentions on individuals' biological systems – for example, assessing whether physiological activity decreases or increases in response to a distant person's intention that someone should become calm or excited.

In a typical PK study, a computer might be connected to a micro–electronic random event generator (REG) or random number generator (RNG) that, by chance alone, produces two different outcomes equally often. The equipment is arranged so the two outcomes are associated with different events that participants witness – for example, one outcome leads to a light bulb getting brighter, the other to it becoming dimmer. The participant's task is to mentally make the light bulb brighter or dimmer. To ensure that the REGs/RNGs produce an unbiased random output, they are also run when no one is there to influence them.

Another form of PK experiment involves participants sitting in front of a computer screen and being asked to increase the output – for example, either raising or lowering a horizontal line.

These kinds of experiment offer an automated protocol, with random targets, determined by machines, and results recorded without human intervention, making fraud almost impossible.

Research: psychokinesis

- Nelson and Radin (1989) reported a meta-analysis of RNG–PK research, comprising 832 experiments, including 258 control studies, by 68 investigators, finding a small but significant effect (51 per cent). This was supported by Jahn *et al.* (2005), who conducted over 1,000 experiments, involving millions of trials, with 100 participants, again finding a small, significant effect, suggesting that under certain circumstances, consciousness interacts with random physical systems.

Figure 12.03 Micro-psychokinesis effects are claimed for dice throwing

- Henry (2005) found that RNG performance is not affected by distance; performance is similar whether participants are next door to the machine or thousands of miles away.

- Radin and Ferrari (1991) performed a meta-analysis on 148 dice-rolling experiments performed by 52 investigators, involving 2.6 million dice throws between 1935 and 1987, finding a small but significant result. However, Hansel (1989) reported that when criteria necessary for a conclusive PK test were applied – having two researchers, true randomisation of targets and independent recorders – none of the tests produced evidence for PK regarded as conclusive. This suggests that significant effects are actually products of flawed methodology.

- Schmidt (1970) asked participants to observe a circle of nine lamps and when one was lit, to try to move it mentally in a certain direction, finding that some participants appeared able to exert an influence, suggesting support for the existence of PK. Schmidt (1976) had similar success with getting participants to influence clicks on a cassette tape generated randomly by a radioactive source, finding that they could be made stronger or weaker by mental effort, producing convincing evidence for the existence of PK.

- Stevens (1999) asked participants accessing a web page to try to control the paths of laser beams, finding more influence over the beams than in a control condition of no mental effort, supporting the notion of PK.

Evaluation

Psychokinesis

- Parapsychologists often complain that the standard of proof required for their studies to be accepted as valid is unfairly higher than in other areas of psychology. However, Abelson (1978) believed that 'extraordinary claims require extraordinary evidence', implying that the strength of evidence needed to establish new phenomena is directly proportional to how incompatible the phenomena are with current beliefs.

- For psychokinesis to be accepted there is a need for conclusive experiments, free of any possible error or fraud, and immune to all sceptical doubt. However, this is not possible, as science only deals with probabilities, not certainties.

- Rao and Palmer (1987) believed that REG experiments can be seen as 'conclusive' experiments, as they minimise, as much as is possible, any chances of fraud or error. Such tests produce significant results, but, somewhat inevitably, are still criticised and not accepted, as although there is evidence for the existence of PK, independent researchers generally cannot replicate findings.

continued ...

...continued

- Schmeidler and McConnell (1958) found that believers of PK produce more supporting evidence on tests of paranormal abilities, and therefore results can be explained as due to participant and researcher bias.
- Radin (1997) believed that the insular nature of scientific disciplines hinders the acceptance of parapsychologists' work by other scientists.
- A pertinent criticism is that of Radin (2003), who asked, if PK exists, why it is not used for human good rather than merely bending spoons, and so on. And why are psychics not becoming extremely rich by picking the correct lottery numbers each week?

Research in focus

One problem with studies of paranormal phenomena (as with most areas of psychology) was the tendency (up to 1975) to only publish studies showing significant results. This creates what is known as the 'file drawer problem', where the possibility arises that journals are only publishing studies with Type I errors.

What are Type I errors? How do they differ from Type II errors? How do psychologists strike a balance between making these two types of error?

Explain in terms of studies of psychic phenomena what effects making Type I errors would have.

Contemporary research

Bem (2010)
Is this evidence that we can see the future?

Parapsychology has had a hard struggle to convince scientists that there is any irrefutable evidence of psychic phenomena, with little in the way of peer-reviewed studies being published. Where significant findings have been found, as with ganzfeld studies, suspicions have centred on faulty methodology and possible researcher bias. However, this peer-reviewed research was conducted by a respected psychologist, with a reputation for running careful experiments, and is published in a respected journal, with scrutiny by esteemed sceptics not identifying any serious flaws.

Aims

To provide tests that mainstream psychologists could readily replicate and evaluate, by conducting a variety of time-reversed versions of established psychological phenomena, so that events generally interpreted as causes happen after tested behaviour rather than before it.

Procedure

A series of experiments involving more than 1,000 student volunteers were conducted over an 8-year period.

Experiment 1: participants were shown a list of words and asked to recall them and were then told to type words randomly selected from the same list.

Experiment 2: a technique was adapted from 'priming', the effect of subliminally presented words on individuals' responses to images – for example, assessing whether participants who were momentarily flashed the word 'ugly' take longer to decide that a picture of a kitten is pleasant than if 'beautiful' were flashed. This procedure was reversed to assess if the priming effect works backwards in time as well as forwards.

Experiment 3: participants were told that an erotic image would appear on a computer screen in one of two positions, and asked to guess which position it would be. The eventual position was selected at random.

continued ...

...continued

Findings

Experiment 1: participants were better at recalling words they would later type.

Experiment 2: the priming effect worked equally well backwards in time as it did forwards.

Experiment 3: participants guessed correctly 53.1 per cent of the time, a statistically significant result.

Conclusions

Evidence is apparent of statistically significant findings of psychic phenomena beyond chance occurrence.

Evaluation

- The methodology is recognised as sound and offers a scientifically verifiable means of assessing the topic area.

- The fact that significant results are found across a range of experiments reduces the chance of the results being a statistical fluke.

- Well-established phenomena, like the ability of aspirin to prevent heart attacks, are also based on similarly small significant effects.

- The findings have so far stood up to scrutiny. One failed replication of the word-recall test has occurred using an online survey panel, which Bem criticised, as it is impossible to know with such a method how much attention participants have paid to a task.

You are the researcher

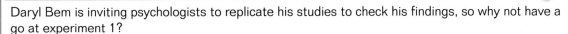

Daryl Bem is inviting psychologists to replicate his studies to check his findings, so why not have a go at experiment 1?

Compile a list of 20 numbered items that are unconnected to each other in meaning or similarity of sound and so on. Read out the list of items to a participant and give the participant 1 minute to recall as many items as possible.

Select words at random from the list – you will need a random number table or computer-generated random numbers to achieve this – and ask the participant to type out those words. Repeat for another 19 participants.

If Bem is correct, participants should recall significantly more words that they later typed. You can deduce this by carrying out a Wilcoxon signed matched ranks test.

Research in focus

Significant findings from studies of psychic phenomena are often questioned in terms of inadequate methodology, and, increasingly, efforts have been made to conduct rigorously controlled studies.

What are double-blind studies and how do they benefit research into psychic phenomena? How do single-blind studies differ from double-blind ones?

Researcher bias is another area of concern. What measures are taken to reduce researcher bias?

Psychology in action

Methodology

Parapsychology, in its struggle to be accepted as a serious scientific discipline, has provided psychology with much improved methodology. The main criticism of parapsychology was that seemingly significant results actually emanate from flawed research practices. Therefore, parapsychology endeavoured to produce watertight research conducted under rigorous conditions. Even if this did not provide evidence of psychic phenomena, it has given psychology much improved methods used in all branches of the subject.

In the 1930s, the Rhines conducted experiments to demonstrate the validity of telepathy, where a receiver would guess the identity of an unseen card looked at by an agent. The card order needs to be randomised, achieved by shuffling, but in fact this is not truly random, and extensive efforts were made to produce random number tables, numbers produced without predictable patterns. Results were not as striking, but were still significant. Attention then turned to the relationship between researcher and participant, and methods were devised to stop information being passed unwittingly, by isolating them from each other, having target cards unknown in advance to either participant or researcher, and having independent verification and analysis of results. Above-chance results became rarer, but still occurred, unless sceptics performed replications, and then significant results were never found. This demonstrated the importance of biased attitudes held by researchers and the need for double-blind techniques. Other controls were introduced; like pre-setting the number of trials so they do not just continue until significant results are found and developing new analytical techniques.

These forms of control are now the norm in psychology, and more rigorously conducted studies lead to more accurate results and thus better practical applications – that is, ones actually of benefit. In 2010, a man shown by several independent US forensic scientists to be 'guilty beyond doubt' of planting a terrorist bomb, was shown to be innocent. Why? Because their supposed objectivity became biased by knowing in advance the 'guilty' results found earlier by esteemed colleagues, and this affected their perception of the evidence. This is just like believers in parapsychology finding significant results while sceptics do not.

Research in focus

Do you understand the concept of randomisation?

Define random numbers? Why would shuffling cards not ensure random selection?

What is a random sample and why is it difficult to achieve in a population of people?

Random sampling does not guarantee a representative sample. Explain why not.

Which sampling method would produce a more representative sample?

Figure 12.04 Random selection of stimuli, necessary in controlled experiments, is not ensured by shuffling cards

You are the researcher

Findings from studies of the paranormal are often dependent on whether researchers are believers or sceptics, suggesting that some form of unconscious bias is occurring. Test this out by performing a correlation as follows.

First, for co-variable one, ask 20 participants to assess on a scale of 1 to 20 (1 being no belief, 20 being strong belief) their degree of belief in the paranormal.

For co-variable two, repeat the procedure for the staring experiment (see page 476), but with each of your participants as the reader. Ask them to test about four sitters each and record the number of successful guesses for the four sitters combined as the participant's score.

Analyse the data with a Spearman's rho and plot the data on a scattergram.

Strengthen your learning

1. Outline the Chinese pseudoscience debate.
2. Why can the study of Basil Shackleton be considered a case of scientific fraud?
3. Construct an elaborated evaluation of issues of pseudoscience and the scientific status of parapsychology – that is, an evaluation where points build on each other to form an effective commentary.
4a. Outline the procedure involved in ganzfeld studies.
4b. Explain the arguments for and against ganzfeld studies supporting the existence of ESP, using research evidence as part of your explanation.
5a. Outline what is meant by psychokinesis and how it is studied.
5b. To what extent does research evidence indicate that psychokinesis exists? Give details.
5c. Aside from research evidence what other evaluative points can be made about the phenomenon?

Assessment Check

1. Outline one issue of pseudoscience. (4 marks)

2. Outline and evaluate methodological issues relating to studies of psychokinesis. (20 marks)

3. Outline issues of pseudoscience. (8 marks)

4. Evaluate methodological issues relating to ganzfeld studies of ESP. (16 marks)

5. Discuss pseudoscience and the scientific status of parapsychology. (24 marks)

Examination guidance

If more than one issue of pseudoscience were outlined in question 1, all would be marked, but only the best one credited. As only an outline is asked for, offering evaluative material would not be creditworthy.

At least two methodological issues need to be outlined in question 2, though describing more than two would not be a good tactic, as only 4 marks are available for the outline. Most effort should be concentrated on the evaluation, where 16 marks are on offer. Suitable evaluative material could focus on the degree of research support for psychokinesis, as well as relevant methodological analysis.

Question 3 only requires descriptive material relating to issues of pseudoscience. If more than two issues were presented, less detail would be expected. Offering descriptive material in response to question 4 would not be creditworthy. A good method of evaluation would be to construct a commentary based on methodological issues that centred around Ganzfeld and psychokinesis studies.

The term 'discuss' in question 5 means to describe and evaluate, and both pseudoscience and the scientific status of parapsychology need to be covered, with a balance achieved between the two to access the top band for the 8 marks available for an outline. An effective evaluation might focus on theoretical considerations, like the divide between science, non-science and pseudoscience.

Explanations for anomalous experience

The role of coincidence and probability judgements in anomalous experience

A coincidence occurs when two unrelated events correspond. Although no obvious relationship exists, a belief forms, creating a cognitive bias, that one causes the other. This can be seen as an explanation of how superstitions arise. The perception of coincidences leads to occult or paranormal claims, supporting the belief system of fatalism, where events are seen as predestined. Coincidences also happen due to shortcuts in information processing, occurring as an attempt to simplify understanding.

Research: coincidence

- Esgate and Groome (2001) found that participants underestimated how big a group of people is required to be for there to be a 50–50 chance of two of them sharing a birthday (it is actually 23), illustrating how people miscalculate and assume that paranormal phenomena are at play.

- Zusne and Jones (1989) calculated the chances of thinking about a known person by chance 5 minutes before learning of their death. In a country the size of the USA, 3,000 adults a year would have this experience, demonstrating how what may seem like a paranormal coincidence can be explained by chance factors.

- Falk (1982) found that when extraordinary coincidences occur, people commit the error of singling that event out and according it significant status, suggesting a bias in cognitive processing.

- Blackmore and Troscianko (1985) found, using coin-tossing trials, that believers in the paranormal are less accurate in making probability judgements than non-believers, underestimating the probability of chance events. This suggests that believers are more likely to consider events as beyond coincidence.

- Falk (1989) found that unlikely coincidences are considered more significant when they happen to us, suggesting an egocentric bias is at work.

Evaluation

Coincidence
- Chopra (2003) believed that the ancient Vedic philosophy that all events can be related to unseen prior causes or associations, no matter how vast or trivial, and that there is therefore no such thing as coincidence, is becoming accepted by scientists.
- Slovic et al. (1982) believed that when unlikely events happen, like a bizarre accident, they serve to remind us of our own mortality.
- The calculation of coincidences is dependent on accurate memory, as track must be kept of how often, when, and so on, apparently associated events have occurred in the past. As memories are reconstructive and subject to error, wishful thinking and suggestion, this may not necessarily be consistently achievable.

Probability judgements

Many people often misjudge the probability of unrelated events occurring and instead come to believe that such events are connected by some paranormal source. For example, a person has a dream that appears in some part to come subsequently true, or someone is thinking about a person, the phone rings and it's that person. Actually the probability of one dream out of all those a person has coming true, or a phone call coming from one person out of all the people thought about isn't large and statistically is perfectly explainable as coincidence. But many people will be convinced otherwise that psychic forces are at play.

The fact that belief in paranormal events has increased seems to suggest that the general public isn't basing its judgements on scientific evidence or reasoning, but instead on the media (with popular TV shows like the X-files), the testimonies of trusted others and the misperception of personal experiences as being due to paranormal phenomena.

There are several cognitive factors that can help to explain why people make incorrect probability judgements and see paranormal forces at play instead of mere coincidence.

Intuitive versus analytical thinking styles

Those with intuitive thinking styles, lacking reasoning and critical thinking so that evidence is not analytically evaluated, have more of a tendency towards paranormal beliefs.

Lindeman and Aarnio (2005) argued that believers in the paranormal make similar cognitive errors, characteristic of children's immature errors of reasoning while they are still learning about how the world works. Therefore, such people believe that thoughts influence objects and that biological processes are not unthinking, unintentional processes, but have intentions and goals. Such thinking is apparent in alternative health treatments, where individuals believe that willpower alters health states. The idea of healing energies has intuitive appeal, especially to those ignorant to or prejudiced against science, and such individuals are much likelier to believe in the paranormal.

Cognitive illusions

Believers in the paranormal seek reasons for events and cannot accept unexplained events as random, meaningless occurrences. Cognitive illusions concern a perceptual style where chance and probability are misperceived, so that when presented with a pattern of occurrences with no explanation, those prone to believing in the paranormal tend to infer that unseen, psychic forces are at work. They also have a poor concept of randomness, reading significance into random patterns.

Illusion of control

Believers in the paranormal have a tendency to perceive random processes as being under personal control, especially if perceived as involving skill.

Confirmatory bias

Believers in the paranormal tend to ignore evidence that refutes their beliefs and overemphasise evidence that confirms them – for instance, concentrating on the parts of horoscopes that come true and ignoring the majority that does not.

Cold reading

Believers in the paranormal are more gullible to 'cold reading', a technique where supposed psychics give strangers the impression that they know lots about them, by using vague, general statements as descriptive of a unique personality.

Research: probability judgements

- Aarnio and Lindeman (1975) investigated the beliefs and thinking styles of superstitious and sceptic individuals, finding that superstitious individuals assigned more physical and biological attributes to mental phenomena, assigned more mental attributes to water, furniture, rocks and other material things, and believed that entities like these have psychological properties, such as desires, knowledge or a soul. This suggests that believers in the paranormal are distinguishable by cognitive errors and intuitive thinking.

- Genovese (2005) found that beliefs in the paranormal among teachers correlated with cognitive errors and intuitive thinking styles, suggesting that cognitive factors are linked to paranormal beliefs, with such beliefs held by teachers being especially important, as they are more able to transmit them to others.

- Langer and Roth (1975) found that early success at a task, like picking lottery numbers, enhanced the illusion of control, making participants believe that skill was involved, supported by a bias in recalling a higher number of successes than there actually was. This illustrates how an illusion of control creates a probability judgement that contributes to a belief in ESP.

- Blackmore and Troscianko (1985) found that believers of paranormal phenomena performed worse than disbelievers on a task involving the generation of a string of random numbers, giving fewer repetitions of the same number than would be expected by chance. This suggests that believers are subject to cognitive illusions that affect ability to determine the probability of events. This was supported by Brugger *et al.* (1990), who found non-believers to be better at generating random numbers than believers, suggesting that they are more cognitively able.

- Paulus (1988) found that believers in the paranormal consider that dreams are predictive, on the basis of a dream event and a future occurrence, demonstrating how such individuals are prone to paranormal beliefs through poor estimation of probabilities.

- Hyman (1977) showed how successful cold readings by a psychic, where general information is identified by audience members as pertaining specifically to them, convinces other audience members of the existence of paranormal forces.

- Musch and Ehrenberg (2002) gave participants the Belief in Paranormal Scale and a battery of probabilistic reasoning tasks, finding a correlation between scores on the Belief in Paranormal Scale and error rates in probabilistic reasoning. However, the relation disappeared when cognitive ability, measured by final grades, was controlled for, suggesting that differences in general cognitive performance rather than specific probabilistic reasoning skills provide the basis for paranormal beliefs.

Evaluation

Probability judgements

- Research does not identify where cognitive factors – such as cognitive illusions and thinking styles involved in paranormal beliefs – originate from. Such factors could be innate or learned. Banziger (1983) found that participants on a parapsychology course emphasising scepticism became more sceptical in their thinking, implying that cognitive styles can be altered by experience leading to a change in probability judgements.

- Although many studies find differences in probability estimation between believers and non-believers, not all do, suggesting that the area is not fully understood or that some studies have used flawed methodology.

- The fact that many humans have cognitive systems that detect patterns where none exist may be explainable in evolutionary terms as a biological device to try to make sense of the world, which bestows a survival value.

Classic research

Wiseman *et al.* (1995)

Eyewitness testimony in the seance room

Much evidence relating to paranormal phenomena consists of eyewitness testimony. However, research indicates such testimony to be unreliable. Research also suggests that observers' expectations and beliefs play a role in the production of inaccurate testimony. Therefore, sceptics might expect trickery from alleged psychics, while believers would not. The researchers here wanted to see whether eyewitness testimony of seances was unreliable and what effect their level of scepticism had.

Figure 12.05

Aim

To assess the reliability of testimony relating to seance phenomena and whether paranormal events could be produced in a modern seance.

Procedure

Twenty-five participants completed a questionnaire assessing whether they believed that paranormal phenomena might occur during seances.

They then attended three seances, where chairs were arranged in a large circle, with various objects – a book, slate, bell and maracas, coated with luminous paint – were placed on a table in the middle of the circle. The medium (an actor) indicated a small luminous ball, suspended on a piece of rope from the ceiling. After turning out the lights, he asked everyone to join hands and concentrate on trying to move the ball mentally, and then try in the same way to move the objects on the table. During the seances, the slate, bell, book and table remained stationary, though in order to have some semblance of psychic phenomena, the maracas were moved by trickery.

Findings

Twenty per cent of participants recalled incorrectly the maracas being examined before the seance.

Twenty-seven per cent of participants recalled at least one of the stationary objects moving in the first two seances.

Seventy-six per cent of sceptics as opposed to 54 per cent of believers did not recall the ball moving.

Fourteen per cent of sceptics as opposed to 40 per cent of believers recalled at least one other object moving.

Twenty per cent of believers compared to 0 per cent of sceptics thought they had seen genuine psychic phenomena.

Conclusions

Eyewitness testimony in seances is unreliable, but more unreliable among believers than sceptics.

Expectations and beliefs can lead individuals to be unreliable witnesses of psychic phenomena.

continued ...

...continued

Evaluation

- The study probably underestimated the degree of unreliability, as the seances only lasted 10 minutes and participants recalled immediately afterwards.
- Unreliable believers would probably tell others of their 'experience', leading to widespread beliefs in the paranormal.
- Assessors should be cautious about eyewitness testimony of alleged psychic phenomena.

Explanations for superstitious behaviour and magical thinking

Superstition

Superstitions are irrational beliefs that objects, actions or circumstances not logically related to a course of events influence outcomes – for instance, that wearing a certain jumper will cause the wearer's football team to win. Superstitions are often linked in this manner to magical thinking and ritual behaviours, and it is believed that if adhered to they will bring about desired results. Superstitions therefore have an element of self-deceit about them, whereby believers of a superstition feel they have a part to play in achieving a goal that is actually outside their sphere of influence. This, in turn, has an emotional component in decreasing anxiety while simultaneously increasing confidence.

Research in focus

In Wiseman's study, a questionnaire was used to assess belief in paranormal phenomena, a popular research method in this area.

Why is a questionnaire a form of self-report?

How do questionnaires differ from interviews and surveys?

Explain how a Likert scale could be used to assess degree and direction of belief in the paranormal.

Give two strengths and weaknesses of questionnaires as a means of assessing belief in the paranormal.

The motivation behind superstitions is a desire for control and certainty, with individuals searching for a rule or explanation of why things happen. The creation of false certainties through superstitions is regarded as better than having no certainty at all, and this is especially so in situations where we want success, like the local football team winning. Individual differences in levels of superstitious behaviour are explicable as some individuals having a greater need for control and certainty, and in this way can be seen to link to personality factors.

Behaviourism explains superstitions as occurring through operant conditioning, either by positive reinforcement, where certain behaviours or objects become associated with pleasurable outcomes, or by negative reinforcement, where behaviours or objects become associated with reducing anxiety levels associated with uncertainty. Superstitions can also be cultural constructions, passed on through socialisation from one generation to another, and varying between cultures.

Research: superstitions

- Skinner (1948) found that pigeons adopted unique body movement superstitions by learning to associate them with rewards of food pellets.

- Lustberg (2004) found superstitions among sportspeople to be beneficial, as they increase confidence, motivation and persistence, thus enhancing chances of winning.

- Fluke *et al.* (2010) conducted questionnaires with 200 undergraduates, finding three reasons for a belief in superstition: to gain control over uncertainties, to decrease feelings of helplessness, and because it is easier to rely on superstitions than coping strategies. This suggests that superstitions fulfil several functions.

- Atsaides (2010) found that Greek superstitions vary not only from island to island, but between the villages on an island. On one island, some people considered bats so lucky that they carried bat bones with them, while other islanders considered bats so unholy as to be avoided at all costs. This suggests that some superstitions may have a cultural purpose in determining in-group/out-group membership.

- Keinan (1994) gave questionnaires to 174 Israelis after the Iraqi Scud missile attacks of 1991, finding that those with the highest stress levels were those who had the greatest belief in superstitions. This supports the idea that superstitions create an illusion in the possessor that they control outcomes and thus would be responsible for missiles hitting or missing targets.

- Whitson and Galinsky (2008) asked participants to recall situations of full or no control and then presented them with scenarios describing important occurrences preceded by unrelated behaviours, like knocking on wood. Participants who recalled situations of no control were more likely to associate the occurrences and unrelated behaviours as being related, suggesting that people who perceive themselves as lacking control over situations are more likely to develop superstitions.

Evaluation

Superstitions

- Although superstitions are irrational and have no basis in fact, they can be seen in a positive manner as increasing and maintaining psychological health through their ability to decrease anxiety levels, while increasing confidence and self-assurance, though Kienan's research (1994) suggests that they can also have a negative impact on health.

- Although superstitions can have an obsessive element to them, comprising a ritualised, repetitive nature, they are not seen as part of obsessive-compulsive disorder under psychiatric classification systems like DSM-IV.

- Cross-cultural superstitions tend to have a basis in fact, like the belief that spilling salt brings misfortune. Salt in ancient times was a rare, valuable commodity, the intake of which was necessary for continued existence; therefore, wasting salt could have negative consequences. This implies that some superstitions have an educational value to them, often instilled through fear.

- In China, the number '8' is considered lucky. Simmons and Schindler (2003) report how the price of many items for sale in China end in an '8', and that any exporters wishing to break into the increasingly lucrative Chinese market should set prices including this superstitious element.

Figure 12.06 Some superstitions have an educational value to them: spilling salt could be costly, as salt was rare, valuable and necessary for life

Magical thinking

Magical thinking has several elements to it, including the belief that all things are connected through paranormal forces. Stevens (2009) also sees magical thinking as investing special powers and forces in things perceived as symbols, with the majority of the world's peoples believing that energy flows connect such symbols with their referent points. The specific content of these symbols is culturally determined, with some symbols found in all cultures, like fire, water and eggs, though they may mean different things in different cultures. Therefore, magical thinking can serve to represent culturally specific and culturally universal symbolism, with paranormal beliefs existing as a shared belief system, serving to bind people together within cultural groupings.

Magical thinking also proposes the *law of similarity*, that things or events that resemble each other are connected in some causal way that defies scientific investigation and explanation, while the *law of contagion* sees things that have been in contact or association with each other, as retaining a connection when separated, for example believing that the bones of saints retain spiritual powers. Many Eastern philosophies contain elements of magical thinking, such as the primacy of the mind over physical matter (see the Chinese pseudoscience debate page 448). There are those also who see religious beliefs as being a form of magical thinking, for example by believing that if prayed to, dead saints have the power to heal incurable diseases.

Like supersititions, magical thinking can be related to cognitive factors and may also act as a coping mechanism for those who have suffered traumatic experiences.

Research: magical thinking

- Lawrence *et al.* (1994) used questionnaires to find a positive correlation between childhood trauma and magical thinking, supporting the idea that belief in the paranormal acts as a coping mechanism for those who have suffered traumatic experiences. This was supported by Perkins and Allen (2006), who found that students who had suffered abuse were more likely to believe in paranormal phenomena associated with personal control, like ESP, but not with phenomena not associated with personal power, like UFOs.

- Irwin (1994) found that children who spent their childhood with an alcoholic parent had stronger beliefs in magical thinking, witchcraft, superstitions and precognitions, again suggesting that paranormal beliefs, including magical thinking, serve a coping function.

- Einstein and Menzies (2003) tested the idea that obsessive-compulsive disorder (OCD) was related to magical thinking. They gave 60 obsessive-compulsive patients several questionnaires to measure their levels of magical thinking, thought-action fusion and obsessive-compulsive behaviour (the magic-ideation scale, the lucky behaviours and lucky beliefs scales, the thought-action-revised scale and the obsessive-compulsive inventory), finding that magical thinking was strongly related to obsessive-compulsive symptoms. This suggests that a tendency to magical thinking underpins the links between beliefs in superstition, thought-action fusion and obsessive-compulsive severity.

- De Craen *et al.* (1996) reviewed six studies published in the *British Medical Journal* and reported that Europeans and Americans had magical thinking beliefs about the suitability and effectiveness of different-coloured pills. Red, orange and yellow pills were thought to have stimulant properties, while blue and green tablets were perceived as having sedative qualities. Specifically, red tablets were seen as having a cardio-vascular effect and orange pills were believed to affect the skin. This suggests a cultural basis to magical thinking beliefs, though some beliefs are cross-cultural, for example red being associated with blood. This was supported by Bonser (1963) who reported that health workers in Chile had found that Mapuche Indians favoured taking red pills, as red had an association with exorcism and thus the pills were perceived as purging illness.

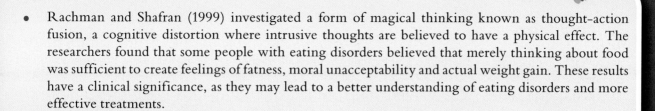

- Rachman and Shafran (1999) investigated a form of magical thinking known as thought–action fusion, a cognitive distortion where intrusive thoughts are believed to have a physical effect. The researchers found that some people with eating disorders believed that merely thinking about food was sufficient to create feelings of fatness, moral unacceptability and actual weight gain. These results have a clinical significance, as they may lead to a better understanding of eating disorders and more effective treatments.

Evaluation

Magical thinking

- Schweder (1997) saw magical thinking, a belief in irrational and non-scientific beliefs, as serving the function of searching for meaningful connections between things, thus serving to increase a sense of certainty and control.

- De Craen et al.'s (1996) research suggests a practical application, in that the pharmaceutical industry should manufacture pills in the colours represented by their magical thinking connotations. For example, heart medication should come in red colours, due to their association with blood. If patients have confidence in the medication they are prescribed, not only are they more likely to take it, but the medication may even be more effective due to kind of placebo effect.

- Magical thinking may actually produce real effects at times. If people believe something to be so, then this increases the chances, through enhanced confidence, motivation and so on that this really will occur. For instance, if a person with religious beliefs who is ill is told by other believers that they will pray for their recovery, then this increases the chances that the patient will actually produce or perceive that they have produced an improvement in their condition.

- Magical thinking often perpetuates itself by people's preference to accept magical thinking explanations even in the face of contradictory scientific evidence. Beyerstein (1997) reports that many patients and even therapists will interpret 'alternative' medicines and practices, which have no basis in fact, as having resulted in a 'cure' even when they were also taking more traditional prescribed medicines that have a scientifically demonstrative effect. The result of this is that beliefs in magical thinking are hard to break down and can have seriously negative effects, such as dangerously ill people refusing treatments that are known to be effective in favour of ones based on magical thinking, as well as sustaining a market for bogus medicines, which may have harmful effects.

Supplementary learning

Why do people believe in astrology?

Astrology is a pseudoscience that sees the relative positions of heavenly bodies as providing information about people's personalities, allowing understanding of the past and present and making predictions for the future.

Groome (2001) argued that with no scientific evidence supporting astrology, it is irrational that people believe in it. However, irrational beliefs interest psychologists, so research was conducted into the phenomenon.

Figure 12.07

Snyder and Schenkel (1975) asked people for their time and date of birth, and presented each with a personality description allegedly based on their horoscope. In reality, everyone was given the same profile; however, most participants believed the profile was accurate. Similarly, French et al. (1991) found that most participants believed that a description of their personality was 'good' or 'excellent', despite the fact that it contained both extremes of each personality dimension – for example, 'at times you are extraverted … while at other times you are introverted'.

These experiments illustrate the *Barnum effect*, where people believe anything about themselves provided it includes vague, general things that most people could identify with – for example, 'you feel some people do not appreciate you enough'. Astrologers also tend to focus on the continued …

...continued

more flattering aspects of the reader's personality, so that individuals are being told what they want to hear.

People possibly accept the principles of astrology unquestioningly because many individuals look for an understanding of their lives and insight into the minds of others. The incomplete answers of psychology are not sufficient for most, who need a simple framework to make sense of the world and those around them. Astrology and beliefs in other phenomena, like superstition, give them the insights, certainty and control over events that bring them comfort and security.

You are the researcher

Does astrology have validity? Astrologers claim that people have distinctive characteristics relating to when in a year they were born, from which predictions can be made. To test this out, assemble a sample of participants, ask them their star signs, and tell them they will hear a description of their star sign personality. By random selection, read half of them the correct description of their star sign and half of them an incorrect description (chosen at random from the other 11 star signs). On a scale of 0 to 10 (0 being 'not descriptive' and 10 being 'very descriptive'), ask them to score how accurate the description is. If astrology is true, the mean score should be higher for the true description group.

What statistical test is needed to analyse the data?

What ethical problem is there with this study and how could it possibly be overcome?

Personality factors underlying anomalous experience

Personality factors concern the characteristics that individuals possess, levels of which contribute to their uniqueness. Psychologists have attempted to see whether particular characteristics are associated with anomalous experiences.

Neuroticism is a personality trait characterised by anxious, moody behaviour and emotional instability, and is a characteristic associated with a belief in the paranormal. This may be due to neurotics finding the paranormal world to be a source of comfort, allowing them to interpret and predict events and thus quell their natural disposition for being overemotional. Such beliefs might also just be a product of the overemotionality of neurotics.

Another personality trait, *extroversion*, has been associated more specifically with ESP abilities. This has been theorised as due to extroverts having lowers levels of arousal in the reticular activating system (RAS) of the brain, making them more amenable to displaying such abilities. However, other research suggests that a link to extroversion is purely a product of flawed methodology.

Another aspect of personality linked to anomalous experience is that of *defensiveness*, cognitive resistance to perceiving situations and information as threatening. Research indicates that individuals who show defensive reactions tend to have lower ESP scores than non-defensive individuals.

Research: personality factors

- Honorton *et al.* (1998) performed a meta-analysis of 60 studies, finding extroversion significantly associated with ESP ability, suggesting a link between personality and psychic ability. However, effects were not consistent across studies; and further analysis, where studies were divided into forced choice/free choice, and whether participants were tested in groups or individually, again revealed a lack of consistent results and that some findings were due to flawed methodology, where participants completed a personality

questionnaire after they had had feedback on their ESP performance, rather than before. This suggests that the apparent ESP/extroversion relationship can be explained by non-paranormal means.

- Honorton (1998) subsequently isolated 12 individual-tested studies comprising 221 auto-ganzfeld trials, finding that all gave a significant result between ESP ability and extroversion, and only one tested extroversion levels after feedback was given. This finding suggests a link between personality and psychic ability.

- Wiseman and Watt (2004) tested the relationship between paranormal beliefs and neuroticism on two widely used types of personality questionnaire, finding with both that high neuroticism scores were associated with a belief in the paranormal, implying a link with personality.

- Williams *et al.* (2007) assessed 279 13–16-year-olds on the Junior Eysenck Personality Questionnaire and the Index of Paranormal Belief, finding that neuroticism was fundamental to individual differences in paranormal belief, with paranormal belief independent of extroversion and psychosis.

- Johnson (1977) used the Defensive Mechanism Test (DMT), where pictures of threatening situations are used to assess perception, finding that individuals who exhibited defensiveness had lower ESP abilities, suggesting that this aspect of personality is linked to paranormal ability.

- Haraldsson and Houtkooper (1992) performed a meta-analysis of Icelandic studies of defensiveness, finding a significant relationship between DMT scores and ESP ability, suggesting that defensive people feel threatened by ESP information and block it out. Watt and Morris (1995) supported this, by measuring defensiveness through individuals' reactions to weak sensory stimuli, finding that defensive individuals had lower ESP scores than non-defensive individuals.

Evaluation

Personality factors

- Watt (2005) perceived the evidence for a defensiveness–ESP relationship as consistent with the theory that ESP information is initially perceived at an unconscious level and that this information is subject to distortions and transformations prior to emergence in conscious awareness. The evidence is also perceived as illustrating how psychological factors can be seen to contribute to an understanding of paranormal phenomena.

- Rattet and Bursik (2000) suggested that the contradictory results found in research into extroversion may be due to methodological issues, like measurement limitations, imprecise operational definitions of what constitute psychic beliefs, and the specific biases of the researchers.

- The relationship between personality and anomalous experience is not a simplistic one. Different personality factors are associated with different aspects of the topic area. Neuroticism is associated with a belief in the paranormal, while extroversion is associated with psychic ability like ESP.

- Extroverts may perform better in tests of ESP ability, purely because they adapt swiftly to the new social situation of the laboratory and are aroused, motivated and comfortable with being tested. Introverts, on the other hand, may not adjust so readily to the testing environment, nor be so activated and engrossed in it.

Strengthen your learning

1a. Outline the role of
   i)　coincidence
   ii)　probability judgements
   in anomalous experience.
1b. To what extent do research studies provide support for the role of coincidence and probability judgements in anomalous experience?
2a. Outline explanations of
   i)　superstition
   ii)　magical thinking.
2b. To what degree are these explanations supported by research evidence?
2c. What other evaluative points, aside from research evidence can be made about these explanations?
3a. Outline how personality factors may affect anomalous experience.
3b. To what extent does research support the idea that personality factors affect anomalous experience. Give details.

Assessment Check

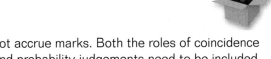

1.　Outline how personality factors may underlie anomalous experience. (4 marks)

2.　Outline the role of coincidence and probability judgements in anomalous experience. (8 marks)

3a. Outline and evaluate explanations for superstitious behaviour. (12 marks)

3b. Outline and evaluate explanations for magical thinking. (12 marks)

4.　Evaluate the role of coincidence in anomalous experience. (16 marks)

5.　Outline and evaluate personality factors underlying anomalous experience. (24 marks)

6.　Outline and evaluate the role of probability judgements in anomalous experience. (24 marks)

Examination guidance

In question 1, only descriptive material would be credited and a 'shorter' outline of how personality factors may underlie anomalous experience is required, as only 4 marks are on offer (compared to question 2. where 8 marks are on offer for a similar outline)

Question 2 also only requires descriptive material, so any evaluative material would again not accrue marks. Both the roles of coincidence and probability judgements need to be included, with a reasonable balance between the two to gain access to the highest band of marks.

Questions 3a and 3b are quite similar in their requirements and mark allocation. Four marks are available for outlining explanations of superstitious behaviour and 8 marks for evaluating them, while 4 marks are on offer for outlining explanations of magical thinking, with 8 marks again for an evaluation.

Only evaluative material is required in question 4, so providing descriptive content wouldn't be creditworthy and would waste valuable examination time.

Question 5 requires a 'longer' version of an outline of personality factors underlying anomalous experience, as 8 marks are up for grabs, with 16 marks for the evaluation, possibly formed around the degree of research support for the explanations.

Question 6 is similar to question 5 in its requirements and mark allocation. There are 8 marks for outlining the role of probability judgements and 16 for evaluating them and again the degree of research support would be a useful means of building an effective evaluation.

Research into and explanations for exceptional experience

Psychic healing

There are many instances of people reporting psychic healing powers, often by 'therapeutic touch', known as 'laying on of hands'. However, other claims have been made for distance healing, where people are treated without physical contact and indeed over large distances. Charismatic religious figures often possess such 'gifts' and attain elevated status.

Psychic healers sometimes use mediums like crystals to supposedly tap into bodily energy fields and sources, though a lot of the theory surrounding such ideas is not backed up with empirical evidence.

Research: psychic healing

- West (1957) reviewed the medical records of 11 cases of miracle cures occurring at the shrine of Lourdes, given official 'miraculous' status by the Catholic Church, finding the records disappointing as crucial information was missing; a similar conclusion was reached by magician James Randi, examining the data later on. Therefore, this is not irrefutable evidence for psychic healing; indeed, the fact at least 6 million people have visited Lourdes in search of miracle cures, suggests that 11 apparent miracles is not that astounding.

- Grad (1959) studied Oskar Estabany, a cavalry officer who discovered healing powers when treating army horses. Mice who had a portion of skin removed recovered faster if treated by Estabany. During his treatments, production of the enzyme trypsin was stimulated, suggesting a biological basis to psychic healing. Eskabany demonstrated his talent on humans, with Krieger (1979) finding that haemoglobin levels were stimulated during his treatments and stayed elevated for a year after, again implying a biological basis.

- Ostrander and Schroeder (1970) documented the abilities of Colonel Alexei Krivorotov, who placed his hands close to patients' bodies, with patients reporting a sensation of heat. However, no change in temperature was found in the healer's hands or the patients' skin, implying that any beneficial effect was the result of suggestive power or a placebo effect.

- Droscher (1971) reported on the phenomenon of musical psychic healing, where vocal music is used to heal. He believed this occurs as humans can hear ultrasonic sounds within their heads and these ultrasonics combine with body chemistry to facilitate healing. However, evidence is lacking to show how this would actually occur.

- Braud and Schlitz (1988) investigated distance healing, asking healers to focus attention on a photograph of a patient for 1-minute periods. The patient would be unaware of this, thus ruling out the possibility of a placebo or suggestive effect. During healing periods it was found that galvanic skin responses (GSR), often associated with activity in the sympathetic nervous system, altered, suggesting a real biological influence.

Figure 12.08 Psychic healers claim to use 'therapeutic touch' to channel healing energy with their hands

Contemporary research

Benson *et al.* (2006)

Study of the therapeutic effects of intercessory prayer (STEP) in cardiac patients

Figure 12.09

Intercessory prayer, praying to God on another's behalf, has been argued to influence recovery from illness, but sceptics claim that such results are due to flawed methodology. The researchers here wanted conduct a scientifically controlled trial of the power of prayer, and assess the role that knowing someone was praying for them would have on seriously ill people.

Aims

To assess whether prayer itself or knowledge that prayer is being provided influences outcome.

To assess whether being certain of receiving intercessory prayer was associated with uncomplicated recovery after coronary artery bypass graft (CABG) surgery.

Procedure

Participants were patients at six US hospitals, randomly assigned to one of three groups:

- 604 participants received intercessory prayer after being informed that they may or may not receive prayer.
- 597 did not receive intercessory prayer after being informed that they may or may not receive prayer.
- 601 received intercessory prayer after being informed they would receive prayer.

Intercessory prayer was provided for 14 days, starting the night before CABG.

The dependent variable was whether complications/major events/death occurred within 30 days of CABG.

Findings

In the two groups uncertain about whether they received intercessory prayer, complications occurred in 52 per cent (315/604) of patients who did receive intercessory prayer, compared to 51 per cent (304/597) who did not receive intercessory prayer.

Complications occurred in 59 per cent (352/601) of patients certain of receiving intercessory prayer, compared with 52 per cent (315/604) of those uncertain of receiving intercessory prayer.

Major events and 30-day mortality were similar across the three groups.

Conclusions

Intercessory prayer has no effect on complication-free recovery from CABG.

Certainty of receiving intercessory prayer is associated with a higher incidence of complications.

Evaluation

- The results suggest that praying has no beneficial effect, but it is unknown if members of the 'not prayed for' groups were prayed for by other people.
- The study cost $2.4 million, most of the money coming from the John Templeton Foundation, which supports research into spirituality. Although negative results were found, this does suggest that there is a desire from a powerful lobby to find evidence of the 'power of prayer'.

Psychology in action

The benefits of psychic healing

There are many who believe, and there is much evidence to suggest, that psychic healing is a sham performed by money-fleecing, attention-grabbing charlatans on vulnerable and deceivable individuals, and that the practice is utterly despicable and needs to be exposed and banned.

However, the alternative way of perceiving psychic healing is in the good it does. Psychic healing may occur because it has some real biological effect; or it may just be a form of spontaneous recovery based on the presence of a caring person reducing anxieties and fears to facilitate healing; or it may be a type of short-term recovery, possibly due to suggestive reasons; or it may be a result of a placebo effect, where a fake treatment can improve a patient's condition simply because the person has the expectation that it will be helpful.

There is also the notion that psychic healing is a cultural concept, alien and frowned on by western culture, but seen as perfectly legitimate and beneficial elsewhere. Mollica (2005) suggested that psychic healers are beneficial in dealing with the widespread trauma occurring during catastrophes such as the Asian tsunami. Patients treated by culturally familiar methods, like psychic healing, often benefit more than with medical treatments, because they are offering 'psychological first aid' that is not intrusive or anxiety creating. So whether it is a real phenomenon or not, psychic healing can be argued to be a psychological force for good.

Evaluation

Psychic healing

- Guinan (2004) reported, after an extensive review of scientific literature, that the Catholic Church's Medical Association has banned the practice of 'therapeutic touch'.

- Psychic healing may occur through some real biological effect; be a form of spontaneous recovery based on the presence of a caring person reducing anxieties and fears to facilitate healing; be a type of short-term recovery due to suggestive reasons; or be a result of a placebo effect where a fake treatment improves a patient's condition because of the expectation that it will be helpful.

- The suspicion exists that many studies were not rigorously controlled and therefore that experimenter effects and demand characteristics occurred. More stringent studies are required, especially replications of earlier studies.

- Medical doctors are educated in how to heal and how such treatments work. However, few psychic healers have prior medical training/knowledge, so how is it possible to heal, not knowing the complexities of the human body? One suggestion, if psychic healing is a real phenomenon, is that psychic healers are in some unconscious way able to help humans tap into natural bodily defences and healing resources.

Out-of-body/near-death experiences

Out-of-body experiences (OBEs) is a term developed as a more bias-free label than 'astral projection' or 'spirit walking', and involves a perception of floating outside one's body, or being able to see one's own body from an exterior place.

OBEs occur as several subtypes. There are *parasomatic* OBEs, where individuals have another body other than their usual one; and *asomatic* OBEs, where individuals feel they have no body. A rare subtype is where an individual feels there is a connecting cord between bodies.

The majority of OBEs occur when people are in bed, suggesting a link to sleep and dream states; they can also occur with some drugs, like ketamine.

Figure 12.10 Out-of-body experiences are also referred to as 'astral projection' and commonly occur in bed

Some experience OBEs as self-willed, while others report being pulled involuntarily from their bodies, usually after a feeling of general paralysis. This suggests that OBEs happen during a borderline stage between REM sleep and arousal, when sleep paralysis occurs and dream images mix with usual sensory input.

OBEs can often be encountered by people having dangerous near-death experiences (NDEs).

Research: out-of-body/near-death experiences

- Blanke *et al.* (2005) found that OBEs were simulated in participants with no history of OBEs by electrical stimulation of the right temporal-parietal brain area, suggesting a biological explanation.

- Ehrsson *et al.* (2007) simulated OBEs using virtual-reality goggles to con the brain into thinking the body was located elsewhere. Participants' real bodies were then touched, and the visual illusion, plus the feel of their bodies being touched, made volunteers believe they had moved outside their physical bodies, suggesting that OBEs are triggered by mismatches between visual and tactile signals.

- Van Lommel *et al.* (2001) studied 344 patients who had been successfully resuscitated after heart attacks; 18 per cent reported near-death experiences, including OBEs, during a period when clinically dead, with little if any brain activity. This implies that continuity of consciousness is possible if the brain acts as a receiver for information generated from memory, and that consciousness exists independently of the brain.

- Irwin (1985) reported that OBEs occur with very low or very high arousal. Green (1968) found that 75 per cent of participants experiencing an OBE had very low arousal, as they were lying down when the episode occurred, while a substantial minority of cases happened during high arousal, like a rock-climbing fall. Other evidence backing up the idea of separate subtypes comes from Poynton (1975), who found similar patterns to Green (1968), using research from different countries.

Figure 12.11 People who have near-death experiences often report moving towards a light or into a tunnel

- Greyson (1997) reported that during cardioverter-defibrillator implantations doctors induce heart attacks to test the device and therefore create a possibility of NDEs occurring. Unexpected random visual targets controlled by a computer were positioned where they could only be seen from above the operating table. During the post-op recovery phase, patients guessed what image was displayed and no results beyond chance occurrences were found.

Evaluation

Out-of-body/near-death experiences

- Blackmore (1982) believed that OBEs occur if a person loses contact with sensory inputs and perceptions occur from elsewhere, while still awake, suggesting that the phenomenon is a dream-state experience.

- One possible practical application of research into OBEs is creating video games that give a sense of high levels of reality. It may also be possible for surgeons to operate on people great distances away, by controlling a robotic, virtual self.

- Blackmore (2007) praised Ehrsson's (2007) research for bringing OBEs into the laboratory, allowing theories of how such phenomena occur to be tested under controlled conditions.

- Moody (1998) reported, after years of studying NDEs, that they were wonderful experiences, typically consist of a buzzing noise, a blissful peace, moving into light and meeting religious-type people. However, this seems to be a very selective view of NDEs, as 15 per cent of people experiencing them describe them as 'hellish' and frightening, suggesting that research in this area may often be invalid due to researcher bias and poor methodology.

- Entering a tunnel is commonly reported with OBEs and NDEs, and often interpreted as a religious experience. However, tunnel-like experiences also occur with epilepsy, falling asleep, meditation and some drugs, suggesting a biological explanation.

- Blackmore (1991) believed that NDEs provide no evidence for life after death, and inform more about consciousness and the brain than events beyond the grave.

Supplementary learning

The phenomenon of unseen stares

It is claimed that some people have the ability to detect unseen stares, and evidence exists to back up this claim. Sheldrake (1998) reported that 20,000 controlled trials of unseen staring involving blindfolded participants, separated from starers by closed windows, showed significant results. However, Baker (2000) stated that it is a product of responding to subtle signals from the environment, while Marks and Colwell (2000) believed that it occurs due to methodological faults, because if feedback is given to participants they get better at detecting staring; proof, the researchers believed, of participants learning predictable sequences in supposedly random presentations.

However, Sheldrake (2000) argued that the standards for 'proof' set by sceptics are so high that it is not really possible for tendencies to be detected, and such strict criteria are not set for other psychological areas. For instance, Baker's (2000) criticism was based on him staring at 40 people engrossed in activities like working at a computer and then asking if they had detected being stared at. Five said they had (12.5 per cent), and Baker confirmed that three had stood up and looked around when he stared at them. But he then added on the criteria of them having to say where he was

continued ...

A treasure trove of material pertaining to 'strange beliefs, amusing deceptions and dangerous delusions' is the Skeptic Dictionary, complete with search engine to just about every anomalous experience possible. Go to www.skepdic.com

...continued

seated when staring at them and further discounted results from two participants, on the basis that one felt that people often stared at her and another claimed psychic powers. But if such people could detect unseen stares, then maybe they would make such claims. Sheldrake agreed that results improve with feedback, but are still significant without them.

The debate is ongoing, but raises an important point that scientists should expect a certain level of stringency in studies of the paranormal before results would be accepted as meaningful, but what should that level be and why should it be any stricter than levels imposed generally in psychology? Should it also be acceptable to 'move the goalposts' and set higher levels of acceptance every time significant results are found?

You are the researcher

People often claim that they have 'eyes in the back of their head' – that is, that they can detect when people are staring at them. To test out this claim, ask a participant 'sitter' to sit in a chair and stare at a non-reflective wall. A 'viewer' stands at least 2 metres behind them and either stares at their head or looks away according to a random schedule. A 'reader' then asks in an emotionless voice, 'Are they staring now?' The viewer then says whether they are being stared at or not. Each viewer has ten trials. By the law of averages, they should get five correct.

Why must the wall be non-reflective? Why must there be a distance of at least 2 metres between sitter and viewer? Why is a reader needed? Why is an emotionless voice used?

Psychic mediumship

Mediums exist in many cultures, often as socially designated practitioners, like shamans, who claim to deliberately alter their consciousness to obtain information or exert influence in ways useful to their social group. Mediums are especially active in the *Spiritualism* movement, apparently communicating messages from the afterlife, often helping people to come to terms with the death of loved ones. There are two general subtypes:

1. **Physical mediums** – physical phenomena are demonstrated at seances, viewable to those sitting with the medium. Spirit people communicate to the living by raps, audible figures and materialised figures.

2. **Mental mediums** – mental phenomena are demonstrated through the mind of a medium. This can occur in four ways:

   - *clairvoyance* (where a medium sees a spirit)

   - *clairaudience* (where a medium hears a spirit)

   - *clairsentience* (where a medium senses the presence and thoughts of a spirit)

   - *trance mediumship* (where a medium is overshadowed by a spirit communicator speaking directly through the medium).

Research: psychic mediumship

- Beischel and Schwarz (2007) assessed the reception by mediums of material about deceased persons received under rigorous experimental conditions. Eight established mediums were used with eight student participant 'sitters', four of whom had lost a parent and four of whom had lost a peer. The mediums, blind to the identities of the sitters and the deceased, each 'read' two absent sitters, with each sitter being 'read' by two mediums. Each sitter then read two itemised transcripts, one intended for

themselves and the other for a paired control, choosing the one most applicable to them. Significantly higher findings were obtained for intended versus control readings, suggesting that some mediums can receive information about deceased people.

- Rock *et al.* (2008) asked eight psychic mediums to independently describe how they experienced receiving information from a discarnate (deceased loved one). Seven common themes were found:
  1. Multi-modal sensory impressions concerning the discarnate
  2. Visual images of the incarnate in the medium's 'mind's eye'
  3. 'Hearing' information from the discarnate in the medium's 'mind's ear'
  4. 'Feeling' the discarnate's illness/cause of death
  5. Experiencing aromas associated with the discarnate
  6. Empathy with the discarnate
  7. Alteration of mood while in contact with the discarnate.

- Rock and Beischel (2008) gave seven mediums counterbalanced sequences of a discarnate reading and a control condition, finding significant differences between the discarnate and control readings with regard to how the person being read was experienced, with an altered state of consciousness apparent during discarnate readings, suggesting that a medium is a conduit enabling a discarnate to communicate with a loved one.

- Schwartz *et al.* (2001) arranged for five mediums to interview a woman who had experienced six significant losses in the last decade. The woman only answered yes or no to questions to cut down on the chances of the mediums using intuitive reasoning. The mediums performed at an accuracy level of 83 per cent, compared to 36 per cent for control interviewers, suggesting a real psychic effect.

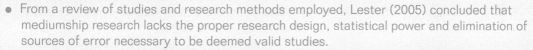

Evaluation

Psychic mediums

- From a review of studies and research methods employed, Lester (2005) concluded that mediumship research lacks the proper research design, statistical power and elimination of sources of error necessary to be deemed valid studies.

- Laboratory-based research into the authenticity of psychic mediumship needs to strike a balance between optimising the mediumship process for both mediums and assumed spirits, in order to increase the probability of capturing the phenomenon if it exists, as well as creating controlled research methods in order to eliminate other explanations.

- The evidence from psychic mediumship is similar to other areas of paranormal experiences, with positive results gained from believers but not from unbelievers, suggesting that results cannot be accepted until replicated by independent observers.

- Research into psychic mediumship raises ethical concerns, as those involved may be grieving for loved ones; therefore, procedures should be applied to eliminate possibilities of harm.

- Kelly (2008) believed that most mediums are not intentional frauds, but exploit vulnerable people emotionally. She believed that psychic mediumship is merely empathetic intuition or 'cold reading', where mediums tell people seemingly amazing facts known only by psychic methods, but which actually misuse statistical probability to make them plausible.

Strengthen your learning

1a. Outline what is meant by the following:
  i)   psychic healing
  ii)   out-of-body/near-death experiences
  iii) psychic mediumship.
1b. For each of the above:
  i)   Outline details of three relevant research studies.
  ii)   Assess to what extent research evidence supports the existence of these as true paranormal phenomena.
  iii) Aside from research evidence, what other evaluative points can be made about them?

Assessment Check

1. Outline one or more research studies into psychic healing. (4 marks)

2. Outline and evaluate research studies into out-of-body and near-death experiences. (20 marks)

3. Outline and evaluate research studies into psychic mediumship. (24 marks)

4. Discuss explanations for one or more of the following i) psychic healing ii) out-of-body/near-death experiences iii) psychic mediumship (24 marks)

5. Outline explanations of psychic healing and psychic mediumship. (8 marks)

Examination guidance

Answers to question 1 should only include descriptive material, not evaluative, and should be of the 'shorter' variety, as only 4 marks are available. Question 2 requires both descriptive and evaluative material, with most focus on the evaluation, as it is worth 16 marks compared to 4 marks for the outline.

Description of research studies in question 3 could attain a maximum of 8 marks and any relevant knowledge displayed, such as procedure, aims, results etc. would be creditworthy. As the focus of the question is on research studies, evaluation of methodology would also gain credit.

Question 4 offers several choices for an answer. Basically the more of the three listed options covered, the less detail would be expected. The term 'discuss' means that explanations have to be both described and evaluated.

Question 5 only requires descriptive material and to access the highest band of marks would require a reasonable balance to be attained between outlining explanations of psychic healing and psychic mediumship.

Summing up

- Anomalous psychology concerns the study of extraordinary behaviour and experience, with experimental studies of the paranormal known as parapsychology.

- Pseudoscience means 'false science' and refers to so-called sciences and scientific practices with little or no scientific basis.

- The Chinese pseudoscience debate concerns the refusal of Chinese scientists to accept traditional non-scientific practices as valid.

- Scientific fraud concerns deliberate fraud, like that by Soal, exposed by Markwick (1979) as a cheat.

- The scientific status of parapsychology has been through several stages and there is an on going debate about how and whether scientific principles can be applied to anomalous experience.

- Ganzfeld studies of ESP are seen by some as providing scientific proof of telepathy, while sceptics believe that evidence can be explained by other means.

- Psychokinesis is the process of moving or otherwise affecting physical objects by the mind, with no physical contact.

- Psychokinesis research regularly produces small but significant results under strictly controlled conditions.

- Coincidences occur when two unrelated events correspond and a cognitive bias forms that one causes the other, which can lead to paranormal experiences, with events seen as predestined.

- Many people also misjudge the probability of unrelated events and believe instead that they're connected by paranormal forces.

- There are several cognitive factors involved in probability judgements, such as *intuitive thinking styles* that lack reasoning, *cognitive illusions* where probability is misperceived, *illusions of control* over random occurrences, *confirmatory bias* towards supporting evidence, and *cold reading* creating gullibility through general statements.

- Superstitions are irrational beliefs that objects, actions or circumstances not logically related to a course of events can influence outcomes.

- Superstitions behaviour is motivated by a desire for a sense of control and certainty.

- Magical thinking sees all things as connected via paranormal forces and can be seen as an explanation for religious beliefs.

- Superstitious behaviour and magical thinking can both be related to cognitive factors and be seen to function as coping strategies.

- The personality characteristic of neuroticism has been linked with beliefs in the paranormal, while extroversion is associated with ESP ability, as well as the trait of non-defensiveness.

- Psychic healing concerns restoration of health through spiritual practices, with some evidence to back its claims and may therefore create some real biological effect.

- Out-of-body-experiences (OBEs) involve a perception of floating outside one's body, or being able to see one's own body from an exterior place.

- OBEs are often encountered by people having dangerous, near-death experiences and may be explainable in biological terms.

- Psychic mediums claim an ability to experience contact with spirits of deceased souls, communicating messages to loved ones through physical and mental means.

- As psychic mediums are found in all cultures, they may fulfil a need in helping people come to terms with the death of loved ones.

13 Psychological research and scientific method

The application of scientific method in psychology	**481**
The major features of science	482
Validating new knowledge and the role of peer review	485
Designing psychological investigations	**489**
Selection and application of appropriate research methods	489
Implications of sampling strategies	492
Issues of reliability	493
Assessing and improving validity	493
Ethical considerations in the design and conduct of psychological research	494
Data analysis and reporting on investigations	**498**
Appropriate selection of graphical representations	498
Probability and significance	500
Factors affecting choice of statistical test	501
The use of inferential analysis	502
Analysis and interpretation of qualitative data	502
Conventions on reporting on psychological investigations	503
Summing up	**510**

Decoding the specification

Examination questions on this part of the specification are not essay-based like most A2 questions. They build on the research methods requirements of the AS specification, though in a more searching and detailed manner. The specification concentrates on what science consists of, how it functions, how it relates to the study of psychology and the ways in which new knowledge can come to be accepted.

Your compulsory examination question on this part of the specification will be based around some stimulus material, such as details of a previous study. You will then be asked questions centred on this material, which will test your knowledge of the area and your ability to use research methodologies – for instance, how to plan, carry out and write up research studies. This can be achieved by using the material in this chapter to build upon your knowledge of research methods learned while studying at AS level and when designing and carrying out mini-practicals.

The application of scientific method in psychology

IN THE NEWS

Adapted from the *Daily Telegraph*, 19 February 2008 © Telegraph Media Group Limited 2008

Peer review: the myth of the noble scientist

Peer review is supposed to combat fraud, but it can just as easily hold back radical discoveries.

Scientific journals are as closed as the Royal Society once was. The gatekeeper is 'peer review', where papers are screened by experts, who judge if the experiments that the manuscripts describe are credible.

But, without having actually witnessed the experiments, how can experts determine that? Reviewers have to trust the authors to tell the truth. Consequently, the most important part of a paper is the name at the top.

If a well-known scientist submits a paper, it will probably be accepted; if an unknown submits one, it will probably not be. Science is a closed club, partly to ensure that only accurate papers are published, but largely to prevent fraud. No fewer than 15 per cent of scientists at the National Institutes of Health (the US government's top health laboratory) admitted to bending data to fit their theories.

But peer review carries dangers. First, it allows dunderheads to block unexpected ideas. Everybody within the scientific community knows of Barbara McClintock, Nobel Prize winner in 1983 for discovering gene jumping.

She was forced to publish her findings informally, in the annual reports of the Carnegie Institution, because she could not persuade peer reviewers to accept them.

Figure 13.01 Peer review: gatekeeper or obstructor of the truth?

Moreover, peer review is slow, allowing unscrupulous reviewers to plunder their competitors' papers and block their publication.

They are still peer-reviewed, but soon reputable scientists will start to publish their own electronic papers. The convenience will be irresistible and validation comes only after publication, when others try to reproduce the work.

Peer review is science's safeguard. It allows for verification of new knowledge and stops flawed or unscientific research from becoming accepted fact. Practical applications are based on scientific knowledge; if this were built on false theories and research, the consequences could be immensely damaging. Yet, as the article above details, peer review is not without its criticisms, and there exists a real possibility that scientists will disregard the process and publish research papers themselves. But for science to be truly objective and worthwhile, a system of checks will always be necessary.

The major features of science

Science is a system of acquiring knowledge through a process known as the *scientific method*, which is defined as the observation, identification, description, experimental investigation and theoretical explanation of phenomena.

The scientific method has three parts to it:

1. Observation and description of a phenomenon or group of phenomena.

2. Formulation of a hypothesis to explain the phenomena. Use of the hypothesis to predict the existence of other phenomena, or to predict quantitatively the results of new observations.

3. Performance of experimental tests of the predictions by several independent experimenters and properly performed experiments.

The use of empirical methods

The most important feature of science is its dependence on *empirical methods* of observation and investigation. This involves observations based on sensory experiences (via the senses) rather than simply on thoughts and beliefs. Therefore, a scientific idea is one that has been subjected to empirical testing by the use of rigorous observations of events and/or phenomena. For science to make sense, there must be an explanation of empirically observed phenomena, achieved by developing theories that can be tested and improved by empiricism.

Science therefore involves making predictions, tested by scientific observations (empirical ones). Such observations are made without bias or expectation by the researcher and are performed under controlled conditions. In this way, theories and hypotheses are validated (found to be true) or falsified (found to be untrue), and it is the belief that this ability to predict and control behaviour under experimental conditions can also be achieved in real-life settings that makes psychology opt for science as its selected path towards the acquisition of knowledge.

Replicability

Confidence in psychological findings is increased by replicating investigations, as part of the validation process. This involves repeating research under the same conditions. It is important that scientific research is written up fully and clearly, so that it can be properly replicated and thus reliability and validity can be established. Fleischmann and Pons (1989) claimed to have created cold fusion, a form of low-energy nuclear reaction, in the laboratory, raising hopes of producing abundant and cheap sources of energy. However, enthusiasm dropped when replications of their experimental technique failed to get the same results. They had either witnessed a separate phenomenon or had made errors in their procedures. Only by replication were scientists able to arrive at this conclusion.

However, due to the fact that *levels of significance* are used to determine the *probability* of results being meaningful (differences in levels of the IV that are beyond the boundaries of chance), the chances of replication of research attaining the same results are not as straightforward as might be imagined (see 'Contemporary research: Miller (2009)' on page 507).

Objectivity, bias and fraud

An important feature of scientific research is that it should be objective, perceived without distortion of personal feelings or interpretation. Objectivity is an integral part of empiricism, where observations are made through sensory experience and not from the biased viewpoint of researchers.

Empirically observed phenomena must be *objective* to be considered truly scientific. In order to diminish the possibility of unconscious bias, researchers use *standardised instructions*, *operational definitions of observed variables* and *physically defined measurements of performance*, such as *double-blind techniques*. If phenomena are observed in a biased fashion, they are *subjective* rather than objective, such as a biased interpretation of answers to an interview.

Such bias is unconscious, with no deliberate attempt by the researcher to produce certain results. For example, results from ganzfeld studies, which test for the existence of ESP (see 'Extrasensory perception – ganzfeld studies' on page 451), tend to match the beliefs of the researcher. Therefore, researchers who believe ESP to be real find results supporting such a belief, while those who are sceptical find results refuting the existence of ESP.

However, there are examples of deliberate fraud by researchers. Cyril Burt was a psychologist famous for his work on the inheritance of intelligence, leading to the formation of the 11+ school entry examination that affected many young people's educational opportunities. However, some of his research, conducted on IQ and twins was deliberately falsified, probably due to Burt's biased, subjective views about the inheritance of intelligence. Therefore, due to a lack of objectivity, false findings occurred, which led to flawed practical applications (see 'Classic research: Burt (1955, 1958, 1966)' below). Research has shown that the Burt affair was not an isolated occurrence, with the incidence of fraud and scientific misconduct worryingly high. *Peer review* has an important role to play here as a 'gatekeeper', stopping the publication of unscientific and flawed research (see 'Contemporary research: Meyer (2004)' on page 487). Replication also helps to show whether research findings are valid.

Classic research

Burt (1955, 1958, 1966)
The heritability of IQ

Cyril Burt was regarded as one of the greatest psychologists of his day and was nicknamed 'the father of the 11 plus', the test used in British schools to select students for various educational destinations. Burt was a great believer in the inheritance of intelligence and supported Spearman's idea of general intelligence, or 'g', on which everyone can be measured and which forms the basis of IQ tests (see 'Spearman's two-factor model' on page 237). As MZ (identical) twins share genetics and environment, Burt was interested in studying separated MZ twins who only shared genetics. If their IQ levels were similar, it would indicate intelligence to be innate. Burt's continuous research in this area went a long way to establishing that heredity plays a much more prominent role in determining intelligence than environment does. This influenced countless others, and their findings and conclusions, as well as impacting on a multitude of lives through his work being used to fashion the education system. Yet the evidence seriously suggests that he was a fraud and concocted a lot of his data.

Figure 13.02 Did Burt actually test 53 pairs of separated identical twins, or did he, as the evidence suggests, fabricate his data?

Aim

To assess the relationship between IQ scores of pairs of individuals of varying genetic similarity.

continued ...

...continued

Procedure

IQ tests were administered to identical (MZ) twins reared together and reared apart, and to non-identical same-sex (DZ) twins reared together. These tests occurred over a number of years, with additional data being added to earlier findings.

Testing was conducted by Burt and two co-workers, Margaret Howard and Jane Conway.

Findings

MZ twins reared together had very similar IQs, of 94.4 per cent.

MZ twins reared apart had similar IQs, of 77.1 per cent.

DZ twins reared together had less similar IQs, of 55.2 per cent.

Table 13.01

YEAR	IQ CORRELATION (%) OF MZs REARED TOGETHER	NUMBER OF PAIRS OF MZs REARED TOGETHER	IQ CORRELATION (%) OF MZs REARED APART	NUMBER OF PAIRS OF MZs REARED APART	IQ CORRELATION (%) OF DZs REARED TOGETHER	NUMBER OF PAIRS OF DZs REARED TOGETHER
1955	94.4	83	77.1	21	?	?
1958	94.4	?	77.1	30+	?	?
1966	94.4	95	77.1	53	55.2	127

Conclusions

Although environment has some input, heredity plays a more prominent role in determining intelligence.

Evaluation

- It is unlikely that Burt was able to find so many separated MZ twins. His 1966 study claims 53 pairs, by far the largest twin study of its kind.

- Kamin (1974), a respected psychologist, stated that Burt's data was not worthy of scientific consideration. This criticism was backed by Jensen (1980), a supporter of the hereditary viewpoint and a previous admirer of Burt, who also found fault with his data.

- After an extensive search, Gillie (1976) failed to find either of Burt's two supposed co-workers and concluded that they were fictitious.

- It is extremely statistically unlikely that as subsequent pairs of twins were added to the data the correlation coefficients would remain exactly the same.

- Fannelli (2009) conducted a meta-analysis of 18 surveys into research misconduct, finding that 2 per cent of researchers admitted falsifying or modifying data in order to get it published, and 33 per cent admitted to questionable research practices; 14 per cent knew of falsification by colleagues they had not reported, and 73 per cent knew of questionable research practices by others they had not reported. This suggests that fraud misconduct is worryingly common within the scientific community, especially as these surveys asked sensitive questions; therefore, the findings are probably a conservative estimate of the true prevalence of scientific misconduct.

Falsification (hypothesis testing)

Part of the verification (validation) process is the idea of falsifiability, where a scientific theory or hypothesis is found to be false. Replication of exact research procedures is the accepted manner of determining this to be so. The psychodynamic approach in psychology, associated with the work of Freud, is criticised for being unfalsifiable. Freud's account of personality allowed him to place interpretations on behaviour that could not be shown to be untrue. For example, Freud might argue that someone behaves in a certain fashion due to events in their infancy, and if the person agreed this to be so, it is seen as supporting Freud. However, if the person disagrees, it is still seen as supporting Freud, as he would argue that they are repressing experiences from their infancy.

The Chinese pseudoscience debate (see page 448) is centred on the acceptance or not of so-called scientific theories based on traditional Chinese philosophies that are irrefutable – that is to say, they cannot be replicated and therefore cannot be validated or falsified. Some in China even argue for the banning of traditional medicines on the basis that they have not been scientifically validated.

Psychology in action

The scientific process and practical applications

Figure 13.03 Relationship counselling is effective because it is based on objective, scientific research

Psychology has provided the world with a multitude of practical applications that benefit individuals and society as a whole. Romantic couples with relationship problems have benefited from psychological counselling; education has been shaped for the better through research into cognitive development; and psychological therapies have removed and reduced the mental anguish that sufferers of mental disorders have endured. But all of this occurs only if the psychological theories that such applications are based on are unbiased and genuinely scientific.

When practical applications are based on subjective, biased beliefs and practices, society does not benefit.

It is not that long ago that the pseudoscience of eugenics, dressed up as scientific fact, unleashed its 'proven' practical applications on society, and in its name thousands in the USA were sterilised for having 'low intelligence genes'. The aim was to benefit mankind by purifying the races, but all of this was based on flawed beliefs and research. As many of those sterilised were black, the accusation can be made that it was actually just racism dressed up as science. Psychology has a responsibility to ensure that research is properly conducted in an unbiased fashion, so that society will truly benefit.

Validating new knowledge and the role of peer review

Peer review is considered fundamental to scientific and scholarly communication and is part of the verification process by which research is deemed to be scientifically acceptable or not. Peer review consists of a system used by scientists to determine whether research findings can be published in scientific journals. The peer review system subjects scientific research papers to independent scrutiny by scientific experts in that field (peers) before a decision is made about whether they can be made public. So important is the peer review system that it is often referred to as 'the arbiter of scientific quality' and is perceived as a 'gatekeeper' or filter system, reducing the chances of flawed or unscientific research being accepted as fact. The peer review system operates on the belief that the status of research results is as important as the findings themselves.

Science is increasingly important in all areas of life, not just psychology, and scientific developments often become the subject of news headlines and public interest. A growing amount of scientific information is being made public, and there is an increasing number of organisations, such as drug companies, promoting and discussing scientific research in the public domain, and it is often difficult to decide which research is worthy of consideration and which is spurious, especially when different scientists argue completely different viewpoints – for example, the very public argument between scientists as to whether the MMR vaccine was safe to use on children.

Over a million research papers are published in scientific journals each year, but although the peer review system is recognised and used by scientists globally as the best means of assessing scientific plausibility, the general public knows little, if anything, about this verification process. However, it is important that the public, especially those who deal with scientific claims, like patient groups, are aware of the concept if they are to avoid the frustration and damage that comes from accepting poor scientific research. Therefore, research needs to have passed public scrutiny before being accepted as true.

The peer review process

During the peer review process, it is usual for several expert reviewers to be sent copies of a researcher's work by a journal editor. These reviewers report back to the editor, highlighting weaknesses or problem areas, as well as suggestions for improvement, if necessary. There are generally four options for reviewers to recommend:

1. accept the work unconditionally

2. accept it as long as the researcher improves it in certain ways

3. reject it, but suggest revisions and a resubmission

4. reject it outright.

Criticisms of peer review

Critics argue that peer review is not as unbiased as it claims. Research occurs in a narrow social world, and social relationships within that world affect objectivity and impartiality. In obscure research areas, it may not be possible to find people with sufficient knowledge to carry out a proper peer review. There are even suspicions that some scientists' ability to consider research in an unbiased and professional manner is compromised by them being funded by organisations with vested interests in certain research being deemed scientifically acceptable. Reviewers have also been accused of not accepting research so that their own studies can be published, and even of plagiarising (copying) research and then passing it off as their own. One way of attempting to address this is to ensure that reviewers are anonymous and independent.

A further criticism is that the power to publish research papers is controlled by elites and sometimes affected by personal jealousies. Therefore, there may be resistance to revolutionary ideas that go against the elite or prevailing views, fitting Kuhn's idea that science does not advance steadily, but by one paradigm (the accepted assumptions of science) being toppled and replaced with another.

Peer review is also a slow process, sometimes taking months or even years to complete.

The consequences of false or unscientific research being accepted as true can be serious, not least because many other scientists' subsequent research may be built on the fact of the original research being accepted as true. Cyril Burt, who falsified research into the heritability of intelligence, was a major figure in the field of intelligence and his research findings, widely accepted by the psychological community as being true, greatly influenced the work of subsequent researchers, who often took his work as a starting point for their own research (see 'Contemporary research: Burt (1955, 1958, 1966) on page 483).

Contemporary research

Meyer (2004)

Intelligent design: the origin of biological information and the higher taxonomic categories

Intelligent design (ID) is an attempt by fundamental Christians to make the biblical story of creationism seem scientifically credible. ID argues that there are complex systems that cannot be explained by evolution, and that the universe is so unimaginably complex and perfect that it must have been created by an intelligent designer, opposing the accepted evolutionary idea of natural selection. Gilchrist (1997) assessed all peer-reviewed scientific journals published since ID was first proposed, finding no articles supporting it, though he found thousands supporting evolution. In 2004, the first peer-reviewed article supporting ID finally appeared in The Proceedings of the Biological Society of Washington *(vol. 117, no. 2, pp. 213–39). The Proceedings is a peer-reviewed biology journal published at the National Museum of Natural History at the Smithsonian Institution in Washington, DC.*

Figure 13.04

Aim

To provide support for a theory of intelligent design by showing that evolutionary biology has not identified a specific causal explanation for the origin of life.

Method

An information-based analysis of evidence relating to the origin of biological form during the Cambrian age of 530 million years ago, where there was a sudden appearance of many new life forms.

Findings

That a host of scientific essays and books have questioned the ability of natural selection and mutation as a mechanism for generating new life forms.

Conclusions

No current theory of evolution can account for the origin of information necessary to build novel animal forms.

Intelligent design is a valid alternative explanation for the origin of biologically higher life forms.

Evaluation

- The journal the article was published in has subsequently disowned the paper, issuing a statement explaining that the Meyer paper did not go through the journal's approved peer review process and does not meet the scientific standards of the journal.

- ID's explanation for its absence from peer-reviewed literature and disowning by this journal is that papers explaining the findings and concepts in support of ID are consistently excluded from the mainstream scientific discourse because ID arguments challenge principles regarded as fundamental by the mainstream scientific community, and that research which points towards an intelligent designer is rejected simply because it deviates from the scientific community's dogmatic beliefs.

- Supporters of ID have yet to offer scientifically testable or verifiable data, and the peer review process can be argued to have fulfilled its role as an efficient gatekeeper, preventing the scientific validation of politically driven pseudoscience.

Research in focus

ID claims to be a scientific theory, yet only Meyer's (2004) study has been published and this was subsequently disowned. Explain the purpose and workings of the peer review system in relation to studies involving ID.

What could be the consequences of flawed research being verified by peer review?

What criticisms are there of peer review?

Psychology in action

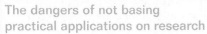

The dangers of not basing practical applications on research

Practical applications are based on objective, unbiased research that is capable of being replicated and has undergone a process of peer review to check its scientific credentials. This ensures that such applications are sound ones and beneficial to society.

When this is not the case, negative consequences can occur. In the 1950s, Chinese leader Mao Zedong observed birds eating the rice crop and decided on a nationwide campaign of eradicating the birds, so that food production would be increased and famine overcome. However, after exterminating millions of birds, the rice crop totally failed. The birds had been consuming the grubs and insects that fed on the rice, not the rice itself. Without the birds, the crop totally failed and millions starved. Mao Zedong's intentions were good ones, but if he had subjected his beliefs to proper scientific research and scrutiny, this disaster would never have occurred.

For a detailed report of what peer review is and does, including a discussion of the criticisms levelled at the process and the pressures on researchers to act dishonestly, go to www.columbia.edu/cu/21stC/issue-1.1/peer.htm

Strengthen your learning

1. Explain what is meant by empirical observation.
2. Outline what is meant by replicability and what its purpose is.
3. What evidence is there that scientific fraud and misconduct do occur?
4. Explain why falsification is regarded as important in science.
5a. Explain what is meant by peer review.
5b. Outline how peer review occurs.
5c. What criticisms of the process are there?
5d. What possible reasons are there for studies relating to intelligent design not being published in peer-reviewed journals?

Assessment Check

1. Outline why science is dependent on empirical methods of observation and investigation. (4 marks)

2. Explain the role of replicability in psychological research. (4 marks)

3. Outline two methods used by investigators to reduce the possibility of bias in research. (6 marks)

4. Outline the major features of science. (10 marks)

5. Outline the process of peer review. (6 marks)

6. Explain two advantages and two disadvantages of peer review. (4 marks)

Examination guidance

All of the above could theoretically be asked as examination questions, though possibly in the context of some stimulus material.

An answer to question 1 could focus on the role of controlled conditions, bias, hypotheses generation, theory testing, and so on, in the acquisition of scientific knowledge.

One mark would be gained in question 2 for explaining what is meant by replicability, with a further three marks available for elaborating on its role, part of which could be fulfilled by use of a relevant example.

Relevant answers to question 3 could focus on standardised instructions, operational definitions, objective measurements, double-blind technique, and so on.

Reference to replicability, objectivity, hypothesis testing and the use of empirical methods could form appropriate ways to answer question 4. Candidates would need to outline at least two features, with less detail expected if more than two features were offered.

Care should be taken with question 5 only to outline the process – for instance, outlining the purpose of peer review would not be creditworthy. In question 6 you will get 2 marks for the advantage part of the question and 2 for the disadvantage.

Designing psychological investigations

Selection and application of appropriate research methods

There are several different research methods, suitable for different types of research. Psychology places an emphasis on scientific methods, so many psychologists may favour an experimental approach, but all methods have strengths and weaknesses, and the best method is often dependent on the research situation. Good research often employs more than one method – for example, a laboratory experiment may be supported by a detailed questionnaire.

Experiments

Experiments are the most scientific form of research and the only method establishing *causality*. Although operating in somewhat artificial conditions, they are probably the best method, where circumstances permit. The laboratory experiment is most preferred, allowing for strict control over variables and conditions, with field and natural experiments occurring in more natural circumstances, but with reduced control. Field experiments use artificially created independent variables, whereas natural experiments use naturally occurring ones.

Key terms

Research methods – experimental and non-experimental means of conducting practical investigations

Sampling – selecting part of a target population for research purposes

Reliability – a measure of consistency within a set of scores and over time

Validity – the degree to which results can be generalised beyond the research setting

Ethical considerations – measures that protect participants from harm and retain their dignity

You are the researcher

Perform an experiment that assesses whether context can affect perception. You will need, from left to right, one bowl of hot water, one of lukewarm water and one of cold water.

Participants place both hands in the middle bowl of lukewarm water. Ask them the question whether the temperature of both hands is the same or different?

Then get them to place their left hand in the hot water and their right hand in the cold water. Then ask them to replace them in the lukewarm water and repeat the question. One hand should feel colder than the other due to the context that the hot and cold water create.

You will need to create a suitable aim, null and experimental hypotheses (one- or two-tailed?), a data sheet and standardised instructions.

Work out the IV and DV, as well as the type of design.

What other features need to be considered, including ethical issues?

Correlations

Correlations are performed when relationships are investigated. They show direction and intensity of relationships, but cannot establish causality or investigate non-linear associations. Correlations are sometimes used when experiments are ethically unsuitable. Correlations can identify areas worthy of further experimental investigation.

You are the researcher

Design and conduct a correlational study testing the prediction that people in romantic relationships will have similar levels of physical attractiveness. The wedding photos pages of local newspapers are a good source of material.

You will need two co-variables and a means of measuring attractiveness in both males and females, as well as an appropriate correlational hypothesis. How many couples will you need to assess?

Think carefully about who will rate the males/females.

Plot your data on a scattergraph and then use a Spearman's rho test for a statistical analysis.

Self-reports

Questionnaires, interviews and surveys gain direct information from participants about themselves. A lot of data is gained in relatively short time periods. Causality cannot be established and there are risks of idealised and socially desirable answers. Interviews require face-to-face scenarios. Self-reports can be used to identify areas worthy of further research by more stringent means.

You are the researcher

Design and conduct either a structured interview or a questionnaire examining differences in male and female attitudes to healthy living. You will need to formulate simple, unambiguous, non-biased questions on attitudes to things like smoking, drinking and eating, as well as questions concerning actual behaviour.

Include both open and closed questions. How would you analyse the responses?

Observations

Observations are conducted when the emphasis is on seeing natural behaviour in a natural environment (though they can be conducted under laboratory conditions too). Causality cannot be established and replication is difficult, but ecological validity is high.

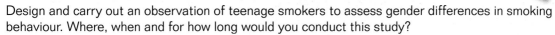

You are the researcher

Design and carry out an observation of teenage smokers to assess gender differences in smoking behaviour. Where, when and for how long would you conduct this study?

Different categories could be assessed, such as number of smokers, amount and types of cigarettes smoked, how much of a cigarette was smoked, and so on.

How would you determine inter-rater reliability?

How would the data be analysed and presented?

What ethical considerations need to be taken into account?

Case studies

Case studies are conducted on one person, or a small group, often to assess unique circumstances. They provide rich, detailed data, but findings cannot be generalised to others, nor can they establish causality.

Supplementary learning

Longitudinal study approach: *Seven Up!*

Most studies provide a 'snapshot' of how participants are now, in terms of their behaviour, attitudes, and so on. This is not necessarily representative of how they are most of the time, nor does it show how they develop such behaviours and attitudes. A useful way of overcoming these problems is to conduct a longitudinal study. As the name suggests, this involves carrying out a study over a long period of time, usually at set intervals, in order to see *trends*, changes over time. As the same group of participants are tested several times, longitudinal studies can be seen to be a type of repeated measures design.

Figure 13.05 Tony, a working-class boy, filmed every 7 years

Perhaps the most famous longitudinal study is the TV series *Seven Up!*, which started in 1964 and films a sample of children born in 1957, following their progress through life with an extensive interview of each participant every 7 years.

As the same participants are used, there are no participant variables (individual differences). However, longitudinal studies take a long time, with no guarantee of useful results, do not show causality and suffer from *atypical sample attrition*, where, over time, participants of one type drop out, calling into question how representative the sample is that remains. In the *Seven Up!* programme, a cross-section of British children was used, working-, middle- and upper-class, male, female, as well as urban and rural-based children. However, over time, the socially advantaged participants have tended to drop out.

To see video clips of 'John', a socially advantaged child, during the *Seven Up!* study, at various points in his life, go to www.youtube.com/ watch?v=BJj-fc6h0fo There are also lots of links to other children featured in the study. The next episode will be in 2013.

Implications of sampling strategies

A sample is a part of a target population used for research purposes. The idea is that what is true for the sample is true for the population from which the sample is taken and represents. There are several sampling methods used in psychology and these entail implications for bias and generalisation.

Sample size usually depends on the size of the target population, the resources available and the sampling method chosen. Larger samples are preferred, but sample size does not necessarily overcome biased sampling techniques. A biased sampling technique allied to a small sample size can invalidate results and such findings cannot be generalised to the target population.

Random sampling

A random sample occurs where members of a target population are selected without bias. This is achieved by names out of a hat or by random number tables. A truly random sample is difficult to obtain, as generally all members of a target population are not available for selection. A random sample is not necessarily representative, because random selection could provide a biased sample – for example, all females – making generalisation difficult.

Opportunity sampling

Opportunity samples are easier to obtain, because use is made of people's availability. Opportunity samples are often biased, as those available may be unrepresentative – for example, all shoppers – and difficult to generalise from.

Self-selected (volunteer) sampling

Volunteer samples are obtained by advertisements or posters, requiring little effort to obtain. Volunteers tend to be certain personality types and therefore unrepresentative. They are often keen to help and more at risk of demand characteristics.

Systematic sampling

Systematic samples are obtained by selecting every 'nth' person – for example, every fifth person. This is unbiased, producing fairly representative samples.

Stratified sampling

Stratified samples select groups of participants in proportion to their frequency in the target population. Individuals for each group (strata) are randomly selected, producing a representative sample. If random sampling is not used for the stratas, it is called *quota sampling*.

Issues of reliability

Reliability refers to consistency. *Internal reliability* concerns the extent to which something is consistent within itself – for example, that all the components of a psychological test measure the same thing. *External reliability* concerns the extent to which a measure of something is consistent with other measures of the same thing.

If findings from research are replicated consistently, they are reliable. There are several ways of assessing and improving reliability.

Reliability is important in itself, but doubly important in that validity cannot be established without reliability being established first, though reliability does not guarantee validity.

Inter-rater reliability

Inter-rater reliability refers to the degree to which different raters/observers give consistent estimates of the same object or phenomenon. It is particularly useful in observational research. If two observers agree to the type of play children are involved in, then they have inter-observer reliability, but if one observer categorises a child as involved in cooperative play, while another observer categorises it as rough-and-tumble play, they do not have inter-observer reliability. A correlation coefficient can sometimes be used to assess the degree of reliability.

Test-retest reliability

Test–retest reliability measures the stability of a test or interview, for example, over time. It involves giving the same test to the same participants on two occasions. If the same result is obtained, then reliability is established.

Assessing and improving validity

Validity concerns accuracy, the degree to which something measures what it claims to. Therefore, validity refers to the legitimacy of studies and the extent to which findings can be generalised beyond research settings as a consequence of a study's *internal* and *external* validity.

Face (content) validity is a simple way of assessing validity involving the extent to which items look like what a test claims to measure.

Concurrent validity assesses validity by correlating scores on a test with another test known to be valid.

Internal validity

Internal validity is concerned with whether the effect observed in the research is due to the manipulation of the independent variable and not some other factor. Internal validity can be improved by minimisation of investigator effects, reduction of demand characteristics, the use of standardised instructions and use of a random sample. These factors ensure that a study is highly controlled, leaving less doubt that observed effects are due to poor methodology. Milgram's electric shock study was internally valid, as participants believed it to be real.

External validity

External validity refers to the extent to which an experimental effect (the results) can be generalised to other settings (*ecological validity*), other people (*population validity*) and over time (*historical validity*). Milgram's electric shock study lacked external validity, as it is not usual to shock people for getting questions wrong, it only used male participants and was a product of its time. External validity can be improved by setting experiments in more naturalistic settings.

Research in focus

From your knowledge of psychological research, give details of studies (other than Milgram) that have attracted criticism in terms of:

- ecological validity
- population validity
- historical validity
- mundane realism.

Ethical considerations in the design and conduct of psychological research

The British Psychological Society's (BPS) code of ethics helps to address all possible ethical considerations when designing and conducting research, so that participants are protected from harm and their dignity remains intact.

If unethical research is conducted, psychology will not have a respected public profile, people will be reluctant to participate in future research, and the subject will not advance or be of positive use. In the past, unethical research occurred, giving psychology a negative profile. The ethical guidelines that follow are in place to try to stop this recurring:

- Informed consent – participants receive all details of intended research, so a considered decision can be made whether to participate. For people below the age of 16 and those incapable of giving informed consent, like the mentally disordered, informed consent is gained from parents or legal guardians. In instances where deceit is inevitable in order that hypotheses are not revealed, participants are fully debriefed, giving them an opportunity to withdraw their data.

- Presumptive consent – informed consent is gained from non-participants, without revealing the hypotheses to the real participants. People similar to the participants are given full details and asked if they would participate. If they agree, it is presumed to be okay to perform the research.

- Prior general consent – this is similar to presumptive consent, but participants agree to not be informed – that is, they agree to be deceived, but without knowing how or when.

- Right to withdraw – participants can withdraw at any point, including withdrawing data after research has finished. No attempts are made to persuade people to continue.

- Deceit – participants should not be misled. Informed consent is not possible where deceit occurs.

- Protection from harm – participants should leave studies in the same physical and psychological state they entered them. Participants should not incur physical or psychological harm. No research procedure or practice should subject participants to levels of risk different to what they would normally encounter. Debriefing helps reduce the risk of harm. If unexpected harm occurs, it is the responsibility of researchers to attend to it – for example, by the provision of counselling, and so on.

- Debriefing – participants are told all details of the research and reassured about their performance. The right to withdraw is emphasised.

- Inducement to take part – participants should not receive rewards to take part, as the ability to rationally consider whether to give informed consent is compromised.

- Confidentiality/anonymity – details of identities and performances should not be made public. Participants must consent to any uses to which research findings will be put before research commences.

- Ethical committees – all facets of potential research are considered by experts and concerned bodies, who decide whether research is ethical and can proceed.

- Cost-benefit analysis – potential costs are compared against potential benefits, to decide whether research should proceed. If benefits exceed costs, research can proceed.

- Observations – people are only observed in circumstances where they would expect to be observed.

Socially sensitive research – implications of the research go beyond the participants used in the study and can potentially negatively affect the lives of identifiable people, by direct effects and through the publicity the research attracts from the media and public – for example, research into 'gay genes' (see 'Classic research: Hamer *et al.* below).

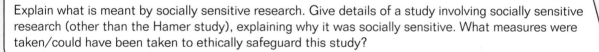

Research in focus

Explain what is meant by socially sensitive research. Give details of a study involving socially sensitive research (other than the Hamer study), explaining why it was socially sensitive. What measures were taken/could have been taken to ethically safeguard this study?

Classic research

Hamer *et al.* (1993)

A linkage between DNA markers on the X chromosome and male sexual orientation

Dean Hamer had spent his career studying the link between genetics and cancer, and cites a mixture of curiosity, altruism and boredom as the reasons for switching to the controversial topic of sexual orientation. The state of genetic research in this area was sufficient to convince him that the scientific study of sex could benefit from advances in genetic mapping, and might make the debates about sexual orientation more scientific and less political. However,

Figure 13.06 Research into the 'gay gene' proved intensely controversial

this was not to prove the case. Hamer's finding of a genetic link to male homosexuality has led to heated arguments, which incorporate political, religious, philosophical and ethical components. Such controversy had not been Hamer's aim, but special care should be taken when conducting socially sensitive research to think of the possible implications of the research. Hamer is not a psychologist and possibly did not realise the malevolence of the genie he was releasing from the bottle, but it was Hamer himself who coined the term 'gay gene', which in retrospect he would admit was a mistake.

continued ...

...continued

Aim

To search for evidence of genetic linkage in male homosexuality.

Procedure

Incidence rates of male homosexuality were assessed in the families of 114 homosexual male participants.

DNA linkage analysis was conducted on a selected group of 40 families in which there were two gay brothers and no evidence of maternal transmission.

Findings

Increased rates of same-sex orientation were found in the maternal uncles and male cousins of participants, but not in their fathers or paternal relatives.

DNA analysis revealed a positive correlation between homosexual orientation and the inheritance of genetic markers on the X chromosome in approximately 33 of 40 sibling pairs (64 per cent). The linkage to markers on Xq28, the subtelomeric region of the long arm of the sex chromosome indicated a statistical confidence level of more than 99 per cent that at least one subtype of male sexual orientation is genetically influenced.

Conclusions

The findings suggest evidence of a genetic factor influencing the development of homosexuality, especially in men with homosexual brothers.

Evaluation

- Sanders et al. (1998) gave further support by finding that 13 per cent of uncles of gay brothers on the maternal side were homosexual, compared to 6 per cent on the paternal side. Some studies have found similar results, while others have failed to replicate the effect.

- The findings inflamed the nature versus nurture debate. Although Hamer had believed the idea of a genetic component would lead to increased understanding and tolerance of homosexuality, it actually led to speculation in the media of the possibility of screening for and aborting 'gay foetuses', to remove 'gay genes' from the gene pool.

- Hamer never dismissed the importance of environmental factors in determining homosexuality, and argued that research into homosexuality should be separate from political and ethical debates. However, science cannot be separated from society, as its findings have a direct impact on it and researchers have a responsibility to predict possible implications of socially sensitive research.

- Hamer defends his use of the term 'gay gene' as a need to find simple terminology to help the public understand this complex field, but the public overreacted to his findings as though they were proof of the biological basis of homosexuality. Researchers often use language that evades general understanding and, again, researchers have a responsibility to ensure that their findings are clearly and unambiguously communicated to the general public.

To read a consideration of the ethical concerns of research into sexual orientation, go to www.udo-schuklenk.org/files/orient.htm

Strengthen your learning

1. Explain under what circumstances the following research methods are used:
   i) experiments
   ii) correlations
   iii) self-reports
   iv) observations
   v) longitudinal studies
   vi) case studies.
2. Outline what is meant by the following:
   i) random sampling
   ii) opportunity sampling
   iii) self-selected sampling
   iv) systematic sampling
   v) stratified sampling.
3. Explain the difference between internal and external validity.
4. Outline what is meant by the following:
   i) inter-rater reliability
   ii) test-retest reliability.
5a. Explain the difference between external and internal validity.
5b. Outline different types of external validity.
6a. Outline what ethical guidelines are in place to try to prevent unethical research occurring.
6b. Why might Hamer's research into the 'gay gene' be considered socially insensitive?

Assessment Check

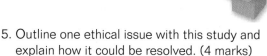

A team of investigators gave a panel of wine experts some unnamed white wines to taste, asking them to choose from a list of terms to describe the wines. All of the experts described all of these wines in terms appropriate for white wines.

The procedure was then repeated with the same number of red wines, but, unknown to the experts, some of these wines were white wines dyed red with an odourless, tasteless substance. All of the experts described all of these wines in terms appropriate for white wines.

1. What were the IV and DV in this study? (2 marks)

2. What type of experiment was used and what was the experimental design? (2 marks)

3. Give one advantage and one disadvantage of this design. (4 marks)

4. Explain why the procedure was performed twice. (2 marks)

5. Outline one ethical issue with this study and explain how it could be resolved. (4 marks)

6. The data generated by this study were of at least ordinal level. What is meant by ordinal-level data? (1 mark)

7. Before being published in a scientific journal, the research report had to be peer reviewed. Outline and evaluate the peer review process. (10 marks)

Examination guidance

The way to earn good marks when answering these types of question is to use the information in the stimulus material coupled with your knowledge of research methods. Give clear, concise and unambiguous answers, and, where multiple marks are available, ensure that elaboration of the answer is provided.

Question 7 requires a description of how peer review occurs and an evaluation, possibly in terms of its strengths and weaknesses.

Data analysis and reporting on investigations

Appropriate selection of graphical representations

Graphs display data in pictorial fashion, permitting an easily understandable alternative to numerical presentations. There are several types of graphs, each used in different circumstances. Graphs should be titled and each axis, horizontal (x) and vertical (y), should be labelled. The vertical axis usually represents the DV (frequency) and looks best if the y-axis height is three-quarters the x-axis width.

Bar charts

Bar charts show data in the form of categories being compared – for example, males and females (see Figure 13.07). Categories are represented by columns on the x-axis, all of the same width and separated by spaces. The use of spaces illustrates that the data on the x-axis is not continuous, but is 'discrete', like the mean scores of different groups, or percentages, totals, ratios, and so on. Bar charts can display two values together – for example, if the male and female groups in Figure 13.07 were divided into two further groups: under and over 20 years of age. Bar charts can be used with words and numbers.

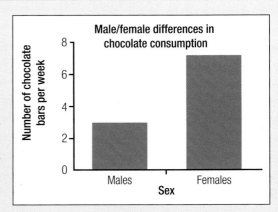

Figure 13.07

Histograms

Histograms and bar charts are similar, but histograms are used for continuous data like test scores, with these continuous values ascending along the x-axis and the frequency of the values shown on the y-axis. There are no spaces between the bars, as the data are continuous. The column width for each value is the same.

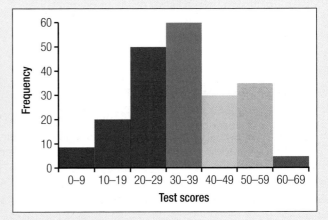

Figure 13.08

Frequency polygons

Frequency polygons are similar to histograms in that the data on the *x*-axis is continuous. A frequency polygon is produced by drawing a line from the midpoint top of each bar in a histogram. The advantage of a frequency polygon is that two or more frequency distributions can be compared on the same graph.

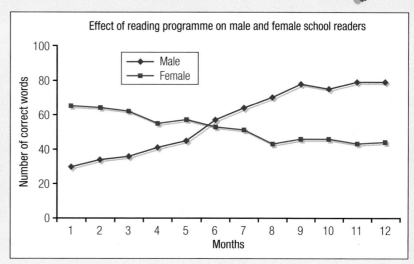

Figure 13.09

Scattergrams

Scattergrams are a type of graph allowing representation of the degree of correlation (similarity) between two co-variables. Scattergrams can display both negative and positive correlations.

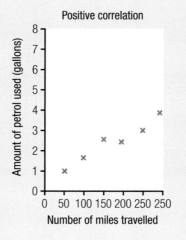
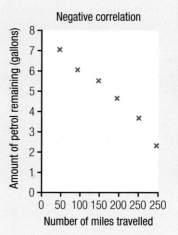

Figure 13.10

Supplementary learning

Meta-analysis: combining the results from lots of previous research

Sometimes research findings seem to suggest one result and other times the opposite. This can be confusing, but the study of human behaviour, by its very nature, is not straightforward. One way to deal with conflicting research findings is to conduct meta-analyses. This is where the results of several studies into the same research hypothesis are combined into a single statistical analysis, with the data provided from these previous studies. Meta-analyses are a good method of finding out what the majority of research findings show, so that general trends can be established. Fannelli (2009) conducted a meta-analysis of 18 studies to find alarming overall rates of researcher misconduct (see 'Classic research: Burt (1955, 1958, 1966)' on page 483).

Probability and significance

Psychological research generally looks for differences or relationships between sets of data. However, of prime importance is whether such differences and relationships are *significant* ones, beyond the boundaries of chance.

If a coin is tossed 100 times, then by the law of averages there should be 50 heads and 50 tails. However, it might be 52 heads and 48 tails, meaning that there is a difference between the two sets of data, but is it beyond the boundaries of chance? Probably not, but how is the cut-off point determined between the two sets of data being significant or insignificant? 55 heads to 45 tails? 60 to 40? This is where the idea of probability comes in.

Probability is denoted by the symbol p and concerns the degree of certainty that an observed difference or relationship between two sets of data is a real difference/relationship or has occurred by chance factors. It is never 100 per cent certainty that such differences and relationships are real ones – that is, beyond the boundaries of chance; this is why it is impossible to prove something beyond all doubt, so an accepted cut-off point is needed, and in psychology, and in science generally, a significance

Figure 13.11 If a coin is tossed 100 times, the expectation would be for 50 heads and 50 tails, but what ratio of heads and tails would be deemed beyond the boundaries of chance?

(probability) level of $p \leq 0.05$ is used. This means that there is a 5 per cent possibility that an observed difference or relationship between two sets of data is not a real difference, but occurred by chance factors. This is deemed to be an acceptable level of error.

On certain occasions, a stricter, more stringent level of significance may be needed – for example, if testing out untried drugs or in new research areas. Then a significance level of $p \leq 0.01$ might be used, meaning that there is a 99 per cent certainty that an observed difference/relationship is a real one, but there is still a 1 per cent chance that it occurred due to chance factors. An even stricter level of $p \leq 0.001$ would mean that there is a 99.9 per cent certainty of a real difference/relationship, but there is still a 0.1 per cent chance that it occurred by chance.

Type I and Type II errors

A Type I error occurs when a difference/relationship is accepted as a real one – that is, beyond the boundaries of chance – and we are wrong because the significance level has been set too high. This means the null hypothesis would be wrongly rejected – for example, if a pregnancy test revealed a woman to be pregnant and she was not. With a 5 per cent significance level, this means, on average, that for every 100 significant differences/relationships found, 5 of them will have been wrongly accepted.

A Type II error occurs when a difference/relationship is accepted as being insignificant – that is, not a real difference/relationship – and we are wrong because the significance level has been set too low – for example, 1 per cent. This means that the null hypothesis would be wrongly rejected – for example, a pregnancy test reveals a woman not to be pregnant when she is.

The stricter the significance level is, the less chance there is of making a Type I error, but more chance of making a Type II error, and vice versa. One way to reduce the chance of making these errors is to increase the sample size.

A 5 per cent significance level is the accepted level, as it strikes a balance between making Type I and Type II errors.

Factors affecting choice of statistical test

When data have been collected, an appropriate statistical test needs to be selected to analyse the data to see whether they are significant or not (beyond the boundaries of chance). In order to decide which statistical test to use, it needs to be decided whether a difference or a relationship between two sets of data is being tested for. Then it must be determined what level of measurement the data is. There are three basic levels of measurement: nominal, ordinal and interval/ratio.

Nominal data

This is the simplest type and involves counting frequency data. For example, how many days of the week were rainy/sunny? How many men/women were there? Tally charts are used to record this type of basic data. With nominal variables, there is a qualitative difference between values, not a quantitative one.

Ordinal data

This involves ranking data into order, with each value being greater/larger/better than another. Rating scales are often used – for example, the finishing places in an athletics race, first, second, third, fourth, and so on. It is known which athletes are better than others, but the distances between individual athletes may be different. The distance between first and second may be shorter than between second and third, and one person's subjective rating of 7 may be very different to another's rating of 7. Ordinal data are more informative than nominal data.

Interval/ratio data

This is the most accurate form of measurement as it uses equal measurement intervals – for example, 1 second in time is the same length as any other second in time. Standardised measurement units, like time, weight, temperature and distance, are interval/ratio measures. The same statistical tests are chosen regardless of whether there are interval or ratio data, therefore they are classified together. Interval data have an arbitrary zero point, whereas ratio data have an absolute zero point. For example, zero degrees temperature does not mean that there is no temperature (interval data), whereas someone with zero pounds in their bank account would have no money (ratio data).

Nominal, ordinal, interval and interval/ratio are ranked in relation to one another, getting gradually more informative each time. The mnemonic NOIR (nominal, ordinal, interval/ratio) can be used to remember this order.

The final factor determining choice of statistical test is whether the research utilises a repeated measures design (including matched subjects) or an independent measures design.

Once these criteria have been established, the appropriate statistical test can be selected (see Table 13.02).

Figure 13.12 The finishing places in a running race, first, second, third, fourth, and so on, provide an example of ordinal-level data

Table 13.02 Choosing the appropriate statistical test

NATURE OF HYPOTHESIS	LEVEL OF MEASUREMENT	TYPE OF RESEARCH DESIGN	
		Independent (unrelated)	Repeated (related)
DIFFERENCE	Nominal data	Chi–square	Sign test
	Ordinal data	Mann–Whitney U test	Wilcoxon (matched pairs)
	Interval data	Independent t–test	Related t–test
CORRELATION	Ordinal data		Spearman's rho
	Interval data		Pearson product moment

The use of inferential analysis

Inferential tests are ones showing how likely it is that patterns observed in sets of data occur by chance, and whether it is possible to infer (deduce) that the same patterns exist in the general population. There are four main tests that the specification requires knowledge of:

1. Chi-squared – used when a difference is predicted to occur between two sets of data; the data are of at least nominal level; and an independent measures design has been used (participants perform only one condition of the experiment). It is also possible to use chi-squared as a test of association (relationship).

2. Mann-Whitney – used when a difference is predicted to occur between two sets of data; the data are of at least ordinal level; and an independent groups design has been used.

3. Wilcoxon signed-matched ranks – used when a difference is predicted to occur between two sets of data; the data are of at least ordinal level; and a repeated or matched pairs design has been used.

4. Spearman's rho – used when a relationship (correlation) is predicted to occur between two sets of data; the data are of at least ordinal level; and the data are pairs of scores from the same person or event.

Statistical analysis produces an *observed* value, which is compared to a *critical* value in order to determine whether the observed value is significant (beyond the boundaries of chance). Critical value tables need to be referenced, taking into consideration such information as whether a hypothesis is directional or non-directional (one-tailed or two-tailed), the number of participants or participant pairs (N) used, and what level of significance is being used – for example, 5 per cent. The Mann-Whitney and Wilcoxon tests require observed values to be equal to or less than the critical value to be accepted as significant, allowing the null hypothesis to be rejected. The chi-squared and Spearman's rho tests require an observed value to be equal to or greater than the critical value to be accepted as significant, allowing the null hypothesis to be rejected.

Analysis and interpretation of qualitative data

Qualitative data is non-numerical, like a narrative of what was said in an interview, or a child's drawing. Such data provide insight into feelings and thoughts that quantitative data cannot. When analysing such data, researchers look for underlying meanings and this can be very subjective, based on the researcher's own interpretation. There are ways of converting qualitative data into quantitative data so that it can be objectively analysed by statistical means. This involves converting the data into categories or themes. *Content analysis* is one such way, involving counting frequencies of occurrences – for example, with children's drawings of a Christmas tree and presents researchers could count the number of presents and

their size categories, and so on. Alternatively, a magazine article about a political speech could be scrutinised for the number of 'positive' words/phrases and the number of 'negative' words/phrases.

When data have been created in this way, they can be presented descriptively by means of words, tables and graphs, and subjected to statistical analysis to test for significant differences or associations.

Conventions on reporting on psychological investigations

Progress in science depends on communication between researchers. It is, therefore, essential to describe the results of research as accurately and as effectively as possible. All psychologists hope to get their research published in eminent peer-reviewed journals and have to write reports according to the conventions of each journal. Although each journal has its own style, the main sections of psychology reports are the same, and written in such a way that *replication* would be possible, allowing others to repeat the research to check results.

It is usual to write up research in continuous prose, in the past tense, avoiding slang terms/colloquialisms and using a clear, unambiguous writing style.

The basic requirements of a report are to communicate:

- what was done
- why it was done
- what was found
- what it means.

There is no single best way to set out a report, but the general format is as follows:

- title
- abstract
- introduction
- method
- results
- discussion
- references
- appendices.

Title

This should be clear, relevant and fully informative.

Table of contents

This is optional, but is best included, along with page numbers.

Abstract

A summary of around 150 words, the abstract generally consists of two sentences each on the theoretical background (previous research), aims and hypotheses, methodology, results, conclusions and suggestions for future research.

Introduction

This details why the study was conducted. General theoretical background, controversies and previous research investigations of the chosen topic are covered. Only relevant material should be used. A 'funnel' technique is employed, starting off with a broad theoretical perspective, which then narrows down to the precise study area.

This section is very much like a 'funnel', whereby it starts off with a broad perspective and should lead on to the more precise aims and hypotheses under study.

Aims

The overall aim(s) are stated clearly, precisely and concisely.

Hypotheses

The experimental/alternative hypotheses and the null hypothesis are stated, precisely and unambiguously. A justification of the direction of hypotheses (one-tailed or two-tailed) is also included, as is the level of significance, which is normally 5 per cent ($p < 0.05$).

Method

This is an outline of what was done. All methodological details are reported so that the study could be replicated. Materials used in the study, like questionnaires and standardised instructions, are included in the appendices. The 'Method' section splits into several subsections:

1. **Design** – includes:

   - choice of method – for example, laboratory experiment
   - choice of design – for example, independent measures
   - choice of techniques – for example, time sampling
   - identification of variables – for example, IV, DV and extraneous variables
   - ethical considerations.

2. **Participants** – includes sampling details:

   - target population described in terms of relevant variables, like age, gender, and so on
   - sampling method – for example, opportunity sampling
   - actual sample, including how many participants and how they were recruited and selected
   - naivety of participants to the purpose of the study and whether any declined to take part or subsequently dropped out
   - allocation of participants to the testing conditions.

Apparatus/materials

This is a description of any technical equipment involved and how it was used. Only materials directly relevant to the investigation are included. Any mark schemes, questionnaires, and so on, go in the appendices.

Standardised procedure

This consists of a step-by-step procedure allowing for replication of the study. It includes details of where the study took place, any standardised instructions and debriefing procedures. If instructions are lengthy, they can be placed in the appendices and are referenced here. Do not repeat material detailed in the method section.

Controls

This should include details of such controls as counterbalancing, random allocation of participants to groups, single- or double-blind procedures, control of extraneous variables, and what steps were taken to avoid bias in the sampling or experimental procedures.

Results

This involves a presentation of what was found in terms of the data collected. This occurs as abbreviated or summary versions of the raw data, written in connected prose, with the support of tables and/or graphs referred to in the text. Names and personal terms are confidential information and therefore not included in any form of results.

Raw data are referenced here and presented in the appendices. One example answer sheet, questionnaire, and so on, is included in the appendices.

Descriptive statistics

Key findings should be described briefly in the most straightforward manner to give readers a chance to 'eyeball' the data.

Numerical statistics, like measures of central tendency (mean, mode or median) and measures of dispersion (range, standard deviation), should be included and results summarised in the most appropriate graphical form. Only one graph should be presented for the same data and should be visually clear and not overly complex.

Tables, graphs, and so on should be clearly titled and labelled and units of measurement specified.

Tables should be numbered and titled above the table, figures and graphs below. Labels on axes should be unambiguous. Do not insert too much information.

Inferential statistics

Reasons for selecting a particular statistical test are given, as well as what it tests for. Actual calculations are referenced here, but placed in the appendices.

The outcome of statistical analyses is given, along with critical table values of the test, the significance level and whether the test was one-tailed or two-tailed.

The outcome is explained in terms of acceptance and rejection of the experimental and null hypotheses.

Discussion

This section explains what the results mean and breaks down into several subsections.

Explanation of findings

Key findings are clearly described in psychological terms that relate to the aims and hypotheses. All findings should be presented, including minor, unexpected and contradictory ones, plus an explanation of what the findings show and why they occurred.

Relationship to background research

Research is presented and discussed in terms of previous research findings presented in the introduction. Aspects of the design that may account for differences in the findings from previous studies are outlined.

Limitations and modifications

Possible sources of error, like flawed measurement techniques, poor sampling, lack of controls and/or poor procedures, and so on, are outlined and discussed. Possible means of rectifying these faults are presented.

Implications and suggestions for future research

Further research studies suggested by the findings of the current one are presented here, as well as other possible ways of testing the hypotheses.

Also presented are any implications and applications that the findings of the present study suggest. These should be specific and precise and not involve general comments such as 'more work needs to be done'. Specific suggestions such as using more participants, eliminating confounding variables such as background environmental noise, and improving standardised instructions are fine, provided it is demonstrated that these factors have affected the findings in some way.

Conclusion

A concise paragraph is presented encapsulating key conclusions drawn from the study.

References

Full details are listed of all references cited in the report. This enables others to research the references if desired. The standard format is as follows:

- **Journal articles** – author's name(s) and initial(s), year of publication, title of article (lower case preferred), title of journal (in full), volume number, page numbers. For example, Shepard, R.N. and Metzler, J. (1971) Mental rotation of three-dimensional objects. *Science*, vol. 23, 701–3.

- **Books** – author's name(s) and initial(s), year of publication, title of book (initial capitals for key words), place of publication, publisher. For example, Wodehouse, P.G. (1917) *The Man with Two Left Feet*. London: Methuen.

- **Chapters in books** – combines aspects of the procedure for journal articles and books (see above), by giving the author of the chapter and their chapter title first, followed by 'In A. Smith (ed.) …', and so on. For example, Cohen, G. (1982) Theoretical interpretations of visual asymmetries. In J.G. Beaumont (ed.) *Divided Visual Field Studies of Cerebral Organisation*. London: Academic Press.

Appendices

Numbered appendices are provided containing full instructions given to subjects, raw data and calculations for statistical analyses, plus other stimulus materials used. Information should be presented clearly and unambiguously.

Contemporary research

Miller (2009)

What is the probability of replicating a statistically significant effect?

Replication involves repeating a study exactly in order to check the results. The idea of falsifiability, where theories can be rejected by being proved not true, is an important concept in science and is one of the main reasons why research reports are written up as they are. And yet, as the following research shows, the chances of being able to predict whether results will be replicated is not as straightforward as might be imagined.

Aim

To assess the probability that if an experiment produces a statistically significant effect, it will be replicated in a follow-up experiment.

Procedure

A mathematical analysis of evidence regarding the probability of attaining similar results in replicated studies was conducted.

Findings

The probability of a statistically significant result being replicated in subsequent research, where the standard 0.05 (5 per cent) probability level was used, varies between 0.18 (18 per cent) and 0.998 (99.8 per cent).

Individual replication probability can actually be less than the Type I error rate, even after getting a significant result in an original experiment.

Conclusions

Replication probability cannot be accurately estimated from results determined by reference to probability levels.

Research findings are not simply accurate or non-accurate; instead, because of the use of significance levels, there is only a *probability* of them being accurate. This means that it is exceptionally difficult to assess the likelihood of a significant result being replicated.

Evaluation

- Researchers must accept the fact that they cannot generally determine the probability of replicating a significant effect.

- Due to the use of significance levels to assess the probability of results being accurate, replication is a much more complex concept than many imagine.

Although textbooks relate the main features of important research studies, there is no substitute for reading the original report write-ups. Go to http://psychclassics.yorku.ca/index.htm to access the website 'Classics in the History of Psychology'. Read through famous psychology papers, which will be of use elsewhere in your studies, but also to see how research is written up and presented.

Strengthen your learning

1. Explain the difference between bar charts, histograms and frequency polygons.
2. Sketch two scattergrams showing a negative correlation between miles travelled and how much petrol is left in a car's tank, and a positive correlation between miles travelled and the amount of petrol used. Remember to appropriately title and label your graphs.
3. Explain what is meant by:
   i) a significance level of 0.05
   ii) a significance level of 1 per cent.
4. Explain what Type I and Type II errors are and under what circumstances they are made.

continued ...

...continued

5. Explain what is meant by the following:
   i) nominal data
   ii) ordinal data
   iii) interval data
   iv) ratio data.
6a. What information is required to decide which statistical test to use?
6b. Explain what is required in order for the following statistical tests to be carried out:
   i) chi-squared
   ii) Mann-Whitney
   iii) Wilcoxon signed ranks
   iv) Spearman's rho.
7. Outline how content analysis is carried out.
8. Why are research reports written up in a conventional way?

Assessment Check ▶

A researcher assessed the evolutionary prediction that women over 35 years old would conceal their age more than males over 35 years of age when seeking heterosexual partners, by counting the number of times that age was revealed in magazine dating advertisements. Five hundred male and female advertisements were assessed. The results are summarised in Table 13.03.

Table 13.03 Number of over-35s not revealing age in classified advertisements

	NUMBER NOT REVEALING AGE	PERCENTAGE NOT REVEALING AGE
Women	350	75
Men	100	20

1. Give an appropriate one-tailed (directional) experimental hypothesis for this study. (2 marks)

2. Under what circumstances is the use of one-tailed hypotheses justified? (2 marks)

3. What type of experimental design has been used? (1 mark)

4. Explain one strength and one weakness of this design. (4 marks)

5. After this study was published, another researcher decided to replicate it. Explain what is meant by replication and what the purpose of the procedure is. (4 marks)

6. The data was of at least nominal level. What statistical test should be used? (1 mark)

7. An opportunity sample was used in this study. Explain one strength and one weakness of this method. (4 marks)

8. After performing this research, the investigator was interested in seeing whether there was a relationship between the age of women and the number of women concealing their age in personal advertisements. Design a correlational study to investigate this, including appropriate details. (7 marks)

continued ...

...continued

Examination guidance

The way to earn good marks when answering this type of question is to use the information in the stimulus material coupled with your knowledge of research methods. Give clear, concise and unambiguous answers, and, where multiple marks are available, as in question 2, ensure that elaboration of the answer is provided.

For question 8, sufficient appropriate details would be needed to gain access to all the marks – for instance, a correlational hypothesis, details of the method used, naming of co-variables, and so on.

Summing up

- Science is a system of acquiring knowledge through a process known as the scientific method, which is defined as the observation, identification, description, experimental investigation and theoretical explanation of phenomena.

- Confidence in psychological findings is increased by replicating investigations to check the results.

- Scientific research should be objective and free from bias, though fraud and misconduct do occur.

- Peer review consists of scrutiny of research papers by experts to establish whether they should be published.

- Peer review acts as a 'gatekeeper' to prevent flawed research being published.

- Peer review is criticised for not being impartial and for some reviewers acting in an unprofessional manner.

- There are several forms of research methods, each suitable for different research situations.

- A sample is a part of a target population and several sampling types exist, each with implications for bias and generalisation.

- Reliability refers to consistency, with internal reliability concerning the extent to which things are consistent within themselves, and external reliability referring to the extent to which a measure of something is consistent with other measures of the same thing.

- Inter-rater reliability concerns the extent to which different raters give similar estimates of the same phenomenon, while test-retest measures the stability of a test over time.

- Validity refers to accuracy, with internal validity concerning whether the research effects are due or not due to the manipulation of the independent variable, while external validity concerns the extent to which results can be generalised to other settings.

- The BPS code of ethics helps to address ethical issues so that participants are free from harm and their dignity protected.

- Different graphs exist to display different types of research data.

- Research differences are accepted as being significant if their probability is beyond the boundaries of chance. The accepted probability level in psychology is 0.05 (5 per cent).

- A Type I error occurs when a difference/relationship is accepted as a real one and is not real.

- A Type II error occurs when a difference/relationship is rejected, but actually does exist.

- There are various statistical tests, with criteria for their use depending on type of hypothesis, type of design and level of data.

- Qualitative data are more subjective, but can be converted to quantitative data by content analysis, where objective categories are created.

- Psychological reports are written up in a set manner to allow for replication.

Index

abnormality
  autism 58–9
  and insomnia 30
  see also psychopathology
absolute deprivation 136
abuse, and magical thinking 466
accommodation 279, 280
addictive behaviour
  causative factors 426–32
  drug abuse 412–13, 414, 415, 418, 428, 429, 430, 432
  gambling 420–5
  models 411–18
  public health campaigns 429, 440–3
  smoking 418–20
  treatments 432–9
  video games 383
adolescents
  gender role schemas 204
  effect of media 378
  and peer pressure 427–8
  relationships 114, 385
  smoking 418, 419, 428, 429
  use of video games 383
adoption studies
  depression 338, 339
  intelligence 269
  schizophrenia 324
adult attachment types 109
advertising 392, 392–5
affordances 53
age *see* adolescents; children; lifespan changes; older people
aggression
  deindividuation 128–32
  and genetics 142–6
  group displays 152–7
  infidelity and jealousy 149–52
  institutional 133–8
  neural/hormonal causes 138–41
  SLT 123–8, 132
  see also violence
agonistic drugs 436
agoraphobia 352, 367
Ajzen, addiction theory 434–5
alcohol
  dependency 134, 427, 429, 436, 437, 442–3
  and sleep 27
amygdala, role in aggression 145, 146, 382
analytical intelligence 242
androgens, and gender behaviour 208

animal phobias 352
animals
  biological rhythms 7, 9
  brain size 266
  conditioned learning 249–53
  ethics of research 10, 23, 35, 144, 177, 254, 260, 413
  generalisation of studies 7, 19, 141, 177, 265, 413
  learning and intelligence 251–60, 262, 264–6
  phobias in 358
animistic thinking 281
anomalous experience (paranormal)
  coincidence 460
  magical thinking 465–6
  mediums 463–4, 476–7
  out-of-body/near death experiences 474–6
  parapsychology 448–58
  and personality 468–9
  probability judgements 461–2
  pseudoscience 448–9
  psychic healing 471–3
  psychic phenomena study 456–7
  and sleep paralysis 37–8, 474
  superstitions 464–5
anonymity 495
antagonistic drugs 436
anti-bullying programmes 308
anti-social behaviour 377–81
  see also aggression; stalking; violence
antidepressant drugs 345–7, 348, 365
antipsychotic drugs 329, 330, 365
anxiety 430, 465
anxiety disorders 352
  explanations 356–64
  symptoms and diagnosis 351–5
  therapies 318, 365–72
anxiolytic drugs 365, 366
apnoea 15, 16, 28–9
apprenticeship hypothesis 262
Argyle, relationship theory 84
arranged marriages 94, 109, 116
assimilation 279, 280
associative visual prosopagnosia study 73–4
astrology 467–8
attachment theory 109–14, 404
attention-distraction hypothesis 394
attentional bias 363
attitudes 388, 389, 390, 391, 392

attraction 81–6, 96–7, 148
attractiveness 97, 391, 399
auditory hallucinations 319, 331, 332
autism 58–9, 302–3, 309, 311
auto-ganzfeld studies 451
aversion therapy 438

babies
  perception studies 59–63
  sleep patterns 1–15, 16
balanced messages 388, 389
Bandura, Ross and Ross, aggression study 124–6
bar charts 498
Barnum effect 467–8
Baron-Cohen, TOM study 302–3
BBC prison study 136
Beck, depression theory 343, 344, 345
behaviour shaping/modification 250
behavioural activation 348–50
behavioural approach
  addictions 415–17, 418, 419, 420, 421
  anxiety disorders 361–3
  depression 342–3
  dieting 169
  obesity 188–9
  psychopathology 315
  relationships 84–5
  sexual selection 95–102
  social learning theory 123–8
  see also behavioural therapies
behavioural beliefs 434
behavioural insomnia 25
behavioural self-control training 438
behavioural therapies 315
  addictions 438
  anxiety disorders 368–70
  depression 349–50
  and OCD 362
bell curve hypothesis 275
Bem, psychic study 456–7
Bennett-Levy, and Marteau, phobias research 360–1
benzodiazepines (BZs) 365, 366, 436
bias
  attentional 363
  cognitive 343–4, 423–4, 460
  egocentric 305–6

political 291, 381
see also cultural bias; gender bias; researcher bias
binocular cues 56, 57
biochemical explanations
abnormality 315
depression 339–42
schizophrenia 325–6
biological approach
addictive behaviour 411–13, 418, 421
aggression 132, 139–46
anxiety disorders 356–7
biological rhythms 2–12
depression 338–9
eating behaviour 172–84, 191–3
OBEs/NDEs 474, 475
psychic healing 471, 473
schizophrenia 323–5
sleep 13–23
sleep disorders 24–39
social cognition 308–11
see also biological therapies
biological preparedness 251, 357
biological rhythms 2–12, 177
see also sleep
biological therapies
anxiety disorders 365–6
depression 345–7
psychosurgery 315, 318
schizophrenia 329–30
biosocial approach, gender 207, 214–19, 220
bipolar depression 335, 336, 339
bisexuality, and gender development 208, 218
BITCH intelligence test 275
blindness recovery studies 63–6
blood phobias 356, 357
bobo doll study 124–6
bodily kinaesthetic intelligence 244
body symmetry 96–7, 100, 101
bottom-up perception theory 50–4
boundary model, dieting 168
Bowlby, attachment theory 109
BPS, ethics code 494
brain
and addiction 413, 416–17
and aggression 145–6
and gender 207, 208, 210
mirror-neuron system 308–11
effect of nutrition 271
in OBEs/NDEs 474
size 265–6
structure and intelligence 262, 263

brain damage, prosopagnosia 72–6
brain-imaging techniques, and eating behaviour 178
brightness constancy 58, 62
British Psychological Society (BPS), ethics code 494
Bruce, and Young, face recognition theory 70–2, 75
bruxism 33–4
bullying 308
Burt, Cyril, fraud 483–4
Buss
infidelity studies 150
mate preferences 214

CAH 207–8, 210, 215
CAIS, and gender identity 208
case studies 491
cataplexy 35
catatonic schizophrenia 320
causality 489, 490, 491
CBT *see* cognitive behavioural therapy
celebrity 396–406
celebrity stalking 403, 404, 405
celebrity worship 400–2
central control 326, 327
central micro-injection 178
centrally processed messages 390
centration 281
chi-squared test 502
children
attachment style 109–11
cognitive development 279–91
gender development 200–15, 221–30
gender dysphoria 216–18
magical thinking 466
moral understanding 292–7
OCD 364
and parents 102–5, 105–8
sleep 14–15, 31, 32
social cognition 298–311
temper tantrums 107
and TV adverts 393, 394
video game addiction 383
Chinese pseudoscience debate 448, 451, 485
chlorpromazine 329
circadian rhythms 2, 3–4, 7, 8, 9, 27
classical conditioning 249–50, 251, 253
and addiction 415, 416, 417, 438
and anxiety disorders 361
and obesity 188, 189
in relationships 84

clozapine 329, 330
cognition *see* cognitive development
cognitive behavioural group therapy 370, 372
cognitive behavioural therapy (CBT) 315
anxiety disorders 370–2
depression 345, 348–9
eating disorders 190, 191
schizophrenia 331–2
cognitive biases 343–4, 423–4, 460
cognitive development
gender development 200–3
moral understanding 292–7
social cognition 298–311
theories 279–91
cognitive dissonance 388, 414
cognitive function, in shift work 12
cognitive illusions 461
cognitive priming 379–80
cognitive psychology
and addiction 419, 421, 423–4, 438–9
eating behaviour 168, 169, 177, 178
face recognition 69–77
gender development 200–5, 229
information-processing theories 237, 240, 241–8
obesity 190–1
perceptual development 56–69
perceptual organisation theories 44–56
psychopathology 315, 326–7, 343–5, 363–4
cognitive shifts, eating behaviour 168
coincidence 460
cold reading 461, 477
Coleman, obesity studies 176–7
collaborative learning 290, 291
collectivist cultures *see* non-western cultures
Colligan, shift work study 12
colour constancy 58, 62
common reward pathway 417
communication
central and peripheral 390
using computers 385–6, 432
communication addiction disorder 432
compulsions *see* obsessive-compulsive disorder
computer games 385
computer mediated communication 385–6

computers, *see also* internet; video games
concrete operational stage 282
concurrent validity 493
conditioning
    and gender development 204, 217
    in intelligence 249–53
    and obesity 188, 189
    in phobias 359
    and relationships 84
conference model 270
confidentiality 495
confirmatory bias 461
conflict
    parental 105–8
    see also aggression; violence
congenital adrenal hyperplasia (CAH) 207–8, 210, 215
Conrod, alcohol intervention study 442
conservation (cognitive development) 282, 284
content analysis 502–3
content validity 493
contingency management 438
continuity hypothesis 109–14
control beliefs 434
conventional morality 294
Coon, TV advertising study 393–4
core sleep model 20
correlations 490
cortical neurons 266
cortisol, and obesity 193
cost-benefit analysis 495
courting 97, 100
covert desensitisation 438
creative intelligence 243
crime 133–4, 145
Crockett, serotonin study 140–1
cross-cultural research 56, 221
    cognitive development 285
    gender roles 208, 213
    perceptual development 66–7
    theory of mind studies 303
crowd behaviour 128–31, 132, 152–7
cultural bias
    cognitive theories 288
    eating behaviour 166
    gender roles 230
    intelligence testing 274–6
    moral development 297
    perspective taking 307
    psychiatric diagnosis 323, 3161–7
cultural factors
    in celebrity 397–8

eating behaviour 164–5
    in mating 101
    in perception 48–9, 66–7, 68
    psychic healing 473
    in relationships 86, 89, 94, 115–19
    researcher bias 119
cultural influences 261
    cognitive development 287
    eating behaviour 161, 166
    gender roles 230–3
    race and intelligence 274
cultural relativism 230
culture bound syndromes 317

Dapretto, mirror neuron study 309
data analysis 498–503
Deady, testosterone study 209
debriefing 494
decalage 282
deCODE genetics, nicotine study 419–20
deep-brain stimulation 366, 367
defensiveness, and paranormal 468, 469
dehumanization 156–7
deindividuation 122, 123, 128–32
delusions 319, 326, 336
Delvenne, prosopagnosia study 73–4
depressed attributional style 344
depression
    and addiction 430
    explanations 338–45
    and insomnia 29, 30
    post schizophrenia 320
    symptoms and diagnosis 335–8
    therapies 318, 345–50
deprivation model of aggression 123, 135
depth perception 51, 56, 66
desensitisation
    in addiction 411
    to violence 380, 381, 384
determinism
    and attachment 115
    celebrity 400
    and eating behaviour 177
    gender theories 214
    intelligence theories 267
    jealousy and infidelity 151
    and phobias 364
    psychometric theories 240
    and relationships 86
    and reproductive behaviour 107, 108
    and sleep 14

diagnosis
    depression 336–8
    psychiatric disorders 315–17
    reliability 315, 316–17, 320–1, 337, 339, 354
    schizophrenia 319, 320–3, 327
    validity 315, 316–17, 321, 322–3, 337–8, 355
Diagnostic and Statistical Manual of Mental Disorders (DSM-IV) 24–5, 315
diathesis-stress model 324, 339, 357
diet
    healthy eating 161, 163, 165–6
    and intelligence 271
    effect of TV adverts 393–4
dieting 167–71, 398
DILS 454
discovery learning 279, 289
discrimination, (conditioning) 250
disequilibrium 279, 280, 292
disorganised schizophrenia 320
disorganised thinking 326
distance healing 471
distance perception 56–7, 66
distant influence on living systems (DILS) 454
distorted thinking 363
disturbances of effect 320
divorce 116, 118
dopamine
    in addiction 411, 415, 416, 417, 418, 421–2
    in depression 340, 345, 346
    in drug treatments 436
    and obesity 191, 192–3
    in OCD 365
    in schizophrenia 325, 326, 327, 329
    in sleep 21
double-bind theory 327, 328
downward drift 328
drug abuse
    influences 428, 429, 430, 432
    models 412–13, 414, 415, 418
    treatments 436, 437
drug maintenance therapy 436
drug therapies 315, 318, 329–30, 345–7, 365–6, 436–7
dual control theory 172, 173
Duck, relationships dissolution theory 89–92
dyadic phase, relationship breakdown 90, 91

e-communication 385–6
E-FIT face recognition system 76
eating behaviours
    biological theory 172–7
    and celebrity 398, 401
    disorders 185–95
    evolutionary theory 178–84
    influences on 160–71
    see also diet
eating disorders 185–95
ecological demands 261, 262–3
ecological validity 493
ECT 315, 330–1, 347–8
EEA 84, 107, 179, 359
egocentric bias 305–6
egocentric speech 286, 287
egocentrism 281, 283, 301, 305–6
Elaboration likelihood model 388,
    390–2
elderly, addictions 429, 430
electroconvulsive therapy (ECT)
    315, 330–1, 347–8
emotional infidelity 149–52
emotions
    in perception 46–7
    and persuasion 389
    in schizophrenia 320
    effect of video games 382
    see also aggression; empathy;
        expressed emotion; mood
empathy
    in CBT treatments 332, 371
    development 304–7
    media influence 378
    mirror neurones 309
    effect of video games 384
empirical methods 482, 483
emulation, in social learning 255
encephalisation quotient (EQ) 266
endogenous pacemakers 2, 8, 9
enhancement, in social learning 255
enrichment 272
Environment of Evolutionary
    Adaptiveness (EEA) 84, 107, 179,
    359
environmental factors
    and intelligence 261, 268–70
    see also nature/nurture debate
Epley, perspective taking 305–6
equilibrium 279, 280
equity theory 88–9
ethical guidelines 494–5
ethical issues 494–5
    addiction 422
    aggression 130
    animals in research 10, 23, 35,
        144, 177, 254, 260, 413

gender dysphoria 220
gender roles 214
gene mapping 273
imposed etics 233
isolation experiments 3
moral development 297
neonatal perception 63, 68
perception 49
phobia treatment 370
prosopagnosia 77
psychic mediumship 477
psychometric theories 240
race and intelligence 276
restored sight studies 66
theory of mind 303
eugenics 241, 274, 448, 485
evolutionary theory
    aggression theory 142, 148–57
    and animal intelligence 260
    and anxiety disorders 357–61
    attraction 83–4
    biological preparedness 251, 357
    and celebrity 398–400
    criticisms 184
    eating behaviours 178–84, 194–5
    and gambling 425
    and gender 207
    gender roles 211–14
    group displays 152–5
    and human intelligence 261–7
    infidelity and jealousy 149–52
    lynch mobs 156–7
    obesity 194–5
    parent-offspring conflict 105–7
    parental investment 102–5
    and probability judgements 462
    sexual selection 95–102, 148
    sleep theories 18–20
exercise, and sleep 20, 22, 23
existential intelligence 245
exogenous zeitgebers 2, 5, 9–12
experimental design 489–94
experiments, types 489
exposure and response prevention
    (ERP) 369, 370
expressed emotion 327, 328, 333
external validity 493
extinction, (conditioning) 250
extra sensory perception (ESP) 449,
    451–4, 458, 468, 469, 483
extroversion, and paranormal 468,
    469
eyewitness testimony, séances
    463–4

face recognition
    prosopagnosia 72–7
    theory 70–2
face recognition nodes (FRNs) 71,
    75
face recognition systems 76
face validity 493–4
facial expressions
    and analysis 70, 74, 75
    and perception 47
facial speech analysis 70
facial symmetry 96, 101, 102
factor analysis 237, 240
false beliefs 301, 302–3
false hope syndrome 168
falsification, in research 485
families
    influence 124, 327, 328, 342
    see also parents
family therapy 333
fandom 397, 400–2
fear see phobias
fear of animals study 360–1
Felliti, sleep eating study 187
Festinger, deindividuation 128
field experiments 489
film see media influence
first-order conditioning 249
flooding (implosion) 369, 370
food
    and insomnia 27
    and mood states 162
    see also diet; eating behaviour
food extraction hypothesis 262
foraging hypothesis 262–3
formal operational stage 282, 285
foster grandparent programmes 270
fraud
    and perception 47
    scientific 448, 449, 450, 483–4
free will see determinism
frequency polygons 499
friendships 84, 92
FRNs 71, 75
functional invariants 280

'g' factor, intelligence 237, 240
gambling 421–5, 431–2
ganzfeld studies 448, 451–4, 483
Gardner, intelligence theory 244–6
Garg, mood and eating research 161
gender, definition 200
gender bias
    dieting 171
    institutional aggression studies
        138

intelligence testing 276
moral development 296, 297
psychiatric diagnosis 3161–7
shift work studies 12
gender consistency/constancy 201–2, 203, 204, 299
gender constancy theory 200–3
gender development
  biosocial approach 214–19
  cognitive developmental theory 200–3
  cultural influences 230–3
  evolutionary explanations 211–14
  gender schema theory 203–5
  hormonal and genetic influences 206–10
  media influence 379
  social influences 221–30
gender dysphoria 207, 216–19
gender factors
  aggression 127, 138, 151
  attachment and relationships 115
  infidelity and jealousy 149–52
  insomnia 30
  mating 97, 101
  in OCD 359
  parental investment 102–5
  in relationships 83, 86, 89
  stalking 404
  effect of stress on eating 162–3
gender identity 200–1, 203, 207, 299
gender roles
  cognitive theory 200–3
  cross-cultural research 208, 213
  cultural bias 230
  evolutionary theory 211–14
  nature/nurture debate 220, 233
  stereotyping 223–6
gender schema theory 200, 203–5
gender stability 200, 202, 203
gene-mapping 270, 273
  and anxiety disorders 356, 357
  and depression 339
  and schizophrenia 323, 324, 325
generalisation
  animal studies 7, 19, 141, 177, 265, 413
  in conditioning 249
  in sleep 17, 28
genetic variation 95
genetic vulnerability 362
genetics
  and addictions 412–13, 413, 419–20
  and aggression 142–4

anxiety disorders 356–7
  and depression 338–9
  and eating behaviour 178
  in gender development 206–7, 217, 219
  and intelligence 261, 268–70
  and narcolepsy 36, 39
  and obesity 191–2
  psychopathology 315
  and schizophrenia 323–5
  and sleepwalking 31, 32, 33
  see also nature/nurture debate
ghost sickness 317
ghrelin 169, 173, 193
Gibson
  food hypothesis 262
  perception theory 50–4
Gibson and Walk study 60–1
giftedness 243
glucose theory 174, 175
gossip 398–9
grandparental investment 103, 104–5
graphs 498
Gregory, perception theory 45–9
Gregory and Wallace 63–4
Griffiths, gambling study 423–4
group behaviour, deindividuation 128–31, 132
group displays (aggression) 122, 152–7
Guildford, intelligence theory 239
Gulevich, Dement and Johnson, sleep study 21–2

habituation, (violence) 380
habituation training 370, 371
Hamer, sexual orientation study 495–6
handicap hypothesis 96, 100
  see also facial symmetry
Hazan and Shaver, attachment study 110–11
healthy eating 161, 163, 165–6
Heber, Milwaukee project 273
Heinz dilemma 293–4
heredity see genetics
heritability 142, 261
hibernation theory 18
histograms 498
historical validity 493–4
holistic approaches 31, 70, 72, 205, 220, 247
holographic biology 448
homosexuality 208, 218, 398
Honorton and Ferrari, precognition

study 452–3
horizon ratios 52
hormones
  and aggression 139–40, 141–2
  and depression 340
  in dieting 169
  and eating 173–4, 176–7
  and gender 206–10, 217, 219
  and obesity 193
  in sleep 12, 14
hostile aggression 123, 133–6
Hovland-Yale model of persuasion 388–9
Huesmann, TV violence study 378–9
human intelligence 261–3, 265–7
  cultural factors 274–6
  and environment 270–3
  and genetics 267–70, 483–4
  information-processing theories 237, 240, 241–8
  psychometric theories 236, 237–41
  theory of mind 257–9
Hunt, cognition study 241
hypodermic effect 392, 395
hypothalamus
  and depression 340
  and obesity 172, 173, 174, 175, 177, 192
  sex differences 207

idiopathic insomnia 25
illusion of control 461
imitation
  in social learning 255
  see also observational learning
implosion 369, 370
importation model of aggression 123, 133–4
imposed etic 230, 276
indirect theory of perception 45–9
individual differences
  and aggression 132
  in cognition study 241
  and dieting 170
individualist cultures see western cultures
inducement 494
inferential tests 502
infidelity 149–52
information-processing theory 237, 240, 241–8, 326
informed consent 494
infradian rhythms 2, 4–5, 6
injection phobias 356, 357

inner speech 286
insecure-avoidant attachment 109, 111, 113, 115
insecure-resistant attachment 109, 111, 113, 115
insomnia 24–31
instinctive drift 252
institutional aggression 123, 133–8
instrumental aggression 123, 133
insulin 175, 193, 340, 342
intelligence 237
    conditioned learning 249–53
    Machiavellian 260
    and meat eating 183
    non-human 251–60, 262, 264–6
    see also human intelligence; intelligence testing
intelligence testing 240–1, 267–76
intelligent design study 487
inter-rater reliability 255, 493
interactionist view 136–7, 144, 220, 273
interdependence theory 89
internal validity 493
internalisation 286
International Classification of Diseases (ICD-10) 315, 317
internet addiction 410, 432
internet advertising 395
internet dating for Muslims 116, 117
interpersonal intelligence 244
interpersonal sex roles 213
intersex individuals 207–8, 210, 215–16
intersexual competition 96, 103, 149
interval data 501, 502
intrapersonal intelligence 245
intrapsychic phase, relationship breakdown 90, 91
intrasexual competition 96, 103, 148
intuitive thinking 461
IQ tests 268
    see also intelligence testing
Irwin and Cressey, importation model 133

jealousy 149–52
    see also sibling rivalry
jet lag 2, 10–11, 27
Jones, Little Peter study 369

Kanizsa illusion 48
Katz and Lazarsfeld, advertising theory 392

Kelly and Thibault, interdependence theory 89
Kendler and Prescott, drug abuse study 412–13
kin selection theory 105
kinaesthetic intelligence 244
Kohlberg
    gender constancy theory 200–1
    moral development theory 292

labelling theory 323, 327, 328
laboratory experiments 489
language, evolutionary function 398
language ability 266, 285
latent learning 253
lateral hypothalamus 172, 173, 174, 175
law of contagion 466
law of effect 250
law of similarity 466
Le Bon, crowd behaviour 128
learned helplessness 342, 343, 344, 359
learned insomnia 25
learning see conditioning; observational learning; social learning; social learning theory
Lee, relationship dissolution model 93, 94
leptin 173, 174, 176–7, 192, 193
Lewinsohn, depression theory 342, 343
lifespan changes, sleep 8, 14, 14–16
limbic system
    and aggression 145–6
    psychosurgery 318
    and schizophrenia 327
linear perspective 51, 52
linguistic intelligence 245
lipostatic theory 174, 176–7
Little Albert study 362
Little Peter study 369
logical intelligence 245
longitudinal studies 491
lynch mobs 156–7

McClintock and Stern, menstrual study 4
McCutcheon and Houran, celebrity study 402
Machiavellian intelligence 249, 260
magical thinking 362, 460, 465–6
major depression 335–6, 340
maladaptive thinking 363, 370
manic depression 335, 336, 339

Mann-Whitney test 502
MAOA (gene) 143–4, 339, 340
MAOIs 345, 346, 365
Markwick, E. scientific fraud study 449
marriage 94, 109, 116–18
Martin and Halverson, gender schema theory 203–5
matching hypothesis 81–2
maternal personality study 209
mathematical intelligence 245
meat preferences 183–4
media influences
    celebrity 396–407
    computers/internet 384–6
    and gambling 431–2
    on gender development 223–6
    on paranormal belief 461
    persuasion 388–95
    on social behaviour 127, 377–81
    video games 382–4
mediums 463–4, 476–7
melatonin 6, 12, 14, 26, 27
memory 460, 463–4
men
    jealousy 149–52
    mating strategies 97–8
    as prisoners 138
    see also gender factors
menstrual cycle studies 4, 5
mental mind maps 263
mere exposure effect 397
meta-analysis 499
meta-representations 326, 327
methadone 436, 437
Miller, significance study 507
Milton, foraging hypothesis 262
Milwaukee project 273
minority ethnic groups, diet 164–5
miracles 471
mirror neuron system 299, 308–11
mob football 153
Moller, handicap hypothesis 96
Money, gender research 210, 215
monoamine oxidase A (MAOA) 143–4, 339, 340
monoamine oxidase inhibitors (MAOIs) 345, 346, 365
monocular cues 56, 57
mood
    and addiction 414
    and eating behaviour 161–3, 168
    and persuasion 389
    see also emotions
moral development 292–7
moral dilemmas 293

moral intelligence 245
morality 293
motion parallax 51
motivation
   and dieting 169
   in perception 47
   and persuasion 392
   in SLT 123–4
multiple intelligences 237, 239
musical intelligence 245, 246
musical psychic healing 471
mutations 95

narcolepsy 35–7
'natural born killers' 146
natural experiments 489
natural selection 95
naturalistic intelligence 245, 246
nature/nurture debate
   food preferences 184
   gender roles 220, 233
   institutional aggression 138
   intelligence 267–76
   perception 49, 56, 68
near death experiences (NDEs)
   474–6
needle phobias 356, 357
negative reinforcement 250
negative schemas 343–4
negative triad 344
neonates 14, 56, 59–63, 181
neonaticide 105
neural mechanisms 139–42, 172–8,
   178, 192–3
neurons, in intelligence 266
neuropeptides 173, 174
neuroticism, and the paranormal
   468, 469
neurotransmitters
   and aggression 139–42, 143, 144
   and eating behaviour 178, 192
   and narcolepsy 36
   in phobias 365
   and schizophrenia 325, 326
   see also dopamine; noradrenaline;
      serotonin
nominal data 501, 502
non-human animals
   conditioning 251–3, 254
   intelligence 251–60, 262, 264–6
non-western cultures
   marriage 94, 116, 117, 118, 119
   morality 297
   perception 68
   relationships 86
   see also western cultures

noradrenaline
   in addiction 422
   in depression 339, 340, 345
   in sleep 14, 21
normative beliefs 434
NREM sleep 7, 15, 28
nucleus accumbens (NA) 417
nutrition see diet; healthy eating

OBEs 474–6
obese mice theory 176–7
obesity 29, 178, 186–95
objectivity 482–3
observational learning 123–8, 204,
   342
observations (experiments) 491, 495
obsessive-compulsive disorder
   explanations 356–7, 358, 359,
      361–2, 362–3, 364
   and magical thinking 466
   symptoms and diagnosis 353, 354,
      356
   therapies 365, 366, 367, 368, 369,
      370, 371, 372–3
obstructive sleep apnoea 28–9
older people, addictions 429, 430
one-trial learning 249, 251
online communication 385–6
operant conditioning 249, 250–1,
   251–2, 253
   and addiction 415, 416, 417, 418,
      421, 438
   and anxiety disorders 361–2
   and depression 342
   and obesity 188, 189
   in relationships 84
Operation Headstart 272
operations, (cognitive) 279, 280
opportunity sampling 492
optic array 45, 51
optic flow patterns 50–1
ordinal data 501, 502
Oswald, restoration theory 20, 22
out-of-body experiences (OBEs)
   474–6

painkillers, addiction 429
paranoid schizophrenia 320
paranormal belief see anomalous
   experience (paranormal)
parapsychology
   ESP studies 449, 451–4, 458
   psychokinesis studies 454–6
   as science 449–50
parasocial relationships 396, 397,
   401, 403

pareidolia 44
parent-offspring conflict 105–8
parental investment 102–5
parents
   influence on gender 215, 216,
      221–3
   relationship with children
      105–11, 115
   and schizophrenia 319
   see also families
Parker, apprenticeship hypothesis
   262
participants in research, rights 494–5
Paz-y-Miño, social dominance
   study 264
peer pressure, and addiction 427–8
peer relationships 114–15, 221
peer review 481, 485–7
penectomised twin 210
perception
   development 56–69
   face recognition 69–77
   theories 44–56
perceptual defence 46
perceptual organisation theories
   44–56
perceptual set 45–9
peripherally processed messages 391
person identity nodes (PINs) 71, 75
personal therapy 331, 332
personality
   and addiction 420, 421, 422,
      426–7
   and insomnia 20
   and obesity study 190–1
   and paranormal experience 460,
      468–9
perspective-taking 299, 304–8
persuasion, media influences
   388–96
Petty and Cacioppo, persuasion
   model 399–402
phase-delay shifts 11, 12
pheromones study 4
phobias
   symptoms and diagnosis 352,
      352–3, 354, 355
   theories 356, 357–9, 360–1, 361,
      362, 363–4
   treatments 70, 365, 366, 367–8,
      368–9, 371
physical attractiveness 97, 391, 397
   see also attraction
Piaget
   cognitive development theory
      280–3, 288–90

theory of morality 296–7
Piaget and Inhelder, egocentrism
  study PINs 71, 75
pleasant event scheduling 348–9
Pleistocene era (EEA) 84, 107, 179,
  359
Plotnik, animal intelligence study
  257–8
political bias, research applications
  291, 381
population validity 493
positive reinforcement 250
post-conventional morality 294–5
post-schizophrenic depression 320
Power-Threat hypothesis 156
practical intelligence 243
prayer, effect 472
pre-conventional morality 294
pre-operational stage 281–2, 283
predator-prey sleep theory 18, 19
prefrontal cortex
  in addiction 411, 430
  in intelligence 240, 266
pregnancy 107, 163
Premack and Woodruff
  theory of mind 258-9, 301
Prentice-Dunn and Rogers,
  self-awareness 129
prestige 399–400
presumptive consent 494
primary depth/distance cues 56, 57
primary insomnia 24–6
primary mental abilities theory
  238–9
primary reinforcement 250
printed media, effectiveness 385,
  389
prior general consent 494
prison simulation study 129–30
prisoner subcultures 133–4
prisons 129–30, 133–6
private self-awareness 129
pro-social behaviour, media
  influence 377–8, 379–81
pro-social reasoning 293
  see also perspective-taking
probability, in statistics 500, 507
probability judgements 460, 461–2
protection from harm 494
pseudoscience 448, 450
  see also anomalous experience
    (paranormal)
psychasthenia 30
psychiatric disorders
  and dieting 170
  gender dysphoria 216–19

and insomnia 27, 30
and SLT 128
  see also psychopathology
psychic healing 471–3
psychic mediums 463–4, 476–7
psychic phenomena see anomalous
  experience
psychical research 449
psychodynamic approach
  and obesity 178, 186–8
  sports events 153, 155
  unfalsifiable 485
psychodynamic therapy 319, 333–4
psychokinesis 454–6
psychological explanations see
  behavioural approach; cognitive
  psychology; social psychology
psychological resource model 426
psychological therapies see
  behavioural therapies; cognitive
  behaviour therapy; psychosurgery
psychometric theories, intelligence
  236, 237–41, 247
psychomotor disturbances 320
psychopathology 314–15
  anxiety disorders 351–72
  depression 335–50
  diagnosis 315–18
  schizophrenia 314, 318–34
  see also abnormality
psychophysiological insomnia 25
psychosurgery 315, 318, 366–8
public health campaigns 429, 440–3
public safety campaigns 395
public self-awareness 129

qualitative data 502

race, and intelligence 274–6
random event generator 455, 456
random number generator studies
  455, 456
random sampling 492
ratio data 501
rational emotive therapy 332
readiness 288, 289
reducing expressed emotion 333
reductionism
  addiction 413
  celebrity 400
  conditioning 254
  gender schema theory 205
  and infidelity 151
  intelligence theories 267
  multiple intelligences 246
  and obesity 195

perception 55
psychometric theories 240, 247
and relationships 86
and reproductive behaviour 107,
  108
and sleep 14, 20, 107, 108
and social cognition 311
reinforcement
  in addiction 415, 416, 417
  in conditioning 221, 250
  in depression 342
  and gender stereotypes 217,
    221–4, 226–7, 228–9
  and needs satisfaction 81, 84–6
relapse prevention model (RP) 169,
  414, 415
relationships
  and childhood experiences
    109–14
  and computers 385
  cultural influences 115–19
  interpersonal sex roles 213
  parasocial 396, 397, 401, 403
  with peers 114–15
  and reproductive behaviour
    95–108
  romantic 80–94, 115–17
  and stalking 404
  with therapists 332
relative deprivation 136
reliability
  of diagnosis 315, 316–17, 320–1,
    337, 354
  of studies 255, 493
REM sleep 6, 7, 8
  age differences 14, 15, 16
  restorative properties 22
  and sleep disorders 31, 33, 35
repetitive behaviours see obsessive-
  compulsive disorder
replication of results 482, 507
report writing 503–6
research applications 485, 488
  addiction 422, 431, 435
  advertising 395
  aggression studies 145
  circadian rhythms 10
  cognitive development 288–91
  conditioning 253, 254
  deindividuation 132
  eating behaviour 166, 191, 195
  enrichment 273
  face recognition systems 76, 77
  ganzfeld technique 454
  gender self-help groups 211
  gene research 146

magical thinking 467
mirror neurons 311
multiple intelligences 246
narcolepsy 39
nutrition and intelligence 271
obesity 191, 195
parapsychology 458
perception simulation 67
perception theory 54, 55
perspective-taking 307
prison aggression 138
psychometric theories 240
relationship dissolution 92
restoration theory 23
restored sight studies 68
shift work and jet lag 12
smoking studies 420
social learning theory 128
stress 431
weight loss 171
research design 489–94
research methodology 489–94
research reports 503–6
researcher bias
    cultural research 119
    paranormal studies 454, 456, 475
    reducing 483
    schizophrenia 324
    video games 384
residual schizophrenia 320
response, in conditioning 249
restoration theory of sleep 14, 20–3
restored sight studies 63–6
restraint theory 167–8
rewards-needs theory 81, 84–6
rewards/costs theory 81, 86–7
Rhine, J.B. and Louisa 449–50, 458
right to withdraw 494
rights of participants 494-5
ritual behaviour (sport) 154
role models 201, 380, 397, 400
romantic relationship
    and attachment style 109–14
    attraction 81–6
    breakdown 89–94
    cultural influences 115–17
    maintenance theories 86–9
Ropar and Mitchell, visual
    constancy study 58–9
Rose, Blackmore and French, sleep
    paralysis study 37–9
Rosenhan, schizophrenia study 322
Russell, menstrual study 5

's' factor, intelligence 237
SAD 5, 9

Saegert, attraction study 82
Sally-Anne experiment 302–3
sampling methods 489, 492
scaffolding 279, 286, 287, 291
scattergrams 499
schemas 279, 280, 326, 343–4
schizophrenia
    description 318, 319
    explanations 323–8
    symptoms and diagnosis 318–23
    therapies 318, 329–34
schizophrenogenic explanations 319
schools, influence on gender
    228–30
Schutzwohl, infidelity study 151
scientific fraud 448, 449, 450,
    483–4
scientific method 482
SCN (superchiasmic nucleus) 8, 14
seasonal affective disorder (SAD) 5, 9
second-order conditioning 249
secondary depth/distance cues 57
secondary insomnia 26–7
secondary reinforcement 250
secure attachment 109, 111, 112,
    113–14
selective serotonin reuptake
    inhibitors (SSRIs) 339, 340, 345,
    346, 365, 372
self-awareness 129, 298–300
self-esteem 299, 317, 427
self-help groups 317
self-perception theory 388
self-recognition 249, 256–7, 298–9
self-reports 490
self-selected sampling 492
Selman, role-taking theory 304
semiotics 286
senses see perception
sensitive guidance 287
sensorimotor stage 281, 282
seriation 281
serotonin
    and aggression 139–41, 143–4
    and depression 339, 340, 345
    and OCD 365
    in schizophrenia 326
    in sleep 14
serotonin behaviour regulation
    study 140–1
SET 81, 86–7
set point theory 168, 174, 175, 177
Seven Up! study 491
sex categorisation 231
sex roles 212
sexual dimorphism 95–6

sexual identity 200, 210
sexual infidelity 149–52
sexual selection 95–102
    and attachment styles 112–14
    and gender roles 212
    and social learning 256
sexy sons hypothesis 100
shape constancy 58, 58–9, 62
Shapiro, sleep studies 20, 22
shift work 2, 8, 11–12, 27
sibling rivalry 106, 107
significance, in statistics 500, 507
Simmons, sperm study 98
simple learning see conditioning
simple schizophrenia 320
single parents 101
situational causes of aggression 133,
    134–6
size constancy 58, 62
Skinner, superstition hypothesis 362
Skinner box 250
Slaby and Frey, gender constancy
    study 201–2
sleep
    lifespan changes 14–16
    stages 6
    theories 18–23
    see also REM sleep; sleep disorders
sleep apnoea 15, 16, 28–9
sleep cycles 6
sleep deprivation 19, 20, 21–2
sleep disorders
    bruxism 33–4
    insomnia 24–31
    narcolepsy 35–7
    sleep paralysis 35, 37–9, 474
    sleepwalking 2, 31–3
sleep paralysis 35, 37–9, 474
sleep-eating 187–8
sleep-state misperception 25, 26
sleeper effect 390, 429
sleepwalking 2, 31–3
SLT see social learning theory
smoking 418–20, 428, 436, 441–2
Soal, telepathic study 449
social causation 327
social cognition
    development 298–311
    mirror neuron system 308–11
    perspective taking 304–8
    sense of self 298–301
    theory of mind 249, 257–9, 299,
        301–3, 308
social complexity 261
social complexity hypothesis (SCH)
    263–5

social exchange theory (SET) 81, 86–7
social identity theory 136
social inoculation 440
social learning 249, 254–6
  see also social learning theory
social learning theory (SLT)
  and addiction 416, 417, 418, 419, 420, 421
  and gender development 200, 217, 221–30
  and media influence 377–8
  and obesity 188
  observational learning 123–8, 204
  and phobias 362
social media addiction 432
social phobias 352, 356, 363, 367, 371
social psychology
  abnormality see psychopathology
  aggression 122–38
  celebrity 396–8
  effect of childhood experiences 109–19
  gender models 214–16
  human reproductive behaviour 95–108
  romantic relationships 80–94
  schizophrenia 327–8
  see also media influence
social role taking 304
social skills training 333, 350
social speech 286
sociobiological approach 81
  relationships 83, 86
sociocultural explanations
  abnormality 315
  addiction 421
  schizophrenia 327–8
  superstition 465
somnambulism (sleepwalking) 2, 31–3
Sousa, OCD study 372
spatial intelligence 245
Spearman, two factor model 237–8
Spearman's rho 502
sperm competition 97, 98–100
spiritualism 449
spontaneous recovery, in conditioning 250
sport, and aggression 152–5
SRY gene 206, 208
SSRIs 339, 340, 345, 346, 365, 372
stage theories
  cognitive development 281–2, 286

face recognition 70
gender development 200–3
moral development 294–5
relationship breakdown 89–94
sleep 6, 15
social role taking 304
stalking 376, 397, 403–6
statistical tests 501–2
Steinke, gender study 225–6
stereotyping, and gender 204–5, 223–6
Sternberg, intelligence theory 242–4
stimulants, and insomnia 27
stimulus, in conditioning 249
stomach contraction theory 172, 174
Strange Situation study 109, 111, 112
stratified sampling 492
stress
  and addiction 414, 430–4
  and eating behaviour 161, 162–3
  and superstition 465
structural encoding 70, 75
structure of intellect model 239
studies
  addiction 411–12, 414–15, 416–17, 419–20, 427, 430
  advertising 394
  affordances 53
  aggression 139, 140, 141, 142, 143–4, 145–6
  attachment styles 112–13
  attraction 81–2, 83
  biosocial theory 215–16
  celebrity 399–400, 400–2
  circadian rhythms 3, 8, 9
  cognitive development 284, 287, 288, 289
  conditioning 251, 252
  cultural influences on gender 231–2
  culture and marriage 117–18
  deindividuation 129–31
  depression 337–8, 338–9, 340–2, 342, 342–3, 344
  depth perception 60–2
  dieting 167–8, 169, 170
  eating behaviour 178
  face recognition 71, 72, 73–6
  food preferences 179–80, 181–2, 182, 183–4
  ganzfeld studies 453–4, 483
  gender identity 201–3, 204–5, 208–9, 210, 213–14, 222–3, 223–6

group displays 154–5
healthy eating 165–6
infidelity 150–2
infradian rhythms 4–5, 6
insomnia 26, 27, 28, 29, 30
institutional aggression 134, 135–6
intelligence in animals 256–7, 259, 260, 262, 264–5
intelligence in humans 266–7, 268, 269, 270–1, 272, 273
intelligence testing 274–5
intelligence theories 237–8, 238–9, 241, 244, 246, 483–4
jet lag 10–11
longitudinal 491
media influence 377–8, 379–80, 381
mirror-neuron system 310
mood 162, 168
moral understanding 295–6
narcolepsy 31–9
OBEs/NDEs 474–5
obesity 187–8, 189, 190–1, 191–2, 192–3, 194
parental relationships 103–5, 106
peer relationships 114–15
perception 45, 46, 47, 48, 51, 52
personality and paranormal 468–9
perspective taking 306–7
persuasion 389, 391–2
planned behaviour theory 435
probability judgements 462
psychic mediums 476–7
psychokinesis 455–6
relationship dissolution 91, 93
romantic relationships 81–2, 84–5, 86, 87, 91, 93, 117
schizophrenia 320–3, 323–4, 325–6, 326–7, 328
self-awareness 300
self-recognition 256–7, 299
SET 86, 87
sexual orientation 495
sexual selection 98–100, 101, 102
shape constancy 58–9
shift work 11–12
sight restoration 63–6
sleep 16–17, 18–22, 26, 27, 29, 30
social influences on gender 227, 229
social learning 255–6
social learning theory 124–7, 222–3
stalking 404–6